M.9

BRITISH THEATRE

BRITISH THEATRE

★

PETER NOBLE

Foreword by

LAURENCE OLIVIER

★

☆

BRITISH YEARBOOKS

22, CHANCERY LANE, LONDON, W.C.2

MADE AND PRINTED IN GREAT BRITAIN BY
KNAPP, DREWETT & SONS LTD.,
KINGSTON-UPON-THAMES & LONDON—w.11762

FOREWORD

☆ *Laurence Olivier*

THE past few years have witnessed a heartening growth of stature in the British Theatre. For the first time in a very considerable period our stage approximates in quality and power to the great Continental theatres as well as to those formidable organizations, the American and Soviet Theatres. The English Theatre possesses a long and inspiring tradition and has had many periods of historic grandeur. Perhaps no other moment has approached in splendour and achievement the glorious Restoration Period, when many notable talents and much vitality and enthusiasm were involved in the rebirth of our theatre. That is, no other moment until now.

The wartime Renaissance in the theatre, not only in London but in all parts of Great Britain, is here to stay. Drama has been brought to the British people, many of whom have seen a play performed for the first time in their lives. And both audiences and standards have demonstrated an appreciable growth, culminating in the successful work of such organisations as the Arts Council and the Old Vic, a company which has a special place in my affections. The Old Vic, with headquarters in London, Liverpool, Bristol and elsewhere, represents a most important step in making the theatre a people's art and a people's pleasure. It has for some time been, in people's minds, our National Theatre ; it is now destined to be in fact.

We have had much talk of a National Theatre in the past, but it should be realised that such a venture requires considerably more than the mere building components. The edifice itself is important, but this is as nothing when compared with the people who are to be concerned with operating such a theatre. It is the human raw material which matters most—the administrators, directors, producers, playwrights, actors, stage managers, designers, painters, technicians and musicians. These form the basis upon which a great and lasting theatre may be founded, and at the present time the English stage is particularly rich in such talent.

And, for the first time in many years, the Government is taking an interest in the theatre. I need not dwell too long on the sterling work of the State-backed Arts Council (formerly known affectionately all over the country as CEMA), which has made possible so much good work in London and the provinces. I am a firm believer in State subsidy for the theatre, although such has been the tremendous public interest in the staging of " good " drama recently that the Arts Council's guarantee against loss has been in most cases unnecessary. Let us hope that this boom in the theatre will continue during the post-war years. May we also hope that the thousands of new audiences who have been attracted to stage plays in the past few years will continue to take pleasure in the great dramatic masterpieces of all time.

But we must not forget new plays. There must be new blood in our theatre if it is to remain healthy, and not the least important of this new blood are the young playwrights. We must encourage writers to work in the theatre medium ; and in this respect I should like to see special playwrights' schools attached to theatres in much the same way that some theatres possess dramatic academies for their acting students.

The success of the Old Vic seasons of repertory would seem to indicate that the repertory system is completely satisfactory in every way. The post-war theatre will surely witness a move towards a further extension of the repertory system, and this is a good thing. Let us hope that the rebirth of our theatre, both in the intrinsic artistic sense and in the fact of the general increase of interest in worth-while plays, will be a feature of post-war Britain. For a nation which loves its theatre is a healthy nation.

INTRODUCTION

" Are we entering into another Elizabethan Age ? There are indications of a glowing renaissance in Britain of culture and invention, science—and art. Never, I doubt, have we seen in the past, in the same year, despite the ' glamour ' of the actor-manager system now gone, four such performances in classic roles as the Richard III of Laurence Olivier, the Hamlet of John Gielgud, the King Lear of Donald Wolfit and, to go outside Shakespeare, the Peer Gynt of Ralph Richardson.

CEMA, the semi-national venture that ensures a preference for cultural entertainment, has made possible the association with Gielgud and Olivier of all-star companies that add lustre to the highest traditions of our stage. There is talent every-where. Is it to be nurtured by the State for the benefit of all ? Or is the old system of private ' enterprise,' or every man for himself, to exploit only the meretricious ? "

HANNEN SWAFFER in the *Daily Herald,*
October, 1944.

Has the theatre in England progressed in any way during the past few years ; and is there any hope for the stage in this country? The answer to both these questions is unquestionably in the affirmative, and in the following pages I hope to show my reasons for assuming that many of the ills befalling the English stage during the years between the two wars have, in the past six years, been shaken off. Collected in the following pages are a number of articles, essays and reviews which form a pattern of activity in the recent years of the British theatre. I make no apology for the continued reiteration throughout of certain basic arguments ; in any case the views expounded have, I am glad to say, become increasingly widespread of late. A mass-movement towards the supporting of a State Theatre and State Opera and Ballet is more than indicated by the widespread public interest and support for such State-aided theatre as already exists.

As a worker in the theatre for some years, both on the stage and behind the scenes, as a member of the audience in theatres in various parts of Europe and as an enthusiast of drama who desires to witness the growth of a truly significant British stage, I would claim the privilege of casting the darts of critical opinion at the theatrical scene in England to-day, and more particularly in the West End of London, since—and this is to be regretted—it is the hub of most stage activity in these Isles. Taking as a criterion the theatres of the United States and the Soviet Union, we see that the theatre of Great Britain does not appear to approach the full grandeur which is its true heritage. This is not because of lack of talent or national genius, but due in part to a very simple fact. I submit that one of the reasons why the theatre occupies a comparatively unimportant part in the lives of the mass of the British people is that, unlike Russia and America, we do *not* include the study of drama in the ordinary school curriculum.

Why this is so must remain a mystery. Some of the arts may have found their way into the more enlightened halls of English learning ; not so the drama. In American high schools a theatre is part of the school building, no college is without its campus playhouse. Similarly in the Soviet Union the young people learn of Gogol, Tchekov, Shakespeare and Gorky as soon as they are able to write. I submit that Chairs of Drama should exist in all English Universities. We perceive that in England, however, the acquisition of most forms of culture is regarded with deep suspicion. "When I hear the word culture I reach for my gun," is reputed to have been said by the notorious Goering—I feel that his words find an echo in the subconscious thoughts of many a leading British educational authority !

Without the basic asset of being taught the history of drama (possibly in conjunction with ordinary classroom history), the younger generation in England is suffering a considerable handicap. Obviously the firm foundation for a truly great theatre is built upon the love of a people for its drama and traditions. But love is barren without understanding ; and to thousands upon thousands of English people the living theatre is an unknown quantity. Nevertheless the position improved beyond all question during the course of the war. In the following pages the reader may note the recorded facts concerning the steady growth in popularity and prestige of CEMA (now the Arts Council), the Old Vic, the independant theatre groups, as well as such interesting recent innovations as the commercial production of " good " plays, and ENSA tours of the accepted dramatic classics (like Strindberg's *The Father* and certain of Shakespeare's plays). Out of the war there has arisen a strong non-commercial theatre which, allied with the finest elements of the commercial stage, will yet create in England a theatre for the people, a theatre which will shoulder proudly the great dramatic traditions of this country.

LONDON. January, 1946.

ACKNOWLEDGMENTS

The author wishes to express his gratitude to JOHN VICKERS, many of whose photographs illustrate this book. Thanks and acknowledgments are also due to Cecil Beaton, Angus McBean, Felix H. Man, Houston Rogers, Edward Mandinian, Gordon Anthony, Russell Sedgwick, Hess, Alexander Bender, Vivienne, and Fred Daniels.

CONTENTS

———

THEATRE REVIEW

 Peter Noble

BLACKOUT IN THE THEATRE
The London Stage, 1939-1942

The outbreak of war found the theatre unprepared. The result was a blackout of the footlights in conjunction with the general lapse into enforced darkness. The Government order to close the theatre came, and every London theatre closed its doors. A great number of people were thrown out of work, thousands more were evacuated, many actors and theatre technicians joined the Forces and Civil Defence Services and the question as to what part the theatre might play in wartime society was left unanswered. Then, after the first shocks of the declaration of war and the blackout gradually wore off, the prerogative of re-opening the playhouses was left in the unsteady hands of individual managements. At first the result was chaos ; the panic was on, but it is pleasant to record that this manifestation was not unduly lengthy. By October half-a-dozen theatres were open and the audiences were beginning to trickle back to Shaftesbury Avenue as the expected air-raids failed to materialise. In accordance with the view that wartime entertainment must contain a maximum of sex-appeal, (an attitude of mind left over from the last war, and, later on, completely disproven in this one) the first theatres to show signs of life were such as the Windmill and the Prince of Wales, each specialising in " non-stop revue," that form of theatrical art which each had made peculiarly its own.

But there were other more encouraging signs of life in the theatre ; the Westminster was the first playhouse to open with a " straight " play when the London Mask Theatre (with a high-quality company, which included Stephen Murray, Robert Harris, Catherine Lacey, Mark Dignam and Michael Denison) staged J. B. Priestley's interesting new work, *Music At Night*, the Embassy opened with a programme of new plays, while Ashley Dukes' gallant Mercury Theatre played to capacity business with Synge's *The Playboy Of The Western World*. At Unity Theatre a political revue, *Sandbag Follies*, was written and produced within forty-eight hours of the commencement of hostilities ; this ran into three successful editions. It could be seen, therefore, that the " avant-garde " theatre, at least, failed to be intimidated by the blackout and, by the New Year, the situation in London's West End, too,

13

had practically retrieved itself. The position during those first few weeks had certainly seemed ominous and, indeed, the majority of the productions which had been running in London at the outbreak of war had packed up and gone on tour. Among the shows which visited the provinces were *The Importance Of Being Earnest, Design For Living, Dear Octopus, Robert's Wife, The Corn Is Green* and *Saloon Bar*, while the Old Vic Company began an extensive tour which brought the drama to thousands who had hitherto never been lucky enough to see a first-rate production of a " good " play.

By Christmas many of the above began to return to the West End, but not before discovering the surprising fact that a large, intelligent and enthusiastic audience actually existed *outside* the capital ! January, 1940, saw the return to town of Noel Coward's *Design For Living* (having its first production in Britain) in which Diana Wynyard, Anton Walbrook and Rex Harrison infused much-needed gaiety into their roles in a play which had been the subject of some adverse criticism when first produced in New York. (Although it had been acted on Broadway by Noel Coward himself, with Lynne Fontanne and Alfred Lunt as the other members of the triangle, many of the New York critics disliked it, especially George Jean Nathan, who devoted several columns to a condemnation of the play). Nevertheless, Coward has always been assured of a rapturous reception in the country of his birth and his brittle *Design For Living* ran at the Savoy for a considerable time.

Conditions in the theatre were by no means back to pre-war normality, however. Many of the shows played matinées only, some of the more enterprising managements announced that their evening performances would commence at six o'clock in order to give people time to get home early, and in most cases seats were reduced to within more reasonable limits (though they were still far too expensive for the general public). An encouraging innovation was that evening dress, the mark of bourgeois respectability, disappeared completely from the stalls and dress circle. More shows continued to come back to town and soon the London theatre scene was further enlivened by the return of the John Gielgud all-star, and wholly delightful, production of Oscar Wilde's *The Importance Of Being Earnest* at the Globe, while the brilliantly-written Elmer Rice indictment of fascism, *Judgement Day*, came to the Phœnix and Esmé Percy and Joyce Redman appeared in a revival of Hsiung's inimitable *Lady Precious Stream* at the Kingsway.

Again, Little Theatres were well in evidence, for Henry Cass's fine modern dress production of *Julius Cæsar* at the Embassy threw into prominence the superb performances of Walter Hudd and Eric Portman ; the Westminster staged Shaw's *Major Barbara*, with Catherine Lacey as the Salvation Army lass, while a new experimental theatre, the Actors' Company, commenced a promising season at the Rudolph Steiner Hall with Alec Guiness's dramatisation of Dickens' *Great Expectations*.

It was at this time that Emlyn Williams chose to produce his new play, *The Light Of Heart*, a drama of theatre-land which, although hokum in the grand manner and bristling with improbabilities, gave Godfrey Tearle the opportunity once more to show what a grand actor he was. His dipsomaniac Thespian and Angela Baddeley's crippled daughter were the performances which contributed mainly to the play's success. Daphne du Maurier's dramatisation of her own novel *Rebecca*, with that intelligent actress Celia Johnson and the late Owen Nares, began a long run in Shaftesbury Avenue, and it was agreeably significant that extreme success rewarded Donald Wolfit's first wartime season of Shakespeare at the Kingsway, where among the plays he produced were *Much Ado About Nothing*, *The Merchant Of Venice*, *Othello*, *Hamlet* and *Twelfth Night*. The response from the public was tremendous, and the Kingsway took the place of the Old Vic in the affections of London's Shakespeare-starved theatregoers.

But plans had been formulating for the re-opening of the Waterloo Road playhouse, and it was not long before the Old Vic Company was playing to capacity at every performance with *King Lear*, acted by a very strong cast, including John Gielgud as the Monarch, Fay Compton and Cathleen Nesbitt as Regan and Goneril, and Lewis Casson, Jessica Tandy, Stephen Haggard and Robert Harris—a galaxy indeed of first-class actors ! It was an outstandingly well-staged production, and the year 1940 also saw a number of other very interesting stagings, including Gay's *The Beggar's Opera*, directed by John Gielgud with Michael Redgrave as Macheath, and Wycherley's *The Country Wife* produced by Miles Malleson and played delightfully by Hermione Baddeley, Ursula Jeans and Alec Clunes, while the Open Air Theatre began a new and highly successful season in the Park. After its premier presentation at the Malvern Festival, the new Bernard Shaw play, *In Good King Charles' Golden Days*, opened in London at the New with Ernest Thesiger, Cecil Trouncer and Alec Clunes ; while another play from the pen of the inimitable Irish master, *The*

15

Devil's Disciple, which under the auspices of the Old Vic had been touring the country since the outbreak of war (along with Goldsmith's *The Good Natured Man,* Shaw's *Saint Joan,* with Constance Cummings, and Norman Ginsbury's *Viceroy Sarah*) came to the Piccadilly with Robert Donat as Dick Dudgeon and a fine cast including Roger Livesey, Milton Rosmer, Rosamund John and Joyce Redman.

The London Mask Theatre, founded by J. B. Priestley and Michael MacOwan, had kept up an extremely high standard once the war commenced, and one was always sure to see an interesting production at the Westminster. Just before the war one of London's outstanding successes had been Eugene O'Neill's *Mourning Becomes Electra,* with Beatrix Lehmann, Laura Cowie and Robert Harris as the tragic triumverate. And, again, it was O'Neill who drew the crowds to the Victoria theatre when Henry Cass directed a moving production of his sombre masterpiece *Desire Under The Elms.* Beatrix Lehmann was magnificent in this trial-piece of modern drama, while Stephen Murray as Eben and Mark Dignam as Ephraim enjoyed considerable successes in extremely difficult roles. Both these actors had established enviable reputations with their work at the Westminster, and it was a great pity that this production of *Desire Under The Elms* marked the end of one of the most worthy attempts to form a permanent home for worth-while drama in London during the past twenty years.

But things were looking up in the West End theatre, and in those dark days, after the Fall of France, Norman Marshall's revue, *Swinging The Gate,* which brought a number of new faces to the Ambassadors, was an outstanding hit, and ran for nearly a year. Hermione Gingold, Walter Crisham, Ronald Millar, Robert Helpmann, Reginald Beckwith, Guy Verney, and many other clever young people helped to enliven for many of us those fateful days in the summer of 1940 with a full measure of satire and wit. Meanwhile at the Old Vic a magnificent production of *The Tempest* saw outstanding performances from John Gielgud as Prospero, Jack Hawkins as Caliban and Marius Goring as Ariel.

On the tiny stage of the Torch Theatre, Irene Hentschel produced a new play by Aimée Stuart. Titled *Jeannie,* it dealt with a little Scotch drudge who inherits £200 and decides to visit Vienna, the city of her dreams. Here she meets a hard-headed Yorkshire business-man who befriends her, and a Viennese aristocrat who proposes to her under the impression that she is an heiress. But

all comes right in the end for Jeannie—in the arms of her Yorkshireman. The central figure was played by a brilliant newcomer,
Barbara Mullen, who conquered London overnight. Eric Portman
gave a sympathetic performance as her prosaic, middle-aged lover,
while Albert Lieven and Tatiana Lieven were excellent Viennese
" types." The play was so successful that it was at once transferred
to Wyndham's, where it had a long and triumphant run. *Jeannie*
put the Torch on the map, and thenceforth a number of interesting
new plays were staged here.

And a new Little Theatre was added to the growing list when,
in Kensington, Herbert Marshall opened his Neighbourhood
Theatre with an unusual staging of an American play, Robert
Ardrey's *Thunder Rock*. It was an immediate success, proving a
great personal triumph for Michael Redgrave, who played
Charleston, and it was later transferred to the West End, where
it became the first wartime play to receive a subsidy from the
Government—the powers-that-be evidently deciding that the
message of the play was indicative of the spirit abounding in this
island during the summer of that most eventful year.

A new phase began in the late summer, however, for air raids
commenced in full force, both by day and night, and once more
the bottom dropped out of the theatre. Again, as at the outbreak
of war, the theatres closed ; indeed, some of them were " blitz "
casualties, and for a time there was little theatrical entertainment
to be found in London. (It is only just to point out that two
little playhouses did not close even during the worst of the raids—
the Windmill and the Left Wing playhouse Unity—theatres with
widely different policies !) It was a great blow to theatregoers
when the Gate, after a fine production of Reginald Beckwith's
interesting Borstal play *Boys In Brown*, was forced to close, owing
to the extremely difficult wartime conditions. The little Villiers
Street playhouse had carved for itself a *niche* in the affections of
London's more discerning theatregoers over a considerable number
of years due to its progressive policy, unusual productions, outstanding direction and high-quality acting. But it became another
air raid casualty.

The first play in London's West End to brave the " blitz "
was André van Gyseghem's production of John Balderston's evergreen *Berkeley Square* at the Vaudeville, a delightful play delightfully acted by Jean Forbes-Robertson and Rosalinde Fuller, with
van Gyseghem in the Leslie Howard role. Later, at the Strand,
Donald Wolfit inaugurated his now-famous policy of " lunch-time

Shakespeare." With an extremely fine cast (which included Cathleen Nesbitt, Irene and Violet Vanbrugh and Rosalinde Fuller) he established an enviable reputation and with his packed matinées he kept the flag of drama flying throughout the worst periods of the daylight raids on London.

The tragedy, distress and damage caused by total war naturally affected the audience-attendance a great deal, while among the legitimate theatres which became air-raid casualties were the Shaftesbury, Queens and Little (all beyond repair), Neighbourhood, Embassy, Torch, Old Vic, Duke of York's, Chanticleer, Court, Sadlers Wells and Kingsway. However, 1941 opened bravely enough with John Gielgud's all-star revival of J. M. Barrie's *Dear Brutus* (in which production that great artiste Margaret Rawlings made her farewell performance before retiring into domesticity in the country.) And, while Gielgud and his gallant company— Roger Livesey, Leon Quartermaine, Nora Swinburne, Margaret Rawlings, Mary Jerrold, Ronald Ward, Muriel Pavlow, Zena Dare, Ursula Jeans and George Howe—performed Barrie's fantasy to packed houses in Shaftesbury Avenue, our leading actress, Edith Evans, was literally stopping the show at each performance of Herbert Farjeon's *Diversion* at Wyndham's, in which her magnificent voice and superb presence enabled her to take intimate revue in her formidable stride. Dorothy Dickson, Bernard Miles, Peter Ustinov, Walter Crisham, Vida Hope, Joan Sterndale Bennett and Joanna Horder were others who distinguished themselves in this gay Farjeon show.

A whole book could be written on this phase of the wartime theatre. For a year or more continuous nightly—and sometimes daily—raids were a commonplace, and although theatre attendances naturally suffered they did not decrease to such a degree that it was impractical to keep the theatres open. On the contrary some London shows played to full houses night after night, and, indeed, many plays had fairly successful runs throughout the worst period of the intensive raids on London.

This experience was duplicated in Birmingham, Manchester, Glasgow and the other provincial cities which had considerable air raid damage. Nightly the bombers came over, and Hitler massed his troops along the coast of Europe ready for invasion, but the reaction generally in this country was one of defiance, an attitude reflected in the theatre. A number of West End plays went on tour, however, and played always to large and enthusiastic provincial audiences. Those productions which remained in London carried on right through the raids. Many theatres equipped themselves with bunks and shelters, and back-stage and below-stage dormitories came into existence at a number of playhouses.

At London's " Folies Bergères," the Windmill Theatre, a whole new existence grew up, a new life conditioned by the raids. The artists lived, worked, slept, performed, relaxed, all in the same building, night after night, day after day. Nightly they continued their performances, and the audience was invited to use the theatre air-raid shelters for as long as they liked—and they did. At the Players' Theatre, Leonard Sachs and his genial band of helpers carried on the shows far into the night and invariably, if the raids were intense, the audience remained in the basement playhouse all night, sleeping in chairs, on improvised bunks, on the bar and on the floor !

The same thing happened at other theatres, not only in London, but in all parts of the country. Actors tirelessly gave impromptu performances right into the small hours to keep up the spirits of audiences imprisoned in the theatre by the danger of bombs and shell splinters outside. Luckily in most cases where theatres were destroyed by bombs the audiences were not present, and the percentage of casualties in theatres during the raids on England was, in fact, remarkably low. During the worst periods some theatres gave matinée performances only, so that Londoners might have time to hurry home for shelter by the time the sirens sounded. But it was noticed that the plays and shows which gave evening performances generally did so to good houses. Theatregoers, on the whole, refused to be intimidated by Hitler's bombs.

A long, dismal, dangerous winter slowly passed, and by Spring of 1941 it seemed that the tide had turned. Raids became less frequent, all theatres opened for evening shows, audiences flowed back, new plays came on and further new productions were planned. The crisis was over.

By the summer of that year the " Battle of Britain " had been won, the air menace over London ceased and one by one many of the shows which had been so successfully touring the provinces again returned to town. Principal among these was S. N. Behrman's witty and amusing play *No Time For Comedy*, which came back to the Haymarket with Rex Harrison, Diana Wynyard and Lilli Palmer in the leading roles. Harrison once more proved what

French Without Tears had demonstrated a few years before, that he is one of our leading actors in the field of light comedy, while Diana Wynyard and Lilli Palmer were excellently cast as the rival protagonists in this most laughable of triangles. After the grim " blitz " period the public were more than ever anxious for their theatre-fare to be gay, light-hearted and tuneful; the best of the revues produced to meet this demand was Leslie Julian Jones' *Rise Above It*, which at the Comedy united the two Hermiones, Gingold and Baddeley for the first time and gave Walter Crisham the opportunity of repeating his revue triumphs of the *Gate Revue* and *Diversion*. All three, plus the inimitable Henry Kendall, combined brilliantly to make the witty *Rise Above It* one of the slickest, funniest shows of the war. *Black Vanities*, at the Victoria Palace, saw Frances Day collaborating in mirth and music with that wonderful comedy team Bud Flanagan and Chesney Allen and with Zoë Gail in close attendance, while *Up and Doing* at the Saville provided uproarous entertainment for many months with a first-rate cast of revue favourites, among whom Leslie Henson, Binnie Hale, Cyril Ritchard and Stanley Holloway all shone brilliantly. It was an interesting psychological development, this return of public favour to revues and musicals. Natural and understandable, of course, was the reaction to the experiences of the grim horror of a London winter during the long period of continual air raids. As if to announce their relief at the cessation of the " blitz," theatregoers flocked to the light comedies, while the above three revues played to deservedly capacity business for a long time.

Bombed out of the Waterloo Road, the Old Vic Company made its headquarters at the New Theatre, where for its first production Tyrone Guthrie and Lewis Casson co-directed *King John*, with Sybil Thorndike, Abraham Sofaer and Ernest Milton in the cast. This was followed by a most successful season of Tchekov's *The Cherry Orchard*, in which Walter Hudd as the gentle poet Trofimov and Athene Seyler as Madame Ranevsky, both gave praiseworthy performances. And, at this time, two of the war's biggest successes began their record-breaking runs—Noel Coward's *Blithe Spirit* and Esther McCracken's *Quiet Week End*. *Blithe Spirit*, with several different casts, has achieved the longest run of any wartime play.

After June 22nd, 1941, when the Soviet Union became our allies in the struggle against German fascism, a wave of pro-Russian sentiment swept through the country, extending to the theatre where, within a short time, the classic Soviet comedy, Valentin Katayev's *Squaring The Circle* (directed by Peter Ustinov), and Afinogenov's *Distant Point* were both seen in the West End. The latter play was particularly successful. André van Gyseghem staged it at the Westminster, where excellent performances were given by Mary Morris, Esmé Percy, Edmund Willard and Guy Verney. Both these plays (and the musical, *Sorotchinski Fair*) aroused a keen interest among the theatre-going public for more plays and shows about life in the Soviet Union, but, although the demand seemed to be there, the theatre managements did nothing to satisfy it until the Old Vic produced Konstantin Simonov's *The Russians*, two years later.

1942 opened in a blaze of glory with the slick Marcel Varnel production of that fast-moving, witty piece by George Kaufmann and Moss Hart, *The Man Who Came To Dinner*, a play freely based upon a character libellously resembling the late Alexander Woollcott, the American literary figure and lecturer. This satirical comedy had all London laughing for more than a year ; it gave Robert Morley the part of his career and his Woollcottian celebrity was indeed a superbly-drawn study of a superbly-written character. Another outstanding American play, seen at the Aldwych, was Lilian Hellman's *Watch On The Rhine*, a moving and brilliantly-acted tragedy written around the disintegration of European culture under Nazism. Anton Walbrook and Diana Wynyard brought great power to their roles, he as Kurt, the German underground worker, she as his loyal American wife ; and *Watch On The Rhine* must be acclaimed one of the most sincere and praiseworthy plays produced in wartime England.

During this time Ivor Novello's perennial musical play, *The Dancing Years*, of which he wrote the libretto, composed the music and played the principal role, continued to be one of the greatest theatrical successes of the war years. Originally produced in 1939, it was taken off when war broke out. Then, later, in a rewritten, modernised version it ran for nearly three years. But J. B. Priestley's satire on the B.B.C., *Goodnight, Children*, which came to the New in early 1942, was not so fortunate. In spite of Naunton Wayne's polished acting, the play failed to draw an audience and it was certainly one of the most spectacular failures of that year. Emlyn Williams' new " blitz " play, *The Morning Star*, however, seemed to catch the public fancy and, with Williams himself and Angela Baddeley in the leading roles, it ran for a considerable time at the Globe (although it was by no means such a good play as Priestley's satirical piece).

Once more Bernard Shaw proved to be a sure-fire box-office success when his delightful play, *The Doctor's Dilemma*, was produced by Irene Hentschel at the Haymarket in the Spring. With a cast which included Vivien Leigh as the delectable Mrs. Dubedat, Austin Trevor, Frank Allenby, Charles Goldner, George Relph and Cyril Cusack (and later Peter Glenville), this witty comedy kept the Haymarket filled for many months and deservedly, for it was a polished and sparkling production. In May the Arts Theatre opened with a policy of " privately presenting " new and classic plays, of the kind usually referred to as " uncommercial," acted by a talented company, of which a nucleus was to appear in each play. Behind this venture was a young actor, Alec Clunes, who, after having distinguished himself in seasons at the Malvern Festival and at the Old Vic, undertook the task of creating in London a new theatre group, a theatre with a definite policy and with the highest possible standards. It must be recorded that both the policy and the standards have remained consistently high since the inception of " The Arts Theatre Group of Actors, under the direction of Alec Clunes." The opening play was Clifford Odets' *Awake and Sing*, previously seen in this country only at a special performance by the Stage Society just before the war. A play of power and beauty, it was acted extremely well by Martin Miller, Lilly Kann, Richard Attenborough, Vivienne Bennett, Harry Ross and Julian Somers, while Alec Clunes' direction was full of strength and subtlety. It was almost an inspiration on Clunes' part to open the new venture with this first-rate American play, a play which undoubtedly possessed certain social implications besides being a moving psychological drama. The founding of this new theatre group at the Arts Theatre in the middle of the war was both courageous and well-timed, and it was considered by many theatre-goers that the appearance in the West End of this permanent centre for high-quality drama ranked as one of the most important theatrical events of the wartime years. The Arts, at any rate, certainly succeeded in filling the gap which had been left by the disappearance of the illustrious Gate Theatre.

An eagerly-awaited production in the summer of 1942 was John Gielgud's *Macbeth*, though many of the critics were not too happy concerning his choice of that distinguished and sensitive actress Gwen Ffrangcon-Davies to play the strong-minded Lady Macbeth. Nevertheless this was in many ways a magnificently-conceived

Macbeth, which, though perhaps not an example of Gielgud at his best, was a brave effort, which showed that our leading actor was not content to rest on well-earned laurels, but was continually striving to increase the prestige of, and to heighten the standards of, the British stage. Here is perhaps the place to point out that Gielgud, one of our finest actors, and indeed one of the best actors in the world to-day, has maintained his high position in the affections of theatregoers during the war with his performances at the Old Vic in *King Lear* and *The Tempest*, as well as his own productions of *The Importance Of Being Earnest* and *Macbeth* (and later, *Love For Love*, and his exciting Repertory Season in 1944). Were any more proof required that Gielgud is an actor of whom England can well be proud, his wartime work for the theatre and for the public has surely proven how inestimable is his value to our theatre as producer, actor and artist.

During 1942 most plays dealing with the war had a scant success—prominent casualties being *Lifeline*, by Norman Lee and Barbara Toy, an authentic and moving story of the Merchant Navy, which, while being skilfully directed (by Michael Redgrave) and credibly acted (by Wilfred Lawson, Arthur Sinclair, Terence de Marney, Guy Verney and Robert Beatty) suffered the same fate as *Salt Of The Earth*, Michael Egan's topical play about Occupied France, which although distinguished by the excellent acting of Milton Rosmer, James Donald and John Slater, yet lasted only a few days at the Vaudeville. It seemed that the " escapist " thriller, like J. Lee Thompson's *Murder Without Crime*, was the type of play which took the public fancy at this time, although Terence Rattigan's *Flare Path* and Mary Hayley Bell's *Men In Shadow* were new war-plays which admittedly became very successful. This was, however, due to obvious reasons—for in the Rattigan play the *locale* was an inn near an airfield, the plot was distinctly novelettish and the characters sufficiently conventional to make it an entertaining confection about the " boys " of the Royal Air Force; while *Men In Shadow* (though quite a gripping melodrama) was merely a clever thriller with a war setting. It derived most of its popularity from its use of that well-used dramatic standby, " the hunted man " ; in this case the hunted were R.A.F. pilots forced down in France and hidden from the Nazis by friendly Frenchmen. John Mills (who co-directed with Bernard Miles) gave a thoughtful and restrained performance as the chief of the hidden fliers, while Hubert Gregg, Ralph Michael and Alice Gachet were all first-rate.

Before the war a young Londoner, James Hadley Chase, had experienced a certain success with a form of sensational novel previously popularised by American writers. With no knowledge of New York or Chicago, apart from the study of films and documents, Chase evolved a type of quick-moving gangster story which soon after the outbreak of war achieved astonishing popularity. These cheap editions of the stories of Chase and others—" shilling shockers," as they were known—sold in their thousands on the bookstalls, the most widely-successful being the notorious " No Orchids For Miss Blandish." Impresario George Black, noting the tremendous popularity of this gangster epic, commissioned Chase to make a play-adaptation, which was produced at the Prince of Wales Theatre with Mary Clare as the fearsome Ma Grisson, Robert Newton as the homicidal Slim and Linden Travers as the ill-fated Miss Blandish. It achieved as great a success as Chase's fast-moving musical play *Get A Load Of This*, produced at the London Hippodrome, with Vic Oliver, a few months previously.

At the Arts Alec Clunes produced another new play, this time by a young British actor-playwright, Peter Ustinov. It was the first he had had produced, though he had been writing plays from the time of his early 'teens (while his translation of Jean Sarment's *Fishing For Shadows* had been seen at the little Threshold Theatre as early as 1940). Dealing with a group of White Russian exiles living in Kensington, *House of Regrets*, was leisurely and brilliant, the characterisation and dialogue indicating that in Ustinov the English theatre had acquired a new playwright of distinct promise. As in most Arts Theatre productions, the acting was on a high level, with a superb gem of character-drawing by John Ruddock as the ageing admiral. Max Adrian's obsessed general, continually drawing up plans to attack the Soviet Union with his beloved cavalry, and the striking portrait of a senile ballet dancer by Noel Willman, were other performances of great power in this production. (Since this time Peter Ustinov has had two other plays produced in London : *Blow Your Own Trumpet* in 1943, which was coolly received by the critics and *The Banbury Nose*, which was one of the outstanding new plays of 1944).

Inexplicable indeed was the lukewarm response which attended the production of Patrick Hamilton's new play, *The Duke In Darkness*, in the autumn of 1942. A far cry from the trunk-crime horrifics of Hamilton's successful thriller *Rope*, this unusual play was " different," moving and strongly dramatic. Dealing with a little-known period in French history, it gave Michael Redgrave the part of his career as the faithful Gribaud, gradually being driven mad by his imprisonment with his royal master in a castle tower. I felt at the time that this play possessed every ingredient for success— intelligent writing, an unusual, intriguing and deeply interesting theme, Redgrave's powerful psychological study of impending madness, and first-class acting by Leslie Banks, Hugh Burden and Walter Fitzgerald. Why then did it fail to achieve a satisfactory run ? I cannot say ; but it is my firm belief that if this play were put into the 1945 repertory of, say the Old Vic, it would prove to be an enormous success. It really has not yet had a fair chance. (Indeed, the same might .be said of any number of worthwhile English plays which did not become an immediate commercial hit).

Claudia, a new American play by Rose Franken with a far slimmer plot and considerably less dramatic interest, on the other hand registered an immediate hit and commenced a lengthy run. Much of its success, however, was due to the really outstanding acting in a virtuoso role of Pamela Brown, a new personality (who had been " discovered " by James Agate in Oxford and "directed" by him in *Hedda Gabler* a year or so before her sensational London *debut*). *Claudia* provided her with the type of family part which possessed almost universal appeal—a nitwit young wife in the throes of early married life—and it made her a star overnight. It was a production of Ibsen's *Hedda Gabler* which drew attention to another overnight sensation, Sonia Dresdel. Having played in repertory theatres all over the country, and appeared on tour with the Old Vic Company at the beginning of the war, Miss Dresdel, armed with a new name, came to the little Mercury Theatre with no advance publicity and within a few weeks she had become a star. Directed by Dermot Cathie, this Ibsen drama drew crowds to Notting Hill Gate to witness Sonia Dresdel's brilliant Hedda. There was no question but that Miss Dresdel possessed that indefinable quality which makes a great star and (less often) a great actress. Her versatility became apparent later on when she played the gay Millament in William Congreve's *The Way Of The World*, and she soon received a number of offers to appear in the West End. But wisely Miss Dresdel decided not to leave the Mercury and she continued there for a further period while preparing to make her first West End appearance in Walter Hudd's production of *Hedda Gabler*.

The little Torch Theatre, an experimental playhouse in Knightsbridge, had already achieved a wartime success with Aimée Stuart's

Jeannie (which, with Eric Portman and Barbara Mullen, was transferred to the West End and later made into a film). It came into the limelight once more when Oxford undergraduate Peter Brook produced here an original and highly interesting version of Christopher Marlowe's *Doctor Faustus*. Brook utilised every inch of his tiny stage and his promising, though modest, production saw performances of quiet power from Leo Biek as Mephistopheles and Frederick Hurdis as Faustus. Peter Brook has since been producing interesting work at the Chanticleer and other "avant-garde" theatres (and, more recently, at Stratford-on-Avon).

American plays continued to be extremely popular in London. (One of them, *Arsenic And Old Lace*, is, indeed, still running at the time of writing). Joseph Kesselring's satirical and unusual play is the story of two benevolent and ancient ladies whose hobby is poisoning elderly and homeless men, but the dialogue is so beautifully written that no accusation of bad taste can be levelled at this comic masterpiece. Treated as a fantasy, it is enormously funny, with one wonderful character (the brother who believes himself to be Teddy Roosevelt) and with comedy acting of a high order from Lilian Braithwaite and Mary Jerrold as the two charming old poisoners. The other American importation in 1942 was *The Petrified Forest*, a Robert Sherwood drama, written some years previously, which provided the late Owen Nares with an opportunity to show how fine an actor he was. Constance Cummings, Hartley Power, Robert Beatty and Harry Ross were others in the cast who were responsible for excellent performances in a play which had many exciting moments, marred only occasionally by rather woolly liberal philosophy. It was the last worth-while play to be produced in the year 1942.

Three years had passed since war had been declared, three years of theatrical ups and down, three years of blackout in the theatre. But the English stage was beginning to find its feet, and in 1943 and 1944 the tentative gropings towards the creation of a theatre of significance, the abortive moves towards the establishment of a really great English theatre began to have something of an effect. In 1944-45 the theatre in London reached full stature. They are, indeed, important years in the history of the English theatre, and have, therefore, been dealt with in some detail. In the succeeding chapters I have examined some of the hopes, ideals, failures and successes of these three years, with the knowledge that the pattern forms the story of what has been termed "the wartime Renaissance in the English theatre."

1943

TURGHENEV, IBSEN AND SHAW

James Agate once told me a great truth ; it was this. If a
play appeals to say, 5,000 average people and also to say, 500
intellectuals, then it is a great and universal work of art. Similarly,
if a play appeals to 5,000 intellectuals and to 500 average people,
then it ranks with *Macbeth*, *Hamlet*, *The Cherry Orchard* and *Hedda
Gabler*. But if 500 intellectuals (how I hate this word) enjoy a
play which has no appeal for the average person, then it *may* be
a great art but not the art which will rank forever with universal
works of art. And, of course, there are hundreds of plays which
have an appeal for the average person and contain nothing of
interest for the highly intelligent playgoer—and there will, no
doubt, be hundreds more. There are at least a dozen of this type
always running in London and probably doing very good business.
You might well ask what I am trying to prove ! All this preamble
brings me to my point that the production of Turghenev's *A Month
In The Country* at the beginning of 1943 had, in my opinion, an
appeal limited mainly to the intelligent and enlightened playgoer.
Directed leisurely by Emlyn Williams, at the St. James Theatre,
the play dealt with the emotions and frustrations of a group of
aristocrats in a country house in the Russia of the Tsars. The
emotional entanglements of Natalia, played by Valerie Taylor,
cause anguish to four other people, and her unhappy love for the
new tutor becomes a source of pain to herself and to others. But
little sympathy can be spared for Natalia, one's pity is reserved
for her lover Rakitin, who stands aside to watch the course of
amorous events with cynical and sometimes pained detachment ;
this has always been an exceedingly difficult role. Michael
Redgrave essayed it with sensitivity ; his was a polished
performance and one which stood head and shoulders above the
others in this thoughtful and interesting comedy of manners and
morals.

In Ted Willis's play *Buster* at Unity Theatre, the scene was
laid in a London slum, and told the story of young street-corner
gangster, Buster, who, upon the impact of war, grows to a sense
of his own responsibility and ends by being awarded the George
Cross for air-raid bravery. Based on an actual real-life story of
an Islington boy, this cleverly conceived play was directed intelligently by Eric Capon and although there was a tendency to

concentrate all subtleties of characterisation upon the figure of Buster (with a consequence that the mother and the International Brigader lost a good deal of their significance) this was partially understandable when the role was in the hands of clever young Alfie Bass, youthful veteran of hundreds of Unity Theatre performances. He was magnificent and made a visit to *Buster* an evening of vital theatre.

Brighton Rock, Graham Greene's absorbing study of homicidal adolescence in pre-war Brighton, was adapted for the stage by Frank Harvey, Jr. ; and Richard Bird's production at the Garrick made it a vivid, exciting play of race-gang feuds, holiday crowds, murder and cockles in London's Coney Island. To say that the adaptation was satisfactory is not altogether true, for it is certain that to transfer into other mediums Greene's literary excursions into the recesses of the criminal mind is a difficult and complex process. Hollywood failed to do it, and although *A Gun For Sale* (the screen version of a Graham Greene novel) was a first-rate film in the same way that *Brighton Rock* was an excellent play, neither contained the true essence of those psychological subtleties which are a distinguishing mark of Greene's books. As Pinkie, the boy-murderer, Richard Attenborough was outstanding. The part was a difficult one and successfully to characterise the warped slum-brat needed insight and experience. Attenborough lacked the latter, though this was not often apparent, but with understanding and a real feeling for the role he created a hateful and pitiful wretch who dominated the stage. Racy and fast-moving, the play abounded with fascinating characters, of which Hermione Baddeley's Ida was the most lovable, the others being, for the most part, gangsters, drunks, sluts and stool-pigeons. William Hartnell was excellent as Pinkie's henchman, a really admirable study of educated inebriety was contributed by Harcourt Williams, and Dulcie Gray's pathetic waitress was a beautifully-drawn character, carefully built up by this clever young actress with skill and subtlety. Altogether this staged excursion into what Arthur Calder Marshall (in an article on Graham Greene, in " Horizon ") calls " Greene-land," constituted an admirable piece of unusual theatre.

If Greene's Pinkie possesses a complex character he resembles an open book compared with Ibsen's Hedda. In *Hedda Gabler*, which the Mercury Players presented at the Westminster, after its initial success at the Mercury Theatre, we are confronted with a woman whose envy and meanness threaten the lives and happiness of others and reduce her to introspection, morbidity and finally to suicide. Possessed of charm, beauty and intelligence, Hedda uses these only to wreck the lives of those around her. She is a woman of repellent fascination in this production, magnificently played by Sonia Dresdel, whose performance put her, at once, in the front rank of our younger actresses. Revolving around her (like moths seemingly anxious to be singed by the flame) are her husband, former lover and would-be lover, each of their lives becoming tragically shadowed through contact with her extraordinary viciousness. Elwyn Brook-Jones, an unusual and exceedingly fine Judge Brack, brought to the part a suavity, menace and tensity which has been lacking in previously witnessed productions of this most absorbing of plays. Walter Hudd produced the Norwegian classic and acted the pitiable Tesman with consummate skill. He is a most satisfying actor who rarely disappoints ; but then neither does the play. One realises again and again that Ibsen, that most brilliant of pre-Freudian playwrights, has written in *Hedda Gabler* one of the greatest psychological studies in modern drama.

George Black's new spectacle, the revue *Strike A New Note*, was bright and cheerful and contained a large proportion of youthful and exuberant talent. The youngsters included Derek Roy, Triss Henderson, Zoë Gail, Maureen Stanley, John Brandon and a host of others, but it was to the inspired comic discovery Sid Field that most of the honours went. He showed that he was a born clown, and as Slasher Green, as an inebriated dude, as a golf amateur, and in others of his extraordinary gallery, he had the audience continuously roaring at his drolleries and facilities of expression. The best things in the show were the Screen Souvenirs, in which Therese Langfield and Alec Pleon were a comic riot, and all the scenes in which Sid Field appeared. His golfing scene vied with his musical-recital sketch for honours, with the Slasher Green number in close pursuit. But in fact everything which Sid Field did was supremely funny. He was, indeed, the comic "find" of the war, and *Strike A New Note* will forever be remembered as the show which introduced this provincial favourite to London audiences.

With a cast, which included some of our leading actors, the revival of Shaw's "Tchekovian comedy" *Heartbreak House*, produced by John Burrell at the Cambridge, promised to be outstanding, but proved to be something of a disappointment. Shaw considers this to be his best play, but I most humbly beg to differ. His central character, Captain Shotover, is a magnificent old man, his lines are the most telling of the play, and Robert Donat played the octogenarian with intelligence, passion and feeling. But the other people at the house-party were an odd collection, and one found little humanity or credibility in any of them, with the possible exception of George Merrit's cynical study of the capitalist (unfortunately only *too* true to life). Edith Evans settled down to give us an entertaining Mrs. Hushabye and Isabel Jeans' beauty and charm still managed to be breath-taking, but the honours went to Deborah Kerr, who achieved the transformation from sweet innocence to cynical womanhood in an extremely intelligent fashion, considering that she had under three hours in which to effect it. Often I had the impression that I was witnessing a Marx Brothers filmic extravaganza, but as Shaw himself calls it a "fantasia," I suppose I must be satisfied that I found enjoyment in some of the grand old man's finest speeches and witty moralisings. Certainly this production saw some of the finest acting encountered on the London stage during the war.

In all, this was a most interesting period in the theatre. The demand for "good" entertainment in the fourth year of war definitely showed itself to be present, and with Shaw, Ibsen, Shakespeare, Barrie and Synge represented, there was really no dearth of drama for the connoisseur. However, there was another aspect. For the thousands of Service men and women who flocked into London in search of week-end entertainment the situation was bleak indeed. (The old ruling against the legitimate theatre operating on Sundays is as out-dated as the bustle. Public opinion is all for Sunday Opening, and M.P.'s should listen carefully to the people on this issue. Then they might, perhaps, play their part towards ensuring that, on Sundays, the British people will be able to enjoy some entertaining and educative theatre as well as certain Hollywood mediocrities).

"THEY CAME TO A CITY"
A Theatrical Revolution

At the beginning of 1943 it was a startling reminder of the lack of creative writers for our theatre when one realised that the number of overworked revivals and American importations outnumbered new British plays by more than three to one—and that of these new

British plays there were less than half-a-dozen produced in more than six months (and one was by an Irishman !).

Inevitably the question arose as to what was wrong with the English theatre, and the answer was the same as it had been for more than twenty years, and, to an extent, still is to-day. At that time I wrote the following : " The West End of London is an amusement centre ; it has no other desire but to amuse—and, of course, to make money. Thus, very few new plays or experiments are undertaken and under the present anarchy—the commercial presentation of drama—it is only to be expected that shows which made money in America (or in the last war) are more attractive to managements than untried plays by new playwrights."

"We in England have very little national culture, and certainly no National Theatre where new playwrights may be encouraged to concern themselves with the stirring events of the time, and where young people from all walks of life may be apprenticed to the profession of dramatic interpretation and creation for the amusement and edification of the majority of our people (who at present hardly go to the theatre at all). Few attempts have been made to present drama to the people ; CEMA is leading the way, with the Old Vic a close second, but this is not enough. If little Eire can support the Abbey Theatre, then surely England, centre of a huge Empire, should be able to support at least one National Theatre where new playwrights, artists and actors would be encouraged to further the progress of the drama and so enable it to take its place—as a stimulant necessity to the full cultural life of the British people?" (It must be admitted, however, that since then the situation has become a good deal brighter).

Of the new plays of 1943, *They Came To A City*, at the Globe, was possibly the most thoughtful, unusual and outstanding piece of work seen on the London stage since *Watch On The Rhine*. Priestley visualises a group of people suddenly, from nowhere, finding themselves at the gate of a strange city. The characters are assorted, splitting up into the class division of workers and non-producers, toilers and parasites—a harsh distinction, but nevertheless true to life in our ruthless twentieth century. It is inevitable that to Joe the stoker, to Alice the waitress, and to Mrs. Batley, the lovable old charwoman, this strange city with its new system, its fine buildings, its abolition of wars, its happy people and its comradely spirit is Paradise itself. To the ageing aristocrat it is all quite bewildering, to the petty-bourgeois clerk it is desirable but

31

unattainable, and to Cudworth, the self-made (and necessarily unscrupulous) business-man it is absolute anathema. Priestley ingeniously leaves much to the imagination and his dialogue is crisp, subtle and telling. Though the play is perhaps lacking the stuff of poetry, it shows a breadth of vision and a fine, poetic imagination in a playwright who does not hesitate to write drama about realities. In a cast which was generally excellent, John Clements was particularly impressive with his superbly vigorous portrait of Joe, while Googie Withers as Alice, Frances Rowe, Raymond Huntley, Ada Reeve, Norman Shelley and A. E. Mathews were all first-class in Irene Hentschel's intelligent production of a play which was revolutionary in theme, sardonically realist and certainly a much-needed breath of fresh air in Shaftesbury Avenue.

The long-awaited *Present Laughter* at the Haymarket was a back-stage story, in the familiar vein in which Noel Coward excels. The characters were the usual odd beings who hang around dressing-rooms and cocktail lounges, and the three acts were concerned with their inanities and obsequities, with special attention to their amorous activities. No playwright could devise this type of play with greater skill than Mr. Coward ; his dialogue was slick, his situations were amusing, and at least one of his characters— delightfully interpreted by James Donald—was quite fascinating. But we were offered nothing new, the plot was practically non-existent and the play, merry prank though it might be, was no more than a series of clever Coward revue sketches.

Of the brilliant Noel as the classic interpreter of the lives, hopes and philosophy of the British people I have long held certain views. *This Happy Breed*, which was presented alternately with *Present Laughter*, confirmed my opinion, which was that Mr. Coward (unlike Mr. Priestley), is completely out of his element when writing a play purporting to deal with realities. During the play one was continually being irritated by his reactionary ideas, and the fact that his working-class people possessed a maid (?) abundant whisky on the sideboard (?) and behaved generally like a set of comic revue characters did not add to the merits of this production. Mr. Coward will certainly have a permanent place in the English theatre, for he is a superbly skilful playwright. His *Hay Fever* will always be considered as a perfect comedy of manners of the 1920's, as Wilde's *Importance Of Being Earnest* is a perfect period piece of the 'nineties. Wilde, however, never attempted to write a serious play about Dublin low-life. He knew his limitations. Mr. Coward evidently does not. *This Happy Breed* showed him to be a dyed-in-the-wool reactionary, a cynical yet diabolically clever word-spinner whose working-class characters were essentially the same unreal, sentimental, stupid, long-suffering, patriotic figures which occurred in middle-class novels of a decade ago. Nevertheless both plays gave Coward an opportunity to demonstrate what a polished actor he is ; Judy Campbell enhanced her growing reputation and those clever young actors, James Donald and Billy Thatcher, were responsible for memorable moments.

At the Arts Theatre *The Old Foolishness*, by the Irish playwright Paul Vincent Carroll, was seen in London for the first time. Already enjoying a high reputation in Ireland and America, Mr. Carroll laid the foundations of a new and greater reputation in England with this play, which dealt with parochial life in a remote Irish village. His story of two brothers in love with the same girl was given unusual twist and variation, his dialogue was at times wild, powerful and lusty, at others quiet and moving. As in the best of Synge and O'Casey there is real poetry in the lines of this play-wright's dramas—and good characterisation. Michael Golden's sober young farmer was an intense and thoughtful study, Barbara Waring was excellent as the city-bred colleen, while Billy Shine was outstanding as Dan, the high-spirited, imaginative poet and rascal. His complete understanding of the role of this " real broth of a bhoy " was at once apparent ; it was indeed the finest single piece of acting seen in London for some years. Dennis Arundell's production of this intelligent new play provoked anticipatory pleasure of the long-promised West End staging of Carroll's famous *Shadow and Substance* (which in 1942 had won the New York Drama Critics' award for " The Best Foreign Play ").

One of the successes of the year (in fact one of the biggest successes of the wartime theatre) was John Gielgud's production of *Love For Love*, William Congreve's classic three-hundred-year-old comedy. It was highly diverting, every member of a distinguished cast was in excellent fettle, and all the performances were beautifully in keeping with the period in this frolic of seventeenth-century manners, modes and morals (or lack of them !). The thin plot concerns a legacy, a father and his two sons widely diverse in person and character, but most of the play's action takes place in someone else's bed. The Congreve wit is sparkling, if occasionally bawdy, and Leslie Banks, Miles Malleson, Cecil Trouncer, Max Adrian, Mr. Gielgud himself and Mesdames Yvonne Arnaud, Marian Spencer, Angela Baddeley, Rosalie Crutchley and Naomi Jacob obviously enjoyed themselves—and so did we. On reflection, one thing is certain— whatever play John Gielgud produces or appears in is always sure to be worth-while. He is indeed a great power for good in the English theatre.

John Drinkwater's *Abraham Lincoln*, revived at the Playhouse by Tyrone Guthrie, might be termed " a quiet play." In the sombre setting of the Civil War we see Lincoln at home, in the White House, at the front—we see him philosophising, we are given an insight into his kindly spirit and over all we catch glimpses of the qualities which contributed to his greatness. Much of the play's moving quality in this Old Vic staging was due to the sincere performance of Herbert Lomas as Lincoln ; while Felicity Lyster, Rosalind Atkinson, Morris Sweden, Noel Willman and Tristan Rawson all acted well in their rather nebulously-drawn roles. With Tyrone Guthrie's production I had only one quarrel. Why was the role of Frederick Douglass, the great Negro writer and lecturer, played by the white actor James Harcourt ? With his burnt-corked face and servile posturings he resembled a minstrel from a seaside concert-party rather than the highly intelligent, beautifully-spoken, proud and dignified man which history records the famous Negro leader to have been. The Negro actor, Robert Adams, would have been far more suitable as this character ; Mr. Harcourt tried hard, but was hopelessly inadequate to play the role of one of history's most distinguished coloured men.

Ashley Dukes's version of the Diderot comedy, *The Mask Of Virtue*, staged at the Mercury, is an amusing little piece about a trollop posing as a maiden of virtue in order to win a Marquis. It was a delightful and scintillating trifle and the very essence of the Gallic spirit was captured in Julian Somers' production. Renée Asherson gave a performance, as the innocent-looking harlot, which was full of grace, wit and subtlety. The part made Vivien Leigh a star in 1935 ; it provided a virtuoso role for Miss Asherson, a clever young actress, with a rare beauty. Her performance was well worth seeing in a very welcome revival.

Of the other revivals there was little that one could say. *Show Boat* was pleasant enough, the Jerome Kern melodies were still lovely, and there was some first-rate singing by Pat Taylor and Gwynneth Lascelles in the colourful show at the Stoll. *The Vagabond King* gave Webster Booth and Ann Zeigler an opportunity

★ **_Robert Donat_** and Rosamund John in Shaw's "The Devil's Disciple", produced by Milton Rosmer, 1939.

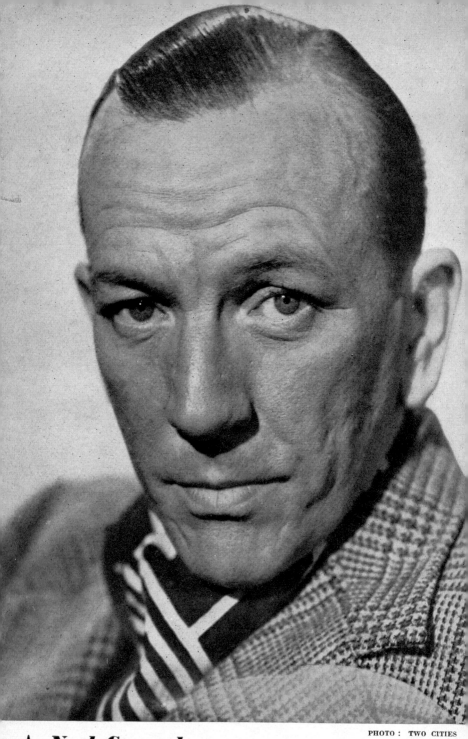

★ *Noel Coward,* whose wartime plays include "Blithe Spirit", "Present Laughter" and "This Happy Breed".

PHOTO : HOUSTON ROGERS

★ *Hermione Gingold*, as Bacchante in the revue
"Swinging The Gate", produced by Norman Marshall, 1940.

★ *Rachel Kempson* and Michael Redgrave in Gay's "The Beggar's Opera", produced by John Gielgud, 1940.

PHOTO : FRED DANIELS

★ *Eric Portman,* who appeared in Aimée Stuart's "Jeannie", produced by Irene Hentschel, 1940.

★ **_Beatrix Lehmann_** and Stephen Murray in Eugene O'Neill's "Desire Under The Elms", produced by Henry Cass, 1940.

★ *James Agate,* dean of dramatic critics, with his favourite Modigliani and his favourite brandy.

PHOTO : TUNBRIDGE-SEDGWICK

★ *Michael Redgrave* and Robert Sansom in Robert
Ardrey's "Thunder Rock", produced by Herbert Marshall,
1940.

to display their vocal talents, and remained the same swashbuckling, fairy tale (and extremely popular) entertainment. The Brieux play, *Damaged Goods*, after a successful tour, opened in the West End and lasted but ten days—which was a pity for, though not entertainment in the true sense, it deserved to be seen by all. Well acted by John Carol, Joan Greenwood and James Dale, the play however failed to attract blasé London audiences, who evidently preferred their propaganda in newspaper rather than dramatic form.

Spring of 1943 was notable for the production in the West End of Priestley's new play and for an opportunity to revaluate Noel Coward's position among British playwrights. It was at least obvious that if only we could discover and encourage a dozen young writers for the theatre, who possessed new ideas, sincerity, political consciousness and a social conscience coupled with but a *third* of Noel Coward's dexterity, feeling for dialogue and technical skill then the future of the English theatre might be assured.

REALISM IN THE THEATRE

The question which seemed to arise continually in the wartime theatre was the oft-repeated " Escapism or realism—which shall it be ? " During the First World War the trend was towards the former—farces, revues, leg-shows and gay comedies were the order of the day—and at the beginning of the recent conflict, after the theatre had recovered from the first impact of war, a similar trend became apparent. This however very gradually gave way, in part, to a more intelligent type of entertainment, and with the formation of new theatre companies under the auspices of CEMA, added to the grand work which was being done by the Old Vic, Unity, Mercury and the Arts (not forgetting H. M. Tennent Ltd.) the situation for the discerning theatregoer became a good deal brighter. Naturally the escapist shows—and some of them were really very good indeed—outnumbered the realist and serious dramas, but the fact was inescapable that, in the summer of 1943, at least a section of the English theatre was holding up a mirror to realities. Encouraging indeed were the attempts of some producers and playwrights to show us real life on our stages, as opposed to the dream-world which we had been accustomed to witnessing during that turbulent period between two wars. The signs of a new trend were apparent in the productions of such new plays as *The Russians*, *The Moon Is Down* and *Living Room*.

At the Playhouse the Old Vic Company was seen in Konstantin Simonov's documentary piece, *The Russians*. Dealing with a section of the Eastern front where the Nazis were occupying a Soviet town, this was stirring drama of the highest order. As the leader of the guerillas, constantly harrying the German troops, Michael Golden gave a first-rate, powerful performance. Here were thrills, realism and excitement, while the acting generally was on a high level— Freda Jackson's Valya was a superb piece of character-drawing, David Carr gave a thoughtful performance as the poet-turned-soldier, while Olga Lindo, Franklyn Dyall and Frederick Horrey were all responsible for moments of rare excitement. They formed part of the pattern which made *The Russians* outstanding theatre.

John Steinbeck's dramatisation of his novel, *The Moon Is Down*, came to the Whitehall with Lewis Casson, Karel Stepanek and Carla Lehmann in the principal roles. It was an intelligent reconstruction of what might happen in any town occupied by the Nazis, distinguished by Steinbeck's careful and realistic drawing of some of the German characters. That many of these Nazis were not themselves fanatical believers in the Hitler terror regime was something which the author credibly illustrated and his classic phrase, " The flies have conquered the flypaper," echoed by Alan Haines as a young Nazi who searches for kindness among the conquered people, was an indication of his beliefs. Was this wishful thinking ? At any rate this dramatisation of Steinbeck's famous novel, given a moving and interesting production by Basil C. Langton, was credibly and restrainedly acted by Karel Stepanek as the Commandant, Lewis Casson as the Mayor, Carla Lehmann and Julian d'Albie.

That entertainment in the strict sense may be derived from a play which is concerned with slums, unemployment, depressed areas, landlordism and condemned property was ably demonstrated in Esther McCracken's play *Living Room* at the Garrick. We view the situation through the eyes of two elderly ladies who own condemned slum property ; when they see their livelihood slipping away, their distress is tempered by their new-found knowledge that the whole system is a vicious circle, of which they are merely a part. The play abounds with thoughtful dialogue and the acting of Louise Hampton and Nellie Bowman, as the two spinsters, was quietly touching. It was, perhaps, not surprising that the author of *Quiet Week-end* could write powerful realist drama like *Living Room*, for before Miss McCracken made a big success with *Quiet Wedding*, she wrote a number of one-act plays, expressing distinct Left-wing sympathies. Living as she had done in that ugly industrial town Newcastle, Esther McCracken had much opportunity to realise the immense social inequalities which existed in our " civilisation." *Living Room* was based on actual cases she had met with in the North, and the characters and central situation were all drawn from real life. This was one of the main reasons for the play's sincerity and refreshing reality. It had a message which Miss McCracken was evidently not afraid to put across the footlights, a message of hope for the underdogs of all countries, a message that the long war would assuredly put a stop to social injustice at home as well as abroad.

At the Ambassadors one of the most welcome events of the season was the return to town of Hermione Gingold and Walter Crisham in the funniest, slickest and cleverest revue since 1941's *Rise Above It* (or in fact since *Buzz Buzz*). Along with the incomparable Crisham and Gingold in *Sweet And Low* was a company of talented youngsters, including Bonar Colleano, Ilena Sylva, Richard Curnock and Brenda Bruce, who all obviously enjoyed themselves hugely in the superbly witty songs and sketches. To choose between Gingold as Brunhilde, as Lilian Braithwaite or as Lucretia Borgia, and Crisham masquerading madly as Valerie Taylor, an American soldier soliloquising before Lincoln's statue, or as a lonely mariner in the crow's nest, was something which I left to other critics. I regarded them as the perfect pair—she the Gilbert to his Sullivan, the Stanley to his Livingstone; together they were sheer bliss. Indeed, they soon became a wartime theatrical institution—their sketch " Poison Ivy " by Denis Waldock being the high-light in an intimate revue *par excellence*.

Henrik Ibsen continued to draw crowds to the Duke of York's Theatre, where Norman Ginsbury's excellent adaptation of *Ghosts* was beautifully acted, especially by Beatrix Lehmann as Mrs. Alving. Like most of Ibsen's women characters, she is extremely complex, but Miss Lehmann succeeded in giving us one of the finest Mrs. Alvings seen in London for many years, an intelligent and moving portrayal of one of modern drama's most interesting figures. She brought a vigour and a nervous energy to the part which made her performance invigorating to watch. As her son John Carol was good and their tense final scene was brilliantly acted and produced. An amusing study of that old rascal Engstrand was contributed by Harry Herbert in Dennis Arundell's production, which deserved to be widely seen. Following the short London season, *Ghosts* went on a tour of the ENSA Garrison Theatres and was an immediate success, proving once again (if proof be needed) that the troops appreciated good drama when they were given an opportunity to see it.

The most eagerly-awaited event of the season, to many London theatregoers, was the return of musical comedy idol Jack Buchanan. He certainly took no chances on the vehicle which served to re-introduce him to the West End, for *It's Time To Dance* at the Winter Garden Theatre was grand musical entertainment, and quite good of its kind. The story, never very important in musical comedy, was something about Jack being mistaken for " The Tiger," an international crook and gigolo. However, the tall, urbane, smiling, good-natured Buchanan succeeded, as all musical comedy heroes do, in rounding up the gang, with the aid of delicious Fred Emney, and, of course, the happy ending, with Jack and Elsie Randolph united, was pleasurably inevitable. Here were grand music and lyrics, the cleverest quips of any show in town, a vigorous performance by Marjorie Brooks and dancing in the superb manner by Buddy Bradley who, accompanied occasionally by Jack Buchanan himself, gave us supreme rhythmic choreography.

It was a far cry from this gay entertainment to the Vaudeville, where Enid Bagnold's complex creation *Lottie Dundass* held sway. Here was no fun and laughter, but madness and murder in a most unusual and gripping play. Lottie, daughter of a homicidal maniac and grand-daughter of a famous actor, derives inherent madness from the one and histrionic ability from the other. Is she a great actress or merely a gifted amateur? This we are never allowed to know, for after one grand farewell performance Lottie dies in her mother's arms. That this initial stage appearance was made possible by the fact that Lottie has murdered the under-study to prevent her going on instead, is perhaps a degree incredible, except that Miss Bagnold's carefully-created character, full of nervous tension and inhibition, is so fascinating as to command belief. Ann Todd's powerful and praiseworthy study as Lottie was no less than brilliant. With this one performance (following upon her success as " Peter Pan " a year before) she entered the front-rank of our worth-while dramatic actresses. Sybil Thorndike as the mother was quietly first-rate, that charming and intelligent young actress Renée Asherson as Lottie's friend was excellent and restrained, while Bruce Winston's little gem as the producer provided a constant delight in this well-acted play written on an out-of-the-ordinary theme.

A number of interesting shows came and went during the early part of the summer of 1943. A tasteful production of Paul Vincent Carroll's *Shadow and Substance* at the Duke of York's, was distinguished by a virtuoso performance from Joyce Redman, but inexplicably the public stayed away from Carroll's masterpiece, which had been a great success in New York a year or so before. Was it because the theme was concerned with the ramifications of Catholicism? Or was it due wholly to the lukewarm reception of the critics? Perhaps it was the wrong time for the London production of a sad and serious religious play? At any rate *Shadow and Substance* deserves a revival, and it is at least certain that it will still continue to be produced in this country twenty years or more from now.

LITTLE THEATRES IN LONDON

In Britain to-day, and especially in London, there are a number of Little Theatres, which are often the meeting ground of amateur and professional actors, bridging a gap which has long been far too wide. Little Theatres, variously called " experimental theatres " or " art theatres," were at first the result of our system of dramatic censorship. In order to circumvent the ban placed on some of the works of Shaw, Brieux and Ibsen in the late nineteenth century, Little Theatres succeeded in giving performances of many such plays to private audiences, forming their own membership theatre clubs for the purpose. But it is in the past few years that these theatres have come out into the open and have been prominent in exerting an influence towards raising the standard of present-day drama ; several plays, later praised universally for their quality, having first been seen in these experimental playhouses.

Just before the outbreak of war the British Drama League was responsible for an encouraging innovation—the formation of a Little Theatre Group—with a committee including Norman Marshall of the Gate Theatre, and Alfred Emmett and Herbert Marshall, two stalwarts of the Little Theatre movement. The British Drama League defines a Little Theatre as " an approved organisation which has for its main purpose the public or private presentation of stage-plays in a theatre of small capacity, or other building owned or leased for the staging of plays." It is heartening to note that no distinction is drawn between amateur and professional theatre groups. Many intelligent professional actors, tired of the conventional West End stage, have taken refuge for a period in a Little

Theatre, where they have often been able to give their best performances under conditions of artistic freedom, not always obtainable in the commercial theatre.

For the point is that the pursuit of profits is not the main object of these groups. They continually endeavour to produce intelligent and worth-while entertainment, new and original plays, using revolutionary ideas of production and presentation. They are not afraid to experiment, the box-office is not their main guide ; and their new ideas have been responsible for the production of much fine drama, as well as interesting innovations in direction and technique. Over forty groups were affiliated to the British Drama League Little Theatre Group in 1939, although the war caused this number to dwindle considerably. However, they still exist in most of the provincial cities and still functioning are the Unnamed Society and the Theatre Union in Manchester, the Middlesbrough Little Theatre, Bradford Civic, Newcastle People's Theatre, Leeds Civic Theatre and Glasgow Unity Theatre, while there are over a dozen in London alone. In the capital, however, the air raids put several Little Theatres out of action (casualties have included the Neighbourhood, Torch, Threshold, Embassy and Gate), but there are several still carrying on. Many of these groups are able, by forming theatre clubs, to give private performances of unlicensed plays and in this way some of the masterpieces of O'Neill, Ibsen and Odets, as well as many new plays by American and Continental playwrights, have been seen in London.

During the war the English theatre was oft-times concerning itself with musical shows, last-war revivals, farces and " non-stop revues." This situation made the existence of these tiny out-of-the-way theatres all the more refreshing, for their plays, staging and acting are infused with a genuine love of the serious theatre. For example, Unity Theatre has in the past few years continued to reflect the lives and conditions of the people on its stages, and has presented excellent productions of realist dramas by Gorky, Afinogenov and Odets, as well as original works by Sean O'Casey, Geoffrey Parsons, Ted Willis and other new dramatists. The Mercury, Q Theatre and Torch have all continued their function of presenting new and classic plays—the Mercury with an admirable season of repertory, including Ibsen and Congreve, the Q with several interesting new productions, and the Torch with plays by such playwrights as Walter Greenwood and Shaw Desmond as well as drama by new writers. Alfred Emmett's gallant little Questors Theatre, an amateur group, kept open uninterruptedly during the war with stagings of the works of Goldsmith, Synge, Thornton Wilder, Ostrovsky, Hsiung and Sudermann, as well as a number of new plays, an original revue and two festivals of one-act plays— an excellent record.

A most encouraging sign was the formation of a number of new Little Theatres during the war. At a period when the commercial theatre was in a state of flux, these vital groups began to make an appearance in the provinces and in London. Herbert Marshall's Neighbourhood Theatre opened auspiciously with his brilliantly-directed *Thunder Rock*, followed by new plays by Norman Ginsbury and Winifred Holtby and it was a great blow for intelligent theatregoers when it was " blitzed." The Threshold, opened by a group of enthusiastic youngsters, led by Elwyn Brook-Jones and Peter Ustinov, delighted theatregoers with out-of-the-ordinary productions of Odets, Cocteau, Sutro, Schnitzler and Sarment before it too suffered air-raid damage. And the Arts Theatre Group of Actors, a co-operative venture under Alec Clunes' direction, soon came to share with Unity and the Mercury the distinction of being the spearhead of the " *avant-garde* theatre movement."

In Hampstead two unique Little Theatres opened soon after the outbreak of war—the Lantern and the Free German Theatre. Both are groups of refugee actors ; the Lantern, directed for a long period by Martin Miller, produces plays and revues in English and German, while the Free German Theatre throughout the war presented a number of scintillating and witty cabarets and revues in the traditions of the Continental cabaret theatres.

Although the Workers' Circle Theatre was bombed out, the East End still has two Little Theatres which offer original theatre-fare. The Jewish Theatre, at the Grand Palais, and later, Folk House, gives performances of classic plays in Yiddish, along the lines of the Maurice Schwarz Group and the Habima Players, and here has been seen some of the best acting in London, while Toynbee Hall Theatre has, in the past few years, staged several one-act play festivals as well as the first English production of the American Living Newspaper, *One Third Of A Nation*, and André Obey's *Noah*, among other good things.

It must be conceded that the Little Theatre Movement played its part in the wartime theatrical revival ; its growth is another encouraging indication that the great traditions of our national drama are being carried forward in these turbulent times. At a period when the purely commercial stage has often eschewed novelty and originality, these Little Theatres have pointed the way to the time (not so far distant, we hope) when drama will be accorded the importance it deserves, and take its rightful place in the cultural life of the people.

A FEAST OF ENGLISH COMEDY

That sensible and most respectable character, Johnny Tarleton, in Shaw's *Misalliance*, gives vent to an opinion held by many when he says " I want to forget. If I buy a book or go to the theatre I want to forget the shop and forget myself from the moment I go in to the moment I come out." In respect of the cinema I am inclined to believe that the majority of filmgoers *do* go to see films in order to forget, in order to get away from things for a brief moment, to forget life's realities and cruelties. But is this true of the theatregoer ? I respectfully submit that, in the main, the wartime theatregoer was not so much concerned with forgetting the outside world as in enjoying the play (which is not always the same thing), being stimulated by the ideas expressed, being amused by the wit of the dialogue, enthralled at the play's message or held in admiration by the acting. There is a difference, for example, in forgetting oneself at an Abbott and Costello trifle and forgetting oneself at a performance of, say, *The Rivals*. The one is dismissed from one's mind immediately, the other provides reminiscence at witty lines, food for thought, admiration for classic construction as well as continual intellectual stimulation long after the performance is over. Yet both are comedies, as were all the plays in the admirable Festival of English Comedy staged at the Arts Theatre in the summer of 1943. With the exception of *The Watched Pot* all the plays were well-known comedy classics, but it is safe to say that all five were worth seeing over and over again for they were not merely humorously escapist—they were plays which provided a stimulant and a tonic amidst much of the artistic mediocrity in Shaftesbury Avenue.

The Constant Couple, George Farquhar's merry and bawdy piece, was the first offering in what proved to be an altogether delightful season. *Love For Love* had already whetted London's appetite for Restoration Comedy, and Alec Clunes' shrewd production lacked none of the former's wit and exquisite staging. That Farquhar's comedy had had no revival for nearly one hundred and fifty years was somewhat surprising, for those extraordinarily fascinating characters Wildair, Smuggler, Vizard and Clincher, deserved better than this scurrilous treatment. Avice Landone as Lurewell, "that woman who is all women," acted with a wit and vitality which was refreshing, while gaily outwitting her was the charming and boisterous Wildair, swashbuckling and likeable rogue, an acting triumph for Alec Clunes, the director of the Festival. He was gloriously and impudently magnificent. *The Constant Couple* was further distinguished by the clever performances of Billy Shine, David Bird, Dorothy Primrose and Derek Birch.

From Restoration Comedy it was a long step to Sheridan's *The Rivals*, for here is no illicit love, philandering and dishonouring. In this Eighteenth Century comedy all the couples are truly constant, all love is really true, and though it does not always run smooth, through subterfuge and masquerade and even a duel to the death, love finds a way in the end. We were introduced once more to that eminent monster Mrs. Malaprop, in whom Avice Landone presented a highly diverting, though perhaps excessively formidable figure and to David Bird's glorious Sir Anthony Absolute of irascible nature and roving eye. When our interest in the romances of the young couples began to flag there was always that completely satisfying actor Denys Blakelock to keep the fun fast and furious with his intelligent and hilarious portrayal of the delightful Bob Acres.

But it was Pinero's mid-Victorian farce, *The Magistrate*, which brought Denys Blakelock to the fore, and deservedly so, for his Mr. Posket, magistrate at Mulberry Street Police Court, was a superb characterisation. Possessed on the one side with a conscience, which to any member of the Bench would be a constant embarrassment, and on the other with a nineteen year-old stepson posing as fourteen (to conceal the real age of the magistrate's second wife) the poor man floundered unhappily in and out of trouble, bringing upon himself the final ignominy of sentencing his own wife to fourteen days' imprisonment! Led into the illicit pleasures of gambling and midnight suppers at hotels by his precocious and provoking son, comically played by Harold Lang, Blakelock made of the bewildered Posket a tremendously funny figure in a comedy which abounded with laughter-provoking types. The two "stout fellahs" of Billy Shine and David Bird brought a priceless air of "Poonah and tiffin" to the scene, while in this Victorian gallery of humour the rascally retainer of Robert Marsden and the jube-jube sucking Mr. Bullamy of Derek Birch were highly entertaining period-pieces.

Having its first London production in this Festival was the Edwardian comedy of manners *The Watched Pot* by H. H. Munro and Charles Maude. Dealing with the efforts of a group of young ladies in a country house to marry off one of their number to the eligible Trevor, the play had obvious resemblances to Wilde, markedly so in its use of so many witty Wildean-like epigrams. Though consistently amusing, it just failed to reach the high standard set by the other plays in the season, but, nevertheless, it deserved to have had earlier productions than this one, which contained a piquant performance by Richard Goolden as Ludovic Bavvel and a grand comic rendering by Avice Landone, as a red-haired widow with persistent matrimonial intentions. That anyone should want to marry Trevor at all was a mystery to me for he seemed a singularly uninteresting young man whose eventual choice of a mate reflected his lack of enterprise. As his mother, Susan Richards, gave a terrifying study of a prudish Edwardian gorgon, while the chief object of her disapproval, beautifully played by Denys Blakelock, was a delicious and diverting character. Blithely and unwittingly Blakelock stole every scene in which he appeared, and he proved once more that he was always a valuable acquisition to this company. One remembers with extreme pleasure the many polished performances given by this unassuming and excellent young actor ; and easily recalls his beautiful light comedy touch in *No Time For Comedy* at the Haymarket in 1941. But it is true to say that Mr. Blakelock carved for himself at the Arts a niche in the affections of discerning theatregoers merely on his work in this Festival of Comedy. Certainly one may submit with safety that Denys Blakelock still remains among the leading comic actors in England to-day.

No festival of English comedy would have been complete without representation from that grand old master Shaw. His *Misalliance* brought us to comparatively modern times, for though it had been written thirty years before, it was delightfully fresh and up-to-date and, in fact, it was a good deal wittier and more thought-provoking than most modern plays. Again the scene was a country house, this time the misalliance was the marriage planned between Hypatia, played by Ruth Buchanan, and spoiled brat Bentley, admirably acted by Harold Lang. To upset all plans there arrived upon the scene a couple of flyers whose plane has crashed into the greenhouse, while the advent of a young Cockney intent upon assassinating the master of the house complicated matters still further. The resultant confusion was delightful, but what followed was of the purest gold—the female acrobat played by Magda Kun, Lord Summerhays in the person of Billy Shine and Tarleton and his son (David Bird and Robert Marsden) discussed in a provocative manner marriage and morals, parents and children, sex and education for almost two hours. That the whole thing was highly entertaining is praise indeed for Alec Clunes' intelligent and witty direction and the really excellent acting of the above (plus Peter Jones, who as the Cockney socialist, was quite brilliant in the best part he had had in the Festival).

The theatregoing public had very little chance to form an opinion about Peter Ustinov's short-lived *Blow Your Own Trumpet*, which Michael Redgrave produced for the Old Vic at the Playhouse. The obviously first-rate talent which Ustinov had displayed in his Arts Theatre success, *House Of Regrets*, caused most of the critics to express astonishment that this time the young man had failed to write a masterpiece comparable with Shaw or Ibsen. Actually the play had a good deal to say for itself (though it was, perhaps, a shade *too* verbose) and it deserved better treatment from the critics. Ustinov assembled a group of frustrated characters in an Italian café and for two acts allowed them to discuss their inhibitions in public. That these people were, in the main, conventional " frustrated types " and that the expounded philosophies were vacillatory and unimpressive, probably accounted for the play's luke-warm reception. Actually it had one brilliantly original character (played magnificently by Elwyn Brook-Jones) and some extremely interesting dialogue, and though it failed to move, even as a static play, it was an intelligent piece of theatre, commanding more attention than a great many of the plays at that time on view in London.

The failure of Tolstoy's *War And Peace*, at the Phœnix, to achieve a success with West End audiences was even more inexplicable. It was a brave experiment. The intricate plot with its many scenes provided a play which was a little top-heavy, and on the whole, lacking in emotion, but the grandeur of its theme, the superb production by Julius Gellner, the acting of Frederick Valk, David Dawson and Peter Illing, and above all, the highly original settings and designs by Hein Heckroth—all these surely deserved better treatment than a run lasting less than a month? It proved at any rate that to experiment on the English stage is a most costly affair and will continue to be the prerogative of brave individuals with a progressive and far-seeing policy.

CONTINENTAL THEATRES

Largely because of the situation in Europe during the past ten years, London has become one of the most cosmopolitan of cities ; actors, musicians and writers have come here from all parts of the Continent to escape the dictatorship which means death to all free art and thought. Many of them have eked out a living for a time by doing menial jobs, but their overwhelming desire has been to take up the threads of their broken careers, and in the end they have shown the vitality of their art by transplanting it into some corner of London.

The Foreign Theatre has now become part of the London scene. During the last few years the capital has certainly developed towards becoming the most international city in the world, and the cream of European culture now finds a home in England with a consequent raising of our general artistic and cultural standards. Wherever a group of Czechs, Austrians, French or Dutch meet there will be found a theatre. Most of these Little Theatres are situated in Hampstead, but in Commercial Road, in London's East End, there exists a Yiddish theatre of the sort which one finds in many Continental towns.

Here nightly are seen comedies, dramas and great classic plays performed before a faithful and regular audience which comes from all parts of London to enjoy the acting of Mark Markov and his Yiddish Players. Markov came to England a few years ago with the famous Maurice Schwarz Company, but when Schwarz left for America, Markov with his wife and leading lady Etta Topel, stayed in London, took over a little East End theatre and both have produced and acted every week since then. The plays vary from week to week. Naturally, Jewish playwrights are most popular with audiences and the plays of Sholem Asch, Richter, Freimann, Peretz and Sholem Alekheim are performed regularly. As a contrast to *The Dybbuk* and *The Golem*, gay modern comedies, some written by members of the group, receive a try-out at this London Yiddish theatre—an example being *The King Of Lampedusa*. The acting is expressive, only a very sketchy knowledge of the language is necessary for one to understand the plays, and the general atmosphere of good-humour among what is probably the most remarkable theatre audience in town, makes a visit to this out-of-the-way playhouse a memorable experience. There is literally nothing else like it in England.

In Hampstead are several Refugee theatres, the most important among them being the Lantern, the Free German, and the Blue Danube. The Czech Theatre has its headquarters at the By Candlelight Club in Maida Vale, while the Free French Theatre (or Théatre Molière as it is called) gives performances on Sundays at various West End theatres. In 1939 a group of Austrian exiles, formerly actors and writers from the Viennese stage, introduced into this country the first " Kleinkunstbeuhne "—" small art stages "—a form of Little Theatre well-known in their native Austria. Their first theatre, at Westbourne Grove, attracted a good deal of attention, so much so that they obtained larger premises and at present are installed in a miniature theatre at Eton Avenue, where plays and satirical revues are performed before a cosmopolitan audience. Called The Lantern, it still shines as brightly as it did in 1939, and is a beacon which attracts all lovers of freedom, as well as theatre-lovers. The actors, obviously, enjoy their work and this enjoyment communicates itself to the audience. Performing with very few props and little scenery, the actors achieve the most breath-taking effects, and though the theatre is small, the shows are first-rate. They have produced a sparkling version of *The Beggar's Opera*, by Bert Brecht, plays by Curt Goetz, Ashley Dukes and Kurt Weill, and the Jaroslav Hasek comedy *The Good Soldier Schweik* among others.

The most recently successful of all the Continental theatres is the Théatre Molière. Since 1940 a great many French actors and actresses have been living and working over here in the Embassy and in other Free French organisations. Over a period of years more than two hundred and fifty performances have been given by them, chiefly in camps, in schools and for various cultural circles, but only in 1943 was it decided to organise regular theatrical productions in French. All the players have been devoting their special gifts to propaganda, more especially to broadcasting. Now they want to do more and this Free French Theatre has been formed to occupy that important place in Anglo-French relations which is so necessary now in the difficult post-war period.

The finest works in French drama are seen on its stages and already they have produced, at their own French Institute Theatre, the plays of Molière, Merimée, Bernard and others. London's considerable French colony is thus able to enjoy productions in the Gallic tongue and this group is rapidly becoming one of London's most interesting theatre ventures. The leading light of the scheme is genial Paul Bonifas (who scored a West End stage success in the play *Men In Shadow*). He has gathered around him a talented company, including Suzie Marquis, Georges Rex, Gyliane Balmaceda, Paul Clarus, Elma Soiron, Rene Poirier and other favourites of the Paris stage. (Many have since returned to France).

In 1943 the well-known painter Kokoschka opened a new and enlarged stage for the Free German Theatre. This talented and enthusiastic group of anti-Nazis acts in political and topical revues, while their celebrated International Cabaret is worth going a long way to see. One of their most successful productions was a political revue, *Gulliver Goes To School*, by Egon Larsen and Frederick Gottfurt, with music by Allan Gray (who composed the score for the Pressburger-Powell film, *The Life And Death Of Colonel Blimp*). Played in a piquant mixture of German and English, all the revues are easy to follow, for the art of these brilliant people is universal. Anne Marie Hase, a famous Berlin cabaret star, can hold an audience of any nationality in her spell, while Ellen Mosner, a clever young actress, Agnes Bernelle, Charlotte Keuter and Gerard Kempinski are others whose work in these " Freie Deutsche Kulter Bund " shows is inimitable.

And that is the word which describes all these Continental theatres—inimitable. Apart from the language differences, there is something entirely unique in the manner in which the plays and shows are presented. The actors have new and exciting styles, the technique is interesting and different, the atmosphere, both off-stage and on, is one of friendliness and comradeship and the gallantry of spirit which distinguishes the members of these groups is something to be marvelled at. Most of the actors, although big names in their own countries, came over to England completely unknown. Theirs has been a hard fight, not only to resume their profession, but to take up work of any kind. Dozens of talented Continental actors have had to take jobs washing dishes, scrubbing floors, waiting at tables and doing menial tasks of all descriptions, while awaiting their chance to do the work they love. And now, after some years in this country, a few of them are at last receiving the recognition which they deserve, not only in these Little Theatres, but also on the West End stage.

In the cast of *Arsenic and Old Lace* at the Strand Theatre was Martin Miller, who for some years acted at the Lantern, as did Tatiana Lieven, who has appeared in *Idiot's Delight* and *Jeannie*, among others. Other Austrian actors regularly appearing on our commercial stage include Gerard Hinze, Frederick Richter, Amy

Frank, Albert Lieven, Anton Walbrook, Irene Eisinger, Maria Elsner, Lilli Palmer and Irene Prador. From the Free German Theatre have come Lilly Kann, Ferdi Mayne, Gerard Kempinski, Agnes Bernelle, Paul Demel and Charles Goldner. And other Continental actors and actresses and producers who have become a part of the London theatrical scene include Alice Gachet, Herbert Lom, Frederick Valk, Sybilla Binder, Marcella Salzer, Josef Almas, Julius Gellner, Karel Stepanek, Carl Jaffé and Wanda Rotha.

They are new personalities, with new ideas, new talents, new blood for the English stage. Their contribution to our theatre is something for which we must thank London's little foreign theatres.

THE CRITIC AND THE THEATRE

The controversy conducted in the columns of the " New Statesman " by Michael Redgrave, Beatrix Lehmann and J. B. Priestley, in the summer of 1943, caused a good deal of comment in the theatre. Some people considered that Redgrave had been ill-advised to address his argument to the critics at a time when his most recent production, *The Wingless Victory*, had yet to be seen by them. This was, I feel, taking rather a poor view of the critics who, on the whole and in spite of past differences, are usually prepared to bestow praise upon a new production irrespective of who is connected with it. That *The Wingless Victory* did not run, as a result of the quality of the notices, was due largely to the fact that most of the critics were, it seemed, irritated not so much by the fact that a Malayan princess could speak intelligently and poetically but by the fact that Maxwell Anderson's language was too high-flown, pretentious, and in fact quite unpoetical. A celebrated dramatic critic went so far as to devote as much space to an ill-tempered attack upon one of America's leading dramatists as he had on a previous Sunday devoted to an eulogy of a witless piece of musical comedy nonsense which he had been pleased to call " a charming musical " ! Surely, after this, the theatregoer might well ask whom he is to believe in these matters ?

The true value of the dramatic critic in England has always been difficult to assess. Except in a very few cases, most of our theatre critics have long decided to take the line of least resistance and to treat the theatre as entertainment only. With this decision I am in part agreement—but I should add that it is surely possible to view a play through an additional angle or two. The theatre should be an integral part of the cultural life of a people ; not only should it be regarded as an entertainment, but also as a contribution to literature, society, art. The fact that a play can function as both cultural *and* entertaining apparently escapes some critics. So easy is it for most of them to put the play into pigeonholes, variously labelled " light entertainment," " dull and uplifting," " good, but slow " or " not for the theatregoer in search of entertainment." But sometimes a play is (all too rarely, I am afraid) both an entertainment and a lasting work of art (as, for example, such different works as *The Cherry Orchard* and, to take a more modern play, *Watch On The Rhine*). Then it becomes a good play, and often a great play, a valuable asset in the movement towards a better appreciation and understanding of our national heritage of drama. This then is the criterion upon which the present writer bases a judgment—does the play move you, does it entertain, does it make you think ?

As Priestley remarked, an earnest out-of-the-ordinary production is rarely praised, for the critics are usually a little afraid of it. Few of them possess any basic ideas about the theatre as a genuine art and as an enduring institution. They have no fundamental desire to witness new experiments or to experience any changes in theatrical or dramatic technique (no theatrical manager dares to produce the plays of William Saroyan over here, for fear of the critical reception). Many of them neither know, nor do they care, about the art of the drama—they function merely as weathercocks for managerial opinion, since it is at least certain that no theatrical management will ever be encouraged to attempt something new or original when to do so is to incur the cool reception of the critics, whose judgments undoubtedly affect that great amorphous body, the theatre-going public. Is the critic to be a buffer between play and public, a mirror or a magnifying glass, an intelligent interpreter or a literary buffoon ? What is his function to-day ? And should he himself be subjected to criticism ? Certainly anyone who doubts that he should must read Sean O'Casey's comments on our dramatic critics in his admirable and hard-hitting book on the English theatre, " The Flying Wasp." Have we at present half-a-dozen dramatic critics in this country who are worthy to follow in the footsteps of Walkeley, Beerbohm, Montague, Shaw ? I think not. At any rate I, never having been on the side of the angels, am invariably finding myself on the side of the rebels. I say then, " more power to the pens of Michael Redgrave, J. B. Priestley, Beatrix Lehmann and any others who have the courage to strike back and to speak up for themselves and for our theatre. It will, in any case, be all the better for healthy argument and any resultant change."

As for the Maxwell Anderson play, *The Wingless Victory* (the cause of the controversy) which had a short-lived run at the Phœnix, I must confess that I found it interesting, thoughtful and certainly deserving of better treatment than that which was accorded it by critics and public. It dealt with the colour-problem (surely as urgent to-day as it was in Salem in 1800 ?) and was concerned with the effect upon a New England town of the home-coming of a young sea captain with his Malayan wife and child. Inevitably the result was tragedy and the play ends with the Malayan girl killing both herself and her child in order to escape from the puritanical tyranny of the narrow-minded bigots who had succeeded in turning her husband's love to doubt. As the princess, Wanda Rotha gave a most moving performance, while André van Gyseghem was unobtrusively excellent as the puritan cleric. Michael Redgrave's production was admirable, the play was full of beauty and glowing with a message to humanity, but *The Wingless Victory* sailed in and out of the Phœnix Theatre without causing a ripple to disturb the West End's smug equanimity.

Considering the above, it seemed therefore inevitable that Mr. Jack Hulbert and Miss Cicely Courtneidge should receive from the critics a deluge of praise, a veritable tidal-wave of enthusiasm for their joint efforts in their new musical comedy *Something In The Air* at the Palace. Actually this piece was often quite funny, largely due to the inspired work of Miss Courtneidge, who is an accomplished artist. And of course Jack Hulbert was as jocularly Hulbertian as usual, while Jean Gillie, Ronald Shiner and Gabriel Brune each took full opportunity when the chance to shine presented itself.

At the Savoy, Firth Shephard continued his triumphal policy of enabling Londoners to see New York stage successes, by presenting the riotous *My Sister Eileen* by Joseph Fields and Jerome Chodorov. Adapted from Ruth McKenney's popular series of stories in that incomparable weekly, " The New Yorker," the play revealed itself as a swift satire on New York's Bohemian quarter. To a basement apartment in Greenwich Village come Ruth and Eileen, fresh from the country. In New York they meet a succession of men, all would-be Lotharios intent upon wooing the fair (though distinctly fluffy) Eileen. Providentially the plain but clever sister, Ruth, steers a hazardous passage through a mass of reporters, prizefighters, amorous landlords and Brazilian cadets to the fairly inevitable happy ending. It was all great fun, the staging was slick, swift and altogether excellent, and each curtain rang down to a roar of laughter. As the sisters, Coral Browne and Sally Gray were quite perfect, while grand comic performances came from Max Bacon, Harry Ross, Virginia Winter and Charles Farrell. *My Sister Eileen* was a fast-moving comedy, grand satirical stuff, full of laughs, hard-boiled humour, distinctly American, but with a wide appeal.

A new play by James Bridie is always an eagerly-awaited theatrical event and his *Mr. Bolfry* at the Playhouse was an atonement for those playgoers who had perhaps been disappointed in his *Holy Isle* at the Arts a few months previously. The latter did not quite " come off " but *Mr. Bolfry* most certainly did. It is concerned with a Calvinist minister, suddenly confronted with a large and extremely real Devil, conjured up by his atheistic niece and a young soldier billettee. Faced with One against whom he has preached for so many years, the minister begins a battle of wits which carries us along joyously for an hour before it ends finally in the defeat of Evil. An intelligently-written and well-constructed fantasia, *Mr. Bolfry* is excellent theatre. Bridie's dialogue is sheer delight and in this production the acting of Alastair Sim as the minister was equalled only by the suave demoniacal charm of the Devil, beautifully acted by Raymond Lovell (afterwards Walter Fitzgerald). But then all the acting here was on a high level, Sophie Stewart and Alfie Bass being particularly excellent in a new play which deserved the high praise it received, for it had something to say, and said it intelligently and amusingly. This was an example of Bridie at the top of his form.

To the Westminster for a short season came a worthy production of Tchekov's *Uncle Vanya*, acted by Norman Marshall's excellent new company. Quiet, moving and interesting, the Russian classic was extremely well acted by Harold Scott, Vivienne Bennett and Frith Banbury. Under the auspices of CEMA, that intelligent director Norman Marshall had formed his own company, with headquarters at the Cambridge Arts Theatre. The object of this group was to produce worth-while plays, both new and classic, and it had been doing excellent work touring the Northern cities. *Uncle Vanya* was its first production to be seen in London and it was well received, for it was impeccably produced, with a first-class Roger Furse *decor*, being a good example of the high-quality work being done by the Norman Marshall company on its tours of the Midland and Northern provincial towns.

WHY NOT A NEGRO THEATRE?

Robert Adams, the West Indian actor, seen on the London stage during the war in such plays as *The House Of Jeffreys, The Little Foxes* and *The Judgment Of Doctor Johnson,* announced his intention recently of forming, as soon as conditions permitted, a theatre of a kind which has never before existed in this country— a Negro Theatre. Adams, a highly intelligent actor and play-wright, is the most talented Negro player in this country; it is his contention that Britain, which rules an Empire containing millions of coloured people, should possess a Negro Theatre in its capital. Why not a Negro Theatre? London, now a highly cosmopolitan centre, has several National Theatres within its do-mains—Czech, Austrian, French, German, Jewish, Dutch—and the Negro Theatre, with coloured actors and actresses appearing in Negro plays, would, indeed, be a worthy addition to London's international theatre scene. In the past, one of the obstacles to the formation of such a theatre has been that there *were* no Negro actors and actresses in this country. But, in fact, at the present time, there are quite a number of talented coloured players in England who would welcome the opportunity to act in worth-while Negro plays in a Negro Repertory Theatre. Nowadays many Negro actors engage in other work rather than spend their time in playing the servile roles of stupid retainers, servants and such-like. But offer them realist roles in new and classic plays, and Londoners would be truly astonished at the wealth of Negro talent which would reveal itself in this country.

Another objection has been that there are no Negro plays, or plays suitable for Negro actors. Robert Adams gives the answer to this when he outlines his programme. When his Negro Reper-tory opens, it is his intention to commence the season with Eugene O'Neill's *Emperor Jones,* with Adams himself playing the role of Brutus Jones (which he created in the television and radio versions). This will be followed by Eugene O'Neill's *All Gods Chillun Got Wings* (last seen in London some years ago, with Paul Robeson and Flora Robson in the leading roles) and a new play by Adams him-self about the Negro revolt in the West Indies. Other plays which, it is hoped, will be included in the repertory are Marc Connelly's *Green Pastures,* C. L. R. James' *Toussaint Louverture,* the American Living Newspaper *Haiti* (which was produced with great success by the Negro Federal Theatre in New York), Eugene O'Neill's *Dreamy Kid,* Richard Wright's *Native Son* and the operetta by

Du Bose Hayward and George Gershwin—*Porgy And Bess*. In addition to the above, there are still available a number of interesting plays about Negro life by Paul Green, Langston Hughes and others, while Herbert Marshall and Fredda Brilliant have written a play about the first Negro Republic, *The Black Emperor*, which would give Adams a magnificent leading part.

In England, apart from the visits of *The Blackbirds*, the all-Negro revues, we have had few opportunities of seeing Negroes in the theatre, but in New York, where there is a considerable black population, there have been for a number of years certain enormously successful Negro productions. Some, like *The Green Pastures* and *Porgy And Bess*, have become stage classics and there are others which seem likely to attain this distinction. Among these are *Native Son*, staged by Orson Welles and John Houseman, in which that fine actor, Canada Lee, gave the most moving performance of the year, *Mamba's Daughters* by Du Bose and Dorothy Heyward, and *Cabin In The Sky* (both distinguished by the inspiring performances of Ethel Waters) and Hall Johnson's *Run Little Chillun*," described by New York critics as " the most ambitious and accomplished drama by a Negro," while *Anna Lucasta*, a production of the Negro Theatre, was one of Broadway's biggest successes recently. And, in addition, there have been the famous Negro versions of the classics. *Macbeth*, directed by Orson Welles and John Houseman, a highly successful production of the Harlem Federal Theatre, was rivalled only by the Chicago Federal Theatre's colourful version of *The Mikado*, with Louis Armstrong and Maxine Sullivan in the cast ; and to these there has lately been added the highly original Negro Theatre production of *A Midsummer Night's Dream*. This latter has been so successful that it has been followed by the New York hit of 1944—*Carmen Jones*, which probably bears little affinity to Bizet's opera *Carmen*, yet is, nevertheless, an exciting and stimulating musical play, with fine acting, singing and dancing from talented Negro artists.

Outside America the Negro Theatre has had only a temporary existence. Some groups have been formed in the West Indies and one or two in Africa, the most successful being the Bantu Theatre, which André van Gyseghem founded in Johannesburg just before the war. However, this no longer functions, and Robert Adams' new venture will possibly be the only Negro Theatre existing within the British Empire. The contribution of the coloured peoples to music and entertainment during the past half-century is inestimable and that the Negro often possesses considerable histrionic talent is a fact now generally accepted by most. It is certainly true that many Negroes have powers of understanding and interpretation not often met with in white actors. A theatre such as Adams is determined to form, giving regular performances in London and the provinces of intelligent plays acted by Negro *and* white actors, would be of unlimited value towards the creation of a wider understanding of the Negro problem. Such a theatre would do a power of good in dispelling colour prejudice. There are immense possibilities in a Negro Theatre existing as an important liberal weapon for the uprooting of basic inhibitions and the sowing of the seeds of tolerance.

For a Negro Theatre is not only a theatre in which the players are all Negroes, or one playing to a Negro audience. Further, it is not a theatre dedicated only to the production of plays of Negro life. Rather is it a theatre in which the best elements of the drama and of progressive thought combine to interpret the life, talents, gifts, racial heritage and burdens of the Afro-American Negro to his fellow countrymen and citizens. The emancipated Negro has now progressed towards the creation of his own art and culture, in painting, sculpture, literature and the dance. The drama has great potential power for good; the Negro Theatre will, assuredly, harness this power in its struggle for artistic and social recognition for the Negro race.

TOWARDS A STATE THEATRE ?

London had not possessed a permanent Repertory Theatre for many years, though some abortive attempts had been made in the past to start one in the West End. But in the fifth year of war, there were already signs that this movement might well develop into prime importance and significance, for some of the leading figures of the English stage, expressing themselves as more than dissatisfied with the existing theatrical conditions, announced their intentions to make attempts at breaking the stranglehold of commercialism. Tired of the tyranny of the star-policy, the long-'run system, the casual labour which is the actor's constant lot, some of the more intelligent and perceptive theatre workers announced plans for the formation of permanent theatres with planned repertoires and definite artistic policies, and with salaries run on a co-operative basis, a system which had already shown good results in managements large and small (notably at the Arts Theatre). The repertory theatre idea began to permeate many influential channels and threatened to spread a good deal farther as the end of the war (and false theatrical prosperity) loomed as an imminent possibility.

Before the outbreak of war the French producer Michel St. Denis formed a theatre along the above lines at the Phœnix, but after only two plays, a Soviet drama and a Shakespeare comedy, he was forced to abandon his programme of production owing to lack of public support. Inexplicable indeed was the group's quick demise for among the gifted people connected with the St. Denis Theatre were Michael Redgrave, Peggy Ashcroft, Rodney Ackland, Basil C. Langton and Marius Goring. It is significant that in wartime all these artists continued in their efforts to create a better theatre. Marius Goring was the co-founder of the Actors' Company, a most interesting theatre group which had its headquarters at the Rudolf Steiner Hall a few years ago ; Basil C. Langton formed his Travelling Repertory Theatre early on in the war and has since done work of inestimable importance up and down the country, operating from the Birmingham Repertory Theatre, while in 1944 Rodney Ackland and Peggy Ashcroft were concerned with the Contemporary Theatre, at the Whitehall. In addition, Michael Redgrave, who had been associated with every forward movement in the theatre in recent years, announced that his own Repertory Theatre would be formed as soon as circumstances permitted. Thus it could be seen that there was beginning to grow up a not inconsiderable movement away from monopoly control of the London theatre and towards the formation of independent theatre groups.

Inevitably the next step to these Repertory Theatres would be State subsidy followed by the establishment of a series of theatres, large and small, in various parts of the country, each running on the lines of the Old Vic. To those who had watched with keen interest the progress of CEMA in its work of taking the drama to the people and in giving workers who have never seen a play the chance to enjoy and understand something of England's great theatrical traditions, these new movements, led by foremost British artists, were a source of hope and inspiration. Indeed, Michael Redgrave's words were echoed by a large body of theatrical opinion when he said : " My desire is to work in a theatre with a planned policy. My own company will be run on a repertory basis, presenting different plays on different evenings and I shall insist on a minimum rehearsal period of four weeks, with of course more if we can get it. We shall perform classic and modern plays and will tour for three months of the year, but the most important thing is that we shall endeavour to work with a definite artistic policy—that of Stanislavsky."

The first production of the Contemporary Theatre, Rodney Ackland's *The Dark River*, at the Whitehall, was however, not all that many of us would have wished it to be. Mr. Ackland, who will always be remembered for that unique and clever play, *Strange Orchestra*, assembled this time a group of shadowy characters in the house of an old school-teacher on the banks of the Thames. Here arrives a former pupil, Catherine, now divorced and in a quandary about her love affair with a young architect (newly returned from the war in Spain) and her friend Gwendolen, stupid and self-centred, with a middle-class mentality (if not morality). In the house the schoolmarm dreams of her son, killed in the First World War, her ageing father dreams of his dead wife, and a famous film director of twenty years ago sits and dreams of rebuilding his career on the reputation of his out-dated successes. Living in this dream-world the characters recreate the past ; the year is 1937 and England is hurtling towards a Second World War but all are oblivious, each has the desire to return to the past while of the present they wish to know nothing. There is a very good basic idea here, but it is difficult to become interested in these people ; the romance of Catherine and the architect is fairly tedious while he, who should be the only real person in the play, is sketchily drawn. In any case the meeting in the last act between ex-husband and lover is as false and manufactured as a situation in English farce yet, in spite of all its faults, Ackland's production of *The Dark River* was worth a visit, for the acting was superb. Peggy Ashcroft gave a sensitive, compelling and finely-drawn study, while the performances of the late Nadine March, Susan Richmond, Ronald Simpson and Wilfrid Walter all dovetailed neatly to form an interesting, though slow-moving piece of theatre. But when, in the second act, Catherine gave a manuscript to her ex-husband, saying : " Publish my memoirs and you can keep the money," I must confess that I gave a rueful smile. If it really were as easy as that I should have published even more volumes of memoirs than James Agate !

Mabel and Denis Constanduros ingeniously managed to string three short sketches into one long one, named it *Acacia Avenue*, and, fortunately, obtained Gordon Harker for the leading role. The result was seen at the Vaudeville. It concerned itself with a suburban family and the holiday abroad which did not come off. This led to some odd complications, for the parents, returning home unexpectedly, found their daughter engaged in a preparation for marital delights which, according to convention, are usually postponed until after a wedding ceremony. However, all was proven to be above board, the misunderstanding was cleared up and we were left at curtain-fall with the knowledge that " a marriage would take place." It was all extremely trite, but fairly amusing, Gordon Harker being particularly good in a part which was for him practically a gift, while the performances of Megs Jenkins and Yvonne Owen were excellent. But the chief delight of the evening was the polished acting of Hubert Gregg, who it seemed would soon be one of our leading actors in the realm of light comedy. For the undemanding theatregoer, *Acacia Avenue* was quite entertaining.

To anyone prepared to journey to Notting Hill Gate, *The Tragedy Of Nan*, by John Masefield, at the Mercury, was well worth the visit. Nan is the daughter of a man hanged for stealing, and living with a friend of her father's she receives from his wife and daughter the proper treatment they consider should be meted out to a " brat of a gallows-bird." Driven frantic by the nagging tongue of the harsh Mrs. Pargetter, Nan is only too ready to be beguiled by the winning ways of handsome Dick, a local farmer. When he, too, humiliates her for being her father's daughter, Nan, in a fit of desperate passion, kills him and wanders off to die in a nearby river. Ironic, indeed, is the discovery that her father was after all innocent of the crime, but the tragedy is predestined ; the old Gaffer, steeped in mystery and folklore, has oft proclaimed to the girl the tragic end which awaits her. This mystical and fascinating character was played here by H. R. Hignett (the originator of the part in 1908) and the ingenious production by Julian Somers, on the Mercury's small stage, was workmanlike and impressive. But it was to Pauline Letts, as the ill-fated Nan, that all honours went ; like her predecessor at the Mercury, Sonia Dresdel, she possessed a supreme stage presence, and a fascinating voice. She resembled Miss Dresdel in one other aspect—she could really *act*.

The John Gielgud production of *Landslide* at the Westminster, was apt to be disappointing, for, in adapting the Julian Luchaire play, the authors Dorothy Albertyn and David Peel, made no allowances for the fact that the original nine characters were French. In *Landslide* (not as good as *Nursery Slopes*, the original title) these bouncing English youngsters seemed to have no real

thoughts in their heads, the whole thing was no more than a " huge
lark " and their back-chat was shallow and tedious. This was a
pity, for there was a good deal of talent in the youthful cast. Dulcie
Gray, and a very fine young actor, John Byron, were excellent as
the only serious-minded members of the stranded party, Miss
Gray's incurable invalid being particularly moving. Others who
did their best with the inadequate dialogue and situation were
Peter Hammond, Sheila Sim, David Peel and Olga Edwardes.
Rolf Gerard's *decor* was first-rate, but it was unfortunate that there
was not more depth in this play, which in spite of a polished production, seemed to miss much of the essential spirit, and certainly
a good deal of the depth, of the Luchaire original.

MIKHOELS POSES A QUESTION

" What, no Shakespeare ? " These were the words of Solomon
Mikhoels, famed Soviet Shakespearean actor (whose *King Lear* is
acknowledged to be one of the finest on the world's stages) when
visiting London in 1943 on his way back to the U.S.S.R. following
a goodwill mission to the U.S.A., accompanied by Colonel Pfeffer,
the Russian soldier and poet. At that time some of us also asked,
"Why, in the greatest city in the world, is there no playhouse
performing all the year round the works of England's greatest
playwright ? Why are the British so bashful about their Bard ?
Where, in point of fact, is the London Shakespeare Theatre ?
Or, for that matter, where is our London National Theatre?"
Echo answers " where?" Like the Beveridge Plan, the schemes
for the State Theatre in our capital have been shelved or abandoned,
more's the pity, and the occasional presentation of Shakespeare
on our stages is left to the not-too-tender care of the commercial
theatre. But certainly the most worthy efforts have come lately
from the Old Vic and from CEMA, which is a significant indication
that State-aided theatre would seem to be the only solution towards
obtaining in our theatre a fuller expression of our national culture
and great theatrical traditions.

But Mikhoels, an Honoured People's Artist from the
greatest State Theatre in the world—the Soviet Theatre—had
cause, indeed, for his bewilderment. Coming from a country
where *Othello*, for example, had one hundred and forty-three
different productions between 1938 and 1941, it was not surprising
that he expected to find, at least, *one* of Shakespeare's plays upon

London's wartime stages ! However, although there were no works of the Bard, the Soviet actor and producer found some other interesting dramatists represented in West End theatres. There might not be Shakespeare, or, incidentally, Shaw, Synge, O'Casey, Ibsen, de Vega, Molière, Racine, O'Neill or Gorky, but there *were* Wilde, Congreve, Barrie, Bridie, Farquhar and Priestley, along with Coward, Rattigan, Ackland and McCracken. So, until the advent of the National Theatre, the discerning theatre-goer had to be thankful for small mercies and take consolation in the good theatre, which was there, if he cared to weed it out.

At the Westminster, Robert Donat commenced his management with a first-rate production of Oscar Wilde's *An Ideal Husband*. Directed with polish by Jack Minster, the fifty-year-old play was full of grace and charm, the sets and costumes by Rex Whistler were sumptuous to gaze upon, and a hand-picked cast performed wonders with Wilde's witticisms (though the actors were not so well served here with witty lines as in certain of his other plays). *An Ideal Husband* is, frankly, melodrama and would appear to be written by Wilde in widely varying moods, the epigrammatic veneer disappearing occasionally to show traces of the more ingenuous ingredients of melodrama such as blackmail, stolen letters, an adventuress and "a man with a past." Wilde always clearly defines his favourite character in each of his plays ; this time it is the charming fop, Lord Goring, who was beautifully played here by Roland Culver. Balancing her wits against him was the soft-voiced blackmailer of Martita Hunt, while the diplomat and his wife, the characterization of whom is not Wilde at his best, were deftly played by Manning Whiley and Rosemary Scott. Most of the humour was supplied by the wittily inane Lady Markby of Irene Vanbrugh, by Esmé Percy as a hearty old clubman and by Peggy Bryan as a pert and presentable Victorian debutante.

The wartime success of George Farquhar's *The Constant Couple*, and William Congreve's *Love For Love*, was a sure indication that theatregoers would find Alec Clunes' production of Farquhar's *The Recruiting Officer*, at the Arts, extremely diverting. And they certainly did. The " pressing " of men into the Queen's Army formed a background for the highly amusing antics of recruiting officer Plume, his sergeant, the rascally Kite, and a rival recruiting captain, rejoicing under the apt nomenclature of Brazen. The roistering Plume has as much success with the women as he has with the men ; and, in fact, as many recruits as he tricks into the Army he leaves behind children to take their places ! He is bold, bad, gallant—in fact, another edition of that other engaging Farquhar creation, Sir Harry Wildair. Trevor Howard gave a masterly rendering of this attractive monster, and his performance was certainly one of the best seen on the London stage during 1943. Helen Cherry's Sylvia was borrowed largely from *As You Like It*, and Miss Cherry, whose Rosalind is among her most successful roles, essayed this eighteenth century Principal Boy with ease and grace. Elwyn Brook-Jones was an enterprising rogue, his magician's scene being particularly good, while boisterous period acting was contributed, in uniform degrees of modest excellence, by Edward Byrne, Jenny Laird, Dorothy Gordon and Robert Marsden.

From Wilde's 1890's to Farquhar's early 1700's—then back to the early 1900's with the revival of Barrie's *The Admirable Crichton*, which came to His Majesty's. The story is too well-known to dwell upon ; suffice it to say that it demonstrates the natural supremacy of a humble butler over his aristocratic master when both are landed on a desert island. It attacks the snobbery and outrageous class-distinction which were more apparent at Barrie's time of writing than doubtless they are to-day, though it is still true to say that a section of our ruling class persists in classifying workers and servants as denizens from another world (excepting, of course, during the period when they are " our gallant boys " in the Services). It is a pity that many critics see only the comedy in Barrie's play. They do not see (or, perhaps, *will* not see) what lies beneath the surface of the play's humour—the tragedy of that unwillingness on the part of our rulers to undergo change of any sort, which is the attitude that has led us to recent disasters. Barry K. Barnes, Diana Churchill, James Harcourt, Jean Compton Mackenzie, Dermot Cathie and Joan Shannon all acted well in a slow but otherwise satisfying production of one of Barrie's lesser works.

Agatha Christie adapted her book *Ten Little Niggers* for the stage, and the entertaining result was seen at the St. James' Theatre. It was an excellent thriller, if one was in a not-too-critical mood, and it, of course, delighted all detective-story lovers. Allan Jeayes was excellent in a made-to-measure part as the mad judge, while Terrence de Marney, Linden Travers and Gwyn Nicholls all acted their " who-dunnit " roles with tensity. But Percy Walsh stole the play with his delightful portrayal of an ex-policeman, blundering like a bull through an evening of mystery and murder. To sum up : December, 1943, saw good revivals of Wilde, Barrie and Farquhar, but no worth-while new plays and a number of indifferent musical shows. One could not help but feel that Professor Mikhoel's question "What, no Shakespeare?" needed a hopeful answer.

1944

SHERWOODIAN CYNICISM—AND ENGLISH PANTOMIME

Inevitably at the beginning of a new year it is found expedient to review the drama of the previous year, first as a guide to and an indication of one's own dramatic standards, and secondly, as a pivot on which to build hopes and ideals for the new theatrical year. In achievement, 1943 had been a most interesting year. First and foremost it saw the production in the West End of Priestley's startlingly original and thought-provoking *They Came To A City*, a play which five years before would have been produced only at Little Theatres like Unity or the Gate, but certainly not for West End audiences. That *They Came To A City* ran for many months in Shaftesbury Avenue was a heartening indication that, in the midst of chaos and world revolution, drama with social implications, real-life theatre with its roots in the lives of the people was potentially able to command large audiences. To assume that, in the fifth year of war, socialism was becoming widely accepted as preferable in every way to fascism-capitalism, was an understatement ; the common people were determined that the old order of things would disappear at the end of the terrible war— and with it the old theatrical order. The demand for good theatre was there, the production of plays like the Priestley allegory, Esther McCracken's *Living Room*, Ted Willis's *Buster*, Konstantin Simonov's *The Russians*, Rodney Ackland's *The Dark River* (almost a brilliant play) as well as the huge success of those grand seasons at the Arts Theatre were most reassuring, while the sterling work of the Bradford Civic Playhouse, Glasgow Unity, Sally Latimer's Amersham Playhouse, Norman Marshall's Company at Cambridge Arts Theatre and elsewhere, the Glasgow Citizens' Theatre, the Old Vic at Liverpool, Basil C. Langton at Birmingham, and CEMA at Bristol's Theatre Royal (and, in fact, in all parts of the country) was proof that our great heritage of drama was in the capable hands of some intelligent, socially-conscious theatre workers. And the situation is much the same to-day. It is to these, and not to the theatrical playboys and their three-act bits of nonsense, that we must look for the salvation of British drama. Perhaps the end of the war will see England taking its place alongside the Soviet theatre, the Continental theatres, the American and Irish theatres among the great and significant theatres of the world?

Two of the leading representatives of the Broadway Theatre, Alfred Lunt and Lynne Fontanne, paid us a visit in December, 1943, and their first production, at the Aldwych Theatre, was Robert Emmett Sherwood's *There Shall Be No Night*. My feelings about their choice were at that time rather mixed. Firstly, the play said very little that was new—it was the well-known story of a country in the throes of war and imminent conquest by the Nazis. And, though the characterization was interesting, it provided few original touches and, indeed, only the superb acting of the Lunts, made *There Shall Be No Night* rank among plays worth seeing.

War floods its way across Europe and the tide reaches Greece ; we are shown the reactions of a famous Greek scientist, winner of the Nobel Prize, a man of ideals and deep humanity to whom all forms of violence are repugnant. At first he is against resistance, but later, when his son, sensitively played by Terry Morgan, joins up, he realises the futility of waiting for death and joins the army as a doctor, only to be killed on the frontier. His wife, a more difficult part, for it has few dramatic highlights, was handled, in this production (by Alfred Lunt), with incomparable skill by Lynne Fontanne. The scene where she told the American reporter of the death of her son was inspiring theatre and Miss Fontanne showed that she was an admirable actress whose presence in London constituted a great asset to our stage. Frederick Lloyd as the ageing uncle and Muriel Pavlow as the frightened mother-to-be were both excellent, while the acting of Alfred Lunt was a continual joy. Lunt's work in this play was the very antithesis of the tight-lipped English style of portraying emotion, and consequently doubly effective. Occasionally his tremendous technique over-shadowed his inspiration so that at times one found oneself, rather reluctantly, admiring his histrionic style dispassionately, instead of being moved by the dialogue or situations. The fact that the Lunts appeared in this Sherwood play for months in America in the same characters, played against a background of the *Russo-Finnish* clash, indicated a certain cynicism in their attitude, which demonstrated further my point about their astonishing technique. For surely Lunt would not have us believe that the strength and emotional range which he demonstrated as a Greek fighting the

Nazis was duplicated a few years before, when he portrayed a Finn fighting against " the wicked Russians " ? The fact that he could so easily slip from one ideological role to another was an able indication that it was only the role and not the play content, ideals or significance (if any) which appealed to him. Anti-Soviet yesterday, Anti-Nazi to-day—is it so simple as that ? The whole affair left a nasty taste in the mouth. But if one left one's memory in the cloakroom there was much to be enjoyed in this Sherwood *opus*, for the acting of the Lunts was a revelation to English theatre-goers, who for years had been brought up on a milk-and-water diet.

It has often been remarked that a play produced after the film version has been generally seen is never so satisfactory, and this was borne out by the Harry Segall play, *Halfway To Heaven*, which came to the Princes early in 1944. It was the play from which was made that really first-rate film *Here Comes Mr. Jordan*, and to those who saw the movie it was at once apparent that the play presented technical difficulties which in Hollywood were easily surmountable. Nevertheless, this production was highly amusing, due to the wonderful comedy performances of Bobby Howes and that amiable clown Sydney Howard. To attempt to describe the plot here would lead to endless complications. Suffice to say that it concerns a boxer who is taken to Heaven before he is actually due for death. It is therefore the job of Mr. Jordan, a sort of celestial chartered accountant, to find for the pugilist another (and similarly muscled) torso, and, when he does, the complications are endless—and hilarious. Bobby Howes in a straight acting role had never been seen to better advantage as Joe, the boxer ; one took him so much for granted and, indeed, failed to realise just how good an actor he was until the final scenes. He was magnificent while, as his bewildered manager, that comic-gestured genius Sydney Howard gave us some of the heartiest laughs of a diverting evening. As Mr. Jordan, impeccable actor J. H. Roberts was quietly first-rate, while Marcel Varnel's production was at all times completely satisfying, in spite of the fact that the play could not hope to compare with the outstanding film version.

From Norwegian dramatist Helge Krog came a new play, *On Life's Sunny Side*, at the Arts. Krog has often been likened to his fellow-countryman Ibsen, but in this play there was more than a hint of Tchekovian construction ; the characters were by no means simple and the dialogue, though at times apt to be pedestrian, was often witty and provoking. To a delightful country estate, peopled by those fortunate enough to live " on life's sunny side," Hartwig, the son, brings his bride Esther, a typist from the city. She is the only touch of real life in these idyllic surroundings, disliked by her mother-in-law and courted by neighbouring ne'er-do-wells. When Hartwig, to test her love, invites her former sweetheart to stay with them, the resultant emotional misunderstandings create comical confusion and, in fact, the last act owes much to Ellisian farce. But what a fine young actress is beautiful Mary Morris. It was a pleasure to see her on the London stage once more, bringing to Esther a warmth, a quality of reality and inner fire which marked her out as an actress and personality of the front rank. The play was distinctly worth seeing for her performance alone, while the admirable cast included Elwyn Brook-Jones, Trevor Howard, Helen Cherry, David Bird, Dorothy Reynolds and Michael Raghan, each of whom was first-rate in this interesting new play.

Take improbability number one—an earl serving as an ordinary seaman, add improbability number two—a duke's daughter as a W.A.A.F. private and mix gently with a stage aristocrat plus that hoary old horror, the stage " gentleman's gentleman." Next throw in the Englishman's supposed conception of a typical American soldier, plus the conventional stage Frenchman along with the final stock ingredient, the trollop with a heart of gold, and there you had the characters of Terence Rattigan's play *While The Sun Shines*, which was produced by Anthony Asquith at the Globe. The situation was the hackneyed and much-beloved theme of three suitors for the hand of one beautiful heroine, with eventual triumph for the " democratically-aristocratic " sailor-earl (also with heart of gold). But it was all much funnier than it sounds, for Rattigan is an extremely clever young man and a gifted, though conventional, playwright. And of course the public loved it, especially those parts where the earl emphasized that he got only one egg a month (in his luxurious Albany flat) and had to rely on the good graces of a chemist's assistant for his razor blades ! But this arrant stupidity apart, one might well have been disappointed that this new play showed no particular improvement on the author's *French Without Tears* of six years before. The acting was slick and polished, especially the performances of Michael Wilding, Ronald Squire, Brenda Bruce, and Hugh McDermott, while I must confess that I admired Eugene Deckers' portrayal of the French lieutenant best of all. Altogether this was the best—or the worst—example of the successful West End commercial play. But whatever else it might be, it was most certainly most entertaining.

73

Unity Theatre made a brave attempt to depict the story of the music-halls upon its pocket-size stage with its production of an extravaganza, *Winkles and Champagne*. The first half consisted of a seventeenth-century burletta, a concert in the early nineteenth century and a beer-garden in the 1870's, but it was in the second half, a reconstruction of a music-hall of the 1900's, that the show really managed to get going. Here the Unity songsters came into their own and excellent singing and fooling by Doris Levenson, Frank Godwin, David Kossof, David Abrahams, Joe Levene and a host of Unity favourites brought the colourful show to a triumphant close. With the rough edges smoothed off during the run of this unusual production, it continued to be the lustiest, and certainly the gayest, show in London. Bernard Sarron's *decor* was as usual, highly original and slickly utilitarian.

Pantomime flourished as usual in 1943-44 with colourful shows at half a dozen theatres. His Majesty's staged the Jack Hylton version of *Cinderella*, with lovely Evelyn Laye as Principal Boy, and a grand array of comedians, including Tessie O'Shea and George Moon, while pretty Natasha Sokolova danced delightfully. It was a long time since London had seen a production of *Humpty Dumpty*, and at the Coliseum several talented people combined to provide classic Christmas entertainment in this " pepped-up " story of the fairy-tale character who " had a great fall." First and foremost in the cast was the West End's finest Principal Boy, Pat Kirkwood, with a lovely figure, a rare beauty and a grand voice, while those comic teams, Nervo and Knox and Naughton and Gold, almost revived the hilarious traditions of the Crazy Gang. It was not every day of the week that one was privileged to see a Dame of the British Empire swinging on a wire through the air, but this is what was happening to Sybil Thorndike at every performance of Esmé Church's production of *Alice in Wonderland* at the Scala. With her in Clemence Dane's version of the Lewis Carroll classic, with music by Richard Addinsell, was Roma Beaumont as Alice, and a fine cast, which included Geoffrey Dunn and Julian Somers. And, of course, the perennial *Peter Pan* was seen at the Cambridge, this time with appealing Glynis Johns in the famous Barrie role, giving the best performance as Peter seen in London since Jean Forbes-Robertson's inspired Peter Pan of some years before.

Another, and much wittier, version of *Cinderella* was produced at the little Players' Theatre by Don Gemmel, who, as one of the Ugly Sisters, gave without doubt one of the funniest pantomime

★ *Mary Morris* and Guy Verney in Afinogenov's
"Distant Point", produced by André van Gyseghem, 1941.

★ ***Rex Harrison,*** who appeared in Coward's " Design for Living", 1940 ; and S. N. Behrman's " No Time for Comedy", produced by Harold French, 1941.

PHOTO: ANGUS MCBEAN

★ *John Gielgud* and Jack Hawkins in Wilde's "The Importance Of Being Earnest", produced by Gielgud, 1940.

★ **Leslie Banks** and Michael Redgrave in Patrick Hamilton's "The Duke in Darkness," produced by Redgrave, 1942.

★ *Edith Evans,* as Queen Elizabeth, in the Herbert
Farjeon revue "Diversion" (first edition produced by George
Benson ; second edition by Walter Crisham, 1940-41).

★ *John Gielgud,* as Mr. Dearth, in Barrie's "Dear Brutus", which he produced in 1941.

PHOTO : ANTHONY

★ *Fay Compton* and Cecil Parker in Noel Coward's "Blithe Spirit", the longest run of the war years, first produced by Coward himself in 1941.

PHOTO : ANGUS MCBEAN

★ *Celia Johnson* and the late Owen Nares in the dramatisation of Daphne du Maurier's "Rebecca", produced by George Devine, 1940.

performances seen in London for many years. Satirising the conventional pantomime in the adaptation by Archie Harradine, this jolly tongue in cheek show had in its cast many favourites of the Players' talented company, including Charlotte Bidmead, Jean Anderson, Heather Boys, Paulette Preney, Joan Sterndale Bennett and Therese Langfield. And this version of *Cinderella* took every opportunity to poke good-natured fun at that peculiarly English institution, the pantomime, with its " hero " who is a girl (the Principal Boy) and the heroine (the Principal Girl), the Dame, who is always a low comedian, the use of modern popular songs in a timeless fairyland setting, the inevitable ballet, the feeble humour and all the other traditional attributes of our seasonal theatrical pastime. Visitors from America and the Continent are continually bewildered by pantomime's peculiarities but it deserves to be conceded a special place in the English theatre.

The transforming of fairy stories and folk-tales into theatrical entertainment, with stock and much beloved characters, is a notably English innovation, duplicated in few other countries. More important than English farce and Old Music Hall, pantomime, our main traditional and national theatrical event, takes place on or about Christmas and is viewed by foreigners with interest and amusement. Set loosely around a fairy-tale like *Mother Goose*, *Cinderella* and *The Sleeping Beauty*, or based upon a nursery rhyme of the kind which tells a definite story—*Humpty Dumpty*, for example —the pantomime has certain necessary characteristics which mark it out from ordinary stage fare. Sometimes the plot may be taken from a folk-story or traditional tale, like *Robinson Crusoe*, but, in any case, a pantomime rarely deals with new characters and situations. Dick Whittington, his Cat, Cinderella and the Ugly Sisters, Jack the Giant Killer, the Giant himself (not forgetting the Beanstalk), the beautiful heroine, the handsome Prince, Snow White and the Seven lovable Dwarfs, Jack and Jill, the Broker's Men, Dandini, Buttons—they are endless and all as popular and endearing to the vast pantomime public, which is by no means confined to adults.

It would take a courageous producer indeed to attempt to create new pantomime characters—but then why should he ? There are many variations on the fairy-tale themes and a *Cinderella* in Nottingham or Birmingham may well differ in a number of respects from the West End version of the same story. One does not look for sanity in pantomimes ; the original story may well be forgotten during production, for, if the stars of the show are two popular comedians, then their parts of the Ugly Sisters or the Brokers' Men may well be built up to become the most important and lengthy parts in the show. The action is stopped at all times for an interchange of backchat between the low comedians or for a comic dance by the Cat or Mother Goose, or even by the Giant! Inevitably there is the aforementioned Principal Girl and, most important of all, the Principal Boy, who is never played by a boy or male actor but always by a lovely girl in conventional tights. Woe betide the producer who would dare to make the Principal Boy other than a girl. But nobody dares to alter the pantomime traditions which go back for scores of years. Most of the famous musical comedy stars of decades past have been famous Principal Boys, and, to a certain extent, this custom exists to-day, so that we find Evelyn Laye, Fay Compton, Pat Kirkwood, Patricia Burke and others occupying this traditional role with the necessary virility.

That the Great British Public should view with equanimity, and even approval, the spectacle of two girls making love on the stage (even though one is attired as a boy), has often been commented upon by visitors to England. In this case the Shakespearean custom of boys playing feminine leads has been reversed —and with considerable success. Most pantomimes possess the traditional Ballet and an important but much-maligned character, the Fairy Queen, who is rarely played seriously and during the past few years has deteriorated into the Comic Relief instead of being a semi-serious Patience Strong figure, continually moralising and waving a rather tired-looking wand. The Harlequinade too is a much-beloved feature and no pantomime would be complete without Harlequin and Columbine in ballet costume gaily dancing a *pas-de-deux*, complete with masks, hot pokers and the other familiar features. The story may often be nonsense—not organised nonsense like that of the revered Marx Brothers—but a sort of inconsequential nonsense which gives the impression that the show has been built haphazardly around the comic personalities. But this time-honoured combination of music-hall and touring revue, replete with a selection of the popular dance tunes of the moment and a number of old and well-tried gags, was prospering during the war, as it does during the Christmas period every year. Seats are always sold out weeks before a performance and the family queues up for hours to " go to the panto."

Classic drama might well wait for an audience. New drama **and** serious stage productions perhaps pass unnoticed and struggle through a three-week's run, but there has always been a huge public for that most popular and inane of English theatrical traditions—the pantomime. Who was it who once said " The British have no culture ? " At any rate they have a sense of the ridiculous.

THE EXPERIMENTAL THEATRE

In 1944 the announcement of the imminent re-opening of the Embassy Theatre in Hampstead and the re-opening of Chanticleer Theatre in South Kensington, coupled with the fact that Hilda Maude (long associated with that pioneer Little Theatre group, " The Playroom Six ") had taken a long lease of the Torch Theatre at Knightsbridge led to the hope that the Little Theatre was, once again, coming into prominence. There were at that time about a dozen in London alone, each had its own individuality, each contributed something worth-while to our theatre. And to-day the Little Theatre movement in England is second in importance only to the considerable Tributary Theatre in America. It was in the United States that the famous Chicago Little Theatre was founded by Englishman Maurice Browne in 1911 ; soon afterwards, in New York, the little Provincetown Playhouse discovered Eugene O'Neill, and the Washington Square Players founded the movement which later developed into the Theatre Guild (the nearest thing in America to a State Theatre on the lines of those which existed in most large European cities before this war).

In England the Little Theatre Movement had its beginnings in the Independent Theatre (founded by J. T. Grein in 1887) and in the Stage Society. In the early part of the present century Harley Granville-Barker took over the Court at Sloane Square and there staged many exciting seasons of " good " drama, while other small groups flourishing at that time included the Mermaid Theatre and the Maddermarket Theatre in Norwich. During the post-war period the rebellion against the strangle-hold of business men upon the theatre took the form of several independent theatre groups functioning separately, each founded with the object of creating individual platforms for the drama, each with conceptions which were different, original and sometimes revolutionary.

Hampstead, centre of so many experimental playhouses in 1925, saw the founding of the Everyman, at first under the direction of Norman Macdermott (and later Malcolm Morley and Milton

Rosmer) and the Embassy, with A. R. Whatmore, as director, and afterwards André van Gyseghem and John Fernald. From humble beginnings in Covent Garden, the Gate, directed by Peter Godfrey (followed by Norman Marshall) went on to create a world-famous centre for drama of an unusually high quality, which earned the little Villiers Street theatre the reputation, which it held for many years, of being the leading experimental theatre in England. Others sprang up in various parts of town—the Portfolio Playhouse, The Players, The Intimate (founded by John Clements), Unity Theatre, André van Gyseghem's Experimental Theatre, Ashley Duke's Mercury, the People's National Theatre (directed by the indomitable Nancy Price), the Q, The Westminster, and others. Worthy of inclusion in this group were the semi-professional and amateur theatres like the Tavistock, Questors and St. Pancras People's Theatre, as well as The Maddermarket, the Unnamed Society and the many dozens of other provincial groups which have made our amateur theatre movement the most vital in Europe.

Wartime brought with it a revival of interest in Little Theatres. Many were formed since the outbreak of war—Herbert Marshall's Neighbourhood, Elwyn Brook-Jones's Threshold, Alec Clunes's Arts Theatre Group, the Actors' Theatre, the Lantern (Free Austrian), the Free German Little Theatre, The Blue Danube, the By Candlelight, and the Austrian Stage. These and other independent theatre groups began to beat the blackout, and at a time when the West End stage offered a great deal of expensive nonsense, some out-of-the-ordinary and interesting theatre-fare was always to be found in these little playhouses. To-day, in addition to the above, Unity Theatre is going from strength to strength, often with first-class productions by amateur actors, while the Mercury, Players', Gateway, Questors, Jack Sherman's Kane Players (who produced an extraordinarily interesting stage version of *Citizen Kane* in 1943) and others are carrying on in the courageous traditions of the independent experimental theatre movement.

The Embassy, long known before the war as an " *avant garde* " playhouse, did magnificent work under its young directors André van Gyseghem and John Fernald, while some years before, the Chanticleer, too, put on several interesting productions, the work of the Webber-Douglas Theatre School. In 1944 it opened again under the direction of Greta Douglas who, with a permanent company of promising young actors, presented interesting programmes of classics as well as new plays. No such thing as a star system prevailed at the Chanticleer (for it is one of the basic tenets of most Little Theatres that team-work and co-operation, plus a belief in the play itself, its message and significance is the only way to create a " piece of theatre "). A play produced to perfection relies mainly upon the dovetailing of all performances ; in any case I strongly contest James Agate's conception of the drama which places so much emphasis upon a central character surrounded by shadowy puppets.

Therefore, it was all the more encouraging for lovers of the theatre to see that Little Theatres were managing to carry on their struggle against theatrical conventions amid a welter of commercialism. One of the most successful of these " private membership theatres " (which are able to circumvent the Lord Chamberlain's censorship of plays) was the Arts Theatre, where Alec Clunes founded a real experimental theatre without stars and with a courageous and intelligent policy. The first to present the work of Helge Krog to this country, the Arts continued its policy with a production of another play not previously seen in London. It was *Don Abel Wrote A Tragedy* by the prolific Quintero Brothers (who have written more than two hundred plays, including, of course, such well-known modern classics as *A Hundred Years Old*). Set in the Spain of the early 1930's, this charming little comedy dealt with the trials and tribulations of a Government clerk, who was so foolish as to write a play and even more foolish as to presume to have it produced on the Madrid stage. The early scenes in his office were very funny, the Civil Service atmosphere being portrayed with bite and pungency. The clerks were each carefully drawn, each cleverly acted ; notably amusing was the stupid Urrutia, played with every ounce of humour extracted from it by Elwyn Brook-Jones (whose Judge Brack was a triumph of the previous year's *Hedda Gabler*).

Middle-aged clerk Don Abel completes his first play ; this goes to his head and he leaves the office for ever—to devote himself to art. When his play has been rejected for the one hundredth and fiftieth time his devotion to art wears a little thin, but by sheer chance and through the kindness of a famous actress his tragedy does at last get a production. Typical of Continental satire and realism is the fact that the play is a failure. Were this by an English playwright Don Abel would almost inevitably have had an overnight success. So back to the office it is, and from what we gather at the final curtain, it is back to *secret* play-writing for the incorrigible Don Abel. It was a very amusing production, with a delightful performance by that clever and sincere actor John Ruddock as Don Abel and intelligent acting by Edward Byrne, Grace Lane, Jonathan Field, David Bird, Tony Quinn, Olaf Pooley and Dorothy Reynolds.

Most plays by Emlyn Williams are worthy of a visit and *The Druid's Rest* was almost up to the standard of his *Night Must Fall*. The atmosphere of an Edwardian Welsh village was admirably caught and, though the plot was slim, the dialogue and characterization were full of interest. A young newcomer, fourteen-year-old Brynmor Thomas, proved to be a discovery and excellent work was contributed by Roddy Hughes, Gladys Henson and Michael Shepley in a comedy which, though not Williams' best work, was nevertheless an amusing little play.

Emlyn Williams is an extremely interesting theatre personality. He is a fine actor, but it is chiefly as a playwright that he has found international fame. What of his wartime output? *The Light Of Heart* was a disappointment; *The Morning Star*, a topical " blitz " play, provided meaty acting parts for Angela Baddeley and Williams himself, but was otherwise completely undistinguished. It is his new serious Welsh play, *The Wind Of Heaven*, which is likely to give Emlyn Williams some claim to be regarded as one of the most significant of modern British dramatists. Certain is it that Williams is completely at home when writing about the people he knows well. *The Corn Is Green*, which deals with Welsh mining life, is probably his best play—and there is potentially a great playwright in Emlyn Williams, who is comparatively young and still capable of writing great drama.

THE BARD COMES INTO HIS OWN

In early 1944 came a bustle of theatrical activity. Every management appeared to have ambitious plans for the New Year and, most important of all, it was promised that the Bard himself would have a hearing on at least two London stages, one of which might well (conditions permitting) have become a permanent London Shakespeare Theatre. At the New Theatre, the Old Vic Company was seen in the production by Tyrone Guthrie and Michael Benthall of *Hamlet*, an eagerly awaited theatrical event by virtue of the seemingly surprising fact that ballet-dancer Robert Helpmann was enacting the role of " the gloomy Dane," a part he had danced many times in the ballet of his own creation. And Donald Wolfit, who for seven years had courageously toured the plays of Shakespeare all over the country, took over the Scala Theatre for a season to present his own productions of Shakespeare's *Hamlet, Othello, Richard III, As You Like It, Twelfth Night* and *King Lear*, as well as plays by Ben Jonson and Henrik Ibsen. Wolfit's season, which featured a different play at each performance, was indeed a true classical repertory season of the kind which exists in all the important theatres of the Soviet Union. His venture was an oasis in the arid theatrical desert, though when one considered that more performances of Shakespeare's works are given in the Soviet Union in one year than in twenty years in England, then even encouraging manifestations such as this could be considered but minute drops in the dramatic bucket.

However, one felt thankful for small mercies (though, in truth, Wolfit's performances could hardly ever be labelled small!). On the contrary, many were a good deal larger than life, which was, I presume, one reason why his *Richard III* was so greatly admired by James Agate, champion of the " great actor " school, as opposed to the " team-work " school, represented by Tyrone Guthrie, among others. Guthrie's conception of *Hamlet* at the New was one which allowed no undue emphasis to fall upon any one character, excepting as was dramatically necessary. Robert Helpmann's performance of Hamlet was remarkably interesting. Though he lacked strength and voice, there was a certain power in his subtle and intellectual approach which resulted in a Hamlet in the correct perspective, as part of the tragic pattern in which the Queen, the King, Ophelia, Laertes and the Prince were analogous one to the other, each equally dependent for life and effect upon the successful dovetailing of characters to form a satisfying dramatic whole.

This *Hamlet* was in many ways a magnificent staging, superbly produced, artfully and artistically lit. All very well, though it might be, for critics to point out that Shakespeare wrote largely for the open-air theatres without consideration of lighting methods, this was after all a 1944 production of a classic play, and Guthrie's and Benthall's collaboration was strictly a modern conception. So, for that matter, was Helpmann's ; his was a weaker, finer, more inhibited Prince. But what he lacked in fire he made up for with his finely-drawn and extremely intelligent study of one of drama's most complex tragic figures. Laurence Hanray's Polonius offered little that was new ; my yardstick was (and still is) the performance of George Howe in John Gielgud's 1935 production. Pamela Brown's Ophelia, Basil Sydney's King, and Geoffrey Toone's Laertes

were effective without being in any way spectacular, but
especially good was Charles Hickman's amusingly original Osric.
Though not, perhaps, to everybody's taste, this Old Vic *Hamlet*
deserved to be widely seen ; it ranked as one of the outstanding productions of Shakespeare seen in London for many years.

Donald Wolfit's *Merchant Of Venice* at the Scala gave us a
Shylock at all times truly pathetic ; his Jew was a most moving
portrayal, while Rosalind Iden's Portia pleasantly combined the
charm of the beautiful heiress with the brisk efficiency of the bogus
counsellor.   Once more the Court Scene intrigued by its obvious
injustice ; the Judge is a mere puppet and one realises very soon
that all the cards are stacked against " the infidel Jew."   The
question arises once more—is the play a condemnation of anti-
Semitism ?   I hope it is, but fear that it is not.   Wolfit's production
was patchy—especially grotesque and jarring to the ear were the
parrot-cries of " the mob " in the Court Scene.   The voices, in
musical comedy unison, sounded like a male voice quartet.

About Wolfit's *Richard III* much has been written in the past.
His hunchback monarch was, I think, the finest performance of his
Scala season in a thoughtful and spectacular production, achieved
in a simple setting.   There was a fire and a dash about his
malignant King which cast into prominence, however, the lack
of virility apparent among the rest of his cast.   Rosalind Iden and
Eugene Wellesley were excellent, but some of the other members of
this gallant company were unfortunately not up to standard and
obviously under-rehearsed ; the season suffered from this quality
of unevenness.

The consistently high level of Arts Theatre plays was demonstrated once more with the production by Catherine Lacey of John
Masefield's *The Witch*.   With a background of Lutheran bigotry,
heresy-hunting and witch-baiting, this drama of fanaticism and
passion was played intelligently to its tragic end.   In a small
Norwegian town, Absalon the pastor is old ; his beautiful young
wife Anne feels herself drawn to her stepson, Absalon's son by a
previous marriage.   The boy falls madly in love with her and she
with him, but a fateful quality surrounds their love ; one hears the
knell of doom as Anne proclaims of this love to her aged husband.
His death in a paroxysm is sufficient to persuade the community
that the girl-wife is a witch ; her own tragic awareness of her
early history does the rest.   The girl is herself convinced that she
is bewitched, but were we, the audience ?   (She was at all times

completely bewitching, at any rate). As Anne, Mary Morris gave, once again, a performance which placed her in the front rank of young actresses on the English stage. No mincing flibberti-gibbet this, but a strong-minded, strange-natured yet completely feminine and understandable creature of moods and fancies. Her looks, her bearing in action and repose, her truly outstanding ability to create atmosphere, all made this young actress a theatre name to conjure with. Splendid acting came also from Abraham Sofaer as Absalon, Richard Wordsworth as his son and Ernest Hare as the drunken cleric, in one of the better stage productions of the war years.

Of Reginald Beckwith's *A Soldier For Christmas*, which came to Wyndham's, one could say little more than that it ably filled the breach made by the departure of Esther McCracken's *Quiet Week-End* to the Middle East. Once more we had the week-end country house, but this time there was a fair amount of quite interesting and often witty dialogue about " the post-war world." The author created at least two very original characters, but to balance this, gave again that much-maligned and hackneyed stage puppet, the Cockney Communist. Portrayed as an elderly charwoman with revolutionary tendencies, she was drawn with as much wit and realism as was used by the "Daily Mail" leader-writer during the Soviet-Finnish campaign. The breezy Canadian soldier, whose presence so upsets the English household, was played with gusty charm by Robert Beatty, but the odd behaviour of the daughter of the house left little that Pauline Letts could do with her. Trevor Howard was cynically brilliant in a thankless role and one could not help admiring the work of Joyce Barbour and Meriel Forbes, but Susan Richmond stole most of the honours with her stinging portrayal of an almost extinct type, the county blue-blood. However, the play was, on the whole, a disappointment to those of us who knew that Mr. Beckwith was capable of writing much better comedies than this.

At this point one felt an urgent need to turn to a dictionary in search of fresh superlatives. None were too many, none more well-deserved than those which could be applied to *Sweeter And Lower*, the new edition of *Sweet And Low*, the intimate revue at the Ambassadors. The wittiest writers in London here assembled what bade fair to eclipsing *Rise Above It* as the finest wartime revue, and with the incomparable Hermione Gingold and Henry Kendall as the stars, this intimate entertainment was obviously set to keep London laughing for years—but definitely. It is, perhaps, not realised just what an accomplished actress is Miss Gingold. Time and time again in this sparkling production she assumed with supreme ease a completely different personality. Her gallery of portraits was endless, and with each new gesture, each new turn of expression and change of voice, the delightful Hermione went from strength to strength, giving a revue performance which had to be seen to be believed. And aiding and abetting her was the delicious Henry Kendall, whose duchess explaining pantomime to an American soldier vied with his elderly ballet-dancer sketch for the title of the funniest revue scene of the war. The group of talented youngsters supporting Gingold and Kendall included the extremely clever Bonar Colleano, the lovely Edna Wood, the subtle Ilena Sylva, the agile George Carden and the suave and humorous Richard Curnock, each one quite obviously a potential star. Certainly their " apprenticeship " under Miss Gingold and Mr. Kendall has stood them in good stead for the future.

UNITY : THE PEOPLE'S THEATRE

" It is the first stirring of the social conscience that must develop itself in the minds of all thinking writers in this country, this urge to express actual conditions through their writings. The relation which an art form bears to the social and economic forces of its time is both immediate and more marked in the case of drama."

With the successful 1944 production of *Winkles And Champagne*, the story of the music halls, Unity Theatre once more leapt into the limelight, as it had done a few months previously with its staging of Lopé de Vega's *Fuente Ovejuna* (seen at the little King's Cross theatre for the first time in England). Theatregoers who were thrilled with the Spanish masterpiece were equally delighted by the lusty and virile quality of Unity's entertaining music-hall show ; many began to ask " Where and how did Unity begin its career as the leading people's theatre in this country ? " The story is, indeed, an inspiring one of struggle, hard work and faith in a theatre which has, for ten years, steadily produced realist stagings of plays depicting faithfully each and every facet of contemporary life.

When young theatre director André van Gyseghem, on a ship bound for Soviet Russia, met some actors from a theatre group called " Red Radio " he was immediately interested to learn of their efforts to achieve a live theatre in London's East End. Proof of their enthusiasm was the fact that they were travelling, as was van Gyseghem, to the International Workers' Theatre Olympiad held that year in Moscow. From this meeting arose further gatherings in London, and finally (with the assistance of its co-founder Herbert Marshall, then returned, after seven years in the Soviet Union) came the formation of "The Rebel Players," a group of worker-actors performing in small halls, on the steps of Trafalgar Square, on the backs of lorries, and in fact anywhere that they could command an audience to witness their "agit-prop" drama and sketches.

In 1936 the group acquired its first Little Theatre, a disused church hall in King's Cross, and decided to name it Unity Theatre. Working at other jobs during the day, the actors rehearsed at night and at week-ends and at last presented the first play in their first premises—Herbert Marshall's staging of *Waiting For Lefty*. The choice of the controversial Clifford Odets play was evidently a good one, for it played to packed houses for months and even had H. G. Wells leaping to his feet at the end of the performance to join in the chorus of actors and audience—"Strike, strike!" A private theatre club, Unity built up its membership to 2,000 with vital performances of new and unusual plays, so that after two years it was necessary to take over another, larger theatre in Goldington Street. Formerly a doss-house and Presbyterian Chapel, the building miraculously grew into a fine little theatre after Unity had sent out a call for assistance to its members. Carpenters, bricklayers, painters and willing helpers of all kinds were found to give their services voluntarily towards the creation of the Workers' Theatre.

In 1937 the new theatre, equipped with the most up-to-date lighting system in Europe, opened with a Soviet play, Pogodin's *Aristocrats*, to an enthusiastic audience of press and public, but it was later on, with the production of Ben Bengal's *Plant In The Sun*, that the name of Unity came into theatrical prominence. Paul Robeson long in agreement with Unity's aims that "true art effectively and realistically presented in the theatre can help the people to move towards the betterment of society," gave up stardom at Drury Lane in order to act with the Unity amateurs in the American strike play, and, during the run of *Plant In The Sun*, membership rose by leaps and bounds. London theatregoers in their hundreds travelled to King's Cross to experience an evening of vital and "different" theatre.

93

With Christmas 1938 came the production which did most to put Unity on the theatrical map—their first " political pantomime " *Babes In The Wood*, a merry musical satire by Geoffrey Parsons and Berkeley Fase, which soon had all London rocking with mirth. The barbed wit of the book, the tuneful and meaningful music and the acting of Vida Hope, Bill Rowbotham, Ann Davies and the others in a huge and talented cast kept crowds queueing at Unity and a result was that membership skyrocketed to more than 7,000 in six months ! Praise from the press was unanimous, at last the theatre was able to expand, and in the summer of 1939 Unity took over the Kingsway Theatre as the first professional Workers' Theatre in England, planning to commence with Herbert Marshall's staging of Geoffrey Trease's *Colony*, with Beatrix Lehmann and Robert Adams. Unfortunately the war upset all plans for this development, and for the time being, Unity operates from King's Cross and has had to shelve the idea of a professional theatre until conditions permit.

At the outbreak of war, when most of the West End theatres seemed stunned, Unity opened immediately with a political revue *Sandbag Follies* (written and produced by Unity Play Department in forty-eight hours) followed by *Turn Up The Lights* and a number of other revues. Thenceforth, through " blitz " and blackout, the enthusiastic worker-actors kept the playhouse open continually throughout the war ; a list of the outstanding wartime plays produced here would, indeed, be long. Many well-known playwrights have had their works performed on Unity's stages. And, in 1941, John Allen's production of Sean O'Casey's great play *The Star Turns Red* prompted James Agate to write " The most vital theatre in London is to be experienced in a back-street theatre in King's Cross—Unity."

During its ten-year career, Unity has always excited the admiration of the progressive elements of the professional stage, and in addition to André van Gyseghem and Herbert Marshall, actors, writers and producers of the calibre of Lewis Casson, John Fernald, Rollo Gamble, Sybil Thorndike, Beatrix Lehmann, Walter Hudd, J. B. Priestley, Michael Redgrave, Rachel Kempson, Rodney Ackland, Patrick Hamilton and a host of others have helped in many ways—acting, producing, advising, lecturing. At all times Unity acts as a bridge between the English professional theatre and the considerable amateur movement ; many of Unity's amateur actors who have given outstanding work here are now acting on the professional stage. Among these are Vida Hope, John Slater, David Green, Alfie Bass, Bill Rowbotham, Harry Ross, Jane Edgeworth and David Dawson, while among the many Unity " discoveries " are Ted Willis, author of *Sabotage* and the successful *Buster*, designer and producer Bernard Sarron, painter Lawrence Gowing, writers Geoffrey Parsons, Leonard Peck and Berkeley Fase, and director Eric Capon (later producer of the Citizens' Theatre, Glasgow, and the Old Vic at Liverpool).

Unity is a unique theatre, even visiting Americans admit there is nothing like it in the U.S.A. It is an independent, self-supporting peoples' theatre with a method of acting and a quality of production often superior to those found on the blasé West End stage. And there are, in addition to the London theatre, about a score of " Unity's " in the provinces, for the Unity Theatre movement has grown amazingly since the days of the " Rebel Players." From September 5th, 1939, onwards, in spite of wartime difficulties, it carried on, ready at the end of the war to play its part in the tremendous task of creating a new and different world. For Unity is a theatre with a purpose, and that purpose has still not yet been achieved.

PRIESTLEY, ABCA—and WOLFIT

Jointly with ABCA (the Army Bureau of Current Affairs), CEMA, in the summer of 1944 presented, at the Playhouse, Priestley's new play *Desert Highway*, produced and performed entirely by men serving in the Army. There had, of course, previously been many all-soldier shows giving concerts at their barracks, there had even been one or two revues put on at London theatres with all-Service casts, but *Desert Highway* was an interesting innovation in that it was the first play to be publicly performed by a group of actors organized within the Army as a production unit. ABCA arose out of the serving soldier's desire to know something about the war, the true problems behind the scenes, the real reasons why he was engaged in the most terrible struggle civilization has ever known, and for some time past this worthy organisation had arranged lectures, study circles and discussion groups to meet the Army's desire for more knowledge. An off-shoot of the scheme was the ABCA Play Unit, under the direction of Major Michael MacOwan (who, just prior to the war, was director of the London Mask Theatre).

The history of the ABCA Play Unit is an interesting one. Michael MacOwan, who left the Westminster Theatre to join up in the ranks, was for over two years in a Light Ack-Ack regiment before becoming Education Officer. Following this he went to the War Office, then to ABCA, where he was encouraged by W. E Williams to consider the production of regular dramatic entertainment for the troops, under the auspices of ABCA and Army Welfare. Major MacOwan, impressed by Suria Magito's production of the American W.P.A. play *One Third Of A Nation*, a Living Newspaper by Arthur Arent, which was staged at Toynbee Hall Theatre in 1942, decided that this technique was ideally suited to play-production for scattered Army units. Therefore, in 1943, he produced a short play, acted by Army personnel, drawn from the Central Pool of Artists, and written by actor Stephen Murray, who was at that time in the London District Theatre Unit, a branch of Army Welfare. The first ABCA Play Unit programme, Murray's *United We Stand*, produced along with *What's Wrong With The Germans?* by factory-worker Miles Tomalin, was a great success and since that time many other productions have been undertaken and many performances given by the Army *for* the Army, the two most interesting of their plays in 1944 being *It Started With Lend-Lease* by Ted Willis and Jack Lindsay, produced by Captain Stephen Murray, and *The Japanese Way* by Bridget Boland and Jack Lindsay, produced by Captain André van Gyseghem. Like ENSA and CEMA, ABCA is a wartime theatrical institution which has served to introduce drama to many who had previously never been to the theatre.

Priestley agreed to write a topical play for the group, dealing with the war in the Middle East, and *Desert Highway* was the result. In many ways it was magnificent theatre and was certainly superbly acted by the cast of soldiers, all formerly professional actors. Against a background of the war in the Syrian Desert, we were introduced to a tank crew, stranded in a hollow, off the beaten track and cut off from the rest of the company. The troopers, all widely differing types, were acted by Stephen Murray as the Jew, John Wyse as the intellectual cynic, Stanley Rose, delightful as a Cockney " old sweat " and George Cooper, Emlyn James and Peter Tuddenham as the Yorkshireman, Welshman and country boy respectively. It would have been difficult to find six more satisfying character-studies in any play on the London stage at that time. Their reactions to their situation, their quarrels, discussions, hopes, philosophies, their comradeship, the bravery of simple men—all these things were portrayed with human feeling and dignity. I was not altogether happy about the second act, a flashback to 703 B.C., being unable to discover a satisfying analogy between the two scenes ancient and modern, and in any case for Priestley's quasi-religious mysticism I had little or no regard. He endeavoured to place what was a straightforward political and social struggle on the misty levels of a spiritual war, a religious crusade. This was, of course, nonsense—even the Government dispensed with that notion early on in the war and Priestley, nothing if not a realist, would have done well to have left that aspect to Organised Religion (which has been pumping out propaganda of a similar sort during every war in which this country has been engaged). But in the third act we were back once more to reality, and a tragic reality it was. As the curtain falls on the stranded soldiers, they are gazing into the air as they hear a plane approaching. " Is it one of ours ? " they are asking, hopefully, as the play ends. *Desert Highway* was a play of great merit ; this and other ABCA plays certainly deserved to be allotted a permanent theatre in London where the best of ABCA (and CEMA) productions might be seen by the general public in London.

Continuing at the Scala his fine efforts to retain a permanent place for Shakespeare on our stages, Donald Wolfit presented an Othello, Hamlet and Touchstone in quick succession, the best of these being the last, proving once again that he was a superb comedian, though not always a completely satisfying tragedian. He was, however, excellent in the early scenes in *Othello*, when his happiness with Desdemona was expressed in the lines (and one believed in them) :—

> " If it were now to die,
> 'Twere now to be most happy ; for I fear,
> My soul hath her content so absolute
> That not another comfort like this
> Succeeds in unknown fate."

Later on, when Othello's jealousy was fanned into flame, when he was in the throes of the misery of his psychological complexities, Wolfit was not quite so effective, though his death scene redeemed his performance. But he was not helped in any way by his Iago, a most unsubtle characterisation by Eugene Wellesley, and, if ever a theatrical truism were just, it is that " Othello needs an Iago." However, the Desdemona of Rosalind Iden, the Roderigo of Richard Goolden, the Emilia of Elizabeth Bayley and the Cassio of Richard

Lyndhurst were all worthy studies in a production which was, on the whole, one of the most satisfying of the Scala season's offerings.

The gay improbabilities of *As You Like It*—the masquerading, the banishment, the deception, the light-hearted love-making—all were underlined here in a gay rendering of the comedy. Rosalind Iden's Rosalind was her best performance of the season, while Wolfit, essentially a comic actor, was thoroughly at home as the Fool. He skipped merrily about, cracked his jokes, indulged in quips, mocked the little country girl with marriage and generally gave a bright and sprightly performance.

Of Wolfit's *Hamlet* there were varied opinions. Most critics agreed that it was an austerity production, monastically simple to such a degree that the setting was not even artistically satisfying. Wolfit took the Prince in his stride—Hamlet is merely another intelligent and effective portrayal in his gallery of Shakespearian characters—but one was not altogether happy with his conception. It was heavy, stolid, lacking grace and poetry, though it had much strength and, indeed, one or two particuarly fine moments. In many ways his Prince was a good deal better than Robert Helpmann's at the New Theatre, although the Guthrie production was far more alive and thrilling. But the difference between the New and Scala staging was not merely one of *decor*. More than ever was it apparent that Wolfit's supporting company was rarely up to the required standard. And it was not always a question of under-rehearsing. Nevertheless, Richard Goolden, Eric Adeney, Dorothy Primrose and Rosalind Iden (the best of his company) all gave consistently good performances at the Scala, and, notwithstanding the various occasional weaknesses displayed, those of us who loved the plays of Shakespeare counted ourselves very lucky in having an actor-manager of the calibre of Donald Wolfit who continued courageously to present, amid wartime difficulties, these many productions of the works of our great national poet.

The Chanticleer, new Little Theatre, opened with a quietly impressive production by Greta Douglas of *A Hundred Years Old* by the Quintero Brothers, beautifully acted throughout by a young and talented cast. Papa Juan's hundredth birthday is an event eagerly looked forward to, not the least by Papa Juan himself. His plans and preparations for bringing his whole family together for the occasion form the basis of this charming play, which is a constant delight. Full of quiet humour, it was nicely acted by John Lindsay, Audrey Fildes and Margaret Gordon. The Spanish atmosphere was captured by a pleasing Harker set, while other

promising young actors in this sunny production included Joy
Harvey, Simon Taylor, Edward Rutherfoord and Roy Siddons.
Many of us hoped that after such an auspicious beginning this
theatre might intersperse its classic programme with an occasional
new play ; and, indeed, a new war-play by Robin Maugham,
He Must Return, was produced later on with conspicuous success and
excellent acting from Laurence Payne, Robert Marsden, Anthony
Wallis and John Garley.

Green And Pleasant Land, a new play by Leonard Peck, was seen
at Unity Theatre. Dealing with the turbulent period of the early
1800's in England, it was a drama set against the background of the
struggle of the Chartists to obtain better conditions for the workers
in the factories. Kate, the wife of a reactionary politician, rebels
against her husband and the class he represents. Her liberal
sympathies are aroused by the workers and her love for Julian, the
Chartist leader, causes many complications. Though the first act
was inclined to be slow, the pace later improved and the last act,
when Kate decided to throw in her lot with the Chartists, was quite
exciting. Excellent performances are given by Anne Davies, Ellis
Solomon, Louie Bradley and Bert Pearl in a play with a strong
political flavour, which just failed to be really good theatre.

One of the theatrical sensations of 1943 was Sonia Dresdel's
Hedda Gabler. A new and vital stage personality, she had to
wait until the middle of 1944 for another opportunity to demonstrate
her remarkable talents (her ill-fated Spring tour of Henry Becque's
witty *Parisienne* evidently being well above the heads of provincial
audiences). The new vehicle was well chosen, though Joan
Morgan's *This Was A Woman* could hardly be labelled a good
play. By no means was it that ; the dialogue was weak, the
character of the daughter was quite unreal, the whole thing was,
in fact, the sheerest melodrama—and at times the lines were
astonishingly banal and stupid. Nevertheless, the part of Olivia
Russell, modern Hedda, was certainly a wonderful role for Miss
Dresdel, and she proved beyond all doubt that she was an actress
unique, resourceful and brilliant. Conquering a slight tendency
to over-act at the beginning of the play, she went on to give a
virtuoso performance in wickedness and cruelty which made
Ibsen's Hedda a simple country girl in comparison. A visit to
the Comedy was essential, if only to see Sonia Dresdel's powerful
acting, although Nova Pilbeam, Lyonel Watts, John Bryning and
Shelagh Fraser were all excellent as various victims of her lust
for power.

Out of more than five hundred entries to the Arts Theatre Competition for New Plays, the prize-winner was *The Two Children* by Peter Powell, a young playwright serving in the Navy. Produced by Alec Clunes and performed at the Arts, it proved to be a quiet, thoughtful and intelligent play, which though at times a little slow, was an entertaining enough study of pre-war county types. Lieutenant Powell's arguments were straightforward and, perhaps, a little unsubtle, but his points were made with wit and wisdom. He showed us a typically English upper-class household dominated by Lady Harriet, an old port-drinking tartar. Her spineless son and daughter-in-law, conventional and county, had a daughter while the local parson had a son ; the two children grew up in an atmosphere of cricket and church, country fetes and the usual round of riding and hunting. How were they equipped to face the outbreak of war in 1939 ? Not at all, said Powell, and his reasons were made plain in this interesting, though leisurely, conversation-piece, well acted by Anne Firth, Dorothy Reynolds, Jean Cadell, Cecil Ramage and Tristan Rawson. The best performance was contributed by that intelligent actor Denys Blakelock, very effective in an unusual role, as the cynical archæologist son. However, the two children of the title were so nebulously drawn that one could not help feeling a minimum of concern for their welfare ; that was the play's main weakness, and neither Alan Haines nor Honor Blake could do much about it.

To return to Donald Wolfit. At the Scala Theatre he was still continuing to present eight productions in repertory, each performance a different play—seven by Shakespeare, one by Ben Jonson. Thus, during each week, Wolfit himself produced and appeared in leading roles in eight completely different plays. He was seen as Hamlet, King Lear, Malvolio, Richard III, Touchstone, Shylock and Othello, as well as that rascally Jonson creation Volpone—an incredible feat, the like of which had not been seen on the English stage for more than a hundred years. But Wolfit took them all in his stride and showed once again that he is, indeed, a unique genius of the theatre, his memory astounding, his technique faultless. In his task of presenting the works of Shakespeare to the masses he is tireless, his love of the theatre is genuine and inspired.

Donald Wolfit is considered one of our outstanding Shakespearean actors. Lear, Shylock and Malvolio are his finest portrayals, in fact his Lear is possibly the greatest rendering of the Bard's portrait of crumbling majesty to be seen in London for many years. For seven years the Donald Wolfit company has performed the plays of Shakespeare and of the Restoration dramatists, as well as modern works, all over the British Isles, and Wolfit himself has done more to keep alive the works of this playwright than any other living actor. Since 1937, when his permanent company was formed, he has toured literally from Lands End to John o' Groats ; hundreds of thousands of people have gained pleasure through his pioneer work, many hundreds of his audiences, indeed, witnessing the plays of Shakespeare for the first time.

For two years before that, Donald Wolfit played leading roles at the Shakespeare Memorial Theatre at Stratford-on-Avon, and it was following his success here that he decided to devote his professional life to the cause of familiarising the British people with the inspired poetry of the greatest English playwright. Set-back after set-back has been his lot since the early years of his nation-wide tours, but in spite of all difficulties, accentuated more during the long years of war, the gallant Wolfit Company has carried on, bringing pleasure to audiences in all parts of the country.

During the war, in 1940, Donald Wolfit presented lunch-time Shakespeare to theatre-starved Londoners, and at the Strand Theatre, during the worst of the air-raid periods, he continued his daily performances of the poet's glorious verse. Apart from other seasons at the St. James's Theatre and the Westminster Theatre, and, of course, the culminating and outstandingly successful season at the Scala, the company principally spent its time touring the provinces, where the name of Wolfit probably means more than it does to London theatregoers. Like Sir Frank Benson before him, Wolfit is a name known up and down the country to all true theatre-lovers.

The practice of retaining a permanent repertory company and a permanent repertory of plays performed on different nights of the season is one which is used extensively in the Soviet Union. (In Russia, of course, Shakespeare is the most revered of playwrights, his works being performed continually throughout the year in a dozen cities). But in England the usual procedure is to run a play for as long as the public will pay to see it before replacing it with another. The disadvantages of this " long-run " system to both actor and audience are obvious and Wolfit eschews this form of commercialism. He prefers to give a different play at each performance and, if possible, a new production of a classic play as often as he can. Thus his actors do not become stale with constant repetition. For instance, to play Iago in *Othello* one night and the Ghost in *Hamlet* the next night, with perhaps a matinée as Sir Andrew Aguecheek in *Twelfth Night* in between, provides the actor with infinite variety, the result being that performances tend to be fresh, the productions each a new and exciting adventure.

That this achieves creditable results was proved during the Scala season. Apart from Wolfit and one or two others, the standard of the company at first was generally not very high. However, as the season progressed, unexpectedly good performances were given by members of the cast who at first seemed to find difficulty in feeling their way through their various roles. Thus at the height of the Scala season Wolfit was supported by some dozen very good actors, who were improving play by play. Among these were Rosalind Iden, Richard Goolden, Brown Derby, Elisabeth Bayley, Dorothy Primrose, Eric Adeney, Roy Dean, Ann Chalkley, Reginald Jarman and Eric Maxon.

Of Donald Wolfit himself much has been said. Suffice to repeat that he is one of our finest actors ; his *King Lear* alone is enough to justify his position among the great ones of the contemporary English theatre. But the pathos underlying his ridiculous Malvolio, his supremely intelligent study of Hamlet, his subtle portrayal of the revengeful Shylock, his jocund Touchstone, the fantastic villainies of his " Crookback Richard," the tenderness of Othello's love scenes with Desdemona, all these (not to mention his memorable study of Jonson's terrifying Volpone) are outstanding personal memories of great Shakespearean seasons by a truly courageous actor and producer. The theatregoers of this country have a good deal to thank Mr. Wolfit for. He is a National Theatre in himself.

REDGRAVE'S " UNCLE HARRY "

The English Theatre is notoriously unenterprising—which is another way of saying that the managements will rarely invest in such a risky venture as a new play by an unknown author, unless, of course, it is " the mixture as before." (Such enterprise as does exist can usually be found only in the smaller non-commercial theatres). An illustration of this lack of imagination was demonstrated by the immense success of *Uncle Harry* at the Garrick. Author Thomas Job, a Welsh schoolmaster, took this play around to a dozen London managements some years before, only to have it rejected by them all. Luckily he had the good sense not to be discouraged by this and to offer his play to America where it was snapped up, later to become a pronounced Broadway success. Then, in 1944, the play found its way back to England and, ironically enough, it must have cost a good deal more to stage it in London at that time than it would have done a few years before when Job was an unknown playwright with a play which was too " unusual," " grim " and " sordid," (so the managements said) to be a success in the West End.

Uncle Harry proved to be a powerful, and occasionally terrifying, play set in a provincial town in the early 1900's. Harry is the pathetic, kindly, middle-aged and frustrated bachelor whose life at home with two possessive and quarrelsome spinster sisters is dreary and oppressive. When his former sweetheart enters his life once more he is galvanized into murder, motivated by growing hatred of his sisterly encumbrances. He arranges the perfect crime, poisons Hester and throws the blame on Lettie. Relentlessly the hand of the law works out the tragic destiny of the wretched woman, but the closing scenes have an unusual twist. When the inhibited Harry, rejected by his sweetheart, finally confesses to his crime, no one will listen to him, the authorities refuse to believe him. Only one knows that what he asserts is the truth—and that is Lettie, who goes to her doom with the realisation that his is the worse fate. Harry remains, a shambling demented figure, wandering along back-streets, telling his story to anyone who will listen. Sombre ? Morbid ? Perhaps, but this production, directed by Redgrave and William Armstrong, was grand theatre with superb acting by Michael Redgrave, Beatrix Lehmann and Ena Burrill. His performance as Harry was the best thing Redgrave had ever done —(it was even more masterly than his Gribaud in *The Duke In Darkness*)—and he leaped to the forefront of English actors with this sensitive and pathetic study of middle-aged ineffectuality. *Uncle Harry* was a play which well repaid a visit, for it had an unusual and fascinating atmosphere which caused it to remain long in the memory.

An exciting month in the theatre also saw the brilliant acting of Donald Wolfit as *King Lear* at the Scala. This season continued to be a tremendous success, proving once again that the public *will* go to see good drama. The great plays of Shakespeare drew great audiences and our thanks went to Wolfit for his courage and faith, both in his repertory policy and in his public. Lear was his finest portrayal (though his Volpone ran it very close) and the mighty character of the aged and demented monarch, as Wolfit presented him at the Scala, was moving and impressive. The Heath Scene showed us a Wolfit who was master of the art of portraying madness satisfactorily, something which few actors are able to achieve. He was magnificently moving. More strength was needed, however, by Anne Chalkley's Regan and Elisabeth Bayley's Goneril; neither had the vehemence nor the capacity for creating the terror which should have been inspired by these roles. But Reginald Jarman's Kent was worthily played and carefully drawn, and Richard Goolden's Fool a gem of characterisation, acted with originality and pathos.

From the demented horrifics of *King Lear* we arrived at the masquerading frolics of *Twelfth Night*, in which Rosalind Iden cavorted deliciously and lightheartedly as a most pleasant and lovely Viola, while Wolfit played Malvolio with dignity, subtlety and occasional touches of pathos. Eric Adeney was Sir Toby Belch, Richard Lyndhurst was Sir Andrew Aguecheek and Dorothy Primrose excellently gay as the merry madcap Maria, while Roy Dean's Feste was his best portrayal in the season—this young actor improved play by play.

What a great work is Ben Jonson's *Volpone*, what a gusty masterpiece! And what a magnificent scoundrel Donald Wolfit made of the sensual Fox of Venice—though here his rascalities were well matched by the fawning obsequities of the parasite Mosca (a clever study by young actor, Brown Derby). In a play, in which the chief character is wholly immoral, nevertheless a moral *is* drawn and the final scenes found Volpone atoning for his many sins while Virtue (in the persons of Rosalind Iden and Richard Lyndhurst) triumphed. Richard Goolden's Corbaccio, Lionel Stevens' Voltore and Eric Adeney's Corvino were all good studies in avarice in one of the best all-round productions of the Scala season.

Murder took the stage once more in Harold Purcell's *The Rest Is Silence* at the Prince of Wales. This play was a reconstruction of the case of the notorious Madeleine Smith, who, in the middle of the last century, was accused of poisoning her lover with arsenic. The verdict was " Not Proven," and Purcell set out to dramatize the events leading up to the trial and to reconstruct the trial itself. Extravagantly produced in flash-back technique, the play was a little over-long and somewhat clumsy, but gave Ann Todd an opportunity of proving once more that she was one of the most interesting young actresses on the London stage. Martin Walker was impeccable as her elderly fiancée, while Karel Stepanek did extremely well to make a credible character out of the sketchily-drawn lover. This " episodic sequence " could not properly, however, be termed a play. The actual story of Madeleine Smith was both holding and dramatic and it is to be hoped that this unwieldy drama is by no means the last word to be written on the extremely fascinating theme of " the Edinburgh poisoner."

The Chanticleer continued its interesting new career by staging Clifford Bax's *The Venetian*, distinguished by an exquisite performance by Audrey Fildes, who demonstrated from her work as the Venetian, that she was a most gifted and promising actress. Geoffrey Dunn as the Cardinal and John Lindsay as the Duke made up a first-rate trio in this very charming period play. Greta Douglas, director of the Chanticleer, followed this with a production of a new play by Lionel Birch *The Orator*, a satire on small-town politics in the turbulent years before the war. The sincere young idealist, who muddles through his speeches, is rejected by the voters in favour of a cynical young waster with the gift of the gab, showing that oratory is preferable to sincerity, as far as politics are concerned. Robert Marsden, Joy Harvey and David Ralph were the chief protagonists in this satirical comedy, which indicated that Major Birch was a playwright with excellent ideas.

The Chanticleer promised for production new plays by Robin Maugham and Wilfred Walter, while the little Gateway Theatre in Notting Hill Gate also announced half-a-dozen new plays ready for presentation. Our unknown young playwrights seemed to be girding up their loins. Certainly it was true to say that the small experimental theatres had done most to encourage new writers, and out of the mass of chaff it was quite likely that one or two golden grains would be discovered.

THE GROWTH OF CEMA

When, a few months after the outbreak of war the Council for the Encouragement of Music and the Arts was founded by the Pilgrim Trust and Lord De La Warr (then president of the Board of Education) no one could have visualised the tremendous advances which this organisation would make during the wartime years. Now, aided by grants from the Treasury, the Arts Council (formerly CEMA) occupies a unique position in England—it is the answer to all critics who affirm that the policy of State-aided theatre is neither practical nor beneficial. In fact, the reverse is the case ; the three CEMA departments of music, art and drama have hurdled innumerable barriers, overcome obstacle after obstacle, and in 1944, each had completed four successful years of bringing to the people of this country the finest contemporary music, art and theatre. It is with the latter that I am primarily concerning myself; I intend to confine this brief appreciation mainly to the activity of CEMA in our theatre during the most critical years in this island's history.

The first Director of Drama, Ivor Brown, had to relinquish his position to become editor of " The Observer." His successor was Lewis Casson, and under his guidance CEMA has blossomed into the full flower of dramatic expression, and it is greatly due to his intelligence and integrity that the organisation has more than fulfilled its early promise. (In 1945 he was succeeded by Michael MacOwan, a most excellent choice).

When CEMA was established in 1940 the immediate problem was the provision of music and drama to meet the conditions of blackout, concentration of workers in new centres and the collapse of existing sources of theatre and music. Throughout the winter of 1940-41 the name CEMA began to be known in all parts of the country, the period of air raids intensified the need for its work and by 1942 it had stabilised itself and was securely placed in the affections of audiences in Wales, Cumberland and the Home Counties. This was a period of consolidation as well as for expansion and the cessation of raids found CEMA in the position for the first time of being able to think in terms of the future. For some while the guaranteeing of existing theatrical companies to help them continue their normal work had been the basis of the Drama Section's work, but gradually a most interesting development has taken place—the creation of a system of plays (as well as concerts and art exhibitions) to be given at Royal Ordnance Hostels in isolated regions. For some time now these R.O.H. Tours have been one of the most widely-successful and enthusiastically-welcomed of all CEMA ventures.

For these hostel workers are part of an enormous untapped source of audience and the Council's work in this direction is possibly the most important single facet of its achievement. By 1943 it had become evident that some form of association with the various touring companies was essential. Obviously the spasmodic sponsoring of limited tours was not completely satisfactory and now the Council's association with companies, instead of being for a particular play or season, is (like that with the symphony orchestras) an arrangement which runs from year to year, covering all the companies' activities. Thus each theatre group, while enjoying complete artistic freedom, will continue to submit its plans for review and discussion at the beginning of each annual period.

Of all these companies the longest collaboration has been with the Old Vic. From the bewildering early days of the war, through these magnificently courageous tours of County Durham and Wales, to the opening of the Old Vic's Liverpool headquarters, the Playhouse, and up to the culminating wondrous 1944-45 season at London's New Theatre, the association of CEMA and the Old Vic has blazed a trail of glory and splendid theatrical endeavour. Exemption from entertainment tax has been granted by the Board of Customs and, necessarily, CEMA companies are all non-profit making, all reserves accumulated being used in ways which are to the advantage of the theatre and the public it serves. The pioneer production in the hostel experiment was the Old Vic's staging of Laurence Houseman's *Jacob's Ladder* in 1942. Its success was such that to-day a regular circuit is in operation and many companies are continuing the task of bringing drama to the people ; included among these are Walter Hudd's Company, Stanford Holme's Company, Norman Marshall's Company, Ashley Dukes' Mercury Players and Basil C. Langton's Travelling Repertory Theatre, while the Pilgrim Players, the Market Theatre and André van Gyseghem's Company are others whose past work in these tours has been invaluable.

The response of factory workers to productions of the plays of Shaw, Goldsmith, Shakespeare, Maugham, Ibsen, Dekker, O'Neill, Wilde, Tchekov, Priestley, Afinogenov and others has been truly amazing. Playing to workers, dozens of whom had previously experienced no contact with living drama, the actors confessed to enjoying a new stimulant and were surprised and delighted with the spontaneous comments and intelligent appreciation of these new audiences. And the steady increase of the size of audiences at the hostels is an indication that the presentation of dramatic productions to the masses constitutes an obvious task for CEMA after the war. It has been the constant experience of actors during these tours to play before a completely unsophisticated audience, unaffected by convention or theatrical prejudice, an audience wonderfully appreciative and capable of boundless understanding and intelligence. Many thousands of such workers have had their first taste of " good " theatre during the past few years ; never again will they be content to sit through second-rate " roadshows " and cheap revues. The people are ready for good drama and post-war possibilities for the Council in this direction will be innumerable.

The Theatre Royal, Bristol, was the first theatre to come under the direction of the Council in its scheme for the decentralisation of the English theatre (ultimately this exquisite little theatre will be presented to the people of Bristol). During the two years in which the Council has presented plays there the artistic level has been higher than any other theatre in England (possible exceptions being Liverpool's Playhouse and Glasgow's co-operative theatre, the Citizens'). Other theatres in the provinces will gradually be added to Bristol's Theatre Royal in the list of Arts Council-controlled playhouses. Thus, with permanent theatres in various parts of the country, with a dozen first-class touring companies " on the road " and with headquarters in London, Wales and Northern Ireland, the Council will be the first to make State-aided theatre a practical success.

But for the war CEMA would not have come into existence and it is up to us who believe in the importance of its work to see that it does not cease to exist now that hostilities have ended. In " The Arts In Wartime," an excellent publication issued in 1944, the Council declared its policy as follows : " The defined purpose of the Council for The Encouragement of Music and the Arts is to maintain the highest possible standard in the arts. The Council is prepared to enlist in this policy the co-operation of theatre companies who have before them the same ideal of service to the community ; which are anxious to spread the knowledge and appreciation of all that is best in the theatre, and thus to bring into being permanent educated audiences all over the country. It is a special aim of the Council to encourage the dispersal of the arts to centres which, mainly for reasons connected with the war, are cut off from enjoying them." This is a worthy purpose and one which has been more than fulfilled. The basic missionary work of the Arts Council will assuredly have endless repercussions. It can—and must—go on.

PRIESTLEY AND LINKLATER

Priestley is one of the most important playwrights of our time and his plays invariably make the headlines and fill the theatres. His successful *Desert Highway* was designed to show us at home the sort of life which was being lived by the men of the Eighth Army in the North African desert. Later on in the year, in response to the oft-repeated question from the troops themselves, Priestley wrote a new play, a comedy called *How Are They At Home ?* It was extremely amusing, and possibly the sort of play which Priestley writes without effort. His fluent pen can doubtless present us with plays of the *genre* of *When We Are Married* at least once a year, while he salts the theatregoer's porridge with an occasional masterpiece in the manner of his *Johnson Over Jordan* and *They Came To A City*.

What do theatregoers prefer ? Well, in Priestley's case, I should say that they have learned to expect a great deal from him. They respect his outspoken opinions, they admire his first-rate ability to present a satisfying dramatic whole and they go to see a new play of his expecting a more-than competently written drama or comedy with a liberal leavening of social content. And they were not disappointed therefore in his new play, for although it was a broad comedy, and a very funny play indeed, there were enough cleverly-imposed sly social digs to ensure a palatable dish for those who were seeking to gain from the theatre something more than mere entertainment. Priestley has never been an after-dinner playwright ; he is essentially a people's dramatist and *How Are They At Home ?* had a universal appeal. (I wish he would allow London theatregoers to see his two plays—*Music At Night*, which had a limited run during the London Mask Theatre's season at the Westminster and which, as I noted earlier, was the first straight play to be produced in London after the outbreak of war, and *The Long Mirror*, which has been seen only in the provinces).

However, his comedy at the Apollo kept London laughing for some months. Many theatregoers seemed to prefer escapist entertainment, so Priestley gave London an " escapist " play. This did not mean that it was not topical. On the contrary, it was full of all the wartime complications in our private lives—the *locale* was a country house with the usual billetees and evacuees, plus an aristocratic factory worker, in the middle of giving an austerity party for her fellow-workers. It was all very amusing, with a beautiful piece of acting by Henry Hewitt as a Civil Servant with a *penchant* for string quartets, and grand performances by Charles Groves as the butler, John Slater as the British private and by Ralph Truman, Patricia Laffan and George Carney.

Eric Linklater's many books have caused him to be regarded as one of our leading literary figures, and rightly so. He has a merry wit which, in the medium of his novels, as well as in his radio plays *The Great Ship*, *The Cornerstones* and *Rabelais Replies* has been communicated to a wide audience. Why was it then that his first and eagerly-awaited stage play, *Crisis In Heaven* at the Lyric, was such a disappointment ? With a background of Elysium, that mythical haven where all the great and famous people through the ages find their way, the possibilities were surely endless ? There seemed to be so much that Linklater could have done, and so little which he actually accomplished. Briefly, the plot concerned itself with a scheme of old Aristophanes to mate Love (Helen of Troy) with Reason (Voltaire), in order to bring forth from this perfect union a Peace which would put an end to the war which has broken out in Elysium. Peace, when it was " born," arrived in the guise of a fully-grown policewoman, and was wedded (to keep Peace permanent) to Courage, *alias* the " British Soldier Through The Ages " ! The situations were not even slightly amusing and Linklater's political naivety was the most apparent fact established by this production. The plot wound its leisurely way through three over-long acts ; there was very little humour, one or two occasional (and very welcome) witty lines, but nothing more. Not one of the famous characters delivered a line which might be said to possess intellectual content, the play drifted along in shallow depths and never really reached deep water. Was that because Linklater reasoned that controversial dialogue might put the play in deep water with the Shaftesbury Avenue audiences ? He dipped his pen in acid once, and then only to deliver a spiteful attack on his own pitiful cardboard representative of those who were not able to reply to his gibes. Linklater was often described by the Press at this time as " the soldier-playwright." Obviously if he had thought less militarily during the conception of this play the result would have been a good deal happier. *Crisis In Heaven* was directed with rare polish by John Gielgud, but in spite of excellent acting by Ernest Thesiger, Nicholas Phipps, Esmond Knight and Deering Wells, the result was a disappointment to those of us who, knowing Linklater's other work, like the celebrated Biblical character, expected so much and received so little.

Strindberg was, in the fourth year of war, becoming popular with the troops ; an ENSA tour of *The Father* had been acclaimed by the soldier-audiences wherever it had been shown. Then in the summer of 1944 the Chanticleer Company produced his little-known *Easter*, a quiet and beautifully-written play, set in Sweden in the early years of this century. The Heyst family live in the shameful shadow of their imprisoned father, an embezzler. The son feels that he is disgraced and the daughter becomes demented with grief ; we see them during the period of Good Friday to Easter Eve, watch their trials, witness their disappointments and their final tribulation. The play, a realistic treatment of a symbolic theme, was directed by Greta Douglas with sympathy and sensitivity. Margaret Gordon gave a performance of great pathos as the mad child, while Robert Marsden, Laurence Payne, Meg Maxwell-Lyte and Joy Harvey all acted with skill.

To the Arts, for a short season, Paul Bonifas brought his Théâtre Molière in a programme which showed that he and his talented company were well able to act skilfully in both English and French. In Molière's *Doctor Without Medicine* (in English) and *Les Prècieuses Ridicules* (in French), the acting of Bonifas and his group proved to possess a wit and charm rarely encountered on the English stage. No knowledge of the language was essential to appreciate Bonifas' antics in the latter play, and among his cast Elma Soiron, Georges Rex, Paul Clarus, Suzy Marquis and René Poirier distinguished themselves with first-rate portrayals. The Bonifas Group should have a permanent London French Theatre ; the actors deserve it, and so do the theatre-going public.

At the Arts was also produced a Sir John Vanbrugh play, brought up to date by Sheridan, and entitled *A Trip To Scarborough*. It was colourful hearty theatre, with fops and grand ladies and intrigues and scandal, and with such delightful names as Sir Tunbelly Clumsy, Tom Fashion, Miss Hoyden, Probe and Loveless embroidering the comical antics of Frith Banbury, delightful as Lord Foppington, and David Bird, a monstrous and heavenly Sir Tunbelly. It was not so much the dialogue here as how it was delivered, and Messrs. Richard Wordsworth, Derek Birch, Edward Byrne and Newton Blick, aided and abetted by Mesdames Betty Jardine, Joan Haythorne, Wenda Rogerson and Laura Smithson combined to perform Sheridan's jolly joke with a great deal of rollicking fun and gusto.

111

NEW PLAYWRIGHTS—AND NEW BOMBS !

In the late summer of 1944 there was scarcely any audience in the London theatre, for the new " secret weapon," the flying bomb, had succeeded in emptying the West End, and the theatres, like all forms of entertainment, were suffering accordingly. Actors and actresses in Shaftesbury Avenue played nightly to sparsely-filled theatres, some plays were taken off and many new productions were indefinitely postponed. Nevertheless, just previous to the appearance of the daily (and nightly) nuisance, there had been certain encouraging aspects of theatrical activity in London. At least three new plays saw their first production, while the Arts, Chanticleer and Open Air Theatre produced brave revivals of classic plays.

The Kate O'Brien novel *The Last Of Summer*, dramatized by playwright John Perry, came to the Phœnix Theatre in a skilful production by John Gielgud. Set in Ireland, it proved to be a story of mother-love, of *The Silver Cord genre*, with Fay Compton giving a powerful and extremely intelligent performance as the woman who exercised all her dominant influence over the weaker-natured son, played by Geoffrey Toone. The first two acts were slow and clumsily-constructed, but this was more than compensated for by a moving third act, in which newcomer Margaret Johnston competed with Miss Compton for acting honours. This was a strange play, not by any means good, but with much in its atmosphere to recommend it, including the acting of the above, and also that of Hugh Burden, Ada Reeve, Hazel Terry and Tony Quinn. The background of Eire just up to the outbreak of war caused one to give way to a certain nostalgia for the works of Eire's greatest playwright, Sean O'Casey. This dramatic genius, creator of the famous *Juno And The Paycock*, *Plough And The Stars* and *Within The Gates* has not allowed any of his later plays to be produced on the London stage (with the exception of *The Star Turns Red*, which he wrote especially for production at Unity Theatre in 1940). This is a sorry state of affairs ; O'Casey's *Purple Dust* and his latest, *Red Roses For Me*, *should* be seen in London. It is, indeed, a sad commentary on the English theatre that a man of real genius will not allow his plays to be produced on our commercial stage.

A new play from the pen of young dramatist Ted Willis is always an event. Both *Sabotage* in 1942 and *Buster* in 1943 showed that he is a writer with a great deal of promise. One felt this

even more upon seeing his latest *All Change Here*, produced by
Herbert Marshall at Unity Theatre. The play was patchy, and
although it contained a great deal of very fine writing, yet his
work still showed a dramatic immaturity. But he is a playwright
with ideas, and he is not afraid to put them on to a stage. Here
he dramatised another theme taken from contemporary events,
basing his play around the life of an ordinary English family, and
more particularly around the lives of the daughters, who were
" clippies." The garage scenes were fast-moving, fascinating
slices of real life. The problems of whether or not to strike in
this particular stage in the war were brought into prominence
as Willis showed us husband and wife in opposition on this vital
question. The last act was by far the best and one was left at
curtain-fall with the certain knowledge that Ted Willis would soon
become a first-rate playwright, for he showed once more that he
had original ideas, high ideals and a tremendous flair for writing
smooth-flowing dialogue. His play was distinguished by some
very good acting from Lilian Hinton as the mother, Jack Clifford
as the father and by Laurence Davies, Helen Henderson and
Norman Cranwell.

One felt that Ronald Millar would also write a very good play
at any moment. His *Murder From Memory* in 1942 was just another
thriller, but his *Zero Hour*, which had a lamentably short run at
the Lyric, was a great deal better in every way. Like Willis,
Millar set his scene on the eve of the opening of operations in
Europe, and, like Willis, his play was one of ideas in conflict rather
than of situation. In fact, Millar and Willis had a good deal in
common—they were both young, both ex-Service men, both
theatre workers, (Millar was an actor, Willis a dramatic critic)
and each had the advantage of possessing political awareness and
a social conscience. *Zero Hour*, which though consisting mainly
of what Ben Jonson would call " a monstrous deal of talk," was,
nevertheless, an interesting play which deserved a better fate than
it received (flying bombs or no flying bombs). It was well acted,
particularly by Walter Fitzgerald as an English fascist, and by
Alan Haines and Gerard Hinze, but London theatregoers,
intimidated by a luke-warm press, preferred to stay away. They
missed a thoughtful play on a topical theme.

The case of *All Change Here* and *Zero Hour* provided an interesting
insight into the workings of the London theatre. The former was
well-produced at Unity, a non-commercial theatre which encourages

new British dramatists, and it was thus ensured of a minimum run of two or three months, during which time the play might be altered, have its rough edges polished off, and generally be improved in production. The latter, however, having failed to make a lot of money in the first three days, was ignominiously withdrawn. The moral was not that *Zero Hour* was the inferior of the Willis play ; it was that only in the non-commercial theatre was the new playwright given anything resembling a real chance. Could one really blame Sean O'Casey for refusing to allow his plays to be put on by West End managements ? The above example surely indicated the bankruptcy of the commercial mind.

Jean Jacques-Bernard is a playwright with a subtle and delicate style, but *The Sulky Fire* was not given an altogether satisfactory translation by John Leslie Frith in Claud Gurney's production at the Arts. It is the story of a returned prisoner-of-war and his gradually-aroused suspicions of his wife's infidelity during his four years' absence. Sensitively written, the play depends a great deal upon the atmosphere and certainly upon the personalities of the two protagonists. As the girl, Nancy Hornsby (who had a great personal success in this role at Liverpool Old Vic a few months before) was almost perfect, but one felt that Michael Golden had been miscast as the husband ; he had an earthy quality in his work which came amiss here. Nevertheless he gave a careful performance, though John Ruddock as his father stole every scene in which he appeared. Ruddock is one of my favourite actors. Of him it can safely be said that he never gives other than a first-class portrayal. He has certainly been responsible for many memorable performances at the Arts Theatre in the past few years.

One upon whom, quite wrongly, I feel, has fallen the mantle of Ibsen, is Norwegian playwright Helge Krog, whose *Happily Ever After* was produced by Greta Douglas at the Chanticleer. It was an interesting play, extremely well-written and conceived, dealing with the loves of a young girl, Sonja, from the period of youthful impetuosity, through the stage of Bohemian free-love to marriage with a business-man ; and then back full-circle to her first love. The character of the girl was most complex, the part an extremely difficult one, but Sheila Burrell gave an excellent performance and showed herself to be a most promising young actress ; while Laurence Payne, the artist, Robert Marsden, the student, and Alan Adair, the business-man, all gave satisfying character-studies as the amorous influences of the various periods of Sonja's eventful life.

★ *John Gielgud,* as Macbeth, in his own production of
Shakespeare's tragedy, 1942.

★ *Vivien Leigh* and Peter Glenville, as the Dubedats, in Shaw's "The Doctor's Dilemma", produced by Irene Hentschel, 1942.

★ ***Constance Cummings,*** who appeared in S. N. Behrman's "Skylark", 1940 ; and in Robert Sherwood's "The Petrified Forest", produced by Norman Marshall, 1942.

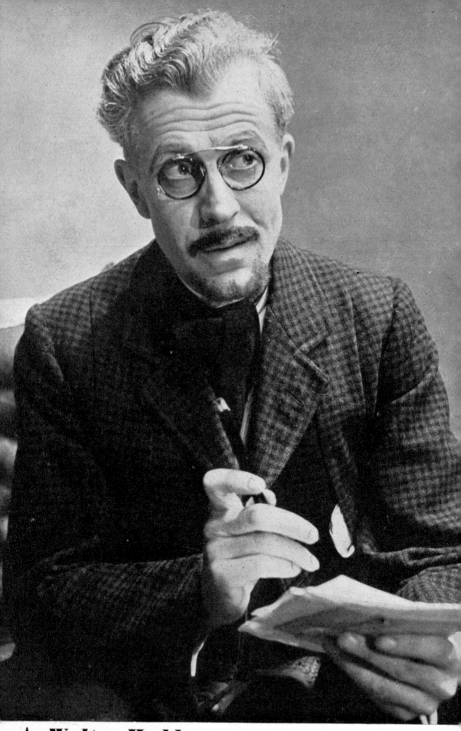

★ *Walter Hudd,* as he appeared in his own production of Ibsen's "Hedda Gabler" in 1943. Hudd was prominent during the war years for his many C.E.M.A. tours.

PHOTO : TUNBRIDGE-SEDGWICK

★ *Max Adrian* and John Ruddock, as the exiled White Russian officers, in Peter Ustinov's tragi-comedy "House of Regrets", produced by Alec Clunes, 1942.

★ *Peggy Ashcroft,* who appeared in "The Importance Of Being Earnest" in 1940, in Rodney Ackland's "The Dark River", 1943, and with John Gielgud, 1944-45.

PHOTO : ANGUS MCBEAN

★ ***Robert Morley*** and Coral Browne in "The Man Who Came To Dinner", by Moss Hart and George S. Kaufman, produced by Marcel Varnel, 1942.

★ *Sonia Dresdel,* who came into prominence in the war years with her performance as Hedda Gabler. She also appeared in "This Was A Woman", and "The Sacred Flame".

A revival of Lonsdale's *The Last Of Mrs. Cheyney* at the Savoy, in the capable hands of director Tyrone Guthrie, proved (surprisingly one felt) to be really excellent light entertainment. It contained a polished study by Jack Buchanan as Dilling, while Coral Browne was superbly high-minded as Mrs. Cheyney. One could hardly expect to be bored when the cast also included such delightful people as Athene Seyler, Austin Trevor, Frances Rowe and James Dale, and indeed this Lonsdale period-piece stood up remarkably well —in any case it was, of its type, quite a good play. And, more important, it was a witty play.

Two examples of CEMA-sponsored productions came to London at this time. To the Lyric, Hammersmith, Walter Hudd brought his company in Thomas Dekker's *The Shoemaker's Holiday*, a rousing, rollicking and very English comedy with grand portrayals from Andrew Leigh, John Raffan, Sheila Macintosh, and Hudd himself. At the Open Air Theatre, the Stanford Holme Company was seen in that masterpiece, *Lady Precious Stream* by S. I. Hsiung, charmingly acted by an excellent cast. It was certainly reassuring to see that CEMA productions were on the whole better produced and acted than many West End plays, not to mention the fact that the works they performed were (and still are) in nearly all cases, eminently superior. In 1944 there were about a dozen of these companies " on the road," and most of them still continue their good work. May we hope that it will soon be possible for Londoners to have a chance to see them *all* in turn ?

CRISIS IN THE THEATRE

It had to be admitted that the theatre was, during the autumn of 1944, in a very bad way. Out of the thirty or more playhouses usually functioning in London's West End, only eight remained open. The reason? Flying bombs—or that, at least, was the immediate cause, but it all went much deeper than that. Every crisis in the last ten years had caused similar repercussions in the London theatre. And this time the audiences let the theatre down—or was it the theatre which let down the audiences ? Maybe it was a little of both. At any rate controversy began to range in the Press concerning the proper role of the theatre in times of emergency. Some writers believed that with three years of prosperity behind them the theatre managements could well afford to play to empty houses, that, in fact, it was their public responsibility to remain open whatever happened. To these critics the managements replied that two

G

weeks of bad houses could quite well cancel out all the profits made during the whole run. " Why should we play at a loss ? " they cried. And in a country where a completely different morality is inspired and created within the hushed circles of " business " there was no effective reply to this. To an extent it was reasonable to submit that if the Government wished the theatres to remain open for the benefit of morale then it should have subsidised the theatres and thus helped to meet losses half-way.

Certainly the Government side-stepped the issue. On the one hand it constantly urged the theatres to remain open while on the other it refused all State aid, or help in financing worthwhile plays to do so. Whichever way one looked at it, the whole business was a sorry mess and a significant reflection on the condition of the theatre in the world's capital. The London theatre had always stewed in conditions which were, to say the least, anarchic and in times of crisis this was revealed as chaos. Nevertheless it would be wrong to imagine that the managements were entirely to blame for the theatrical collapse. The flying bombs did indeed keep audiences away from the theatre and it was problematical that, even if the bulk of the theatres had kept open, whether they would attract reasonable attendances. The public deserted the theatre and who could blame them ? For the actors however it was a horrifying experience to play nightly to a tiny number of people scattered in various parts of the house, and that was the unfortunate lot of some of the casts of plays which remained open until the end of the " blitz."

The brighter side of the penny revealed that this decentralization of the theatre as a result of the air attacks on London was another step in the move towards the realization of a nation-wide theatre with playhouses in every town, and opera houses and civic theatres in the principal provincial cities. At the beginning of the war, then later, during the 1940-41 raids, and again in 1944, the provinces were given the chance to see well-produced shows with good casts. The urge for good theatre exists outside London. Thousands of people have seen stage plays for the first time since the Old Vic and CEMA have been sending out first-rate touring companies to outlandish places like Wales and Cumberland, and with the encouragement and continuation of their work, the beginnings of a re-birth in the provincial theatre at last seem to be hopefully apparent.

The only new production during the worst of the raids was a revival of John Drinkwater's comedy *The Bird In Hand* at the

Arts Theatre, where director Alec Clunes was determined to carry
on whatever happened. This play, of 1920 vintage, deals with
the efforts of a trio of guests in an old country inn to convince
the bigoted innkeeper, Thomas Greenleaf, that he should desist
from attempting to dictate to his daughter about her private life.
The guests are an elderly K.C., a commercial traveller in sardines,
and a jolly young plutocrat with Socialist sympathies ; between
them and in three amusing acts they ensure that true love runs
smooth. Greenleaf is an irritating, lovable old publican, strictly
a child of his time. Herbert Lomas was perfect in the role, which
he created in the original production, and grand performances
were given by Frith Banbury, George Bishop and Katherine
Boutall while, in the scene-stealing role of Blanquet, Andrew Leigh
was excellent. The lovers were played by Felicity Lyster, from
the Old Vic, and Richard Stapley (a young newcomer with considerable charm). Alec Clunes produced and the very good *decor*
was the work of Maise Meiklejohn.

Other plays which continued to run in London for the duration
of the raids were *How Are They At Home* ? at the Apollo, *This Was
A Woman* at the Comedy, *Blithe Spirit* at the Duchess, *While The
Sun Shines* at the Globe, *Last Of Mrs. Cheyney* at the Savoy, *Arsenic
And Old Lace* at the Strand, *Twelfth Night* (with Ernest Thesiger
as Malvolio) at the Open Air Theatre, and *Miss Julie* at the Chanti-
cleer. That scintillating revue *Sweeter And Lower* still continued
to pack houses at the Ambassadors, while the Windmill Girls and
Phyllis Dixey held the fort of " real art " at the Whitehall and
Windmill Theatres.

A HOPE FOR THE THEATRE

The occasional wartime evidences of internal controversy in
the English theatre was, perhaps, a healthy sign. It indicated
at least that some of the more intelligent actors were sitting up
and taking notice that our theatre possessed certain shortcomings
which had prevented it from attaining the stature of others such
as the Soviet theatre and the Irish theatre. Michael Redgrave,
Peter Ustinov, Beatrix Lehmann and J. B. Priestley all, at different
times, leaped into print with their varying criticisms of our theatre,
and their contributions were valuable and illuminating—in two
senses. Much of what they said was only too painfully true, but
that these theatre workers should be concerning themselves about
their job and its future was significant. So many of our actors

and actresses were content to go on acting in mediocre plays,
unfortunately too many of our playwrights were being encouraged
to write them. Neither writer nor interpreter considered it would
seem that there was any purpose in entering into a serious discussion
on the English theatre. Both continued to turn out technically
first-rate (and often third-rate) work while vehemently denying
that they had any part to play in that great outside world beyond
the footlights. This blind contentment with conditions was a
barrier which had to be broken down ; it was this apathy which
had been one of the factors contributing towards our gradual
theatrical decline during the years immediately preceding the war.

But all the blame should not have been laid at the feet of the
actors. Encouraging, indeed, that the number of politically-aware
and socially-conscious theatre workers had grown daily. With
war conditions spotlighting every anomaly in the business, more
and more young actors and actresses were beginning to ask questions
and to think more deeply about general theatrical conditions.
Wartime, too, had seen the growth of the actors' trade union
into considerably more than a bargaining power and, certainly,
the part which British Actors' Equity will play in the future in
the re-orientation of our theatre is inestimable. When Equity
began its long and difficult task the chief opposition came not
only from the business men who control the theatres, but from
those stage players who said " It is impossible to organise artists !
They are individuals. Trade unionism is all right for the factories,
but not for the stage." Well, they have been proven wrong, and
though the job is by no means finished, those actors who tend to
think individually and act collectively have gradually assumed
greater importance and influence.

Peter Ustinov has recently said that the failure of our present
theatre to attain stature as a satisfying art form is because the four
groups who contribute towards its success or failure—namely, the
theatre workers, the audience, the men who put up the money
and the critics—are not pulling their weight. He thus appears
to spread the blame equally over these four groups. Michael
Redgrave, on the other hand, tends to blame the critics. Along
with such theatre workers as Walter Hudd, André van Gyseghem,
Beatrix Lehmann and Herbert Marshall, I humbly submit that
the change *must* come from the top, that is, from the men who
own the theatres and control the productions which are seen on
their stages. If the spirit of enterprise, as Ustinov says, has deserted

our playwrights, this is surely due to the fact that enterprise, daring and courage are words practically unknown to the managers who are in the position to employ or commission the playwrights. " The theatre has never known such prosperity as now," they cry in defence, and to a certain extent that is true. But that it is only temporary is something which has escaped notice and the absence of a long-term policy in the commercial theatre (or, for that matter, of any policy at all) is often only too apparent.

But I have headed this chapter " A Hope For The Theatre " because I firmly consider that post-war plans for the theatre will be exciting and altogether progressive. Various reasons contribute to my belief. Firstly, a great new audience has grown up which previously had never known the live theatre—both ENSA and CEMA are responsible for much of this. Of the latter organisation I have often written ; as the Arts Council it still goes from strength to strength, bringing first-rate productions of classic plays to workers in factories in all parts of the country and its development in the post-war period into a travelling branch of State Theatre is of course inevitable, its influence valable. Recently the Co-operative Movement entered into the theatrical sphere. The People's Entertainment Society during the past few years presented a number of London successes, including *They Came To A City* (with H. M. Tennent), *Ten Little Niggers* (with Farndale) and *How Are They At Home ?* (with Jack Hylton), and they have made a number of plans to send out touring companies to every provincial city where there is a co-operative movement (and that means almost every English town). The P.E.S. has already bought theatres in various parts of the country and thus adds itself to CEMA, creating a formidable *bloc* of worth-while non-commercial theatre organisations, formed to combat the decay of the commercial theatre in England.

And that is not all. The Old Vic, with headquarters in Liverpool and at the New Theatre, London, successfully inaugurated a policy of real repertory, in the style of the Soviet theatre, choosing, for its first three productions, *Peer Gynt, Arms And The Man* and *Richard III*, playing on alternating evenings through the season. But the artistic bankruptcy of the long-run system was not only spotlighted by the Old Vic but also by John Gielgud, whose company opened at the Haymarket with a programme consisting of *Hamlet, Love For Love* and *The Circle*, also played in nightly repertory. Thus the focal points of State-aided theatre and the commercial theatre

both demonstrated that the first blows towards the rebuilding of the
English theatre were being struck. And with the growing power of
the Arts Council and others becoming daily more obvious, it thus
seemed that we were indeed witnessing the beginnings of a
new movement in the theatre.

It was the Arts Theatre which again defied the flying bombs,
to present Alec Clunes's production of that delightful Carlo Goldoni
comedy *Mine Hostess*, which though a favourite with Soviet
audiences, is rarely seen in England. The translation by Clifford
Bax was altogether admirable and lost not a fraction of the gaiety
of the original. Light, airy and quite enchanting, the play deals
with the efforts of the pretty hostess of an inn to make a self-
confessed misogynist fall another victim to her womanly wiles. The
hussy in this case was Judy Campbell, the woman-hater Baliol
Holloway, and both acted well. Miss Campbell as Mirandolina
was a roguish and captivating creature and we could hardly blame
the Knight for his final surrender, even though she did leave him
high and dry in the end in order to marry her valet. It was
Mr. Holloway however who was most successful in capturing in his
performance the atmosphere of the period, though Newton Blick,
Dorothy Reynolds and Joan Sterndale Bennet gave entertaining
comic studies in a most amusing and diverting production.

ENSA AND THE DRAMA

With the outbreak of war, the Theatre Royal, Drury Lane, one
of the oldest theatres in London and on whose boards stalked the
ghosts of past glories, became transformed overnight into an
immense dramatic factory, for it was requisitioned as the headquarters of the Entertainments National Service Association, branch
of the Navy, Army and Air Force Institutes—in other words, ENSA.
From Drury Lane since that time has flowed a continuous stream
of organised entertainment units, produced and rehearsed in the
Theatre Royal and dispatched to play their admittedly vital part in
Britain's war effort.

From the very beginning the Drama Section of ENSA came
under the direction of Henry Oscar, well-known actor and
producer, and it was under his guidance that the provision of plays
for the Army, Navy and Air Force grew to its present-day pro-
portions. In the midst of a general theatrical collapse in September,
1939, the Drama Section began a long and difficult period of
valuable and constructive work. The first ENSA play to be sent

out was Frank Harvey, Jr.'s *Saloon Bar*, which commenced a four-weeks' tour of camp-sites. This play, from this modest beginning, attained three continuous years playing in England alone, with various changes of cast. For a play to be performed all over this country for three years, never in the same place twice, was indeed an achievement and an indication of the enormity of the whole task. Those faithful stand-bys, *Night Must Fall* and *While Parents Sleep* were the first productions to be sent to the B.E.F. in France in the early days of the war and ENSA continued to send regular companies to the men of the Services in England and on the various fronts. At the close of 1944 there were four such companies touring Egypt, playing at different camps and towns every night, while a permanent ENSA Repertory Company in India kept six plays continuously in the repertory and organised tours to various sections of the India and Burma fronts. In addition, there were more than a dozen companies touring England at the same time, two more were covering Northern Ireland while half-a-dozen others covered the shifting fronts in France, Holland and Belgium.

It seems inconceivable that this immense organisation began with an office in Drury Lane, a blank blotting pad—and Henry Oscar. But it is to his boundless energy and enthusiasm that much of the success of ENSA's Drama Section can be credited. Single-handed, and often encountering what seemed to be insuperable difficulties, he procured plays, producers and casts and organised them into home and overseas tours, with the result that since 1940 literally hundreds of productions of all types of plays were produced under his able guidance to be sent to the troops. Henry Oscar may well look back on his work during the first five years of war with satisfaction. It was a difficult task, the handicaps involved were tremendous ; nevertheless these ENSA plays succeeded in their job of bringing pleasure to millions of fighting men and their value towards the heightening of morale was inestimable.

In autumn, 1939, at a time when the English theatre was, to all intents and purposes, non-existent, Oscar and his producers laid the basis of what for a considerable period was the sole instrument for the provision of drama to the Forces. And the plays themselves gradually showed a tendency to improve in quality. Farces, thrillers and light comedies were, naturally, still prime favourites, but indicative of the general improvement in taste and gradual changing of standards was the fact that ENSA tours of Shakespeare, Ibsen, Shaw and Strindberg were received with enthusiasm, and little opposition, in camps and garrisons in all parts of the country. Thus, in spite of the criticism often levelled against it, ENSA succeeded to a degree in bringing drama to numbers of soldiers, to whom before the war the theatre was an unknown quantity ; and it may be conceded that ENSA, like CEMA, has played its part in creating that great new post-war audience which will be thirsting for good drama and demanding the nation-wide theatre which the State (which brought it to them during the war) can provide in times of peace.

In addition to the productions prepared at Drury Lane, there existed since 1940 a kind of " lease-lend " system, by which West End successes followed the London run by undertaking tours under the auspices of ENSA. In this way many of the best-known " names " of the English stage were seen in fit-ups on camp sites in Cornwall, in Northumbrian church halls, in converted barns in the Highlands and on the stages of ENSA-constructed Garrison Theatres from Aldershot to Gibralter. The provincial Repertory Theatres, too, became part of the scheme and the Repertory companies of Dundee, Birmingham, Colchester and Glasgow, and many others, were sent out as complete units to Ack-Ack Batteries and out-of-the-way R.A.F. sites. And it was the rank and file of the English theatre which rallied wholeheartedly behind ENSA. Repertory actors in London and the provincial cities unselfishly gave their services for months and even years at a time, some even from the outbreak of war until 1944. In fact it was by no means the stars who were most important in linking the soldier with his home through the means of dramatic entertainment. Certainly more truthful is it to record that it was the work of these thousands of capable yet often unknown actors who contributed in the main towards the staging of hundreds of successful productions of nearly two hundred different plays (as widely diverse as *Love In A Mist*, *The Father*, *Saloon Bar* and *Man And Superman*) since ENSA began its wartime career.

THE OLD VIC: TOWARDS A NATIONAL THEATRE

The splendid brilliance of the 1944-45 Old Vic Repertory Season at the New Theatre and the attendant acclaim, which was its well-deserved lot since the opening nights, augered well for similar seasons in future. To those of us who for many years had been continually advocating the creation of a National Theatre, the season was a living example of its practical possibilities. The Old Vic *was* in effect London's National Theatre ; it would, at any rate, suffice until the dream itself became realisation. The plays which were chosen to open the season were Ibsen's *Peer Gynt*, Shaw's *Arms And The Man* and Shakespeare's *Richard III*, a representative choice from three of the great masters of drama. Other classic plays were planned to be added to the repertoire in due course and the season was for many people the most exciting and heartening theatrical event of the war. More than that, it was a significant prelude of a new movement in the English theatre, for two other leading West End managements soon followed by announcing their intention of presenting repertory seasons in London. Thus it seemed the artistic barrenness of the long-run system was gradually becoming apparent, and the standard of excellence of the Old Vic Season undoubtedly threw into greater prominence the shoddy production and low artistic level of some long-running West End " successes."

To translate Ibsen's unwieldy masterpiece into terms of an alive dramatic whole is a formidable task, but Tyrone Guthrie was aided here by the really admirable English version by playwright Norman Ginsbury, and the production rose to heights of great power in its moving presentation of one man's journey through life. Whether or not *Peer Gynt* is just this, or a moral dissertion or an allegory, it is certainly great poetic drama, in which Ralph Richardson gave a performance which placed him in the front-rank of modern actors. The callow selfishness of the idle dreamer Peer gave place to the satisfied smug facade of the middle-aged business man, while this in turn showed Peer in the final sequence as a lonely, embittered and desperately fearful old man, returned at last to the scenes of his childhood. The wheel had turned full circle and the little boy revealed himself once more, as Peer sat on the ground in the final scene, reflectively stripping the skins off the onion. In all three phases Richardson was superb ; Peer Gynt is one of the testing roles of drama, the actor literally *does* run the whole gamut of emotion throughout its length. And Richardson was brilliant, powerful and moving, while the Aase of Sybil Thorndike, the Troll King of Nicholas Hannen, the Woman in Green of Margaret Leighton, the Solveig of Joyce Redman, the Button Moulder of Laurence Olivier and the really excellent team-work of Harcourt Williams, Vida Hope, Sydney Tafler and Morris Sweden all dovetailed to form a deeply significant and often inspiring performance of a great and soul-stirring play.

In direct contrast was the light-hearted fooling of Laurence Olivier and Ralph Richardson in Shaw's *Arms And The Man*, one of his less-serious pieces, set in the Ruritania of the early 1900's. What would have seemed to be a witty broadside against militarism resolved itself into a merry morality-piece with a great deal of amusing and edifying dialogue spoken and acted beautifully by Messrs. Laurence Olivier, Ralph Richardson, Nicholas Hannen and Morris Sweden and Mesdames Sybil Thorndike, Margaret Leighton and Joyce Redman. John Burrell's production managed successfully to combine the occasionally varied acting styles of the participants in this comedy ; the Sergius of Laurence Olivier many times veered dangerously towards burlesque, as did Joyce Redman's saucy and audience-conscious Louka. And Ralph Richardson's " chocolate cream soldier " was often in direct contrast to these, while Nicholas Hannen's Bulgarian Blimp occasionally approached caricature. But these were small points of criticism, indeed, in a play which was a constant joy to watch. The production moved swiftly, and with the triple assets of delightful Doris Zinkeisen settings, the satisfying comedy-work of the talented cast and the intelligent direction of Mr. Burrell, this 1944 version of Shaw romped home to a triumphant final curtain.

The John Burrell production of *Richard III* reached heights of magnificence unequalled even by the wonderful Troll Scene, Boyg Scene and Lunatic Scene of *Peer Gynt*. It was the finest staging of a Shakespeare play seen in London for many years. In every way it was superb. It had in Laurence Olivier a Richard whose diabolical cunning, hypnotic eye, treachery, villainy and sheer downright devilry were presented intelligently and, most important this, credibly. That Olivier's conception of this most complex character differed from some of the greatest actors of Crookback Richard in no way reflected upon his final success. He was certainly the finest Richard III of our generation ; in his fiery, quicksilver performance there were moments bordering upon genius, unforgettable moments in a truly titanic production. Two of these still stay in my memory. Who could forget the scene when, after being spat upon by the contemptuous and sorrowing widow Anne, Richard with consummate skill and subtle, honeyed inflections, wheedled her round to accepting him, her husband's murderer, in the role of suitor ? In previous productions the acting had rarely convinced me in this most difficult of scenes, but Shakespeare's superbly skilful writing coupled with acting of the highest order brought this moment to vivid life. And again, the scene when Richard heard that he was to be crowned king was surely unforgettable ? As he leaped out of the chapel window, tossing the Bible over his shoulder, we saw the swiftly shifting emotions cross his face—satisfaction, jubilation, triumph! Then, quick as a flash, he drew himself up in flushed arrogance and, turning with imperious dignity, bade the astonished courtiers kneel to their new king. It was in such instances that Olivier revealed himself as a subtle and inspired actor. He acted not only with voice and gesture but also with face and eyes and the whole of his body. This then was a Richard III to be seen and long remembered; his was a performance fit to rank him with the great ones of the English stage. To Nicholas Hannen's Buckingham, Sybil Thorndike's Margaret, Joyce Redman's Anne and Sydney Tafler's Catesby was well-deserved honour conceded ; Harcourt Williams, Margaret Leighton, George Relph, Michael Warre, Charles Leno, Nancy Nevinson, Morris Sweden and the rest of this first-rate company combined in their varied and excellent ways towards the creation here of a triumphant and memorable dramatic production.

To be able to write honestly and sincerely that this Repertory Season was the most important single event in the wartime theatrical scene was indeed to my great personal satisfaction. To Tyrone Guthrie, John Burrell, Ralph Richardson and Laurence Olivier and all those who planned and worked to bring this great season of drama to successful fruition went the grateful thanks and praise of all intelligent theatregoers. That there was hardly an empty seat during the entire season should once more prove that the British people are thirsting for " good " theatre and will not be satisfied until there are a dozen Old Vics—and more ! During five years of war the work of the Old Vic has earned for it a high place in the affections of lovers of the drama. Since being " blitzed " out of its Waterloo Road headquarters, this company has continued to present and produce only the highest quality work in London, in Liverpool and on its tours of Wales and the North. Wartime has intensified the need for " good " theatre and the Old Vic has carried on in the highest traditions of its founder, the late Lilian Bayliss. The London season of 1944-45, the beginning of great things, was the high-point culmination of five years of brave and courageous work in the wartime theatre.

The absence of new plays in the Old Vic programme was a point quickly noted by critics, but the reason for the dearth of new playwrights may surely be laid at the door of the commercial managements who have consistently rejected the new, the different, the revolutionary and the thoughtful among plays submitted to them for production. In the rare instances when a management has taken a chance, it has backed out of its commitments and taken the play off after only a few performances, if it has not proved an *immediate* box-office success. Nevertheless there are a small number of young playwrights whose finest work is yet to be seen on our stages and who, in spite of setbacks, are continuing to write the best plays of which they are at present capable. One of this number is Peter Ustinov ; I see no reason at all why his *The Banbury Nose*, produced at Wyndham's in late 1944, should not have been included in the Old Vic repertory. It represented a great improvement on his earlier work and was a witty and extremely worth-while comedy. Certainly the play, while not being a masterpiece, could have acquitted itself well in such company as Shaw and Ibsen.

The first hurdle, that of writing the play backwards, was taken in the young playwright's stride, and fascinating was the manner in which he unrolled his canvas from back to front while preserving the qualities which made it a satisfactory dramatic whole, as intelligent as it was stimulating. Mr. Ustinov once more made the vagaries of old age his main target. He had done it before in *House Of Regrets*, and again in his one-act play *Beyond*, and here he assailed the crumbling resistance of near-senility with well-aimed darts of satire at the conservatism, stubbornness, hypocrisy and general futility of age. Coupled with this he launched a most telling broadside against family tradition. The Banbury nose of the title belonged to the family of Hulme-Banbury, who came over with William the Conqueror and beget a long line of sons, all soldiers except one. This one, the last of the Hulme-Banbury's was the most nebulously-drawn of all the play's characters. As, we assume, he purported to be the mouthpiece for echoing Ustinov's own rebellious urges, one was inclined to experience a tinge of disappointment at the general weakness of argument displayed by this character as well as with the slipshod logic of his philosophy. Again the depth and profundity of much of this playwright's work seemed to be marred by these occasional faults. However, *The Banbury Nose* was, notwithstanding, one of the finest new plays seen in London in 1944 and showed twenty-three-year-old Peter Ustinov to be the most promising British playwright of the war.

The acting in Norman Marshall's thoughtful production was generally excellent. Roger Livesey emulated his *Colonel Blimp* performance with his most skilful interpretation of a military martinet through four different generations, while Ursula Jeans in a pastel-shade role was quietly excellent. Lyn Evans, Alan Trotter, Michael Shepley, Isolde Denham and Eric Maturin were all very good as the Banburys, but it was to Hugh Burden that most of the acting honours fell. His sensitively-acted study of the curate drew attention to Burden as one of the cleverest of our young actors.

At the Aldwych Theatre Marcel Varnel produced a strong, intelligent American play, *Tomorrow The World*, which faced up to post-war problems in Germany. "What are we to do with the Germans?", is a question which has been posed many times (and answered by Lord Vansittart and others). In this play the authors, James Gow and Arnold d'Usseau, set the scene in a Middle West town where to the home of a kindly, liberal-minded college professor comes a German boy, son of the professor's old Heidelberg friend, Carl Bruckner. But Emil, the boy, is not by any means his father's son, in fact, he has been taught to hate the memory of his anti-Nazi father. This strutting little horror, his mind poisoned with Nazi ideology, presents a pretty problem to the American household. He is cunning, deceitful, vicious, cruel and cowardly; at twelve he is a veteran of evil for he has been taught that kindness and tolerance are signs of weakness and that the theory of the "Master Race" is borne out by American ineffectuality. What is to be done with him and with thousands like him? Education, psychological treatment, the gradual substitution of a new set of values—these are part of the remedy, according to the authors. And we were left at curtain-fall with the knowledge and reassurance that Vansittartism can never work in practice. *Tomorrow The World* was a valuable and intelligent play and certainly a worth-while contribution from the theatre to post-war plans for a permanent world peace.

As Emil, fourteen-year-old David O'Brien was magnificent; he was easily the theatrical "find" of 1944. Angela Glynne was also excellent as the little American girl while as her father, the professor, Robert Harris was quite outstanding. He gave a performance of sincerity, charm and intelligence, recalling his many acting triumphs at the London Mask Theatre some years before. Elizabeth Allen, Lilly Kann and Julien Mitchell contributed fine studies in what was a worth-while play.

REAL REPERTORY

The Festival of English Comedy, which Alec Clunes staged at the Arts in 1943, had certain repercussions. It was the first large-scale experiment undertaken for a number of years in attempting to establish a real Repertory Theatre permanently in London. By real repertory I mean the system of retaining a number of plays in a theatre's repertory, a different play being seen at each performance. Thus all the plays in the programme are kept in circulation throughout the season while new productions are constantly being added to the repertoire, in the style of the Continental theatres. For instance, the Old Vic Company, whose policy at the New achieved success beyond all expectation, added new plays to the repertory as the season continued. And at the Haymarket the Gielgud Company followed suit with a programme of plays by Shakespeare, Congreve and Maugham, played alternately throughout the season by an all-star group of actors, other plays later being added during the season.

The commendable modesty which John Gielgud demonstrated in his billing outside the Haymarket Theatre was emulated inside. It is perhaps not realised to what degree has been Gielgud's accomplishments towards the betterment of the English stage during the past ten years or so. Beyond all question he has raised the standards of acting and production in our theatre. He has employed only the finest actors and actresses in all his ventures and never does he allow undue prominence to be given to his own name. The high point of his distinguished career was the 1944 Haymarket season of repertory.

Once more he gave us an inspiring *Hamlet*, a sparkling (if occasionally disappointing) production of *The Circle*, and a production of *Love For Love* which for wit, polish and gaiety had been unparalleled in the wartime theatre scene. Acknowledged as the foremost verse-speaker on our stage, Gielgud went all out for the beauty of the lines in George Rylands' straightforward production of *Hamlet*. In many ways it was not so interesting as the Guthrie-Benthall staging at the New some months before, but to enjoy to the full the rich and glorious verse of our finest playwright spoken with passion and beauty by one of our finest actors, then this *Hamlet* should not have been missed. Here was great acting. Among the first-rate company, those who distinguished themselves in the plays of this memorable season were Leslie Banks, Peggy Ashcroft, Yvonne Arnaud, Cecil Trouncer, Miles Malleson, Marian Spencer, Max Adrian and George Woodbridge.

Somerset Maugham's plays wear extremely well. His *The Circle* was one of the mainstays of the Haymarket season, while his delightful comedy, *The Breadwinner*, drew record-breaking audiences to the Arts, where Leonard Sachs, the producer and

Denys Blakelock, " the breadwinner," combined to create a comedy rich in satire (more than a degree bitter for Maugham reflects in all his work his noted misogynistic outlook). James Agate in his " Sunday Times " column considered that Blakelock's outstanding acting success in this role " made the evening and spoilt the play," because Maugham's middle-aged stockbroker is designed as a dull creature, lacking in understanding and possessing no sense of humour. In fact this esteemed critic went so far as to head his article " Denys Blakelock Ruins a Play ! " How wrong he was. That Blakelock made of the stockbroker, who decides to leave his family and go off and enjoy himself for a change, a diverting, likeable and wholly charming fellow was surely the correct approach ? How better to throw into prominence the inanity and egotism of his family ? The point which Maugham continually makes is that they are not likely to detect a subtle sense of humour and a modest charm in their father whom they despise simply because he is of a different generation. And, while there is no indication that there father is a bore (except in their eyes), Maugham supplies an abundance of evidence that the contrary is the case. Mr. Blakelock's outstanding performance was rich in humour, and was both thoughtful and logical, and to the connoisseur it stood out as a piece of acting of the highest quality. For two years Denys Blakelock had maintained a perfection of subtlety and intelligence in his work at the Arts Theatre. For those who asserted that he was only a supreme comic actor one felt obliged to remind playgoers of his moving and pathetic study as Sam in *Awake and Sing* a few years before.

In the wartime years the novels of Anthony Trollope seemed to undergo a revival in popularity. His works had also been heard on the radio in serial form and in late 1944 Vera Wheatley dramatised his " Last Chronicles of Barset," which was produced at the Lyric under the title of *Scandal At Barchester*. To transfer Trollope's country chronicles to the stage required considerable dexterity. His novels possess a leisurely and human quality which is found difficult to adapt adequately into a play. Nevertheless the story of the perpetual curate of Hogglestock who is wrongly accused of theft was so well acted by Felix Aylmer, Olga Lindo, Milton Rosmer, Dennis Price, Audrey Hesketh and Dorothy Hyson that it became a play which was graceful, full of charm and interest, in fact, admirable entertainment for the discerning playgoer. (It was the first production of Una Plays, a theatre group headed by Michael Redgrave and Robert Helpmann).

Another encouraging move in an extremely interesting
theatrical year was made at the historical Lyric Theatre, Hammersmith, where a season of Bernard Shaw's plays in real repertory
began. Among the plays which were produced in nightly
repertory were *Too True To Be Good, Village Wooing, Candida, The
Dark Lady Of The Sonnets* and *Pygmalion*. Ellen Pollock and Michael
Golden were the producers of this Shavian season, while the company
included Michael Golden, Nigel Clarke, Richard Goolden, Patricia
Hilliard, Wallas Eaton, Joan Craft, John Leather, Edward Byrne,
and, of course, Ellen Pollock, whose Eliza Doolittle was the best of
her several performances. Other Shaw plays were promised as
additions to the repertoire, so that for the first time since the war
began London possessed two Shakespeare Theatres (the New and
the Haymarket) and a Shaw Theatre (the Lyric). The public
response to this new venture indicated something that the success
of the New and Haymarket seasons had already pointed to—a great
new public for worth-while theatre.

To conclude this chapter here is a quotation from the " Daily
Telegraph " of November 30th, 1944. Under the heading
" Shakespeare War-Time Boom " occurs the following :—

" Shakespeare is enjoying greater popularity in London to-day
than he has experienced in any war since the Napoleonic era.
About 37,000 people have paid to see the first thirty-three performances of Mr. Laurence Olivier's *Richard III* in the Old Vic
repertory at the New Theatre.

" Mr. John Gielgud's *Hamlet* at the Haymarket has already been
seen by more than 23,000 players.

" These figures represent a degree of popularity unrivalled by
Shakespeare in wartime since Edmund Kean made his sensational
debut at Drury Lane in 1814. It is a curious coincidence that
Kean's most popular roles were Hamlet and Richard III. In
his first season when he touched heights of popularity he never
afterwards reached, he played Richard to average receipts of £562
and Hamlet to £512.

" His Othello, which was reckoned his finest performance,
brought a house nearly £100 less than his Richard. Even Kean's
Richard, however, only three-quarters filled the theatre, whilst
both Mr. Olivier and Mr. Gielgud are playing to packed houses.

" It is estimated that in his first season about 50,000 people
saw Kean's Richard. Before Christmas (1944) this figure will

have been exceeded by Mr. Olivier's performance, Mr. Gielgud has already passed the 14,000 who saw Kean's Hamlet."

WHERE ARE OUR PLAYWRIGHTS?

The fact that the new Peter Ustinov play *The Banbury Nose* was taken off after a comparatively short run led one to ask whether the theatre-going public really wanted new plays. It was, of course, an excellent thing to find that the New, Haymarket and Hammersmith Lyric were invariably full up at each performance. But it was significant that while the programme contained plays by Shakespeare, Shaw, Ibsen, Congreve and Maugham, there was not included even one new play by a new playwright. That the great classics were given new life on the London stage and that these seasons of real repertory were achieving wide success in no way minimised the danger. The English theatre cannot stand still, and though there is a vast store of treasure among the dramatic masterpieces of the world, new blood, new talent is necessary in order that the English drama shall progress into full flower. Many times it has been asserted that new British playwrights are rarely given a real chance, but then the question does arise as to where new playwrights are to be discovered?

Small indeed is the number of professional playwrights in this country. Many plays are written annually by writers who have had little or no connection with the theatre. Some of them are badly written, clumsily constructed and obviously show inexperience. Eventually they are returned to the would-be playwrights without a word of explanation and without advice, criticism or help. It may well be argued that managers, producers and play-readers (such as they are) in the commercial theatre, have scarcely time to read the submitted plays, let alone return a detailed criticism. And, in the main, this argument is valid. Many play-producing concerns are one-play ventures; while the existing play is on there is very little preparation made for the future. Thus no money can be spent on reading and considering plays which might never be given production. Obviously then a system of play-reading may only exist in the case of a permanent theatre venture (the type of theatre, in fact, the establishment of which is continually being advocated by true lovers of the theatre such as Tyrone Guthrie, Michael MacOwan, J. B. Priestley and others). Thus is established another strong argument for State-aided theatre. Only when young writers can be encouraged and given

139

opportunities by a progressive theatre with a far-seeing, long-term policy shall we in England see the beginnings of a vital national theatre, presenting plays by new playwrights.

Peter Ustinov's play, an intelligent and extremely worth-while effort, ran only for a comparatively short time. It seemed that, as a commercial work, it had certain shortcomings. Nevertheless, I am certain that it would have been turned into a considerable success were it presented by a State theatre, nursed carefully, included in a programme of repertory and generally given a *real* chance to make its mark. And that is what should happen to the work of all our young playwrights. Only in this way can we ensure a steady flow of new plays, *some* worth-while plays and, perhaps, a masterpiece.

During the latter part of 1944 there were no new plays produced, but a number of interesting revivals, including Noel Coward's *Private Lives* at the Apollo, which was quite amusing, even though much of the humour was out-dated. The petty squabbles, disputes and stand-up fights of two useless idlers may have constituted entertaining theatre in 1930, but things have changed since then, not the least in the theatre, and a 1944 definition of this play might easily be " much ado about nothing." Nevertheless, it was very well acted by John Clements, a shade Cowardesque, Kay Hammond, extremely Hammondesque, and by Peggy Simpson and Raymond Huntley, excellent in the unsympathetic role of the stodgy Victor. The production, by John Clements, was slick and the sets were sumptious, but there was something of an air of decadence about these stagey people. One felt that it was not possible to care less about Elyot and Amanda, they were quite obviously spoiled, selfish and of no particular use, either to themselves or to society generally. But the play was redeemed by a number of quite funny lines, in the Coward manner, including the classic " Women should be beaten regularly—like gongs." So should some playwrights.

At the Lyric, Hammersmith, the Bernard Shaw Repertory Season began well with Ellen Pollock's production of *Too True To Be Good*, not one of G.B.S.'s best plays, but still miles ahead of most modern efforts in wit and originality of both dialogue and construction. Shaw breaks all the rules of the theatre, yet none can be said to break them more successfully. In the first act we were introduced to the chief characters, but at curtain-fall Richard Goolden, as The Germ, told the audience that although the play was now virtually over the characters would resume the stage for the next two acts for the purpose of a discussion. And, in fact, this is exactly what happened! However, the resultant conversation was so stimulating that one soon forgot the lack of plot and the unconventional construction and revelled in the wit of the Irish master.

Ellen Pollock was outstanding as the amorous centre of attraction, Michael Golden was impressive as the unbelieving cleric, while Edward Byrne as his atheistic parent made the most of the play's best speeches and gave a fiery and passionate delivery of some of the lengthiest diatribes in modern drama. Patricia Hilliard's poor little rich girl, John Leather's eccentric private, Nigel Clarke's artistic officer and Wallace Eaton's intellectual sergeant were all interesting studies in this production.

Eugene O'Neill's waterfront story *Anna Christie* has not been seen in London for many years. The role of Anna is, indeed, a difficult one and constitutes a testing piece for young actresses. Flora Robson scored a considerable success at the Westminster some years ago as O'Neill's tragic heroine. And Dorothy Reynolds, a clever young actress who had previously been seen in many character parts in Arts Theatre productions, made a very good showing as Anna. Hers was an intelligent and moving effort, matched in mood by Ernest Jay's Chris, which was beautifully acted. It was that fine young player Trevor Howard, however, who leaped into the theatrical limelight once again with his fiery, passionately Irish and idealistic stoker, Matt. What a superb actor he is. Laurence Payne's bored barman and Anne Marie Hase's aged harridan completed a collection of interesting waterfront studies.

THE END OF THE LONG RUN?

The outstanding single feature of the most successful theatrical year of the war was the return to favour of the repertory system. In the Old Vic Company at the New Theatre and the John Gielgud Company at the Haymarket, London acquired in one week two first-rate repertory theatres.

For two hundred years the theatre has pursued the policy of the long run (with occasional experiments in repertory, such as the historic Frohman season, directed by Harley Granville-Barker at the Duke of York's over forty years ago) and this system has been responsible for many of the ills attending the modern English stage. Now, at last, it would seem that the thin end of the repertory wedge has been prised under the mountain of managerial implacability, and the deserved success of the New, Haymarket and Hammersmith Lyric (not forgetting the Arts), has forced into the open the vexed question of long runs versus repertory. The former has long been part of the theatrical scene, but it was not always so. More than two hundred years ago Covent Garden and Drury Lane were the only theatres permitted by law to produce straight plays, thus possessing virtually a theatrical monopoly. Catering for the entire London playgoing public, both these theatres had of necessity to produce a number of different plays, sometimes more than fifty a season, and keep them in their repertoire. Each night a different play would be given, so that it was quite usual for the theatregoer to see at Drury Lane as many as eight plays in one week—such as *King Lear*, *Hamlet*, *Richard III* and *Othello* along with Jonson's *Volpone*, Farquhar's *The Constant Couple* and Vanbrugh's *The Provoked Wife*, with possibly a few curtain-raisers thrown in for good measure ! This dwarfs even the Gielgud and Old Vic seasons ; the amount of hard work, enthusiasm and versatility demonstrated gives an indication of the vitality of the seventeenth and eighteenth-century London theatre. (Nevertheless, the present-day record of Donald Wolfit, who plays eight leading Shakespearean roles during one week, compares favourably with Garrick's total of twelve parts in one month at Drury Lane).

The long run system, as we know it, came into being with the passing of the Theatre Act of 1843, which put an end to the previous situation of the Covent Garden—Drury Lane joint monopoly and resulted in an immediate increase of theatres presenting straight plays. Thenceforth each new theatre kept its one play running, and soon Londoners were able to choose their plays from upwards of a dozen different theatres, with the result that the repertory system gradually reached its demise. It was claimed by the managements that commercially and artistically the long run policy was superior, but this was, and still is, questionable. Certainly the actor may affirm with truth that a long run means stagnation, boredom, a deadly lack of interest in the part and in the play, resulting in eventual artistic barrenness. The constant repetition, the same dialogue, moves and business tend to make the performance dull and lacking in inspiration. This is, however, not the fault of the actor, who can hardly be expected to play the same part every night for six months or more without getting stale.

But happily the tyranny of the long run is at last being threatened. It has held sway for more than two hundred years and only now has the actor finally rebelled. Ballet audiences and opera audiences have become accustomed to repertory. The response to the wartime repertory seasons would seem to indicate that theatre audiences will also become accustomed to the idea, while the generally high standards of the productions of both companies demonstrates that the actor responds to a system which means for him a variety of parts large and small, a constant testing of his dramatic powers and a means of ensuring that his versatility becomes apparent to a public long accustomed to type-casting in the theatre. If actors of the eminence of Laurence Olivier, Leslie Banks, Ralph Richardson, John Gielgud, Sybil Thorndike, Peggy Ashcroft and the others who have shown their faith in repertory continue to have their way it seems likely that we shall be enjoying *real* theatre in London for some time to come. We are witnessing, as Hannen Swaffer has said, the beginnings of a renaissance in the English theatre ; sincere theatre-lovers will echo his expressed hope that the post-war years will not see a return to the ultra-commercialised, take-a-chance, slump-boom, hit-flop theatre of the years between the wars.

Both the New and Haymarket had auspicious additions to their repertoires. The Old Vic's staging of *Uncle Vanya*, a play of atmosphere, from the pen of the sensitive poet and schoolmaster, Anton Tchekov, provided an opportunity for Laurence Olivier to show once more in his characterisation of the doctor, Astrov, a subtlety and intelligence which marks him as the outstanding actor of his generation. The lazy sultriness of the country estate was captured in John Burrell's production which, though tending to err on the side of slowness, was nonetheless notable for its concentration upon the relevant psychological details which make the play a powerful study of human foibles and frailty. The approach of Ralph Richardson to the role of the inhibited and embittered Vanya was careful, skilful and thoughtful, if a trifle robust at times, and into the Telyegin of George Relph, the Yelena of Margaret Leighton and the Sonya of Joyce Redman one felt that a reasonable amount of understanding had been poured. To an audience not over-accustomed to *Uncle Vanya* the tragi-comedy was inclined to become a comi-tragedy, but the next generation of theatre-goers will distinguish more easily the truths and lessons of this quiet masterpiece, which is sociological criticism at its most telling.

A curiously ironic choice for mid-winter was Nevill Coghill's staging of *A Midsummer Night's Dream* at the Haymarket. Few messages here, but ever present the poetry and enchantment of Shakespeare's immortal fairy-tale. The dropping of Mendelsohn's time-honoured musical score, the casting of John Gielgud as Oberon and Max Adrian as Puck were questionable improvements upon the usual procedure of production, but Leon Quartermaine, Marian Spencer and Francis Lister scored as the nobles while the Quince of Miles Malleson and the Bottom of Leslie Banks were superbly comic additions to their already formidable roster of characters.

This theatrical quarter saw the presentation of half-a-dozen new plays, most of them disappointing. The most amusing was Terrence Rattigan's *Love In Idleness* at the Lyric, a light-hearted variation on the *Hamlet* theme. Three of the new plays presented problems. Rattigan showed us a Cabinet Minister whose quiet *ménage* with an attractive widow is threatened with destruction on the coming upon the scene of her son, newly arrived from Canada. The problem here was real enough, but the playwright presented no solution and the play tailed off disappointingly. The supreme acting of Lynne Fontanne and Alfred Lunt, however, was enough to make this comedy well worth seeing. The problem in *The Years Between* by Daphne du Maurier, at Wyndham's, arose from the conflict between a returned husband, believed dead for three years, and his wife, who in the years between has built a new life; but again the play did not satisfactorily resolve the issue and the final act was disjointed and aimless. Clive Brook made an auspicious return to the London stage and Nora Swinburne acted the wife with sympathy and assurance. But it was almost as much of a disappointment as Frederick Lonsdale's *Another Love Story* at the Phœnix. One could hardly fail to display a certain lack of interest in the problem presented here, which was whether the hero should be allowed to marry into a rich Long Island family or resume relations with one of his former victims (if someone as attractive as Judy Campbell could thus be labelled). Anton Walbrook was definitely not at his best in light comedy and the talents of a number of other people were wasted on this what must be termed a tedious and witless trifle.

Anna Neagle made her return to the stage in an adaptation of Jane Austen's *Emma* at the St. James's. It had a certain charm, as did Barrie's whimsical piece *Quality Street*, which opened the blitzed Embassy once more; it was delightfully acted by Jean Forbes-Robertson and Linden Travers. Among other new plays were *Laura* at the St. Martin's and Vernon Sylvaine's *Madame Louise* at the Garrick. In the former Vera Caspary and George Sklar failed to write a part interesting enough for Sonia Dresdel, who is a powerful actress and thrives on strong meat, while in the latter Mr. Sylvaine provided Alfred Drayton and Robertson Hare with the types of roles in which they have previously endeared themselves to farce audiences. (Trousers were conspicuously absent).

Whatever one felt about religion it is certain that even the most cynical of theatregoers could hardly fail to be moved by *The Wind Of Heaven* by Emlyn Williams, at the St. James's. Williams had, in this play, written his best work since *Spring 1600* or *He Was Born Gay* (both eminently superior in every respect to the more successful *The Light Of Heart* or *Morning Star*). He took as his theme the coming of a second Messiah to a tiny Welsh village in the 'nineties. To the Welsh valley comes Ambrose Ellis, circus owner and successful impresario, in search of a dwarf who is reputed to make music from thin air. The " freak " proves to be Gwyn, the son of Bet, a servant girl, whose shining quality of faith is one of the most inspiring aspects of this most carefully drawn of all the Welsh playwright's many dramatic creations.

The transformation of Ambrose from hard-bitten cynicism to final, unwilling belief in the uncanny power of the child was beautifully drawn, and well-acted by Emlyn Williams. Both he and Diana Wynyard were responsible for some touching moments. In a quieter vein her sensitive acting proved the perfect medium of balance to his more necessary tendency to flamboyancy, in a character who was drawn slightly larger than life. Miss Wynyard was superb. And, as the humble, self-effacing and faithful Bet, Megs Jenkins gave one of the best stage performances of 1945, a perfect portrayal in dignity and sincerity of a modern Madonna. In an excellent cast Herbert Lomas, Barbara Couper and Arthur Hambling were responsible for moments of first-rate theatre, in a play which was one of the most skilfully-written and impeccably-acted plays seen in London for many years. It was, indeed, a triumph for Emlyn Williams.

STAGE MARRIAGES

A feature of the English theatre a decade or so ago was the popular practice of husbands and wives appearing together on the stage. Many famous combinations graced the boards in the late nineteenth century, among the most well-remembered being the

Bancrofts, the Martin Harveys, the Bensons, the Forbes-Robertsons, Fred Terry and Julia Neilson, Marie Tempest and Graham Browne, the Boucicaults and the Maudes. Two hundred years ago it was a procedure for managers of stock companies to engage for a season a husband and wife as leading players. And in the eighteenth century it was quite usual for half-a-dozen married couples to be appearing at Drury Lane and Covent Garden at the same time. But through the years all this has changed, and with the demise of the great actor-managers in the late nineteenth century, husband-and-wife teams became less and less prevalent.

Present-day husband-and-wife theatrical teams include Sybil Thorndike and Sir Lewis Casson, Roger Livesey and Ursula Jeans, Cyril Ritchard and Madge Elliot, Diana Churchill and Barry K. Barnes, Helen Cherry and Trevor Howard, Ann Ziegler and Webster Booth, and Rachel Kempson and Michael Redgrave (who were seen together in *Jacobowsky And The Colonel*, a new American play, produced at the Piccadilly in the summer of 1945). While, of course, Vivien Leigh and Laurence Olivier bid fair to becoming England's Royal Family of theatreland. At the Phœnix Miss Leigh was seen giving the finest performance of her career in the truly inspired Laurence Olivier production of *The Skin Of Our Teeth*, and at the Lyric that incomparable team Mr. and Mrs. Lunt delighted Londoners during the first few months of 1945 in the Rattigan comedy *Love In Idleness*.

Are these family teams a good thing for the theatre? It would seem that the answer is overwhelmingly in the affirmative, both theoretically and in actual practice. One of the principal reasons for the success and popularity of the Soviet theatre is the long-held system of permanent companies playing in repertory, for it is certain that constantly acting together brings to the actors concerned a knowledge of each other's styles, method, technique and is an invaluable aid to the polish of the finished production. Permanent companies, such as the above, have been formed only too rarely in England in the past, but in 1944 and 1945 repertory companies in the West End of London have brought to theatre-goers a vision of the splendour which might well be attendant on the theatre of the future. At any rate these seasons revealed that astonishingly fine results may be achieved by actors accustomed to working together, and being used to each other's personalities and styles of acting. Thus, to a lesser degree, it seems apparent that such a team as Alfred Lunt and Lynne Fontanne would bring to their roles a depth of understanding and mutual sympathy of a kind beneficial to the play and to the theatre as a whole.

The Lunts are, of course, the first names which spring to the tongue when discussing stage marriages, for their outstanding acting achievements on both sides of the Atlantic have placed them in a class of their own. In this country Sybil Thorndike and Lewis Casson are perhaps the most famous of our stage couples, having appeared in a number of interesting and intelligent productions in the past thirty years. And, at the Piccadilly, Mr. and Mrs. Michael Redgrave, who had previously appeared together in *The Beggar's Opera* and *Uncle Harry*, were seen in the new S. N. Behrman play from Franz Werfel's well-known novel. *Jacobowsky And The Colonel* is set in France at the time of Dunkirk and the Fall of Paris, and is concerned with an exciting trip across France to the Channel and so to England by an arrogant, feudal-minded Polish officer and his companion, a " professional refugee," S. L. Jacobowsky. Primarily a study in character, the play demonstrates the triumph of the Jew's kindliness, tolerance and resourcefulness over the selfish arrogance of the Polish Blimp. But the setting of a comedy in the tragic period of Europe's collapse seemed likely to incur the criticism of a section of playgoers to whom the spectacle of refugees, civilian bombing, swaggering Gestapo and Nazi " tourists " brought to mind anything but humorous memories. And it is problematical whether this was the correct psychological moment to treat the complex Continental scene of the past few years as a background for intrigue in the combined manner of Ouida and Eric Ambler. Nevertheless this was a good play, a sensible play and, on the whole, an entertaining play. The Werfel sense of situation and character, combined with Behrman's grim witticisms ensured an interesting evening of theatre, well acted by Michael Redgrave, Rachel Kempson, Karel Stepanek, Esmé Percy, Frith Banbury and David Bird.

Russian playwrights Gogol and Ostrovsky were recently represented in London. Gogol is rarely seen here, while *The Storm* has been for many years Ostrovsky's only representation on the London stage. The Chanticleer in Kensington staged his *Wolves And Sheep*, a gay little comedy, and *Larissa*, a Tchekov-like tragi-comedy of life in a provincial town on the Volga in the middle of last century. Both demonstrated why Ostrovsky is considered one of the most popular dramatists in the Soviet Union. *Wolves and Sheep* was an exceedingly well-constructed comedy, produced by Greta Douglas, with intelligent performances by Olive Layton, Robert Marsden and Lucille Gray ; while *Larissa*, a curiously compelling play, gave many opportunities to Jacqueline Gelsthorp and Joseph James, two promising new players.

The Gogol comedy, *The Government Inspector*, was given the character of a sixth-form revel in the John Fernald production at the Arts, but it was extremely amusing, providing a satirical insight into the inefficiency and corruption of the Tzarist provincial regime. Geoffrey Dunn gave a mannered, highly comic rendering of the impoverished gambler mistaken for the government inspector, while Morris Sweden as the mayor was excellent as a small-town dignitary, and Peter Cresswell, John Garside, Gibb McLaughlin, Nuna Davey and Natasha Sokolova had amusing moments as the other participants in the fast-moving Russian farce.

Ivor Novello's 1945 spectacle, *Perchance To Dream*, at the London Hippodrome, was rivalled for splendour, magnificence and general three-ring-circus effect by the Robert Nesbitt extravaganza, *The Night And The Music* at the Coliseum. Both were splendiferous, colourful, breath-taking, colossal. The hackneyed highwayman situations in the Novello play were matched by the hoary jokes of Vic Oliver. But in the matter of lack of taste and wit the Coliseum show won easily. The admirable mechanics made possible by the revolving stage, and the hypnotic mass of colour and girls, however, ensured that this top-heavy musical registered an immense success, thus demonstrating the remarkable catholicism of British theatregoers.

THORNTON WILDER'S MASTERPIECE

What do theatregoers really demand from the theatre ? Do they go primarily to be amused, entertained, coddled ? Or do they demand more serious fare—plays to make them think, plays dealing with problems of real life, psychological plays, plays with educational value, plays which point a message to humanity ? Certain is it that a vast number of playgoers ask nothing more than to be entertained, and should a message or two be thrown in for good measure so much the better, providing it does not unduly interfere with the plot. Any playwright attempting to break the bonds of theatrical convention is taking a chance of alienating public taste, which by and large has remained constant throughout the past decade. However, the wartime rebirth of the theatre has attracted a new and potentially much larger public, which possesses no preconceived notions of theatrical offerings ; it is this enormous public which possibly will help to influence public taste in the direction of new experiments in our theatre. An audience of inexperienced play-goers may, for example, on seeing Thornton Wilder's *The Skin Of Our Teeth* have entered more wholeheartedly into the genial spirit of make-believe than a sophisticated audience, more accustomed to conventional stagings. But it is true to say that the Wilder play, like all masterpieces, has in implication and design a universal appeal.

When *The Skin Of Our Teeth* was first produced in New York it is reported that a section of the audience walked out during the intermission and did not return. The London production, directed by Laurence Olivier at the Phœnix, also caused much bewilderment and controversy, though I am not aware that anything so drastic as a mass walkout was at any time perpetrated. At each performance one heard murmurs of mystification from the audience as the crazy pattern of unconventional happenings unfurled themselves before the startled eyes of playgoers accustomed to an evening of traditional theatre, theatregoers unaccustomed to witnesing drama of a kind likely to upset their mental equilibrium.

And this Thornton Wilder play is so *different* as to do just that. It is a comedy and yet a tragedy, both a morality play and the wildest of farces, it is moving, it is uproarious, it is social commentary, it is nonsense *a la* Brothers Marx, it is sincere, it is facetious—in short, the author of " The Bridge of San Luis Rey " and " Our Town " has here written a drama which may be all things to all men. Here is a dramatic work which obeys no rules, yet abides by the first rule of the theatre—to entertain. Here is a piece of theatre which, while rattling along merrily at breakneck speed for two and a half all-too-short hours, also manages to obey yet another equally important dramatic rule—to educate. To entertain, to educate, to provide an exciting evening of originality, wit and wisdom and outstanding poetry—all these things *The Skin Of Our Teeth* succeeds in doing. It is the supreme morality play, since the moral insinuates itself subtly into our consciousness what time we are chuckling at Wilder's quiet wit or laughing uproariously at the antics of Sabina, who shares with the Antrobus family the epoch-making sensation of representing, for the purposes of the play, the whole human race since the beginning of the world.

For that is the crux of this apparently crazy comedy. Mr. and Mrs. Antrobus represent Eternal Man and his Mate, Sabina is the

Eternal Siren or Other Woman, Henry and Gladys are the varying qualities of Youth, each experiencing the frustrations, disasters and triumphs which have been the lot of Man since that curiously persistent mammal learned to walk and, more important still, to think and feel.

That this most sensitive of American playwrights should choose the comic strip technique for presenting his thesis is not surprising. Wilder is a keen philosopher; he knew that his ideas would be certain of getting across to his audience if they were presented amusingly, excitingly and, above all, with originality. He succeeds in his purpose, which is to make us think, to reflect on life and death, on human happiness and progress and the barriers which lie in the path of its true fulfilment. It is safe to say that everyone in the audience can profit from seeing the play. There was more good sense in the apparent nonsense than in any dozen other plays to be seen in London in 1945 ; both amusement and edification are to be gained from this most original work.

Scorning a realist staging Wilder has made use of that expressionism which in the 1920's stormed the theatres of Europe, and which is associated in many playgoers' minds with gloom. But here this expressionism has a purpose—to point theatrically the admittedly formidable attempt to put the whole story of civilisation on a stage, and to achieve dramatic highlights by the use of expressionistic effect rather than reality. Lest the above should seem to claim for Wilder's play a certain serious headmasterish quality, let me at once affirm that here was the wittiest, funniest, most unusual piece of stage-craft seen in England for many years. Unconventional to a sometimes astonishing degree, nevertheless, this gay concoction, which applied a " little revue " technique to a theme worthy of Greek drama, was all entertainment. Laurence Olivier indicated by his subtle handling of a complex production and by intelligent touches of direction an awareness and complete understanding of Thornton Wilder's purpose. This was a skilled directorial achievement, helped not a little by the high-quality acting of a hand-picked cast.

To write that Vivien Leigh as Sabina achieved an acting triumph is, perhaps, an understatement. Her delightful quicksilver performance was the best thing she had ever done in the theatre. Representing the *femme fatale* through the Ice Age, the Deluge and the Reconstruction, Miss Leigh gaily picked a triumphant pathway, occasionally stepping daintily out of character to inform a delightedly startled audience that the play was meaningless, her own role stupid and that they had far better spend their time in the bar ! Vivien Leigh took advantage of what was the acting part of a lifetime to give a delightful and unquestionably brilliant performance.

Joan Young, so excellent in *Our Town* a year or so previously, gave a moving performance in a quieter vein as Mrs. Antrobus, patient, tolerant, kindly, lovable—the eternal Mother and Wife. Cecil Parker (bearing an astonishing resemblance to the late John Barrymore) played Mr. Antrobus with power, vigour and sensitivity. As Henry (otherwise Cain), the epitome of neo-fascism, Terry Morgan was excellent ; his scenes with Cecil Parker were intensely moving, while the dynamic moment when he stepped out of character to reveal himself as a frightened neurotic, will remain long in the memory. Among a large, hard-worked cast Ena Burrill, Pamela Conroy, Michael Lynd and Sidney Monckton distinguished themselves in a memorable production of a great play.

John Webster's grim piece of Grand Guignol *The Duchess Of Malfi*, was an addition to John Gielgud's admirable Haymarket season. In this little-known Elizabethan drama, horror is piled upon horror—incest, strangulation, lust, murder most foul. It is problematical whether *The Duchess* will be given another revival for some years, for it has no particular interest, except, perhaps, an historical one, to a modern audience. Nevertheless, it is a gusty melodrama, which gives opportunities for supreme studies in villainy. John Gielgud was a first-rate Ferdinand, while from Cecil Trouncer came a perfect piece of period acting as the arch-villain Bosola. The object of their most foul intentions was played beautifully by that most delicate of actresses Peggy Ashcroft, for whose splendid performance as The Duchess of Malfi, this horrific masterpiece would bear witnessing a second time. In the strong company Leslie Banks, Leon Quartermaine, Marian Spencer, Miles Malleson and John Blatchley were each outstanding.

GRAND GUIGNOL

Stage studies in the macabre are invariably certain to be successful. The thriller, dramatic standby of the commercial stage, has long been a favourite with audiences, and in August, 1945, the lover of the gruesome found much on the London stage to entertain him. In the early 1920's Sybil Thorndike and Lewis

Casson inaugurated a chilling season of Grand Guignol at the Little Theatre, and for sheer, unadulterated terror this season has remained supreme until recently. Ellen Pollock, who was behind the excellent Bernard Shaw Season at the Hammersmith Lyric in 1944, produced and appeared in a series of short horror plays at the Granville, Walham Green, a few months later. Her fellow-producer, John Hanau, and her fellow-actors Richard Goolden, Anne Firth, Gordon Edwardes, Edith Sharpe and Anthony Baird combined with Miss Pollock to stage with gusto some of the plays which had thrilled London in the 1920's, along with a number of new ones written for this 1945 season.

The Granville became a permanent home for the horror play, maintaining the system of theatrical specialisation which is generally to be commended. Audiences learn what to expect from a theatre which specialises, and just as the farce-minded invariably visit the Comedy and the musical-comedy lovers know that their favourite stage-fare may usually be seen at the Coliseum or Hippodrome, so those 1945 playgoers with a taste for drama that was gruesome made the trek to Walham Green. However, it became apparent that the terror plays which one saw at the Little in 1923 and those staged at the Granville in 1945 were horrifics with a difference. For in the intervening score of years novelists and playwrights had, it seemed, " discovered " psychology. The psychological thriller took the place of the other cruder kind, and in recent years playwrights in this country have developed this particular form of play to quite an astonishing degree. Wolcott Gibbs, erudite dramatic critic, writing in that slick weekly " The New Yorker," refers to " the psychological melodramas at which the British are so adept." And it is certainly true that British plays in the *genre* of *Rope, Gaslight, Love From A Stranger, Suspect, Ladies In Retirement* and *Brighton Rock* have earned for our playwrights a niche in international dramatic literature. Our playwrights would appear to have established a tradition. The greatest contributor to horror in literature is, of course, the American Edgar Allan Poe, many of whose stories would dramatise excellently. But the heritage of dramatic flesh-creepers seems to have been handed down to playwrights on this side of the Atlantic, and more especially in Britain. The late Edgar Wallace wrote a number of essays in Grand Guignol of which the most notable is *The Case Of The Frightened Lady*. This play, along with two other Edgar Wallace thrillers, toured our provincial cities in 1945 with considerable success. Horror pays dividends. And Edward Percy's

study of blackmail, arson and murder *The Shop At Sly Corner* was
being enacted in the tradition of the great blood-curdlers by Keneth
Kent, Cathleen Nesbitt and Victoria Hopper at the St. Martin's,
where it seemed likely to remain for many months to follow. The
Granville Theatre thus had no corner in crime. And in Shaftesbury
Avenue a psychological melodrama, *Duet For Two Hands*, at the
Lyric, was one of London's 1945 successes. Written by Mary
Hayley Bell, author of *Men In Shadow*, it provided meaty roles
for her husband John Mills and that brilliant young actress Mary
Morris.

Duet For Two Hands was a gripping drama on an unusual and
absorbing theme. A young poet loses his hands in an accident and
by a miracle of surgery is given two new ones. A diabolically clever
surgeon performs the operation, using—a fiendish touch this—the
hands of a man who has been hanged for murder. Stephen Cass,
the poet, feels the new hands growing to life as the months pass.
Gradually he senses, in their nervous twitching and stretching, a
new power, a subtle urge to fulfil a strange destiny. He feels
himself possessed by the personality of the former owner of his hands,
the dead man seems to call to him. They are strong hands, with
long powerful fingers, continually straining—but for what?

Is it possible for the hands of the dead man to affect the mind
of Cass? Medical science, which has not yet succeeded in grafting
complete limbs on to maimed bodies, says no. But Mary Hayley
Bell said yes; and so persuasive were her dramatic powers, so
intriguingly worked-out her thesis, that we found ourselves absorbed
in spite of ourselves in the sheer fantastics of her plot. Actually
the fundamentals of her theme are by no means new. Conrad Veidt
appeared in a German film, *The Hands Of Orlac*, as far back as
1924. He played the role of an artist who has a murderer's hands
grafted on to his stumps, after which he develops homicidal
tendencies. The film was re-made by Karl Freund in Hollywood
in 1935 with the late Colin Clive as the sensitive artist whose whole
life is distorted by his new hands, and Peter Lorre as the demented
surgeon.

But in *Duet For Two Hands* the surgeon was by no means a
simple case of madness, and the play has a number of new and
original facets. Elwyn Brook-Jones made of Doctor Sarclet a
wholly fascinating figure. Realisation of his strange and sadistic
nature, though not always of his motives, gradually filters into the
audience consciousness as the play pursues its sombre pattern.

He is a curiously pathetic character ; the psychological subtleties of his complex nature being given eloquent expression by Brook-Jones. Reminiscent of the late Frank Vosper, this young actor was mannered, inconsistent, powerful. He broke all the rules yet by sheer power of personality compelled attention. His work in this play indicated that in Elwyn Brook-Jones the English stage had acquired a talented actor whose future might be considerable.

John Mills gave an impeccable performance. As the tortured poet he was at all times master of his extremely difficult role, and was responsible for some superb moments of terror. In setting the play in the remote Orkney Islands in the period 1904, Miss Hayley Bell enlisted all possible topographical aid in establishing an eerie atmosphere, even into the sun-drenched living room of the doctor's lonely house. His daughter was an elfin figure, strange, inhibited, fey, steeped in Orkneys twilight. Added to this she had the odd fortune to fall in love with Cass, whose hands once belonged to the dead man she first loved.

It said a good deal for the quality of the acting of Mary Morris that she brought credibility to the part of Abigail. She is an actress with beauty, grace, personality and a first-rate acting ability. *Duet For Two Hands* made her a West End "name" overnight—and rightly so. Elspeth March played the doctor's sister with charm, though the character was inclined to be indistinctly drawn. The setting, by co-producer Anthony Pelissier, was one of the best seen in London for many years. He was certainly to be congratulated on the fine *decor* of an unusual play which deserved to be seen for the high quality acting of John Mills, Mary Morris and Elwyn Brook-Jones.

Firth Shephard, indomitable producer of American successes, did not in *Chicken Every Sunday* at the Savoy quite hit the bullseye. On the face of it any play which gives opportunities for a variety of family characterisation, such as *You Can't Take It With You*, should be fairly certain of success. But, though Angela Baddeley's Arizona boarding house was full of incident, and contained guests as varied as Red Indians and ex-yodellers, the play did not come off. It was about as American as Nelson's Column. Nevertheless Frank Leighton, Kathleen Boutall, Alison Leggat and Miss Baddeley herself did their utmost to make it mildly entertaining. There were a number of incidents involving children which were in questionable taste ; the play would have been improved if these had been eradicated.

PHOTO : CECIL BEATON

★ *Robert Donat,* as Captain Shotover, and Deborah
Kerr as Ellie Dunn, in Shaw's "Heartbreak House", produced by John Burrell, 1943.

H

★ **Donald Wolfit,** as Volpone in Ben Jonson's comedy, 1943. Wolfit has appeared in and produced most of Shakespeare's plays during the past eight years.

★ ***Frederick Valk*** as Othello, and Bernard Miles as
Iago in the Old Vic Company's production, directed by
Julius Gellner, 1942.

★ ***Richard Attenborough*** and Martin Miller in
"Awake And Sing," produced by Alec Clunes, as the first
production of the Arts Theatre Group of Actors, 1942.

PHOTO : JOHN VICKERS

★ **_Anton Walbrook_** and Diana Wynyard in Lilian Hellman's "Watch On The Rhine", produced by Emlyn Williams, 1942.

★ *Valerie Taylor* and Isolde Denham in Turghenev's "A Month In The Country", produced by Emlyn Williams, 1943.

★ *Pamela Brown,* who appeared in "Claudia" in 1942, "Hamlet" and "Madeleine" in 1944, and "Death Of A Rat", produced by Murray Macdonald, 1946.

PHOTO : VIVIENNE

★ *Emlyn Williams,* whose plays in the past few years have included "The Light Of Heart", "Morning Star", "Druid's Rest" and "The Wind of Heaven".

THE HISTORICAL PLAY

The historical play is as old as the theatre itself. The passion playlets, earliest-known forms of drama, were re-enactments of historic religious happenings, while at the present time historical plays tend to form a growing proportion of our theatre-fare. And every generation has created its own specialists in the art of re-writing history to suit the ends of drama. Shakespeare's monumental gallery of history's great figures ranges from Egypt's queen to England's merry, many-wived monarch, from France's ineffectual Dauphin to England's crookback Richard, from Rome's ill-starred Cæsar to our own Bluff King Hal. The extent to which Shakespeare distorted history to serve his own dramatic purposes, and his justification for so doing, have both been debated often in the past three hundred years. The camps are sharply divided. On the one side are those who affirm that the drama of actual events is far superior to the fictionised substitute. The opposers declare that great art requires more than an ability for documentation and that the unvarnished truth can be extremely dull when presented on a stage.

To an extent the identical arguments serve for all forms of drama. Indeed it may be interesting to note that the same controversy similarly divides our makers of documentary films. Some directors aim at presenting on the screen actual events in the lives of the people *exactly* as they are experienced (the Soviet Union has been particularly successful in films of this kind). Others directors and producers, who have tried this method and found it wanting, argue that real life must be dramatised if it is going to be portrayed on a screen in a way calculated to hold the interest of the filmgoer. In short, they claim that screen characterisation must be slightly larger than life.

But, *revenons a nos moutons* (as one of our most distinguished dramatic critics would inevitably phrase it), and realise that the problem is common to the film and theatre. As an advocate for many years of realism in the theatre, it goes hard for me to have to say that, in the case of the historical play, the method for the play-wright of occasional varnishing would appear to be more satis-factory than the method of trying to work only with plain facts. The fictionising gloss does more than cover a multitude of sins; it makes a play out of the drama of real life. I therefore favour the former, believing that the dramatist's coating over historic personages and incidents, so long as possible distortion of essential truths is

J

limited to the barest minimum, tends to result in the better theatrical effect.

To take a case in point. Two plays seen in London in 1945 dealt with the same figure, the Prince Regent of England, afterwards George IV. One, for purposes of the plot, distorted considerably the character of the young Prince Regent, and this whitewashing failed to lend credibility to the play, which ran in the West End for only a short while. The other, Norman Ginsbury's *The First Gentleman*, at the Savoy, was a brilliant piece of work— and historically accurate, as far as I am aware. No doubt Mr. Ginsbury has drawn his principal character slightly larger than life, which is all to the good, as the success of the play demonstrates ; but there is strictly no whitewashing. *The First Gentleman* is magnificent history, supreme theatre, unquestionable entertainment for all playgoers. It deals with the later period in " Prinny's" career, when, separated from his wife and surrounded by mistresses and enemies, he awaits his father's death, so that he might ascend the throne he has coveted so long.

When the play opens, the obese, vain peacock of a prince is trying to marry off his daughter, Princess Charlotte, to the Prince of Orange. George endeavours to persuade his daughter that this would be a " good " marriage, but her heart is with the penniless Leopold of Saxe-Coburg, and Charlotte refuses to abide by her father's wishes. She flees to the country home of her mother, exiled from the Court many years before, and from her retreat the high-spirited girl defies her angry father. Prinny, anxious at all costs to be popular with his own people, finally sees that to give in would perhaps bring him the love and affection of his subjects. Charlotte and Leopold are thus married soon afterwards and are happy at last while the Prince Regent anxiously awaits the appearance of a son, heir to the throne.

Unhappily Charlotte dies in childbirth, the child is still-born and this last blow finally ends George's long-held hopes for a line of kings descending from him. We leave the gross, ill-tempered, insensitive creature being fitted into his corsets as he prepares to attend the funeral of his daughter ; and such is the subtlety of Mr. Ginsbury's writing that we feel pity mixed with loathing for this broken, corpulent, creature. Robert Morley gave what must be termed a virtuoso performance as the Prince Regent. No other actor in England to-day could have equalled the magnificence of his portrayal. This was a king, this was a man, this was acting of the very front rank. Wendy Hiller was equally fine as Charlotte, combining a fire and an attack in her acting which is so often lacking on the West End stage. In Norman Marshall's well-produced and lavishly-mounted production Philip Friend, Wilfrid Walter, Amy Frank, Una Venning and Robert Beaumont all gave excellent performances in a play about which Norman Ginsbury has cause to be extremely proud.

The other success of the month was a play of an entirely different kind. *No Room At The Inn*, by Joan Temple, produced by Anthony Hawtrey at the Embassy, was also a realist play, based on actual events, but events considerably nearer our hearts than the vanities of past princes. It was concerned with the problems of evacuation and of foster-parents, problems which as we saw from our newspapers at that time, were still prevalent and pressing. In a " safe " town a weak and harassed billetting officer puts another child into the house of a vicious harridan, who acts as foster-mother to four other evacuees, in order to escape conscription. The children are unkempt, dirty and undernourished. We see the sweet little girl transformed in this environment to a cunning, filthy urchin ; we witness with real horror these unfortunate " Dead End kids " growing up in squalor, their whole outlook and behaviour coloured by ill-treatment. The play ends with the murder of the woman as she lies on her bed in a drunken stupor—in the final, powerful scene two of the children creep up to her room and hold a pillow over her face until she coughs out her last choking gasp.

This was grim, moving, dramatic theatre, finely acted by a first-rate cast. Freda Jackson as Mrs. Voray was superbly and horrifyingly realistic, while Joan Dowling and Mary Kimber as two of the children, Tony Quinn as the billetting officer, and Ruth Dunning and Ursula Howells were all praiseworthy. It was good news to hear that the Arts Council had decided to send this play on a provincial tour to enable it to be seen by a wider public.

A double event took place at the Westminster. Robert Donat returned to the stage after an absence of over two years ; and Walter Greenwood, celebrated author of *Love On The Dole*, wrote the vehicle for his return. It was a comedy, titled *The Cure For Love*, a flimsy trifle concerning a soldier's return to his Lancashire home and the encumbrance of a fiancée he does not love. Donat was perfectly at home in a part which fitted him like a glove and in no way taxed his talents, while Renée Asherson gave a quietly first-rate performance as the London evacuee who finally captured his heart. Marjorie Rhodes, Charles Victor and Joan White were the other protagonists in this amusing little comedy, which kept the Westminster filled with Donat and Greenwood admirers for many months.

Among the new plays seen in London during the same period was one from America, *Kiss And Tell*, by F. Hugh Herbert, at the Phœnix. One could partially understand this comedy's success in New York, but to London audiences the whole thing seemed to be rather a poor joke which did not come off, and which in any case went on for far too long. The producer, John Fernald, seemed more at home at the Arts, where he also directed an interesting revival of Ibsen's *A Doll's House*, with Jenny Laird as Nora and Cyril Luckham as the unctious Torvald. In a careful and intelligent production the work of Harold Scott as Dr. Rank and Dorothy Black as Mrs. Linden was worthy of note.

THE BRITISH DRAMA LEAGUE—
" Guardian Angel of the Amateur Actor "

One of the most virile amateur theatre movements exists in this country. It is on a par with those in the Soviet Union and the U.S.A., other great theatregoing nations. Yet it is only a comparatively recent development and the organisation which can be said to have guided and nurtured the British amateur theatre to its present prominence is the British Drama League, founded just over twenty-five years ago.

The desire to " play-act " is an instinct in the human being, which shows itself at first in the dressing-up antics of children. Later on in school plays and pageants, on the village green or in the school hall, this passion for acting reveals itself even more strongly. Most people like to act. Many people think they can act. But acting is an arduous profession, the training is long and difficult, the struggle for fame heartbreaking. Therefore thousands of young people, who daily concern themselves with the mundane tasks of clerks, shop assistants, salesmen, hairdressers and so on, sublimate this desire to act by doing so in groups in their leisure hours.

Thus they are able to express themselves on the stage while not having to saddle themselves with the problem of earning a living by acting. Every town and hamlet in the British Isles possesses a theatre group of some sort, while many towns have several amateur dramatic societies where rivalry is keen. All the people who act, design, produce and help in any way in a production of one of these societies are already fully occupied in a hard day's work in a factory, office, shop or home. But their parts are learnt in their lunch-times, their movements rehearsed in their coffee breaks. At night and at week-ends they meet, sometimes for months on end, to prepare a production which may have only one or two performances to an audience largely composed of friends and relations.

But it is not the number of performances which are given, but the quality which matters most ; and the standard of amateur acting in Great Britain has increased considerably in the past twenty years. There are more than 30,000 drama societies function-ing in Great Britain and Northern Ireland in normal times ; many of these have an extremely high standard and some have achieved professional level. The British Drama League, functioning from a pleasant, green-doored house in Fitzroy Square, directs and guides most of these societies, lends them sets of published plays, sends them lecturers and producers, arranges drama festivals in various parts of the country to sharpen the spirit of friendly com-petition. In fact it is difficult to conceive what would have happened to the thousands of amateur actors and societies *without* the help of the B.D.L.

In the autumn of 1918 the Workers Educational Association was conducting a series of play-readings. Among this audience was Geoffrey Whitworth, who thought how fine it would be to encourage further amateur play-readings and to provide a focus of revival in all aspects of the art of the stage. He thereupon set at once to the task of planning the formation of the what was later to be called the British Drama League. Among the band of pioneers who helped in the formation of the League were Lena Ashwell, Else Fogerty and W. J. Turner, while the defined objects of the League was " the encouragement of the art of the theatre, both for its own sake and as a means of intelligent recreation among all classes of the community."

Later, the strengthened League went ahead on two platforms of theatre endeavour. The first was to aid in the establishment of a National Theatre, the second was to promote and assist any efforts being made in the development of acting, drama and the theatre wherever they might exist. Thus there grew up a body of enlightened men and women who aided in every way the attempts of young people to band themselves together for the purpose of acting in their own productions. And gradually a great movement has grown up, a national movement in every sense of the word, the British Amateur Theatre Movement. In 1923 the number of groups affiliated to the League was three hundred and sixty, in 1939 it numbered many thousands. The organisation has grown to such an extent that in 1937 thirteen thousand complete sets of plays were sent out to societies functioning from Huddersfield to Cardiff, and as far apart as the Cumberland heights and the Cotswold hamlet—in fact in all parts of the British Isles.

In 1927 the first National Drama Festival was organised. Since then dozens of drama festivals have taken place in London, the Midlands, Scotland and Northern Ireland. Lectures on the theatre have been arranged in most of the provincial towns. Advice is given as to the kind of plays to produce, detailed criticisms of new plays by young playwrights are sent out from the League in dozens. The League's own magazine "Drama" has built up a wide circulation, and not only among the members of the B.D.L. Gradually from Fitzroy Square was developed a great band of theatre enthusiasts, actors by the thousand, new audiences in their tens of thousands. Geoffrey Whitworth's dream has come true. The Arts Council has helped to make England a nation of theatregoers. The British Drama League has helped to make us a nation of actors. Both organisations are at one in the idea of building a National Theatre. Whitworth and his gallant band have had the idea for years; now, maybe with the assistance of the Arts Council, some definite plan may be put forward for the establishment in London and the provincial cities of a *chain* of National Theatres, putting good plays and good acting within the reach of the great majority of the British people.

For the people demonstrated during the war that the theatre is in their blood. In spite of the call-up, the evacuation of thousands, the long hours in the factories and all the other difficulties—in spite of all these things thousands of amateur societies continued to function. Indeed, many new ones grew up. Wherever a Civil Defence group was stationed, or a Home Guard regiment quartered, there grew up an amateur theatrical group. When a body of evacuated civil servants arrived in a lonely Welsh town, within a week a new play was in the process of production. And everywhere, helping, advising, sending parcels of plays and books on the theatre, keeping in touch with these new groups as well as with the established societies was the British Drama League.

At a time when boredom and listlessness were the lot of the British people drama proved an effective antidote. And, later, when danger threatened, when Nazi bombers circled the skies, the production of plays by community groups helped to bolster morale and take the mind off immediate horrors. Within the Army new groups grew up. The League supplied the plays, and by 1942, nearly three hundred Service Units were affiliated. In the sphere of " Holidays At Home," the League was also active, taking a prominent part in the promoting of dramatic entertainment under this scheme.

Amateur acting has been in the past the outcome of the enthusiasm of a few persons who have gathered around them other enthusiasts. Such enthusiasts still exist in various parts of the country. For example, there is James B. Bisset, well-known North London amateur producer and lecturer. His group, the Amateur Repertory Theatre, has, in three years, produced nearly thirty plays ; of these seven were new plays by unknown playwrights. Each member of the society works by day, some as long as twelve hours. But, like so many hundreds of other amateur groups, Bisset's A.R.T. has carried on. And, in times of war as well as peace the British Drama League, guardian angel of the amateur actor, has also carried on.

Twenty-six years ago a few enthusiasts sat on wooden boxes and talked of the formation of a body to encourage the love and pursuance of drama. To-day the outcome of that meeting is the national British Drama League, unique and well-loved organisation. In the next few years the public's interest in the theatre is bound to be on the increase. And in the task of creating the new audiences and of canalising and guiding the activities of amateur actors and producers the League will be well in evidence. Not the least of its endeavours will be its work on the scheme for the formation of State-aided Civic Theatres, which it originally put forward in 1942. To the work of the creation of further community theatres the energies of the League are now actively bent.

WAR PLAYS

The Second World War demonstrated again a fact which was shown clearly during the Great War—that war plays do not achieve wide popularity until the war is over. During the past few years a number of plays dealing with various facets of the war were staged in London with scant success. *Happy Few, Desert Rats, Oflag 3, Salt*

Of The Earth, Lifeline, Escort—these were a few of the war plays which had short runs. None of these met with public approval, though at least two of them were really excellent dramas. And it was the same in the last war.

Soon after the Great War quite a few war plays achieved success, notable among these being *Tunnel Trench* and the famous *Journey's End*. It seemed then, as now, that the inevitable reaction which sets in during the aftermath of war brings with it a new appreciation of plays dealing with war's problems, especially those which probe deeply the causes of war and face up to post-war difficulties. But during a war this kind of stage-fare just does not ring the bell. In this war there were certainly such hits as *Flare Path* and *Men In Shadow*, though in both cases the war was merely a background to the plot, the one novelettish, the other melodramatic. But many of the others which dealt with war at sea, at home, on the various fronts—these marked up red in the account books. Will they do so in a few years ?

Indications are that the contrary will be the case. It is quite possible that there are any number of *Journey's End's* still waiting to be written, still dormant in the minds of playwrights in the Services until such times as the ideas and dialogue flow easily on to paper. I predict that we shall be seeing more and more new plays about returning soldiers adjusting themselves to new conditions. Daphne du Maurier wrote *The Years Between* in 1944. It ran at Wyndham's for a considerable time, providing a meaty role for film star Clive Brook as the British officer who returns to his wife after being missing for three years. The play concerned itself with the well-to-do classes, but W. Chetham Strodes' new play, *Young Mrs. Barrington*, staged at the Winter Garden in the autumn of 1945, centred around a suburban family in the same situation.

Here is an ordinary, pleasant middle-class family living in Edgware, Streatham or Beckenham—the fussing, kindly and possessive mother, the untidy, lanky, mechanically-minded son, the serious New Statesmanish daughter and the eldest son, the apple of his mother's eye, who has returned from several years' overseas service with the R.A.F. War seems to have made little change in him, but it has made considerable alterations in the character of his young wife. Hers is the double task of getting used to this strange young husband and of trying to establish their married independance in the face of motherly interference. For the young Mrs. Barrington the problem is the same as for any amount of re-united married couples. Plays such as this might well be valuable ammunition in the fight to see that the broken threads of war-torn marriages are mended.

Leueen MacGrath played the strong dramatic role of the young wife, and she made the most of it. Tom Gill was the attractive, restless flyer, while Elliot Mason was outstanding as his fussing, lovable mother. Excellent performances were given by Margaret Barton and Peter Hammond as the younger members of the family, and Joan Haythorne's friendly neighbour was a beautiful piece of acting in an extremely well-acted play.

We had, at that time, three plays on similar themes running in London—*The Years Between, The Cure For Love* and *Young Mrs. Barrington.* Maybe at a later period other, and perhaps better, plays about the returned warrior will have added themselves to the list? On the fact of it, a drama dealing with a troop hospital behind the Burmese lines would not have appeared to be very entertaining. But John Patrick's *The Hasty Heart,* at the Aldwych, on that very same theme succeeded in being one of the most moving productions seen in London for some time. Producer Murray Macdonald was responsible for an excellent job in this story of a proud, friendless little Scot, who arrives at the hospital and proceeds to upset the other inmates until they learn that, unbeknown to himself, he has only six months to live. They tease him, pity him, buy him a kilt, and learn to love and admire him. This strange, perverse character comes to life in the hands of Emrys Jones, who gives a fine and moving performance as the Scot.

Among the gallery of inmates clever studies were contributed by Jerry Verno, Frank Leighton and Orlando Martins, while Margaretta Scott's nurse, the only woman in the cast, was coolly lovely, sympathetically drawn and well-acted in a war play which seemed most likely to beat the war-play bogey. *A Bell For Adano* at the Phœnix, adapted by Paul Osborn from John Hersey's great novel, was a war play with a difference. It tells the story of a little Italian town taken over by the Americans after the collapse of the Mussolini regime. The townsfolk are despondent, the food and transport situations are difficult, some of the former fascist officials are hoping to retain their power—in short, here are real problems for the conquerors. How to breathe a semblance of life and self-respect into people desperately in need of food, water, comforts, materials is the main task of Major Joppolo of the United States Army.

Fitted by virtue of his Italian ancestry, and of his tolerance, sympathy and keen understanding of the people, for the task of rehabilitating the town, Joppolo finds obstacles in his path, among his own bureaucrats as well as the townsfolk. He surmounts difficulty after difficulty and helps to replace the famous Adano bell (melted down by the Germans for arms months previously). But no sooner is this symbol of decency in place, no sooner is order and self-respect restored to the town, no sooner has he gained the affection of the Italian people, than Joppolo is recalled. The play ends as the young officer leaves the town to face punishment for disobeying orders. As he takes his farewell of the townspeople the new bell of Adano tolls, ringing in a new way of life for the people.

Here then was a great theme. And Osborn did a fine job with Hersey's admirable book, making this a play of power and sincerity, finely directed by American producer Henry C. Potter. As Joppolo Robert Beatty gave the finest performance of his career. He was perfectly cast, giving a clean-cut, sincere rendering of a fine character, the best thing he had done on the London stage since *The Petrified Forest*. Other good performances were given by Frederick Valk, Bonar Colleano, Jr., Milo Sperber, Sebastian Cabot, Gerard Kempinski, Arnold Marlé and Victor Rietti in a play which deserved not to be missed.

Big Boy at the Saville was a show, however, which might easily be given a miss. The talents of Richard Hearne and Fred Emney were wasted on a slim plot and ludicrously unfunny dialogue, but Carol Raye and Edward Baxter sang and danced delightfully and were obviously worthy of better things. But not even the inspired antics of Richard Hearne could save this musical comedy from mediocrity.

Two Little Theatres re-opened in late 1945—the Torch, with a seldom-performed play by Ibsen, *Rosmersholm*, and the Mercury with a new play, *The Old Man Of The Mountains*. In Basil Ashmore's production at the tiny Knightsbridge Theatre Joan Miller was outstanding as Rebecca West, that strange Hedda Gablerish figure, while Esmé Percy's unctuous Ulric Brendel had some fine moments. Other plays presented at the Torch by the London Theatre Group included James Joyce's interesting study *Exiles*, distinguished by a sensitive performance by Hermione Hannen.

The policy at the Mercury, inaugurated by Martin Browne's Pilgrim players, was the presentation of new plays by poets. Once the platform of such poets as T. S. Eliot, the Mercury began by staging plays by poets Norman Nicholson and Ronald Duncan, Christopher Fry, Anne Ridler and others. Nicholson's *The Old Man Of The Mountains* proved to be the story of Elijah set in modern Cumberland. It was full of high-flown dialect verse, beautifully spoken by Robert Speaight as Elijah, Henzie Raeburn, Frank Napier and Martin Browne, who also produced on the tiny stage with skill.

COWARD AT THE CROSSROADS

One of the most eagerly awaited events of the 1945-46 season was Noel Coward's revue *Sigh No More*, which opened at the Piccadilly in August. Remembering Coward's considerable reputation in the field of revue-writing, many found his new musical *mèlange* disappointing for a variety of reasons. *Sigh No More* lacked wit, contained not one clever sketch, was wholly pre-war and quite unreal, had at least one scene which was in questionable taste, lacked cohesion and was over-long. In fact it was the theatrical epitome of the mouse which was brought forth, amid much puffing and blowing, by the mountain of fable.

A certain amount of one's disappointment may have been due to the build-up, the advance publicity, which claimed for Coward's show the distinction of being the high-water mark of all time in the realms of light theatrical entertainment. The casting of this revue took many weeks of careful sifting. The master himself made the final choice. He chose the principals, the designers, the choreographers, the singers, the dancers, the chorus, the orchestra. He himself produced *Sigh No More* and launched it on an eager West End audience. But even the most rabid Noel Coward fans were not really happy about the Coward lyrics, songs, and humour here displayed. The question arose : has the playwright reached a turning point ?

Coward has been for many years a centre of controversy. There are those that affirm that he is among our finest playwrights ; others class him low down among the also-rans. Undoubtedly he is brilliantly versatile and in his varying capacities as actor, playwright, librettist, composer and producer he has been responsible in the past for a great deal of excellent work. To English drama he has contributed at least one good play, *Hay Fever*, for our lighter theatre he has written *Bitter Sweet*, *Private Lives*, some excellent melodies, as well as a number of near-successes like *Operette* and

Conversation Piece. Of his theatrical failures *Sirocco*, *Home Chat* and *Point Valaine* spring to mind—but, on the whole, even his mediocre work has been acclaimed far in excess of its deserts.

He once wrote a very good play, *Post Mortem*, which was in the nature of an attack on war, and the conditions of modern society in general. So far, it has never been produced, but it is certainly a much more thoughtful piece of writing than most of his popular plays. For example, his *Cavalcade*, an inferior piece of work, was extremely successful, though this was possibly because it was outrageously jingo and embarrassingly nationalist, at a time when nationalist spirit ran high. But Sean O'Casey, distinguished dramatist and critic, described the play as " a tawdry piece of work, a halfpenny-worth of bread to an intolerable deal of sack," and many critics are inclined to agree with him.

Be that as it may, Noel Coward is an institution in the theatre. Everything he does is news. When he enters the motion picture field he does so in style ; acting in, producing, writing and directing one of the finest British films ever made—*In Which We Serve*. His *Blithe Spirit* has enjoyed one of the longest runs of any plays in London. His ten-year-old *Private Lives* was successfully revived at the Apollo in 1945. At the age of forty-five, Coward has, indeed, accomplished a great deal.

What of his future ? Apart from *Blithe Spirit*, he has in the past ten years written *Present Laughter*, an amusing trifle, and *This Happy Breed* (an attempt to create a "Cavalcade " of the years between the two wars). The latter was a shoddy piece of work, abounding in false sentiment, patronising airs, shallow philosophy. Lacking completely any perception as to the real lives of the common people, it was out of touch with reality, reactionary to a degree. Its characters were puppets, the dialogue was unreal. It was made quite plain in *This Happy Breed* that Mr. Coward does not understand the working class and that, in any case, he dislikes them intensely. This contempt for the common people of this country is, in fact, made obvious in all his work. It was even apparent in his revue *Sigh No More* when, in one pointless and particularly unfunny number, he delivered a vicious attack on a typical working class family, and incidentally, on the new Government.

Coward stands for all the things which the war has brought an end. What will he do in the new world which we are now trying to build from the ruins of the old ? He is essentially a pre-war playwright. But so great is his skill, so impeccable his play-construction, so versatile his talents, so quicksilver his mind that it is possible that he may adjust himself to future conditions.

One thing is clear. Anything which Noel Coward writes will attract attention from a large public, to whom his name is a kind of magic. Any play, revue or operetta bearing his signature will achieve a successful run. Coward is a commercial success. He, therefore, does not have to write down to his public, and, should he be responsible for a play with a serious theme, this would also become as successful as, for example, the mediocre *Sigh No More*. George Bernard Shaw did not begin to write plays until he had reached the age of forty; he did not have a success until many years later. Is it, perhaps, possible that Coward has *his* best work in front of him ? He once wrote the following : " The great problem for the young dramatist is whether to set out from the very first writing what managers require from him, or to concentrate on creating what he requires of himself. The latter is by far the more difficult course to pursue, but in the end, provided he is backed by genuine ability, infinitely more satisfactory."

This is as true to-day as when Noel Coward wrote this some years ago in the preface to his " Three Plays." Will he heed his own advice ? The future for this brilliant man is rich with possibilities. Were he to take stock of the new life being built around him, were he to realise that 1946 is not 1926, or even 1936, were he to harness his skill to the writing of worth-while drama on the great themes of modern problems, then assuredly his work would take on a new dignity, assume a much-longed-for depth. His best play *Post Mortem* was written after the first World War. Surely the Second World War provides themes strong enough for stirring and inspiring drama ? Noel Coward is a great power in the English theatre. May we hope soon that the term " great " will also be applied to his writings.

His revue *Sigh No More* had some amusing moments in the first half, but tailed off lamentably in the second part. The joy of the evening was Joyce Grenfell, whose gallery of comic studies was superb, while Madge Elliot and Cyril Ritchard did their excellent best with their not-very-good material. Graham Payn, our leading *jeune premier*, sang and danced delightfully, but clever Cliff Gordon was given few opportunities to show what a brilliant mimic he could be. The show was well-dressed, lavish, colourful— Mr. Coward however could do much better than this.

CLASSICAL REVIVAL

The 1945-46 Old Vic season at the New, like the previous year's season, proved to be a riotous success. " House Full " boards were on view at every performance here of the great plays of Shakespeare, Sophocles and Sheridan. And, just round the corner from St. Martin's Lane, there had not been a single vacant seat at the Arts since the commencement of the Festival of English Drama, which included plays by Shakespeare, Sheridan, Shaw, Pinero and Farquhar. Wartime had certainly witnessed a classical revival, and the move towards the staging of dramatic classics would appear to have had something of a continuance in popularity in the immediate post-war period.

Lending itself particularly well to this movement was the system of real repertory, which enables a theatre group to present the plays of different historical periods on alternate evenings during the season, thus providing both a relaxation for the actors and a fillip to new audiences. It is by now generally agreed that long runs are crippling to artistry. The actors dread each performance after the play has been running for three months—with a consequent drop in performance standards. Real repertory (as distinct from the " weekly rep." of some provincial and suburban theatres) provides the actors with variety, enables them to come freshly to each new role.

Thus, at the Old Vic, Laurence Olivier varied his ancient, withered Justice Shallow in *Henry IV—Part Two* with the dashing Hotspur in *Part One*, and alternated the comic Puff in *The Critic* with that great figure of tragedy, Oedipus, in the Sophocles drama. Similarly, at the Arts, Alec Clunes essayed such diverse dramatic disguises as Sir Harry Wildair in *The Constant Couple*, Charles Surface in *The School For Scandal* and the Prince in *Hamlet*.

Undoubtedly the Arts Theatre is the acknowledged leader of London's Little Theatres. Since Alec Clunes became theatre director in 1942, this little playhouse just off Charing Cross Road, has been the mecca of all serious-minded playgoers. A number of new plays have been produced and many excellent revivals of little-known classics. Audience and standard have appreciably increased since the Arts Theatre Group of Actors presented its first staging, *Awake And Sing*, in the summer of 1942.

Presented in the Arts Festival of English Drama repertory were five plays—Shaw's *Getting Married*, Farquhar's *The Constant Couple*, Sheridan's *The School For Scandal*, Pinero's *The Thunderbolt* and

Shakespeare's *Hamlet*, each one a masterpiece of its period, each admirably staged and acted. The producers were Judith Furse, Christopher Fry, Peter Streuli and Alec Clunes ; the actors included Clunes, Margaret Vines, Olga Lindo, Derek Birch, Mark Dignam, Dorothy Primrose, Roy Malcolm, Julian d'Albie, Alan McClelland, Dorothy Reynolds and Chris Castor.

Alec Clunes was a superb Prince in Judith Furse's production of *Hamlet*. He was the finest Hamlet seen in London for many years, bringing to the role a grace and virility, a fine sensitivity and a rare intelligence. His rendering of the great tragic figure was youthful, manly, fiery, sardonic, sensitive, intensely moving. His handling of the " O what a rogue and peasant slave am I " speech was masterly, and I have yet to see a more brilliant rendering of the " To be or not to be " and " Pronounce me this " speeches. Outstanding were Hamlet's scenes with Ophelia, the Play Scene and the Closet Scene, with Gertrude, played finely by Olga Lindo. Mark Dignam's Claudius was dignified, sensual and powerful, while Peter Streuli, Newton Blick and Dorothy Primrose each distinguished themselves in this masterly production of a great play. But the evening was Alec Clunes' triumph—and rightly so. At once he leaped forward into the very front rank of our young actors, and proved, once again, that he obviously possessed a brilliant future in the theatre.

Sir Arthur Wing Pinero's play *The Thunderbolt* demonstrates a refreshing solidity of plot in these days of slim central themes and shows his remarkably deft hand at work on half-a-dozen diverting character studies. The play is a study of a family, the Mortimores of Linchpool. Human weakness—and strength—is the subject of *The Thunderbolt*, and it is indeed a thunderbolt to the family when, having practically spent their legacy from a dead brother, they discover that the money is not rightfully theirs.

Marcus Insley, Olga Lindo, Julian d'Albie and Dorothy Primrose were formidably Philistine in this Peter Streuli production, while Roy Malcolm's intensely moving study of the " weakling " of the family had moments of great pathos. As his low-born wife, accustomed to the humilities of family snubs, Dorothy Reynolds gave a tender emotional performance, full of light and shade. Margaret Vines, excellent as Helen, and Gordon Davies, upheld a slight love interest ; but the play is mostly powerful stuff which makes modern theatregoers curious to see more of the works of the great Edwardian dramatist, whose comedy *The Magistrate* was one

177

of the hits of the Arts Festival of English Comedy two years before. Brian Haines and Bertram Shuttleworth were a capital pair of lawyers, the former giving his best performance of the season as the deliciously correct old family advisor.

No Festival of English Drama would be complete without representation from that grand old master George Bernard Shaw, and his play *Getting Married* was chosen as representative of his timely wit and sagacity. Like most of his works, this one rambled along with a minimum of movement and a maximum of talk. But what talk ! And what diverting characters ! I do believe that Mrs. George is my favourite Shaw creation, and how beautifully was she played by Olga Lindo, an actress long known to be blessed with wit and charm.

The marriage ceremony was put up as an Aunt Sally and knocked down repeatedly throughout the play, which consists of two acts in which the arrival of Mrs. George is talked about, and a third act in which the fabulous lady actually puts in an appearance with disastrous and highly amusing results. Mark Dignam's sensible prelate was an indication of how to be a first-rate actor without being showy. The fine delivery and dignity of this actor made him indeed a great asset to the Arts company. Notable also were Alan McClelland's St. John Hotchkiss, Julian d'Albie's General, Newton Blick's Collins, Brian Haines' Sykes and Marcus Insley's Soames.

The boisterous Farquhar farce, *The Constant Couple*, was revived in 1943 by Alec Clunes for the first time in more than a hundred and fifty years, and it was with extreme pleasure that theatregoers welcomed the further revival of this bawdy piece in the new Festival. What a great comedy actor is Clunes ! He strode through scene after scene with gusty good humour ; his magnificent voice and ebullient personality being enough to relegate the other actors to a two-dimensional background. But that he does not do so is a triumph, firstly to the production as a whole and also individually to Margaret Vines for an entrancing Lady Lurewell, to Julian d'Albie for Smuggler, to Derek Birch for Standard and to Dorothy Primrose for the virtuous Angelica.

Particularly outstanding was Margaret Vines, whose work generally in this Festival was of an exceptionally high standard. Her Lurewell vied with her Lady Teazle for dazzle, wit and intelligence, and in a totally different vein her Helen in the Pinero drama was a restrained and quietly admirable performance. In

Sheridan's *The School For Scandal*, produced by Christopher Fry, her quarrel scenes with Sir Peter Teazle were beautifully done, and her deft touch was responsible for the success of many amusing scenes. Among the plotters, scandalmongers and tattlers, one recalled with pleasure the Backbite of Marcus Insley, the Crabtree of Bertram Shuttleworth, the Mrs. Candour of Chris Castor, the Lady Sneerwell of Dorothy Reynolds and the Careless of Gordon Davies.

Alec Clunes here played Charles Surface. Costume comedy is his *mètier*, and his impish sense of humour was well in evidence, especially in the scenes with Peter Streuli, an excellent Sir Oliver. This is Sheridan's best comedy, though his *The Critic* and *The Rivals* (also on view in London at that time) run it very close. Perhaps these three, along with Sheridan's admirable version of Vanbrugh's *A Trip to Scarborough*, will form the basis for a Richard Brinsley Sheridan Repertory Season at some time in the future? Such a possibility provokes anticipatory delights.

So much for the Arts Theatre Festival of English Drama, a brilliantly successful season, which showed that on a modest outlay a repertory season of " good " plays might be launched at a London theatre. Furthermore, events in 1944 and 1945 proved beyond doubt that a large and intelligent audience awaited such ventures, the audience which crowded the Old Vic, the Haymarket and Arts and all the Little Theatres which sprang up in London during the war.

At the Gateway, Irene Edouin kept the flag of drama flying in 1945, introducing some new plays, new actors and new directors, of whom two in particular, Mary Duff and Richard Taylor distinguished themselves with productions of Frank Vosper's *People Like Us* and J. B. Priestley's *The Long Mirror* respectively. Greta Douglas transferred her successful company from the little Chanticleer in Kensington to a new experimental playhouse off Baker Street. Meanwhile her production of Euripides' *The Trojan Women* at the Lyric, Hammersmith, brought back Marie Ney to the London stage after too long an absence, and gave Eileen Herlie an opportunity to show that she was one of the most promising young actresses on the English stage.

Notting Hill Gate possessed a veritable covey (or is it herd ?) of Little Theatres. In addition to the Gateway, Basil Ashmore's London Theatre Group were functioning with fair success at the recently-formed Lindsey, where among the new plays presented

179

here in 1945 were *The Red Horizon* by Sir Osbert Sitwell and R. J. Minney and *Tomorrow Will Be Different* by Paschoal Carlos Magno, with a varied group of actors, including Esmé Percy, Ernest Milton, Ellen Pollock, Kenneth Morgan, Mavis Walker, Violet Farebrother and Hermione Hannen. And not more than a step from the Lindsey was the Mercury, where Martin Browne's Pilgrim Players were to be seen in their interesting season of poets' plays. While Norman Nicholson's *Old Man Of The Mountains* presented the story of Elijah and Ahab in a modern Cumberland setting, Ronald Duncan's *This Way To The Tomb* was a more ambitious work, consisting of a masque and anti-masque based on the theme of the legend of St. Anthony. Robert Speaight, Frank Napier, Henzie Raeburn, Pamela Alan and Norman Tyrrell were outstanding in both plays under the able directorial hand of Martin Browne.

HAS OUR THEATRICAL TASTE IMPROVED?

A well-known dramatic critic once remarked that public taste has not improved since the great days of the famous actor-managers. This statement is, however, not borne out by facts. A comparison between the theatre-fare of World War One and World War Two would quickly indicate strong division of standards, in favour of the latter. One of my friends, a well known theatrical manager, often impresses upon me that the period between 1914 and 1920 was " the Golden Age " of musical comedy. He remarks upon this with undisguised nostalgia, but I submit that it is open to question whether one should regret the passing of the musical comedy era.

Our fathers point with pride to such " classics " as *The Maid Of The Mountains*, *No, No, Nanette*, *The Desert Song*, *The Vagabond King*, *The Chocolate Soldier*, *Rio Rita* and others of that *genre*. No doubt, in their time, these musical shows were pre-eminent, but it is with the minimum of sorrow that many of us witness the passing of what must surely be one of the least intelligent, though innocuous, of all theatrical entertainments. The key-word is of course "entertainment," for nobody would deny that all of the above aim at nothing more than being just that. They had their place during the last war and, to a much lesser extent, they occupy a niche in the modern theatre.

But we have surely grown up since the Great War. Taking at random a few musical comedy titles from those popular on the London stage during this period one encounters such naiveties as *High Jinks*, *Please Help Emily*, *Mother Machree*, *When Love Creeps In Your Heart* and *Mother's Sailor Boy*. And in the realm of " drama," one notes that the current successes bore such titles as *At A Step-Mother's Mercy, Ashamed Of The Man She Married, Because Love Made You Mine, The Black Sheep Of The Family, If Love Were All, Just A Little Pair Of Shoes, The Light That Leads Me Home, A Spanish Minx* and *We Can't Be As Bad As All That.* Upholders of the old school will probably echo the sentiments of the last-named play. But the fact remains that the theatregoer of 1916 in search of stimulating and edifying plays, either by contemporary dramatists or by such acknowledged masters as Shaw, Synge and Will Shakespeare himself would appear to have had a very lean time.

It is my contention, therefore, that our taste *has* indeed improved from one war to another. In the past six years many thousands of people have become playgoers for the first time. The Second World War brought not only a political and economic upheaval, but laid the foundations for a number of great social changes, particularly in relation to art and culture. Not only has the audience increased, but the standard of shows has also increased appreciably. Far be it from me to suggest that our theatre entertainment should be always of one kind. There will always be those who prefer Max Miller to J. B. Priestley—and why not? There will always be audiences for musical comedy as well as for the dramatic classics. Shakespeare will continue to have such formidable rivals as Sid Field and Hermione Gingold. And this is as it should be, for only the catholic theatregoer is assured of continual excitement in the modern theatre. Opera, ballet, musical plays, farces, revues, bedroom comedies, extravaganzas, burlesques, tragedies, thrillers, psychological dramas—take your choice; samples of each may usually be seen in our great cosmopolitan capital.

At the risk of being labelled an intellectual snob, I would say that the great new audiences which during the war flocked to repertory seasons of the classics at the New, Haymarket, Arts and elsewhere demonstrated clearly a re-orientation in audience outlook. Undoubtedly we have grown up. Furthermore it is quite obvious that the boom in " good " plays will continue so long as there is an Old Vic, and such actors and producers as a Laurence Olivier, an Alec Clunes, a Tyrone Guthrie, a John Gielgud, a John Burrell, a Peggy Ashcroft, to name but a few of the great figures of the British Theatre. And although Londoners would scorn a tatty musical comedy and would pass right by any theatre advertising such once-popular "epics" as *When Love Creeps In Your Heart* they certainly go in large numbers to see Cicely Courtneidge, Sid Field, Jack Hulbert, Tommy Trinder, Bobby Howes and Jack Buchanan. For these are giants of the lighter stage, just as the Oliviers and Richardsons are the giants of the more serious side of the British theatre.

So don't let them fool you. When your parents tell you of " the good old days," when they point with pride to the long running *Belle Of New York* or *Gypsy Princess*, remember that times have changed, and changed for the better. We have become more sophisticated, more discerning and—dare one say it?—more intelligent. Not since the lustiest days of the Restoration Playhouse have we had such a healthy theatre. For the first time in many years the British stage can really take its place alongside the greatest theatres of the world. We may always have with us our musical comedies, our pantomime, and our witless English farces, but we also possess the dignity and grandeur of a serious theatre, conscious of its power and determined to play its part in the building of a new life.

Dignity was indeed the keynote of the 1944 and 1945 Old Vic seasons. Not the pompous dignity of a Malvolio, but the mixed humility and pride which is true dignity. It would seem difficult to surpass the glories of 1944's season, of Ralph Richardson's Peer Gynt, Laurence Olivier's Richard III, Sybil Thorndike's Aase, and Joyce Redman's Louka. But for sheer excellence, for inspirational production and acting the 1945 season gave us hope and confidence anew in our great new theatre. John Burrell produced *Henry IV, Parts I and II*, with skill, and marshalled a hand-picked cast to form a pattern of historic pageantry. Both the plays are generally considered among Shakespeare's lesser works. They are chiefly known as vehicles for the monstrous and jocund Falstaff, who is here superbly impersonated by Ralph Richardson, one of the greatest comedy actors of our generation. He is at his best, and his best is supreme, in the scenes with Bardolph, Poins and Prince Hal at the tavern, while in *Part II* he reaches great heights of both comedy and pathos in his memorable moments with Justice Shallow and Doll Tearsheet.

Laurence Olivier played the roles of the fiery Hotspur in *Part I* and the aged Shallow in *Part II* with equal facility. Endowing Hotspur with a most attractive and logical stammer, he impressed upon the audience the personality of this dreamer and soldier, lover and leader as no other actor playing this part has done in living memory. Not a highly rewarding role at most times, Harry Hotspur became a living human being, colourful and likeable, in the hands of our finest young actor. One will not easily forget the tenderness of his love scenes with Lady Percy, delicately played by Margaret Leighton, nor his brittle sense of humour in the Glendower episode, nor the inspired pathos of his death scene. This was great acting indeed, calling forth even further tributes to Olivier's talent.

Both he and Richardson were at the top of their respective forms in their scenes together in the second half of *Henry IV*. Falstaff merrily leads on to further bragging tales the " lean and slippered pantaloon " Shallow, who reminiscing on one single day spent with Falstaff in London thirty years before, brings to his boasting such lavish descriptions of metropolitan orgies as to make even such an accomplished liar and braggart as the Fat Knight himself blench with astonishment mixed with admiration. Ralph Richardson was a glorious Falstaff, the finest performance of his considerable career.

Joyce Redman's Doll Tearsheet mingled a Dublin accent with a throaty, gin-soaked timbre to her voice, successfully on the whole, though her scenes with Falstaff appeared to be under-produced. Sybil Thorndike, neglected somewhat in *Part I*, came into her own in the second part, for her querulous Mistress Quickly was a constant delight. A revelation during this season was the acting of Michael Warre who, having distinguished himself in one or two minor roles in 1944, made an excellent job of Prince Hal in both parts. Nicholas Hannen, Harcourt Williams, Sydney Tafler, George Relph and Miles Malleson were the other bastions in a strong company, while one might safely predict that next season would find John Garley, George Rose and Joseph James playing parts more requiring the talents which each obviously possessed.

If *Henry IV* was an indication of Ralph Richardson's comic genius, then the double bill of Sophocles' *Œdipus* and Sheridan's *The Critic* was an even further indication, should any be required, of Laurence Olivier's truly remarkable versatility. To come straight from playing the tragic Œdipus and to assume the Rowlandson nose of the comic Puff ; to step so blithely from drama to the realms of farcical comedy, and to do so with wild success, indicated more fully the genius of our finest young actor. This was Olivier's night and he took it with both talented hands.

Sophocles' tragedy of *Œdipus*, fated by the gods to kill his father and marry his own mother has been with us almost 2,500 years. The sombre story holds no particular moral, and points only the inevitability of destiny. The supreme tragedy of the young Œdipus, gradually coming to the realisation that the prophets were right and that he has indeed killed his own father and wed his mother, shows not so much the frailty of human nature, since both deeds were done unknowingly. Rather is this the pinnacle point of horror, the supreme tragedy, the inevitable hand of Fate. As such it remains a formidable theme, and the role of the accursed king is a hurdle attempted by the great actors of every decade. Laurence Olivier succeeded triumphantly, and gave us moments of sheer terror and flashes of genuine pathos. This was great dramatic acting.

From the temples of ancient Thebes we were jerked with a pleasurable start to the stage of the eighteenth-century Drury Lane Theatre. Miles Malleson's production of Sheridan's farce, *The Critic*, was a worthy complement to the Greek tragedy. We had watched soberly and with deep interest the torment of a tortured soul ; now we lost ourselves in the diverting antics of Mr. Puff, hack journalist and would-be playwright.

This comedy was full of good moments. One remembers with pleasure Puff's description of his trade, Sir Fretful Plagiary's angry insistence upon his own tolerance—this character was beautifully played by Miles Malleson—the delightful " ham " acting of Tilburina and her Confidant, and Puff banging his head against the wall as the actors mangle his beloved lines.

But it would be invidious to select either scenes or performances in a team-work production so slick and altogether excellent. Nevertheless Olivier's Puff could not be praised too much. Here was an actor who really worked ; by look, gesture, voice, movement, Olivier from inside the skin of this miserably bad playwright, showed us with fun and subtlety the bombast, vanity and unconscious humour of one of Sheridan's most amusing creations. The spectacle of Laurence Olivier being carried upwards by a piece of scenery, being lowered on a wire, fired at by a cannon and catapulted on to the stage from the very top of the proscenium arch will remain long in the memories of the Old Vic audience.

In a large and more than capable cast one remembered with pleasure the Dangle and Sneer of George Relph and George Curzon, the Confidant of Joyce Redman, the Whiskerandos of Sydney Tafler and the Sir Christopher Hatton of George Rose ; and last, but certainly not least, the Lord Burleigh of Ralph Richardson who spoke no word but nodded his way across the stage with mute brilliance. Here was great nodding indeed.

I referred above to the opposing types of theatregoers. Pursuing this subject further, let us cast a critical eye over the lighter side of the 1945 London stage, where such figures as Courtneidge and Trinder, Drayton and Hare, Lynn and Askey reign in comical splendour, transporting theatregoers into ecstatic admiration. *Under The Counter*, by Arthur Macrae, with music by Manning Sherwin, spotlighted the inimitable Cicely Courtneidge as one of the greatest of modern clowns. She possesses the rare quality of drollery, she can switch effortlessly from burlesque to real sentiment, the tear is always ever ready behind the smile. Miss Courtneidge is high-spirited, gay, witty and extremely funny in everything she does. A thin story of an actress with a Black Market mind served to keep her on the stage for most of this three-hour show, and who would want better?

Thorley Walters sang and clowned charmingly as an Under Secretary at some ministry or other—I was never sure which one—and one may surmise that his brand of appeal will find him a place among light comedy stars of the future. Hartley Power, Cyril Raymond, Irene Handl and Jeanne Stuart contributed to the fun of a show which was good entertainment, and which contained some of the loveliest Manning Sherwin music heard on the stage since the Hulbert-Courtneidge musical, *Something In The Air*.

Jack Buchanan returned to town in a new revue *Fine Feathers*, at the Prince of Wales' Theatre. It was a fair show, quite amusing, with a tremendous discovery in Ethel Revnell, a bouncing, vital comedienne with a Gracie Fields quality. Both she and Duggie Wakefield were extremely funny. Jack himself sang and danced nonchalantly, putting to effective use the charm with which he has been luckily endowed, but he should have thought twice about continuing to sing the number called " When Will They Liberate London ? " which was in such bad taste as to be embarrassing. On the evening the present writer saw *Fine Feathers*, Mr. Buchanan fumbled his words while singing this extraordinary song. He would have done well to forget them more often.

Richard Brinsley Sheridan, playwright and wit, was fully represented in the London theatre in the autumn of 1945. His comedy *The Rivals*, produced by Edith Evans and William Armstrong, at the Criterion, was a colourful and gay production, enlivened by the magnificent Mrs. Malaprop of Edith Evans herself. It was a great pleasure to see the beautiful little Criterion open again as a theatre, and what better play than this comedy of errors to set it once more on its career as the historic playhouse in the heart of Piccadilly Circus. Reginald Beckwith was a delightfully droll Bob Acres and shared with Miss Evans the triumph of the evening. Audrey Fildes, Anthony Quayle, Peter Cushing and Morland Graham were other jovial participants in this well-dressed Sheridan romp.

MARATHON PRODUCTIONS, BAX AND O'CASEY

By January, 1946, the number of London productions with over a hundred performances to their credit was becoming alarming. Sixteen shows had chalked up the century, each looked like achieving another hundred performances with ease, while at least another score of productions seemed to be settling down for their first hundred. It was the season of long runs. *Blithe Spirit* had registered almost two thousand performances, *Arsenic And Old Lace* had nearly reached one thousand three hundred, while each of *Sweeter And Lower*, *While The Sun Shines* and *Happy And Glorious* were well on their ways to the thousand mark.

London's only new plays at the beginning of 1946 were to be seen at the political playhouse, Unity Theatre in King's Cross, and at the experimental theatre, the Swiss Cottage Embassy. The first was *God Bless The Guv'nor*, by Ted Willis (adapted from Mrs. Henry Wood), a period burlesque which went on just a little too long. It attacked the twin " evils " of drink and trade unionism, and the audience were invited to join in the cheers for the honest young employer's son and to jeer the villainous trade union organiser. Quite good, clean fun, the play had the advantage of excellent settings by Bernard Sarron and admirable acting by Joe Levene, Frederick Billany, Mark Chaney and Elsie Chisnall. Not the best of Unity's productions it, nevertheless, had a number of amusing moments and, at any rate, it was " different."

Now The Day Is Over by Gerald Savory and Charles Freeman, at the Embassy, was a new play based on Savory's admirable novel " Behold This Dreamer." The dramatisation did not quite come off, but this production was distinguished by the excellent performances of Bill Rowbotham as an imbecile, and Beatrice Varley as his kindly aunt. In a Liverpool suburb a series of shocking murders occur. The imbecile boy is suspected and his guilt seems almost certain until the inevitable Scotland Yard man comes up from London and tracks down the real killer, a sex maniac lodging in Auntie B's house. Terence de Marney gave a mannered, bravura performance as the genial, cocky, popular Charlie. It was a powerful piece of acting, with some horrific moments in the last act. But whereas a novel may satisfactorily present the complexities of a sex murderer's mind, it is extremely difficult to bring this out in dialogue, and that was the play's main fault. Owing a little to *Night Must Fall*, it had much of interest for the playgoer in search of the unusual. At least it was a *new* play, and for that reason alone it deserved to be seen.

Emlyn Williams re-wrote his ten-year-old comedy *Spring 1600*, and produced it himself at the Lyric, Hammersmith. This is a charming piece, concerned with Richard Burbage, famous 17th Century actor, the man who opened the Globe Theatre, with *Twelfth Night*, a new play by a young playwright called William Shakespeare !

Andrew Cruickshank gave a swashbuckling, amusing study as the gallant Dick Burbage, while Jessica Spencer as Ann Byrd, who disguises herself as a boy in order to play opposite her hero Burbage, offered us a performance which should make her a future West End name to conjure with. She acted with charm and freshness, showing herself to be a young actress possessing a lovely quality.

Somerset Maugham's powerful drama *The Sacred Flame*, was revived at St. Martin's, with Sonia Dresdel in the famous role of Nurse Wayland. It was the best thing she had done since *Hedda Gabler*, and certainly proved her to be one of our finest actresses, with an unequalled power for moving an audience to deep emotional reaction.

Mary Hinton's mother, Mary Martlew's wife, and Ian Lubbock's restrained study of the invalid flyer, were all praiseworthy performances in a play which clearly demonstrates Maugham's keen dramatic sense.

February saw a new play by Clifford Bax, whose historical plays *The Rose Without A Thorn* and *The Venetian* have earned him a considerable reputation as a dramatist on historical themes. The play was *Golden Eagle*, a drama written around the life and times of Mary Queen of Scots. To many Bax enthusiasts it proved disappointing. While it may conceivably have read well, and indeed, possessed many lovely passages, it seemed dramatically insufficient, the production was stagey and slow. The character of Mary is fascinating, and Claire Luce tried hard to bring life to the part. She was, however, handicapped by the play.

Torin Thatcher brought a manly quality to the part of Bothwell, David Read played Darnley, and John Byron was excellent as the secretary Rizzio. But he was hardly helped by his role. It was never made clear if he really *was* Mary's lover ; he was given a hump and made to look quite unattractive in this production. Yet surely for Rizzio to have had such power and influence over a woman who was so notoriously promiscuous is an indication that Mary and he *were* lovers ? It was never made clear in *Golden Eagle*, and the same may be said of the part of Darnley. Was *he* in love with Mary ? One would never believe so from seeing the play.

At times confusing, at other times slow, nevertheless the play had one great asset—the acting of beautiful Claire Luce as the ill-fated Queen. Everything she did was in keeping with the character of this strange, wayward Mary, at times lovable, at other times proud, cunning, a born intriguer, a ruthless and ambitious woman. Many times Miss Luce saved the play from being dull.

Sean O'Casey is something of a stormy petrel of modern drama. His plays *Juno And The Paycock*, *The Plough And The Stars* and *Within The Gates* are world-famous. He is one of the great ones of the contemporary stage. A stern critic of the West End theatre, he has for several years refused to allow his new plays to be performed in London, relenting only in 1940, when he wrote *The Star Turns Red* for production at Unity Theatre. In 1945 the Old Vic produced his *Purple Dust* at Liverpool, and in early 1946 Una Plays (whose directors include Bronson Albery, Michael Redgrave and Robert Helpmann) produced his new play at the Embassy.

This was quite a theatrical occasion, and the tragi-comedy justified the public interest, for it was a magnificent piece of dramatic poetry, beautifully conceived, written with an Irishman's passion and a poet's fervour. The central character is Ayamonn, a Shakespearean student who is also a strike leader, a fiery, idealistic figure, or as Synge would say " a lovely man." We see him enacting Shakespeare's roles in the privacy of his own mean room. But in the Dublin streets he plays the greatest role of his life, as he leads the strikers to the picket line. He is killed by the police, and the last act, with the religious factions quarrelling over his coffin, is superb writing in the most ironic O'Casey vein.

There are so many good moments in this excellent Ria Mooney production, so many memories of an evening of beauty that one is perforce to choose only two for illustration. Who will forget the scene on the Dublin embankment when the wretched flower girls and the unemployed loungers are suddenly touched with the magic of a brooding Irish evening? Their cares are forgotten, their rags vanish. For a moment they are happy, laughing, dancing folk, led by the jovial Ayamonn, played by Kieron O'Hanrahan, and the beautiful flower girl, charmingly played by Norrie Duff. And the final scene in the quiet churchyard between the old fiddler and the two Protestant vergers will also stay long in the memory.

Here then was vital theatre, with performances of great power, especially by Kieron O'Hanrahan, Maureen Pook, Tristan Rawson and a newcomer of comic genius, Eddie Byrne, who should never be allowed to return to Ireland.

THREE NEW PLAYS OF 1946

Of three interesting new plays by British playwrights, produced in London in March, one was quite simply escapist, one presented a social problem in an intelligent and diverting manner, and one was frankly and unashamedly propagandist. Of the three, the first was perhaps the best entertainment, although the second ran it close as good theatre, well acted and presented. The third? Well, one was forced to admit that whereas all art may be propaganda—as Voltaire once said—all propaganda is certainly not art. And Montagu Slater's new play at the Scala, with a singularly powerful theme and a great sweep of characterisation, just failed to come to life as a " piece of theatre," to use Gaston Baty's favourite phrase.

Some theatregoers found much of interest in *Century For George*, the first presentation of a new theatre group called " Theatre '46 " in their season at the Scala, and produced by Julius Gellner. Others disliked it immensely. The theme is industrial unrest, the drama is played through a period of a hundred years in the life of a family in " Coketown." The story traces the rise of trade unionism, from the days when to be a union member was a crime to these days of more enlightened relations between capital and labour. Interwoven into this formidable theme is a love story of three generations, in each of which the same genial figure re-appears. The " George " of the play's title is a militant trade unionist in 1850, a dispirited ex-Serviceman in the doldrums of the 1920's, and a lusty, class-conscious Eighth Army soldier in the modern sequences.

Symbolic of man's struggle for full industrial emancipation, George is a fine character, superbly played by Bernard Miles, with Jenny Laird, John Blythe, Arthur Hambling, Beatrice Rowe, and Jean Shepheard in close attendance, Blythe being particularly good in a difficult and sketchily-drawn role. Slater's main fault was that he seemed to have attempted to bite off a great deal more than *three* playwrights could possibly chew. His writing failed to encompass successfully the grandeur of the main idea. Well-intentioned, it needed to be pruned, tightened, lightened.

Warren Chetham Strode's *The Guinea Pig*, produced by Jack Minster at the Criterion, presented a minimum of theatrical faults. It dealt intelligently and sympathetically with a problem, it was good theatre, and solid entertainment throughout. To a public school comes Walthamstow boy Derek Blomfield, to an atmosphere of well-to-do gentility. His working-class origin and accent mark him out as a target for the snobbish, tradition-ridden housemaster, enacted with skill by that superb actor Cecil Trouncer ; but the efforts of a " progressive " young master prevent ultimate distress for our humble hopeful. At curtain fall he is adjusted to the school, and the school to him.

The boy's parents were finely played by Joan Hickson and Duncan Lewis. No caricature here, but honest-to-goodness character drawing on a level with the bitter, sardonic portrait of the housemaster, and the shadowy character of the spineless head-master, a diplomatic background figure. For the benefit of theatregoers demanding amorous activity at some stage in the proceedings there was a flimsy love interest supplied by Rachel Gurney and that intelligent young actor Robert Flemyng. *The Guinea Pig*, like his previous *Young Mrs. Barrington*, indicated that in Chetham Strode we had a dramatist of considerable potentialities. His work showed depth, lucidity, style. He had the skill of con-struction and the sureness of touch of a Priestley, Maugham or Ackland.

John Perry, another promising new dramatist, first came on to the London theatre scene a year or two before with his drama-tisation of Kate O'Brien's novel " The Last of Summer," a story fairly difficult to transfer to a stage. In spite of the acting of Fay Compton, Hugh Burden and Margaret Johnston, the play failed. But its fate was not shared by Perry's adaptation of Francis Brett Young's *A Man About The House*. This production possessed three main pillars of strength : it was a well-constructed play, with excellent comedy, and good, economic dialogue throughout : it possessed those admirable actors Flora Robson and Basil Sydney : and the direction of William Armstrong was eminently successful in achieving speed, diversion and tension in what might have been a meandering, though interesting, psychological essay.

Flora Robson gave a magnificent performance as a spinster from Wolverhampton, who, with her middle-aged sister, settles down in a villa in Capri (Ivor Brown, in " The Observer," wittily referred to her as a "Wolverhampton Wanderer"). No sooner are the sisters established in the house than the genially sinister butler, Salvatore (whose relations with the former owner, an elderly colonel, seem to have been dubious, to say the least) begins to woo the elder Miss Isit. And with favourable results, for the cold, unemotional English lady thaws in the Sicilian sun, and in spite of her sister's protests she marries the scheming *major domo*.

Salvatore follows wooing and winning with an attempt at poisoning but this time is not so successful, for the intervention of a doctor, an old friend of the family, averts the final tragedy. The last-act scenes, with Miss Robson giving a harrowing performance of a woman suffering from the slow effects of arsenical poisoning, are horrifyingly realistic ; while Basil Sydney's Salvatore is a masterly study in naive lechery and villainy. Wyndham Goldie brings an antiseptic breath of Harley Street efficiency to the leisurely Italian scene, while Betty Sinclair, Ernest Thesiger and Frank Tickle are effective and wholly realistic.

This play, like the two others, demonstrates that we possess in England the best raw material for building the world's most significant theatre, for we certainly have some of the greatest actors and finest producers in the world today. Perhaps tomorrow we shall produce some great dramatists ?

BIOGRAPHICAL INDEX

British Theatre

ACKLAND, RODNEY. Actor, playwright and producer. Born London, 1908. Studied for the stage at the Central School of Dramatic Art, making his first appearance in *The Lower Depths* (Gate, 1924). Subsequently in repertory at Oxford, Edinburgh, etc. ; then on tour in a number of plays. Among his own plays are *Improper People, Dance With No Music, Strange Orchestra, After October,* etc. Among his adaptations are *The Old Ladies* and *Crime And Punishment.* In 1943 he produced his own play, *The Dark River,* at the Whitehall. Has recently been writing and producing films for the Ministry of Information. In 1945 collaborated on *Cupid And Mars* (with Robert Newton).

ADAMS, ROBERT. Actor and producer. Born Georgetown, British Guiana, 1909. Formerly a teacher and headmaster at schools in various parts of the West Indies. Acted extensively on the amateur stage in Jamaica. Made his first professional appearance in London in *Stevedore* (Embassy, 1935). He has also appeared in the West End in *Toussaint L'Ouverture, You Can't Take It With You, He Signed His Name, Emperor Jones,* etc. In 1939 he appeared in *Colony* at Unity Theatre. He has recently acted in *The House Of Jeffreys* (Playhouse, 1942), *The Little Foxes* (Piccadilly, 1942), *The Judgment Of Dr. Johnson* (Arts, 1943), on tour in *Aloma Of The South Seas,* etc. In 1944 formed the Negro Repertory Theatre and with it appeared in and produced *All God's Chillun* at Colchester (in association with the Repertory Company). In 1946 appeared in *All God's Chillun* (Unity Theatre).

ADRIAN, MAX. Actor. Born Ireland, 1903. Studied for the stage at Stedman's School of Dramatic Art, making his first appearance on the stage in *Katja The Dancer* (Gaiety, Isle of Man, 1926). Made his first appearance in London in *The Squall* (Globe, 1927). 1930-32 with Northampton Repertory Company. Made his first appearance in New York in *First Episode* (Ritz, 1934). Among the plays in which he has acted in London are *This Desirable Residence, The Impresario From Smyrna, Immortal Garden, The Composite Man, The Bat, Peter Pan,* etc. Joined the London Mask Theatre in 1938 and appeared in *Troilus And Cressida, Marco Millions, The Will, The Doctor's Dilemma,* etc. In 1940 appeared in *The Country Wife* (Little), followed by *Warn That Man* (Garrick, 1941-42), *Light And Shade* (Ambassadors, 1942), *The House Of Regrets* (Arts, 1942), *Love For Love* (Phœnix, 1943). Joined John Gielgud Company and appeared in the Repertory Season at the Haymarket in the latter play, and also in *Hamlet, The Circle, A Midsummer Night's Dream* and *The Duchess Of Malfi,* 1944-45. Appeared in *Our Betters,* 1946.

AKED, MURIEL. Actress. Born Bingley, 1887. Studied for the stage at Liverpool Repertory Theatre, making her first appearance here in *Alice-Sit-By-The-Fire,* 1916. Remained at Liverpool until 1923, making her first appearance in London in *The Rose And The Ring* (Wyndham's, 1923). Subsequently appeared in London in *Uncle Vanya, Rosmersholm, Hindle Wakes, Macbeth, A Doll's House, The Lady With The Lamp, Murder On The Second Floor, People Like Us* and many others. Thenceforth in the West End in *After All, Autumn Crocus, Gay Love, Sixteen, Love From A Stranger, A Ship Comes Home, Autumn,* etc. In 1943 appeared in *Cradle Song* (Lyric) ; then in 1945, *The Gay Pavilion* (Piccadilly).

ALLEN, ADRIANNE. Actress. Born Manchester, 1907. Studied for the stage at the Royal Academy of Dramatic Art, making her first appearance in *Easy Virtue* (Duke Of York's, 1926). Subsequently in London in *The Country Wife, Lost Property, An American Tragedy, Potiphar's Wife, Happy Families* and others. Then in *Private Lives,* after which she made her first appearance on the New York stage in *Cynara* (Morosco, 1931). Then in London in *Never Come Back, The Shining Hour, Till The Cows Come Home, Plan For A Hostess,* etc. In 1939 she appeared in *We At The Crossroads.* Recently in *Flare Path* (Apollo, 1942-43). *Dear Evelyn,* 1946.

194

★ *Ann Todd,* who appeared in Enid Bagnold's "Lottie Dundass", produced by Irene Hentschel, 1942, and in Harold Purcell's "The Rest Is Silence", produced in 1943.

★ *Alec Clunes* as Sir Harry Wildair and David Bird as Smuggler, in Farquhar's comedy, "The Constant Couple", revived after 150 years by Alec Clunes, 1943.

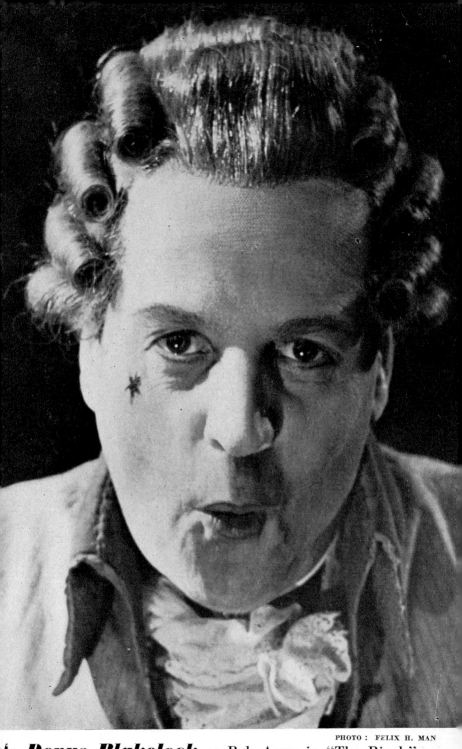

PHOTO : FELIX H. MAN

★ *Denys Blakelock* as Bob Acres in "The Rivals",
produced by Noel Iliff for the Arts Theatre Festival of
English Comedy, 1943.

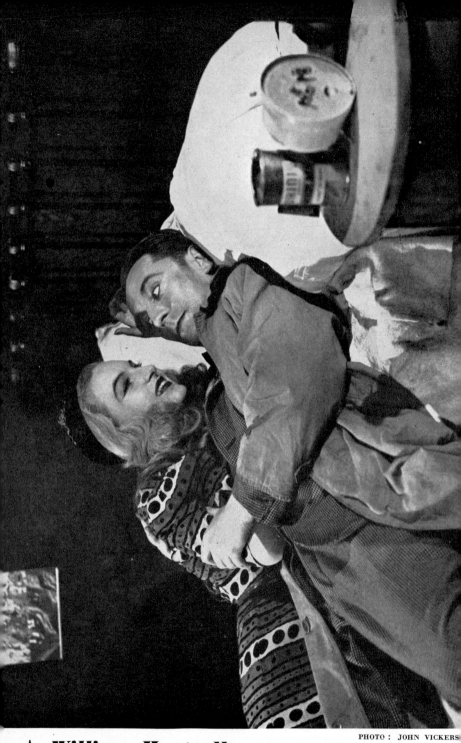

PHOTO : JOHN VICKERS

★ **William Hartnell** and Virginia Winter in Frank Harvey's dramatisation of Graham Greene's novel "Brighton Rock", produced by Richard Bird, 1943.

PHOTO : EDWARD MANDINIAN

★ **_Roland Culver_** as Lord Goring, and Peggy Bryan as Mabel Chiltern in Wilde's "An Ideal Husband", produced by Jack Minster, 1943.

PHOTO: FELIX H. MAN

★ *John Carol* as Oswald, and Beatrix Lehmann as Mrs.
Alving in Ibsen's "Ghosts", produced by Dennis Arundell
in 1943.

Abraham Sofaer and Mary Morris in John Masefield's "The Witch", produced by Catherine Lacey, 1944.

★ **Sid Field,** comedy discovery of the war years, as he appeared in George Black's revue, "Strike A New Note", produced by Robert Nesbitt, 1943.

ALLAN, ANNE. Actress. Born Calcutta. Came to England, educated at Westonbirt and studied at the Acton-Bond Dramatic School. Made her first appearance on the stage with Northampton Repertory Company in 1937, then first appeared in London in *Magyar Melody* (His Majesty's, 1939). Since then in *New Faces*, 1940, *The Admirable Crichton*, 1943, *A Murder For A Valentine*, 1944, etc. Recently : *Three's A Family* (Saville, 1945).

ALLEN, ELIZABETH. Actress. Born Skegness, 1910. Married to W. J. O'Bryen. Made her first appearance on the stage in *The Taming Of The Shrew* with the Old Vic Company (Lyric, Hammersmith, 1927) ; subsequently in *The School For Scandal, Much Ado About Nothing, Henry V*, etc. Also acted in London in *Michael And Mary, Oh, Daddy ! The Iron Woman, The Innocent Party, Quiet Wedding*, etc. Recently in *Punch Without Judy* (New), *Tomorrow The World* (Aldwych), and on tour, 1944-46.

ALLEN, JACK. Actor. Born Sandbach, Cheshire, 1907. Educated Rugby and Cambridge. Married to Ruth Dunning. Formerly engaged in industry, he joined Liverpool Repertory Company in 1931, remaining until 1933. He made his first appearance in London in *Jealousy* (Fortune, 1933). Then in *Sweet Aloes*, after which he appeared at the Malvern Festival and in a number of West End productions, including *People In Love, Poison Pen, Three Blind Mice*. From 1939 to 1945 : served in H.M. Forces. On being invalided out he appeared in *Myself A Stranger* (Embassy), *Fit For Heroes* (Embassy and Whitehall), *It Happened In New York*, on tour. In 1946 he appeared in *The Quick And The Dead* (for the Repertory Players) (Savoy), *Frieda* (Westminster), etc.

ALLENBY, FRANK. Actor. Born Tasmania, 1898. Made his first appearance on the stage in *The Marriage Of Kitty* (Melbourne, 1917), subsequently acting in Australia until 1923, when he first appeared in London in *Good Gracious, Annabelle*, followed by *The Conquering Hero, The Torch Bearers, The Letter, Peter Pan, Bird In Hand, The Ivory Door, The First Mrs. Fraser, Death Takes A Holiday*, etc. Also in *Flat To Let, Dangerous Corner, Sweet Aloes* and many others. Recently in *The Doctor's Dilemma* (Haymarket, 1942-43), *Emma* (St. James's, 1944-45), *The Gay Pavilion* (Piccadilly, 1945), etc.

ANDREWS, ROBERT. Actor. Born London, 1895. Made his first appearance in 1906 at the Strand Theatre in *Share Acres* ; subsequently appeared in *A Royal Family, The Lost Heir, Enemy Of The People*. First appeared in America in 1911. Among other plays in which he has acted in London are *Pygmalion, Secrets, Morals, Hay Fever, The Cat's Cradle, Mr. Pim Passes By, The First Mrs. Fraser, Fresh Fields, Murder In Mayfair, Full House, After Dark*, etc. Recently : in *The Nutmeg Tree* (Lyric, 1941). In *Perchance To Dream* (London Hippodrome, 1945).

ARDEN, NEAL. Actor. Born London. Studied for the stage at the Royal Academy of Dramatic Art, making his first appearance on the stage on tour in *The Truth Game* and *Jonah And The Whale*, etc. 1939-41 served in H.M. Forces, after which joined the B.B.C. In 1942 he appeared in *Blossom Time* (Lyric), *Night Of The Garter* (Strand). Then in *The Lilac Domino* (His Majesty's, 1944). Recently appeared in *Wait My Love* (Q, 1945), *Zoo In Silesia* (Embassy, 1945), etc.

ARMSTRONG, WILLIAM. Producer. Born Edinburgh, 1882. Educated Edinburgh University. First appeared 1908 at Stratford Memorial Theatre in *Henry V*. Was with Glasgow Repertory Company, then toured United States in *Milestones*. Played leads at Liverpool Repertory Theatre, 1914-16. Has appeared in London in *A Midsummer Night's Dream, King Henry IV, Man and Superman, Abraham Lincoln, Hedda Gabler*. Director at Liverpool Repertory Theatre, 1923-44, and Assist. Director Birmingham Repertory Theatre. Has produced many plays in the West End. Recently *Old Acquaintance* (Apollo), *Claudia* (St. Martin's), *Pink String And Sealing Wax* (Duke of York's), *Uncle Harry* (with

L

Michael Redgrave) (Garrick), *The Circle* (for John Gielgud's Repertory Season) (Haymarket), *The Glass Slipper* (St. James's), etc. 1945 : directed *The Rivals* (with Edith Evans) (Criterion) ; *Man About The House* (Piccadilly, 1946).

ARNAUD, YVONNE. Actress. Born Bordeaux, 1892. Formerly a pianistic child prodigy. Made her first appearance on the stage in 1911 in *The Quaker Girl* (Lyric) ; subsequently in *The Girl In The Taxi, L'Enfant Prodigue, Jerry, The Naughty Princess, Tons Of Money, A Cuckoo In The Nest, And So To Bed.* First appeared in New York in 1927. Other plays in which she has appeared in London include *Mischief, By Candlelight, Canaries Sometimes Sing, The Improper Duchess, Henry V, Plan For A Hostess.* In 1941 in *The Nutmeg Tree.* In 1943 appeared in *Love For Love* (Phœnix.) Recently with the John Gielgud Company in *Love For Love* and *The Circle* (Haymarket, 1944-45).

ARUNDELL, DENNIS. Actor and producer. Born London, 1898. Made first appearance on stage at Lyric, Hammersmith, in 1926 in *Riverside Nights.* Joined Old Vic, 1933, and appeared in *Cherry Orchard, The Tempest, Macbeth, Love For Love, Measure For Measure.* Also appeared in the West End in *Touch Wood, Mary Tudor, A Month In The Country, Busman's Honeymoon* and others. Recently appeared in *Gaslight* (Apollo). Has produced over 60 plays, including, recently : *The Old Foolishness* (Arts), *Ghosts* (Duke of York's, 1943), etc. 1944 : On tour in *The House On The Bridge.* 1945 : producing for ENSA, etc.

ASHCROFT, PEGGY. Actress. Born London, 1907. Studied at the Central School of Dramatic Art. Made first appearance on the stage at Birmingham Repertory Theatre in 1926 in *Dear Brutus.* Played in London in 1927 in *The Return* ; subsequently in *The Way Of The World, Easter, A Hundred Years Old, Jew Süss, Othello, The Breadwinner.* In 1932 joined Old Vic Company and appeared in *She Stoops To Conquer, The School For Scandal, Mary Stuart, The Merchant Of Venice.* Among other plays in which she has appeared are *Romeo And Juliet, The Seagull, High Tor* (in New York, 1937). Joined John Gielgud in 1938 and played in *Richard II, The School For Scandal, The Three Sisters, The Merchant Of Venice.* Later with Michel St. Denis Company in *The White Guard* and *Twelfth Night* at the Phœnix. In 1940 : *The Tempest* (Old Vic). Recently : *The Importance Of Being Earnest* (Phœnix, 1940), *Cousin Muriel* (Globe, 1940), *The Dark River* (Whitehall, 1943). Joined the John Gielgud Company and has appeared in *Hamlet, A Midsummer Night's Dream* and *The Duchess Of Malfi* (Haymarket, 1944-45).

ASHERSON, RENEE. Actress. Born London. Educated London and Switzerland. Studied for the stage at The Webber-Douglas Dramatic School, making her first appearance with the Birmingham Repertory Theatre. Then she joined the Old Vic Company and appeared in *The Tempest* (Old Vic, 1940). In 1941 appeared in *The Rose Without A Thorn* (Tavistock), *King John* (New), etc. In 1942 appeared in *A Midsummer Night's Dream* (Westminster). Also on tour with the Old Vic in *The Witch* and *Othello*, in which she also appeared at the New in 1942. In 1943 she acted in *Lottie Dundass* (Vaudeville). In 1945 appeared in *The Cure For Love* (Westminster) ; *Romeo and Juliet* (King's, 1946), etc.

ATKINS, ROBERT. Actor and producer. Born London, 1886. First appeared in 1906 for Herbert Tree in *King Henry IV* at His Majesty's, subsequently in *Hamlet, Richard II, Twelfth Night,* etc., until 1909. Toured with Forbes-Robertson in Britain and to the United States, and also with Sir Frank Benson. Appeared with the Old Vic and also Stratford Memorial Theatre, later becoming stage director, then producer. Produced *Peer Gynt* for the first time in England. Toured his own company in 1925 and has since toured and played in every one of Shakespeare's plays. Has staged numerous Shakespearean productions in London and all the plays produced at the Open-Air Theatre, 1933-39. During the war he toured with his own company and produced seasons at the Open Air

Theatre and at the Westminster. 1944 : Appointed producer, Stratford-on-Avon Memorial Theatre. 1945 : Producer at Stratford, and Director, Open Air Theatre, London, etc. 1946 : Produced " *Golden Eagle* " (Westminster).

ATTENBOROUGH, RICHARD. Actor. Born Cambridge, 1923. Married to Sheila Sim. Studied for the stage at the Royal Academy of Dramatic Art, making his first appearance in *Goodbye, Mr. Chips* (Intimate, Palmer's Green, 1941) ; followed by *Cottage To Let* and *Ah, Wilderness*. Made his first appearance in the West End in *Awake And Sing* (Arts, 1942), followed by *Twelfth Night* (Arts, 1942), *The Little Foxes* (Piccadilly, 1942), *Holy Isle* (Arts, 1943), *Brighton Rock* (Garrick, 1943). Since 1943 has been serving with the R.A.F.

AUDLEY, MAXINE. Actress. Born London, April 29th, 1923. Married to Leonard Cassini. Educated at Westonbirt, after which she went to America, studied at Tamara Daykarkanova School of Acting. She returned to England and studied at the London Mask Theatre School, making her first appearance in *A Midsummer Night's Dream* (Open Air, 1940). She then appeared in Robert Atkins's Season of Shakespeare at the Westminster in 1942 ; then on tour in *Room For Two*, after which she appeared in *Spanish Village* (Unity, 1943). In 1944 she toured for the Old Vic in *Arms And The Man*. 1945-46 appeared at Salisbury Garrison Theatre in *Ghosts* and *The Two Gentlemen Of Verona*.

AYLIFF, H. K. Producer. Born South Africa. First appeared in London in 1908 in *Pete* at the Lyceum. Subsequently in *When Knights Were Bold, Chains, Fanny's First Play, At Mrs. Beam's*. Producer, Birmingham Repertory Company from 1922. Has produced among others : *Heartbreak House, Back To Methuselah, Candida, Mary Stuart, Rosmersholm*. Producer at many of the seasons at Malvern Festival. Recently produced *Music At Night, The Last Trump, Geneva* (all at Malvern in 1938). In 1940, *In Good King Charles's Golden Days* (New). 1945 : Produced *The Cure For Love* (for Robert Donat) at the Westminster, etc. ; also *So Brief The Spring*, 1945-46.

AYLMER, FELIX. Actor. Born Corsham, 1889. First appeared at the Coliseum, 1911, in *Cook's Man*, then with Fred Terry and Sir Herbert Tree. Joined Birmingham Repertory Company in 1913. Later appeared in London in *Madame Sand, Abraham Lincoln, The Green Cord* and many others. To New York in 1922 to act in *Loyalties*. Among other plays in which he has appeared in the West End are *Misalliance, The Philanderer, The Doctor's Dilemma, The Terror, Bird In Hand, Strife, The Voysey Inheritance, Saint Joan, Heroes Don't Care, Waste, Power And The Glory, The Flashing Stream*, etc. Recently : Appeared in *Scandal At Barchester* (Lyric, and Wyndham's, 1944-45).

BADDELEY, ANGELA. Actress. Born London, 1904. Married to Glen Byam Shaw. First appeared at Old Vic in 1915 in *Richard III*, subsequently in *A Winter's Tale, Make Believe, The Beggar's Opera, The Insect Play, The Rivals, The Wild Duck* and many others. In 1926 to Australia. Among other plays in which she has appeared in the West End are *Marigold, A Hundred Years Old* and *The School For Scandal*. To South Africa in 1931 ; on returning to London appeared in *The Rose Without A Thorn, Sheppey, Night Must Fall* (also in New York, 1936). Returned to London in *Pride And Prejudice* ; then in *The Three Sisters, The Merchant Of Venice, Dear Octopus, The Importance Of Being Earnest*, etc. Recently : *The Light Of Heart*, 1940, *The Morning Star* (Globe, 1941-42), *Love For Love* (Phœnix, 1943), *It Depends What You Mean* (Westminster, 1944), *Chicken Every Sunday* (Savoy, 1945). On tour in *A Doll's House*, 1945-46. In 1946 appeared in *The Winslow Boy*.

BADDELEY, HERMIONE. Actress. Born Broseley, 1906. Made her first appearance in London in *La Boite a Joujou* (Court, 1918). Subsequently appeared in London in *Make Believe, The Knight Of The Burning Pestle, The Likes Of*

'*Er, The Fledglings, The Punch Bowl, The Co-Optimists Of* 1924, etc. Subsequently
in *On With The Dance, Nine To Eleven, Still Dancing, Cochran's Revue Of* 1926,
Queen High, Lord Babs, Excelsior, The Shanghai Gesture, etc. Also in London
in *Tobias And The Angel, After Dinner, Ballyhoo, The Greeks Had A Word For It,
Why Not Tonight ? To And Fro, Floodlight, Nine Sharp* and others. In 1939
appeared in *The Little Revue,* which ran until 1940, after which she appeared in
The Country Wife (Little, 1940). Then in *Rise Above It* (Comedy, 1941-42),
Sky High (Phœnix, 1942), *Brighton Rock* (Garrick, 1943). She then toured in
the Middle East with Leslie Henson's *Gaieties,* returning to London in *Cinderella*
(Winter Garden, 1944-45), followed by *Gaieties* (Winter Garden and Saville,
1945). In 1946 appeared in *Grand National Night* and *Don't, Mr. Disraeli.*

BAKER, JOHN. Actor. Born Newport, Mon., 1917. Educated at Westminster
School. Made his first appearance on the stage in *Chu The Sinner* (Embassy,
1937), then in repertory at the Intimate, Palmers Green, and in various productions
at Q. From 1939-43 he served in H.M. Forces. On being invalided out he
appeared in *An Ideal Husband* (Westminster), followed by *This Time It's Love,*
on tour. Recently : In *Alice In Wonderland* (Palace, 1944-45), *Emma* (St. James's)
and *The First Gentleman* (New and Savoy, 1945-46).

BANBURY, FRITH. Actor. Born Plymouth, 1912. Educated Stowe and
Oxford. Studied for the stage at Royal Academy of Dramatic Art ; making his
first appearance in *If I Were You* (Shaftesbury, 1933), subsequently toured in
Richard of Bordeaux in 1934. Then played in London in *The Dark Tower, Hamlet,
The Good Young Man* and others. Appeared with Robert Morley and Peter Bull
at the Perranporth Summer Theatre, 1936-37-38 ; then in *Goodness, How Sad* at
the Vaudeville, 1938-39. Among the other shows in which he has recently
appeared are *Follow My Leader* (Apollo, 1940), *New Faces* (Comedy, 1940 and
Apollo, 1941), *New Ambassadors Revue* (Ambassadors, 1942), *Jam To-day*
(St. Martin's, 1942), *Light and Shade* (Ambassadors, 1942), *A Trip To Scarborough*
(Arts, 1943), etc. Joined Norman Marshall's Company in 1943 and appeared in
The Idiot on tour, and in *Uncle Vanya* (Westminster, 1943). In 1944 appeared in
Bird In Hand (Arts and St. Martin's), then in *Jacobowsky And The Colonel*
(Piccadilly, 1945). Appeared in *While The Sun Shines* (Globe, 1946).

BANKS, LESLIE. Actor and producer. Born West Derby, 1890. Made first
appearance on stage in 1911 with F. R. Benson's Company in *The Merchant Of
Venice.* Toured 1913-14 in United States and Canada. Appeared in New York
1914 in *Eliza Comes To Stay.* First appeared in London in 1914 in *The Dangerous
Age.* After the last war joined Birmingham Repertory Company ; then at
Everyman appeared in *Major Barbara, Candida,* etc. Among the other plays in
which he has appeared in London are *Fanny's First Play, The Young Idea, R.U.R.,
Quinney's, The Lady With The Lamp, Emma Hamilton, Springtime For Henry,
Service, Clive Of India, The Two Mrs. Carrolls, Goodbye Mr. Chips.* Has produced
plays in London and New York. Also in *Cottage To Let* (Wyndham's), *The
Duke In Darkness* (St. James's, 1942). Joined John Gielgud Company and has
appeared in *Love For Love, Hamlet, A Midsummer Night's Dream, The Duchess
Of Malfi* (Phœnix and Haymarket, 1943-45). Then in *Grand National Night,*
1945-46.

BANNERMAN, KAY. Actress. With the Old Vic Company at the beginning of
the war, on tour, and in London. In 1942 she appeared in *The Merchant Of Venice*
(New), then toured with the Old Vic until 1944, when she appeared in *Guilty*
(Lyric, Hammersmith). Recently : In *Myself A Stranger* (Embassy, 1945), *The
Gambler* (Embassy, 1945). With Harold Brook she wrote *Fit For Heroes,* produced
at the Embassy, and on tour 1945.

BARBOUR, JOYCE. Actress. Born Birmingham, 1901. Married to Richard
Bird. Made her first appearance on the stage in *To-night's The Night* (Gaiety,

1915); subsequently in London in *Irene, Now And Then, Sally, London Calling,* etc. First appeared in New York in *Havoc* (Maxine Elliot, 1924), returning to London in *The Punch Bowl,* followed by *Queen High, Evergreen, Words And Music, Hay Fever, The Greeks Had A Word For It* and others. More recently in the West End in *The Two Bouquets, George And Margaret,* etc. In 1940 in *Spotted Dick* (Strand), followed by *Saloon Bar* (Wyndham's, 1941), *Let's Face It* (Hippodrome, 1943), and *A Soldier For Christmas,* 1944-45. Appeared in *Blithe Spirit* (Duchess, 1945).

BARNARD, IVOR. Actor. Born London, 1887. Studied for stage with F. R. Benson. Made first appearance at Belfast Theatre Royal, 1908, in *Don Quixote,* subsequently toured in England. With Birmingham Repertory Theatre, 1913-16. Among plays in which he has appeared in London are *The Skin Game, Will Shakespeare, The Vortex, Berkeley Square, The Bird In Hand* (also in New York, 1929-30), *The Crime At Blossoms, Grand Hotel, Strife, The Seagull,* etc. Recently: *The Dark River* (Whitehall, 1943), *The Bird In Hand* (St. Martin's, 1944).

BARNES, BARRY K. Actor. Born London, 1906. Married to Diana Churchill. Studied at the Royal Academy of Dramatic Art. First appeared on London stage in *Paul I* (Court, 1927), subsequently in repertory. Among the many plays in which he has appeared in the West End are *Merchant Of Venice, The Silver Tassie, The Barretts Of Wimpole Street.* In 1932 toured Australia with latter play. Returned to London and appeared in *The Late Christopher Bean, Spring Tide, The Ascent Of F.6, Thank You, Mr. Pepys* and others. Recently: *The Body Was Well Nourished* (Lyric, 1940), *On Approval* (Aldwych, 1941), *The Admirable Crichton* (His Majesty's, 1943). In 1945 appeared at the Embassy in *Tomorrow's Eden.*

BARROW, JANET. Born Bedford. Educated in Brussels. Trained for the stage under Rosina Filippi, making her first appearance at the Royal Court Theatre. She has a long and varied experience on the stage in this country. Recently in *The Devil's Disciple* (Piccadilly, 1940), *Shephard's Pie* (Princes, 1941), *The Grand Manner,* on tour, *Lottie Dundass* (Vaudeville, 1943), *Arsenic And Old Lace,* on tour, 1944-45.

BARRY, MARIA. Actress. Born London, 1920. Married to Michael Law. Made her first appearance on the stage in *Anything Goes* (Palace, 1935), then on tour in musical shows and in shows at the London Casino. She made her first appearance in " straight " drama in *The Playboy Of The Western World* (Mercury, 1939-40). After this she studied for the stage under John Fernald at the London Mask Theatre School. Subsequently in repertory in Brixton and Watford, after which she joined the Norman Marshall Company, appearing in *The Gay Lord Quex* (Cambridge Arts). In 1943 she joined the Market Theatre on tour for CEMA in *Back To Methuselah* and *Twelfth Night.* In 1944 appeared in *Don Abel Wrote A Tragedy* (Arts), *The Rest Is Silence* (Prince of Wales). Recently in *Madame Louise* (Garrick, 1944-46).

BARTON, MARGARET. Born London, May 27th, 1926. Studied at the Royal Academy of Dramatic Art, making her first appearance in *Pink String And Sealing Wax* (Duke of York's, 1943). Then in *It Depends What You Mean* (Westminster, 1944-45). Recently: *Young Mrs. Barrington* (Winter Garden, 1945-46), *Dear Ruth* (St. James's, 1946).

BASS, ALFIE. Actor. Born London, 1915. Began acting in boy's clubs at the age of 13 and became the youngest producer for the London Federation of Boys' Clubs. Then joined Unity Theatre in 1936, and appeared in *Waiting For Lefty, Where's That Bomb, The Aristocrat, Plant In The Sun* and *Distant Point,* etc., and in many revues. In 1943 appeared in *Buster* at Unity and later at the Arts.

Made his debut on the professional stage when he appeared in *Mr. Bolfry* (Playhouse, 1944). Also appeared in *The Alchemist* and *He Who Gets Slapped* (for the Old Vic) (Liverpool Playhouse, 1944). 1945-46 : With the Old Vic Company at Liverpool.

BAX, CLIFFORD. Playwright. Born London, 1886. Among his plays are *Polly, Midsummer Madness, Upstream, Mr. Pepys, Socrates, The Venetian, The Rose Without A Thorn, The House Of Borgia, The Impresario From Smyrna* (adaptation). In 1945 he published a book, " Whither The Theatre ? " His adaptation of Goldoni's *Mine Hostess* was produced at the Arts in 1944.

BAXTER, EDWARD. Actor and dancer. Born Clifton, Bristol, 1916. On the stage since a child, he made his professional appearance in a concert party at Weston-super-Mare in 1936, after which he appeared in repertory and in many musical productions on tour and in *Van Damm's Revue* (Garrick) until he joined the Army in 1940. He served in H.M. Forces until 1943, when he was invalided out, appearing in *Flying Colours* (Lyric). Then in *The Gypsy Princess* (Saville, 1944), *Big Boy* (Saville, 1945-46), etc.

BAXTER, JANE. Actress. Born 1909. Studied for the stage under Italia Conti. First appeared in *Love's Prisoner* (Adelphi, 1925), subsequently in *Peter Pan, A Damsel In Distress, The Middle Watch, To Have And To Hold, George And Margaret* and many others. Recently : *Living Room* (Garrick, 1943), *While The Sun Shines* (Globe, 1943-45).

BAYLEY, HILDA. Actress. Born London. Made her first appearance in *The Yellow Jacket* (Duke of York's, 1913) ; subsequently in London in *The Great Gamble, Grumpy, The Laughter Of Fools, The Thirteenth Chair, Carnival, Othello* and many others. Also in the West End in *The Way Things Happen, The Dark Angel, Intimate Enemies, Thunder In The Air* and many others. In 1939 she appeared in *Interlude* (Duke of York's). Recently : In 1942 in *Little Women* (Westminster), etc. In 1945 in *Kiss And Tell* (Phœnix).

BEATON, CECIL. Artist, photographer and designer. Born 1904. Educated at Harrow. Has designed the decor for a number of ballets including *Le Pavillon, Apparitions*. Also designed the Cochran revues *Streamline* and *Follow The Sun*. Recently designed the costumes for *Heartbreak House* (Cambridge, 1943), and designed the settings for *Crisis In Heaven* (Lyric, 1944), *Lady Windermere's Fan* (Haymarket, 1945), *Dandy Dick*, 1946, *Our Betters*, 1946, etc.

BEATTY, ROBERT. Actor. Born Hamilton, Ontario, Canada, 1909. Educated University of Toronto. Came to England in 1937 and studied at R.A.D.A., making his first appearance on the London stage when he under-studied Raymond Massey and walked on in *Idiot's Delight* (His Majesty's). He then appeared in *To Love And To Cherish* (Kingsway) and *Grouse In June* (Criterion, 1939). Recently acted in *Lifeline* (Duchess, 1942), *The Petrified Forest* (Globe, 1942-43), *A Soldier For Christmas* (Wyndham's, Vaudeville and Playhouse, 1944). In 1945 appeared in *Laura* (St. Martin's), *Love From A Stranger* (Gateway) and *A Bell For Adano* (Phœnix).

BEAUMONT, ROBERT. Actor. Born London, October 15th, 1923. Educated Cranbrook School, Kent. Made his first appearance on the stage with the Old Vic in *The Merry Wives Of Windsor* (New, 1942). Remained with the Old Vic, appearing in *Othello* (New, 1942), *The Merchant Of Venice*, 1943, *Abraham Lincoln* (Playhouse, 1943), and *The Russians* (Playhouse, 1943). Then joined the Old Vic Company at Liverpool, appearing in *Six Characters In Search Of An Author, Noah* and *Androcles And The Lion*, etc. In 1944 he appeared in *Hamlet* for the Old Vic, at the New. Then on tour in *There Shall Be No Night*. Recently : In *Alice In Wonderland* (Palace, 1944-45), *The School For Scandal* and *Pride And Prejudice* (Oxford Playhouse, 1945), *The First Gentleman* (New and Savoy, 1945-46).

BEAUMONT, ROMA. Actress. Born London, 1914. Studied under Italia Conti. Made first stage appearance at Holborn Empire in *Where The Rainbow Ends*, subsequently appearing in musical shows and cabaret. Among the West End plays in which she has appeared are *Mr. Whittington, Crest Of The Wave, The Dancing Years* (Adelphi, 1939-43). In 1940 appeared in *Black Velvet* (Hippodrome). Recently: *Alice In Wonderland* (Scala, 1943), *Perchance To Dream* (Hippodrome), 1945.

BECKWITH, REGINALD. Actor and playwright. Born York. Made his first appearance on the London stage at the Grafton, and afterwards at the Gate Theatre, where he appeared in many productions of Norman Marshall. Also in the West End in *The Gate Revue* (Ambassadors), *Follow My Leader* (Apollo, 1940), *Swinging The Gate* (Ambassadors), etc. 1940-44 B.B.C. War Correspondent returning to stage in *The Rivals* (Criterion, 1945). Is the author of much revue material and of the following plays : *Adults Only, Lysistrata, Boys In Brown* and *A Soldier For Christmas*, etc.

BELL, MARY HAYLEY. Playwright and actress. Born Shanghai, China, 1914. Married to John Mills. Educated in England. Studied for the stage at the Royal Academy of Dramatic Art. Toured Australia with Fay Compton in *Victoria Regina* and other plays. Was for three years with Sir Seymour Hicks and then appeared in *Tony Draws A Horse*, both in London and New York, 1939. Among her plays are *Men In Shadow*, 1942, and *Duet For Two Hands*, 1945.

BENNETT, PETER. Born London, September 17th, 1917. Educated Malvern College. Studied for the stage at Royal Academy of Dramatic Art, making his first appearance in *The Pleasure Garden*, Folkestone, 1936. He first appeared in the West End in *The Misanthrope* (Ambassadors, 1937), followed by *The Zeal Of Thy House, The Western Chamber, Macbeth, Lady Precious Stream* and in seasons at the Open Air, 1937-38-39. In 1940 he appeared in *Chu Chin Chow* (Palace), followed by *Peter Pan* (Adelphi, 1941), and season at the Open Air, 1942. Recently: In Robert Atkins's Shakespearean Season (Westminster, 1942), appearing in *A Midsummer Night's Dream, The Merchant Of Venice* and *Henry IV (Part I)*. Also in *Peter Pan* (Cambridge, 1943), *War And Peace* (Phœnix, 1943), *Macbeth* (Lyric, Hammersmith, 1944), *The Golden Fleece*, on tour, 1944-45, *The Alchemist* and *The Spinster Of South Side* (both at King's, Hammersmith, 1945), also in *Zoo In Silesia* (Embassy).

BENNETT, VIVIENNE. Actress. Born Poole, 1905. Studied at the Royal Academy. First appeared on stage in a sketch at the Coliseum ; subsequently in repertory at Northampton, Cambridge, Dublin and Birmingham. Among the plays in which she has appeared in London are *The Faithful Heart, Six Characters In Search Of An Author, One More River, Counsellor At Law*. Joined Old Vic in 1935 and played in *Othello, Major Barbara, Henry IV, Peer Gynt, Julius Cæsar, The Three Sisters, Macbeth, King Lear*. Other plays in which she has appeared in London are *Night Must Fall, People At Sea, Coriolanus, Private History, They Fly By Twilight*, etc. 1940-43 toured with her own company, The Market Theatre, and has also appeared in *Awake And Sing* (Arts), *Twelfth Night* (Arts), *Holy Isle* (Arts), *Macbeth* (Lyric, Hammersmith), *Uncle Vanya* (Westminster) and several CEMA productions. 1944-45 : On tour in *The House On The Bridge* and *Hidden Horizon*. Appeared in *The Circle Of Chalk* (Arts, 1945). Then on tour in Europe in *Julius Cæsar*, etc. Appeared in *Murder On The Nile* (Ambassadors, 1946).

BENSON, GEORGE. Actor and producer. Born Cardiff, 1911. Studied at Royal Academy. Made first stage appearance at the Malvern Festival, 1929, in *Cæsar and Cleopatra*. Appeared in London, 1930, in *Charlot's Masquerade* (Cambridge), subsequently in *Wonder Bar, Love For Love*. Then toured Australia and Egypt in 1932-33. Other shows he has appeared in include *Mary Read, No More Peace, The Two Bouquets, The Comedy Of Errors, Distant Point, Nine*

Sharp, She Stoops To Conquer, The Little Revue. In 1941 produced *Diversion* (Wyndham's). In H.M. Forces, 1941-45. Appeared in *Better Late,* 1946.

BERNARD, CARL. Actor. Born London, 1909. First appeared on the stage in pantomime at the Palladium in 1928 and thereafter appeared in several musicals for Albert De Courville and revues for Archie De Bear. Toured England and South Africa for two years with Dennis Neilson-Terry and Mary Glynne. Then appeared in London in *Grand Guignol* (Little) and in *Craig's Wife,* before touring South Africa again in vaudeville. Was director of Hull Repertory Theatre for three years and has appeared in repertory at Newcastle and Bradford, etc. Has also acted in London in *Please Teacher, Certainly Sir, Bobby Get Your Gun,* etc. Since the war, acting with the B.B.C. Drama Repertory Company, leaving to appear in *One Room* (Apollo, 1943), and on tour in *Gather No Moss, Lovely To Look At,* etc. In 1945 appeared in *Is Your Honeymoon Really Necessary* (Duke of York's), and on tour in *Through The Door.* 1945-46 : On tour Europe in " *The Lovely Lady* ".

BIRCH, DEREK. Actor and producer. Born London, 1906. Educated Brighton College. Made his first appearance on the stage in *The Lottery* (Playroom Six, 1928). Then appeared in repertory at Manchester and elsewhere. Also appeared in London in *The Housemaster, Clive Of India, The Unguarded Hour,* etc. After invalided from Army, announcer for B.B.C. In 1943 appeared in *Androcles And The Lion* (Arts), then joined the Festival Company at the Arts, appearing in *The Rivals, The Constant Couple, Misalliance* and *The Magistrate.* In 1944 in *A Trip To Scarborough* (Arts), then in *The Magistrate* (St. Martin's). Has produced a number of plays, including *The Rochdale Pioneers* for the People's Entertainment Society, *Robin Of England* (Unity, 1945) and *Gaslight* for ENSA tour, 1945. Joined the Arts Drama Festival Company, appearing in *The Constant Couple, Hamlet* and *The School For Scandal* (Arts Theatre, 1945-46).

BIRD, RICHARD. Actor and producer. Born Liverpool, 1894. Married to Joyce Barbour. Made first appearance on the stage with the Liverpool Repertory Theatre, 1918, and stayed there until 1920. To London and appeared at the Everyman. Then in *The Shewing-up Of Blanco Posnet* (Queen's). Subsequently appeared in London in *Widower's Houses, Havoc* (and in New York, 1924), *Candida, The Ghost Train, The Fanatics* (in New York, 1927), *The Sacred Flame, Dangerous Corner, The Dominant Sex, Night Alone,* etc. In 1940 appeared in *Once A Crook* (Aldwych). In 1941 appeared in *Love In A Mist* (St. Martin's). Recently appeared in *The Lady From Edinburgh* (Playhouse, 1945-46). Among the plays he has recently produced in London are *George And Margaret, Room For Two, They Fly By Twilight, Heaven And Charing Cross, Women Aren't Angels, Cottage To Let, Once A Crook, Love In A Mist, Warn That Man, Brighton Rock, Quiet Week-End, Dubarry Was A Lady, No Medals* and *Madame Louise.*

BLAKE, GREY. Actor. Born London, 1917. Educated St. Paul's. Married to Ruth Grundy. Made his first appearance on the stage in repertory at Worthing, where he continued to play for three years. First appeared in London in *To Kill A Cat* (Aldwych, 1938), followed by appearances in *Johnson Over Jordan* and *Berkeley Square* (Vaudeville, 1940). 1940-43, served with the R.A.F. Recently appeared in *This Was A Woman* (Comedy, 1944), *Emma* (St. James's, 1945), *This Land Of Ours* (Q, 1945), etc.

BLAKELOCK, ALBAN. Actor. Born May 17th, 1897. Educated Felstead and Cambridge. He made his first appearance in London in *The Ballad Monger* (Coliseum, 1923). Since then he has been engaged extensively in productions in England, on tour and abroad. Recently : *Wild Decembers, The Silver Tassie* and *Toad Of Toad Hall,* etc. Also in *Heaven And Charing Cross* (St. Martin's, 1939), *The Nutmeg Tree* (Lyric, 1941), *Macbeth* (Piccadilly, 1942), *A Month In The Country* (St. James's, 1943), *Fighter's Calling,* on tour, 1944 ; *Arms And The Man* (for the Old Vic), on tour, 1945 ; and *Myself A Stranger* (Embassy, 1945).

BLAKELOCK, DENYS. Actor and producer. Born London, 1901. Studied at Royal Academy of Dramatic Art. Made his first appearance on the stage in *Sacrifice* (Prince of Wales, 1920) ; subsequently in *You Never Can Tell, Abraham Lincoln, The Lash, The Silver Cord, Red Sunday, A Bill Of Divorcement.* Among the other West End plays in which he has appeared are *The Unquiet Spirit, Insult, The Merchant Of Venice, The Brontës, The Black Eye, Short Story, Yes And No, Comedienne.* Recently : *Awake And Sing, Twelfth Night, Maria Marten, The Watched Pot, Androcles And The Lion, The Rivals, The Breadwinner, The Two Children* (all at the Arts), *The Magistrate* (St. Martin's). Recently produced *Don Abel Wrote A Tragedy* (Arts) and *A Trip To Scarborough* (Arts), etc. In 1945 appeared in *Lady Windermere's Fan* (Haymarket).

BLOMFIELD, DEREK. Actor. Born London, 1920. Educated Egerton House and Merchant Taylors. Made his first appearance on the stage as a child in *What Happened To George* (Savoy, 1934). Has also appeared in *Housemaster* (Aldwych, 1936-38), *Other People's Houses* (Ambassadors, 1941-42). Appeared in repertory at the Intimate, Palmer's Green, and Windsor, etc. Then in *Happy Few* (Cambridge, 1944), *The Magistrate* (St. Martin's, 1944). Recently appeared in *While Parents Sleep* (Whitehall, 1945), *The Guinea Pig* (Criterion, 1946).

BOULTER, ROSALYN. Actress. Born Burton-on-Trent, 1916. Studied at Central School of Dramatic Art. Made first appearance in 1935 in *Clive Of India* (Arts) ; subsequently in London in *A Midsummer Night's Dream, Love's Labour's Lost, Our Own Lives, Children To Bless You, The Tempest, As You Like It, The Housemaster,* etc. First appeared in New York in 1937 in *George and Margaret.* Returned to London in *Ghosts For Sale, Number Six,* etc. Recently in *French For Love* (Criterion, 1940), *Another Love Story* (Phœnix, 1944), *The Assassin* (Savoy, 1945).

BOXER, JOHN. Actor. Born London, 1909. Studied at Royal Academy of Dramatic Art. First appeared on stage in 1928 in *The Dark Path* (Savoy) ; subsequently in *Secrets,* then a season at the Embassy, followed by *The Crime At Blossoms, The Young Idea, Strife, Escape Me Never, The Wind And The Rain* and other plays in London. First played in New York in 1935 in *Escape Me Never.* Other West End plays in which he has appeared include *The Merchant Of Venice, Macbeth, The Boy David, George And Margaret.* In 1940 in *Women Aren't Angels* (Strand). 1940-45 : In H.M. Forces. Recently appeared with A.B.C.A. Play Unit at Arts, 1945.

BRAITHWAITE, LILIAN. Actress. Born Ramsgate. Formerly an amateur ; made her first professional appearance on tour in South Africa in 1897 in *The Merchant Of Venice.* First appeared in London in 1900 in *As You Like It,* subsequently joined F. R. Benson's company, toured with George Alexander, then at St. James's, 1901-06 in *The Wilderness, Liberty Hall, The Importance Of Being Earnest, As You Like It,* etc. Later in the West End in *The School For Scandal, The Flag Lieutenant, Lady Windermere's Fan, The Miracle, Mr. Wu, Peter Ibbetson, The Merchant Of Venice, Julius Cæsar,* etc. Then in *A Bill Of Divorcement,* subsequently in *The Vortex* (and in New York, 1925), *The Silver Cord, The Truth Game, Symphony In Two Flats* (also in New York, 1936), *After All, Flat To Let, Fresh Fields, Family Affairs, Full House, Lady Of La Paz, Bats In The Belfry, Comedienne, Tony Draws A Horse,* etc. Then in *A House In The Square* (St. Martin's, 1940), *Ducks And Drakes* (Apollo, 1942). Recently : *Arsenic And Old Lace* (Strand, 1942-46).

BRANDT, IVAN. Born London, 1903. Formerly an architect. First appeared on the stage in 1927 in *The Flame* (Playroom Six); subsequently toured with Charles Macdona in Bernard Shaw plays. Joined Birmingham Repertory Company in 1928. Made first appearance in New York in 1929 in *Rope,* later in London acted in *Down Our Street, The Venetian, Death Takes A Holiday, The Rose Without A Thorn,*

The Miracle, Many Women, Dinner At Eight and others. Then in *The Wind And The Rain, The Bat, Susannah And The Elders, Portrait Of A Lady*, etc. Recently: *Panama Hattie* (Piccadilly, 1943-44), *Murder On The Nile* (Ambassadors, 1946).

BRIDIE, JAMES. Playwright. Born Glasgow, 1888. Among his plays are *The Anatomist, Tobias And The Angel, Jonah And The Whale, A Sleeping Clergyman, Mary Read* (with Claude Gurney), *The Black Eye, Storm In A Teacup* (adaptation), *Susannah And The Elders, The Last Trump, Holy Isle, Mr. Bolfry, It Depends What You Mean*, etc. With Paul Vincent Carroll he is a director of Glasgow Citizen's Theatre. In 1945 he wrote *The Forrigan Reel*.

BRIGGS, HEDLEY. Actor, producer and designer. Born Birmingham, 1907. Made his first appearance on the stage in *Two Shepherds*, 1921, with the Birmingham Repertory Company, with whom he stayed until 1926. During this period he made his first appearance in London in *The Christmas Party* (Regent, 1922). From 1927-29 he acted and designed at the Festival Theatre, Cambridge. Subsequently mainly designing until 1934, after which he appeared at the Gate Theatre and designed all the settings from 1934 to 1935. He has appeared in London also in *Maya, Misalliance, Charlot's Char-A-Bang, The Witch Of Edmonton* (for the Old Vic, 1936), *Tobacco Road, Serena Blandish, The Shoemaker's Holiday* and others. In 1940 he appeared in *Swinging The Gate* (Ambassadors). Among the West End plays which he has designed are *A Kiss In Spring, Yours Sincerely, Lysistrata, Parnell, Mr. Gladstone, The Painted Smile*, etc. In 1938 he produced *Nine Sharp* and *The Little Revue*, 1939 (for which he also designed the costumes and scenery). In 1940 he produced *New Faces* (Comedy and Apollo, 1941). In 1944 he designed the settings for *A Soldier For Christmas* (Wyndham's). Since 1941 in Royal Navy. Appeared in *Tomorrow's Child* (Lyric, Hammersmith, 1946).

BROCK, CECIL. Actor. Born Dublin, 1915. Educated Jesuit College, Belvedere. Studied for the stage at the Abbey, Dublin, making his first appearance there in *Œdipus*, 1933. In 1934 he joined the Gate Company and made his first appearance in London with this company in *Hamlet* (Westminster, 1935). Also in London in *Armlet Of Jade* (Westminster, 1936), *The Moon In The Yellow River, Youth's The Season* and *Juno And The Paycock* (Saville, 1937). He returned to Dublin, appearing for a season at the Gate, 1940, then at Belfast Opera House, 1942-43, after which he appeared for a season at Glasgow Citizen's in 1943. Recently: In *Daughter Janie* (Apollo, 1944), *A Night In Venice* (Cambridge, 1945), then on tour with Roger Livesey and Ursula Jeans in the Middle East, 1946.

BROOK, CLIVE. Actor. Born London, 1891. Made his first appearance on the London stage in 1920 in *Just Like Judy* (St. Martin's); subsequently toured in *The Harbury Pearls* and others. Following his appearance in *Clothes And The Woman* at the Ambassadors in 1921, he commenced a long film career in London and Hollywood. Recently returned to the London stage in *The Years Between* (Wyndham's, 1945-46).

BROOK, LESLEY. Actress. Born Folkestone, 1917. Studied for the stage at Royal Academy of Dramatic Art, making her first appearance with the Croydon Repertory Company in 1935. Has also appeared at the Open-Air Theatre, Stratford-on-Avon Memorial Theatre and in London in *Grief Goes Over, Power And Glory, Dangerous Corner*, etc. Recently appeared in *Halfway To Heaven* (Princes, 1943), *Private Lives* on tour, *Madame Louise* (Garrick, 1945-46).

BROOK-JONES, ELWYN. Actor. Born Sarawak, Borneo, 1911. Educated Winchester and Oxford. Made his first appearance on the stage in 1932 and has since appeared in more than a dozen repertory companies in all parts of England. In 1940 he founded the Threshold Theatre for new playwrights and new actors. He made his first appearance on the West End stage in *Hedda Gabler* (Westminster, 1942), and then appeared in *Blow Your Own Trumpet* (for the Old Vic) (Playhouse),

Claudia (St. Martin's), *The Recruiting Officer* (Arts), *On Life's Sunny Side* (Arts), *Don Abel Wrote A Tragedy* (Arts). In 1944 toured in *Tomorrow's Eden.* In 1945 appeared in *Duet For Two Hands* (Lyric).

BROWN, PAMELA. Actress. Born London, 1918. Married to Peter Copley. Studied for the stage at the Royal Academy of Dramatic Art, making her first appearance as Juliet at Stratford-on-Avon Memorial Theatre. After this season she toured South Africa in *The Amazing Dr. Clitterhouse*, returning to London in *A Midsummer Night's Dream* (Open Air). Was for a time with the Oxford Playhouse ; then joined Old Vic Company to appear in *The Taming Of The Shrew* and *She Stoops To Conquer.* Acted in 1937-38 at the Perranporth Summer Theatre. More recently rejoined Oxford Repertory Company, appearing in *The Seagull, Rain, Romeo and Juliet, Ghosts, Hedda Gabler*, etc. Joined B.B.C. Repertory Company, then toured in *Golden Boy.* In 1942 appeared in *Claudia* (St. Martin's), *Hamlet* (for the Old Vic Company) (New, 1943), *Madeleine* (for Norman Marshall Company) (Lyric, Hammersmith, 1944). Joined Old Vic at Bristol, 1946.

BROWNE, CORAL. Actress. Born Melbourne, Australia, 1913. Made first appearance at Comedy, Melbourne, in *Loyalties* in 1931 ; subsequently played in *The Calendar, Hay Fever, Let Us Be Gay, Hedda Gabler, Children In Uniform*, etc. Came to London in 1934 and appeared in *Lover's Leap* (Vaudeville). Also played in *Mated, Basilisk, This Desirable Residence, Heroes Don't Care, The Taming Of The Shrew, The Great Romancer, The Gusher* and others. Recently : In 1940 appeared in *Believe It Or Not* (New), *The Man Who Came To Dinner*, 1942-44, *My Sister Eileen*, 1944, and *The Last Of Mrs. Cheyney*, 1944-45 (all at the Savoy).

BROWNE, IRENE. Actress. Born London, 1896. First appeared in London at the Queen's in 1910 in *Robert Macaire* ; subsequently in *Hamlet*, etc. With H. B. Irving Company toured Australia for three years. Re-appeared in London in 1915 in *The Dummy* ; subsequently in *My Lady Frayle, Too Many Cooks, The Gay Lord Quex, Diplomacy, No, No, Nanette.* To New York in 1928 to appear in *The Happy Husband.* In 1931 appeared in London in *Cavalcade.* Among other West End shows in which she has played are *Conversation Piece, Children To Bless You, Call It A Day*, From 1936-40 on New York stage. Recently on London stage in *Blithe Spirit* (Duchess) and *Alice In Wonderland* (Palace), etc.

BROWNE, LAIDMAN. Actor. Born Newcastle-on-Tyne, 1896. First appeared on the stage with Newcastle Repertory Theatre in 1925 in *Doormats*, played leading parts here until 1931. Appeared in London with his company in 1931 at Regent. With the Stratford-on-Avon Festival, 1933. At the Alhambra, 1934, in *Henry V*, then in *Julius Cæsar* and *The Merchant Of Venice.* Among other West End shows in which he has appeared are *A Man's House*, 1066 *And All That, Mademoiselle, The Winter's Tale, Twelfth Night, The Tempest, The Silent Knight, To Love And To Cherish.* Since 1940 : Acting with B.B.C. Repertory Company.

BROWNE, E. MARTIN. Producer and actor. Born Zeals, Wilts, 1900. Married to Henzie Raeburn. Made his first appearance on the stage in *David* (Regent, 1927) ; thenceforth acted in America until 1930. Appeared in London in *Murder In The Cathedral* (Mercury, 1935 and Duchess, 1936). Made his first appearance in New York in the same play (Ritz, 1938). Then appeared in London in *Trumpeter Play, Blind Man's Buff, The Family Reunion* (Westminster, 1939), etc. Among the plays he has produced in London are *Murder In The Cathedral, Mutiny, Panic, In Theatre Street* and *The Family Reunion.* Since the outbreak of war he has been acting and producing with his own company, " The Pilgrim Players " (latterly in association with CEMA). In 1945 he became director of the Mercury Theatre, where he produced a number of plays by poets, including *The Old Man Of The Mountain, This Way To The Tomb, Tangent, The Shadow Factory* and others.

BROWNE, MAURICE. Actor, producer and playwright. Born Reading, 1881. He is known as the founder of the Little Theatre movement in America, as he produced many plays at Chicago Little Theatre from 1912 onwards. He has also produced in London and New York. He made his first appearance on the London stage in *Creditors* (Arts, 1927), followed by *The Unknown Warrior, Othello, The Bear Dances, Muted Strings* and many others. In addition to acting, he has also produced (and presented) a number of plays in London, including *La Prisonnière, The Unknown Warrior, Journey's End, Hamlet, The Venetian, White Secret,* etc. In 1942 he appeared in and produced *School For Slavery* (Westminster). He is the author of many plays, including *The King Of The Jews, The Wife Of William Flavery* and also *Wings Over Europe* (in collaboration with Robert Nichols).

BRYAN, HAL. Actor. Born Tansley, Derbyshire, 1898. Made his first stage appearance in concert party at Skegness, followed by seasons at Blackpool, etc., with the *Fol-de-Rols*. Made his first appearance in the West End in *Miss Hook Of Holland* (Daly's), then in *Savoy Follies, White Horse Inn, Strike Up The Music* and many others. Recently *Flying Colours* (Lyric, 1943), *The Quaker Girl* (Stoll, 1944), *Aladdin* (Cambridge, 1945-46).

BRYAN, PEGGY. Actress. Born Birmingham, 1916. Studied for stage at London Academy of Music and Drama. Made first appearance on stage in 1937 in *A Midsummer Night's Dream* (Winter Garden); subsequently in *April Clouds, The Tempest, Glorious Morning, The Springtime Of Others,* etc. Recently in *Jupiter Laughs* (New, 1941), *The Ideal Husband,* 1943-44, and *Yellow Sands,* 1945 (both at the Westminster).

BRYNING, JOHN. Actor. Born London, 1913. Studied for the stage at Royal Academy of Dramatic Art, making his first appearance in *Theme Song* (Shilling Theatre, 1934). Among the plays in which he has appeared in London are *Oscar Wilde, Gate Revue Of* 1936, *The Good Young Man* and *French Without Tears.* With B.B.C. Repertory Company, 1941-42. Recently appeared in *This Was A Woman* (Comedy, 1944), *A Midsummer Night's Dream* (Open Air, 1945), *Tomorrow Will be Different* (Lindsey, 1945). On tour in *Desert Highway,* 1946.

BUCHANAN, JACK. Actor, producer and manager. Born Helensburgh, Scotland, 1891. Made first London appearance at Apollo in 1912 in *The Grass Widows,* then in *A Mixed Grill, Tonight's The Night, Bubbly, Wild Geese, The Trump Card, Battling Butler* and many others. To New York, 1924, in *Charlot's Revue Of* 1924, after which he produced and appeared in many shows in both London and New York. These include *Toni, Charlot's Revue* 1926, *Sunny, That's A Good Girl, Wake Up And Dream, Stand Up And Sing, Mr. Whittington, The Flying Trapeze* and *This'll Make You Whistle.* Recently played in pantomime and *It's Time To Dance* (Winter Garden, 1943), and *The Last Of Mrs. Cheyney* (Savoy, 1944-45). In 1942 he produced *Waltz Without End* (Cambridge). In 1945 he appeared in *Fine Feathers* (Prince of Wales).

BULL, PETER. Actor. Born London, 1912. Educated at Winchester. Formerly a journalist. He made his first appearance on the stage in 1933 in *Escape Me Never* (in London and New York), then appeared in *The Boy David,* after which he founded the Perranporth Summer Theatre in 1936. He had subsequent seasons here in 1937 and 1938, transferring Robert Morley's play, *Goodness, How Sad!* to the Vaudeville in 1938. Since the outbreak of war has been serving with the Royal Navy.

BURCH, JOHN. Actor and playwright. Born Blackpool, September 6th, 1900. He was formerly a concert singer and appeared in many musical shows from 1925-36. He made his first West End appearance in *A Little Bit Of Fluff* (Ambassadors, 1942-43), followed by *The Fur Coat* (Comedy, 1943-44). Recently: in *Off The Camden Road* (Torch, 1946). He has written a number of plays, including *The Palmist* (Arts, 1937) and *Truth Is Stranger* (which he produced and appeared in at the Torch, 1946). In *Century For George* (Scala, 1946), etc.

BURDEN, ANNA. Actress. Born in Ceylon. Educated at St. Philomena's Convent, Carshalton. Studied for the stage at R.A.D.A., making her first appearance in *Sixteen* (Criterion). Retired from the stage on the outbreak of war, returning in 1941. She later joined the Glasgow Citizen's Theatre, after which she appeared in *Brighton Rock* (Garrick, 1943), then acted for a season at the Open Air Theatre, Regent's Park, 1943, and at Stratford-on-Avon Memorial Theatre, 1944. Then acted in *The Simpleton Of The Unexpected Isles* (Arts, 1945). Subsequently joined Open Air Theatre and appeared in *As You Like It* and *A Midsummer Night's Dream*, 1945. Appeared in *Myself A Stranger* (Embassy, 1945).

BURDEN, HUGH. Actor and playwright. Born Ceylon, 1913. Educated Beaumont College. Made his first appearance on the stage in *Saint Joan* (Croydon Repertory Theatre, 1933), then on tour and in repertory until 1936, when he made his first appearance in the West End in *The Frog* (Princes). Has also acted in London in *A Party For Christmas* (Haymarket, 1938), before serving in H.M. Forces, 1939-41. Recently in *The Duke In Darkness* (St. James's, 1942), *Quiet Week-End* (Wyndham's, 1942), *The Young And Lovely* (Arts, 1943), *The Last Of Summer* (Phœnix, 1944), *The Banbury Nose* (Wyndham's, 1944), *The Critic* (Arts), etc. In 1945 he appeared in *While The Sun Shines* (Globe), *The Years Between* (Wyndham's), *Myself A Stranger* (Embassy). Among his plays are *The House In Dormer Forest*, *The Young And Lovely* and *Myself A Stranger* (in collaboration with Caro Burden). In 1945 he appeared in *The Gambler* (Embassy).

BURKE, PATRICIA. Actress. Born Milan, Italy, 1917. Daughter of Marie and Tom Burke. First appeared on stage at Gate in 1933 in *I Hate Men*; subsequently at Open Air Theatre. Has also played in London in *Nymph Errant*, *Dark Horizon*, *A Man's House*, *Lady Precious Stream*, *Spring Tide*, *Climbing*, *Take It Easy*, *Hide And Seek*, *Happy Returns*, etc. In 1940 appeared in *Up And Doing* (Saville). Recently in pantomime and *Big Top* (His Majesty's, 1942), *The Lisbon Story* (Hippodrome, 1943-44). Appeared in *Stage Door* (Saville, 1946).

BURNS, HELEN. Born London, 1920. Studied for the stage at Royal Academy of Dramatic Art, making her first appearance in London in *A Doll's House* (Everyman, 1942). Also in *They Walk Alone* (Everyman, 1942), *Light And Shade* (Ambassadors, 1942), *Hedda Gabler* (Mercury and Westminster, 1943), *Cradle Song* (Apollo, 1944), etc. Recently: On tour for CEMA in *Twelfth Night*, *Candida*, *You Never Can Tell*. In 1945 she appeared in *Little Eyolf* (Embassy) and also in *Spring 1600* (Lyric, Hammersmith, 1945-46).

BURRELL, JOHN. Producer. Born Naini Tal, India, 1910. Educated Shrewsbury and at the Royal College of Art. 1934-39 director of productions, Barn Theatre, Shere; 1937-39, producer, assistant director, and director of decor for the London Theatre Studio. 1941-44 drama producer with the B.B.C. In 1943 he produced *Heartbreak House* (Cambridge). In 1944 he joined the Old Vic Theatre Company, and produced *Richard III*, *Arms And The Man* and *Uncle Vanya* (New, 1944-45). In 1945 he produced (for the Old Vic) *Henry IV* (*Parts I and II*) (New, 1945-46). In 1945 was appointed chairman of the Old Vic Theatre Company.

BURRILL, ENA. Actress. Born Uruguay, 1908. Made first appearance in London at Everyman in 1928 in *The Silver Box*; subsequently in *Living Together*, *Evergreen*. Joined Liverpool Repertory Company in 1932 and remained until 1935. Returned to London in *Worse Things Happen At Sea*, then in *Noah*, *Coincidence*, *Private Company*, *The Road To Rome*, *People In Love*, *Crest Of The Wave*, *We At The Crossroads* and others. Recently in *Uncle Harry* (Garrick, 1944-45), *The Skin Of Our Teeth* (Phœnix, 1945).

BYNG, DOUGLAS. Actor. Born Nottinghamshire, 1893. Made his first appearance at Hastings in 1914. Toured in *The Girl In The Taxi* in 1915, then appeared in London at the Gaiety in *Theodore And Co.* Other West End shows he has played in include *Yes, Uncle, Crystals, On With The Dance, Cochran's Revue* 1926, *This Year Of Grace, Wake Up And Dream, Cochran's* 1930 *Revue, Stop—Go,* and many others. In 1941 in *Strike Up The Music* (Coliseum) and also *Fine And Dandy* (Saville, 1942). Recently in pantomime; *Flying Colours* (Lyric, 1943), etc.

BYRNE, EDWARD. Actor. Born County Armagh, Ireland, 1914. Made his first appearance on the stage at the Gate, Dublin, in 1935, and thereafter in many plays in various parts of Ireland. Made his first appearance in London in *The Old Foolishness* (Arts, 1943). Subsequently in *Shadow and Substance* (Duke of York's), *Ghosts* (Duke of York's), *The Recruiting Officer* (Arts), *Don Abel Writes A Tragedy* (Arts). Appeared in the Bernard Shaw Season at the Lyric, Hammersmith, 1945, and also in *Father Malachy's Miracle* (Embassy). Then on tour in *Shadow And Substance* and *The Great Adventure,* 1945.

BYRON, JOHN. Actor. Born Kowloon, China, 1912. Educated at Epsom College. Studied for the stage at Royal Academy of Dramatic Art. Made his first appearance with Adeline Genée's Company, State Theatre, Copenhagen, 1932. Has appeared in London in *Ballyhoo* (Comedy, 1932), subsequently with Sadlers Wells Ballet Company, 1933-36. With the Ballet Rambert 1937, then in *Charlot's Revue* (Vaudeville). Also in *Hide And Seek* (Hippodrome, 1937), *Under Your Hat* (Palace, 1939). Since the war has appeared in repertory at Liverpool, and then at Oxford Playhouse until 1941. With the R.A.F. 1941-43. On being invalided out played *Romeo* at Oxford, then appeared in *Landslide* (Westminster, 1943). Joined Stratford-on-Avon Festival Company in 1944, appearing in *Hamlet, A Midsummer Night's Dream, As You Like It, Volpone,* etc. Appeared in *The Rivals* (Salisbury Garrison Theatre, 1944) and in *The Gay Pavilion* (Piccadilly, 1945). Recently appeared in *Macbeth,* etc. (Oxford Playhouse, 1945).

CADELL, JEAN. Actress. Born Edinburgh, 1884. Made her first appearance on the stage at Scala in 1906 in *The Inspector General,* then with George Alexander's Glasgow Repertory Company. First played in London in 1911 in *The Chair Of Love* (Court), subsequently in dozens of plays in England and America. These include *The Little Minister, Daddy Long Legs, The Old Lady Shows Her Medals, Mary Rose, John Gabriel Borkman, At Mrs. Beams, Quality Street, Evergreen, Wild Violets, The Old Ladies, The Black Eye, The Boy David, Suspect* and *Pygmalion.* At Malvern Festival in 1938 appeared in *Music At Night* (and at the Westminster in 1940). Recently: *The Importance Of Being Earnest* (Phœnix), *Macbeth* (Piccadilly), *The Two Children* (Arts, 1944), *Tomorrow The World* (Aldwych, 1945), and on tour 1945-46.

CALTHROP, G. E. Artist and designer. Born Ashton, Devon. Her first stage designs were for *The Vortex* (Everyman, 1924); subsequently she designed for *On With The Dance, Easy Virtue, Hay Fever, Home Chat, This Year Of Grace* and many others. Also designed *Private Lives, Autumn Crocus, Bitter Sweet, Cavalcade, Words And Music, Conversation Piece, Mademoiselle, You Can't Take It With You, Operette,* etc. She also designed several productions on Broadway, including *Design For Living, Point Valaine* and *Excursion.* Has also designed settings for *Blithe Spirit* (Piccadilly and Duchess), *There Shall Be No Night* (Aldwych), *Present Laughter* and *This Happy Breed* (Haymarket), *Emma* (St. James's. Also designed costumes for *The Gay Pavilion* (Piccadilly). Designed sets for *Alice In Wonderland* (Palace, 1944), and *Sigh No More* (Piccadilly, 1945), etc.

CAMPBELL, JUDY. Actress. Born Grantham. Made her first appearance in repertory at her father's theatre, Peterborough, 1935. Then appeared in repertory at Coventry, Brighton, and at the Festival Theatre, Cambridge. In 1939 played with Liverpool Repertory Company. Made her first appearance in London in *New Faces* (Comedy, 1940). She has also appeared in *Ducks And Drakes* (Apollo, 1942), *Lady Behave* (His Majesty's, 1941), *Watch On The Rhine* (Aldwych, 1942-43), *This Happy Breed* and *Present Laughter* (Haymarket, 1943), *Mine Hostess* (Arts, 1944), and *Another Love Story* (Phœnix, 1944-45).

CAPON, ERIC. Producer. Born London, 1911. Educated at Radley and Cambridge. Founded and directed Barn Theatre Studio, Sonning, 1934-37. First produced in London at Unity Theatre, being responsible for the productions of *Distant Point*, 1940, *Buster, Spanish Village*, 1943, etc. Producer at Glasgow Citizen's Theatre, 1943-45. Has also produced *As You Like It* and *Merchant Of Venice* (Open Air Theatre, 1945), and *Romeo And Juliet* (C.E.M.A. and Old Vic tour). Appointed producer for the Old Vic at Liverpool Playhouse, 1945-46, producing *Purple Dust, The Man Behind The Statue*, etc.

CARDEN, GEORGE. Actor, dancer and choreographer. Born Moree, Australia, 1918. Educated in Sydney. Made his first appearance on the stage in *White Horse Inn*, Sydney, and thereafter in many productions there, before coming to England in 1939. Made his first appearance on the London stage in *Revuedeville* (Windmill, 1940). Then appeared in *Lady Behave* (His Majesty's, 1941), *Sky High* (Phœnix, 1942), *It's Foolish But It's Fun* (Coliseum, 1943), *Sweet And Low* (Ambassadors, 1943-44). Recently in *Sweeter And Lower* (Ambassadors, 1944-46). Has produced dances for the following shows : *Sweeter And Lower, Anglo-Russian Merry-Go-Round, Keep Going, Gaieties*, and a number of tours, such as *By Jupiter* and *Sweeter And Lower*. In 1945 collaborated on the dance productions of *Sigh No More* (Piccadilly).

CAREY, JOYCE. Actress and playwright. Born London, 1898. Daughter of Lilian Braithwaite. Studied for stage under Kate Rorke. Made first appearance on the stage at Queen's in 1916 in *Henry V* ; subsequently in London in *Mr. Wu, The Aristocrat, Nothing But The Truth, The Merry Wives Of Windsor, A Midsummer Night's Dream, The Tempest, Little Women*. Other West End plays in which she has appeared include *The Young Person In Pink, The Romantic Young Lady, The Charm School, Dear Brutus*. Went to New York to act in *Easy Virtue* in 1925. From 1927 to 1933 played continuously on the American stage. Returned to London in *As You Like It* ; subsequently in *The Rivals* and *Sweet Aloes*. From 1935 until 1939 she acted in London and New York in *Tonight At* 8.30, *Spring Meeting, The Importance Of Being Earnest* and many others. Recently in *This Happy Breed* (Haymarket, 1943), *Blithe Spirit* (Duchess, 1944-46), etc. Among her plays are *Sweet Aloes* and *A Thing Apart*.

CARL, JOSEPH. Designer. Born Vienna, 1906. Studied art at the Arts and Crafts School in Vienna. Also appeared on the stage in Vienna since 1929. He came to England in 1938 and has since designed settings for *The Dancing Years, Black Velvet, Black Vanities, The Little Dog Laughed, Arc De Triomphe, Ghosts, A Night In Venice, Gay Rosalinda, Jacobowsky And The Colonel, Perchance To Dream, Big Boy* and many others.

CARNEY, GEORGE. Actor. Born Bristol, 1887. Made his first appearance on the stage in 1906 in *Aladdin* (Nottingham Theatre Royal) ; subsequently on music-hall stage. On London stage in 1907 at Holborn Empire and remained in variety until 1926, then toured in South Africa and Australia. Appeared in New York in 1932 in *The Good Companions*, then at Queen's in 1936 played in *Red Night*. Other plays in which he has acted are *When We Are Married, Ma's Bit O' Brass, Heaven And Charing Cross*. In 1940 in *Come Out To Play* (Phœnix). Recently: *How Are They At Home?* (Apollo, 1944).

CAROL, JOHN. Actor. Born London. Among the plays in which he has appeared in London are *Oscar Wilde, Boys In Brown* (Gate, 1940), *Salt Of The*

Earth (Vaudeville, 1942), *Ghosts* (Duke of York's, 1943), *The Shop At Sly Corner*
(St. Martin's, 1945), etc.

CARPENTER, FREDDIE. Dancer and producer. Born Melbourne, Australia,
November 15th, 1909. Educated Sydney Commercial School. Made his first
appearance on the stage in 1924 as principal dancer in musical productions in
Sydney and Melbourne. Then he appeared in New York in *Almanack* (Erlanger,
1928), after which he made his first appearance in London as a dancer at the
Palladium, 1929. From 1930 he appeared in many West End shows, including
Follow A Star, Bow Bells, Yours Sincerely, Tulip Time, Let's Go Gay and many
others. Again back in New York in *I'd Rather Be Right* (Music Box, 1937).
Since 1934 he has produced dances for West End shows, including *Tulip Time,
And On We Go, Maritza, The Dancing Years, Funny Side Up, Up And Doing*
and *Lady Behave.* From 1941-44 he served with the R.A.F. Recently he has
produced dances for *The Love Racket* (Victoria Palace, 1943), *The Lilac Domino*
(His Majesty's, 1944), *Irene* (His Majesty's, 1945), *Big Boy* (Saville, 1945-46).
He also co-produced Leslie Henson's *Gaieties* (Winter Garden, 1945), etc.

CARR, JANE. Actress. Born Whitley Bay, 1909. First appeared on stage in
1928 in *Anthony And Anna* (Newcastle Playhouse) ; subsequently in London at
the Q Theatre in *The Penalty*, 1930. On tour with Jevan Brandon-Thomas
Company, then in London in *The Jack Pot, Savoy Follies, Let's Go Gay, The
Squeaker, Money Talks*, etc. Recently : *Waltz Without End* (Cambridge, 1942-43),
How Are They At Home? (Apollo, 1944).

CARROLL, PAUL VINCENT. Playwright. Born Dundalk, Ireland, 1900.
Among his plays are *Things That Are Cæsar's, The White Steed, Shadow And
Substance, The Strings, My Lord, Are False, The Old Foolishness, The Wise Have
Not Spoken.* With James Bridie is director of Glasgow Citizen Theatre.

CARTEN, KENNETH. Actor. Born London, 1915. Educated Chillon.
Switzerland. He made his first appearance on the stage in *Charlot's Masquerade*
(Cambridge, 1930). Then in *Wonder Bar, Words And Music, Gay Love, Please,
Streamline*, etc. In 1935 appeared in *Tonight At* 8.30, making his first appearance
in New York in the same plays (National, 1936-37). Then in London in *French
Without Tears, Floodlight, Operette.* Returned to New York in 1939 in *Set To
Music* (Music Box). Recently in London in *Ladies Into Action* (Lyric), *Black
Vanities* (Victoria Palace, 1942), *Strike A New Note* (Prince of Wales, 1943),
Alice In Wonderland (Palace, 1944-45).

CASS, HENRY. Actor and producer. Born London, 1902. First acted in London
at the Embassy in 1931 in *The Nelson Touch*, then in *The Macropulos Secret,
Sensation, Precious Bane, Cloudy With Showers.* Producer, Croydon Repertory
Company, 1932-34. Then joined Old Vic and produced *St. Joan, Major Barbara,
Peer Gynt, Julius Cæsar, The Three Sisters, Macbeth, The School For Scandal,
Richard III, St. Helena, The Taming Of The Shrew, King Lear*, and others. Among
other plays he has produced in London are *Muted Strings, Night Alone, Women Of
Property, To Love And To Cherish*, etc. In 1939, *Alien Corn* (Wyndham's), *Julius
Cæsar* (Embassy and His Majesty's). In 1940, *Desire Under The Elms, Abraham
Lincoln* and *Cornelius* (Westminster). Produced *Murder Without Crime* (Comedy,
1943), *Acacia Avenue* (Vaudeville, 1944), *The Young And Lovely* (Arts, 1944),
The Philanderer (Arts, 1944). In 1945 he produced *It Happened In New York.*

CASSON, ANN. Actress. Born London, 1915. Daughter of Sir Lewis Casson
and Dame Sybil Thorndike. Made her first appearance on the stage in 1921 in
A Christmas Carol (Lyric) ; subsequently in London in *The Trojan Women,
Quality Street, Medea.* Toured South Africa, 1928-29, with her parents. On
returning to London played in *Mariners, Jane Clegg, The Roof, Mrs. Siddons,
The Seven Deadly Virtues, Mrs. Warren's Profession, Man And Superman,
Pygmalion, Hippolytus, George And Margaret, The Trojan Women*, etc. During

★ **_Roger Livesey_** and Ursula Jeans in Peter Ustinov's "The Banbury Nose", produced by Norman Marshall, 1944.

★ *Beatrix Lehmann* and Michael Redgrave, as Lettie and Harry, in Thomas Job's "Uncle Harry", produced by Redgrave and William Armstrong, 1944.

★ *John Clements* and Googie Withers in J. B. Priestley's "They Came To A City", produced by Irene Hentschel, 1943.

PHOTO : FELIX H. MA

★ *Trevor Howard* and Helen Cherry in Farquhar's
"The Recruiting Officer", produced by Alec Clunes, 1944.

★ *Anna Neagle*, who made her return to the London
stage in Gordon Glennon's dramatisation of Jane Austen's
"Emma", produced by Jack Minster, 1945.

★ *Clive Brook*, who returned to the English stage, after many years in Hollywood, in "The Year's Between", produced by Irene Hentschel, 1945.

⭐ *Graham Payn* and Pat Taylor in the musical comedy "Irene", produced by William Mollison, 1944.

PHOTO : JOHN VICKERS

★ *Lilian Braithwaite* and Mary Jerrold, as the two delicious old poisoners, in Joseph Kesselring's "Arsenic And Old Lace", produced by Marcel Varnel in 1942.

the war toured with her parents in the Old Vic Company. In 1941 in *King John* (New), etc. Recently appeared in *St. Joan* (Lyric, Hammersmith, 1945 and in 1946).

CASSON, SIR LEWIS. Actor and producer. Born Birkenhead, 1875. Married to Dame Sybil Thorndike. Created a knight in 1945. Made his first stage appearance in 1903 in *A Winter's Tale* (Royalty), then in *Julius Cæsar*, etc. At the Court with Harley Granville-Barker, 1904-07. With Miss Horniman's Company at Gaiety, Manchester, 1908-09 ; then with Charles Frohman Repertory Company in *Justice, Chains, Trelawny Of The Wells* (Duke of York's, 1909). First appeared in New York in 1910 in *Smith*. Appointed producer at Gaiety, 1911-13 ; then producer at Glasgow Royalty, 1914-15. After the war he appeared in London in *The Provoked Wife*, followed by *The Chinese Puzzle, The Trojan Women, Medea, Candida*. Produced season of Grand Guignol at the Little, 1920-22 ; subsequently producing and/or acting in *The Cenci, Cymbeline, Jane Clegg, St. Joan, Henry VIII, Granite, Macbeth*. From 1927-28 with the Old Vic, then toured South Africa with his wife in *Medea, The Silver Cord, Jane Clegg* and *St. Joan*. Re-appeared in London in *Major Barbara* in 1929 ; subsequently in *Late Night Final, The Painted Veil*, after which he toured Egypt and Australia. Other West End plays which he has produced or acted in include *Diplomacy, Ballerina, Nurse Cavell, Victoria Regina* (New York, 1935), *Six Men Of Dorset, Judgment Day, I Have Been Here Before*. For many years has been connected as producer for Old Vic and organised extensive wartime tours with Dame Sybil Thorndike. In 1940 in *King Lear* (Old Vic). Recently appeared in *King John* (New), Old Vic tours, 1940-41, *The Moon Is Down* (Whitehall, 1943), *St. Joan* (King's, Hammersmith, 1945). Has also produced, among others : *King Lear* (Old Vic), *The Man With A Load Of Mischief* (Mercury), *St. Joan* (King's, Hammersmith), *Jane Clegg* (Lyric, Hammersmith). From 1942 to 1945, Director of Drama, Council for Encouragement of Music and the Arts (CEMA, now the Arts Council). Appeared in *St. Joan, Romeo and Juliet*, etc. (King's, 1946).

CASTOR, CHRIS. Actress. Born British Guiana. Studied for the stage at the Guildhall School of Music and under Kate Rorke. Made her first appearance on the stage playing juvenile leads in Mrs. Patrick Campbell's Company, then in repertory at Sheffield, and at the Court in London. Also appeared in *Once In A Lifetime, Paganini, The Barretts Of Wimpole Street, The Brass Paperweight*, etc. During the war she left the stage, returning in *Macbeth*, CEMA tour, afterwards appearing in *Fanny's First Play, The Witch, Don Abel Wrote A Tragedy* (Arts, 1943-44). In 1945 she joined the Arts Festival of Drama, appearing in *The School For Scandal, The Thunderbolt, Getting Married, The Constant Couple*, etc. (Arts), and on tour, 1945-46.

CATTO, MAX. Playwright. Born Manchester, 1907. Among his plays are *French Salad, Green Waters, They Walk Alone, Punch Without Judy* and *Gather No Moss*.

CELLIER, FRANK. Actor and producer. Born Surbiton, 1884. Made his first stage appearance in Reigate in *Sweet Lavender*, 1903 ; subsequently on tour with Ian Maclaren and Edward Terry, and then in West Indies with repertory of Shakespearean and classical plays. First appeared in London in *Cheer Boys Cheer* (Princes, 1914), then in *The Merchant Of Venice*, after which he toured in America and South Africa, reappearing in London in 1920 in *Pygmalion*. Other West End plays in which he has acted include *Madame Sand, Othello, The Winter's Tale, Twelfth Night, The Mask And The Face, The Man With A Load Of Mischief, Mary Rose, Mozart* (New York, 1926), *Aren't We All, The School For Scandal*. In 1934 appeared in *The Rivals*, then in *Biography, The Mask Of Virtue, Punch Without Judy, Under Your Hat*, etc. Has also produced a number of plays. Recently appeared in *Quiet Week-End* (Wyndham's, 1941-44). Produced *This Time It's Love*, 1943, etc.

British Theatre

CHAPMAN, EDWARD. Actor. Born Harrogate, 1901. First appeared at Nottingham Repertory Theatre in 1924 in *Trilby*; then in London at Court in *The Farmer's Wife*, 1925. Spent nearly three years with Birmingham Repertory Company, until 1927 when he acted in London in a number of plays, including *The Taming Of The Shrew, The Constant Nymph, The Good Companions, Jonah And The Whale, Napoleon, Candida, People At Sea*. With Old Vic in 1938-39, appearing in *A Midsummer Night's Dream, She Stoops To Conquer, An Enemy Of The People* and *The Taming Of The Shrew*, etc. In 1940 he appeared in *As You Are* (Aldwych). Demobilised 1946 and appearing in *National Velvet*.

CHERRY, HELEN. Actress. Married to Trevor Howard. She joined Robert Atkins' Company in 1942, appearing in *A Midsummer Night's Dream* (Westminster). In 1943 she appeared in *As You Like It* (Open Air), *The Recruiting Officer* (Arts), *On Life's Sunny Side* (Arts, 1944), etc. Recently: Joined the Festival Company at Stratford-on-Avon in 1944, appearing in *As You Like It, A Midsummer Night's Dream*, etc. In 1945 she appeared in *The Two Mrs. Carrolls* (Embassy) and *Fit For Heroes* (Embassy, etc.). In *The Sacred Flame* (Westminster, 1946).

CHURCH, ESME. Actress and producer. Born 1893. Studied at the Royal Academy of Dramatic Art. Made her first appearance on the stage in 1913 in *Playgoers* (St. James's); subsequently on tour in France and Germany with Lena Ashwell with whose company she stayed from 1920-28, playing scores of leading parts. Then she joined the Old Vic, appearing in *As You Like It, Love's Labour's Lost, Hamlet, Macbeth*, etc. 1931, producer at Croydon. Among the other plays in which she has acted in London are *Dangerous Corner, The Lake, Nurse Cavell, The Hangman* and *Rosmersholm*. Joined Old Vic in 1936 as head of the School of Acting; has since often produced for Old Vic. In 1941 acted in *King John* (New). Now producer, Bradford Civic Playhouse. Recently produced *The Firstcomers* (Civic), *Alice In Wonderland* (Scala, 1943, and Palace, 1944), etc.

CHURCHILL, DIANA. Actress. Born London, 1913. Married to Barry K. Barnes. Studied for the stage with Kate Rorke. Made her first appearance at Royalty in 1931 in *Champion North*; then in *The Flight Of The Arrow, The Streets Of London, The Second Man*. 1933-34, with Oxford Repertory Company. Among the other plays in which she has acted in London are *The Rivals, The Country Wife, Love In A Mist, The Dominant Sex, The Composite Man, Wise Tomorrow, Yes And No, Tony Draws A Horse*. Since the war she has been touring extensively with her husband. Recently: In 1940 appeared in *As You Are* (Aldwych), *The Body Was Well Nourished* (Lyric, 1940), *On Approval* (Aldwych, 1941), *The Admirable Crichton* (His Majesty's, 1943), *Tomorrow's Eden* (Embassy, 1945).

CLARE, MARY. Actress. Born London, 1894. Made first appearance on stage in 1910; subsequently in London in 1912 in *A Posy And A Ring* (Globe). Other plays include *Oliver Twist, David Copperfield, Love For Love, The Provoked Wife, Will Shakespeare, The Skin Game, White Cargo, Kismet, The Constant Nymph*. In 1929 toured South Africa, returning to London in *Moloch*, then in such plays as *Sea Fever, The Midshipmaid, Cavalcade, No Way Back, After October, Story Of An African Farm, Heaven And Charing Cross, Macbeth*, etc. Recently: *Ladies In Retirement* (St. Martin's, 1940-41), *Other People's Houses* (Ambassadors, 1942), *No Orchids For Miss Blandish* (Prince of Wales, 1942-43), *Appointment With Death* (Piccadilly, 1945).

CLARENCE, O. B. Actor. Born London, 1870. Made his first appearance on the stage in music hall, 1880, then in *The People's Idol* (New Olympic, 1890). Subsequently with Sir Frank Benson's Company, also with Ben Greet, touring in the provinces and in Africa until 1902. Has been seen in London in *The School Girl, The Arm Of The Law, The Merchant Of Venice, The Voysey Inheritance, The Winter's Tale, Dombey And Son, The Great Gay Road*, and many others. Also in the West End in *Kipps, The Inferior Sex, Strife, The Will, A Kiss For*

228

Cinderella, Nothing But The Truth, Caste, The Enchanted Cottage, You Never Can Tell, and many others. Since then in *St. Joan, The Cherry Orchard, The First Year, Henry VIII,* etc., in London, and in many plays in New York. Since 1930 he has appeared in London in *The Gay Princess, The Old Bachelor, Caravan, Heartbreak House, Youth At The Helm, Farewell Performance, Climbing, Hamlet,* and many others. In 1940 appeared in *As You Are* (Aldwych), followed by *The Cherry Orchard* (New, 1941). In 1944 in *Guilty* (Lyric, Hammersmith). In 1945 appeared in *It Depends What You Mean* (Westminster), etc.

CLARK, JAQUELINE. Actress. Born London, 1916. Studied for the stage at Royal Academy of Dramatic Art, making her first appearance in *Josephine* (His Majesty's), then in *Robert's Wife* (Globe), and others. Made her first appearance in New York in *Delicate Story* (Henry Miller), followed by *Blithe Spirit* (Morosco, 1941-42). Returned to London in *A Month In The Country* (St. James's, 1943), then on tour with Emlyn Williams in *Blithe Spirit,* on the Continent, 1944. Recently in *Blithe Spirit* (Duchess, 1945), etc.

CLARKE, NIGEL. Actor. Born Epsom, 1895. First appeared on stage with Benson in 1920 in *The Merchant Of Venice* ; stayed with this company until 1924. Then appeared in London in *Where The Rainbow Ends* (Holborn Empire). Toured in *Mary Rose,* acted in *Hamlet* (Haymarket), then on tour with Benson until 1928. Appeared with the Birmingham Repertory Company in London at the Court in *Macbeth, Back To Methuselah, The Taming Of The Shrew,* etc. From 1929-31 directed Epsom Little Theatre. Among other West End plays he has acted in are *Versailles, Getting Married, Lady Patricia.* In 1939 with Donald Wolfit Company. Then in *The Merry Wives Of Windsor* (Strand, 1940). With the Robert Atkins Company at the Westminster, 1942. In 1944 appeared in the Bernard Shaw Repertory Season at the Lyric, Hammersmith, in *Dark Lady Of The Sonnets, Candida, Too True To Be Good, Pygmalion.* In 1945 he appeared in *The Simpleton Of The Unexpected Isles* (Arts).

CLEMENTS, JOHN. Actor and producer. Born London, 1910. Made first appearance on the stage in 1930 in *Out Of The Blue* (Lyric, Hammersmith) ; then in London in *She Stoops To Conquer, The Beaux' Stratagem, The Venetian, Salome.* Toured with Ben Greet's Company, 1931-32. Then acted in London in *Hamlet, The Master Builder, Napoleon, Nichevo,* before founding, in 1935, the Intimate Theatre, Palmers Green. Here he produced and acted in over a hundred productions until 1940. In 1940 appeared in *Alien Corn* (Wyndham's) ; *Skylark* (Duchess, 1941) ; *They Came To A City* (Globe), produced and appeared in *Private Lives* (Apollo), produced *Oh, Josephine,* on tour. Formed his own company with Kay Hammond in 1946, producing *Marriage A La Mode, The King-Maker,* etc.

CLUNES, ALEC. Actor and producer. Born London, 1912. Had considerable amateur experience and was for a time acting and producing at the Tavistock Little Theatre. Made his first professional appearance on the London stage in *The Immortal Garden* (Rudolf Steiner, 1933), after which he appeared with Croydon Repertory Theatre and on tour with Ben Greet. Appeared with the Old Vic Company, 1934-36, in *As You Like It, Hamlet, Peer Gynt, Julius Cæsar, The Three Sisters, Richard III, St. Helena, King Lear, A Winter's Tale, Love's Labour's Lost, The Country Wife* and others. Subsequently in the West End in *Hell-For-Leather, George And Margaret, The Road To Ruin, The Taming Of The Shrew, Yes, My Darling Daughter, Richard III* (for the Old Vic, 1937), *Queen Christine, I Killed The Count,* etc. In 1938 appeared in *Music At Night, The Last Trump* and *St. Joan* at the Malvern Festival, and in 1938 appeared in *The Taming Of The Shrew, Othello, Much Ado About Nothing, Coriolanus* and others at the Stratford-on-Avon Memorial Theatre. In 1940 he appeared in *The Country Wife* (Little), followed by *In Good King Charles' Golden Days* (New). In 1942 he founded the Arts Theatre Group of Actors, where he has since produced and acted continuously. In 1942 he produced *Awake And Sing, House Of Regrets,*

Androcles And The Lion, etc. In 1943 he produced *The Constant Couple, The Magistrate, The Watched Pot* and *Misalliance* (in the Arts Festival of English Comedy). Subsequently produced *The Recruiting Officer, The Two Children, Bird In Hand, Mine Hostess* and a number of others. In 1945, he produced *The Constant Couple* (for the Arts Festival of English Drama). He has also produced *The Magistrate* and *Bird In Hand* (both at St. Martin's, 1945). Among the plays in which he has appeared at the Arts are *Magic, The Swan Song, Androcles And The Lion, Don Juan In Hell, The Constant Couple* and *Mine Hostess*. In 1945 he appeared in *The Constant Couple, The School For Scandal* and *Hamlet* (for the Arts Festival of Drama).

COKE, PETER. Actor. Born Southsea, 1913. Studied for stage at Royal Academy of Dramatic Art. First appeared on stage in *The Man In Dress Clothes*, then with Margate Repertory Company. Also acted in *Do You Remember, Ladies And Gentlemen, The Great Romancer, Bonnet Over The Windmill, Death On The Table, The Intruder* and others in the West End. In H.M. Forces, 1940-46.

COLEMAN, BASIL. Actor. Born London, 1917. Studied for stage under Elsie Fogerty and at the Old Vic School of Acting. Made his first appearance on the stage in *As You Like It* (Old Vic, 1938); then in *Private History* (Gate, 1938), later touring the Mediterranean with the Old Vic, 1939. Since the war has appeared in *King Lear* (Old Vic), *Othello* (New, 1942), *Six Characters In Search Of An Author* (Liverpool Old Vic), etc. Recently appeared in *Alice In Wonderland* (Scala, 1944, and Palace, 1945). Also in *John Gabriel Borkman* (Chanticleer) and *Jacobowsky And The Colonel* (Piccadilly, 1945). Then joined London Theatre Group and appeared in *Rosmersholm* (Torch, 1945).

COLERIDGE, ETHEL. Actress. Born South Molton, 1883. First appeared on stage in 1905 in *Carmen* (Coronet); then in *My Lady's Dress, Milestones, The Rising Generation, Rookery Nook, Thark, Plunder, A Cup Of Kindness, Laburnum Grove, Black Limelight, When We Are Married*, etc. In 1940 appeared in *Women Aren't Angels* (Strand). Recently: *A Murder For A Valentine* (Lyric), *Warn That Man* (Garrick), *The Lady From Edinburgh* (Playhouse, 1945).

COLIN, IAN. Actor. Born May 16th, 1912, Livingstone, Rhodesia. Educated Rhodes University, South Africa. He made his first appearance on the stage in South Africa in *Journey's End*, 1930, afterwards coming to London to appear in *Ballerina, Admirals All, Paganini*, etc. From 1939-44 in H.M. Forces, returning to the stage in *Uncle Harry* (Garrick, 1944-45). Recently in *Desert Rats* (Adelphi, 1945).

COLLEANO, BONAR (Junior). Actor. Born New York, 1925. Educated in London and on the Continent. Toured for many years in America and Europe with his family, " The Colleanos," in variety and in the circus, etc. He made his first appearance on the legitimate stage in *Sweet And Low* (Ambassadors, 1943), followed by *Sweeter And Lower* (Ambassadors, 1944). In 1945 he appeared in *Strike It Again* (Prince of Wales's). Recently acted in *A Bell For Adano* (Phœnix, 1945). In 1946 he appeared in *While The Sun Shines* (Globe).

COMPTON, FAY. Actress. Born London, 1894. Made first appearance in 1911 in *The Follies* (Apollo) until 1913, then in *Who's That Lady?, To-night's The Night* (New York, 1914), *The Only Girl, The Bells, Peter Pan, Cæsar's Wife, Mary Rose* and others. Also played in *Quality Street, Secrets, Hamlet, Liliom, The Constant Wife, Autumn Crocus*. Has appeared in a number of pantomimes and the following plays, among others, *Indoor Fireworks, Murder In Mayfair, A Midsummer Night's Dream, Call It A Day, Julius Cæsar, A Winter's Tale*. In 1937-38 toured Australia, returning to London to act in *Drawing Room, Hamlet*, etc. Recently: *King Lear* (Old Vic, 1940), *Blithe Spirit* (Piccadilly and Duchess), *The Little Foxes* (Piccadilly), *The Last Of Summer* (Phœnix, 1944), *No Medals* (Vaudeville, 1945-46).

COMPTON-MACKENZIE, JEAN. Actress. Born New York City. Educated in U.S.A. and Canada. Married to Arthur Howard. She made her first appearance on the stage in her father's company at the age of four. Began her professional career when she was sixteen at the Copley Theatre in Boston. She came to England and studied under Fay Compton, after which she appeared in repertory at Edinburgh, Cheltenham, Eastbourne, Brighton and Guernsey. Recently she appeared in London in *No Orchids For Miss Blandish* (Prince of Wales, 1942), *The Admirable Crichton* (His Majesty's, 1943), *Tradesmen's Entrance*, on tour, 1944, etc. Recently with the Rock Theatre Company on tour, and at the Rudolf Steiner, 1945, in *Man And Superman*, etc. In 1946 she toured Egypt and India with the Middle East Festival Company.

COPLEY, PETER. Actor. Born London, May 20th, 1915. Educated Westminster. Married to Pamela Brown. Studied for the stage at the Old Vic School, 1932-33, after which he worked in repertory at Leeds and Oxford. Appeared for a season at the Dublin Gate, then toured South America. He has appeared in London in *Viceroy Sarah, Golden Arrow, Goodbye, Mr. Chips*, etc. In 1939 he was producer at Worthing Repertory Theatre. 1940-41 in the Royal Navy. Recently with the Old Vic Company, has appeared in *Henry IV (Parts I And II)* and *The Critic* (New, 1945-46).

COTES, PETER. Actor and producer. Born Maidenhead, 1915. Studied for the stage under Italia Conti, making his first appearance in *The Windmill Man* (Victoria Palace). Subsequently as a child actor in *The Great God Brown, Anne One Hundred, Caravan, The Ugly Duchess, The Breadwinner, Peter Pan*. Then acting in films for some time. On tour in *Rise Above It*, 1940-41, *Thunder Rock*, 1941-42, *Golden Boy*, 1942-43, etc. In 1943 appeared in *Peter Pan* (Winter Garden), then in *Tomorrow's Eden*, on tour 1944. Also appeared in London in *The Last Stone* (Phœnix, 1944). In 1945 acted in *Offlag* 3 (Q), etc. Has produced a number of plays on tour, including *Squaring The Circle, Ridgeway's Funfare*, etc., and also produced at Worthing and Tunbridge Wells Repertory Theatres. In 1945 produced *Angel Street* (Scala) and *Happy And Glorious*, for CEMA. In 1946 founding New Lindsey Group.

COURTNEIDGE, CICELY. Actress. Born Sydney, 1893. Married to Jack Hulbert. First appeared on stage in 1901 in *A Midsummer Night's Dream* (Princes, Manchester). First seen in London, 1907, in *Tom Jones* (Apollo), subsequently in *The Arcadians, The Pearl Girl, A Lucky Escape, Ring Up*, etc. First appeared in New York in *By The Way*, 1925, returning to London in the same play, followed by *Lido Lady, Clowns In Clover, Hide And Seek*, etc. In films for some years, returning in *Under Your Hat* (Palace, 1938-39). Recently in *Full Swing* (Palace, 1942), *Something In The Air* (Palace, 1943-44). In 1945 in *Under The Counter* (Phœnix).

COUPER, BARBARA. Actress. Born London, 1903. Married to Howard Rose. Studied under Kate Rorke and at Royal Academy of Dramatic Art. First appeared on the stage in 1925 in *The Boy Next Door* at Norwich, subsequently in London in 1928 in *The Power Of Darkness* (Arts). Has also acted in London in *La Prisonnière, Wild Justice, Napoleon, Dear Brutus, Crime And Punishment, Distinguished Gathering*, etc. In 1936 with Stratford-on-Avon Festival. Then appeared in London in *Paradise Lost, The Ascent Of F.6*, etc. For some time during the war was with the B.B.C. Repertory Company. Recently: *The Judgment Of Doctor Johnson* (Arts, 1943), *The Wind Of Heaven* (St. James's, 1945).

COWARD, NOEL. Actor, playwright, composer and producer. Born Teddington, 1899. Made his first appearance on the stage at Little in 1911 in *The Goldfish*; subsequently in the following, among others: *The Great Name, Where The Rainbow Ends, Peter Pan, Charley's Aunt, Saving Grace, The Knight Of The Burning Pestle, I'll Leave It To You, The Young Idea, London Calling, The Vortex* (also in New

231

York, 1925), *The Constant Nymph, This Year Of Grace* (New York, 1928), *Private Lives* (also in New York, 1931), *Design For Living* (New York, 1933), *Conversation Piece, To-night at 8.30* (also in New York, 1936). Recently acted in *Blithe Spirit* (Piccadilly, 1941), *This Happy Breed* and *Present Laughter* (Haymarket, 1943). Is the author of the following plays and shows : *I'll Leave It To You, The Young Idea, London Calling* (in collaboration), *The Vortex, Charlot's Revue Of 1924* (in collaboration), *The Rat Trap, Fallen Angels, Hay Fever, Easy Virtue, The Queen Was In The Parlour, This Year Of Grace, Bitter Sweet, Cochran's 1931 Revue, Cavalcade, Words And Music, Design For Living, Conversation Piece, Point Valaine, To-night At 8.30, Operette, Blithe Spirit,* (still running in London), *This Happy Breed, Present Laughter, Sigh No More,* etc. In 1945 *Blithe Spirit* was on at the Duchess, *Private Lives* at the Apollo, and *Sigh No More* at the Piccadilly. He deputised for Cyril Ritchard in *Sigh No More,* September, 1945.

COWLEY, ERIC. Actor. Born Southsea, 1886. Made his first appearance on the stage in *I Dined With My Mother* (Savoy, 1913). Then in *The Merchant Of Venice, Peg O' My Heart, Where The Rainbow Ends, A Kiss Or Two, One Night In Rome, Othello* and many others. Then on tour in America and South Africa, after which he appeared in London in *The Happy Husband, The Merry Wives Of Windsor, Dear Brutus, Let Us Be Gay,* etc. Made his first appearance in New York in *Petticoat Influence* (Empire, 1930), after which he toured America until 1933. Since then has appeared in London in *Up In The Air, Hay Fever, Touch Wood, Out Of The Dark, Bats In The Belfry, Can We Tell,* etc. In 1939 appeared in *Grouse In June,* then in *The Bare Idea* (Comedy), *Nap Hand* (Aldwych, 1940). Then in *On Approval* (Aldwych, 1941), *Rebecca* (Queen's, 1942), etc. In 1943-44 appeared in *Ten Little Niggers* (St. James's), then in *Thirteen To The Gallows,* on tour, 1945. Also in *Zoo In Silesia* (Embassy, 1945).

CREAN, PATRICK. Actor. Born June 27th, 1911. Married to Helen Christie. Educated St. Anthony's, Eastbourne and St. George's College, Weybridge. Made his first appearance on the London stage in *Casanova,* 1932, after which he appeared in repertory in various parts of England and Ireland. Appeared for a season at the Stratford-on-Avon Memorial Theatre, 1937 ; then in London in *Cyrano De Bergerac.* He toured Canada in 1939 in *Charles The King,* afterwards making his first appearance in New York in *Geneva,* 1940. Recently in the West End in *Quiet Week-End* (Wyndham's, 1943), afterwards joining the John Gielgud Repertory Company, appearing in *Hamlet, A Midsummer Night's Dream,* etc. (Haymarket, 1944-45).

CRISHAM, WALTER. Actor, dancer and producer. Born Worcester, Massachusetts, U.S.A., 1906. Made first appearance on stage in New York in 1924 in *The Music Box Revue* ; subsequently in *Sweet Adeline.* First appearance in London in 1932 in *Ballyhoo* (Comedy), then in *Nymph Errant, Why Not To-night ? Hi Diddle Diddle, Spread It Abroad, Careless Rapture, Crest Of The Wave, The Gate Revue, Swinging The Gate,* etc. Recently : *Rise Above It* (Comedy, 1941), *Diversion* (Wyndham's), *Sky High* (Phœnix, 1942), *Sweet And Low* (Ambassadors, 1943), *Gaieties* (Saville, 1945). He also produced *Diversion* in 1941 and *Sky High* in 1942. In 1946 he appeared in *The Time Of Your Life* (Lyric, Hammersmith).

CRUICKSHANK, ANDREW. Actor. Born Aberdeen, December 25th, 1907. First appeared on the stage in the provinces in 1926, making his first appearance in London in *Othello* (Savoy, 1930). Then on tour for four years, after which he made his first appearance in New York in *Richard Of Bordeaux* (Empire, 1934). Also in London in *Victoria Regina, Mary Tudor* and many plays at the Gate, including *Oscar Wilde, Lysistrata* and *Mr. Gladstone.* In 1938 joined the Old Vic Company, appearing in *Macbeth, Othello, A Midsummer Night's Dream, Man And Superman, Hamlet* and *The Rivals.* In 1939 he toured Egypt and the Continent with the Old Vic, also appearing in *Hamlet* at the Lyceum, and also at Elsinore.

Since the outbreak of war he has been in H.M. Forces, making his reappearance on the stage in *Spring 1600* (Lyric, Hammersmith, 1945-46).

CRUTCHLEY, ROSALIE. Actress. Born London, 1920. Educated London and Paris. Made her first appearance on the stage with the Liverpool Repertory Company in 1932, remaining until 1938. Appeared with H. M. Tennent Repertory Company at Glasgow and Edinburgh, 1940. With Oxford Repertory Company, 1940-42. Made her first appearance in London in *Love For Love* (Phœnix, 1943), subsequently appearing with John Gielgud Company in *The Circle* and *A Midsummer Night's Dream* (Haymarket, 1944-45).

CULVER, ROLAND. Actor. Born London, 1900. Studied at Royal Academy of Dramatic Art. First acted at Hull Repertory Theatre in *Peter And Paul*, 1924 ; subsequently first appeared in London at the Scala in 1925 in *Forbidden Fluids*. Among other plays in which he has appeared in London are *Gentlemen Prefer Blondes, Knight Errant, 77, Park Lane, Suspense, Dance With No Music, John O' Dreams, Black Coffee, Distinguished Gathering, French Without Tears*, etc. In 1940 in *On Approval* (Aldwych), *Believe It Or Not* (New). Recently : *An Ideal Husband* (Westminster, 1943-44), *Another Love Story* (Phœnix, 1944).

CUMMINS, PEGGY. Actress. Born Dublin, Ireland, 1925. Made her first appearance on the stage at the Gate, Dublin, 1932 ; subsequently playing at the Abbey and Gate. Appeared in London in *Junior Miss* (Saville, 1942), and *Alice In Wonderland* (Palace, 1945), *Temporary Ladies* (Q). In 1945 went to America.

CUMMINGS, CONSTANCE. Actress. Born Seattle, Washington, U.S.A., 1910. Married to Benn Levy. First appeared on stage in 1926 in San Diego in *Seventh Heaven* ; then appeared in New York in *Treasure Girl*, 1928. Subsequently in *The Little Show, This Man's Town*, etc. First appeared in London in 1934 in *Sour Grapes* (Apollo), then in *Accent On Youth* (New York, 1934), *Young Madame Conti* (London and New York, 1936-37), *Madame Bovary* (New York, 1937). Also acted on the London stage in *Goodbye, Mr. Chips, The Jealous God*, etc. In 1939 on tour with the Old Vic Company in *Romeo And Juliet, St. Joan*, etc. Then acted in London in *Skylark* (Duchess, 1941), *The Petrified Forest* (Globe, 1942-43). In 1946 she appeared in *Men Must Weep*.

CURNOCK, RICHARD. Actor. Born London, 1922. Studied for the stage with Italia Conti, making his first appearance in *Peter Pan* (Palladium, 1934). Toured with Sir John Martin Harvey in *Great Expectations* and *The Only Way*, appearing in *Great Expectations* (Westminster, 1935). Has also appeared in London in *Where The Rainbow Ends, The Boy David, Lady Precious Stream*, etc. In 1940 in repertory at Cork ; 1941, with Newcastle Repertory Company, and 1942 with Birmingham Repertory Company. Appeared in *It Happened In September* (St. James's, 1942), followed by *Sweet And Low*, 1943, and *Sweeter and Lower*, 1944-46 (both Ambassadors).

CUSHING, PETER. Actor. Born Kenley, Surrey, 1914. Educated in London, where he studied art and trained as an architect. In 1935 he made his first appearance on the stage at Worthing Repertory Theatre, where he stayed for three years. Then visited Hollywood, where he appeared in films, and also in a number of Theatre Guild Productions on Broadway. He returned to England in 1942 and appeared in *Private Lives* on tour for a year. Made his first appearance in London in *War And Peace* (Phœnix, 1943), after which he toured in *The Fifth Column*. Recently in *Happy Few* (Cambridge, 1944), *While The Sun Shines* (Globe, 1945), *The Rivals* (Criterion, 1945-46).

DALE, JAMES. Actor. Born London, 1887. Studied for stage at Guildhall School of Music and Drama. First appeared in Birmingham in *As You Like It*, 1908 ; later in London in *Marriages Of Mayfair* (Drury Lane). Subsequently with Fred Terry and Julia Neilson Company, acting in London and New York,

1909-11, then in London in *The Popinjay, The Little Café,* etc. Toured with
Cyril Maude in America, 1913-15; then in London in *Cyrano De Bergerac,
Henry V, The Storm, Grumpy* and many others. Among the many West End
plays in which he acted are *Heartbreak House, She Stoops To Conquer, Loyalties*
(New York, 1922), *Hassan* (New York, 1924), *The Last Of Mrs. Cheyney* (U.S.A.,
1927), *The House Of The Arrow, The Only Way, She Passed Through Lorraine,
Miracle At Verdun, The Green Bay Tree* (New York, 1933), *Arms And The Man.*
Has played at Stratford-on-Avon Festival 1920, 1936 and 1938 and also with the
Old Vic, 1936 and 1940. Acted with the Open Air Theatre, 1942. Recently
appeared in *The Cherry Orchard* (New, 1940), *Thunder Rock* (St. Martin's, 1941),
Tobias And The Angel (Open Air, 1942); *Damaged Goods* (Whitehall, 1943),
Last Of Mrs. Cheyney (Savoy, 1944-45), *The Barretts Of Wimpole Street* (Q), 1945,
etc. Toured the Continent in *Julius Cæsar,* 1945-46.

DALL, EVELYN. Actress. Born January 8th, New York City. Made her
first stage appearance in New York, afterwards appearing in various productions
in America. In 1937 appeared in *Parade* for the Theatre Guild. In London has
appeared in *Present Arms* (Prince of Wales, 1940), *Something For The Boys* (Coliseum
1944), *Follow The Girls* (His Majesty's, 1945-46), etc.

DALLAS, JULIAN. Actor. Born London, 1921. On being invalided out of the
R.A.F. he appeared in repertory at the Intimate, Palmers Green. Then made his
first appearance in the West End in *House Of Regrets* (Arts, 1942), followed by
The Fur Coat (Comedy, 1943), *Cradle Song* (Apollo, 1944), etc. In 1944 he
joined the Old Vic Company at Liverpool, remaining until 1945, appearing in
Point Valaine and others. Recently in *Offlag 3* (Q), etc.

DANE, CLEMENCE. Playwright and novelist. Born Blackheath. Formerly an
actress. Among her plays are *A Bill Of Divorcement, Will Shakespeare, The Way
Things Happen, Granite, Mariners, Wild Decembers, Moonlight Is Silver, The
Happy Hypocrite* (adaptation), *Herod And Marianne.* Recently: *Alice In
Wonderland* (adaptation), etc.

DARE, PHYLLIS. Actress. Born London, 1890. First appeared on stage in
1899 at the Coronet in *Babes In The Wood,* subsequently in London in *Bluebell
In Fairyland, The Belle Of Mayfair, The Arcadians, Peggy, The Girl From Utah,
Miss Hook Of Holland* and many others. Then in the West End in *Lido Lady,
Aren't We All?, Call It A Day,* etc. Recently: *Other People's Houses* (Ambassadors
and Phœnix, 1941-42), *June Mad* (on tour on the Continent, 1945).

DARE, ZENA. Actress. Born London, 1887. Made her first appearance on the
stage at the Coronet in *Babes In The Wood,* 1899, then toured with Sir Seymour
Hicks in *An English Daisy,* later appearing in London in *Sergeant Brew, The
Catch, Lady Madcap, The Beauty Of Bath,* etc. Reappeared on the stage in 1926
in *The Last Of Mrs. Cheyney,* then in *The Second Man,* after which she
toured South Africa with her own company in 1928-29. She has appeared in
London in *The First Mrs. Fraser, Peter Pan, Proscenium, Murder In Mayfair,
Careless Rapture, Spring Meeting* and others. Recently: *Dear Brutus* (Globe,
1941), *Alice In Wonderland* (Scala, 1944), *Watch On The Rhine* (Aldwych), *Another
Love Story* (Phœnix, 1945), etc. In *Perchance To Dream* (Hippodrome, 1946).

DAVIES, BETTY-ANN. Actress. Born London, 1910. Made her first
appearance at the Palladium when she was fourteen, subsequently appearing in
*One Dam Thing After Another, Mr. Cinders, Little Accident, Follow Through,
After Dark* and others. She left the stage for five years to work in films, returning
in *Nine Sharp* (Little, 1938). Since then she has appeared in *The Little Revue,*
1939-40, *New Faces* (Comedy and Apollo, 1940 and 1941), *The New Ambassadors
Revue* (Ambassadors, 1942). In 1942 she appeared in *Light And Shade*
(Ambassadors). Then in *Morning Star* (Globe). She toured in the latter with

Emlyn Williams, also playing in *Night Must Fall*. In 1944 she appeared in *Blithe Spirit* (Duchess). Then in *Dear Evelyn*, 1946.

DAVIES, JOAN. Dance producer. Born London, 1908. Made her first appearance in variety in 1916, continuing as a dancing act until 1932, when she began producing dances in London. Her productions include *No, No, Nanette, Careless Rapture, Balalaika* and many others. Recently *Happy And Glorious* (Palladium), *The Night And The Music* (Coliseum), *Fine Feathers* (Prince of Wales), etc.

DAY, FRANCES. Actress. Born U.S.A., 1912. On the stage in America; then on the London stage in 1932 in *Out Of The Bottle* (Hippodrome). Subsequently in the West End in *Cold Blood, How D'You Do?, Nymph Errant, Jill Darling, Floodlight, The Fleet's Lit Up, Black And Blue*. Recently: in *Black Vanities* (Victoria Palace, 1941-42), *Dubarry Was A Lady* (His Majesty's, Phœnix, 1942-43) *Peter Pan* (Stoll, 1945). To America in 1945. In 1946 appeared in *Evangeline* (Cambridge).

DEAN, BASIL. Producer, actor and manager. Born Croydon, 1888. Married to Victoria Hopper. First appeared on the stage in *The School For Scandal* (Cheltenham Opera House, 1905); subsequently in repertory at the Gaiety, Manchester. On London stage in 1909 in *The Vale Of Content* (Coronet), then in *Lucifer*. Director of Liverpool Repertory Theatre, 1911-13. During Great War was head of Entertainment Section of Navy and Army Canteen Board. Since then has produced a number of plays in London, many under his own management, including *The Skin Game, The First And The Last, Will Shakespeare, Loyalties, R.U.R., Hassan, Rain, The Vortex, Young Woodley, The Circle Of Chalk, The Constant Nymph, Autumn Crocus, Touch Wood, The Sun Never Sets, Call It A Day, Johnson Over Jordan* and many others. Since the outbreak of war has been Director of Entertainments National Service Association, Drury Lane.

DEAN, ROY. Actor. Born London, 1925. Trained to be an architect, then studied to be an opera singer. Joined the Donald Wolfit Company on tour and made his first appearance with this company in London in 1941 at the St. James', playing in *Twelfth Night, King Lear* and others. 1944: Season at Intimate, Palmers Green. In 1945 appeared in *The Lady From Edinburgh* (Playhouse).

DE CASALIS, JEANNE. Actress and playwright. Born South Africa, 1897. Studied at Comédie Francaise, and with Komisarjevsky. First appeared on the stage in France and then in New York. First acted in London in 1921 in *Deburau* (Ambassadors); subsequently acting in New York, Paris and London. In 1924 appeared in *The Man Of Destiny*, followed by *Fata Morgana, Arms And The Man, Charlot's 1928 Revue, Payment Deferred*. Among the other West End plays in which she has appeared are *Success Story, The Mask And The Face, The Mask Of Virtue, Serena Blandish, Behold The Bride*. Recently: *The Fur Coat* (Comedy 1943. Her plays include *Dearly Beloved Wife* and *St. Helena* (with R. C. Sherriff).

DE MARNEY, DERRICK. Actor. Born London, 1906. First appeared on stage in 1923 and in London 1926 in *All The King's Horses* (Globe). Subsequently in the West End in *Romance, Maya, The Hairy Ape, Young Woodley, Martine, The Matriarch* (New York, 1930), *The Faithful Heart, Miracle At Verdun*. Founded in 1932 the Independent Theatre Club (with Terence de Marney). Also acted in London in *The Tudor Wench, The Young Mr. Disraeli, The Scarlet Pimpernel*, etc. 1940-45: Producing and acting in films.

DE MARNEY, TERENCE. Actor, producer and playwright. Born London, 1909. First appeared on stage in London in *The Crown Jewels* (Coliseum, 1923), then in *A Fairy Tale, Brewster's Millions, Treasure Island, The Lady Of The Camelias*. Toured South Africa in 1930 in *Journey's End*. Returned to London in *The Iron Woman*; then in 1932 opened Independent Theatre Club (with his brother

Derrick). Subsequently appeared in London in *Romeo And Juliet, Miracle In America, Murder In Motley, Sonata, Wanted For Murder, Walk In The Sun*, etc. Recently appeared in *Lifeline* (Duchess, 1942), *Ten Little Niggers* (St. James's, 1943-44), *The Crime Of Margaret Foley* (Embassy, 1945). Is the author (with Percy Robinson) of *Whispering Gallery, Wanted For Murder, The Crime Of Margaret Foley*, etc. Produced *Appointment With Death* (Piccadilly, 1944), *Now The Day Is Over*, 1945. Appeared in the latter (Embassy, 1946); and *Dear Murderer*, 1946.

DEMEL, PAUL. Actor. Born May 14th, 1903, in Brno, Czechoslovakia. Made his first appearance on the stage in Vienna 1922. He appeared in Prague, Breslau, Vienna, etc., from 1922 until 1939, when he came to England. He made his first appearance on the London stage in *The Doctor's Dilemma* (Haymarket, 1943). Recently in *Madame Louise* (Garrick, 1945-46).

DENHAM, ISOLDE. Born London, 1920. Married to Peter Ustinov. Studied for the stage under Michel St. Denis at the London Theatre Studio, making her first appearance on the stage in *The House In Dormer Forest* (Barn Theatre, Shere). She understudied Celia Johnson in *Rebecca* (Queen's, 1940) and subsequently appeared in this play on tour with Owen Nares. In 1940 appeared in *Fishing For Shadows* (Threshold), followed by *The Springtime Of Others* (Arts, 1942), *Murder From Memory* (Ambassadors, 1942). In 1943-44 appeared in *A Month In The Country* (St. James's), after which she joined the Old Vic Company at Liverpool, appearing in *The Rivals* and many others. In 1944 she appeared in *The Banbury Nose* (Wyndham's) ; then in *The Lady From The Sea* (Arts, 1946).

DENHAM, REGINALD. Actor, playwright and producer. Born London, 1894. First appeared on stage in 1913 in *Joseph And His Brethren* (His Majesty's). Then with Benson for two years, after which he played for J. B. Fagan, 1919-20, at the Court. Acted continuously on the London stage until 1922, subsequently acting and producing. Then produced a number of plays in London, including *If Four Walls Told, Fata Morgana, The Moon And Sixpence, Rope, Jew Süss, Windfall* and many others. With Edward Percy, he has written *The Last Straw, Suspect, Give Me Yesterday, The Distant Hand, Ladies In Retirement*. Has recently been producing plays in New York.

DESMOND, FLORENCE. Actress. Born London, 1907. Trained as a dancer and first appeared on the stage in 1916 in *Babes In The Wood* (Strand). Then in *On With The Dance* in 1925. Also in London in *This Year Of Grace* (and in New York in 1928), *The Student Prince, Charlot's Masquerade, Savoy Follies, Why Not To-night ?, Streamline, Seeing Stars, Choose Your Time*, etc. Recently in pantomime ; also in *Funny Side Up* (His Majesty's, 1940), *Hi-De-Hi* (Palace, 1943-44).

DEVINE, GEORGE. Actor and producer. Born London, 1910. Educated Winchester and Oxford. Made his first appearance on stage in 1932 in *The Merchant Of Venice* (St. James's), then in *Evensong*, etc. With Old Vic, 1932-33, playing in *Cæsar And Cleopatra, The School For Scandal*, etc., then in London in *Magnolia Street, The Voysey Inheritance, Hamlet, Noah, Romeo and Juliet*. Joined John Gielgud Company in 1937 and played in *Richard II, The School For Scandal, The Three Sisters, The Merchant Of Venice*. Also acted in the West End in *The White Guard, Twelfth Night* (in Michel St. Denis Season), *Rhondda Roundabout* and others. 1936-40, producer and manager of the London Theatre Studio. In 1939 co-produced *The Tempest* (Old Vic) and produced *Great Expectations* (Rudolf Steiner Hall). Since then in H.M. Forces.

DEVLIN, WILLIAM. Actor. Born Manchester, 1911. Educated Stonyhurst and Oxford. Married to Mary Casson. Acted with the O.U.D.S., then in 1933-34 studied for stage at Embassy School of Acting. Made his first appearance on London stage in 1934 in *Nurse Cavell* (Vaudeville), then in the West End in *Queen Of Scots, King Lear, Hamlet, Noah*. With Old Vic 1935-36 in *Peer Gynt, The*

Three Sisters, Julius Cæsar, Macbeth, Richard III, St. Helena, King Lear, etc. Also acted on the London stage in *The Tiger, As You Like It, The Ascent Of F.6, Mr. Gladstone, I Accuse, The Trojan Women, Mourning Becomes Electra, Coriolanus, The White Guard, Twelfth Night, Weep For The Strong.* Since 1940 in H.M. Forces, producing and acting for ENSA in the Middle East. In 1946 joined Old Vic Company at Bristol.

DICKSON, DOROTHY. Actress. Born Kansas City, U.S.A., 1896. First appeared on the stage in New York in *Oh Boy* in 1917 ; subsequently played in London in 1920 in *London, Paris And New York,* subsequently in *Sally, Patricia, Charlot's* 1925 *Revue, Peter Pan, The Ringer, Tip-Toes, Charivara, Hold Everything, Wonder Bar, Casanova.* More recently in *Stop Press, Spread It Abroad, Careless Rapture, Crest Of The Wave, Henry V, The Scarlet Pimpernel.* Recently : *Fine And Dandy* (Saville, 1940), *Diversion* (Wyndham's, 1941), etc. In *Crisis In Heaven* (Lyric, 1944). In 1946 she appeared in *Our Betters.*

DIGNAM, MARK. Actor. Born London, 1909. Married to Georgia Mackinnon. Joined the Ben Greet Company in 1931, and toured Britain and the United States. Made his first appearance in London in *Macbeth* (Kingsway, 1932), then acted in London in *A Cup Of Happiness, Henry V, Libel, Everyman, Hamlet.* At Westminster Theatre, 1936-37, appeared in *The Wild Duck, Waste, Crooked Cross, Uncle Vanya, Heartbreak House, Anna Christie, A Month In The Country, Hamlet.* With the Old Vic 1937 he appeared in *Pygmalion, Measure For Measure* and *Richard III.* Then at the Westminster in *Mourning Becomes Electra, Volpone, The Zeal Of Thy House, You Never Can Tell* and *Marriage.* First appeared in New York in 1938 in *Oscar Wilde.* Returned to London in *Mourning Becomes Electra* (New), then in *Desire Under The Elms* (Westminster, 1940). 1940-44 in H.M. Forces. Recently appeared in *The Simpleton Of The Unexpected Isles* (Arts). In 1945 joined the Arts Festival Company, appearing in *Hamlet, Getting Married, The Thunderbolt.*

DIXON, ADELE. Actress. Born London, 1908. Studied for the stage at Royal Academy of Dramatic Art, making her first appearance in 1921 in *Where The Rainbow Ends* (Apollo) ; then in London in *The Happy Ending, The Sport Of Kings, Leonce And Lena.* In 1927 she went to Egypt with the Robert Atkins Company, appearing in *Twelfth Night, The Merchant Of Venice, Measure For Measure, Othello.* Returned to London and acted with the Old Vic 1928-30 in *Love's Labour's Lost, As You Like It, Macbeth, The Merry Wives Of Windsor, The Rivals, Henry VIII, Romeo And Juliet, A Midsummer Night's Dream, The Imaginary Invalid, Macbeth,* etc. Among the other West End plays in which she has appeared are *The Good Companions, Wild Violets, Give Me A Ring, Three Sisters, Youth At The Helm, Anything Goes, Between The Devil* (New York, 1937), *The Fleet's Lit Up,* and many others. Recently : *All Clear* (Queen's, 1940), *The Merchant Of Venice* (Westminster, 1942), *Crisis In Heaven* (Lyric, 1944), *Babes In The Wood* (His Majesty's, 1944).

DOLMAN, RICHARD. Actor. Born London, 1895. First appeared on the stage in 1923 in *Stop Flirting* (Shaftesbury), then in London in *On With The Dance, Merely Molly, Lady Mary, Merry Merry, Here Comes The Bride, Stand Up And Sing, Three Sisters, Jack O' Diamonds, Going Places,* etc. In 1942 he appeared in *Twenty To One* (Victoria Palace), then in *The Lilac Domino* (His Majesty's, 1944). In 1945 appeared in *Gay Rosalinda* (Palace).

DONALD, JAMES. Actor. Born Aberdeen, 1917. Educated Edinburgh University. Studied for the stage with Michel St. Denis at the London Theatre Studio, making his first appearance in London in *The White Guard* (Phœnix, 1938), followed by *Twelfth Night,* etc. In 1939 appeared in *Great Expectations* (Rudolph Steiner), after which he joined the Old Vic Company, appearing on tour and at the New in *The Cherry Orchard,* etc. In 1942 he appeared in *Salt Of The Earth*

(Vaudeville). Joined the Noel Coward Company in 1943, appearing in *Present Laughter* and *This Happy Breed* (Haymarket). In H.M. Forces 1943-46.

DONAT, ROBERT. Actor. Born Manchester, 1905. Studied for the stage with James Bernard. Made his first appearance on the stage in 1921 in *Julius Cæsar* (Prince of Wales, Birmingham), was a member of Sir Frank Benson's Company, 1924-28, also in repertory at Manchester, Wakefield and Huddersfield. First appeared in London in 1928 in *The Merry Wives Of Windsor* (Wimbledon), subsequently with Liverpool Repertory Company and the Cambridge Festival Theatre. Has also acted in London in *The Liar, The Witch, Precious Bane, A Trip To Scarborough, Salome, A Sleeping Clergyman, Mary Read, Red Night*, etc. Joined the Old Vic in 1939 and toured in *The Good-Natured Man, Romeo And Juliet* and *The Devil's Disciple*, appearing in the last-named at the Piccadilly in 1940. Recently acted in *Heartbreak House* (Cambridge, 1943). Took over the management of the Westminster in 1943; and in 1945 appeared there in *The Cure For Love*.

DOONAN, ANN. Actress. Born London, 1922. Educated St. Guilda's Convent and in Paris. Married to Jack Cooper. Made her first appearance on the stage in *The Sleeping Beauty* (Leeds, 1940), subsequently in *Blossom Time* (Lyric, 1941), *Flying Colours*, on tour, 1942-43, *Hearts Are Trumps* (with Hermione Baddeley), on tour, 1943.

DOUGLAS, ROBERT. Actor. Born Bletchley, 1909. Married to Dorothy Hyson. Studied at the Royal Academy of Dramatic Art, making his first appearance on the stage in *The Best People* (Bournemouth, 1927), then acted in London in *Many Waters* (Kingsway, 1928). Subsequently played in *Mrs. Moonlight, A Bill Of Divorcement, Many Waters* (in New York, 1929), *The Last Enemy* (also in New York, 1930), *Suspense, Badger's Green, After All, Brief Moment* (New York, 1931), *Men In White, Theatre Royal, Most Of The Game* (New York, 1935), *No Exit, Kind Lady, The Springtime Of Others*, etc. Since the outbreak of war has been serving in the Royal Navy.

DRAYTON, ALFRED. Actor. Born Brighton, 1881. Married to Enid Sass. First appeared on the stage in *The Beloved Vagabond* (Cardiff, 1908), then in London in *Peter's Mother* (Haymarket, 1909). Subsequently acted in *The Scarlet Pimpernel, A Little Bit Of Fluff, A Temporary Gentleman, Dear Brutus, Our Betters*, and many others. Has also appeared in the West End in *These Charming People* (New York, 1925), *The Lash, Peter Pan, Double Dan, The High Road* (also in New York, 1928), *The Calendar, The Old Man, Tell Her The Truth, Mr. Whittington, Aren't Men Beasts, A Spot Of Bother, Banana Ridge* and others. Recently: In 1939 in *Spotted Dick* (Strand), *Women Aren't Angels* (Strand, 1940-41) *She Follows Me About* (Garrick, 1943-44). *Madame Louise* (Garrick, 1945-46).

DRESDEL, SONIA. Born in Yorkshire. Educated at Aberdeen. Made her first stage appearance in repertory at Northampton. For some time was in repertory at Harrogate, then 1939-40 toured with Old Vic Company in *The Devil's Disciple*, etc. Made her first appearance in London in *King John* (for the Old Vic) (New, 1941), then in *Hedda Gabler* (Mercury, 1942). This was followed by *The Way Of The World* (Mercury, 1942) and a new production of *Hedda Gabler* (Westminster, 1943). In 1943 appeared in *Parisienne* (St. James's), in 1944 acted in *This Was A Woman* (Comedy). Then in 1945, *Laura* (St. Martin's), *Wait, My Love* and *Green Laughter* (both at Q). Recently: *The Sacred Flame* (St. Martin's and Westminster, 1945-46).

DUKES, ASHLEY. Playwright, dramatic critic and producer. Born Bridgwater, 1885. Married to Marie Rambert. Among his plays are *Civil War, The Man With A Load Of Mischief, One More River, House Of Assignation*; has done a number of translations from the French and German, including *From Morn Till Midnight, The Machine Wreckers, Mozart, Such Men Are Dangerous, Jew Süss, Elizabeth Of England, Vintage Wine* (with Sir Seymour Hicks), *The Mask Of Virtue, Mandragola*. Founded the Mercury Theatre in 1933 and has managed it since that time, producing seasons of new plays and classics. In 1945 he was appointed Director of Drama of the German Theatre. He is also English Editor of " Theatre Arts."

DUNN, GEOFFREY. Actor. Born London, 1903. Educated City of London School. His first stage appearance was in *Twelfth Night* (Bath, 1925). Made his first appearance in London in *Gloriana* (Little, 1925). Thenceforth in many productions in London and elsewhere. In 1939 appeared in *An Elephant In Arcady* (Savoy). Recently in *The Streets Of London* (Orpheum, 1942) and *Light And Shade* (Ambassadors, 1942), *Androcles And The Lion* (Arts), *Alice In Wonderland* (Scala, 1943), *Twelfth Night*, CEMA tour, 1943, *The Quaker Girl* (Coliseum), *The Venetian* (Chanticleer, 1944) and *The Glass Slipper* (St. James's, 1944-45). In 1945 appeared in *The Italian Straw Hat* and *The Government Inspector* (both at the Arts). In 1945 in *The Forrigan Reel* (Sadlers Wells). Reappeared in *The Glass Slipper* (St. James's, 1945-46), *The Thracian Horses* (Lyric, 1946).

DUNNING, RUTH. Actress. Born May 17th, 1911, Prestatyn, N. Wales. Married to Jack Allen. Educated Sale High School. Made her first appearance on the stage in *Love On The Dole* (Garrick, 1938), followed by *Can We Tell*, *Gentleman Unknown*, *Hundreds And Thousands*, *Uneasy Living*, etc. During the war she left the stage, returning in *The Russians* (for the Old Vic) (Playhouse, 1943). Recently : *Temporary Ladies* (Q, 1945), *No Room At The Inn* (Embassy, 1945), and on tour, 1946.

DYALL, FRANKLIN. Actor and producer. Born Liverpool, 1874. Married to Mary Merrall. First appeared on the stage in 1894 in *The Masqueraders* (St. James's), after which he remained with George Alexander for some time. Appeared in London also in *Hamlet*, *The Merchant Of Venice*, *Prisoner Of Zenda*, *Henry V*, *Monsieur Beaucaire*, *Romeo And Juliet*. Toured U.S. in 1905-06, returning to London in *King Lear*, *John Gabriel Borkman*, *A Doll's House*, *Hedda Gabler*. Toured with Martin Harvey in *The Only Way*, etc., then to America with Marie Tempest, returning to London in *Armageddon*. Among the other West End plays in which he acted are *The Taming Of The Shrew*, *Richard III*, *Grierson's Way*, *Medium*, *At Mrs. Beam's*, *Magda*, *Peter Pan*, *White Cargo*, *The Ringer*, *The Silent House*, *The Limping Man*, *The Master Builder*, *Strife*, *Julius Cæsar*, *The Merchant Of Venice*, *The Mask And The Face*, *Tovarich*, *Œdipus Rex*, *Panic*, *The First Legion*, *Idiot's Delight*, *Number Six*, etc. Recently with Old Vic in *The Russians* (Playhouse, 1943), on tour in *White Cargo*, and on tour with Edgar Wallace Repertory Company 1945. Then on tour in *Trilby*, 1945-46.

EATON, WALLAS. Actor. Born London, 1917. Educated at Cambridge. Made his first appearance on the stage in *Indoor Fireworks* (Cambridge Arts, 1937). First appeared in London in *Murder In The Cathedral* (Duchess, 1937), followed by *The Comedy Of Errors* (Mercury), etc. Recently : In 1940 appeared in *The Body Was Well Nourished* (Lyric). 1940-43, served with H.M. Forces. On being invalided out he appeared in a season of Bernard Shaw plays at the Lyric, Hammersmith, 1944-45 ; then in *The Copy* (Arts, 1945), *The Skin Of Our Teeth* (Phœnix, 1945), *Tomorrow's Child* (Lyric, Hammersmith, 1946).

EDDISON, ROBERT. Actor. Born Yokohama, 1908. Educated Charterhouse and Cambridge. Joined the Festival Theatre, Cambridge, in 1930, appearing in *Lady Audley's Secret*, then in London in *Comus* (Arts, 1930). In 1931 with Huddersfield Repertory Company, then with Westminster Company in *The Anatomist*, *A Pair Of Spectacles*, *Six Characters In Search Of An Author*, *Tobias And The Angel*. 1932-34, with Croydon Repertory Theatre, then at the Open Air Theatre. Among the many plays in which he has appeared in London are *Family Affairs*, *Macbeth*, *King Lear*, *Peer Gynt*, *Spring Tide*, *Yes And No*, *Ghost For Sale*, *Tobias And The Angel*, *Number Six*, *A Midsummer Night's Dream*. Also appeared often at the Players'. In 1940 appeared in *All Clear* (Queen's). Since 1940 has been in Royal Navy. Appeared in *The Kingmaker*, 1946, etc.

EDWARDS, GEOFFREY. Actor. Born London, 1911. Educated University College. Studied for the stage at the Royal Academy of Dramatic Art, making his first appearance in *Cæsar and Cleopatra* (Malvern Festival, 1929). Subsequently with Liverpool Repertory Theatre, where he remained for four years. Made his first appearance in London at the Open Air Theatre, Regent's Park, where he stayed for three seasons. Among the plays in which he has appeared in the West End are *Spring Tide, A Doll's House, The Master Builder, Candida, The Island, Out Of The Picture, Susannah And The Elders,* etc. In 1942 appeared in *The Doctor's Dilemma* (Haymarket), followed by *Quiet Week-End* (Wyndham's, 1943). In 1944 he appeared for a season with the Glasgow Citizen's Theatre. On tour in *Desert Highway*, 1945-46.

EDWARDS, G. GRAVELEY. Actor and dramatic author. Born January 24th, 1896. Educated at Charterhouse and Oxford. Made his first appearance on the stage with the O.U.D.S. in *Antony And Cleopatra*. Has appeared on the stage professionally since 1922 ; was with the Old Vic 1925-27. Since then has appeared in many London productions. Recently : *Magic* (Arts, 1942), *Holy Isle* (Arts, 1943), *Don Abel Wrote A Tragedy* (Arts, 1944), *Emma* (St. James's, 1945). Among his plays are *Last Hour* and *Great Cats Play Chess*.

EDWARDES, OLGA. Actress. Born in South Africa. Married to Nicholas Davenport. Educated University of Capetown. Made her first stage appearance in London at the Open Air Theatre, 1935. Subsequently in repertory and on tour with Esmé Percy in Bernard Shaw plays, 1939. Also appeared in *Peril At End House* (Vaudeville, 1940). Joined Stratford-on-Avon Festival Company, 1942. With B.B.C. Repertory Company, 1942-43 ; appeared in *Landslide* (Westminster, 1943), etc. In 1945 she appeared in *Mrs. Warren's Profession,* (Torch). In 1946 in *Grand National Night.*

EGAN, MICHAEL. Playwright. Born Kilkenny, Ireland, 1895. Educated at St. Mary's College, Dundalk, and University of London. Among his plays are *The Dominant Sex, Private Company, Art And Craft, To Love And To Cherish Salt Of The Earth.*

ELLIOTT, MADGE. Actress. Born London, 1898. Married to Cyril Ritchard. Made her first appearance on the stage in the ballet at His Majesty's, Sydney, in 1912. Then in Sydney in *The Blue Bird, The Girl In The Taxi, Going Up,* etc. First appearance in London in *Better Days* (Hippodrome, 1925), then in *Bubbly, Lady Luck, Love Lies, The Love Race.* From 1932-36 she was acting in Australia, returning to London in *Spread It Abroad*, followed by *Cinderella, The Constant Sinner,* etc. In 1940 appeared in *Swinging The Gate* (Ambassadors). Recently in *Big Top* (His Majesty's, 1941), *The New Ambassadors Revue,* 1942, *The Merry Widow* (His Majesty's, 1943), *Sigh No More* (Piccadilly, 1945-46).

ELLIS, MARY. Actress. Born New York, 1899. Made her first appearance on the stage at Metropolitan, New York, in *Suor Angelica,* 1918, then in New York in *The Blue Bird, Louise, The Merchant Of Venice, Casanova, Rose Marie, The Dybbuk, Crime And Punishment, The Taming Of The Shrew, Becky Sharp, Children Of Darkness.* First acted on London stage in *Knave And Queen* (Ambassadors, 1930), then in *Strange Interlude, Queer Cattle, Double Harness, Music In The Air, Glamorous Night, Farewell Performance, The Innocent Party, The Dancing Years* (from 1939-41) and others. Recently : *Arc de Triomphe* (Phœnix, 1943), with the Old Vic in Liverpool, 1943-44, in *Point Valaine,* etc. Then in *The Gay Pavilion,* (Piccadilly, 1945).

ELLIS, WALTER. Playwright. Born London, 1874. Educated King's College. Among his plays are *Cupid And The Captain, A Little Bit Of Fluff, The Hawleys Of The High Street, Almost A Honeymoon, Glass Houses, Bedtime Stories* and *Shooting Stars.* In 1943 he wrote and produced *Sleeping Out* (Piccadilly). In 1945 wrote and produced *Lovely Lady* for a Continental tour.

EMNEY, FRED. Actor. Born in London, 1900. First appeared on the stage in *Romance* (Duke of York's, 1915), then toured in musical comedy. 1920-31, in American vaudeville, returning to England to appear in variety, then in London in *Mr. Whittington, The Flying Trapeze, Seeing Stars, Swing Along, Going Greek, Running Riot,* etc. In 1940 appeared in *All Clear* (Queen's). Recently: *Big Top* (His Majesty's, 1942), *Up And Doing* (Saville), *It's Time To Dance* (Winter Garden, 1943), *Goody Two Shoes* (Coliseum, 1944), *Big Boy* (Saville, 1945).

EUSTREL, ANTONY. Actor. Born London. Made his first appearance on the stage in *The Dybbuk* (Royalty, 1927), after which he went to Egypt with a Shakespearean Company. Appeared in *Macbeth* (Court), and others in Sir Barry Jackson's season. Also in London in *Back To Methuselah*, afterwards appearing in Paris, Antwerp, Brussels, Frankfurt, etc. Other plays in which he has appeared in London include *The Lady Of The Camelias, Jonah And The Whale, Night's Candles, Richard Of Bordeaux* and *King Of The Damned*, and a season at the Gate Theatre. Then in *Balalaika, Paprika,* etc., after which he appeared in repertory at the Intimate, Palmers Green, 1942-44. Recently appeared at the Memorial Theatre, Stratford-on-Avon, 1944 and 1945, in *The Taming Of The Shrew, Antony And Cleopatra, Othello, Much Ado About Nothing, Henry VIII, Romeo And Juliet, She Stoops To Conquer,* etc. In 1946 he joined the Donald Wolfit Company, appearing in *Othello, Hamlet* and *Cymbeline* (Winter Garden).

EVANS, CLIFFORD. Actor and producer. Born Cardiff, 1912. Married to Hermione Hannen. Studied for the stage at Royal Academy of Dramatic Art, making his first appearance in *The Witch* (Embassy, 1930). 1931-32, toured Canada with Norman Page's Company; on his return appeared at the Embassy, then in repertory at Folkestone and Croydon. First acted in the West End in *Gallows Glorious* (Shaftesbury, 1933), then in *The Distaff Side, The Tempest, Twelfth Night*. To New York in *The Distaff Side*, 1934, returning to London in *The Ante Room*. Then in *Hamlet* in New York, 1936, returning to London in *Ghosts*; subsequently in the West End in *The Emperor Of The World, The Doctor's Dilemma* and others. Recently: Produced *What Every Woman Knows* (Lyric, 1943). Since 1943 in H.M. Forces, acting and producing at Garrison Theatre, Salisbury, etc.

EVANS, EDITH. Actress and producer. Born London, 1888. Made her first appearance on the stage in *Troilus And Cressida* (King's Hall, Covent Garden, 1912), then in London in *Hamlet, Milestones, The Conference, The Dead City, The Player Queen, The Merchant Of Venice, My Lady's Dress, Heartbreak House, The Laughing Lady*. Has also acted in the West End in *The Merry Wives Of Windsor, The Way Of The World, Getting Married, Back To Methuselah, A Midsummer Night's Dream*. Joined Old Vic, 1925-26, and appeared in *The Merchant of Venice, Richard III, The Taming Of The Shrew, Measure For Measure, Antony And Cleopatra, The Merry Wives Of Windsor, She Stoops To Conquer, As You Like It, The Shoemaker's Holiday, Much Ado About Nothing, Romeo And Juliet,* Also acted in London in *Caroline, Rosmersholm, The Beaux' Stratagem, Napoleon's Josephine, The Lady With A Lamp* (also in New York, 1931). At Malvern Festival she appeared in *The Apple Cart, Heartbreak House,* then in London in *Delilah, The Old Bachelor, Othello, Evensong* (also in New York, 1933), *Once In A Lifetime, The Late Christopher Bean, Viceroy Sarah, Romeo And Juliet,* (New York, 1934), *The Old Ladies, The Seagull*. With the Old Vic, 1936, in *The Country Wife, As You Like It* and *The Witch Of Edmonton*. Also appeared in London in *The Taming Of The Shrew, Robert's Wife* and *The Importance Of Being Earnest* (Globe, 1939, and Phœnix, 1940). Also in *Cousin Muriel* (Globe, 1940). Recently in *Diversion* (Wyndham's, 1941), *Old Acquaintance* (Lyric, 1942), *Heartbreak House* (Cambridge, 1943), acting and producing at Salisbury Garrison Theatre, 1944. In 1945 appeared in (and co-produced) *The Rivals* (Criterion).

EVANS, LYN. Actor. Among the plays in which he has appeared in London recently are *Jupiter Laughs* (New, 1942), *Androcles And The Lion* (Arts, 1942),

Whitehall Follies (Whitehall, 1942), *The Druid's Rest* (St. Martin's, 1944), *Banbury Nose* (Wyndham's, 1944), *Desert Rats* (Adelphi, 1945).

EVEREST, BARBARA. Actress. Born London, 1890. First appeared on the stage in *The Voysey Inheritance* (Kingsway, 1912) ; then in London in *Damaged Goods, The Cost, Our Boys, Sacrifice, The Dead City, The Ordeal, Ariadne, The Idiot, Cradle Song, The Kingdom Of God.* With Old Vic in 1928, appearing in *Romeo And Juliet, The Merchant Of Venice* and *The School For Scandal.* Has also acted in the West End in *The Apple Cart, The Wild Duck, Fanny's First Play, Pygmalion, Lover's Meeting, Children In Uniform, Viceroy Sarah, Sixteen, Vicky, Pride And Prejudice, Time And The Conways, Walk In The Sun, The Ascent Of F.6,* etc. Since 1939 has been acting in Hollywood and New York, returning to London in 1945.

FARLEY, FREDERICK. Actor. Born London, 1914. Formerly a publisher, he made his first stage appearance at the Oxford Playhouse in 1937. Has also appeared in repertory at Leeds, Harrogate and Windsor. In 1941 he appeared in *Skylark* (Duchess). Then joined Norman Marshall's Company at Cambridge, and on tour. In 1945 he appeared in *Chicken Every Sunday* (Savoy). 1945-46 : In *Under The Counter* (Phœnix).

FARRELL, CHARLES. Actor. Born Dublin, 1901. Made his first appearance on the stage at Detroit in 1912 ; then in London in *The Crown Diamond* (Coliseum, 1921). Subsequently in the West End, appeared in *The Nervous Wreck, The Black Ace, In The Zone, Cape Forlorn, Street Scene, Smoky Cell, Vile Bodies, Whistling In The Dark, Mary Read, The Amazing Dr. Clitterhouse, The Bowery Torch, The Sun Never Sets,* and others. Recently : *My Sister Eileen* (Savoy, 1944).

FAY, W. G. Actor and producer. Born Dublin, 1872. First appeared on stage in *Eileen Oge* (Queen's, Dublin, 1891) ; then in 1902 founded the Irish Company. Later took up management of Dublin Abbey (with Miss Horniman) and acted in *The Well Of The Saints, Riders To The Sea, The Playboy Of The Western World,* etc. Played in New York and Chicago in 1908, and since that time has appeared extensively in Dublin and London. Among the plays in which he has appeared in London are *The Merry Wives Of Windsor, Society, General John Regan* and *Trelawney Of The Wells.* Has been producer at Abbey, Nottingham Repertory, Q, Arts, Birmingham Repertory, and in the West End. Also appeared more recently in *The Shadow Of The Glen, Mary Read, Storm In A Teacup, Moonshine, Spring Meeting,* etc. Recently in *The Tempest* (Old Vic, 1940), *Twelfth Night* (Arts, 1942), *Ducks And Drakes* (Apollo, 1942), *The Well Of The Saints* (Arts, 1943), *Chicken Every Sunday* (Savoy, 1945), etc.

FERNALD, JOHN. Producer. Born California, 1905. Educated at Oxford. Married to Jenny Laird. Formerly a dramatic critic, then stage manager of *Journey's End* in 1928-30. Has produced many plays in London since then, including *She Passed Through Lorraine, Wild Justice, Sixteen, The Dominant Sex, Let's Go Gay, The House Of Borgia, Distinguished Gathering, No Exit, The Provoked Wife, Oscar Wilde, Only Yesterday,* etc. Produced extensively at the Embassy and also at the Westminster, and was principal of the London Mask Theatre School of Acting, 1939-40. Then in the Royal Navy until 1944. In 1945 produced *The Government Inspector* (Arts), *Letters To A Lady* (Embassy), *A Doll's House* (Arts), *Kiss And Tell* (Phœnix), *Arms And The Man,* CEMA tour, etc. Engaged in production for the Reunion Theatre, 1946.

FFRANGCON-DAVIES, GWEN. Actress. Born London, 1896. Made her first appearance on the stage in 1911 in *A Midsummer Night's Dream* (His Majesty's), then in London in *The Glad Eye, The Immortal Hour,* etc. Joined Birmingham Repertory Company in 1921, then acted in London in *Mary Stuart, Back To Methuselah, Bethlehem, King Lear, Romeo And Juliet, A Midsummer Night's Dream, Cæsar And Cleopatra, The New Morality, The Doctor's Dilemma,*

PHOTO : EDWARD MANDINIAN

Robert Helpmann as Hamlet in the Old Vic Company's production, directed by Tyrone Guthrie and Michael Benthall, 1944.

PHOTO : JOHN VICKERS

★ *Alastair Sim* and Sophie Stewart in James Bridie's "Mr. Bolfry", produced by Sim in 1943.

PHOTO : JOHN VICKERS

★ ***Walter Crisham,*** Ilena Sylva, Hermione Gingold
and Bonar Colleano, Jr., in a John Jowett sketch from the
revue "Sweet and Low", produced by Charles Hickman,
1943.

★ *Hermione Gingold* and Henry Kendall in an Alan Melville sketch from "Sweeter And Lower", produced by Charles Hickman, 1944.

PHOTO : G.H.W.

★ *Nora Swinburne,* who appeared in "Dear Brutus", 1941, and later in "Something In The Air", "Watch On The Rhine", "A Month In The Country", "The Years Between".

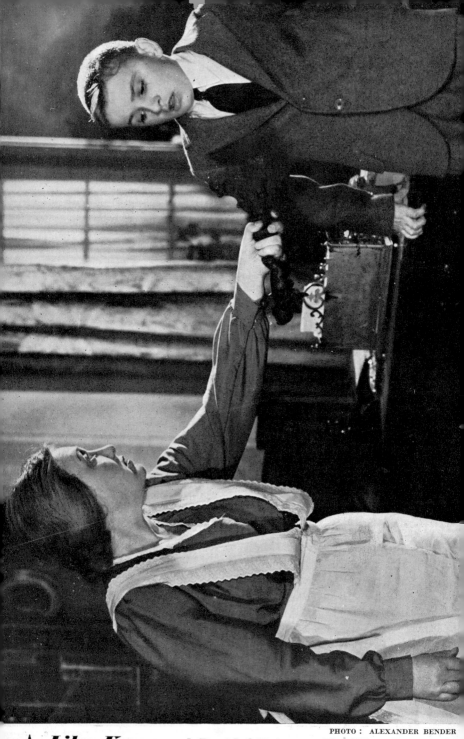

★ **_Lily Kann_** and David O'Brien, as Emil Bruckner, in "Tomorrow The World", by James Gow and Arnold d'Usseau, produced by Marcel Varnel, 1944.

PHOTO : CECIL BEATON

★ *Alfred Lunt and Lynne Fontanne* in
Robert Sherwood's "There Shall Be No Night", produced by
Lunt. They appeared in "Love In Idleness", 1944-45.

★ *Robert Morley* and Wendy Hiller as Princess
Charlotte and the Prince Regent, in Norman Ginsbury's
"The First Gentleman", produced by Norman Marshall,
1945.

Pygmalion, Man And Superman, Easter, The Lady With A Lamp, Macbeth, A Doll's House, Hamlet, The Barretts Of Wimpole Street, Precious Bane and many others. Also appeared in the West End in *Richard Of Bordeaux, Queen Of Scots, Flowers Of The Forest, Justice, Close Quarters, Charles The King, He Was Born Gay, The Three Sisters, Henry V, Gaslight,* etc. Recently in *The Importance Of Being Earnest* (Phœnix, 1940), *Macbeth* (Piccadilly, 1942), and later touring South Africa with her own company (in association with Marda Vanne).

FIELD, ALEXANDER. Actor. Born London, 1892. Made first appearance on stage at Manchester Gaiety in *Westward Ho,* 1913 ; acted in London in same part, subsequently touring provinces for several years in all kinds of plays. Among the plays in which he has acted in London are *Monica, Intimate Enemies, The Crooked Billet, The House Of The Arrow, Journey's End, The Good Companions, The Streets Of London, They Came By Night, The Amazing Doctor Clitterhouse* (New York, 1937), *Lady With Designs.* Recently : *Thunder Rock* (St. Martin's, 1941), *The Merry Widow* (His Majesty's, 1943), *No Medals* (Vaudeville, 1944).

FIELD JONATHAN. Actor. Born 1912. Educated Rouen. Studied to be a pianist and has been musical director in London at the Little, Duke of York's, Vaudeville, Playhouse, etc. Has also written original scores for a number of London productions, including *The Insect Play* and *Alice In Wonderland.* He made his first appearance on the stage with the Old Vic in 1934, remaining until 1936 ; then on tour with the Macdona Players, 1937. Recently appeared in *The Devil's Disciple* (Piccadilly, 1939-40), *Don Abel Wrote A Tragedy* (Arts, 1944), *Three's A Family* (Saville, 1944), *The Magistrate* (St. Martin's, 1945), etc. Recently produced *Thirteen To The Gallows,* on tour, *Doctor Syn,* on tour, etc.

FIELD, SID. Actor. Born Birmingham. For a number of years he was well-known on the variety stage. In 1943 he made his debut in West End revue in *Strike A New Note* (Prince of Wales's). In 1945 he appeared in *Strike It Again* (Prince of Wales's).

FIELDING, MARJORIE. Actress. Born Gloucester, 1892. First appeared on stage in a tour of *His House In Order* in 1913 ; then a tour in various plays until 1924, when she joined Bristol Little Theatre, remaining until 1926. She then played with Liverpool Repertory Company from 1926 until 1934, making her first appearance in London in 1932 in *The Silver Cord* (Embassy). On leaving Liverpool she joined Gladys Cooper and Raymond Massey in a tour of Canada and America, playing in New York in 1934 in *The Shining Hour* and in the same part in London in 1934 at the St. James's. Has also acted in London in *Noah, Romeo And Juliet, Till The Cows Come Home, Old Music, People At Sea, Quiet Wedding,* etc. Recently in *Quiet Week-End* (Wyndham's).

FILDES, AUDREY. Actress. Born Liverpool, 1921. Studied for the stage at the Old Vic School of Acting and joined the Old Vic Company in 1942 at Liverpool. Among the plays in which she appeared here were *Shirley.* She remained with the Old Vic until 1944, when she joined the Greta Douglas Company and made her first appearance in London in *A Hundred Years Old* (Chanticleer). Then in *The Venetian* and *He Must Return* (both at Chanticleer), after which she rejoined the Old Vic at Liverpool, appearing in *Scandal At Barchester, Uneasy Laughter, Hamlet* and many others. In 1945 she appeared in *The Rivals* (Criterion).

FIRTH, ANNE. Actress. Born Westcliff-on-Sea, 1918. Studied for stage under Eileen Thorndike at Embassy School of Acting, and made her first appearance on the stage in 1935 in *Ada* (New). Subsequently appeared in *Romeo And Juliet,* then in 1936 played with Bournemouth Repertory Company. Among the plays in which she has acted in London are *The Crooked Cross, Because We Must, Crisis, Ladies And Gentlemen, Bonnet Over The Windmill, Quiet Wedding,* etc. Acted in *After The Dance* (St. James's, 1939). Recently : *It Happened In September* (St.

James's, 1942), *The Last Of Mrs. Cheyney* (Savoy, 1944), *The Two Children* (Arts, 1944), *Grand Guignol* (Granville, 1945).

FITZGERALD, JOHN. Born London, November 25th, 1919. Educated at Harvey Grammar School, Folkestone. After serving in the Army until 1941, he made his first appearance on the stage at Northampton Repertory Theatre in *Robert's Wife*, 1942. Subsequently appeared in repertory at York, Tunbridge Wells and Palmers Green. Made his first appearance in the West End in *Hamlet* (for the Old Vic) (New, 1944), after which he toured the Continent in repertory, also appearing at the Madelèine, Paris, 1944-45. Recently in *A Bell For Adano* (Phœnix, 1944-45), *Spring 1600* (Lyric, Hammersmith, 1945-46).

FITZGERALD, WALTER. Actor. Born Keyham, Devonport, 1896. Studied for the stage at the Royal Academy of Dramatic Art, making his first appearance in *The Wheel* (Great Yarmouth, 1922). Toured with Mrs. Patrick Campbell, 1922-24, then first acted in London in *The Likes Of 'Er* at the Century with the Lena Ashwell Players, with whom he stayed until 1927. Toured Canada with Sir John Martin-Harvey, 1929-30, then in London played in *Debonair, Let Us Be Gay, Black Coffee*, before touring Canada again. First appeared in New York in *Evensong*, 1933, returning to London to play in *Clear All Wires*, then in the West End in *Sheppey, Young Mr. Disraeli, Someone At The Door*, *1066 And All That, The Emperor Of Make-Believe*. Toured South Africa with Sir Seymour Hicks in 1936. Other plays in which he has appeared in London include *Poison Pen, Under Suspicion, Death On The Table*. Recently in *No Time For Comedy* (Haymarket, 1941), *Murder Without Crime* (Comedy), *The Duke In Darkness* (St. James's, 1942), *Lifeline* (Duchess, 1942), *Mr. Bolfry* (Playhouse, 1944). Then on tour in *Under The Gooseberry Bush* (*The Astonished Ostrich*), 1945.

FLEMYNG, ROBERT. Actor. Born Liverpool, 1912. Educated Haileybury. Made his first appearance on the stage in *Rope* (Truro, 1931); then in London in *The Anatomist* (Westminster). Joined Liverpool Repertory Company in 1932, remaining until 1935. Among plays in which he has appeared in London are *Worse Things Happen At Sea, Accent On Youth, Wisdom Teeth, French Without Tears* and *Banana Ridge*. First appeared in New York in *Spring Meeting*, 1938, and also acted there in *No Time For Comedy*. Since the outbreak of war in H.M. Forces. Appeared in *The Guinea Pig* (Criterion, 1946).

FLETCHER, WILFRED. Actor and producer. Born London, 1890. Studied for the stage at Royal Academy of Dramatic Art. Was for three years with the Benson Company, making his first appearance in *The Ware Case* (Wyndham's); thereafter in many productions in London and the provinces. Recently with the Donald Wolfit Company at the Strand, 1941. Produced *Immortal Garden* (Westminster, 1941). Appeared in *Androcles And The Lion* (Arts, 1943), *Macbeth* (Lyric, Hammersmith, 1944), etc. Producer, Gateway Theatre, 1944-45.

FORBES, BRYAN. Actor. Born London, 1926. Studied for the stage at the Royal Academy of Dramatic Art, making his first appearance on the stage in *The Corn Is Green* (Intimate, 1942). Also appeared here in *The Maitlands*, 1943. Toured in *Fighter's Calling* and *Flare Path*, 1944, subsequently playing in repertory at Worthing, 1945. Joined Embassy Theatre Company, appearing in *Quality Street*, 1945. Then serving with H.M. Forces.

FORBES, MERIEL. Actress. Born London, 1913. Married to Ralph Richardson. First appeared on stage with her father's (Frank Forbes-Robertson) company in *The Passing Of The Third Floor Back*, on tour, 1929. Made her first appearance in London in *Porcupine Point* (Gate, 1931). She then joined Birmingham Repertory Company, after which she played in London in *Dinner At Eight*, followed by *First Episode, This Side Idolatry, Angel, The Dark Tower, Red Night, The Amazing Dr. Clitterhouse, I Killed The Count* and others. With Old Vic in 1938 she appeared in *The Rivals*. In 1940 she appeared in *The Women* (Strand). Recently in *A Soldier For Christmas* (Wyndham's, 1944-45).

FORBES-ROBERTSON, JEAN. Actress. Born London, 1905. Married to André van Gyseghem. First appeared on stage in 1921, in Natal, in *Paddy The Next Best Thing* in her mother's company; later with this company toured Australia and New Zealand. Made her first appearance in London in *Dancing Mothers* (Queen's, 1925); subsequently in the West End in *Uncle Vanya, Don Juan, Berkeley Square, Romeo And Juliet, Peter Pan* (each Christmas, 1927-34), then in 1928 joined the Old Vic. She has also acted in London in *The Constant Nymph, The Man I Killed, Little Eyolf, Hedda Gabler, Measure For Measure, Twelfth Night, Strange Orchestra, As You Desire Me, Rosmersholm, St. Joan* and many others. Appeared in New York in *Promise*, 1936, returning to London in *A Midsummer Night's Dream*, 1937. Also played in the West End in *Time And The Conways, Peter Pan* and many others. Recently in *Berkeley Square* (Vaudeville, 1940-41), *Twelfth Night* (Arts, 1942), *Quality Street* (Embassy, 1945). With York Festival Company 1945, appearing with this company in *The Spinster Of South Street* (King's, Hammersmith), etc. In 1945 she appeared in a programme of Grand Guignol plays at the Granville.

FOX, LEE. Actor. Born Thornaby-on-Tees, Yorks, 1912. Educated at Middlesbrough and at Birmingham University. Made his first appearance on the stage with the Birmingham Repertory Company in 1935; subsequently appeared in repertory theatres in all parts of the country. 1940-41, served in H.M. Forces. On being invalided out he made his first appearance in London in *Holy Isle* (Arts), followed by *Merchant Of Venice* (for the Old Vic) (New, 1943), then appeared in *Uncle Harry* (Garrick, 1944-45). Recently appeared on tour in *Lady Windermere's Fan.*

FOX, WILLIAM. Actor. Born Manila, 1911. Married to Patricia Hilliard. Studied for the stage under Elsie Fogerty at the Central School of Dramatic Art, then made his first appearance on the stage in *The Breadwinner* (Vaudeville, 1930), followed by *A Knight Passed By, Dangerous Corner*, etc. With Old Vic, 1932-33, appearing in *As You Like It, The Tempest*, etc. Has also acted in London in *Night's Candles, The Rose Without A Thorn, First Episode, Precipice, Line Engaged, Someone At The Door, Dusty Ermine, Young Madame Conti* (also in New York, 1937), *I Have Been Here Before, Under Suspicion* and others. Since the outbreak of war in H.M. Forces. In 1945 he formed Reunion Theatre, to aid ex-soldier actors to regain a footing in the profession. In *Exercise Bowler* (Arts, 1946).

FRENCH, HAROLD. Actor and producer. Born London, 1897. First appeared on the stage in 1912 in *The Winter's Tale* (Savoy); subsequently in *Twelfth Night, A Midsummer Night's Dream.* Was a member of Liverpool Repertory Company and Birmingham Repertory Company, after which he appeared in London in *The Blue Lagoon, Lido Lady, Virginia, The Gay Princess, Night Of The Garter* and many others. Among the West End plays he has produced are *Youth At The Helm, French Without Tears, Blondie White, Design For Living*, etc. Recently: *Ladies Into Action* (Lyric), *No Time For Comedy* (Haymarket), etc.

FRITH, JOHN LESLIE. Actor and playwright. Born London, 1889. Educated in London and Paris. Studied for the stage at the Royal Academy of Dramatic Art, making his first appearance in *Cæsar And Cleopatra* (Drury Lane, 1913). Subsequently appeared with the Old Vic and in many productions in London and elsewhere. Recently in *A Soldier For Christmas* (Wyndham's, 1944), *While Parents Sleep* (Whitehall, 1945). He has translated eight plays by Jean-Jacques Bernard, also adapted plays by Guitry, Gignoux, and Roger-Marx.

FULLER, ROSALINDE. Actress. Born Portsmouth, 1901. After some experience of concert work she appeared on the legitimate stage in *What's In A Name?* (New York, 1920), then in *The Champion, Hamlet*, etc. In 1923 she joined the Provincetown Players and appeared in *The Farmer's Wife, Love For Love* and a number of other plays. In 1927 she first appeared in London in

The Squall (Globe) ; subsequently in the West End in *The Unknown Warrior, The Enemy, The Three Sisters, Arms And The Man, Man And Superman, The Philanderer, Misalliance.* Has also acted in London in *Martine, First Episode, Miss Julie, Fritzi, Murder On Account,* etc. In 1938 joined the Donald Wolfit Company, appearing in *The Merchant Of Venice, Much Ado About Nothing, As You Like It, Othello, Macbeth,* etc. In 1940 appeared in *Chu Chin Chow* (Palace). Then in 1941 acted in *Berkeley Square* (Vaudeville) and with Donald Wolfit Company (Strand). Then toured in *Desire Under The Elms, Gaslight, Jane Eyre,* etc. In 1944 toured in *This Was A Woman* ; in 1945 toured in *The Crime Of Margaret Foley,* and also toured in *Madame Bovary.*

FRIEND, PHILIP. Actor. Born Horsham, 1915. Educated Bradfield College. Made his first appearance on the stage in *Glamorous Night* (Coliseum, 1935). Subsequently in *Careless Rapture* (Drury Lane, 1936). Made his first appearance in New York in *French Without Tears,* 1937, returning to London to appear in *Pygmalion* (Haymarket, 1938). In 1941 appeared for a season with Aberdeen Repertory Company. Recently acted in *Pink String And Sealing Wax* (Duke of York's, 1943-44) and on Continental tour in 1945. Appeared in *The First Gentleman* (New and Savoy, 1945-46).

FURBER, DOUGLAS. Dramatic author. Born London, 1885. From 1917 to 1926 he was engaged as an actor ; then author of many London productions, including *A To Z, That's A Good Girl, Stand Up And Sing, Mr. Whittington, The Flying Trapeze, Nine O'clock Revue* and many others. Has contributed to countless revues, and in collaboration has written *Swing Along, Going Greek, Running Riot, Hide And Seek, Me And My Girl, Wild Oats* and *Sitting Pretty,* and many other West End shows. More recently : *Up And Doing, Fine Feathers, Big Boy,* etc. (He is the author and co-author of more than seventy musical plays and revues, as well as many famous songs).

FURSE, JUDITH. Actress and producer. Born Deep Cut Camp, Camberley, 1912. Made her first appearance on the stage in a pageant at Wembley Stadium, 1924. Appeared at Perranporth Summer Theatre, 1936 to 1939. Made her first appearance in London in *Goodness, How Sad* (Vaudeville, 1938). 1944-45, producing at the Arts Theatre. Among her recent productions are *Hamlet* and *Getting Married* (for the Arts Festival of English Drama); *Dutch Family* (Arts, 1946).

FURSE, ROGER. Designer. Born Ightham, 1903. Has designed settings in London for *Anna Christie, Victoria Regina, The Lady From The Sea, Oscar Wilde, Karl And Anna,* etc. ; and *Othello, Hamlet* and *The Taming Of The Shrew* for Old Vic, 1938-39. From 1936-39 was associated, as art director, with Perranporth Summer Theatre. Recently : Designed settings for *King Lear* (Old Vic), *Rebecca* (Queen's), *Uncle Vanya* (Westminster), *The Duchess Of Malfi* (Haymarket), *The Skin Of Our Teeth* (Phœnix) and other plays in London. 1941-45, with the Royal Navy. In 1945 he designed the costumes for *Henry IV* for the Old Vic, at the New.

GADD, RENEE. Actress. Born Argentine, 1908. Studied under Kate Rorke, then made first appearance in *Hassan* (His Majesty's, 1924). Subsequently in *Rose Marie, Lady Be Good, Funny Face, Black Coffee, Lover's Meeting, Money For Jam* and others. Went to United States to appear in *And Be My Love* (Ritz, 1934), then toured in United States and Canada with Barry Jones and Maurice Colbourne. After playing in *Living Dangerously,* she returned to London in *Great Expectations* (St. Martin's, 1936). Also appeared in London in *And The Music Stopped, Money Talks,* etc. Recently in *Skylark* (Duchess, 1942), *They Came To A City* (Globe, 1943-44).

GAIL, ZOË. Actress. Born Capetown, South Africa, 1921. Educated Parktown Convent, Johannesburg. Married to Hubert Gregg. Trained as a ballet dancer. Came to England 1938 and made her first appearance in *New Faces* (Comedy, 1940, and Apollo, 1941). Subsequently in *Black Vanities* (Victoria

Palace, 1941-42), *Sky High* (Phœnix, 1942), *Let's Face It* (Hippodrome, 1943), *Strike A New Note* (Prince of Wales's, 1944), *Happy And Glorious* (Palladium, 1945).

GARSIDE, JOHN. Actor. Born Manchester, 1887. Studied for the stage at the Royal Academy of Dramatic Art, making his first appearance in 1911 in *The Admirable Crichton*; then with Liverpool Repertory Company. First acted in London in 1920 in *The Higher Court*, then at the Everyman for a period. From 1921-23 with Old Vic as actor and designer, and again from 1924-28. Has also acted in London in *Such Men Are Dangerous, Jew Süss, Othello, The Devil's Disciple, Salome, The Rose Without A Thorn, Richard Of Bordeaux, Miracle At Verdun, Ten Minute Alibi, Distinguished Gathering, Whiteoaks, Professor Bernhardi, Lady Precious Stream, Victoria Regina, The Family Reunion* and others. Joined the Old Vic on tour in 1940. Appeared in *King John* (New). Recently : *Uncle Harry* (Garrick, 1943-44), *The Italian Straw Hat* (Arts, 1945), *The Government Inspector* (Arts, 1945), etc.

GELLNER, JULIUS. Producer. Born Prague, 1899. Studied for the stage at Prague and subsequently acted in Berlin and other parts of the Continent. First began his career as producer in Munich, 1923, later becoming chief producer and managing director of the Munich Kammerspiele. From 1933-38 was chief producer Prague Theatre. Came to England and from 1941-45 was a producer in the B.B.C. European Service. Has also produced plays in London, including *Othello* (for the Old Vic) (New, 1942), *War And Peace* (Phœnix, 1943), *They Also Serve*, on tour, 1944, *Close Quarters*, for CEMA tour, 1945. He produced *Century For George*, and *Let Tyrants Tremble*, for "Theatre '46" (Scala, 1946).

GENN, LEO. Actor. Born London, 1905. Educated City of London School and Cambridge. First appeared on stage in *A Murder Has Been Arranged* (Eastbourne, 1930). With Leon M. Lion Company appeared in London in the same part at the Royalty, 1931, and also in *No. 17, Tiger Cats, Champion North, While Parents Sleep*. Then in *Ballerina, Clive Of India*, etc., then with the Old Vic from 1934 until 1936, appearing in *Antony And Cleopatra, Richard II, Much Ado About Nothing, Julius Cæsar, Peer Gynt, St. Joan, Major Barbara, Macbeth, The School For Scandal*, etc. Also acted in London in *The Children's Hour, Twelfth Night, Henry V, St. Helena* and others. Went to Elsinore in 1937 with the Old Vic, in *Hamlet*, returning to London to appear in *The Flashing Stream*. To New York in 1938 to play the same part, returning to London in *Juggernaut*. Since the outbreak of war in H.M. Forces.

GEORGE, RICHARD. Actor. Born London, June 3rd, 1898. Educated at Cambridge. Went to Canada and made many appearances on the stage with the Theatre Arts Guild. Made his first appearance in England in *Androcles And The Lion* (Q, 1934). Then in many plays in London, including *Black Limelight, Troilus And Cressida, Gentleman Unknown, Hamlet* (also at Elsinore), etc. In 1939 appeared in *Great Expectations* (Rudolf Steiner), *Desire Under The Elms* (Westminster), *Rebecca* (Queen's, 1940). Since 1941 has been engaged in films extensively.

GERARD, ROLF. Artist and designer. Born Berlin, 1909. Studied art in Paris and Berlin. Studied medicine at Heidelberg and obtained M.D. at Basle. In 1936 came to England and was assistant to Oliver Messel at the Old Vic. Has designed settings and costumes for *Big Top* (His Majesty's, 1941) and for many Arts Theatre productions, 1942-45. Also designed *Landslide* (Westminster, 1943), etc. In 1945 designed *The Constant Couple* (Arts), *Better Late, Big Ben*, etc.

GIELGUD, JOHN. Actor and producer. Born London, 1904. Studied for the stage at Lady Benson's School and at the Royal Academy of Dramatic Art, making his first appearance on the stage in *Henry V* (Old Vic, 1921), then in *King Lear, Wat Tyler, Peer Gynt*. At the Regent in 1923 appeared in *The Insect Play*,

Robert E. Lee, then in *Charley's Aunt, Romeo And Juliet*, etc. Joined J. B. Fagan's Company at Oxford Playhouse, 1924-25 ; then in London played in *The Orphan, The Vortex, The Cherry Orchard, The Seagull, The Tempest, The Three Sisters, The Constant Nymph.* Went to New York in 1928 in *The Patriot*, returning to London to play in *Ghosts.* Also in the West End in *The Skull, The Lady With A Lamp, Red Sunday.* Joined Old Vic in 1929, appearing in *Romeo And Juliet, The Merchant Of Venice, The Imaginary Invalid, Richard III, A Midsummer Night's Dream, Macbeth, Hamlet, The Tempest, Julius Cæsar, Androcles And The Lion, Antony And Cleopatra*, etc. On the reopening of Sadlers Wells, 1931, played in *Twelfth Night, Arms And The Man, King Lear, Much Ado About Nothing.* Then appeared in the West End in *The Good Companions, Musical Chairs, Richard Of Bordeaux* (which he also produced). Subsequently produced and/or appeared in a number of plays, including *The Maitlands, Hamlet, Noah, Romeo And Juliet, The Seagull.* Went to New York in 1936 to play *Hamlet*, returning to London to appear in *He Was Born Gay.* From 1937-38 he appeared with his own company at the Globe in *Richard II, The School For Scandal, The Three Sisters, The Merchant Of Venice.* Then in *Dear Octopus, The Importance Of Being Earnest* ; played *Hamlet* at Elsinore in 1939. Since the war has acted and produced continuously. At the Old Vic, 1939-40 played in *The Tempest* and *King Lear*, then in *The Importance Of Being Earnest* (Phœnix, 1940), *Dear Brutus* (Globe, 1941), *Macbeth* (Piccadilly, 1942) and *Love For Love* (Phœnix, 1943). In 1944 appeared in the latter, and in *The Circle, A Midsummer Night's Dream, Hamlet, The Duchess Of Malfi*—all at the Haymarket in the Gielgud Repertory Season. Has also recently produced *Ducks And Drakes, Landslide, Cradle Song, Crisis In Heaven, Lady Windermere's Fan, The Last Of Summer*, etc. In 1945 went to Burma with his company, playing in *Hamlet* and *Blithe Spirit.*

GIELGUD, VAL. Playwright and producer. Born London, 1900. Educated Rugby and Oxford. Among his plays are *Self, Chinese White, The Double Man* (with Eric Maschwitz), *Red Triangle, I May Be Old-Fashioned* and *Africa Flight.* Has produced a number of plays in London, including *Tread Softly, The Road To Ruin, Punch And Judy.* Has been Director of Drama, B.B.C., for a number of years ; also producing and acting in radio plays. In 1944 he produced *Happy Few* on tour. In 1945 he produced *This Land Of Ours* (Q). With John Dickson Carr he wrote *Thirteen To The Gallows*, on tour, 1945.

GILL, TOM. Actor. Born Newcastle, 1916. Educated Royal Grammar School, Newcastle. Made his first appearance on the stage in *Treasure Island* at Newcastle Repertory Theatre. Among the plays in which he has played in London are *Antony And Anna, Cornelius, The Last Straw, Goodbye, Mr. Chips.* In 1943 appeared in *A Month In The Country* (St. James's). In 1945 in *Young Mrs. Barrington* (Winter Garden).

GINGOLD, HERMIONE. Actress. Born London, 1897. Studied for the stage under Rosina Filippi, making her first appearance in *Pinkie And The Fairies* (His Majesty's, 1908) ; later in *The Merry Wives Of Windsor*, etc. At the Old Vic in 1914 played in *The Merchant Of Venice*, then in London in *The Dippers, From Morn To Midnight, One More River, Hotel Universe, This World Is Ours, Spread It Abroad, In Theatre Street*, etc. In 1938 played in *The Gate Revue* at the Gate, and later at the Ambassadors. Has also appeared in *Swinging The Gate* (Ambassadors, 1940), *Rise Above It* (Comedy, 1941), *Sky High* (Phœnix, 1942), *Sweet And Low*, 1943-44, and *Sweeter And Lower* (Ambassadors, 1944-46).

GINSBURY, NORMAN. Playwright. Born London, 1903. Educated Grocer's Company School and London University. Is the author of *Viceroy Sarah, Walk In The Sun, The King Could Not Sleep, The First Gentleman, The Firstcomers.* Has also adapted the following Ibsen plays : *Ghosts, An Enemy Of The People, A Doll's House* and *Peer Gynt.* With Winifred Holtby wrote *Take Back Your*

Freedom; and adapted *The Gambler* (from Dostoievsky). In 1944 his version of
Peer Gynt was produced by the Old Vic Company (New), his version of *Ghosts*
was revived at the Duke of York's. In 1945 *The First Gentleman* was staged at
the New and Savoy, *The Gambler* at Embassy, his version of *A Doll's House*
(Winter Garden, 1945-46), etc.

GLENVILLE, PETER. Actor and producer. Born London, 1913. Educated
Stonyhurst and Oxford. Was President of the O.U.D.S., making his first
appearance on the professional stage in 1934 in *The Swan* with the Manchester
Repertory Company. In 1935 appeared in London in *Rossetti*, followed by
Twelfth Night, Man And Superman, The Hangman. With Stratford-on-Avon
Festival, 1936, playing in *Romeo And Juliet, The Taming Of The Shrew*, etc.
In 1939 with the Old Vic in *The Taming Of The Shrew.* 1940-41, appeared in
Light Of Heart (Apollo and Globe). 1942-43, in *The Doctor's Dilemma* (Hay-
market). 1944-45, Director of the Old Vic Season, Liverpool, producing *John
Gabriel Borkman, Point Valaine, School For Scandal, His Excellency The
Governor* and *Lisa.* Also appeared in *Hamlet, Uneasy Laughter* and *The Alchemist.*
Adapted *Lisa* from Turghenev. In 1945 appeared in London in *Duet For Two
Hands* (Lyric). Produced *The Time Of Your Life* (Lyric, Hammersmith, 1946).

GODFREY, PHILIP. Actor. Born London, 1895. Made his first appearance
in vaudeville in 1911. From 1918-22 on tour with Bernard Shaw Repertory
Company. Since then he has appeared in various theatres in London and in the
provinces. Also with Leon M. Lion's Company at the Theatre de L'Odeon, Paris.
For many years he has been seen at the Players' Theatre. In 1943 he appeared in
Heartbreak House (Cambridge), etc. He is the author of " Back Stage " (Harrap,
1933). Appeared in *Century For George* (Scala, 1946), etc.

GOLDEN, MICHAEL. Actor. Born Dublin, 1913. Made his first appearance
on the stage at Abbey, Dublin, 1930 ; subsequently touring in Shakespearean
companies in Ireland and the British Isles. Made his first appearance in London
in *Don Juan In Hell* (from *Man And Superman*) (Arts, 1942). Has also appeared
in *The Russians* for the Old Vic, 1943, *The Old Foolishness* (Arts), *The Dark River*
(Whitehall, 1943), *The Sulky Fire* (Arts, 1944). Also appeared and produced at
the Bernard Shaw season at the Lyric, Hammersmith, 1944. Has acted in *Guilty*
(for the Old Vic) (Lyric, Hammersmith, 1944), then on tour in *Wuthering Heights*,
1944-45. Appeared in *Macbeth* (Oxford Playhouse, 1945), etc. Then with Glasgow
Citizen's Theatre, 1945-46.

GOLDIE, WYNDHAM. Actor. Born Rochester, 1898. Made his first appearance
on the stage in *The Story Of The Rosary* (Theatre Royal, Chatham, 1922) ;
subsequently in London in *Peter Weston* (Comedy, 1924). Then in several tours,
after which he joined Liverpool Repertory Theatre from 1927-34. Appeared in
London in *Sixteen, Summer's Lease, The Unguarded Hour, Parnell, The King's
Pirate, Autumn, Asmodée, Nina*, etc. Since the outbreak of war in H.M. Forces.
He re-appeared on the stage in *A Man About The House* (Piccadilly, 1946).

GOLDING, LOUIS. Novelist and playwright. Born Manchester, 1895. Educated
at Oxford. Has written a number of novels and films. His plays include (in
collaboration with A. R. Rawlinson), *The Miracle Boy* and *Magnolia Street.* Other
of his plays are *The Song Of Songs* and *Symphony Of Youth.*

GOLDNER, CHARLES. Actor. Born Vienna, 1900. Studied for the stage in
Vienna and worked extensively in theatres in Germany, Austria, Holland and
Czecho-Slovakia. Came to England and has appeared in *Once A Crook* (New),
The Doctor's Dilemma (Haymarket, 1942), *Watch On The Rhine* (Aldwych,
1943-44), *Three Waltzes* (Princes, 1945), and on tour 1945-46.

GOOLDEN, RICHARD. Actor. Born London, 1895. Educated Charterhouse
and Oxford. Was a member of the O.U.D.S., made his first appearance on

professional stage with J. B. Fagan's Oxford Repertory Company in *Heartbreak House*, 1923, remaining there until 1926, interspersed with appearances in London. First acted in London in 1925 in *A Comedy Of Good And Evil* (Ambassadors) ; subsequently in *The Cherry Orchard, Riverside Nights, The Kingdom Of God, The Lady With A Lamp, The School For Scandal, Hamlet,* etc. Has also acted at the Stratford-on-Avon Festival, the Festival Theatre, Cambridge, and the Masque Theatre at Edinburgh and Glasgow. In London acted in *Love's Labour's Lost,* etc., and *Twelfth Night* and *Henry VIII* (for Old Vic), *An Enemy Of The People, Dear Brutus, The Alchemist, The Dominant Sex, Bees On The Boatdeck, The Country Wife, Heartbreak House, A Midsummer Night's Dream, Charley's Aunt, Grouse In June,* etc. 1940-41, broadcasting in *The Old Town Hall,* and touring in *Fair And Warmer.* Then in *The Old Town Hall* (Winter Garden, 1942), *King Lear* (St. James's, 1943), tour of *Easy Living, The Watched Pot* (Arts, 1943), with Donald Wolfit Shakespearean Company, Scala, 1944, with Bernard Shaw Repertory Season, Lyric, Hammersmith, appearing in *Too True To Be Good* and *Pygmalion.* In 1945 appeared in *King Lear* and *Macbeth,* with Donald Wolfit (Winter Garden). Then in a season of Grand Guignol, Granville. Recently in *The Circle Of Chalk* (Arts), *The Proposal* (Lindsey), etc. Appeared in *The Land Of The Christmas Stocking* (Duke of York's, 1945-46) ; *See How They Run* (Comedy, 1946).

GORDON, CLIFF. Actor. Born Llanelly, 1920. Made his first appearance on the stage in variety at the Palladium, 1934. In 1937 appeared in *Charlot's Non-Stop Revue* (Vaudeville). In H.M. Forces, 1939-40. Then in *Up And Doing* (Saville, 1940-41), *The Man Who Came To Dinner* (Savoy, 1942-43), *Sky High* (Phœnix, 1943), followed by a season of acting and writing at the Windmill, 1943-44. Recently appeared in *Sigh No More* (Piccadilly, 1945-46).

GORDON, GAVIN. Actor. Born Ayr, Scotland, November 24th, 1901. Educated Rugby. Studied singing at the Royal College of Music and in Milan, 1925-26. He made his first appearance on the stage in *La Vie Parisienne* (Lyric, Hammersmith, 1929). He has also been seen in London in *Pride Of The Regiment, Jolly Roger, Hansel And Gretel, By Appointment, St. Helena, No More Peace,* etc. More recently in *Swing Along, Going Greek, Running Riot,* all at the, Gaiety. In 1943 he appeared in *Magic Carpet,* (Princes), after which he appeared on tour for ENSA in France, Belgium, Holland, Italy and N. Africa ; then in *Cinderella* (Adelphi, 1945-46).

GORING, MARIUS. Actor and producer. Born Newport, Isle of Wight, 1912. Studied for the stage under Harcourt Williams and at the Old Vic Dramatic School. First appeared at the Old Vic in *A Midsummer Night's Dream,* 1929, then toured the Continent with the English Classical Players. From 1932-34 with Old Vic, appearing in *The School For Scandal, Macbeth, Romeo And Juliet, Twelfth Night, The Tempest, The Cherry Orchard, Henry VIII, Measure For Measure, Love For Love, The Voysey Inheritance.* Then acted in the West End in 1934 in the latter play, subsequently touring in France with the Campagnie des Quinze. Appeared in London also in *Noah, The Hangman, Mary Tudor, The Happy Hypocrite, The Wild Duck.* Again with Old Vic, 1936-37, playing in *The Witch Of Edmonton, Twelfth Night, Henry V, Hamlet.* Subsequently in the West End in *Satyr, The Last Straw, Surprise Item, The White Guard.* In 1939 produced *Nora,* appeared in and produced *Lady Fanny* and appeared in *Nina,* and *Hamlet* (in London and Elsinore). In 1939-40 appeared with Old Vic in *The Tempest* ; and in *Great Expectations* (Rudolf Steiner). Then with the B.B.C. European Service, 1940-45.

GRAHAM, MORLAND. Actor. Born Partick, Glasgow, 1891. Made first appearance on stage in 1908 in *The Merchant Of Venice* (Town Hall, Rutherglen). First appeared in London in *Campbell Of Kilmhor* (Coliseum, 1923). Toured from 1924-31 ; then joined Westminster Theatre, playing in *The Anatomist, Six Characters In Search Of An Author, Tobias And The Angel, The Kingdom Of God.* Has also played in *Richard Of Bordeaux, Love's Labour's Lost,* before joining the Old Vic in 1932, appearing in *Romeo And Juliet, A School For Scandal, The Cherry Orchard, Love For Love* and others. Also in *As You Like It* and *A Midsummer Night's Dream* at Open Air ; then *Harvest In The North, The Black Eye, Green Waters, George And Margaret* (New York, 1937), *The Merchant Of Venice, The Man In Half Moon Street*. Recently in *As You Are* (Aldwych and Whitehall, 1940), *The Doctor's Dilemma* (Haymarket, 1941-43), *Distant Point* and *Noah* (Glasgow Citizen's Theatre, 1943), *Three's A Family* (Saville, 1944-45), *The Rivals* (Criterion, 1945-46).

GRANGER, STEWART. Actor. Born London, 1913. Married to Elspeth March. Educated Epsom College. Studied for the stage at the Webber-Douglas School of Dramatic Art, making his first appearance on the stage at Hull Repertory Theatre, after which he appeared in repertory at Birmingham, where he stayed for two years. He made his first appearance in London in *The Sun Never Sets* (Drury Lane, 1938), and subsequently he appeared in the West End in *Serena Blandish* and *Autumn*. In 1940 appeared in *The House In The Square* (Ambassadors), after which he toured with Robert Donat in *To Dream Again*. In 1941 he appeared in *Rebecca* (Queen's). Recently toured the Continent, with Deborah Kerr, in *Gaslight*, 1945.

GRAVES, DIANA. Actress. Educated Westonbirt. Married to Michael Gough. Studied for the stage with the Old Vic, making her first appearance on the stage in *Pride And Prejudice*. Recently in *Margin For Error* (Apollo), *Wingless Victory* (Phœnix), then on tour for CEMA in *The Brontës*. In 1945 appeared on tour in *Hidden Horizon*, then on tour for the Old Vic in *Romeo And Juliet*. In 1946 appeared in *A Doll's House* (Winter Garden).

GRAVES, GEORGE. Actor. Born London, 1876. First appeared on stage in Portsmouth in *The Shop Girl*, 1896, and then in London in 1898 in the same play. Also in the West End in *The School Girl, The Merry Widow* and in many pantomimes. Then in *Houp La !, The Blue Mazurka, Lilac Time,* revivals of *The Merry Widow, The Vagabond King, Me And The Girl,* etc. In 1943 again played Popoff in *The Merry Widow* (His Majesty's). In 1945 appeared in *Me And My Girl* (Victoria Palace).

GRAVES, PETER. Actor. Born London, October 21st, 1912. Educated at Harrow. Made his first appearance on the stage in *Streamline* (Palace, 1934). More recently appeared in *The Dancing Years* (Drury Lane and Adelphi, 1939), *Arc De Triomphe* (Phœnix, 1943-44), *Gay Rosalinda* (Palace, 1945-46).

GRAY, DULCIE. Actress. Born in Kuala Lumpur, Malaya. Married to Michael Denison. Came to England and studied for the stage at the Webber-Douglas School of Drama. In 1937 appeared in repertory at Aberdeen, followed by repertory in Edinburgh, Glasgow and Harrogate. Made her first appearance in London at the Open Air in 1942 in *A Midsummer Night's Dream*, followed by *Twelfth Night*, etc. Recently in *The Little Foxes* (Piccadilly, 1942), *A Midsummer Night's Dream* (Westminster, 1943), *Brighton Rock* (Garrick, 1943), *Landslide* (Westminster, 1943). Then appeared in *The Lady From Edinburgh* (Playhouse, 1945) ; *Dear Ruth* (St. James's, 1946).

GRAY, JENNIFER. Actress. Born Hankow, China. Educated Westonbirt. She made her first appearance on the stage in *Dreams And Ditches* (Piccadilly). Also in *In Theatre Street* (Mercury), *The Corn Is Green*, on tour, *This Happy Breed* and *Present Laughter* (Haymarket, 1943), *Blithe Spirit* (Duchess, 1944), *How Are They At Home ?* (Apollo, 1944), *Another Love Story* (Phœnix, 1945). On tour in Europe in *Love In Idleness*, then in *Dandy Dick*, 1946.

GRAY, LINDA. Actress and singer. Born Harrogate, Yorks. Studied to be a singer and appeared with the D'Oyly Carte Company in London and New York. Also appeared in *Follow The Sun* (Adelphi), *The Two Bouquets, Operette, An*

Elephant In Arcady, and at Glyndebourne and at the Covent Garden Opera House, etc. In 1940 appeared in *The Beggar's Opera* (Haymarket), *Fun And Games* (Princes, 1941), *Wild Rose* (Princes, 1941-42), *Junior Miss* (Saville, 1942-44). Recently : *Merrie England* (Princes, 1945-46).

GRAY, LUCIELLE. Actress. Born Liverpool. Studied for the stage at Eliot-Clarke's School of Drama. Made her first appearance on the stage in repertory at Southport, after which she appeared in repertory at Felixstowe and Halifax. She then studied for two years at the Royal Academy of Dramatic Art, after which she made her first appearance in London in *War And Peace* (Phœnix, 1943), then in *The Tragedy Of Nan* (Mercury, 1944), *Wolves And Sheep* (Chanticleer, 1945), *Strange Orchestra*, and *Britannia Of Billingsgate*, on tour in Europe, 1946.

GRAY, SALLY. Actress. Born London, 1917. Studied at the Fay Compton School of Dramatic Art, making her first appearance on the stage in *All God's Chillun Got Wings* (Gate, 1930). Subsequently appeared in the West End in *Bow Bells, Jill Darling, Over She Goes, The Gay Divorce* and many others. In 1940 she appeared in *Funny Side Up* (His Majesty's) and *Lady Behave* (His Majesty's, 1941-42). In 1944 she appeared in *My Sister Eileen* (Savoy).

GREENWOOD, JOAN. Actress. Born London, 1921. Studied for the stage at the Royal Academy of Dramatic Art, making her first appearance in *Le Malade Imaginaire* (Apollo), followed by *Little Ladyship, The Women* (Lyric, 1940), *Peter Pan* (Adelphi, 1941), etc. Recently in *Damaged Goods* (Whitehall), *Heartbreak House* (Cambridge, 1943). Then joined the Donald Wolfit Company appearing in *Hamlet* on tour. In 1945 appeared at the Playhouse, Oxford, in *The School For Scandal, A Doll's House* and *Cæsar and Cleopatra.* In *It Happened In New York*, on tour 1945-46.

GREENWOOD, WALTER. Playwright. Born Salford, December 17th, 1903. Well known as novelist and screenwriter also. His plays include *Love On The Dole* (with Ronald Gow), *Give Us This Day, The Practised Hand* and *My Son, My Son.* In 1945 he wrote *The Cure For Love* and *So Brief The Spring.*

GREGG, EVERLEY. Actress. Born Bishop Stoke, 1903. Studied for the stage at the Royal Academy of Dramatic Art, making her first appearance in *Easy Virtue* (Duke of York's, 1926). Subsequently in London in *The Matriarch, Private Lives, Grand Hotel, Dance With No Music, Conversation Piece*, etc. Appeared in New York in 1935 in *Point Valaine*, returning to London in *Tonight At* 8.30 (Phœnix), then in *The Constant Wife, Design For Living, On The Frontier*, etc.

GREGG, HUBERT. Actor. Born London, 1914. Married to Zoë Gail. Studied for stage at the Webber-Douglas School of Dramatic Art, making his first appearance on the stage in *Martine* (Ambassadors, 1933). Then with Birmingham Repertory Theatre, and with Open Air Theatre, 1934, playing in *As You Like It, The Tempest, Romeo And Juliet, Twelfth Night.* Has also appeared in London in *The Alchemist, Hamlet* (Old Vic) and with Open Air Theatre in 1935 and 1936 in *As You Like It, Love's Labour's Lost, The Tempest, Twelfth Night, Comus*, etc. Played in London in *Henry V* and *Much Ado About Nothing*, 1936-37, and then appeared in New York in *French Without Tears*, subsequently playing the same part in London in 1938. Then appeared in *After The Dance* (St. James's, 1939). During the war was with B.B.C. European Service, then in H.M. Forces. Since being invalided out he has appeared in *Men In Shadow* (Vaudeville, 1942), *Acacia Avenue* (Vaudeville, 1943) and *While The Sun Shines* (Globe, 1945).

GREGORY, SARA. Actress. Born in Sydney, Australia. Studied for the stage at the Royal Academy of Dramatic Art, making her first appearance in *Cinderella*, Scunthorpe. Recently appeared in *The Vagabond King* (Winter Garden, 1942), *The Waltz Dream*, on tour, 1943, *A Midsummer Night's Dream* (Westminster), *Goody Two Shoes* (Coliseum, 1944-45) and *The Glass Slipper* (St. James's, 1945-46).

GREW, MARY. Actress. Born London, 1902. Studied for stage with Elsie Fogerty and Kate Rorke, making her first appearance in *We Moderns* (Fortune, 1925); subsequently in London in *The Donovan Affair, The Combined Maze, Hindle Wakes, Justice, Loyalties, Welded, The Father, Typhoon, Ghosts, Street Scene* and others. Appeared with the Masque Theatre in Glasgow in 1928 and again in Edinburgh in 1931. Then in London in *The Life Machine, The Left Bank, Hurricane,* etc. Retired from stage owing to ill-health, returning in 1944 in *This Was A Woman* (Comedy). In 1945 toured on the Continent as Eliza in *Pygmalion.* Her play *John O' Dreams* (adaptation from the French) was produced at the Little in 1930.

GRIFFITH, HUBERT. Playwright and dramatic critic. Born London, 1896. Among his plays are *Tunnel-Trench, Red Sunday, The People's Court* and the following adaptations : *Youth At The Helm, Nina, Return To Yesterday, Young Madame Conti* (with Benn Levy), *Distant Point,* etc. Dramatic critic : " Sunday Graphic."

GROVES, CHARLES. Actor. Born Manchester, 1875. First appearance on stage in *Little Goody Two Shoes* (Court, 1888), then with Miss Horniman's Gaiety Company from 1913-16. Appeared in London in *The Rotters, Ghosts, French Leave, Heartbreak House, Treasure Island, The Farmer's Wife, Hit The Deck, The Ringer, The Merry Wives Of Windsor, Major Barbara, Thank You, Mr. Pepys, Behind The Blinds* and many others. Recently: *How Are They At Home?* (Apollo, 1944), *The Last Stone* (Phœnix, 1945). In 1946 appeared in *Grand National Night.*

GROVES, FRED. Actor. Born London, 1880. First appeared on stage in London in *In Days Of Old,* 1899, followed by three years with Martin Harvey and eight years with Fred Terry and Julia Neilson in England and the United States. Has also acted in London in *The Mayor Of Troy, Vanity Fair, Tom, No. 17, The Donovan Affair, Quest, This Year Of Grace, Wake Up And Dream, Cavalcade, Fresh Fields, Aren't Men Beasts, Lady With Designs* and many others. In 1940 in *Cousin Muriel* (Globe). Recently : *Cottage To Let* (Wyndham's, 1940), *Goodnight Children* (New, 1942), *Rain* (St. Martin's, 1942), *Crisis In Heaven* (Lyric, 1944), *Three Waltzes* (Princes, 1945).

GRUNDY, RUTH. Actress. Born Blackheath, 1919. Married to Grey Blake. She trained for the stage at the Embassy School of Acting, making her first appearance in *Touch Wood* (Embassy). Thenceforth in repertory at Worthing, Leeds, Bournemouth and Harrogate, and on tour in *Housemaster.* She made her first appearance in London in *Berkeley Square* (Vaudeville, 1940), followed by *Other People's Houses* (Ambassadors, 1942), *Tradesmen's Entrance,* on tour, 1943, etc. Recently appeared in *The Shop At Sly Corner* (St. Martin's, 1945), *Happy And Glorious,* on CEMA tour, 1945-46.

GUINNESS, ALEC. Actor and playwright. Born London, 1914. Married to Merula Salaman. Studied for stage under Martita Hunt and at the Fay Compton School of Dramatic Art, making his first appearance on the stage in *Libel* (Playhouse, 1934). Then played in London in *Queer Cargo, Hamlet, Noah, Romeo And Juliet, The Seagull.* Joined Old Vic in 1936 and appeared in *Love's Labour's Lost, As You Like It, The Witch Of Edmonton, Twelfth Night, Henry V,* etc. (also appearing in *Hamlet* at Elsinore). Joined John Gielgud's Company in 1937, appearing in *Richard II, The School For Scandal, The Three Sisters, The Merchant Of Venice.* Then with Old Vic in 1938, acting in *Trelawney Of The Wells, Hamlet, The Rivals, The Ascent Of F.6.* In 1940 appeared in *The Tempest* at the Old Vic, and in his own adaptation of *Great Expectations* at the Rudolf Steiner. Then in *Cousin Muriel* (Globe). 1941, toured in *Thunder Rock.* Since 1941 in H.M. Forces.

GUTHRIE, TYRONE. Producer. Born Tunbridge Wells, 1900. Educated Wellington and Oxford. Made his first appearance on stage at Oxford in 1924, thenceforth as producer with the Scottish National Players, 1926-27, and at Cambridge Festival Theatre for Anmer Hall, 1929-30. With Hall came back to London to be producer at the Westminster. Produced *The Anatomist* and *Dangerous Corner* in 1932, then produced for Old Vic, 1933-34. Also produced *Sweet Aloes* and *Mary Read* in London. Since 1936 has been associated with the Old Vic. Director of Old Vic and Sadlers Wells, 1936-45. Among his many Old Vic productions since 1940 are *The Cherry Orchard, Abraham Lincoln, The Russians* ; also produced *The Last Of Mrs. Cheyney* (Savoy, 1944) and *Peer Gynt* for Old Vic, 1944-45, *The Alchemist* (Liverpool, 1945), etc. Resigned from Old Vic in 1945.

HAINES, ALAN. Actor. Married to Wenda Rogerson. In 1940 he appeared at the Alexandra Repertory Theatre, Birmingham, remaining here until 1942, when he made his first appearance in London in *Whiteoaks* (Comedy). Since then he has appeared in *The Moon Is Down* (Whitehall, 1943), *The Two Children* (Arts, 1944), *Zero Hour* (Lyric, 1944), *The Lady From Edinburgh* (Playhouse, 1945-46), etc.

HALE, BINNIE. Actress. Born Liverpool, 1899. Made her first appearance on the stage in *Follow The Crowd* (Empire, 1916) ; then in *Houp La !, Fair And Warmer, The Kiss Call, Katinka, The Odd Spot, No, No, Nanette* and many others. Also in the West End in *Sunny, Mr. Cinders, Nippy, Bow Bells, Give Me A Ring, Yes Madam, Rise And Shine, Home And Beauty, Magyar Melody* and many pantomimes. In 1940 in *Up And Doing* (Saville). Recently : *Flying Colours* (Lyric, 1943), *Cinderella* (Winter Garden, 1944-45), etc. In *Aladdin* (Cambridge, 1945-46).

HALE, SONNIE. Actor. Born London, 1902. Made his first appearance on the stage in 1921 in *Fun Of The Fayre* (London Pavilion) ; subsequently in London in *The Punch Bowl, Mercenary Mary, Queen High, One Dam Thing After Another, This Year Of Grace, Wake Up And Dream, Evergreen, Hold My Hand* and many others. Recently : *Come Out To Play* (Phœnix, 1940), *A Knight Was Bold* (Piccadilly), *The Maid Of The Mountains* (Coliseum, 1942), and also in pantomime. In 1945 appeared in *That'll Be The Day*, on tour.

HALL, CAMERON. Actor. Born Hull, 1897. Made his first professional appearance with the Rupert Lister Repertory Company in 1919, after which he spent many years touring the provinces and also Newfoundland and the West Indies. Made his first appearance in New York in *Young Madame Conti*, 1937, also in *Come Across*, 1938. Appeared in London in *Death On The Table* (Strand, 1938), *Behind The Schemes* and *The Midshipmaid*, 1939. Recently in *As You Are* (Whitehall, 1940), *Women Aren't Angels* (Strand, 1941), *The Man Who Came To Dinner* (Savoy, 1942-43), *The Critic* and *The Italian Straw Hat* (Arts, 1944-45), *Chicken Every Sunday* (Savoy, 1945), *Fifty-Fifty*, (Strand, 1946).

HALSTAN, MARGARET. Actress. Born London, 1879. She made her first appearance on the stage in *Trilby* (Haymarket, 1895). Subsequently in London in *The Liars, You Never Can Tell*, etc., after which she toured with F. R. Benson and George Alexander. Then in London in *The Importance Of Being Earnest, Romeo And Juliet, An Enemy Of The People, Twelfth Night, Othello, Arms And The Man, How He Lied To Her Husband* and many others. Then in *As You Like It, The Provoked Wife, Brown Sugar, Sweet Lavender, Escape, Charles And Mary, The Young Idea*. Then appeared in *Vintage Wine, Distinguished Gathering, Alice Through The Looking Glass*, etc. Recently in *The Admirable Crichton* (His Majesty's, 1943). In 1944 she appeared in a season of Bernard Shaw plays at the Lyric, Hammersmith. In 1945 in *Big Boy* (Saville).

HAMBLING, ARTHUR. Actor. Born Reading, 1888. First appeared on stage in *Old Heidelberg* (King's, Hammersmith, 1912), then to New York in *Eliza Comes To Stay*. He returned to London in the same part in 1914. Has also played in the West End in *Easy Money, Marigold, Autumn Crocus, Napoleon, A Sleeping Clergyman, Androcles And The Lion, Bees On The Boatdeck, Spring Tide, The*

Last Straw,Goodness How Sad and many others. In 1941 acted in *Distant Point* (Westminster). In 1942 in *Holy Isle* (Arts). In 1943 acted in *The Russians* (for the Old Vic) (Playhouse). Recently : *The Wind Of Heaven* (St. James's, 1945).

HAMILTON, DOROTHY. Actress. Born London, 1897. Made first appearance on the stage at Blackpool in *The Dancing Mistress,* 1914 ; then on tour in South Africa, Australia, India and the Far East. Made her first appearance in London in 1923 in *Good Gracious, Annabelle,* subsequently in the West End in *The Torch Bearers, Hay Fever, Emma Hamilton, Passing Brompton Road, On Approval, Service, Sheppey, This Side Idolatry, Cornelius, Sweet Aloes, Jane Eyre, Autumn, Design For Living,* etc. In 1940 in *Jeannie* (Wyndham's, 1940). Recently : *Acacia Avenue* (Vaudeville, 1943-44), *No Medals* (Vaudeville, 1944-45).

HAMILTON, PATRICK. Playwright. Born London, 1904. Among his plays are *Rope, John Brown's Body, Gaslight, The Duke In Darkness, Ethel Fry,* and an adaptation from the French, *The Procurator Of Judea.*

HAMMOND, KAY. Actress. Born London, 1909. Studied at Royal Academy of Dramatic Art making her first appearance on stage in *Tilly Of Bloomsbury* (Regent, 1927) ; subsequently in London in *77, Park Lane, Nine Till Six, Dance With No Music, Evergreen, Women Kind, Three-Cornered Moon* and many others. Also in the West End in *Youth At The Helm, Sauce For The Goose, Bees On The Boatdeck, French Without Tears,* etc. Recently : In 1941, *Blithe Spirit* (Piccadilly and Duchess), *Private Lives* (Apollo, 1945). In 1946 she formed a company, with John Clements, and appeared in *Marriage A La Mode, The King-Maker,* etc.

HAMMOND, PETER. Actor. Born London, 1925. Educated at Harrow School of Art ; studied to be a stage designer. Appeared in repertory at Llandrindod Wells, and at the Intimate, Palmers Green. First appeared in the West End in *Junior Miss* (Saville, 1942). Then in *Landslide* (Westminster, 1943), followed by a tour of *Happy Few.* In 1945 appeared in *Laura* (St. Martin's), *Young Mrs. Barrington* (Winter Garden).

HAMPTON, LOUISE. Actress. Born Stockport. First appeared on stage in *Belphegor* (Manchester) ; subsequently toured in Australia, Egypt, etc. Has acted in London in *Brown Sugar, If Four Walls Told, The Silver Cord, Secrets, The Winter's Tale, The Importance Of Being Earnest, The Adding Machine, A Kiss For Cinderella, Quinneys, The Cat's Cradle, Passing Brompton Road, Aren't We All, The Father, Nine Till Six* and many others. Also in the West End in *Payment Deferred, The Man I Killed, Ghosts, The Late Christopher Bean, Lady Precious Stream, The Two Mrs. Carrolls, Spring Tide, Wanted For Murder, Give Me Yesterday, The Mother* and many others. In 1942 in *Salt Of The Earth* (Vaudeville). In 1943 appeared in *Living Room* (Garrick). Recently : *Letters To A Lady* (Embassy, 1945).

HANAU, JOHN. Producer. Born Cologne, 1909. Educated in Rome. Was a publisher and film director until 1932 when he came to England. 1937-39 director-producer World-Window Technicolor films. In 1942 became managing director of the Arts Theatre Group of Actors. 1943-44 producer-director Henley Repertory Theatre. In 1945 became producer-director " Grand Guignol " Season, Granville, Walham Green ; and then director of productions, Granville, 1946.

HANDL, IRENE. Actress. Born London, 1901. Studied for stage at the Embassy School of Acting, making her first appearance on the stage in *Night Alone* (Embassy, 1937), then in *George And Margaret, Never Say Goodbye, A Star Comes Home* and others. Recently : In 1945 appeared in *See How They Run* (Comedy), *Great Day* (Playhouse), *Under The Counter* (Phœnix), *Mr. Bowling Buys A Newspaper* (Embassy, 1946).

HANNEN, HERMIONE. Actress. Born London, 1913. Married to Clifford Evans. Studied for the stage at Royal Academy Dramatic Art, making her first appearance on the stage with Nicholas Hannen's Company in *The Breadwinner* (Cairo, 1932) ; subsequently touring in Australia and the Far East. First appeared in London in *The Voysey Inheritance* (Sadlers Wells, 1934), then in *Uncle Vanya, Hamlet, The Dangerous Age, The Silent Knight,* etc. Joined the Old Vic in 1938, playing in *Hamlet, Man And Superman, The Rivals,* later touring with Old Vic on Continent and in Egypt. Recently in *Othello* (New) (for the Old Vic), 1942, etc. In 1945 joined the London Theatre Group, appearing in *Exiles* (Torch) and in *Tomorrow Will Be Different* (Lindsey). In 1946 joined the Mercury Company.

HANNEN, NICHOLAS. Actor and producer. Born London, 1881. Studied for the stage under Rosina Filippi, making his first appearance on the stage in *The Girl In The Train* (Vaudeville, 1910) ; subsequently in London in *Gypsy Love, The Dancing Mistress, The Dynasts, The Doctor's Dilemma* (New York, 1915), *Cyrano De Bergerac, The Trojan Women, Candida,* etc. In 1920 joined the Everyman Company ; in 1921 acted in the Grand Guignol Company at the Little. Also acted in London in *The Dover Road, The Gay Lord Quex, Twelfth Night, A Midsummer Night's Dream, The Conquering Hero, Much Ado About Nothing, No. 17, Granite, Many Waters, Red Sunday, The Skin Game, The Importance Of Being Earnest* and many others. Has, in addition, appeared in *Othello, Accent On Youth* (London, 1934, and New York, 1935), *Waste, Candida, People Of Our Class, Weep For The Spring,* etc. In 1940 in *King Lear* (Old Vic). In 1941 in *The Cherry Orchard* (New). In 1942 in *Macbeth* (Piccadilly), *What Every Woman Knows* (Lyric, 1943). In 1943 in *The Rest Is Silence* (Prince of Wales). In 1944 joined the Old Vic Company, appearing in *Peer Gynt, Richard III, Arms And The Man* at the New (and on the Continent, 1945). In 1945 rejoined the Old Vic Company, appearing in *The Critic* and *Henry IV, Parts I and II,* etc. (New, 1945-46).

HANRAY, LAWRENCE. Actor. Born London, 1874. First appeared on the stage in *Hamlet* (Ipswich, 1892) ; then in London in *The Prodigal Daughter,* subsequently touring the provinces and in the Far East and Australia. In London appeared in *The Witch, Above Suspicion,* etc. From 1911-16 with Liverpool Repertory Company. Then acted in the West End in *Billeted, Tilly Of Bloomsbury,* etc. In 1920 joined the Everyman Theatre Company, subsequently appearing on the London stage in *The Faithful Heart, Justice, Loyalties* (New York, 1922), *The Rising Generation, The Lie, Doctor Knock, The Cherry Orchard, Medea, The Father, Escape* (New York, 1927), *Living Together,* etc. Also in London in *Rasputin, Liberty Hall, The Silver Box, The Hairy Ape, The Rose Without A Thorn, Ghosts, On The Rocks, Serena Blandish,* etc. In 1942 appeared in *Goodnight Children* (New). In 1943 in *The Dark River* (Whitehall), *Madeleine* (Lyric, Hammersmith, 1944). Recently : *Hamlet* (for Old Vic) (New), *A Hundred Years Old* (Intimate), *Yellow Sands* (Westminster), etc. In 1945 in *The Glass Slipper* (St. James's).

HARBEN, JOAN. Actress. Born London, 1909. Studied at the Royal Academy of Dramatic Art, making her first appearance on the stage in *The Bridge* (Arts, 1927), after which she acted in *The Unknown Woman* and toured Egypt with Robert Atkins' Company. Appeared in London also in *Quality Street, Measure For Measure, The Merry Wives Of Windsor, Third Time Lucky, Milestones,* etc. With Old Vic, 1930-31, playing in *The Tempest, The Jealous Wife, Antony And Cleopatra, Richard II, Twelfth Night.* Also in London in *A Pair Of Spectacles, Evensong, The Voysey Inheritance, Pride And Prejudice,* etc. Recently : *A Soldier for Christmas* (Wyndham's, 1944-45), *Love From A Stranger* (Gateway, 1945).

HARCOURT, JAMES. Actor. Born Headingly, 1873. First appeared on stage in *The Geisha* (Belfast, 1902), then touring until 1913, when he appeared in London in *Alice In Wonderland* (Comedy). From 1919-31 was with Liverpool Repertory Company in more than 100 productions. Has acted in London in *Laburnum*

Grove, Cornelius, Anthony And Anna, People Of Our Class, Tony Draws A Horse
and many others. Recently : *Why Not Tonight?* (Ambassadors, 1942), *Abraham Lincoln* (for the Old Vic) (Playhouse, 1943), *The Admirable Crichton* (His Majesty's, 1943), *Yellow Sands* (Westminster, 1945), etc.

HARDWICKE, SIR CEDRIC. Actor. Born Stourbridge, 1893. Married to Helena Pickard. Studied at the Academy of Dramatic Art, making his first appearance on the stage in *The Monk And The Woman* (Lyceum, 1912). Subsequently toured in the provinces and South Africa. Joined the Old Vic in 1914 and acted in many productions. Then in Birmingham Repertory Company from 1922 until 1924. Among the plays he has appeared in on the London stage are *The Farmer's Wife, Cæsar And Cleopatra, Hamlet, Othello, Yellow Sands, The School For Scandal, Back To Methuselah, Show Boat, The Apple Cart, Getting Married, The Barretts Of Wimpole Street, Heartbreak House, The Late Christopher Bean, Tovarich* and many others. Acted in New York, 1936-39, in *Promise, The Amazing Dr. Clitterhouse, Shadow And Substance,* etc. Then in Hollywood, 1940-44. Came back to London in 1944 to play in *The House On The Bridge* on tour, and in *Yellow Sands* (Westminster, 1945). Returned to New York, in autumn, 1945.

HARDY, BETTY. Actress. Born Lincoln, 1904. Studied at Royal Academy of Dramatic Art ; first appeared on the stage on tour in 1926-27 in *Peg O' My Heart.* Then in London, 1928, in *Glamour* (Embassy), followed by *Down Our Street, The Good Companions, The Anatomist, Jonah And The Whale, Wild Justice, Ballerina, Mary Read, A Doll's House, Hedda Gabler, People Of Our Class,* etc. With Stratford-on-Avon Festival, 1939, in *As You Like It, Twelfth Night, Richard III, Othello, Cornelius.* With Oxford Repertory Company in 1939. Recently : In B.B.C. Repertory Company, 1940-42, *Watch On The Rhine* (Aldwych, 1942-43). Then on tour in *Tomorrow's Eden,* 1944. Joined the Old Vic Company in 1944 and appeared in *Uncle Vanya,* etc.

HARE, ERNEST. Actor. Born London, 1900. First appeared on the stage in *Jig Saw* (Hippodrome, 1920) ; then with Stratford-on-Avon Festival, 1924, and again from 1926-32. He then toured the provinces, United States and Canada, joining Old Vic in 1933, and appearing in *Henry VIII, Twelfth Night, The Tempest, Love For Love* and *Macbeth.* Has also played in London in *Mary Read, Mary Tudor, Parnell,* etc. With Old Vic 1936-37 in *The Witch Of Edmonton, Hamlet, Henry V* and *Twelfth Night* (and acted in Elsinore in *Hamlet*). Has also acted in London in *Richard II, The Merchant Of Venice, The School For Scandal, Spring Meeting,* etc. Rejoined Old Vic in 1938, appearing in *Trelawney Of The Wells, Hamlet, The Ascent Of F.6* and others. 1939-42, with Old Vic Company on tour and also in London in *The Merchant Of Venice, King John, Othello, The Merry Wives Of Windsor* (all at the New). When the Old Vic took over Liverpool Playhouse he appeared in *Six Characters In Search Of An Author, Androcles And The Lion* and *Abraham Lincoln.* Recently in *The Witch* (Arts, 1943), toured in *Fighters Calling,* then joined the John Gielgud Company at the Haymarket, 1944-45, appearing in *Hamlet, A Midsummer Night's Dream, The Duchess Of Malfi.* In 1945 went to Burma with John Gielgud Company in *Hamlet.*

HARE, ROBERTSON. Actor. Born London, 1891. First appeared on stage in London in *Œdipus Rex* (Covent Garden, 1912), subsequently touring in the provinces. Began a long career of Aldwych farces in 1923 in *Tons Of Money,* followed by *A Cuckoo In The Nest, Rookery Nook, Thark, Plunder, A Cup Of Kindness, Turkey Time, Dirty Work,* etc. Has also acted in London in *Aren't Men Beasts!, A Spot Of Bother, Banana Ridge,* etc. In 1940 in *Spotted Dick* (Strand) and many others. In 1941 appeared in *Women Aren't Angels* (Strand). Recently : *She Follows Me About,* 1943-44 ; *Madame Louise* (Garrick, 1944-46).

HARKER, GORDON. Actor. Born London, 1885. Married to Christine Barry. Made his first appearance in London in *Much Ado About Nothing* (Imperial, 1903); subsequently acted with Oscar Asch until 1913. After the war acted in London in *The Garden Of Allah, Quality Street, The Ringer, Major Barbara, The Calendar, Suspense, The Case Of The Frightened Lady, The Phantom Light, Hyde Park Corner, The Frog, Number Six, The Gusher* and many others. Recently: *Saloon Bar* (Wyndham's, 1940), *Once A Crook* (Aldwych, 1940, and New, 1941), *Warn That Man* (Garrick, 1941-42), *Acacia Avenue* (Vaudeville, 1943-44), touring in *The Case Of The Frightened Lady*, 1945. Appeared in *The Poltergeist*, on tour, 1946.

HARRIS, ROBERT. Actor. Born Somerset, 1900. Educated at Oxford. Studied at Royal Academy of Dramatic Art, making his first appearance on the stage in *The Will* (St. Martin's, 1923). Subsequently in *Fledglings, The Way Things Happen, A Midsummer Night's Dream*, etc. First acted in New York in 1925 in *Easy Virtue* and later in *The Sacred Flame*. In London appeared in *The Marquise, The Amorists, The Silent Witness* and many others. Joined the Old Vic in 1931, appearing in *King John, The Taming Of The Shrew, A Midsummer Night's Dream, Henry V, Julius Cæsar, Twelfth Night, Hamlet*, etc. Also in the West End in *Richard Of Bordeaux, Strange Orchestra, The Wind And The Rain, Storm In A Teacup*. To New York in 1937 to play in *Candida*, returning to London to join the London Mask Theatre Company, appearing in *Mourning Becomes Electra, Troilus And Cressida, Marco Millions* and *The Family Reunion* (Westminster, 1937-39). Then in *After The Dance* (St. James's, 1939). In 1940 he appeared in *King Lear* (Old Vic), *Music At Night* (Westminster). Then 1940-44 with B.B.C., returning to the stage in *Tomorrow The World* (Aldwych, 1944-45). Appeared in *Death Of A Rat* (Lyric, Hammersmith, 1946); then joined Stratford-on-Avon Festival Company.

HARRISON, KATHLEEN. Actress. Born Blackburn, 1898. Studied at Royal Academy of Dramatic Art, making her first appearance on the stage in Eastbourne in *The Constant Flirt*, 1926. Acted in London in 1927 in *The Cage* (Court), followed by *Happy Families, Badger's Green, Jane's Legacy, Lover's Meeting, Line Engaged, Night Must Fall, I Killed The Count, Comedienne, The Corn Is Green* and many others. Recently: *The Corn Is Green* (Piccadilly, 1940), *Ducks And Drakes* (Apollo, 1942), *Flare Path* (Apollo, 1942-43).

HARRISON, REX. Actor. Born Huyton, 1908. Married to Lilli Palmer. First appeared on the stage in 1924 in *Thirty Minutes In A Street* with Liverpool Repertory Theatre, where he stayed until 1927. Made his first appearance in London at the Everyman Theatre, *Getting George Married*, 1930, subsequently touring in *After All, Other Men's Wives, Road House*. Then acted in London in *Another Language, Anthony And Anna, Man Of Yesterday, Short Story*, etc. Appeared in New York in 1936 in *Sweet Aloes*, returning to London in *Heroes Don't Care*. Then in *French Without Tears*, 1937-38, and in *Design For Living* (Haymarket and Savoy, 1939-40). In 1941 played in *No Time For Comedy* (Haymarket). Then in R.A.F., 1942-44. In 1945 he went to Hollywood.

HAWK, JEREMY. Actor. Born Johannesburg, May 20th, 1917. Educated Harrow. Made his first stage appearance on tour in *Housemaster*, 1939. Then in *New Faces* (Comedy, 1940), *Ladies In Retirement* (St. Martin's, 1940-41), *Twelfth Night* (Arts, 1942) and *The Springtime Of Others* (Arts, 1942). From 1942-46 in H.M. Forces.

HAWKINS, JACK. Actor. Born London, 1910. Studied for stage with Italia Conti, first appearing in *Where The Rainbow Ends* (Holborn Empire, 1923). Then played in London in *St. Joan, The Cenci, Young Woodley, Beau Geste*. Acted in America in *Journey's End*, 1929, returning in 1930 to appear in *The Breadwinner*; subsequently in the West End in *Autumn Crocus, While Parents Sleep, Service, As You Like It, A Midsummer Night's Dream, Twelfth Night, Comus, The*

Maitlands, The Frog, Much Ado About Nothing, A Winter's Tale, Autumn, Dear Octopus (New York, 1939). Played in *Hamlet* in London and Elsinore, 1939. Then in *The Tempest* and *King Lear* (Old Vic, 1940). 1940-45, in H.M. Forces, acting and producing for ENSA in the Far East.

HAWTREY, ANTHONY. Actor and producer. Born Claygate, 1909. Son of Sir Charles Hawtrey. Made his first appearance on the stage in *The Lady Of The Camelias* (Garrick, 1930), then joined Old Vic, 1930-31, after which he toured South Africa with Dennis Neilson-Terry. From 1934-35 with Liverpool Repertory Company. Appeared in London in *Power And Glory* (Savoy), *The Mother* (Garrick), *Inquest* (Duke of York's), etc. In 1940 appeared in *Outward Bound* (New), *Wuthering Heights* and *Jane Eyre* for CEMA. Recently : In *Happy Few* (Cambridge, 1944), *Green Laughter*, on tour. In 1945 became director of the Embassy Theatre, producing *Quality Street, The Skipper Next To God*, etc.

HAWTREY, CHARLES. Actor and producer. Born Hounslow, 1914. Studied for stage under Italia Conti, making his first appearance on the London stage in *Bluebell In Fairyland* (Scala, 1927). Subsequently in London in *Where The Rainbow Ends, Street Scene, Peter Pan, Your Number's Up, Bats In The Belfry, Members Only, Happy Returns, The Taming Of The Shrew* (Old Vic, 1939), etc. Recently appeared in *Counterfeit* (Duke of York's, 1940), *New Faces* (Comedy and Apollo, 1940-41), *New Ambassadors Revue* (Ambassadors, 1941), *Scoop* (Vaudeville, 1942). Then in *Old Chelsea* (Princes, 1943), *Merrie England* (Winter Garden, 1944). Made his first appearance in variety at Victoria Palace, 1945. Has produced a number of plays at Torch and Q Theatres, including *Alice In Wonderland* and *Oflag 3*, 1945.

HAYE, HELEN. Actress. Born India, 1874. Made her first appearance on the London stage in 1898 in *The Gypsy Earl* (Adelphi), thenceforth on tour in the provinces with Ben Greet and F. R. Benson. Subsequently appeared in London in *Hamlet, Twelfth Night, Above Suspicion, Hedda Gabler, The Great Adventure, Kipps, The Will, Fanny's First Play, Cæsar's Wife* and many others. Then in *The Skin Game, Secrets, Jack Straw, The Sea Urchin*, etc. Made her first appearance in New York in *The Last Of Mrs. Cheyney* (Fulton, 1925). Afterwards in London in *Fresh Fruit, A Damsel In Distress, After All, Let Us Be Gay, The Dubarry, Sixteen, Moonlight Is Silver, Golden Arrow, The School For Scandal* (Old Vic, 1936), *The Constant Wife*, etc. More recently in London in *The Housemaster, Paprika, The Western Chamber*, etc. In 1939 she appeared in *The Family Reunion* (Westminster) and *Pygmalion* (Haymarket). In 1941 she appeared in *The Nutmeg Tree* (Lyric). In 1943 in *Damaged Goods* (Whitehall).

HAYES, GEORGE. Actor. Born in London, 1888. Made his first appearance in Nottingham in *Hamlet*, 1912 ; then in London in *Hamlet* (Drury Lane, 1913). He toured the United States with Forbes-Robertson, and later with Sir Herbert Tree, returning to London in 1919 in *L'Aiglon* (Globe). Has also acted in London with the Everyman Company and later with the Old Vic Company, from 1923 until 1925. In 1926, he toured South Africa, returning to London in *The Beaux' Stratagem*, followed by *Paul I, La Prisonnière*, etc. In 1928 joined Stratford-on-Avon Festival Company, remaining until 1930. Toured United States in 1928-29 and again appeared at Stratford in 1930, playing in *Romeo And Juliet, Othello, Much Ado About Nothing*, etc. Has also acted in London in *The Ringer, Getting Married, Alice In Wonderland, The Golden Toy, Peter Pan, Paganini, Thank You, Mr. Pepys, The White Guard* and *Twelfth Night* (both with Michel St. Denis Season, Phœnix, 1938), *Johnson Over Jordan* (New and Saville, 1939), etc. Recently : Acted at Stratford-on-Avon Memorial Theatre, 1942 and 1944. In 1945 he appeared in *A Midsummer Night's Dream, The Merchant Of Venice*, at the Open Air.

HAYTHORNE, JOAN. Actress. Born London, 1915. Educated Eastbourne and in Paris. Made her first appearance on the stage with a French company, then studied for the stage at the Royal Academy of Dramatic Art, making her first appearance in England with the Manchester Repertory Company, 1934. Remained with this company until 1938. Then in repertory at Birmingham, before making her first appearance in London in *An Ideal Husband* (Westminster, 1943). Then acted in *The Philanderer* (Arts), *A Trip To Scarborough* (Arts), *The Rivals* (Garrison Theatre, Salisbury), etc. In 1945 acted in *Great Day* (Playhouse), *Young Mrs. Barrington* (Winter Garden).

HELPMANN, ROBERT. Actor, dancer and choreographer. Born South Australia, 1911. First appeared on the stage in Adelaide as solo dancer in 1923 and continued as principal dancer for J. C. Williamson until 1928. Came to London in 1931 and joined Sadlers Wells Ballet Company, remaining as principal dancer since that time. Has also appeared on the legitimate stage in London in *Precipice* (Savoy), *Stop Press* (Adelphi), *A Midsummer Night's Dream* (Old Vic), *The Insect Play* (Playhouse), *The Taming Of The Shrew* (Old Vic) and others. Recently in *Swinging The Gate* (Ambassadors, 1940). He played Hamlet (for the old Vic) in 1944 at the New. He is also well-known as a choreographer, among his ballets being *Hamlet, Comus, Miracle In The Gorbals* and *Adam Zero*.

HENSON, GLADYS. Actress. Born Dublin, 1897. Made her first appearance on stage in 1910 in *Alice In Wonderland* (Savoy); subsequently in the West End in *Buzz, Buzz, London, Paris and New York*, etc. Retired from stage until 1933 when she appeared in New York in *Design For Living*, returning to London in *Hay Fever* (Shaftesbury, 1933). Has also appeared in *Three Sisters*, and *Point Valaine, George And Margaret* (both in New York, 1935-37), *Operette, Set To Music* (New York, 1939-40), etc. Recently in London in *The Morning Star* (Globe, 1942), *Druid's Rest* (St. Martin's, 1944), etc.

HENSON, LESLIE. Actor and producer. Born London, 1891. Was formerly with a concert party, making his first appearance in London in *Sinbad The Sailor* (Dalston, 1910). Subsequently in the West End in *Nicely Thanks, Tonight's The Night* (and in New York, 1914), *The Admirable Crichton, Kissing Time, Sally, Kid Boots, Lady Luck, Funny Face, Follow Through, A Warm Corner, It's A Boy, Nice Goings On, Lucky Break, Seeing Stars, Swing Along, Going Greek, Running Riot* and many others. Has produced and presented many of the above productions in London. Recently: *Fine And Dandy* (Saville), *Up And Doing* (Saville, 1940-41). 1943-44: With *The Gaieties* he went to the Middle East, returning to London to appear in this revue at the Winter Garden and Saville, 1945. In 1945 he toured the Continent with his own concert party.

HEARNE, RICHARD. Actor. Born Norwich, 1909. Appeared in circus and variety with his parents. Made his first appearance on the London stage in *Dick Whittington* (Hippodrome, 1932), then in *Nice Goings On, Lucky Break, The Flying Trapeze, Seeing Stars, Swing Along, Going Greek, Running Riot*, etc. In 1940 in *Shephard's Pie* (Princes), then in *Up And Doing* (Saville, 1940-41), *Wild Rose* (Princes, 1941), *Fun And Games* (Princes, 1941-42) and other revues and pantomimes. In *Panama Hattie* (Piccadilly, 1944), *Goody Two Shoes* (Coliseum, 1944-45), *Big Boy* (Saville, 1945-46).

HENTSCHEL, IRENE. Producer. Born London, 1891. Married to Ivor Brown. Studied for the stage at R.A.D.A., made her first appearance on the stage in *The Fool And The Wise Man* (Princes, 1912). Subsequently in *Thérèse Raquin, The Eldest Son, Potash And Perlmutter*, etc. Joined the Lena Ashwell Players in 1919, acting and producing until 1925. Has also produced in London *The Unquiet Spirit, The Springtime Of Others, Eden End, Close Quarters, Anthony And Anna, Hedda Gabler, A Doll's House, Candida, Time And The Conways, Walk In The Sun, Punch Without Judy* and others. Among the plays she has recently produced are *On Approval, The Doctor's Dilemma, The Nutmeg Tree, They Came To A City, Lottie Dundass, Ten Little Niggers* and *The Years Between.* In 1946 she produced *Dandy Dick,* etc.

HERVEY, GRISELDA. Actress. Born Plomesgate, 1901. First appeared on the stage in 1919 with the Sir Frank Benson Company on tour; subsequently on the London stage in *The Pilgrim Of Eternity* (Duke of York's, 1921). Has also appeared in London in *The Enchanted Cottage, The Rivals, Easy Virtue, Berkeley Square, The Fanatics, By Candlelight, The School For Scandal, The Faithful Heart, The Rose Without A Thorn, The Philanthropist, The Island, The Robust Invalid* and many others. Recently: With the B.B.C. Drama Repertory Company.

HESLOP, CHARLES. Actor. Born Thames Ditton, 1883. First appeared on stage in *Kitty Grey* (Isle of Man, 1903); subsequently touring and running his own concert party. Toured Australia, 1923-25. Made his first appearance in London in *Easy Come, Easy Go* (Garrick, 1926), then in *Alice In Wonderland, The Co-Optimists, The Dubarry, After Dark, Streamline* and many other revues, musical comedies and straight plays. Has also acted in London in 1066 *And All That, The Last Of The Ladies.* Toured Australia 1936-37, returning to the West End in *On We Go* (Savoy), subsequently in *Paganini, The Laughing Cavalier,* 8.45 *And All That,* etc. Recently: *Revue Des Allies* (Prince of Wales, 1940), *Nap Hand* (Aldwych), *This Time It's Love* (Comedy, 1943), etc. In 1945 in *That'll Be The Day,* on tour.

HEWETT, CHRISTOPHER. Actor and singer. Born April 5th, 1922, in the Federated Malay States. Came to England and made his first appearance on the stage at the age of six in *The Sleeping Beauty.* Educated Beaumont College, then studied singing for two years, after which he served in the R.A.F. from 1938-41. More recently he appeared in *The Devil Without,* on tour, *Thunder Rock,* on tour, then at Oxford Playhouse, 1942 and 1943. Then on tour in *More New Faces,* after which he made first appearance in London in *The Merry Widow* (His Majesty's, 1943). Appeared in *Sweeter And Lower,* (Ambassadors, 1944-46).

HEWITT, HENRY. Actor. Born London, 1885. Made his first appearance on the stage in *A Midsummer Night's Dream* (Adelphi, 1905). Joined Sir Herbert Tree's Company until 1908, when he became a member of H. B. Irving's Company. He has acted in London in *The Lyons Mail, The Merry Wives Of Windsor, Romeo And Juliet, The Recruiting Officer, Little Women, Julius Cæsar, The Country Wife, The Wandering Jew, The Way Of The World, The Fanatics, The Matriarch, The School For Scandal, Hamlet, Dirty Work, The Green Bay Tree, The Rivals, As You Like It, Twelfth Night,* etc. Among the other plays in which he has appeared are 1066 *And All That, The Bat, People In Love, Official Secret, Little Stranger,* etc. In 1940 appeared in *Tony Draws A Horse* (Comedy). Then in 1943 played on tour in *Is Your Honeymoon Really Necessary?* In 1944 acted *How Are They At Home?* (Apollo), then toured with *The Lady From Edinburgh* on the Continent and afterwards at the Playhouse, 1945-46.

HICKMAN, CHARLES. Actor and producer. Born Snaresbrook, 1905. Studied for the stage at Royal Academy of Dramatic Art, making his first appearance on the stage in *Aren't We All* (Globe, 1923). Then on tour until 1927, when he acted in *The Price* at Q, before joining the Everyman Theatre Company in 1927. Has also acted in London in *Easter, The Clandestine Marriage, Bird In Hand* (also in New York, 1929, and on tour in the United States, 1930), *The Silent Witness, Bed Rock,* etc. With Old Vic in 1932. Among the other West End plays in which he has appeared are *For Ever, Viceroy Sarah, Elisabeth Of Austria, Ten Minute Alibi, The Return Of Peter Grimm,* etc. 1939-40: Producing in Edinburgh. In 1940 he produced a season of English comedies at the Vaudeville Theatre. In 1941 he appeared in *Big Top* (His Majesty's). In 1944 he acted (for the Old Vic) in *Hamlet* (New). Among the other plays he has recently produced in London are *Sweet And Low, Sweeter And Lower, Keep Going, Daughter Janie, The Lady From Edinburgh, Young Mrs. Barrington, The Vicar Of Wakefield*, etc. In 1946 he produced *Song Of Norway*.

HICKS, PATRICIA. Actress. Born Epping. Studied for the stage at Royal Academy of Dramatic Art, making her first appearance on the stage in *A Midsummer Night's Dream* (Open Air, 1939). More recently in *Tobias And The Angel* (Open Air, 1943), on tour with *Arsenic And Old Lace*, 1944, *The Assassin* (Savoy, 1945), *Arsenic And Old Lace* (Strand, 1945-46).

HICKS, SIR SEYMOUR. Actor, playwright and producer. Born Jersey, 1871. Married to Ellaline Terriss. First appeared on the stage in *In The Ranks* (Islington, 1887); subsequently in *The Ticket Of Leave Man, True Heart*, etc. Went to America in 1889 with the Kendals, reappearing in London in 1891 in *Aunt Jack*. He has appeared in scores of plays in England and America, including *The Transgressor, The Shop Girl, Cupboard Love, The Masked Ball, Alice In Wonderland, Scrooge, Quality Street, Bluebell In Fairyland, Edmund Kean, The Beauty Of Bath, Captain Kidd, Garrick, Broadway Jones, Sleeping Partners, Adam And Eve, The Man In Dress Clothes*, etc. He has also acted in London in *The Love Habit, The Guardsman, Mr. What's His Name, The Gay Adventure, It's You I Want, Vintage Wine, The Miracle Man, The Last Trump, Peter Pan, You're Telling Me* and many others. Is the author of the following plays : *Bluebell In Fairyland, This World Of Ours, The Price Of Silence, Sleeping Partners, Captain Kidd*, etc., and the following adaptations : *The Man In Dress Clothes, The Love Habit, Mr. What's His Name, Vintage Wine* (with Ashley Dukes) and many others. Since the outbreak of war has been in the Middle East for ENSA.

HICKSON, JOAN. Actress. Born Northampton, 1906. Studied for stage at the Royal Academy of Dramatic Art, making her first appearance on the stage in London in *The Tragic Muse* (Arts), then in *A Damsel In Distress, The Middle Watch, The Crime At Blossoms*, etc. From 1931-33 with Oxford Repertory Company, after which she appeared in London in *Summer's Lease, Distinguished Gathering, Murder Gang, The Gusher, It's A Wise Child* and many others. Recently : In 1940 appeared in *As You Are* (Aldwych). With the Walter Hudd Company on tour in *Village Wooing*. Also in London in *The Proposal* (Arts, 1942), *See How They Run* (Comedy, 1944), *Great Day* (Playhouse), *Appointment With Death* (Piccadilly, 1945). In *The Guinea Pig* (Criterion, 1946).

HIGNETT, H. R. Actor. Born Ringway, 1870. First appeared on the stage in 1893 in *Julius Cæsar* with F. R. Benson ; subsequently acting with this company until 1901. Has appeared in London in *If I Were King, Hamlet, As You Like It, Electra, Strife, King Lear, The Tragedy Of Nan, The Golden Fleece, The Dynasts, Peter Ibbetson, The Naughty Wife, Othello, Fanny's First Play* and many others. Has toured in South Africa and all over the British Isles. Other plays in which he has acted in the West End include *The Second Mrs. Tanqueray, Old English, The Cenci, Thérèse Raquin, Julius Cæsar, Richard Of Bordeaux, Men In White, Till The Cows Come Home, Bedtime Story, Romeo And Juliet, Power And Glory*, etc. In 1938 appeared with the Malvern Festival Company ; then in London in *Geneva* and *Number Six*. Recently : *The Tragedy Of Nan* (Mercury, 1943), *Halfway To Heaven* (Princes, 1943), *Emma* (St. James's, 1945).

HILLER, WENDY. Actress. Born Bramhall, Cheshire, 1912. Married to Ronald Gow. Studied for the stage as a student with the Manchester Repertory Company, making her first appearance there in *The Ware Case*, after which she played small parts and became assistant stage manager. In 1932 she toured in *Evensong*, then in 1932 on tour in *Love On The Dole*, in which play she first acted in London at the Garrick in 1935, also in New York in 1936. In 1936 with the Malvern Festival in *St. Joan* and *Pygmalion*. Recently appeared in *Cradle Song* (Apollo), toured in *Twelfth Night* with the Walter Hudd-CEMA Company, then in *The First Gentleman* (New and Savoy, 1945-46).

HILLIARD, PATRICIA. Actress. Born Quetta, India, 1916. Married to William Fox. Studied for the stage at the Royal Academy of Dramatic Art, first appearing in *The Copy* (Q, 1935), then in London in *A Family Man, Call It A Day, Up The Garden Path, I Have Been Here Before, Under Suspicion, The Distant Hand*, etc. Recently : *Wuthering Heights*, on tour, 1944, the Bernard Shaw Season at the Lyric, Hammersmith, appearing in *Too True To Be Good, The Dark Lady Of The Sonnets, Candida*, 1944-45 ; *No Medals* (Vaudeville, 1946).

HINDLE, WINIFRED. Actress. Born November 26th, 1900. Educated in Switzerland and studied for the stage at Royal Academy of Dramatic Art. Made her first appearance in *The Naughty Wife*, on tour, after which she appeared in repertory in Birmingham, Manchester, Edinburgh and Hull. Made her first appearance in London in *The Cup Of Happiness*. More recently appeared in *The Light Of Heart* (Globe, 1939), *The Morning Star* (Globe, 1941-42), *A Month In The Country* (St. James's, 1943), *A Soldier For Christmas* (Wyndham's, 1944), *Under The Counter* (Phœnix, 1945-46).

HINTON, MARY. Actress. Born London, 1896. First appeared on the stage in *Monsieur Beaucaire* in Australia, 1925. Then in England toured with Sir Seymour Hicks in *Mr. What's His Name*, after which she joined the Liverpool Repertory Company, 1927-28. Acted in London in *Payment* (Arts, 1928), then in *The Immortal Lady, While Parents Sleep, The Roof, Family Affairs, Mary Tudor, Waste, Bonnet Over The Windmill, Mary Goes To See* and many others. Also appeared in the West End in *The Masque Of Kings, Private History, The Intruder*, etc. Recently : *The Springtime Of Others* (Arts, 1942), *Claudia* (St. Martin's, 1942-44), *Great Day* (Playhouse, 1945). She appeared in *The Sacred Flame* (St. Martin's and Westminster, 1945-46).

HINZE, GERARD. Actor. Born Berlin, 1904. Educated on the Continent. Made his first appearance on the stage in 1922, subsequently appeared in Hamburg, Berlin, Vienna, Zurich and Odessa. For a long period ran his own theatre in Odessa, and also produced in Hamburg. On the outbreak of war spent one year in a German concentration camp, finally coming to England where he appeared in *Flare Path* (Apollo, 1941-43). He has recently acted in *Zero Hour* (Lyric, 1944), and *Appointment With Death* (Piccadilly, 1945), *The Shouting Dies* (Lyric, Hammersmith, 1945), *Dutch Family* (Arts Theatre, 1946).

HODGE, MERTON. Playwright. Born Gisborne, New Zealand, 1904. Among the plays he has written are *The Wind And The Rain, Grief Goes Over, The Island* and the following adaptations : *Men In White, The Orchard Walls, Story Of An African Farm*.

HOEY, IRIS. Actress. Born London, 1885. Studied at the Royal Academy of Dramatic Art, first appearing on the stage in *The Tempest* (His Majesty's, 1904). Subsequently in the West End in *The Geisha, The Merry Wives Of Windsor, The School For Scandal, Madame X, Baby Mine, The Pearl Girl, To-night's The Night*, (in New York, 1914), *The Belle Of New York, The Man From Toronto, Just A Girl, Summer Lightning, Sylvia, Tell Me The Truth, The Rivals* and many others. She has also appeared in *The Man In Possession, Belinda, The Age Of Youth, The Young Idea, Dinner At Eight, Twelfth Night, The Comedy Of Errors, Mary Read, The Alchemist, The Country Wife, Uneasy Living*, etc. Recently : *The Blue Goose* (Comedy, 1941), *Actresses Will Happen* (Apollo, 1941), *Peter Pan* (Winter Garden, 1943), *Pink String And Sealing Wax* (Duke of York's, 1943-44), etc. In 1945 appeared in *The Vicar Of Wakefield*.

HOFFE, MONCKTON. Playwright. Born Connemara, Ireland, 1880. Formerly an actor, he has written a number of plays, including *The Missing Hand, The Little Damozel, The Faithful Heart, Pomp And Circumstance, The Crooked Friday, Many Waters*, and the adaptations *Carminetta* and *The Blue Mazurka*.

HOLDEN, JUNE. Actress. Born Heysham, September 21st, 1922. Studied at the Royal Academy of Dramatic Art. She made her first appearance on the stage at the age of four, and her first West End appearance in *Bluebell In Fairyland* (Scala, 1935). She appeared in two seasons of Shakespeare at the Open Air Theatre, on tour in *More New Faces, Lady Behave, Nine Till Six*, etc. On tour in Europe in *Saloon Bar*, 1945. Recently in *The Lady From Edinburgh* (Playhouse, 1945), *Peter Pan* (Scala, 1945-46).

HOLLES, ANTONY. Actor. Born London, 1901. Educated at Latymer. Made his first appearance on the stage in *Son And Heir* (Brighton, 1916), then in London in *Charley's Aunt* (St. James's, 1916). Also acted in *Little Women, Carnival, A Family Affair*, etc. Toured Australia in 1925-27, then appeared in New York in *Diplomacy*, 1928. Has also acted in London in *Two Women, Take A Chance, See Naples And Die, Sheppey, Libel, The Ghost Train, The Composite Man, I Killed The Count, Tony Draws A Horse*, etc. Recently : *Scandal At Barchester* (Lyric and Wyndham's, 1944-45) ; *Song Of Norway* (Palace, 1946).

HOLLOWAY, BALIOL. Actor. Born Brentwood, 1883. First appeared on the stage in *The Merchant Of Venice*, on tour, 1898 ; subsequently on tour in Shakespearean companies until 1903, when he first appeared in the West End in *The Man And His Picture* (Kingsway). 1907-12, with the Benson Company ; then appeared in London in *Androcles And The Lion, The Witch, The Tragedy Of Nan, The Merchant Of Venice, Henry V*, etc. 1921-25, appeared with the New Shakespeare Company at Stratford-on-Avon. Subsequently in London in *The Alchemist, Twelfth Night, Richard III, The Country Wife* and many others. Made his first appearance in New York in *Cyrano De Bergerac* (Century, 1924). 1925-27, with the Old Vic Company. In 1928 toured Canada and, on his return, acted in London in *The School For Scandal, Major Barbara, Hamlet, Treasure Island, Measure For Measure, The Merry Wives Of Windsor*, etc. More recently in the West End in *Julius Cæsar, The Silver Box, The Cathedral, The Rivals, Diplomacy*, and many others. Appeared with the Stratford-on-Avon Festival Company in 1934 and at the Open Air Theatre, 1935-36 in *As You Like It, A Midsummer Night's Dream, Love's Labour's Lost, Henry VIII* and others. Then in the West End in *Œdipus Rex, The Road To Ruin* and many others. Recently : Appeared with Stratford-on-Avon Festival Company, 1942, in *The Merchant Of Venice*, etc., and in 1943 in *Henry V, King Lear, The Critic*, etc. In 1944 he appeared in *Mine Hostess* (Arts), *Peter Pan* (Cambridge) and *Jenny Jones* (Hippodrome, 1944-45). Subsequently with the York Festival Company in *The Spinster Of South Street, The Confederacy* and *The Alchemist*.

HOLLOWAY, STANLEY. Actor. Made his first appearance on the stage in *Kissing Time* (Winter Garden, 1919). He was a member of the original " Co-Optimists " from 1924-27. Has also appeared in the West End in *Hit The Deck, Sons Of The Sea, The Co-Optimists Of* 1930, *Savoy Follies, Three Sisters, All Wave, London Rhapsody* and numerous pantomimes. Recently : In *Fine And Dandy* (Saville), *Up And Doing* (Saville, 1940-41). Since 1942 he has been extensively engaged in filming.

HOLLOWAY, W. E. Actor. Born Adelaide, South Australia, 1885. Made his first appearance on the stage in Johannesburg in *Othello* 1911. With Matheson Lang toured South Africa and the Far East until 1912 ; then with his own company toured until 1921 in the Far East. Came to England in 1921 and toured the provinces until 1926. First appeared in London in *Napoleon* (New, 1932); subsequently in *As You Like It, A Midsummer Night's Dream, The Tempest, Maternité, Clive Of India, A Man's House, Henry IV*. Appeared at the Open Air Theatre 1936, 1938 and 1939. Also acted in London in *Dracula, Triumph, Henry V, Macbeth, Much Ado About Nothing* and *Pericles*. Recently : *With* Basil Langton's Travelling Repertory Theatre, on tour and at Birmingham

Playhouse. Also in *The Moon Is Down* (Whitehall, 1943). With the Stratford-on-
Avon Festival Company, 1944 and 1945. In *Romeo and Juliet* (King's, 1946).

HOLME, STANFORD. Actor and producer. Born St. Jean de Luz, France,
1904. Married to Thea Holme. First appeared on the stage in *The Rattlesnake*
(Shaftesbury, 1922), then in *The Green Goddess*. With the Ben Greet Players from
1924 to 1928. Then toured the provinces in *Rookery Nook* and *Thark* before
becoming producer of Oxford Repertory Company, 1931-39. Has acted in London
at the Open Air Theatre in 1938 in *The Tempest, Twelfth Night, Lysistrata, As
You Like It*. Since the war has been touring with the Stanford Holme-CEMA
Company and has also appeared in *The Cherry Orchard* (New, 1941), *Magic*
(Arts), *The Proposal* (Arts, 1942), *Lady Precious Stream* (Open Air Theatre, 1944),
She Stoops To Conquer (Orpheum), etc. Recently with his own company, for
CEMA, touring *Village Wooing, Man Of Destiny, She Stoops To Conquer, Lady
Precious Stream, Sheppey* and *Twelfth Night*, 1943-45. In season at King's, 1946.

HOLME, THEA. Actress. Born London, 1907. Married to Stanford Holme.
Studied for the stage at the Central School of Dramatic Art under Elsie Fogerty,
making her first appearance on the stage in *A Midsummer Night's Dream* (Richmond,
1924). With the Ben Greet Players in 1924-25, appearing in England and Paris.
Toured the provinces in *Rookery Nook* and *Thark*, 1927-28, then went with this
company to United States, 1929-30. She has also appeared in London in *Leave It
To Psmith* (Golders Green, 1930), after which she acted in the West End in *She
Passed Through Lorraine, Hamlet, I Lived With You, The Cathedral, Wild Decembers,
Beau Brummell, Private Room, Royal Baggage, For Ever, The Convict, Lady
Precious Stream, Black Swans* and many others. Has also appeared in *As You
Like It, St. Joan, Reunion In Vienna*, etc. In 1942 appeared in *Macbeth* (Piccadilly).
Recently with Stanford Holme Company touring for CEMA in *She Stoops To
Conquer*, etc. Also in *Lady Precious Stream*, Open Air Theatre, 1944.

HOMAN, DAVID. Designer. Born Oslo, Norway, 1907. Has designed costumes
and scenery for many West End plays, including *Children In Uniform, Admirals
All, Living Dangerously*. From 1934-37 designing many productions at the
Embassy. Also *A Spot Of Bother, Night Alone, Hide And Seek, The Last Straw,
Plan For A Hostess, Comedienne, Tony Draws A Horse*, etc. 1939-40: Designed
a number of productions for the London Mask Theatre at the Westminster,
including *Music At Night, Major Barbara, Desire Under The Elms*, etc. Since
1940 in H.M. Forces.

HONER, MARY. Actress and dancer. Born London, 1914. Married to Peter
Bell. Studied dancing under Espinosa, Legat, Nicholeva, Harold Turner. Made
her first appearance on the stage in *Bluebell In Fairyland* (Scala, 1927), also in
London in *Aladdin* and *The Gay Hussar*. In 1935 joined the Sadlers Wells Ballet
Company, remaining until 1943. Also appeared in *Rise And Shine* (Drury Lane).
Since 1943 has appeared with the Robert Atkins Company at the Open Air Theatre.
Also with the Stratford-on-Avon Festival Company, 1944 and again in 1945.

HOPPER, VICTORIA. Actress. Born Vancouver, Canada, 1913. Married to
Basil Dean. Studied for the stage at the Webber-Douglas School. First appeared
on the stage in *Martine* (Webber-Douglas, 1933), which was transferred to the
Cambridge. Then in London in *Three Sisters, Cornelius, Comus, The Melody
That Got Lost* and others. Also acted in *Autumn, The Boy David*, etc. In 1939
appeared in *Johnson Over Jordan* (New). Recently: *The Shop At Sly Corner*
(St. Martin's, 1945-46).

HORNE, DAVID. Actor and producer. Born Balcombe, 1898. Educated Eton
and Sandhurst. Married to Ann Farrer. First appeared on the stage in his father's
company (Anmer Hall) in 1925; then in London in *Billeted* (Royalty, 1926).
Also in London in *The Awful Truth, A Month In The Country, The Cradle Song
The Beaux' Strategem, The Kingdom Of God, Young Woodley, Journey's End,*

and many others. Has also acted in the West End in *The Roof, Insult, A Doll's House, The Life Machine, Hamlet* (in New York, 1931), *Jonah And The Whale, Antony And Cleopatra, Richard II, Duet In Floodlight, The Philanthropist, Love From A Stranger, Dusty Ermine, Suspect, Robert's Wife, Lot's Wife, The Importance Of Being Earnest,* etc. In 1941 appeared in *Under One Roof* (St. Martin's). Recently : *Pink String And Sealing Wax* (Duke of York's, 1943), *The Last Of Mrs. Cheyney* (Westminster, 1944) and touring with his own company.

HORNE, KENNETH. Playwright. Born London, 1900. Educated King's College. Among his plays are *Half A Million, Miss Cinders, Yes And No, Tree Of Eden, The Good Young Man, Wasn't It Odd?* and *Jane Steps Out.* Recently: *Love In A Mist* (St. Martin's, 1942).

HORNSBY, NANCY. Actress. Born London, 1910. Married to Claud Gurney. Studied for the stage at Royal Academy of Dramatic Art, making her first appearance on the stage in *Hamlet* (Haymarket, 1931). Subsequently in *Gallows Glorious, The Mocking Bird.* With Croydon Repertory Company in 1932, and in 1933-34. Joined the Old Vic Company in 1934 and appeared in *Antony And Cleopatra, Richard II, Much Ado About Nothing, The Three Sisters, The School For Scandal,* etc. During 1936 in repertory at Edinburgh and Glasgow ; then appeared in London in *Spring Tide, Women Of Property, Bulldog Drummond Hits Out,* etc. Recently : With Old Vic Company, Liverpool, 1942-43. Also in *The Sulky Fire* (Arts, 1944).

HOWARD, SYDNEY. Actor. Born Yeadon, Yorkshire, 1885. First appeared with a concert party in 1912, subsequently toured in revue and musical comedy. Made first appearance on the London stage in *Box O' Tricks* (Hippodrome, 1919), afterwards touring in revue in the provinces, and in South Africa. In the West End appeared in *Hit The Deck, Funny Face, The Co-Optimists, Heads Up, It's A Boy, Night Of The Garter, Half-A-Crown, Anything Goes, Wild Oats* and many others. Recently : *Shephard's Pie* (Princes, 1940-41), *Fun And Games* (Princes, 1941-42), *Night Of The Garter,* (Strand, 1942), *Magic Carpet* (Princes, 1943), *Halfway To Heaven* (Princes, 1943), *Dandy Dick,* 1945-46.

HOWARD, TREVOR. Actor. Born September 29th, 1915, Brantford, Ontario. Married to Helen Cherry. Studied at R.A.D.A. Appeared on the London stage in *French Without Tears* (Criterion, 1936-38), then in repertory at Colchester, Harrogate, etc. Appeared at the Stratford-on-Avon Festival, 1939. From 1940-43 in H.M. Forces. Returned to the stage in *The Recruiting Officer* (Arts, 1943). Then in *On Life's Sunny Side* (Arts, 1943), *A Soldier For Christmas* (Wyndham's, 1944), *Anna Christie* (Arts, 1945).

HOWE, GEORGE. Actor. Born Valparaiso, 1900. Educated Harrow and Oxford. Studied for the stage at the Royal Academy of Dramatic Art, making his first appearance in *Robert E. Lee* (Regent, 1923). Subsequently appeared at Stratford-on-Avon, 1924, and with Birmingham Repertory Company, 1925. Since then in London in *The Firebrand, Rosmersholm, The Squall, Charlot's Revue Of 1928, Beau Geste,* etc. With the Old Vic, 1930-31, acting in *The Tempest, The Jealous Wife, Twelfth Night, King Lear,* etc. Thenceforth in the West End in *Richard Of Bordeaux, Miracle At Verdun, Peter Pan, Queen Of Scots, Romeo And Juliet, Hamlet* and *The Lady Of La Paz.* With the Old Vic in 1937, appeared in *Hamlet* and visited Elsinore in the same play. Joined the John Gielgud Company appearing in *Richard II, The School For Scandal, The Three Sisters* and *The Merchant Of Venice* (Queen's, 1937-38). More recently in *An Elephant In Arcady, Marco Millions, Sugar Plum* and others. In 1939 appeared in *Hamlet* in Denmark, returning to London in *The Importance Of Being Earnest* ; in 1941 appeared in *Dear Brutus* (Globe). In 1942 in *Salt Of The Earth* (Vaudeville), then in *A Night In Venice* (Cambridge, 1944-46). Recently produced *The Italian Straw Hat* (Arts, 1945).

HOWES, BOBBY. Actor. Born London, 1895. Made his first appearance on the stage at the Battersea Palace in a Boy Scout scena ; then toured in variety theatres and with concert parties until 1923. In the West End acted in *The Little Revue Starts At Nine* (Little, 1923), then in *Six Cylinder Love, The Punch Bowl, The Blue Kitten, The Blue Train, The Yellow Mask, Mr. Cinders, For The Love Of Mike,* and many others. Also appeared in London in *Tell Her The Truth, Yes, Madam, Please Teacher, Hide And Seek, Bobby Get Your Gun,* etc. Recently : *All Clear* (Queen's, 1940), *Let's Face It* (Hippodrome, 1942-43), *Halfway To Heaven* (Princes, 1943) and in variety at Victoria Palace, 1945. In 1946 he appeared in *Here Come The Boys,* (Saville).

HOWLETT, NOEL. Actor and producer. Born Maidstone, 1901. First appeared on the stage at Folkestone in 1925, subsequently in repertory and on tour until 1935. Producer at Hull, Watford and Margate Repertory Theatre. First appeared in London in *England Expects* (Embassy, 1936), then in *Professor Bernhardi, The Tiger, Charles The King, George And Margaret* and others. Since the outbreak of war, producing and acting for ENSA in the Middle and Far East.

HSIUNG, S. I. Playwright. Born Nanchang, China, 1902. Educated Peking University. Among his better-known plays are *Lady Precious Stream, The Western Chamber* and *The Professor From Peking.*

HUDD, WALTER. Actor and producer. Born London, 1898. Made his first appearance on the stage in *The Manxman* (Aldershot, 1919) ; subsequently toured in the provinces and in South Africa and the Far East. First appeared in London in *Ancient Lights* (Everyman, 1923), then in *The Way Things Happen, We Moderns, Hamlet, The Ghost Train, Their Wife,* etc. With Sybil Thorndike toured South Africa, 1928-29. Has also acted in London in *Hedda Gabler, Too True To Be Good, Richard Of Bordeaux,* etc. Toured America in 1930 in *Journey's End.* Other plays in which he has appeared in the West End are *On The Rocks, Viceroy Sarah, Lover's Leap, Youth At The Helm, England Expects, Goodbye To Yesterday, Geneva,* etc. In 1940 appeared in *Follow My Leader* (Apollo). Appeared in *Thunder Rock* (St. Martin's, 1941), then in Old Vic tour of *The Time Of Your Life.* Acted in Old Vic production of *The Cherry Orchard* (New, 1941). Recently in *A Man With Red Hair* (St. Martin's, 1942), *Twelfth Night* (Arts, 1942). Since 1942 has been touring extensively with his own company for CEMA. His productions include *Hedda Gabler, Twelfth Night, The Shoemaker's Holiday, Mine House, Candida* and *You Never Can Tell.* Appeared in his own production of *Village Wooing* (Orpheum, 1942) and also in *Hedda Gabler* (Westminster, 1943), *The Shoemaker's Holiday* (Lyric, Hammersmith, 1944), *Little Eyolf* and *The New Morality* (Embassy, 1945), etc. In 1946 he toured the Continent.

HULBERT, CLAUDE. Actor. Born London, 1900. Educated at Cambridge. Married to Enid Trevor. First appeared on the stage in a music-hall show at Bradford in 1920 ; subsequently in London in *Fantasia* (Queen's, 1921). Also in *Primrose, Tell Me More, Kid Boots, Sunny, Oh Kay!, Dear Love, Follow A Star* and many others. Acting in films 1932-39. Then in *Worth A Million* (Saville). Recently in *Panama Hattie* (Piccadilly, 1943-44). Entertained troops in Africa 1945.

HULBERT, JACK. Actor, dramatic author and producer. Born Ely, 1892. Educated Westminster and Cambridge. Married to Cicely Courtneidge. Studied for the stage at the Central School of Dramatic Art, making his first appearance on the professional stage in *The Pearl Girl* (Shaftesbury, 1913) ; later in *The Cinema Star, The Arcadians, See Saw, Bubbly,* etc. Also appeared in London in *Lord Richard In The Pantry, Pot Luck, The Little Revue Starts At Nine, By The Way* (also in New York, 1925), *Lido Lady, Clowns In Clover, Follow A Star, Folly To Be Wise,* etc. From 1931-38 acting in films, reappearing on the stage in *Under Your Hat* (Palace, 1938-39). Recently in *Full Swing* (Palace, 1942-43), *Something In The Air* (Palace, 1943-44). Among his productions are *By The Way, On With The Show, Lido Lady, Clowns In Clover, Hide And Seek, Under*

Your Hat, Full Swing, Something In The Air, etc. Is also part-author of many of the above. In 1945 produced *Sweet Yesterday* (Adelphi), *Under The Counter* (Phœnix), etc. In 1946 he appeared in *Here Come The Boys*, (Saville).

HUNT, HUGH. Producer. Born Camberley, 1911. Educated Marlborough and Oxford. Was a member of the O.U.D.S., producing *King Lear* at the New in 1933. In 1934 produced at Norwich Maddermarket ; then at Croydon Repertory Theatre, 1934-35. Also produced in London *King Lear, Rose And Glove, Children In Uniform, Othello*, etc., at the Westminster in 1935. Since 1935 has been producing regularly at the Abbey, Dublin. Also produced *The White Steed* in New York, 1939 and *Shadow And Substance* at the Duke of York's, London, in 1943. Appointed producer for the Old Vic at Bristol, 1946.

HUNT, MARTITA. Actress. Born in Argentine, 1900. Studied for the stage under Lady Benson, making her first appearance on the stage in 1921 with the Liverpool Repertory Company. Made her first appearance in London in *The Machine Wreckers* (Kingsway, 1923). Then in *A Doll's House, The Cherry Orchard, The Three Sisters, Potiphar's Wife, Rasputin* and many others. Also acted with the Old Vic, 1929-30 in *Romeo And Juliet, The Merchant Of Venice, The Imaginary Invalid, Richard II, A Midsummer Night's Dream, Julius Cæsar, Hamlet*, etc. Subsequently in the West End in *Topaze, Twelve Hours, Autumn Crocus, Fresh Fields, The Distaff Side, A Midsummer Night's Dream, Moonlight Is Silver, Frolic Wind, The Seagull, Wise Tomorrow, Othello* (Old Vic, 1938), *The Marriage Of Blood*, etc. In 1939 joined the Actor's Company, appearing in *Great Expectations* (Rudolf Steiner), subsequently on tour with John Gielgud's Company in *Dear Brutus*. Recently : *An Ideal Husband* (Westminster, 1943-44).

HUNTLEY, RAYMOND. Actor. Born Birmingham, 1904. Made his first appearance on the stage with the Birmingham Repertory Company in 1922, remaining here until 1924. First appeared in London in *Back To Methuselah* (Court, 1924), then toured in *The Farmer's Wife* and in repertory until 1927. Played *Dracula* in London, then toured 1928-30 with this play in America. Made his first appearance on the New York stage in *The Venetian Glass Nephew* (Vanderbilt, 1931), returning to England to play in repertory at Birmingham, Edinburgh and Glasgow. Appeared in London in *Clear The Wires, Clive Of India, The White Guard, Cornelius, Richard III, St. Helena, Bees On The Boat-deck, Young Madame Conti* (and in New York, 1937), *The First Legion, Time And The Conways, Glorious Morning, When We Are Married, Rhondda Roundabout* and many others. In 1940 appeared in *Rebecca*. Also in *They Came To A City* (Globe, 1943), *Private Lives* (Apollo, 1944-45), tour of *Oh Josephine*, 1945.

HUTCHESON, DAVID. Actor. Born Craigmore, Scotland, 1905. Educated Tonbridge. Made his first appearance on the stage in *The Lash* (Q, 1926). Subsequently in *Meet The Wife, The Yellow Mask*, etc. . To New York in 1929 in *Sons O' Guns* (Imperial), *Meet My Sister* (Shubert), *Free For All* (Manhattan), returning to London in *Strange Orchestra* (St. Martin's, 1932). Also in the West End in *Mother O' Pearl, Nice Goings On, Happy Week-End, Lucky Break, Gay Masquerade, This'll Make You Whistle, And On We Go*, etc. Since the outbreak of war in H.M. Forces.

HUTCHINSON, HARRY. Actor. Born Dublin, Ireland, 1892. Made his first appearance on the stage at the Queen's, Dublin, in *A Daughter Of Ireland*, 1911. Then made his first appearance in London in *The Playboy Of The Western World* (Court, 1912), after which he acted with the Abbey Theatre, Dublin, until 1916. First appeared in New York in *Patriots*, 1913. From 1916-20 toured with the Irish Players, playing in London and New York, and also toured in Australia. Appeared in London in *Juno And The Paycock, The Playboy Of The Western World, The Plough And The Stars, The Shadow Of A Gunman*, then toured the United States in 1927-28. Also in London in *General John Regan, The Anatomist*

Ourselves Alone, The Moon In The Yellow River, Parnell, Ah Wilderness, Oscar Wilde, The Phantom Light and many others. Since the war he has been acting with the B.B.C. Repertory Company; and in 1943 appeared in *Shadow And Substance* (Duke of York's).

HYSON, DOROTHY. Actress. Born Chicago, U.S.A., 1915. Married to Robert Douglas. On the stage as a child since 1927, then studied at the Royal Academy of Dramatic Art. Subsequently appeared in *Flies In The Sun* (Playhouse, 1933), and *Saturday's Children, Touch Wood, Ringmaster,* etc. On New York stage in *Most Of The Game* (Court, 1935), returning to London in *Pride And Prejudice* (St. James's, 1936). Also in London in *To Have And To Hold, The Melody That Got Lost, Three Blind Mice, A Midsummer Night's Dream, Only Yesterday,* etc. Recently : In 1941 appeared in *Under One Roof* (St. Martin's), *Pink String And Sealing Wax* (Duke of York's, 1943), *Scandal At Barchester* (Lyric and Wyndham's, 1944-45), *Lady Windermere's Fan* (Haymarket, 1945).

IDEN, ROSALIND. Actress. Born in Manchester. Daughter of Ben Iden-Payne, director of Stratford Memorial Theatre, 1936-40. She trained as a dancer under Karsavina, then acted with the Arts League Travelling Theatre for the next six years. Has been leading lady in the Donald Wolfit Company since 1939, appearing in London seasons at St. James's, Vaudeville, Scala, Winter Garden and Westminster in such plays as *Hamlet, The Merchant Of Venice, Twelfth Night, Much Ado About Nothing, Othello, The Master Builder, King Lear* and many others.

ILIFF, NOEL. Actor and producer. Born London, 1902. Educated St. Edmund's School, Canterbury. Made his first appearance on the stage in *The Man Who Ate The Popomack,* Cambridge Festival, 1928. Then on tour and in various repertory companies, including a season at the Gate, Dublin. In Dublin produced *King Lear, Ghosts, The Pleasure Garden,* etc. At Oxford produced *The Circle Of Chalk, Pygmalion,* etc., and at the Festival Theatre, Cambridge, *The Silver Tassie, Uncle Vanya, John Gabriel Borkman, The Importance Of Being Earnest,* etc. In London has produced at the Grafton and Q, and also *A Comedy Of Good And Evil* at the Gate. In 1940 he appeared in *A House In The Square* (St. Martin's). Recently produced *The Rivals* for the Arts Theatre Festival of Comedy, 1943. Since 1940 has been producing for the B.B.C.

INGHAM, MICHAEL. Actor. Born Nottingham, 1922. Educated Claysmore. Made his first appearance on the stage in a children's matinée (Rudolf Steiner Hall, 1930), after which he appeared as a juvenile in a number of shows in 1940 and again in 1941. Appeared at Stratford-on-Avon with the Shakespeare Festival Company, appearing in many of Shakespeare's plays and also in *The Doctor's Dilemma* and *Candida.* From 1941-44 served with the R.A.F. On being invalided out he joined the Greta Douglas Company and appeared in *St. Joan, Richard II* and *The Taming Of The Shrew* (Open Air Season, Liverpool, 1944). Then appeared in *The Rivals* (Salisbury Garrison Theatre, 1944). Recently appeared in *The Critic* (Arts, 1944), and in *As You Like It, The Merchant Of Venice* and *A Midsummer Night's Dream* at the Open Air Theatre, Regent's Park, 1945.

IRELAND, ANTHONY. Actor. Born Peru, 1902. Studied for the stage at the Royal Academy of Dramatic Art, making his first appearance on the stage in *The Rivals* (Lyric, Hammersmith, 1925). Subsequently toured with Phyllis Neilson-Terry; then appeared in London in *The Three Sisters, The Combined Maze, The White Chateau, Thérèse Raquin, Rope, The Importance Of Being Earnest,* etc. Also in London in *The Nelson Touch* ; then in New York in *The Sex Fable* (Henry Miller, 1931). Other West End plays in which he has appeared are *Richard Of Bordeaux, Ten Minute Alibi, Othello, Duet In Floodlight, The Lady Of La Paz, The Taming Of The Shrew, The Flashing Stream* (and in New York, 1939). In 1940 appeared in *The Light Of Heart* (Apollo and Globe) ; then in H.M. Forces. Has written a play, *Byron In Piccadilly.* In *Dear Evelyn,* 1946.

IRVING, ELLIS. Actor. Born Sydney, Australia, 1902. Married to Sophie Stewart. Made his first appearance on the stage in *Macbeth*, Tasmania, 1923 ; then with a Shakespearean Company until 1927. Toured Australia with Renée Kelly and Margaret Bannerman until 1930, when he came to London to appear in *Marigold* (Kingsway) (also in New York, 1930). Toured Canada with Sir Barry Jackson, 1931-32, returning to London in *Once In A Lifetime*. Also in the West End in *Spring, 1600, Whiteoaks, Antony And Cleopatra, The Boy David, Satyr, Macbeth* (for Old Vic), *Death On The Table*, etc. Recently : *Mr. Bolfry* (Westminster, 1944), *My Sister Eileen* (Savoy, 1944), *The Vicar Of Wakefield*, 1945.

IRVING, LAURENCE. Artist and designer. Born London, 1897. Designed sets and costumes for *Vaudeville Vanities*, 1926 ; also *Heat Wave, The Good Companions, Clive Of India, Murder In The Cathedral, Banana Ridge, The Sun Never Sets*. Has also worked on films in Hollywood. Recently designed *Three Waltzes* (Princes), *The First Gentleman* (New and Savoy), etc.

ISHAM, GYLES. Actor. Born Lamport, 1903. Educated Rugby and Oxford. Was a member of the O.U.D.S., making his first appearance on the professional stage in *And So To Bed* (Huddersfield, 1927). First acted in London in *The Spook Sonata* (Strand, 1927). Was with J. B. Fagan at Oxford in 1927 and went with him to New York, appearing in *And So To Bed, The Queen's Husband, The Cherry Orchard*. Returned to England to appear in *Such Men Are Dangerous*, 1928. Joined Old Vic in 1929, then Stratford-on-Avon Festival Company in 1930, touring with this company in the United States until 1932. Has also appeared in London in *Justice, This Side Idolatry, A Rose Without A Thorn, Family Affairs*, etc. To Hollywood in 1935, returning in *The Admirable Crichton* (Embassy, 1935). Then in *The Dog Beneath The Skin, Lady Precious Stream, Henry VIII, The Tempest, Twelfth Night, As You Like It, Love's Labour's Lost*, etc. Also in London in *Old Music, A Midsummer Night's Dream* ; then with Stratford-on-Avon Festival Company in 1938. In the West End in *Macbeth* and *The Ascent Of F.*6 (Old Vic, 1939). Since the war in H.M. Forces.

JACKSON, SIR BARRY. Producer. Born Birmingham, 1879. Is the founder and director of the Birmingham Repertory Theatre, founded in 1913 and still successfully operating to-day. Among the plays first produced under his auspices are *Abraham Lincoln, Back To Methuselah, The Farmer's Wife, Yellow Sands, Bird In Hand*, etc. Since its foundation Birmingham Repertory Theatre has produced over 500 plays and operas. Sir Barry has also produced seasons at the Court, Kingsway, Haymarket, etc., and was director of Malvern Summer Festivals, 1929-37. Adapted plays, *Too Clever By Half* from Griboyedov, *The Doctor's Delight* from Molière. Produced at Birmingham Repertory Theatre, 1944-45 and recently resumed active directorship of this theatre. In 1946 became director of Stratford-on-Avon Memorial Theatre.

JACKSON, FREDA. Actress. Born Nottingham, 1909. First appeared on the stage with the Nottingham Repertory Company in 1934, remaining until 1936. First appeared in London in 1936 in *The Sacred Flame* (Q), then toured in *Night Must Fall*. Joined Old Vic 1936, and played in *The Country Wife, As You Like It*, etc. Also in London in *Judgment Day, The Silent Knight*, etc. Rejoined Old Vic in 1938, appearing in *Trelawney Of The Wells, Hamlet, The Rivals*. Toured with Old Vic in 1939 on the Continent and in Egypt. In 1939-40 appeared in *Judgment Day* (Strand). Joined Stratford-on-Avon Festival Company, 1940, appearing in *The Taming Of The Shrew* and *The Rivals*, etc. Joined Old Vic Company, 1941-42, appearing in *Othello* and *The Merry Wives Of Windsor* (New, 1942). With the Old Vic, 1942-43, appearing in *The Seagull*, and later in *The Russians* (Playhouse, 1943). In 1944 toured in *Tomorrow's Eden*. Appeared in *No Room At The Inn* (Embassy, 1945) and *Tomorrow's Eden* (Embassy, 1945), and on tour with *No Room At The Inn*, 1945, etc.

JAY, ERNEST. Actor. Born London, 1893. First appeared on the stage in *Are You A Mason?* (Penge, 1917), subsequently touring and in repertory at Liverpool and Plymouth until 1926. Made his first appearance in London in *The Ghost Train* (Prince of Wales, 1926) ; then toured Canada until 1929. Has acted in London in *The Flying Fool, Cynara, Payment Deferred.* Appeared in New York in *The Good Companions,* 1931, returning to London in *Man Overboard.* Also in the West End in *Orders Are Orders, Clear All Wires, Whistling In The Dark, Admirals All, Aren't Men Beasts, The Amazing Dr. Clitterhouse* (New York, 1937), *Blondie White, Frozen Glory, Little Ladyship, Punch Without Judy,* etc. Appeared in *The Gentle People* (Strand, 1939), and *Punch Without Judy* (New, 1940). From 1940-43 acted with the B.B.C. Drama Repertory Company. In 1944 acted in *The Breadwinner* (Arts) and in *Anna Christie* (Arts), then in *The Critic* and *Leonce And Lena* (Arts, 1945). Recently in *The Shop At Sly Corner* (St. Martin's, 1945-46).

JEANS, ISABEL. Actress. Born London, 1891. Made her first appearance on the stage in *Pinkie And The Fairies* (His Majesty's Theatre, 1909) ; then in *Richard II, The Greatest Wish, The Darling Of The Gods,* etc. Toured United States, 1915-16, with Harley Granville Barker, returning to London in *The Mayor Of Troy* (Haymarket). Has also appeared in London in *Chu Chin Chow, The Man Who Married A Dumb Wife, Volpone, Fanny's First Play, Arms And The Man, Twelfth Night, At Mrs. Beam's* and many others. Also in *The Eye Of Siva, Hassan, The Country Wife, The Rat, The Rivals, The Man With A Load Of Mischief, Conflict, La Prisonnière, The Road To Rome, The Man In Possession* (also in New York, 1930), *Counsel's Opinion, Springtime For Henry,* etc. Among the other West End plays in which she has appeared are *On Approval, Spring,* 1600, *Full House, The Happy Hypocrite, Mademoiselle.* Acting in Hollywood, 1937-40. In 1940 appeared in *Ladies Into Action* (Lyric). Recently : In London in *Home And Beauty* (Playhouse, 1942-43), *Heartbreak House* (Cambridge, 1943), *Lady Windermere's Fan* (Haymarket, 1945-46).

JEANS, RONALD. Dramatic author. Born Birkenhead, 1887. Was one of the founders of the Liverpool Repertory Theatre. Has written a number of plays and revues, including *The Cage, Buzz Buzz* (with Arthur Wimperis), *Charlot's Revue Of* 1924, *Lido Lady, Charlot's Masquerade, Clowns In Clover,* etc. Part-author of *London Calling, Streamline, Follow The Sun,* etc. Has also written the plays, *Lean Harvest, Bow Bells, The Composite Man, Ghost For Sale,* etc. In 1938, with J. B. Priestley, he founded the London Mask Theatre at the Westminster, which operated until 1940.

JEANS, URSULA. Actress. Born Simla, India, 1906. Married to Roger Livesey. Studied for the stage at the Royal Academy of Dramatic Art, making her first appearance on the stage in *Cobra* (Nottingham, 1925). Subsequently in London in *The Firebrand* (Wyndham's, 1926), then in *Escape, The Second Man, Passing Brompton Road, The First Mrs. Fraser,* etc. Also in *Grand Hotel, I Lived With You,* before going to New York to appear in *Late One Evening* (Plymouth, 1933). Joined Old Vic in 1933, acting in *The Cherry Orchard, Twelfth Night, Henry VIII, Measure For Measure, Love For Love, The Tempest* and *The Importance Of Being Earnest.* Also appeared in London in *Lover's Leap, Vintage Wine, Short Story, The Country Wife, The Children's Hour, They Came By Night, People Of Our Class.* Rejoined Old Vic in 1939 to act in *She Stoops To Conquer, The Enemy Of The People* and *The Taming Of The Shrew.* Then in *The Country Wife* (Little 1940). In 1941 appeared in *Dear Brutus* (Globe). Toured with Roger Livesey in *The Taming Of The Shrew.* Then in *Watch On The Rhine* (Aldwych, 1943). Appeared in *The Banbury Nose* (Wyndham's, 1944). In 1945, with Roger Livesey, she toured the Middle East with ENSA Festival Company in *The Barretts Of Wimpole Street, Pygmalion, It Depends What You Mean,* etc.

JEAYES, ALLAN. Actor. Born London, 1885. First appeared on stage in *The School For Scandal* (Folkestone, 1906) ; then in London in *Priscilla Runs Away* (Haymarket, 1910). Then played in the West End in *Typhoon, Milestones, Hamlet, Cyrano De Bergerac, Peter Pan, Medea, The Bat, Candida, Major Barbara, Fanny's First Play, The Little Minister* and many others. Also in *And So To Bed, The Spook Sonata, The Letter* (New York, 1927), *The First Mrs. Fraser, Service, Bees On The Boatdeck, The Jealous God,* etc. 1940-43 : Acting with the B.B.C. Repertory Company. Then in *Ten Little Niggers* (St. James's, 1943), *The Years Between* (Wyndham's, 1944-46).

JEFFERIES, DOUGLAS. Actor. Born London, 1884. Made his first appearance on the stage in *Jeanne d'Arc* (Strand, 1907) ; then touring the provinces for several years. First appeared in London in *The Man Who Was* (Palace, 1912). Later in *Dear Brutus,* then with Everyman Repertory Company in *Candida, Mary Stuart, The Philanderer,* etc. Also in London in *Oliver Cromwell, The Importance Of Being Earnest, The Three Sisters, Liliom, Exiled.* Toured America in *Bird In Hand,* returning to London in *The Bond,* 1930. Then in the West End in *Street Scene, Lean Harvest* ; with the Old Vic, 1931-32 ; *The Lake, Men In White, Hervey House, Dusty Ermine, The Taming Of The Shrew, Judgment Day, Victoria Regina, The Silent Knight,* etc. Recently : *Rebecca* (Queen's, 1940), *The Petrified Forest* (Globe, 1942-43), *While The Sun Shines* (Globe, 1943-46).

JENKINS, MEGS. Actress. Born Birkenhead, 1917. Was an amateur for many years before joining Liverpool Repertory Company in 1933, where she remained until 1937. Made her first appearance in London in *The Story Of An African Farm* (New, 1938), also in *Heaven And Charing Cross* (St. Martin's, 1939), *The Light Of Heart* (Apollo and Globe, 1940-41). 1942-43 : Appeared in *Light And Shade* (Ambassadors), *The Drunkard* (Arts) and *Shadow And Substance* (Duke of York's). Recently : *Acacia Avenue* (Vaudeville, 1943-44), *The Glass Slipper* (St. James's, 1944-45), *The Wind Of Heaven* (St. James's, 1945).

JERROLD, MARY. Actress. Born London, 1877. Made her first appearance on the stage in *Mary Pennington* (St. James's, 1896) ; subsequently with the Kendals, 1902-05. Also acted in *Under The Greenwood Tree, Nan, The Fountain, Trelawney Of The Wells,* etc. Has also appeared in the West End in *Rococo, Idle Women, Milestones, Disraeli, The Young Person In Pink, Mary Rose* and many others. Then in *The Sport Of Kings, The Lavender Ladies* ; toured South Africa and Australia, 1926-27 with Dion Boucicault. Also in London in *The Constant Wife, The Sacred Flame* (also in New York, 1928), *Devonshire Cream, Britannia Of Billingsgate, Another Language, Laburnum Grove, The Old Ladies* and many others. More recently in *Children To Bless You, Climbing, Yes And No, People Of Our Class.* In 1941 appeared in *Dear Brutus* (Globe). Also in *Ducks And Drakes* (Apollo, 1941), *Arsenic And Old Lace* (Strand, 1942-46).

JESSEL, PATRICIA. Actress. Born Hong Kong, China, 1920. Studied for the stage under Italia Conti, making her first appearance in *Peter Pan,* 1933. In 1935 joined Richmond Repertory Company, then 1937 joined Manchester Repertory Company. Joined Stratford-on-Avon Festival Company and appeared here in 1943 and again in 1944 in *Twelfth Night, The Merry Wives Of Windsor,* etc. In 1945 appeared on tour in *The Golden Fleece,* then joined Donald Wolfit Company, appearing in *Macbeth* (Winter Garden, 1945) ; subsequently on tour with Wolfit.

JOHNS, GLYNIS. Actress. Born Pretoria, South Africa. Educated in London, making her first appearance on the stage in *Buckie's Bears* (Garrick, 1935). Later in London in *St. Helena, The Children's Hour, The Melody That Got Lost, Judgment Day, A Kiss For Cinderella, Quiet Wedding,* etc. 1941-43 : *Quiet Week-End* (Wyndham's), then in *Peter Pan* (Winter Garden, Cambridge, 1943-44).

JOHNS, MERVYN. Actor. Born Pembroke, South Wales, 1899. Studied for the stage at the Royal Academy of Dramatic Art, making his first appearance on the stage in *Far Above Rubies* (Comedy, 1924). Also in repertory at Bristol, then toured in South Africa, 1926-27. From 1927-34 acting and producing at Bristol Little Theatre ; then in London in *Hyde Park Corner, The Provoked Wife*, etc., and in *The Merry Wives Of Windsor* and *A Midsummer Night's Dream* (both at Open Air Theatre, 1937). Also in the West End in *Time And The Conways, Comedienne, The Doctor's Dilemma, Rhondda Roundabout*, etc. In 1939-40 appeared in *Saloon Bar* (Wyndham's). Then in R.A.F., 1940-42 ; subsequently extensively engaged in filming. Recently touring in J. B. Priestley's *The Golden Fleece*.

JOHNSON, CELIA. Actress. Born Richmond, 1908. Married to Peter Fleming. Studied for the stage at the Royal Academy of Dramatic Art, making her first appearance on the stage in *Major Barbara* (Huddersfield, 1928). Subsequently appeared in London in *A Hundred Years Old* (Lyric, Hammersmith, 1928), then in *The Artist And The Shadow, Debonair, Cynara, The Circle, Death Takes A Holiday* and others. Went to New York to appear in *Hamlet* (Broadhurst, 1931), returning to London in *Punchinello* (Globe, 1932). She has also acted in the West End in *The Man I Killed, Ten Minute Alibi, Another Language, The Key, The Wind And The Rain, Pride And Prejudice, Old Music, Sixth Floor*, etc. In 1940 appeared in *Rebecca* (Queen's).

JONES, BARRY. Actor. Born Guernsey, 1893. Made his first appearance on the stage with Sir Frank Benson's Company at Leeds, 1921 ; then played for a time at Stratford-on-Avon Memorial Theatre. Also toured in America and Canada, appearing in New York in *Man And The Masses*, 1924, and *The Constant Nymph*, 1926. Appeared in *The Road To Rome* (New York, 1927-28), then with Maurice Colbourne toured Canada and the United States until 1931. He returned to London and appeared in *The Queen's Husband* (Ambassadors, 1931), after which he toured Canada and appeared again in New York in *And Be My Love*, 1934. On returning to London acted in the West End in *Moonlight Is Silver, Glamorous Night, Promise, Charles The King, Lover's Meeting, Comedienne, The Doctor's Dilemma*, etc. Since the war : in H.M. Forces. In 1945, with Godfrey Tearle, he went to Rome with the ENSA Festival Company, appearing in *The Rivals, The Circle, Pygmalion*, etc.

JONES, EMRYS. Actor. Born Manchester, 1915. Among the plays in which he has appeared in London are *Macbeth*, with John Gielgud (Piccadilly, 1942), *Holy Isle* (Arts, 1943), *Flare Path* (Apollo, 1943-44), *Letters To A Lady* (Embassy, 1945), etc. Recently appeared in *The Hasty Heart* (Aldwych, 1945-46).

JONES, GRIFFITH. Actor. Born London, 1910. Educated London University. Studied for stage at Royal Academy of Dramatic Art, first appearing on the stage in *Carpet Slippers* (Embassy, 1930). Subsequently in London in *Vile Bodies, Ourselves Alone, Richard Of Bordeaux, The Rats Of Norway*, etc. Acted in New York in *Escape Me Never* (Shubert, 1935), returning to London in *After October*, followed by *Farewell Performance, Gertie Maude, Operette, Marco Millions, Behold The Bride*, etc. In 1940 appeared in *Believe It Or Not* (New). 1940-44 : In H.M. Forces. In 1945 appeared in *Lady Windermere's Fan* (Haymarket).

JONES, MARY. Actress. Born Rhayader, Wales, 1915. Studied for stage at Central School of Dramatic Art, first appearing on the stage with The Greater London Players. Then acted in London in *Ten Minute Alibi, Grief Goes Over*, before playing in repertory at Cardiff. Also in London in *Come Out To Play*, then toured the Continent in Shakespeare Company and appeared in Paris in *George And Margaret*. Made her first appearance on the New York stage in *Time And The Conways* (Ritz, 1938), returning to London to play in *Can We Tell, To Love And To Cherish*, etc. In 1941 toured in *They Walk Alone* ; later toured in *This Was A Woman, Through The Door*, etc. Appeared in *Stage Door* (Saville, 1946).

JONES, PETER. Actor. Born Wem, 1920. Made his first appearance on the stage in *The Composite Man* (Wolverhampton, 1937), then first acted in London in *The Doctor's Dilemma* (Haymarket, 1942). Also in *The Imaginary Invalid* (Westminster, 1943), after which he joined the Arts Theatre Festival Company to appear in *Misalliance, The Rivals, The Watched Pot,* etc. Recently appeared in *The Rest Is Silence* (Prince of Wales, 1944), *How Are They At Home?* (Apollo, 1944), *The Simpleton Of The Unexpected Isles* (Arts, 1945), *The Italian Straw Hat* (Arts, 1945), then on tour in *The Golden Fleece,* 1945.

JONES, LESLIE JULIAN. Dramatic author. Born London, 1910. Educated Margate College. Wrote material for the first non-stop revue at the Windmill and twenty-one numbers for the revue which opened the rebuilt Prince of Wales. Among his revues are *Come Out Of Your Shell* (Criterion, 1940), *Rise Above It* (Comedy, 1941), *It's About Time* (Comedy, 1942), *Whitehall Follies* (Whitehall, 1943). Has also written numbers for other revues, including *Sweet And Low* (Ambassadors). In 1943-44 went to Middle East for ENSA, writing and producing revues at Cairo Opera House. In 1945 returned to London and wrote the revue *That'll Be The Day* (which he produced and presented in association with James Lavall). Wrote lyrics etc. for *Better Late* (Apollo, 1946).

JOWETT, JOHN. Actor and writer. Born Wednesbury, Staffs, 1921. Educated Shrewsbury and Cambridge. Served in H.M. Forces, 1940-42, afterwards appeared in *Maria Marten* (Arts, 1942-43), *Love For Love* (Haymarket, 1943), *This Time It's Love* (Comedy, 1944), etc. He has also contributed to the revues *Sweet And Low, Strike It Again, Happy And Glorious, Keep Going, Henson's Gaieties,* and to the show *Jenny Jones,* etc.

KANN, LILLY. Actress. Born Peitz, Nr. Berlin. Had extensive experience on the stage in Dresden, Frankfurt and Berlin. Came to England and made her first appearance on the London stage in *Awake And Sing* (Arts, 1942). Recently appeared in *Blow Your own Trumpet* (for Old Vic) (Playhouse, 1943), *The Cradle Song* (Apollo, 1944), *Tomorrow The World* (Aldwych, 1944-45).

KEEN, MALCOLM. Actor. Born Bristol, 1887. Made his first appearance on the stage in *Ulysses* (His Majesty's, 1902), after which he toured the provinces until 1915. Was with Martin Harvey, 1915-16. Also acted in London in *The Skin Game, A Bill Of Divorcement, The Gay Lord Quex, R.U.R., Hassan* and many others. Among the other West End plays he has appeared in are *Fata Morgana, Rain, Hamlet, One More River, Peter Pan,* etc. Appeared in New York in *Jew Süss,* 1930, returning to England to play in *Hamlet* (Haymarket). Subsequently in London in *The Silent Witness, Precious Bane, The Nelson Touch,* then joined Old Vic, 1932-33, acting in *Cæsar And Cleopatra, As You Like It, Macbeth, The Merchant Of Venice, She Stoops To Conquer, Cymbeline, Romeo And Juliet, Mary Stuart,* etc. Subsequently in London in *Heritage, Maternité, Libel, Justice, The Unguarded Hour* and others. Again to New York in 1936 to play in John Gielgud's *Hamlet,* returning to act in *Treasure Island,* 1937. Also in *Paprika, Hamlet* (for Old Vic), *The Man In Half Moon Street,* etc. In 1940-41 appeared in *The Body Was Well Nourished.* Recently in *Shadow And Substance* (Duke of York's), *The Maid Of The Mountains* (Coliseum, 1943). In 1944 acted in *A Murder For A Valentine* (Lyric). Then in *Pink String And Sealing Wax* (Duke of York's, 1944). Toured Continent with the ENSA Festival Co., 1946.

KELLY, JUDY. Actress. Born New South Wales, Australia, 1913. Studied for stage in Sydney, making her first appearance on the stage there in *The Rising Generation* (Arts, 1930). Came to England in 1932 to appear in films; made her first appearance on the London stage in *Courtship Dance* (Q, 1934). Subsequently in *A Ship Comes Home,* then toured South Africa, 1937. Has also appeared in *Take It Easy, Ring Off Please, King Of Nowhere, Windfall, Bridge Of Sighs,* etc. In 1940 acted in *Believe It Or Not* (New), *Women Aren't Angels*

★ **_Ralph Richardson_** as Peer, in Ibsen's "Peer Gynt", produced by Tyrone Guthrie for the Old Vic Repertory Season, 1944-45.

★ *Laurence Olivier* as Crookback Richard, in Shakespeare's "Richard III", produced by John Burrell for the
Old Vic Repertory Season, 1944-45.

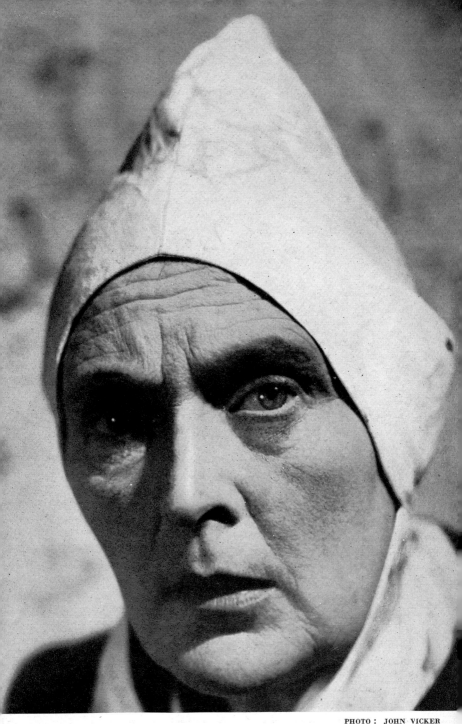

★ *Sybil Thorndike* as Aase, in "Peer Gynt", 1944-45.

★ *Nicholas Hannen* as the Troll King, Margaret Leighton as the Woman in Green and Ralph Richardson as Peer in "Peer Gynt", 1944-45.

★ *Ralph Richardson* as Bluntschli, and Laurence Olivier as Sergius in Shaw's "Arms And The Man", produced by John Burrell for the Old Vic Repertory Season, 1944-45.

★ **_Ralph Richardson_** as Vanya, and Laurence Olivier as Astrov in Tchekov's "Uncle Vanya", produced by John Burrell for the Old Vic Repertory Season, 1944-45.

★ *Flora Robson,* who returned from Hollywood to appear in the Old Vic Company's production of "Guilty" in 1944, and "Man About the House", 1946.

PHOTO : ALEXANDER BENDER

★ *John Clements* and Kay Hammond as Elyot and Amanda in Noel Coward's "Private Lives", produced by Clements in 1945.

(Strand, 1941), and _Warn That Man_ (Garrick, 1942). Recently : _The Crime Of Margaret Foley_ (Embassy, 1945). Then on tour in _Under The Gooseberry Bush_, 1945, which came to the St. James's in 1946 as _The Astonished Ostrich_.

KEMPSON, RACHEL. Actress. Born Dartmouth, 1910. Married to Michael Redgrave. Studied for the stage at the Royal Academy of Dramatic Art, making her first appearance on the stage in _Much Ado About Nothing_ (Stratford-on-Avon Memorial Theatre, 1933). Then acted in London in _The Lady From Alfaqueque_ (Westminster, 1933), after which she rejoined the Stratford-on-Avon Festival Company in 1934, acting in _Twelfth Night, The Tempest, Love's Labour's Lost, Romeo And Juliet_, and others. Played with Oxford Repertory Company in 1935, and Liverpool Repertory Company, 1935-36. Has also appeared in London in _Love's Labour's Lost, Volpone, The School For Scandal, The Shoemaker's Holiday_, etc. Recently : In _The Beggar's Opera_ (Haymarket, 1941), _The Wingless Victory_ (Phœnix, 1943), _Uncle Harry_ (Garrick, 1944), _Jacobowsky And The Colonel_ (Piccadilly, 1945).

KENDALL, HENRY. Actor and producer. Born London, 1897. Educated City of London School. Made his first appearance on the stage in _Tommy Atkins_ (Lyceum, 1914), subsequently appearing in _Business As Usual_. With the Old Vic in 1915, then in the West End in _Cyrano De Bergerac, French Leave, Where The Rainbow Ends, The Circle, Threads, Arms And The Man, East Of Suez, Havoc, As You Like It, Charlot's Revue_ 1924, _Tunnel Trench_, etc. Made his first appearance in New York in _Naughty Cinderella_, 1925. Has also appeared in London in _The Silent House, The Road To Rome, The Flying Fool, The Ghost Train, Charlot's Masquerade of_ 1930, _A Murder Has Been Arranged, Someone At The Door_ and many others. More recently in _Bats In The Belfry, This Money Business, Room For Two, Punch Without Judy_, etc. Appeared in _Rise Above It_ (Comedy, 1941), _Scoop_ (Vaudeville, 1942), _The Fur Coat_ (Comedy, 1942-43), _A Little Bit Of Fluff_ (Ambassadors, 1943), toured in _The Grand Manner_. Recently appeared in _Sweeter And Lower_ (Ambassadors, 1944). Among the plays he has recently produced are _Rise Above It_ (Comedy), _Other People's Houses_ (Ambassadors), _Scoop_ (Vaudeville), _This Was A Woman_ (Comedy), _See How They Run_ (Comedy), _Great Day_ (Playhouse), and _The Shop At Sly Corner_ (St. Martin's).

KENDALL, WILLIAM. Actor and producer. Born London, 1903. Made his first appearance on the stage in _Stop Flirting_ (Queen's, 1923) ; subsequently in _London Life, Old Heidelberg, March Hares, Downhill, Liliom, The Rat, That's A Good Girl, The Command Performance, Mr. Whittington, This'll Make You Whistle_ and many others. Made his first appearance in New York in _Between The Devil_ (Imperial, 1937). Since the outbreak of war in H.M. Forces.

KENT, KATHLEEN. Actress. Born Chelsea, February 24th, 1913. Educated St. Margaret's School. Studied for the stage at Royal Academy of Dramatic Art. Made her first appearance on the stage as a dancer at the Aldwych Theatre, after which she appeared in repertory at Norwich, etc. Has recently been seen in London in _Watch On The Rhine_ (Aldwych, 1943), _There Shall Be No Night_ (Aldwych, 1944), _Love In Idleness_ (Lyric, 1945), _The Trojan Women_ (Lyric, Hammersmith, 1946).

KENT, KENETH. Actor. Born Liverpool, 1892. Studied for the stage at the Royal Academy of Dramatic Art, making his first appearance in _All Men Are Fools_ (Comedy, 1912). Was with Miss Horniman's Company at Manchester in 1915 and thenceforth appeared in London in a number of plays, including _Lucky Jim, Hindle Wakes, Charley's Aunt, The Thirteenth Chair, The Charm School_, etc. Also in the West End in _The Dippers, St. Joan, Summer Lightning, The Constant Nymph, The Wrecker, Sea Fever, Proscenium_, etc. Joined the Old Vic Company in 1935, acting in _Peer Gynt, Macbeth, Julius Cæsar, The Three Sisters_ and others. Also in London in _St. Helena, Muted Strings, To Have And To Hold, Give Me_

Yesterday, etc. Recently : On tour in *The Man With Dark Glasses*, etc. In 1942 appeared in *Full Swing* (Palace), etc. In *The Shop At Sly Corner* (St. Martin's, 1945-46).

KENTON, GODFREY. Actor. Born London, 1902. Married to Vivienne Bennett. Studied for the stage at Royal Academy of Dramatic Art, making his first appearance in *Mr. Garrick* (Brighton, 1922). Subsequently in London in *The Blue Bird* (Duke of York's, 1922) ; then with Lena Ashwell, 1925-27, and at Stratford-on-Avon, 1925-26. Joined Nottingham Repertory Company, 1928-29, and again in 1929-30. With Old Vic in 1928. Then in London in *Episode, Twelfth Night, One More River, The Moon In The Yellow River, Henry IV, The Happy Hypocrite, After October*, etc. With Stratford-on-Avon Company in 1937, then in New York in *Time And The Conways*, 1938. Also acted in London in *Give Me Yesterday, Goodbye, Mr. Chips* and others. 1940-44 : In H.M. Forces. In 1944 joined the Donald Wolfit Company, appearing at the Winter Garden, 1945 and 1946.

KERR, RONALD. Actor and producer. Born London, 1905. Educated City of London School. Studied for the stage at the Royal Academy of Dramatic Art, making his first appearance on the stage in *The Farmer's Wife* (Court, 1924). Subsequently with Sybil Thorndike's Company appearing in London, and on tour in the provinces and South Africa, and in Paris in *Macbeth, St. Joan, Justice Of Israel, Medea* and others. Then joined Leon M. Lion in 1928 as stage director, and appeared in *Exiled* and *This Way To Paradise* (St. Martin's), also stage directing at Daly's, Royalty and Garrick Theatres. In 1931 he joined Sir Barry Jackson's Company, as actor and producer on tour and at Birmingham. In 1934 toured with Emile Littler and produced. Then in London in *Cabbages And Kings* (Ambassadors, 1936). Produced a number of plays at the Q, People's Palace and Embassy Theatres. In 1938 he appeared at the Malvern Festival. Then producer at Intimate Theatre, Palmer's Green, 1941-46.

KING, BRIAN. Actor. Born Surrey, 1917. Formerly engaged as a stage designer, he made his appearance on the stage in repertory, after which he was with the R.A.F., 1939-43. Since then in repertory at Sheffield, on tour in *Emma, No Orchids For Miss Blandish* and others. Then on tour in *Jane Eyre*, after which he toured in *St. Joan*, 1945. Made his first appearance in the West End in *Off The Camden Road* (Torch, 1945).

KING, SIDNEY. Actor. Born London, 1910. Educated Hull Grammar School. Made his first appearance on the stage in 1923 in Fred Terry-Julia Neilson's Company, in *The Scarlet Pimpernel*. Then in repertory in Newcastle and Windsor, after which he appeared in London in *Charley's Aunt* (Haymarket, 1939), *Ladies In Retirement* (St. Martin's, 1940-41), *Warn That Man* (Garrick, 1942), *Aren't Men Beasts* (Garrick, 1943), *Mr. Bolfry* (Playhouse, 1944), *Young Mrs. Barrington* (Winter Garden, 1945-46), etc.

KIRBY, MAX. Actor. Born London, April 24th, 1907. Made his first stage appearance in *No, No, Nanette*, 1928, after which he played Jack Buchanan parts in a number of tours. Made his first stage appearance in New York in *Bitter Sweet*, later also played there in *The Good Companions*. More recently appeared in London in *Night Of The Garter* (Strand, 1942), *It's Time To Dance* (Winter Garden, 1943), *Another Love Story* (Phœnix, 1944-45), *Fine Feathers* (Prince of Wales, 1945-46).

KNIGHT, ESMOND. Actor. Born East Sheen, 1906. Married to Frances Clare. Made his first appearance on the stage in *The Merchant Of Venice* (Old Vic, 1925). He toured with Russell Thorndike in 1926 and joined the Old Vic in 1927. Has also appeared in London in *Thunder On The Left, To What Red Hell ?, Improper People, The Man I Killed, Hamlet, Waltzes From Vienna* and many others. Also in *Volpone, Wild Violets, Three Sisters, Streamline, The Insect Play, Night Must*

Fall, Wise Tomorrow, Van Gogh, The Melody That Got Lost. Joined Michel St. Denis Company in 1938, appearing in *Twelfth Night* (Phœnix). Then with Wilson Barrett, acting and producing with his own company at the King's, Hammersmith, 1938-39. On the outbreak of war he joined the Royal Navy, being invalided out in 1943. Recently appeared in *Crisis In Heaven* (Lyric, 1944), *Three Waltzes* (Princes, 1945). Then in *Romeo and Juliet,* etc. (King's, 1946).

KONSTAM, ANNA. Actress. Born London, 1914. Studied for the stage at the Royal Academy of Dramatic Art. Then in repertory for two years. She has appeared in London in *Saloon Bar* (Wyndham's, 1940), *Once A Crook* (Aldwych, 1941), *Love In A Mist* (St. Martin's, 1941-42). She appeared with the Stratford-on-Avon Festival Company in 1943 in *King Lear, Henry V, Othello* and *A Winter's Tale.* Recently in *The Vicar Of Wakefield,* 1945.

LACEY, CATHERINE. Actress and producer. Born London, 1904. Made her first appearance on the stage in *The Thirteenth Chair* (Brighton, 1925); subsequently in the same play in London in the same year. Also in *Cock O' The Roost,* before touring South Africa in 1927-28. Then with Liverpool Repertory Company, 1929-30. Appeared in London in *The Venetian,* before going to New York to appear in the same play at the Masque, 1931. Has appeared in London also in *Fire, The Green Bay Tree, Night's Candles, The Three Musketeers, Ladies In Waiting, The Maitlands,* etc. Joined Stratford-on-Avon Festival in 1935. Then in London in *The Black Eye, King Lear, Waste, Judgment Day, The Unquiet Spirit,* etc. With Westminster Company, 1938-39, appearing in *Dangerous Corner, Marco Millions, The Family Reunion* and *Candida.* In 1939 also appeared at St. James's in *After The Dance.* In 1940 appeared in *Music At Night* (Westminster), *All's Well That Ends Well* (Vaudeville). In 1942 in *The School For Slavery* (Westminster). In 1943, *The Young And Lovely* (Arts). In 1943-44 in *She Follows Me About* (Garrick). Subsequently in *Jane Clegg* (Lyric, Hammersmith, 1944) and touring the Continent in *The Case Of The Frightened Lady,* 1945. Has produced a number of plays in London, including *The Witch* (Arts), *On Life's Sunny Side* (Arts).

LAFFAN, PATRICIA. Actress. Born London, 1919. Studied for the stage at Webber Douglas School of Drama, making her first appearance on the stage in *The Beggar's Opera* (Oxford, 1937). Toured in *The First Mrs. Fraser,* 1941. Made her first appearance in London in *Androcles And The Lion* (Arts, 1943), then appeared in *Twelfth Night* with Walter Hudd-CEMA tour, etc. In 1944 played in *How Are They At Home?* (Apollo). Recently on tour in *Hidden Horizon,* 1945. Appeared in *They Came To A City* (Oxford, 1946).

LAING, DAVID. Actor. Born Belfast, 1915. Began his theatrical career in travelling Shakespeare Companies, then appeared for a season at the Gaiety, Dublin. Came to England and appeared in repertory in Harrogate, before joining the tour of *The Doctor's Dilemma,* 1942. He made his first appearance in the West End in *The Man Who Came To Dinner* (Savoy, 1942-44), then on tour with *Aloma Of The South Seas,* followed by a season of repertory at the Intimate, Palmers Green. Then in 1944 he appeared in *This Was A Woman* on tour, *No Room At The Inn* (Embassy, 1945), then on tour in *Madame Bovary,* etc.

LAIRD, JENNY. Actress. Born London. Married to John Fernald. Made her first appearance on the stage with Brixton Repertory Company in 1937. Then first appeared in West End in *Comedienne* (Haymarket, 1939), also in *A Party For Christmas* (Haymarket), *Goodness How Sad* (Vaudeville), *This Money Business* (Garrick). Joined London Mask Theatre Company and appeared in *Music At Night* (Westminster, 1940), also *Major Barbara* and *Cornelius.* Recently appeared in *The Judgment Of Dr. Johnson* (Arts, 1943), *The Recruiting Officer* (Arts, 1943), *Mr. Bolfry* (Westminster, 1943), *A Doll's House* (Arts, 1945). Season at Scala, 1946.

LANDSTONE, CHARLES. Playwright and manager. Born Vienna, 1897. Was manager for Grein's Cosmopolitan Theatre, 1928-31, then associated with

Embassy, Everyman, Fortune, etc. Has been business manager and manager of most London theatres, including Open Air Theatre, 1938 and 1939. In 1940 managed *All's Well That Ends Well* (Vaudeville), and *Berkeley Square* (Vaudeville). Associated with the Old Vic and Sadlers Wells, 1941-42. In 1942 became Assistant Drama Director of CEMA and, since 1942, general manager of Theatre Royal, Bristol, the first completely State-aided theatre to operate in England. From April, 1945 : Deputy Drama Director, Arts Council of Great Britain. Among his plays are : *Behind Your Back*, *Ruby Morn* and *On A Summer's Day*.

LANE, LUPINO. Actor and dramatic author. Born London, 1892. Made his first appearance on the stage in 1896, then in London in 1903. Has toured all over the world in vaudeville. Among the West End plays in which he has appeared are *Watch Your Step*, *What A Catch*, *Brighter London*, *The Ziegfeld Follies Of* 1924, *Silver Wings*, *The One Girl* and many pantomimes, etc. More recently in *The Golden Toy*, *Twenty To One*, *Me And My Girl*, etc. Took over management of Victoria Palace and has appeared there in *Twenty To One*, 1942, *La Di Da Di Da*, 1943, *Meet Me Victoria*, 1944, *Me And My Girl*, 1945, etc.

LANG, JULIA. Actress. Born London, 1921. Married to Bill Shine. Studied for the stage at the Westminster School of Acting, making her first appearance on the stage at the Players' Theatre in 1940. From 1941-43 acted with the Market Theatre (on tour under the auspices of CEMA). Then on tour in *She Follows Me About*, 1943, after which she appeared in *Blithe Spirit* (Duchess, 1944-45). Recently joined Birmingham Repertory Company and has appeared in *She Stoops To Conquer* and *Juno And The Paycock*, etc. In *Lady From The Sea* (Arts, 1946).

LAUCHLAN, AGNES. Actress. Born London, 1905. Studied for the stage at R.A.D.A., making her first appearance in *St. Joan* (New, 1924). Joined Lena Ashwell in 1926 and the Everyman Company in 1928, appearing at this theatre in *The Eldest Son*, *Comrades* and *Ginevra*. Has also appeared in London in *Street Scene*, *The Heir*, *Romeo and Juliet*, *The Dover Road*, *The Cathedral*, etc. Then in *A Midsummer Night's Dream* and *The Tempest* (Open Air, 1933), followed by *The Country Wife*, *Our Own Lives*, *Heartbreak House*, *Sarah Simple*, *Ghost For Sale*, *Windfall*, *Sugar Plum* and many others. At the outbreak of war appeared in a revival of *Dear Octopus* (Adelphi), then in *The Country Wife* (Little, 1940). In 1941 toured in *Blithe Spirit* with Ronald Squire ; subsequently appearing in the same play at the Duchess for a year. Joined the Old Vic Company at Liverpool Playhouse in 1944, appearing in *Lisa*. Then in *Romeo and Juliet*, etc. (King's, 1946).

LAURIE, JOHN. Actor and producer. Born Dumfries, Scotland, 1897. Studied for the stage at the Central School of Dramatic Art, making his first appearance in *What Every Woman Knows* (Dumfries, 1921). Subsequently appeared in London in *The Merry Wives Of Windsor* (Old Vic, 1922), then with Old Vic until 1925, after which he joined Stratford-on-Avon Festival Company. Also played in London in *Macbeth*, *Henry V*, *Enchantment*, etc. With Stratford-on-Avon Festival, 1927, Old Vic, 1928, Court Theatre Company, 1930. Among the plays in which he has appeared in London are *The Improper Duchess*, *And So To Bed*, *Napoleon*, *All's Well That Ends Well*, *The Tudor Wench*, *The Rivals*, *The Country Wife*, etc. Joined Open Air Theatre, 1934, and again in 1935, appearing in *The Tempest*, *A Midsummer Night's Dream*, *As You Like It*, etc. In 1936 appeared in *Rosmersholm*, *Hedda Gabler*, *Bees On The Boatdeck*, before touring South Africa in 1937. Also in London in *Surprise Item*, *Operette*, *White Secrets*, etc. Then in Stratford-on-Avon Festival, 1939, in *Othello*, *Richard III*, *Coriolanus*, etc. In 1943 appeared in *Heartbreak House* (Cambridge). In 1945 produced *Hamlet* and others for Perth Drama Festival. Also produced for the Pilgrim Players, etc.

LAWSON, WILFRID. Actor. Born Bradford, 1900. Made his first appearance on the stage in *Trilby* (Brighton, 1916). From 1919-28 acting in repertory in various parts of the British Isles. First appeared in London in *Sweeney Todd*, with Tod Slaughter at Elephant and Castle, 1928; subsequently in London in *Arms And The Man, Pygmalion, The Philanderer, The Doctor's Dilemma, Misalliance, Fanny's First Play* (and others in seasons of Shaw at the Court, 1929-31). Also in the West End in *Heartbreak House, Evensong, Gallows Glorious, The Golden Toy, Antony And Cleopatra* (for Old Vic), *The Barretts Of Wimpole Street*, etc. With Malvern Festival Company, 1935, in *Volpone*, etc. First appeared in New York in *Libel* (Henry Miller, 1935), then on New York stage until 1937. Has also acted in London in *The King's Pirate, I Have Been Here Before* (also in New York, 1938), *Bridge Head*, etc. In 1942 appeared in *Lifeline* (Duchess) and later in *The Streets Of London* (Cambridge, 1942).

LAWTON, FRANK. Actor. Born London, 1904. Married to Evelyn Laye. First appeared on the stage in *Yes!* (Vaudeville, 1923); subsequently in *The Odd Spot, The Last Of Mrs. Cheyney, Young Woodley, The Roof, The Last Enemy, Michael And Mary, London Wall* and many others. Also acted in *The Wind And The Rain* (New York, 1934), and subsequently in New York in *Promise, French Without Tears*, etc., before returning to London to appear in *Quiet Wedding* (Wyndham's, 1938). 1940-45: with H.M. Forces. Then, in 1945, on tour with Evelyn Laye in *Three Waltzes*.

LAYE, EVELYN. Actress. Born London, 1900. Married to Frank Lawton. Made her first appearance on the stage in *Mr. Wu* (Brighton, 1915), and in London in 1916 in the revue *Honi Soit*. Subsequently in pantomime; then *The Beauty Spot, The Shop Girl, The Merry Widow, Madame Pompadour, The Dollar Princess, Lilac Time, New Moon*, etc. Appeared in New York in *Bitter Sweet* (Ziegfeld, 1929), and also in London, 1931. Has also acted in the West End in *Helen, Give Me A Ring, Paganini*; then in New York in *Between The Devil*. In London has also appeared in various pantomimes. In 1940 in *Lights Up* (Savoy). Then in *The Belle Of New York* (Coliseum, 1942). Recently: In *Sunny River* (Piccadilly, 1943), *The Three Waltzes* (Princes, 1945), and on tour, with Frank Lawton.

LEAVER, PHILIP. Actor and dramatic author. Born London, 1903. Studied for the stage at Royal Academy; first appearing on the stage on tour, 1924, subsequently in London in *The Constant Nymph* (New, 1926). Also in the West End in *Grand Hotel, Clive Of India, St. Joan* (for Old Vic, 1934), *Return To Yesterday, Young Madame Conti* (also in New York, 1937), *Judgment Day, Out Of The Picture, Blind Man's Buff, Windfall*, etc. Since the outbreak of war with the B.B.C. Is the author of *Tomorrow Will Be Friday, Three Set Out, Causes Unknown* and other plays; also many radio plays and features. 1945: Wrote the book of *Sweet Yesterday* (Adelphi).

LEE, BERNARD. Actor. Born London, 1908. Studied for stage at R.A.D.A., making his first appearance on tour in *White Cargo*; subsequently in repertory at Manchester, Cardiff, and at the Regent, King's Cross. Also appeared in London in *Appearances, Love For Sale, The Tudor Wench, The Terror, Ten Minute Alibi*, etc. Then in *Murder In Motley, Distinguished Gathering, Murder Gay, Young Madame Conti, The Gusher*. Went to New York to act in *If I Were You* (Mansfield, 1938), returning to London in *People Of Our Class*, followed by *Number Six*, etc. Since the outbreak of war in H.M. Forces. In 1946 appeared in *Stage Door* (Saville).

LEGGATT, ALISON. Actress. Born London, 1904. Studied for the stage at Central School of Dramatic Art, making her first appearance on the stage in *Judas Iscariot* (Scala, 1924). Then in London in *A Kiss For Cinderella*, afterwards with Stratford-on-Avon Festival Company, 1925. Also in London in *Many Waters, The Fanatics, Fear, Mrs. Moonlight, Nine Till Six*, and many others. Subsequently acted in the West End in *Cavalcade, The Rose Without A Thorn, Eden End, Tonight At 8.30, Geneva*, etc. Recently: *Chicken Every Sunday* (Savoy, 1945), *Duet For Two Hands* (Lyric, 1945).

British Theatre

LEHMANN, BEATRIX. Actress. Born Bourne End, 1903. Studied for the stage at R.A.D.A., making her first appearance on the stage in *The Way Of The World* (Lyric, Hammersmith, 1924). Subsequently in the West End in *The Green Hat, An American Tragedy, The Adding Machine, Byron, All God's Chillun Got Wings, Hoppla, The Silver Tassie, Brain, Late Night Final, Wild Decembers* and several others. Also acted in London in *The Wandering Jew, The Tudor Wench, Success Story, The Master Builder, Eden End, The Witch Of Edmonton, Mourning Becomes Electra, They Walk Alone,* etc. In 1940 appeared in *Desire Under The Elms* (Westminster), followed by *Close Quarters* (Apollo, 1941) and *Jam To-day* (St. Martin's, 1942). Recently played in *Ghosts* (Duke of York's, 1943), *Uncle Harry* (Garrick, 1944). In 1945 acting and producing for the Arts Council. Toured the Continent, with Walter Hudd, in 1946.

LEIGH, ANDREW. Actor and producer. Born Brighton, 1887. First appeared on the stage with the Benson Company in *The Merry Wives Of Windsor* (Worthing, 1908), remaining with this Company until 1913. Toured South Africa, 1913-14, then with Old Vic, 1915-16. Has also appeared in London with Old Vic in 1920-22, then in 1923 with Lena Ashwell Players. From 1924-29 acting and producing with Old Vic. Produced in New York, 1930, returning to London to play in *Tomorrow, The Silver Box,* etc. Toured Canada with Sir Barry Jackson, 1931-32 ; then in London in *The Streets Of London, Strife, The Tempest, The Little Man, Androcles And The Lion, Lady Precious Stream, Paganini, Everyman, Othello, She Stoops To Conquer* and dozens of other plays. More recently in *The Three Sisters, Henry V, Climbing,* etc. In 1937-39 producing at Stratford-on-Avon. Recently : *It's Time To Dance* (Winter Garden, 1943), *The Merchant Of Venice* (for Old Vic) (New, 1943), *The Shoemaker's Holiday* (Lyric, Hammersmith, 1944), *Bird In Hand* (Arts, 1944), etc.

LEIGH, VIVIEN. Actress. Born Darjeeling, India, 1913. Married to Laurence Olivier. Studied for the stage at the *Comédie Francaise* and at the R.A.D.A., making her first appearance on the stage in *Giusta,* (Q Theatre, 1935). Then in the West End in *The Mask Of Virtue* (Ambassadors), followed by *Richard II, The Happy Hypocrite, Henry VIII, Because We Must, Bats In The Belfry.* Went to Elsinore in 1937 to act in *Hamlet* and *A Midsummer Night's Dream.* In 1938 played in *Serena Blandish* (Gate). Recently : In 1942 *The Doctor's Dilemma* (Haymarket), *The Skin Of Our Teeth* (Phœnix, 1945).

LEIGHTON, MARGARET. Actress. Born Barnt Green, Warwickshire, 1922. Educated Church of England College, Birmingham. Made her first appearance on the stage at the Birmingham Repertory Theatre in *Laugh With Me,* 1938. With the Travelling Repertory Theatre, 1941 to 1942, on tour and in Birmingham. Joined Birmingham Repertory Theatre, 1942, remaining until 1944, appearing in *The Little Minister, Heartbreak House, The Taming Of The Shrew, As You Like It* and many others. In 1944 joined the Old Vic Company, appearing in *Arms And The Man, Richard III, Peer Gynt* and *Uncle Vanya* (New, 1944-45). In 1945, toured the Continent with the Old Vic Company, then appeared at the New in *Henry IV (Parts I and II), Œdipus Rex* and *The Critic,* 1945-46.

LEIGHTON, FRANK. Actor. Born Sydney, Australia. Educated in Sydney. Made his first appearance on the stage in *Lilac Time* (Sydney, 1926) ; thenceforth appeared on the stage in Sydney and Melbourne for the next ten years (as well as serving for three years in the Australian Navy). Made his first appearance in London in *The Fleet's Lit Up* (Hippodrome, 1937). He also appeared in *Shephard's Pie* (Princes), *Fun And Games* (Saville), *Wild Rose* (Princes). In 1942 appeared in *Junior Miss* (Saville), then in 1944 appeared in *Irene* (His Majesty's). In 1945, acted in *Chicken Every Sunday* (Savoy), *The Hasty Heart* (Aldwych), etc.

LEISTER, FREDERICK. Actor. Born London, 1885. First appeared on the stage in *A Country Girl*, 1906 ; then on tour until 1913. Made his first appearance in London in *The Indian Mutiny* (Princes, 1913), then in *The Little Minister, Peter Pan*, etc. After the war joined Lena Ashwell as producer and actor, remaining until 1922. Has also acted in London in *Outward Bound, The Green Hat, La Prisonnière, Knight Errant, To What Red Hell?, The Man At Six, Murder On The Second Floor, White Horse Inn*, etc. First appeared in New York in *Evensong* (Selwyn, 1932). Then in London in *The Late Christopher Bean, Viceroy Sarah, This Desirable Residence* ; and in New York in *Dark Victory* and *Libel*. Has also acted in London in *Farewell Performance, The Housemaster* (also in New York, 1938), *Lady Fanny*, etc. Also appeared more recently in *The Nutmeg Tree* (Lyric, 1941), *The Cradle Song* (Apollo, 1944). Recently in *No Medals* (Vaudeville, 1944-46).

LETTS, PAULINE. Actress. Born May 1st, 1917, Loughborough, Leics. Married to Geoffrey Staines. Educated Collegiate School, Leicester, after which she studied for the stage at the Royal Academy of Dramatic Art. She made her first appearance in *Twelfth Night* (Prince of Wales, Cardiff) in 1936, after which she appeared in repertory at Coventry and York. In 1938 she appeared for a season at the Memorial Theatre, Stratford-on-Avon, after which she played for a season at York. She made her first appearance in London in *The Tragedy Of Nan* (Mercury, 1943). Recently in *A Soldier For Christmas* (Wyndham's, 1944), *Stage Door* (Saville, 1946).

LEVY, BENN W. Playwright. Born London, 1900. Educated Repton and Oxford. Married to Constance Cummings. Among his plays are *This Woman Business, Mrs. Moonlight, Art And Mrs. Bottle, Evergreen, Springtime For Henry, If I Were You* (in collaboration with Paul Henry Fox), *The Jealous God*. Also adapted the following : *A Man With Red Hair, Topaze, Young Madame Conti* (with Hubert Griffith), *Madame Bovary*, etc. Since the outbreak of war : in Royal Navy. In 1945 became a Member of Parliament.

LILLIE, BEATRICE. Actress. Born Toronto, Canada, 1898. Made her first appearance on the stage in variety in Chatham ; then appeared in London in the revue *Not Likely* (Alhambra, 1914). Subsequently in the West End in *Now's The Time, Oh Joy !, Up In Mabel's Room, Pot Luck, The Nine O'Clock Revue*, etc. Then appeared in New York in *Charlot's Revue of 1924* (Times Square), and thenceforth divided her career between London and New York. She has also appeared in London in *Charlot's Revue Of 1925, Charlot's Masquerade Of 1930, Please, Happy Returns*, etc. In New York has played in *Charlot's Revue Of 1926, She's My Baby, This Year Of Grace, The Third Little Show, Too True To Be Good, At Home Abroad, The Show Is On, Set To Music* and others. In 1940 appeared in London in *All Clear* (Queen's), in 1941 appeared in *Big Top*, the Cochran revue, at His Majesty's. Then acted in New York until 1944, when she toured in England in *Staff Dance*. Appeared in *Better Late* (Garrick, 1946).

LIND, GILLIAN. Actress. Born India, 1904. Married to Cyril Raymond. Made her first appearance on the stage in *The Risk* (Strand, 1922), subsequently playing in London in *The Man Who Ate The Popomack, Alf's Button, From Morn To Midnight, Distinguished Villa, Many Waters, The Constant Nymph, The Field God, Maya, A Man With Red Hair, Alibi, The Calendar* and many others. Also in the West End in *On The Spot, A Trip To Scarborough, The Rose Without A Thorn, The School For Husbands, Spacetime Inn, Clive Of India, No Exit*, etc. At the Vaudeville, 1936, played in *Green Waters* ; then in *To Have And To Hold, Goodbye, Mr. Chips*, etc. Recently : *Cottage To Let* (Wyndham's, 1941), *A Man With Red Hair* (St. Martin's, 1942), *Goodnight Children* (New, 1942), *Emma* (St. James's, 1945). Appeared in *The Quick And The Dead* (Repertory Players, 1946).

LINDEN, JOYCE. Actress. Born London, August 25th, 1923. Educated King's House, Highgate. Made her first appearance on the stage in repertory at Watford, followed by repertory at Windsor, etc. Then in numerous tours, including *Wuthering Heights* and *Vintage Wine*. In 1943 she made her first appearance in London in *Gay Follies* (Cambridge), then in *The Rest Is Silence* (Prince of Wales, 1944), *Young Mrs. Barrington* (Winter Garden, 1945-46), etc.

LINDO, OLGA. Actress. Born London, 1898. Made her first appearance on the stage in *The Sleeping Beauty Re-awakened* (Drury Lane, 1913); subsequently in London in *Sealed Orders*; on tour, 1917-21; then in the West End in *If Four Walls Told, The Ballad Monger, R.U.R., The Will, The Fool, Rain, The Best People* and many others. Also in London in *Othello, The Merchant Of Venice, Enchantment*. Season of Grand Guignol (Little, 1928), *The Stranger Within*, etc. Toured South Africa, 1930-31, returning to London in *Naughty Cinderella*. Also in the West End in *Many Women, The Bear Dances, Viceroy Sarah, The Skin Game, White Cargo, Wise Tomorrow, Cymbeline, Banana Ridge, Jitta's Atonement*, etc. Recently: *Jam To-day* (St. Martin's, 1942), *A Little Bit Of Fluff* (Ambassadors, 1943), *The Russians* (for the Old Vic) (Playhouse, 1943), *Scandal at Barchester* (Lyric and Wyndham's, 1944), *Great Day* (Playhouse, 1945). In 1945 joined the Arts Theatre Group of Actors, appearing in *Hamlet, Getting Married, The Thunderbolt*, etc. (Arts).

LION, LEON M. Actor and producer. Born London, 1879. Made his first appearance on the stage in *True Blue* (Olympic, 1896); subsequently toured with Forbes-Robertson and with George Edwardes. Appeared in London in *The Scarlet Pimpernel, The Beloved Vagabond, The Merchant Of Venice, The Merry Wives Of Windsor, Trilby, The Master Builder, Within The Law, The Doctor's Dilemma* and many others. Also in London in *The Chinese Puzzle, The Faithful Heart, The Silver Box, Justice* and many others. Subsequently in the West End in *No. 17, Escape, Justice, Loyalties, Libel, The Skin Game, Lady Precious Stream, Strange Family* and others. In addition to producing most of the plays in which he has appeared, he has also produced in London, such plays as *The Fanatics, Many Waters, To What Red Hell?, The Skin Game, Street Scene, Libel, Awake And Sing*, etc. Since the outbreak of war has been touring the provinces in various plays. In 1944 he was seen in *Jane Clegg* (Lyric, Hammersmith). In 1945 he toured in *Thirteen To The Gallows*, after which he retired from the stage.

LIPSCOMB, WILLIAM. Playwright. Born Merton, Surrey, 1887. Among his plays are *Persecuting Peter, Clive Of India* (with R. J. Minney), *Thank You Mr. Pepys* (adaptation), etc. Recently wrote *The Gay Pavilion* (Piccadilly, 1945).

LIPTON, CELIA. Actress and vocalist. Born Edinburgh, December 25th, 1923. Formerly a singer; she made her first appearance on the legitimate stage in *Black And Blue* (London Hippodrome, 1940). Also appeared in London in *Get A Load Of This* (Hippodrome, 1942-43), *Jack And Jill* (His Majesty's, 1943-44), *The Quaker Girl* (Coliseum, Stoll, and on tour, 1944-45), *Peter Pan* (Scala, 1945-46).

LISLE, LUCILLE. Actress. Born Melbourne, Australia, 1912, making her first appearance on the stage at the age of four in *Dick Whittington*; then in many plays in Melbourne and on tour in Australia. First appeared in New York in 1930 in *Stepdaughters Of War* (Empire), then on tour in United States with Jane Cowl. Also played in New York in *A Widow In Green* and *Alice Sit-By-The-Fire*, before coming to London in 1933 to appear in *Another Language* (St. James's). Thenceforth in London in *The Late Christopher Bean, Lady Precious Stream, Anthony And Anna, Twelfth Night* (in Michel St. Denis season at the Phœnix, 1938), *Behind The Curtain*, etc. During the war was for a considerable period with the B.B.C. Drama Repertory Company.

LISTER, FRANCIS. Actor. Born London, 1899. Studied for stage at R.A.D.A., making his first appearance in *The Flag Lieutenant* (Haymarket, 1914). Subsequently in London in *The Private Secretary, You Never Can Tell, The Tempest, A Family Man, If Four Walls Told*, etc. Went to New York to appear in *Mary, Mary, Quite Contrary* (Belasco, 1923), returning to London to appear in *The Fake*. Thenceforth in the West End in *Tarnish, Lullaby, Aloma, The Queen Was In The Parlour, Quality Street, Mary Rose* and many others. Again acted in New York in *Dishonoured Lady* (Empire, 1930), returning in *Let Us Be Gay*, followed by *Take A Chance, The Nelson Touch, Richard Of Bordeaux* and others. Went back to New York in 1934 and acted continuously in America until 1939. In 1942 appeared in London in *Macbeth* (Piccadilly). Recently in London has appeared in *Heartbreak House* (Cambridge, 1943), then with the John Gielgud Company at the Haymarket, appearing in *A Midsummer Night's Dream, The Circle* and *Hamlet*, 1944-45. Toured the Continent in *Julius Cæsar*, 1945-46.

LISTER, MOIRA. Actress. Born South Africa, August 6th, 1923. She made her first appearance on the stage at the age of six, in South Africa and studied acting under Amy Coleridge. She also appeared in South Africa on tour in *Vintage Wine*, after which she came to England and appeared in London in *Post Road* (Shaftesbury, 1936). She returned to Africa and appeared in a number of plays, including *Puppet's Party, Pawns In The Game, The Women, The Russians* (and many productions of Leontine Sagan). In 1943 she returned to London and appeared in *Six Pairs Of Shoes* (Playhouse, 1944). In 1945 she appeared at the Memorial Theatre, Stratford-on-Avon, in *Romeo And Juliet, Othello, Twelfth Night, She Stoops To Conquer* and *Henry VIII*. Recently joined the John Clements-Kay Hammond Company appearing in *The King-Maker, Marriage A La Mode*, etc., (St James's, 1946).

LIVESEY, BARRIE. Actor. Born London, 1904. Made his first appearance on the stage in *Crooked Usage* (Apollo, 1921); subsequently in *Life Goes On, The New Moon, The Private Secretary, Frailties*, etc. Appeared in New York in *The Father* (49th Street, 1931), returning to London in *Caravan*; then in *Follow Me, Love For Love* (for Old Vic, 1934), *Queer Cargo, Busman's Honeymoon*, etc. Also in the West End in *White Secrets, Behind The Blinds* and others. 1940-44: In H.M. Forces. In 1945 he appeared in *Dear Murderer* (Granville).

LIVESEY, JACK. Actor. Born Barry, Wales, 1901. First appeared on the stage in *Tiger's Cub*, Tottenham, 1916; subsequently on tour with Sir George Alexander. Made his first appearance in the West End in *The Private Secretary* (Savoy, 1917), then on tour in the provinces, and in India and South Africa until 1927, when he went to America to act in *Yellow Sands* (Fulton), after which he toured the United States until 1928. Has also appeared in London in *The Enemy, Show Boat, The New Moon, The Three Musketeers, The Ringer, Musical Chairs, The Merchant Of Venice* and many others. More recently in *Family Affairs, Lady Precious Stream, The Insect Play, The Gusher*, etc. Recently in *The Lisbon Story* (Hippodrome, 1942-43).

LIVESEY, ROGER. Actor. Born Barry, Wales, 1906. Married to Ursula Jeans. Was a pupil of Italia Conti, making his first appearance on the stage in *Loyalty* (St. James's, 1917). Then in *The Windmill Man, If Four Walls Told, The Man In The Next Room, Fata Morgana, The Cuckoo In The Nest*, etc. From 1926-29 touring in West Indies and South Africa. Then in London in *Sensation, Musical Chairs, The Farmer's Wife*, after which he joined the Old Vic Company, 1932-34. Subsequently in *Martine, Sour Grapes, Lady Precious Stream, Storm In A Teacup*, etc. Made his first appearance in New York in *The Country Wife* (Henry Miller, 1936), then in *Storm In A Teacup* (Guild, 1937), after which he returned to London to appear in *Spring Meeting*. Joined Old Vic again in 1939, acting in *An Enemy Of The People* and *The Taming Of The Shrew*. In 1939 appeared in

299

The Devil's Disciple (Piccadilly), then in *Dear Brutus* (Globe, 1940-41), touring, with Ursula Jeans, in *The Taming Of The Shrew*, etc. Then in *Watch On The Rhine* (Aldwych, 1943). Recently in *The Banbury Nose* (Wyndham's, 1944). In 1945, with Ursula Jeans, he toured the Middle East, with ENSA Festival Company, in *Pygmalion, The Barretts Of Wimpole Street, It Depends What You Mean*, etc.

LLOYD, FREDERICK. Actor. Born London, 1880. Studied for the stage at R.A.D.A., making his first appearance on the stage in *Lady Ben* (Comedy, 1905); then with Vedrenne-Barker Company, 1905-07, after which he toured United States, 1907-08. Then with Lewis Waller and Charles Frohman Companies until 1912, when he toured America once more. In 1918-24 touring United States; then touring Australia until 1925, when he reappeared in London in *The Bright Island*. Has since acted in the West End in *A Doll's House, Outward Bound, The Constant Wife, Ghosts, By Candlelight, After All*, etc. Also in *Topaze, Napoleon, Richard Of Bordeaux, The Maitlands, Jill Darling, Romeo And Juliet* and many others. More recently in *The Seagull, As You Like It, The Taming Of The Shrew*, and with the Gielgud Company in *Richard II, The School For Scandal, The Three Sisters* and *The Merchant Of Venice* (Queen's, 1937-38). Also in London in *The Corn Is Green*, 1938-39. Resumed his part in the latter play, Piccadilly, 1940, *The Morning Star* (Globe, 1942). Recently: *War And Peace* (Phœnix, 1943), *There Shall Be No Night* (Aldwych, 1943-44).

LOHR, MARIE. Actress. Born Sydney, Australia, 1890. Made her first appearance on the stage in *The World Against Her*, Sydney, 1894, and acted in other plays here before appearing in London in *Shock-Headed Peter* (Garrick, 1901). Thenceforth in the West End in *White Magic, Colonel Newcombe, My Wife*, etc., and acting extensively with the Kendals, 1902-07. Also in London in *The Admirable Bashville, The School For Scandal, Hamlet, The Silver King, The Ware Case, L'Aiglon, The Laughing Lady* and many others. Appeared in New York in *A Voice From The Minaret* (Hudson, 1922), returning to London in *The Return*. Thenceforth in *The Love Game, Peter Pan, Beau Geste, Berkeley Square, Dandy Dick, The Breadwinner* (also in New York, 1931), *Casanova, Peter Pan* (Palladium, 1934), *Aren't We All?, Chase The Ace, Call It A Day, And On We Go*, etc. Recently: *Other People's Houses* (Ambassadors, 1941-42).

LOMAS, HERBERT. Actor. Born Burnley, 1887. Studied at the Academy of Dramatic Art, making his first appearance in *The Winter's Tale* (His Majesty's, 1906). Was associated with Miss Horniman's Company, Manchester, from 1909 to 1914. After the war he went to America and appeared in *The Skin Game* (Bijou, 1920), and also in *Hindle Wakes* (Vanderbilt, 1922). From 1924-27 was with Liverpool Repertory Company, then in London with Everyman Company until 1928. Subsequently played in *Bird In Hand* in London and New York, 1928-29. Has also acted in the West End in *Inquest, The Nelson Touch, The Green Bay Tree, The Tudor Wench, Harvest In The North, The Hangman, The Frog, Glorious Morning* and many others. In 1940 appeared in *In Good King Charles's Golden Days* (New). In 1941 in *When We Are Married* (Vaudeville), also in *Actresses Will Happen* (Apollo). More recently in *Holy Isle* (Arts, 1942), *Abraham Lincoln* (for Old Vic) (Playhouse, 1943), *Crisis In Heaven* (Lyric, 1944), *Bird In Hand* (St. Martin's, 1944), *The Wind Of Heaven* (St. James's, 1945).

LORD, PETER. Actor. Born Hove, 1921. Educated Brighton College and London University. Made his first appearance on the stage in *Twelfth Night*, Bristol, 1939. Then in H.M. Forces, 1940-43, afterwards making his first West End appearance in *The Admirable Crichton* (His Majesty's, 1943). Also in *The Last Of Summer* (Phœnix, 1944), *Uncle Harry* (Garrick, 1944-45), *The Skin Of Our Teeth* (Phœnix, 1945), then on tour in *Madame Bovary*, 1945-46, etc.

LOVELL, RAYMOND. Actor. Born Montreal, Canada, 1900. Educated at Cambridge. Made his first appearance on the stage in *East Lynne*, Dundalk, 1924, then first acted in London in *Gossip* (Q, 1930). Thenceforth producing and acting at Leeds and Bradford until 1933, after which he ran repertory theatres at Bournemouth and Southampton. Has appeared in London in *Maternité*;, *The Queen Who Kept Her Head*, *Queer Cargo*, *The King's Pirate*, *Volpone*, *Whiteoaks* and others. Also in the West End in *Can We Tell ?*, *Private History*, *The Mother*, etc. Recently : *The Rose Without A Thorn* (Tavistock, 1940), *Jupiter Laughs* (New, 1941), *Murder Without Crime* (Comedy, 1942-43), *Arc De Triomphe* (Phœnix, 1944), *Laura* (St. Martin's, 1945), *Fit For Heroes* (Whitehall, 1945).

LUBBOCK, IAN. Actor. Born London, 1917. Made his first appearance on the London stage in *The Blue Goose* (Comedy, 1940), then in repertory at Oxford, Windsor, Intimate, etc. Also acted in *Salt Of The Earth* (Vaudeville, 1942), *An Ideal Husband* (Westminster, 1943), *Appointment With Death* (Piccadilly, 1945), *Oflag 3* (Q, 1945), *Kiss And Tell* (Phœnix, 1945). Appeared in *The Sacred Flame* (St. Martin's and Westminster, 1945-46).

LUCE, CLAIRE. Actress. Born New York, 1903. Studied dancing and appeared with Texas Guinan's dancers. Made her first stage appearance in the play *Little Jessie James* (Longacre, 1923), then in *Dear Sir, The Music Box Revue, No Foolin', The Ziegfeld Follies Of 1927*, etc. First appeared in London in *Burlesque* (Queen's, 1928), then in New York and London alternately. She has acted in London in *Gay Divorce, Vintage Wine, Gay Deceivers, Follow The Sun, No Sleep For The Wicked, Of Mice And Men*, etc. At the outbreak of war she went overseas with the first ENSA Concert Party, continuing this work until 1941. Then she joined Robert Atkins Company and appeared in *The Taming Of The Shrew* and *Henry V* (Open Air, 1941), after which she took *The Taming Of The Shrew* on an ENSA tour. Appeared in Perth and Dundee Repertory Theatres in *A Doll's House, Sadie Thompson* and *Anna Christie*, returning to America in 1942. In 1944 came back to England to appear in *Blithe Spirit* for U.S.O. tour of American Forces. In 1945 joined Stratford-on-Avon Festival Company to appear in *Antony And Cleopatra, Much Ado About Nothing, Twelfth Night* and *The Merry Wives Of Windsor*. Appeared in *It Happened In New York*, 1945-46 ; *Golden Eagle*, 1946.

LYEL, VIOLA. Actress. Born Hull, 1900. Studied for the stage at Guildhall School of Drama, making her first appearance on the stage at the Old Vic, 1918. Subsequently she toured with Ben Greet and appeared in repertory at Liverpool and Birmingham. Appeared in London in *The Farmer's Wife, Yellow Sands, Morning, Noon And Night* ; then acted in New York in *Murder On The Second Floor*, 1929. Also in London in *Milestones, Getting Married, Strife, It's A Wise Child, Duet In Floodlight, Lady Precious Stream, Pride And Prejudice, Sarah Simple*, etc. Joined Old Vic in 1938 to appear in *Coriolanus* ; afterwards in the West End in *Lot's Wife, After The Dance* (St. James's, 1939), etc. Recently : *The Man Who Came To Dinner* (Savoy, 1942-43). Joined Stratford-on-Avon Festival Company in 1944 and again in 1945, appearing in the latter season in *Antony And Cleopatra, The Merry Wives Of Windsor, King Henry VIII, Othello*, etc. Appeared in *The Shop At Sly Corner* (St. Martin's, 1946).

LYNN, RALPH. Born Manchester, 1882. First appeared on the stage in 1900, then in the provinces and on tour in the United States. First appeared in London in *By Jingo* (Empire, 1914) ; afterwards in *Hanky Panky, Topsy Turvy, Tons Of Money* and many others. Appeared in a long succession of farces at the Aldwych, including *A Cuckoo In The Nest, Rookery Nook, Thark, Plunder, A Cup Of Kindness, A Night Like This, Turkey Time, Dirty Work* and many others. Thenceforth on tour, and in many films. Recently : *Nap Hand* (Aldwych, 1940), *Rookery Nook* (St. Martin's, 1942), *Is Your Honeymoon Really Necessary* (Duke of York's, 1944-46).

LYNNE, CAROLE. Actress. Born London. She has appeared recently in the West End in *Swinging The Gate* (Ambassadors, 1940), *Black And Blue* (Hippodrome, 1941), *Old Chelsea* (Princes, 1943), *Cinderella*, 1944. Also in 1944 appeared in *Jill Darling* (Saville). Recently in *Jenny Jones* (Hippodrome, 1944-45).

McCALLIN, CLEMENT. Actor. Born London, 1913. Studied for the stage at R.A.D.A., making his first appearance in *Hollywood* (Grafton, 1931), then on tour and in repertory at Festival, Cambridge, and Lyceum, Edinburgh. Then played in London in *Richard Of Bordeaux*, after which, in 1935, he joined the Old Vic, appearing in *Peer Gynt, Julius Cæsar, Macbeth, Richard III, St. Helena,* etc. Also in London in *The Lady Of La Paz, The Crooked Cross,* etc. Joined Stratford-on-Avon Festival Company in 1937, appearing in *Henry V, Cymbeline, King Lear, A Midsummer Night's Dream, A Winter's Tale.* Joined Donald Wolfit Company and toured until 1938, when he joined Birmingham Repertory Company, remaining here until 1939. In 1939 appeared in *The Gentle People* (Aldwych). Recently : In H.M. Forces since the outbreak of war.

McCRACKEN, ESTHER. Actress and playwright. Born Newcastle, 1902. Was formerly an actress, appearing with Newcastle Repertory Theatre for eight years. Wrote several one-act plays, then *Quiet Wedding,* produced at Richmond in 1938 and later at Wyndham's. Other plays include *Counter Attraction, White Elephants, Quiet Week-End, Living Room* and *No Medals.* In 1945 she produced *Living Room* at the Garrick.

McDERMOTT, HUGH. Actor. Born Edinburgh, 1908. Married to Daphne Courtney. Travelled round the world 1936-38 making *Travel Talks* with James Fitzpatrick. Made his first appearance on the London stage in *Death On The Table* (Strand, 1938), followed by *Grouse In June* and *Margin For Error.* Recently appeared in *The Man Who Came To Dinner* (Savoy, 1942-43), *While The Sun Shines* (Globe, 1943).

McGRATH, PAT. Actor. Born London, July 24th, 1914. Educated Brompton Oratory. Studied to be a ballet dancer, making his first appearance on the stage in *Coppelia,* Sadlers Wells Ballet Company, 1933. Then in *Please, Why Not Tonight ?, On Your Toes, Hide And Seek* and other London musicals. In H.M. Forces, 1939-43. Recently appeared in *The Quaker Girl* (Coliseum, Stoll) and on tour, 1944-45.

McLAUGHLIN, GIBB. Actor. Born Sunderland. Made his first appearance on the stage in *The Arcadians* in 1911, followed by *Princess Caprice* and others. Long career in films 1920-45. Recently appeared on the stage in *Waste* (Westminster, 1940), *House Of Regrets* (Arts, 1942), *The Moon Goes Down* (Whitehall, 1943), *The Recruiting Officer* and *The Philanderer* (Arts, 1944), *The Italian Straw Hat* and *The Government Inspector* (Arts, 1945). Recently appeared with York Festival Company in *The Alchemist* and *The Spinster Of South Street,* 1945. Also in the latter play, King's, Hammersmith, 1945.

McLEOD, GORDON. Actor. Born December 27th, 1884, Ivybridge, Devon. Educated Canada and Geneva. Trained for the Navy and served in the Merchant Service for four years. Went on the stage in a fit-up company in South America, and has since appeared extensively in America and England. His recent appearances include *Charles The King, It Happened In September* (St. James's, 1943), *The Sacred Flame* (St. Martin's and Westminster, 1945-46), etc.

MACDONALD, MURRAY. Producer. Born Glasgow, 1899. Commenced his career as an actor with the Scottish National Players in 1919 ; then on tour and in repertory until 1931. Made his first appearance in London in *Mrs. Fischer's War* (Ambassadors, 1931), then in *Vile Bodies,* after which he joined the Old Vic in 1933. His first production in London was *Viceroy Sarah* (with Tyrone Guthrie) ; others include *Love From A Stranger, The Road To Rome, The Bat, Judgment Day, Robert's Wife, People Of Our Class, Comedienne, Goodbye, Mr. Chips,* etc. 1940-45 : In H.M. Forces. Recently producing for the Army at the Garrison Theatre, Salisbury. Also produced *The Hasty Heart* (Aldwych, 1945). Now producing at the Lyric, Hammersmith, *The Shouting Dies,* etc. Produced *Stage Door* (Saville).

MACGINNIS, NIALL. Actor. Born Dublin, 1913. Made his first appearance on the stage in Dublin in 1931 ; then in repertory at Sheffield and on tour in Ireland until 1933. With the Dublin Gate Company, 1933-34. First appeared in London in *A Man's House* (New, 1934), then in repertory at Oxford until 1935. Also played in London in *Hamlet, Anna Christie, A Month In The Country, Macbeth, Volpone, Moonshine, Spring Meeting*, etc. In 1939 played in *Of Mice And Men* (Apollo).

MACGRATH, LEUEEN. Actress. Born London, 1916. Educated Farnborough Convent College, and in Brussels. Made her first appearance on the stage in *Raffles* (Hastings Repertory Theatre, 1934). Made her first appearance in London in *Tovarich* (Lyric, 1935), followed by *Pride And Prejudice, French Without Tears* (which ran for two years), etc. Recently : In *Saloon Bar* (Wyndham's, 1940-41), *Salt Of The Earth*, 1942, *Blossom Time* (Lyric, 1942), *Flare Path* (Apollo, 1942-44). In 1944-45 toured the Middle East and the Continent in *Blithe Spirit*, with Emlyn Williams. Appeared in *Young Mrs. Barrington* (Winter Garden, 1945).

MACOWAN, MICHAEL. Producer. Born London, 1906. Educated at Haileybury. Studied for the stage at R.A.D.A., making his first appearance on tour with the Macdona Company. Then in London in *A Month In The Country, Young Woodley, Milestones*. From 1930-31 with the Gate Theatre Company, then with Hull Repertory Company as producer in 1932-34, after which he produced several plays at Croydon Repertory Theatre. From 1935-36 produced for Old Vic (and directed the Dramatic School). Producer at Westminster Theatre, 1936-40. Productions here and elsewhere include *A Month In The Country, The Wild Duck, The Crooked Cross, Uncle Vanya, Heartbreak House, Hamlet, Mourning Becomes Electra, Volpone, Troilus And Cressida, Marco Millions, Miss Julie, Bridge Head, After The Dance*, etc. Since the outbreak of war in H.M. Forces. Recently : Director of the Play Unit of the Army Bureau of Current Affairs, 1943-45. Appointed Drama Director of the Arts Council of Great Britain, 1945.

MACRAE, ARTHUR. Actor and dramatic author. Born London, 1908. Studied under Italia Conti, making his first appearance on the stage in *Peter Pan* (St. James's, 1921). Studied at R.A.D.A. from 1925-27, thenceforth appearing in repertory at Bristol, Glasgow and Edinburgh. Also acted in London in *Dance With No Music, Song Of The Drum, Sea Fever, The Young Idea, Cavalcade, Three Cornered Moon, Dusty Ermine*, etc. First appeared in New York in *George And Margaret* (Morosco, 1937). Then in London in *Sugar Plum, The Ascent Of F.6*, etc. Recently appeared in *No Time For Comedy* (Haymarket, 1941). Then in the Royal Air Force, 1941-45. Has written a number of plays, including *Flat To Let, Indoor Fireworks*, and is part-author of *Town Talks, Under Your Hat, Full Swing*, etc. In 1945 he wrote *Under The Counter* (Phœnix).

MAKEHAM, ELIOT. Born London, 1882. Studied for the stage under Rosina Filippi, making his first appearance in *Mr. Popple*, Chesterfield, 1910. Subsequently in London in *The Maker Of Dreams* (Vaudeville, 1910), then with Miss Horniman's Company at Manchester, 1912-13. During the war organised concert parties ; was with " Splinters " Company until 1924. Also in London in *Easy Money, Contraband, Mr. Pickwick*, etc. Appeared in New York in *Bird In Hand* (Masque, 1929). Then in London in *Late Night Final, Treasure Island, I Lived With You, Three Sisters, Follow The Sun* and many others. Also in *A Ship Comes Home, Money Talks, The Mother*, etc. Recently : *Tobias And The Angel* (Open Air, 1943), *Waltz Without End* (Cambridge, 1942-43), on tour in *Acacia Avenue*, 1944-45.

MALLALIEU, AUBREY. Actor. Born Liverpool, 1873. Made his first appearance on the stage in 1881 in *Across The Continent*, Leicester ; then in London in *With Flying Colours* (Adelphi, 1899). Then on tour in the provinces and in Australia and Canada. Also acted in London in *The Desperate Lovers, The Apple Cart, Cabbages And Kings, The Queen Who Kept Her Head, There's*

Always Tomorrow, A Butterfly On The Wheel, Glass Houses and many others. Recently : In *Three's A Family* (Saville and Winter Garden, 1944-45).

MALLESON, MILES. Actor, playwright and producer. Born London, 1888. Educated Brighton and Cambridge. Studied for the stage at the Academy of Dramatic Art, making his first appearance in *Justice*, Liverpool, 1911 ; then in London in *Interloper* (Royalty, 1913). Subsequently in the West End in *Fanny's First Play, Twelfth Night, The School For Scandal, The Lost Leader, The Merchant Of Venice, The Tempest, She Stoops To Conquer* and many others. Also in *David Garrick, The Rivals, The Beggar's Opera, Riverside Nights, The Beaux' Stratagem, The Old Batchelor,* etc. From 1932-41 extensively engaged on writing and acting in films. In 1940 he produced *The Country Wife* (Little). Returned to the stage in *Love For Love* (Phœnix, 1943), subsequently joined John Gielgud Company at the H~ymarket, appearing in *A Midsummer Night's Dream, The Duchess Of Malfi* and *Hamlet,* 1944. In 1945 joined the Old Vic Company to act and produce. Produced *The Critic,* and appeared in *Henry IV* (*Parts I and II*), *Œdipus* and *The Critic* (New, 1945-46).

MALTBY, H. F. Actor and playwright. Born Cape Colony, 1880. Made his first appearance on the stage in *The Sign Of The Cross*, Aberystwith, 1899 ; then with the Ben Greet Players, Miss Horniman's Company and many others. Is known chiefly as a playwright and among his well-known plays are *The Laughter Of Fools, The Rotters, A Temporary Gentleman, For The Love Of Mike, Fifty-Fifty* and *The Shadow.* Recently wrote *The Wanglers.*

MANNHEIM, LUCIE. Actress. Born Berlin, 1905. Married to Marius Goring. First appeared on the stage while still at school in *Old Heidelberg,* 1920 ; subsequently appeared in Hanover, Konigsberg and Berlin, where she acted extensively from 1924-34. Came to England and made her first appearance on the London stage in *Nina,* (Criterion, 1935). Has also appeared in *Girl Unknown, The Last Straw, The Countess Maritza,* etc. In 1939 appeared in *A Doll's House, Lady Fanny* and a revival of *Nina.* Since the war has been broadcasting extensively with the B.B.C. European Service.

MARCH, ELSPETH. Actress. Born in London. Studied for the stage under Elsie Fogerty at the Central School of Dramatic Art. Married to Stewart Granger. Made her first appearance on the stage in *Jonah And The Whale,* 1931. Subsequently acted extensively with the Birmingham Repertory Theatre, and at several Malvern Festivals, etc. In 1940 appeared in *The Playboy Of The Western World* (Mercury), *The House In The Square* (Ambassadors, 1941), then working for American Red Cross until 1944. Recently appeared in *Duet For Two Hands* (Lyric, 1945).

MARKHAM, DAVID. Actor. Born Wick, 1913. Studied for the stage at R.A.D.A., making his first appearance in *The Swan,* Manchester, 1934. Then in London in *All Rights Reserved* (Criterion, 1935), followed by *Red Night, The Astonished Ostrich, Robert's Wife* and others. In 1939 appeared in *Only Yesterday* (Playhouse). Then on tour in *Family Portrait,* followed by a tour with the Old Vic Company, playing in *She Stoops To Conquer, Twelfth Night, Trilby, The Kingdom Of God* and *The Cherry Orchard.* Recently with the Old Vic Company at Liverpool Playhouse, and also with Oxford Repertory Company, 1943-44. In 1945 joined the London Theatre Group and appeared in *Rosmersholm* (Torch). Then with the Old Vic Company, (Liverpool Playhouse, 1945-46).

MARLE, ARNOLD. Actor. Born Prague. Studied for the stage under Alexander Strakosch ; making his first appearance on the stage in the provinces, after which he acted with Max Reinhardt in Berlin. Then for twelve years in Munich, after which he acted and produced at Hamburg. Made his first appearance in London in 1933 at the Duke of York's, with the Leopold Jessner Company, after which he acted in Amsterdam and Prague. Came to England in 1939, and acted and produced at the Free German Theatre, 1940-43. Recently he has appeared in *Blow Your Own Trumpet* for the Old Vic (Playhouse, 1943), then he joined the Old Vic in Liverpool in 1944, appearing in *John Gabriel Borkman, Uneasy Laughter, School For Scandal*, etc. In 1945 he appeared in *A Bell For Adano* (Phœnix). Then in *The Time Of Your Life* (Lyric, Hammersmith, 1946).

MARSDEN, ROBERT. Actor. Born London, 1921. Educated Wycliffe College. Made his first appearance on the stage with Warrington Repertory Company in 1939. With the London Mask Theatre Company in 1940, after which he appeared with the Stratford-on-Avon Festival Company in 1941. 1942-43 with B.B.C. Drama Repertory Company; then appeared in *The Judgment Of Dr. Johnson* (Arts, 1943), joined Arts Theatre Festival Company, to act in *The Rivals, Misalliance, The Constant Couple*, etc. In 1944 joined the Greta Douglas Company at the Chanticleer, appearing in *The Orator, He Must Return, The Trojan Women, The Provoked Wife, The Infernal Machine, John Gabriel Borkman, Larissa* and many others. In 1945 he appeared in *The Trojan Women* (Lyric, Hammersmith).

MARSHALL, HERBERT P. J. Producer. Born London, January 29th, 1906. Married to Fredda Brilliant. In 1930 went to U.S.S.R. and worked in Moscow on Soviet films, and also as producer of the Moscow Foreign Workers' Theatre. Returned to England in 1937 and was co-founder of Unity Theatre. Here he produced *Plant In The Sun*, with Paul Robeson, *Waiting For Lefty*, etc. In 1940 he founded Neighbourhood Theatre, producing *Thunder Rock*, also at Globe. In 1941-42 producer for the Old Vic, directing *Time Of Your Life, The Beggar's Opera*, etc. Since 1943 has been in charge of production for Soviet Film Agency, producing, editing and directing dubbed versions of Soviet films.

MARSHALL, NORMAN. Producer. Born India, 1901. Educated at Oxford. Formerly a journalist and actor; joining Cambridge Festival Theatre Company as stage director in 1926. His first production was *The Rumour*, Cambridge, 1927, which was followed by many other productions at the Festival and at Leeds Civic Playhouse. He took over the Festival, 1932-34; then assumed directorship of the Gate, in London, producing, among others, *Victoria Regina, Parnell, Oscar Wilde, The Children's Hour, Asmodée, Of Mice And Men*. He has also produced and presented plays in the West End and in New York. In 1940 produced *Cousin Muriel, Swinging The Gate*; and the *Jersey Lily* and *Boys In Brown* (Gate). Joined H.M. Forces in 1939, returning to the theatre in 1942. Has since produced *Petrified Forest* (Globe, 1942). In 1943 formed his own company, in conjunction with CEMA, and produced, among others, *Uncle Vanya* (Westminster, 1943), and *Madeleine* (Lyric, Hammersmith, 1944). Recently produced *A Soldier For Christmas* (Wyndham's), *The Banbury Nose* (Wyndham's), *Three Waltzes* (Princes) and *The First Gentleman* (New and Savoy, 1945). Produced *Better Late*, 1946.

MARTLEW, MARY. Actress. Born Atherton, Manchester. Educated Brentwood and Switzerland. Studied for the stage in Geneva, and in London at the R.A.D.A. She made her first appearance on the stage in *Second Shot* (Q), after which she was seen in *Party For Christmas* (Haymarket, 1938), *As You Like It* (Adelphi), etc. Then in *School For Slavery* (Westminster, 1942), *A Midsummer Night's Dream, Twelfth Night* and *The Taming Of The Shrew* (Open Air, 1942), *Claudia* (St. Martin's, 1942-44), *Something In The Air* (Palace, 1944), then on tour in Europe, 1945. Recently *The Sacred Flame* (St. Martin's, 1945-46).

MASON, ELLIOT. Actress. Born Glasgow, 1903. Studied for the stage with the Scottish National Players and first appeared in *The Old Lady Shows Her Medals* Glasgow, 1922. Subsequently appeared in London in *A Valuable Rival* (Coliseum, 1923), then with the Scottish Players until 1932. First appeared in New York in *The Lake* (Beck, 1933), then in London in *Touch Wood, Grief Goes Over, No Exit, Sweet Aloes, Blondie White, A Kiss For Cinderella, Little Ladyship*, etc. In

1940 appeared in *As You Are* (Aldwych), *The Light Of Heart* (Apollo and Globe), followed by *The Morning Star* (Globe, 1941), etc. Recently in *The Glass Slipper* (St. James's, 1944-45), *The Young Mrs. Barrington* (Winter Garden, 1945).

MASON, JAMES. Actor. Born Huddersfield, 1909. Married to Pamela Kellino. Educated Marlborough and Cambridge. Made his first appearance on the stage in *The Rascal*, Aldershot, 1931. Subsequently acted in London in *Gallows Glorious* (Arts and Shaftesbury, 1933), then with Old Vic Company, 1933, in *Twelfth Night, The Cherry Orchard, Measure For Measure, Love For Love*, etc. In 1934 and 1937 appeared at Dublin Gate Theatre. Also acted in London in *Parnell, The Road To Rome, Bonnet Over The Windmill, Sixth Floor*, etc. In 1941 appeared in *Jupiter Laughs* (New). In 1943 toured for ENSA in *Jeannie*, etc.

MATHEWS, A. E. Actor. Born Bridlington, 1869. Commenced his career as a call boy and then stage manager in 1886, and thenceforth on tour in Africa and Australia. In London appeared in *The Star Of India, A Pair Of Spectacles, Betsy, Alice-Sit-By-The-Fire, The Silver Box, Peter Pan* and dozens of others. First appeared in New York in *Love Among The Lions* (Lyceum, 1910). In London has also acted in the following, among others : *Diplomacy, Peg O' My Heart, Nothing But The Truth, Bulldog Drummond* (and in New York, 1921), *Beggar On Horseback, The Last Of Mrs. Cheyney, The Happy Husband, The First Mrs. Fraser, The Breadwinner, Short Story.* Also in many plays in New York until 1939. Among other plays in which he has appeared in the West End are *Satyr* and *Ghost For Sale.* Recently : *They Came To A City* (Globe, 1943-44), *Another Love Story* (Phœnix, 1944-45). In *A Play For Ronnie*, 1946.

MATURIN, ERIC. Actor. Born India, 1883. Educated at Tonbridge. Made his first appearance on the stage in *The Second In Command* (Haymarket, 1901), subsequently touring extensively on the provinces and in the United States and Canada with Forbes-Robertson. First acted in New York in *Under The Greenwood Tree* (Garrick, 1907). Thenceforth acting both in London and New York. Has appeared in the West End in *The Parisienne, The Happy Island, The Gilded Pill, The Elder Son*, etc. In 1919 appeared in the West End in *The Governor's Lady* ; subsequently in *Lonely Lady, Heartbreak House, Loyalties, The Prisoner Of Zenda, Beggar On Horseback, The Green Hat, Flotsam, Macbeth* and many others. Also in London in *The Roof, Lady Windermere's Fan, The Gay Adventure, A Present From Margate, Espionage, Double Error, Bats In The Belfry, I Killed The Count*, etc. In 1940 appeared in *The Silver Patrol* (New). Recently : *The Banbury Nose* (Wyndham's, 1944).

MAUGHAM, W. SOMERSET. Playwright and novelist. Born Paris, 1874. Educated King's School, Canterbury, and Heidelberg University. Among his well-known plays are *Lady Frederick, Jack Straw, Our Betters, Cæsar's Wife, Home And Beauty, The Circle, The Letter, The Constant Wife, The Sacred Flame, The Breadwinner, For Services Rendered* and *Sheppey.*

MAXWELL, MEG. Actress. Born London, 1921. Educated Normanhurst Court. Studied for the stage at Webber-Douglas School, after which she appeared in repertory at Rugby, Perth, and two years at Birmingham Repertory Theatre under H. K. Ayliff. In 1944 she joined the Greta Douglas Company, appearing in *Hundred Years Old, The Orator, Love And How To Cure It*, etc. (Chanticleer). Recently in *The Glass Slipper* (St. James's, 1944-45), *The Wind Of Heaven* (St. James's, 1945).

MAYNE, FERDY. Actor. Educated Frensham Heights School. Studied for the stage at R.A.D.A. Made his first appearance on tour with the Greater London Players in *Libel*, 1936, afterwards appearing in repertory at Croydon, Brighton, etc. Made his first appearance in the West End in *Too Famous For Words* (Arts, 1937), then with the Old Vic, after which he was engaged in film production until the outbreak of war. From 1939-45 he was with the European Section of the

B.B.C., also making several stage appearances in London. Recently in *Watch On The Rhine* (Aldwych, 1943), *The Russians* (for the Old Vic) (Playhouse, 1943), *The Gambler* (Embassy, 1945), etc. In 1945-46 he appeared at Watford Repertory Theatre, then in *Gin Palace* (Gateway, 1946).

MEASOR, BERYL. Actress. Born China, 1908. Studied for stage at R.A.D.A., making her first appearance in *Take A Chance* (Whitehall, 1931). Then in repertory at Worthing, Croydon and Hull, after which she appeared in the West End in *Hemlock, Children In Uniform, Murder Gang, Night Alone, People Of Our Class, Can We Tell* and many others. Recently : In *Blithe Spirit* (Duchess). In 1943 in *Present Laughter* (Haymarket) ; *Now The Day Is Over* (Embassy, 1946).

MELFORD, AUSTIN. Actor, dramatic author and producer. Born Alverstokes, 1884. Made his first appearance on the stage in *The Silver King*, Manchester, 1889. First appeared in London in *The Never Never Land* (King's, Hammersmith, 1904); then on tour until 1910, when he appeared in London in *The Whip*, followed by *Ben Hur, Quality Street, Going Up, Sally, Battling Butler*, etc. Was a member of the Co-Optimists, 1922-27 ; also appeared in the West End in *Lucky Girl, A Warm Corner, It's A Boy, Night Of The Garter* and many others. From 1934-40 engaged in writing and directing films. He is the author of *It's A Girl*, etc., and part author of *Battling Butler, It's A Boy, Night Of The Garter* and many others. He has also staged many of the above plays in London. In 1940 he produced *Nap Hand* (Aldwych), etc. Recently staged *Chicken Every Sunday* (Savoy, 1945).

MELFORD, JACK. Actor and producer. Born London, 1899. Made his first appearance on the stage in *The Silver King*, Birmingham, 1912, then in London in *The Thief* (King's, Hammersmith, 1917). Subsequently in London in *Charley's Aunt, Pot Lock, Stop Flirting, Her Cardboard Lover, Mr. Cinders* and many others. Also in *Night Of The Garter, Youth At The Helm, Behind Your Back*, etc. In 1940 he appeared in *Silver Patrol* (New), after which he joined the B.B.C. until 1942. Recently : *Skylark* (Duchess, 1942), *Night Of The Garter* (Strand, 1942-43), *Tonight's The Night, See How They Run* (Comedy, 1945), *Happy Birthday*, on tour 1945-46, etc. Co-produced *Make It A Date* (Duchess, 1946).

MERRALL, MARY. Actress. Born Liverpool. Married to Franklin Dyall. Made her first appearance on the stage in *Cinderella* (Marlborough, Holloway, 1907). Thenceforth on tour in the provinces and in the United States and Canada (with Cyril Maude). Made her first appearance in New York in *The Second In Command*, 1913. From 1915-16 with Birmingham Repertory Theatre. In 1918, with Franklin Dyall, produced and acted at Dublin Abbey. Has also appeared in London in *Other Times, The Speckled Band, Medium, The Lie, The Green Goddess, Loose Ends* and many others. Also in *Macbeth, Little Eyolf, Sybarites, Canaries Sometimes Sing* (in New York, 1930), *Lovers' Meeting, The Master Builder, She Stoops To Conquer, Theatre Royal, The Children's Hour, Post Road, Goodness, How Sad*, etc. In 1940 appeared in *Ladies In Retirement* (St. James's), then on tour in *French For Love*. In 1941 toured in *Play With Fire* and *Rebecca*, subsequently appearing in the latter play at the Strand in 1942. Since then has appeared in *The Little Foxes* (Piccadilly, 1942) and on tour in *Suspect* and *Arsenic And Old Lace*, 1944. In 1945 she appeared in *The Gambler* (Embassy). Also in *The Quick And The Dead* (Repertory Players—Savoy, 1946).

MELVILLE, ALAN. Dramatic author. Born Edinburgh, 1910. Educated Edinburgh Academy. From 1936-40 : producer and script writer, B.B.C. Has contributed to many West End revues, including *Rise Above It, Sky High, Scoop, Sweet And Low, Sweeter And Lower* and *Sweetest And Lowest*. Has been in the R.A.F. since 1941.

MICKLEWOOD, ERIC. Actor. Born in London, 1911. Studied for the stage under Elsie Fogerty at the Central School of Drama, making his first appearance, Malvern Festival, 1934. Has appeared in London in *Nine Sharp* (Little), *New*

Faces (Comedy and Apollo, 1940-41), *Rise Above It* (Comedy, 1941), *Pink String And Sealing Wax* (Duke of York's, 1943), *The Glass Slipper* (St. James's, 1944-45).

MIDDLETON, JOSEPHINE. Actress. Born Nashville, Tennessee. Educated in London. Made her first appearance on the stage at the Kingsway in 1908. Has since appeared extensively in Europe and America. Her recent West End plays include *Lot's Wife, Peril At End House, Crisis In Heaven, House Of Regrets,* etc. In 1945 she appeared in repertory in Dundee and Perth.

MILES, BERNARD. Actor. First appeared on stage in London at the Players' Theatre. Was seen by Herbert Farjeon, who gave him his first West End part in *The Little Revue* (Little, 1938). He subsequently appeared in *Thunder Rock* (Neighbourhood and Globe, 1940), *Diversion* (Wyndham's, 1941), *Othello* (for the Old Vic) (New, 1942), etc. In 1942 he co-directed and appeared in *Men In Shadow.* Toured in his own play, *They Also Serve,* 1945. Season at the Scala, 1946 appearing in *Century For George, Let Tyrants Tremble !,* etc.

MILLAR, RONALD. Actor and playwright. Born Reading, 1919. Educated Charterhouse and Cambridge. Made his first appearance on the stage in *Swinging The Gate* (Ambassadors, 1940). With Royal Navy, 1941-42. Then appeared in *War And Peace* (Phœnix, 1943), *Mr. Bolfry* (Westminster and Playhouse, 1943-44), *Murder For A Valentine* (Lyric), *Zero Hour* (Lyric, 1944). Recently in *Jenny Jones* (Hippodrome, 1945), and touring in *Hidden Horizon,* 1945. Among his plays are *Murder From Memory* (produced at Ambassadors, 1942) and *Zero Hour* (produced at Lyric, 1944). He appeared in *The Sacred Flame* (St. Martin's and Westminster, 1945-46). Wrote play *Frieda* in 1946.

MILLER, CAMERON. Actor. Born October 1st, 1908, Oxford. Educated Magdalen College School. He made his first professional appearance in *Macbeth,* 1928, afterwards in repertory at Croydon, Oxford, and at the Malvern Festival. In H.M. Forces, 1940-45, after which he became producer at Leicester Repertory Theatre. His recent plays in London include *Mrs. Warren's Profession* (Torch, 1945), *People Like Us* (Gateway, 1945), *Spring* 1600 (Lyric, Hammersmith, 1945-46).

MILLER, HUGH. Actor and producer. Born Berwick-on-Tweed, 1889. Made his first appearance on the stage in *The Prisoner Of Zenda,* Glasgow, 1911 ; then in London in *All For Love* (Shaftesbury, 1922). Appeared in Chicago in *The Dybbuk,* 1925, and in New York in *Pickwick,* 1927. Acted in America until 1933, when he returned to England to join Birmingham Repertory Company. Has appeared in London in *Counsellor At Law, The Moon Is Red, The Alchemist, Nina, The Two Mrs. Carrolls, Girl Unknown, Idiot's Delight, The Doctor's Dilemma* and many others. In 1942 appeared in *The Little Foxes* (Piccadilly). Then in *The Rest Is Silence* (Prince of Wales, 1944). Produced *Jenny Jones* (Hippodrome, 1944), Season of Grand Guignol at the Granville, 1944-45, *Sweet Yesterday* (Adelphi, 1945-46).

MILLS, JOHN. Actor and producer. Born Suffolk, 1908. Married to Mary Hayley Bell. First appeared on the stage in *The Five O'Clock Girl* (London Hippodrome, 1929), then on tour in the Far East. Also acted in London in *Charley's Aunt, Cochran's* 1931 *Revue, London Wall, Cavalcade, Words And Music, Give Me A Ring,* etc. Subsequently in *Jill Darling, Red Night, Aren't Men Beasts, Floodlight, Pelissier's Follies Of* 1938. Joined Old Vic, 1938-39, appearing in *A Midsummer Night's Dream* and *She Stoops To Conquer.* Then in the West End in *We At The Crossroads* and *Of Mice And Men.* At outbreak of war joined H.M. Forces, being invalided out in 1942. Recently appeared in *Men In Shadow* (which he produced with Bernard Miles) (Vaudeville, 1942-43), *Duet For Two Hands* (which he produced with Anthony Pelissier) (Lyric, 1945).

MILNE, A. A. Playwright. Born London, 1882. Educated Westminster and Cambridge. Among his plays are *Make-Believe, Mr. Pym Passes By, The Truth About Blayds, The Dover Road, The Ivory Door, Michael And Mary, Sarah Simple* and *Gentleman Unknown.*

MILTON, BILLY. Actor. Born London, 1905. Made his first appearance on the stage in *The Devil's Disciple* (Regent, 1926), subsequently in the West End in *White Birds, Will O' The Whispers,* etc. Made his first appearance in New York in *This Year Of Grace* (Selwyn, 1928), returning to London to play in *Bitter Sweet.* Then in *Bow Bells* (London, 1932), *Gay Divorce* (in Melbourne, 1933), *Fools Rush In* (New York, 1934). Also in London in *Members Only, Worth A Million,* etc. Since the war with the B.B.C. Recently appeared in *The Quaker Girl* (Coliseum, 1943-44).

MILTON, ERNEST. Actor. Born San Francisco, 1890. Married to Naomi Royde-Smith. Made his first appearance on the stage in *The Climax,* Newport, 1912, then appeared in New York in *Joseph And His Brethren* (Century, 1913). Made his first appearance in London in *Potash And Perlmutter* (Queen's, 1914), thereafter appeared in the West End in a number of plays, including: *Ghosts, Salome, Romeo And Juliet, Candida,* etc. With Old Vic Company in 1918-20 appearing in *Hamlet, Everyman, The Merchant Of Venice, Richard II,* etc. Also appeared in London in *Loyalties, Dulcy, The Lady From The Sea, Trelawney Of The Wells, Henry IV, The Dybbuk* and many others. Toured Egypt with Robert Atkin's Company in 1927 and rejoined Old Vic in 1928, playing in *Romeo And Juliet, King Lear, The School For Scandal,* etc. Also in London in *Rope* (and in New York, 1930), *Little Eyolf, Death Takes A Holiday, Grand Hotel, Dizzy, Paganini* (his own play), *Timon Of Athens, Victoria Regina, On The Frontier* and many others. In 1941 appeared in *King John* (New). Recently: *Murder From Memory* (St. Martin's, 1942), *A Winter's Tale* (Open Air, 1944), *Macbeth* (Lyric, Hammersmith, 1944), *Dombey And Son* (King's, Hammersmith, 1945), *Red Horizon* (Lindsey, 1945).

MINSTER, JACK. Actor and producer. Born London, 1901. Made his first appearance on the stage in *Pygmalion,* Croydon, 1920 ; then in London in *If Winter Comes, The Return Of Sherlock Holmes,* etc. With Liverpool Repertory Company, 1926-28 ; then toured in Canada with Sir Barry Jackson. Was producer for Hull Little Theatre, 1935-38. Has also produced at Q, Intimate, Richmond, etc. Since the war with the B.B.C. Then recently produced *An Ideal Husband* (Westminster, 1943), *Emma* (St. James's, 1944), *Perchance To Dream* (Hippodrome, 1945), *The Guinea Pig* (Criterion, 1946).

MITCHELL, JULIAN. Actor. Born Glossop, 1888. Made his first appearance on the stage in 1906 in Blackburn ; then a tour in the provinces until 1928, with his own repertory company. First appeared in London in *The Squeaker* (Apollo, 1928), and has also played in the West End in *Love On The Dole, Miss Smith, Power And The Glory, Traitor's Gate, Candida, Rhondda Roundabout,* etc. Recently: *The Little Foxes* (Piccadilly, 1942), *The Judgment Of Dr. Johnson* (Arts, 1943), *A Murder For A Valentine* (Lyric, 1944), *Tomorrow The World* (Aldwych, 1944-45).

MITCHELL, YVONNE. Actress. Born London. Educated Battle Abbey and St. Paul's. Made her first appearance on the stage in *Great Expectations* (Rudolf Steiner, 1940), after which she appeared in repertory at Oxford, etc. Then in *The Moon Is Down* (Whitehall, 1943), *Cradle Song* (Apollo, 1944), then repertory at Birmingham and Oxford in *Pygmalion, Six Characters In Search Of An Author, Winterset,* etc.

MOLLISON, CLIFFORD. Actor. Born London, 1897. Made his first appearance on the stage in *Billy's Fortune* (Criterion, 1913) ; subsequently in London in *A Safety Match, Loyalties, R.U.R., The Lilies Of The Field, The Will,*

The Likes Of 'Er, London Life, A Midsummer Night's Dream, etc. Also in the West End in *The River, The Girl Friend, Here Comes The Bride, White Horse Inn, Out Of The Bottle, High Temperature, Gay Deceivers, Twenty To One, Balalaika, To Kill A Cat* and many others. In 1940 appeared in *Lights Up* (Savoy). Since 1940 with H.M. Forces. In 1946 he appeared in *Can Can*.

MOLLISON, HENRY. Actor. Born Dundee, 1905. Made his first appearance on the stage in London in *Young Woodley* (New, 1928). Subsequently in London in *I'm Wise, Sons O' Guns, Cochran's* 1931 *Revue, London Wall, Hocus Pocus, Ballyhoo, Richard Of Bordeaux* (also in New York, 1934). In 1939 toured Australia in *Idiot's Delight*. From 1939-45 a prisoner-of-war in Germany. Since being repatriated he has appeared on tour in *Under The Gooseberry Bush*.

MOLLISON, WILLIAM. Producer. Born London, 1893. Made his first appearance on the stage in *Dante* (Drury Lane, 1903). Subsequently acted with Sir Herbert Tree, 1912-14. After the war he toured South Africa until 1924, producing and acting. Then he staged a number of plays in London, including *No, No, Nanette, The Girl Friend, Hit The Deck, Murder On The Second Floor, Sons O' Guns, Wonder Bar* (in New York, 1931, along with *Meet My Sister*), *Tell Her The Truth, Give Me A Ring, Richard Of Bordeaux* (New York, 1933), *Jill Darling*, etc. Also produced such West End plays as *Gay Deceivers, Going Places, Seeing Stars, The Laughing Cavalier, Bobby Get Your Gun, Magyar Melody* and many others. Since 1940 he has produced a number of plays, including *French For Love, Ladies In Retirement, Lady Behave, The Love Racket, The Merry Widow, Panama Hattie, Irene, Happy Few*. In 1945 produced *Merrie England* (Princes), etc.

MONKMAN, PHYLLIS. Actress. Born London, 1892. Made her first appearance on the stage as a dancer in *Lady Madcap* (Prince of Wales, 1904), then in *The Belle Of Mayfair, Butterflies, The Quaker Girl, The Monte Carlo Girl* and many others. 1913-16, principal dancer at Alhambra ; then acted in London in *See Saw, Bubbly, The Co-Optimists, Charlot's* 1924 *Revue, Downhill, Lady Luck, The Co-Optimists Of* 1930, *The Jack-Pot, Rhyme And Rhythm, Stop Press, The Two Bouquets, Operette, Rain* and a number of pantomimes. In 1940 she appeared in *Present Arms* (Prince of Wales), then with her own company on tour for a year. Since then she has appeared in *Rose Marie* (Stoll), *Keep Going* (Palace, 1944), on tour in *Flare Path*, etc. In 1945 on tour with *Sweeter And Lower*.

MORELL, ANDRE. Actor. Born London, 1909. First appeared on the stage with a touring repertory company in *Good Morning, Bill*, 1934 ; and later appeared in repertory at Margate and New Brighton. Made his first appearance in London in *Call It A Day* (Globe, 1936). Also in the West End in *They Came By Night, The Last Straw*, etc. With the Old Vic Company, 1937-38, appearing in *Trelawney Of The Wells, The Rivals, Hamlet* ; subsequently touring with the Old Vic in Egypt. In 1939-40 appeared with the Old Vic Company in *The Tempest*, etc. Since then with H.M. Forces.

MORGAN, DIANA. Dramatic author. Born Cardiff, 1913. Married to Robert McDermott. Studied for the stage at Central School of Drama, making her first appearance on the stage in *The Soldier And The Gentlewoman* (Vaudeville, 1933). Then with Cambridge Festival Company, 1933-34. Appeared in London in *The Country Wife, The Comedy Of Good And Evil, Parnell*, etc. Is part author (with her husband) of *This World Of Ours, Bats In The Belfry, The Gate Revue*, etc. Is also part-author of *Spread It Abroad, Members Only, The New Ambassadors Revue, Swinging The Gate*, etc. She is the author also of *The House In The Square, Three Waltzes*, etc.

MORGAN, KENNETH. Actor. Born London, 1918. Educated at Farnborough and in Germany. Made his first appearance on the stage in *Peter Pan* (Palladium, 1933), then in *Richard Of Bordeaux* (New, 1934). Also appeared in *Treasure*

Island (Stratford-on-Avon), *Private History* (Gate, 1938), *The Taming Of The Shrew*, for Old Vic, 1939. Then played in *Follow My Leader* (Apollo, 1940), and joined Old Vic Company on tour in 1940. With H.M. Forces 1941-44, returning to the stage in *Easter* (Gateway). Has also made several appearances at the Intimate and Q Theatres. Touring in *The Man Who Wrote Murder*, 1945 ; and *Ill Wind*, 1946.

MORGAN, TERRY. Actor. Born London, 1921. Studied for the stage at R.A.D.A., making his first appearance in *The Astonished Ostrich*, Windsor, 1942 ; then spent two years with the London District Theatre Unit (Central Pool of Artists, H.M. Forces), after which he played in repertory at Windsor, Farnham, Letchworth and Oxford. Made his first appearance in London in *There Shall Be No Night* (Aldwych, 1943-44). Recently in *The Skin Of Our Teeth* (Phœnix, 1945), *The Trojan Women* and *Death Of A Rat* (Lyric, Hammersmith, 1945-46).

MORLEY, MALCOLM. Actor, playwright and producer. Born Aldershot, 1890. Educated at Harrow. Made his first appearance on the stage in New York in *Hamlet* in 1911, subsequently acting in America until 1921, when he appeared in London in *Moleskin Joe* (Ambassadors). Also in London in *The Yellow Jacket, Charles I, The Secret Agent*, etc. Producer and actor at the Everyman, 1926-31, producing, among others, *The Father, The Master Builder, Ghosts, Little Eyolf* and *The Storm*. Has also produced at Nottingham, Oxford, etc., and at the Embassy, London. Has written a number of plays, including *The Emperor Of Make-Believe*, and several books on the theatre. During the war has been on tour with his own company in *Pygmalion*, etc. In 1940-41 acting and producing, Stratford-on-Avon Memorial Theatre. Appeared in *Under One Roof* (St. Martin's, 1941), then produced at Birmingham, Richmond and Windsor. 1944-46, producing at Oxford Playhouse.

MORLEY, ROBERT. Actor and playwright. Born Semley, 1908. Educated Wellington College. Studied for the stage at Royal Academy of Dramatic Art, making his first appearance in *Treasure Island* (Strand, 1929). Subsequently on tour and with J. B. Fagan at Oxford, 1931-33, and with Norman Marshall at Cambridge Festival, 1933. With Peter Bull formed Perranporth Summer Theatre in Cornwall and appeared here, 1935-38, in a variety of roles. Has acted in London in *Oscar Wilde, The Great Romancer, Pygmalion* (for the Old Vic), etc. Made his first appearance in New York in *Oscar Wilde* (Fulton, 1938). In 1941 on tour in *Play With Fire*. In 1942 appeared in *The Man Who Came To Dinner* (Savoy), then on tour in *Staff Dance*. In 1945 he appeared in *The First Gentleman* (New and Savoy). Among his plays are *Short Story, Goodness, How Sad* and *Staff Dance*.

MORRIS, MARY. Actress. Born Fiji Islands, 1915. Studied for the stage at the R.A.D.A., making her first appearance in London in *Lysistrata* (Gate, 1939). She then acted and produced at the Barn Theatre, Oxted, after which she acted in *Squaring The Circle* (Vaudeville, 1942), *Distant Point* (Westminster, 1942), *St. Joan* (Winter Garden). Recently on tour in *They Walk Alone* and *Wuthering Heights*, 1944. Appeared in *The Witch* and *On Life's Sunny Side* (Arts), then in *Duet For Two Hands* (Lyric, 1945-46).

MORRIS, PHYLLIS. Actress. Born London, 1894. Educated at Cheltenham Ladies College. Made her first appearance on the stage with the Charles Macdona —Bernard Shaw Company ; then appeared in London in *Service, Music In The Air, Call It A Day*, etc. With the Old Vic Company, 1939-40, on tour of Wales and Durham, returning to London in *Ladies In Retirement* (St. James's, 1940-41), *Alice In Wonderland* (Scala, 1943). Then joined B.B.C. Repertory Company. Recently appeared in *Holy Isle* (Arts, 1943), *Flare Path* (Apollo, 1942-44), and on tour, 1945.

MORSE, BARRY. Actor. Born London, 1919. Studied for the stage at R.A.D.A., making his first appearance in *Charley's Aunt*, Bradford, 1937. From 1937-41 he appeared in repertory at Bradford, Leeds, Croydon, Peterborough, Nottingham, Coventry, Sunderland, Newcastle, Harrogate, etc. Made his first appearance in London in *School For Slavery* (Westminster, 1942). Has also appeared in the West End in *Escort* (Lyric, 1942), *War And Peace* (Phœnix, 1943), *Crisis In Heaven* (Lyric, 1944) and *The Assassin* (Savoy, 1945).

MULLEN, BARBARA. Actress. Born Boston, U.S.A., 1918. Married to John Taylor. Was for a time singing and dancing in New York cabarets. Came to England and studied for the stage at the Webber-Douglas School of Dramatic Art. She made her first appearance on the stage in *Jeannie* (Torch and Wyndham's, 1940-41). In 1943 she appeared in *What Every Woman Knows* (Lyric). Appeared in *So Brief The Spring*, 1945-46.

MURRAY-HILL, PETER. Actor. Born Bushey Heath, 1908. Married to Phyllis Calvert. Educated Westminster and Cambridge. Made his first appearance on the stage in *Old Heidelberg* (Edinburgh, 1933), then in London in *Dark Horizon* (Daly's, 1934). Has also acted in the West End in *Hamlet, Broomstick, Romeo And Juliet, Peter Pan,* etc. Was with Cardiff Repertory Company in 1935, also the Brandon-Thomas Repertory Company at Edinburgh and Glasgow in 1935, and with the Newcastle Repertory Company in 1936. Has also appeared in London in *Suspect, Ladies And Gentleman, The Merry Wives Of Windsor, Julius Cæsar, The Tempest, The Comedy Of Errors, The Winter's Tale, This Money Business, The Last Train South, Punch Without Judy,* etc. Recently : *Watch On The Rhine* (Aldwych, 1942-43).

MURRAY, STEPHEN. Actor. Born Partney, Lincs, 1912. Studied for the stage at Royal Academy of Dramatic Art, making his first appearance on the stage in *Much Ado About Nothing* (Stratford-on-Avon Memorial Theatre, 1933). First acted in London in *Cabbages And Kings* (Ambassadors, 1933), then with Birmingham Repertory Company, 1934-35, and at Malvern Festival in 1934 and 1935, appearing in *Doctor Faustus, The Marvellous History Of St. Bernard, Mutiny, Volpone, Misalliance,* etc. From 1936-37 appeared at the Westminster in *A Month In The Country, Waste, Crooked Cross*. With Old Vic, 1937-38, appearing in *Henry V, Pygmalion, Measure For Measure, Othello, Coriolanus, The King Of Nowhere,* etc. Has also appeared in London in *Ghosts, Tobias And The Angel*. From 1938 to 1940 with the London Mask Theatre Company at the Westminster, appearing in *Troilus And Cressida, Dangerous Corner, Marco Millions, The Will, The Doctor's Dilemma, Bridge Head*. In 1939-40 appeared in *Desire Under The Elms* and *Abraham Lincoln*. Then joined H.M. Forces. Recently acting and producing for A.B.C.A. Play Unit. Was seen in London in 1943 in *Desert Highway* (Playhouse) (a production of A.B.C.A., CEMA and Army Welfare). In 1945 he toured the Continent with the A.B.C.A. Play Unit.

NEAGLE, ANNA. Actress. Born London, 1904. Married to Herbert Wilcox. Made her first appearance on the stage in *Charlot's Revue* (Prince of Wales, 1925), subsequently in London in *Rose Marie, The Desert Song, This Year Of Grace, Wake Up And Dream* (also in New York, 1929), etc. Also in the West End in *Stand Up And Sing* ; and *As You Like It, Twelfth Night* (both at the Open Air Theatre). In 1937 appeared in *Peter Pan*, then went to Hollywood. Returned to England, 1941, and appeared in *Emma* (St. James's, 1945).

NESBITT, CATHLEEN. Actress. Born Cheshire, 1889. Studied for the stage under Rosina Fillipi, making her first appearance on the stage in *The Cabinet Minister* (Court, 1910). Subsequently acted in *John Gabriel Borkman*, then joined the Irish Players, making her first appearance in New York with them in *The Well Of The Saints*, 1911. Then in London in *The Escape, The Winter's Tale, General John Regan, Quality Street, Quinneys* (also in New York, 1915).

She appeared in New York and Chicago from 1915 to 1919, after which she returned to London in *The Merchant Of Venice*. Thenceforth in London in *The Duchess Of Malfi, Antony And Cleopatra, Loyalties, The Doctor's Dilemma, Hassan* and dozens of others. Also acted in London in *The Constant Nymph, A Bill Of Divorcement, The Calendar, After All, The Case Of The Frightened Lady, Children In Uniform, Richard III, Love On The Dole, The Two Mrs. Carrolls,* etc. Then in *Thou Shalt Not——, Land's End,* etc. In 1939 toured Egypt with the Old Vic Company, and also appeared at the Open Air in *Much Ado About Nothing* and *Pericles*. In 1940-41 appeared in *King Lear* (Old Vic), *On Approval* (Aldwych) and *Outward Bound* (New), then on tour in *We Are The People* and *The Man In Dark Glasses,* 1942. Appeared in *Murder For A Valentine* (Lyric, 1944), then on tour with the Edgar Wallace Repertory Company in *The Case Of The Frightened Lady* and *The Calendar,* 1944-45. Recently appeared in *The Shop At Sly Corner* (St. Martin's, 1945-46).

NESBITT, ROBERT. Producer. Born London, 1906. Married to Iris Lang. Among the shows he has produced in London are *Ballyhoo, Hi-Diddle-Diddle, Stop-Go, Take It Easy* and *Black And Blue*. In 1940 produced *Up And Doing* (with Leslie Henson). In 1941 produced *Black Vanities, Blossom Time, Gangway, Fine And Dandy, Wild Rose*. Recently : *Strike A New Note, Strike It Again, The Night And The Music,* etc. In 1945, *Fine Feathers,* etc.

NEWTON, ROBERT. Actor. Born Shaftesbury, Dorset, June 1st, 1905. Made his first appearance on the stage in *Henry IV*, Birmingham, 1920, remaining here for three years. First appeared in London in *London Life* (Drury Lane, 1924). Subsequently in *Her Cardboard Lover, Byron, Bitter Sweet,* etc. Made his first appearance in New York in *Private Lives* (Times Square, 1931). From 1932-34 he acted and produced at the Shilling, Fulham, after which he appeared in the West End in *The Greeks Had A Word For It, Miss Julie, Whiteoaks,* etc. In 1937 he appeared in *Hamlet* at the Old Vic. Recently : in *No Orchids For Miss Blandish* (Prince of Wales and Apollo, 1942). Appeared in *So Brief The Spring,* 1945-46.

NORFOLK, EDGAR. Actor. Born Bradford, 1893. First appeared on the stage in *Nell Gwynn*, Scarborough, 1912, then in London in *Peter Pan* (Strand, 1916). Subsequently in *Macbeth, Emma, Quality Street*. With Birmingham Repertory Company, 1923-24. Toured Australia in 1928. Has also appeared in London in *The Berg, Typhoon, The Man At Six, Hawk Island* and many others. Appeared with the Malvern Festival Company in 1931. Then in London in *A Trip To Scarborough, Sensation, Spacetime Inn, The Distaff Side, This Side Idolatry,* etc. Also in *The Dark Tower, No More Ladies,* then made his first appearance in New York in *Dark Victory* (Plymouth, 1934). Thenceforth in London and New York in *Family Affairs, Eden End, The Taming Of The Shrew, The Great Romancer, Poison Pen, Comedienne* among others. From 1940-44 acted with the B.B.C. Drama Repertory Company. Recently appeared in *Great Day* (Playhouse, 1945), *A Doll's House* (Arts, 1945), *Fit For Heroes* (Embassy), etc.

NOVELLO, IVOR. Actor, dramatic author and composer. Born Cardiff, 1893. Educated at Oxford. Made his first appearance on the stage in *Deburau* (Ambassadors, 1921), thenceforth in London in *The Yellow Jacket, The Rat, Iris, Downhill, The Firebrand, Liliom, The Truth Game, Symphony In Two Flats,* etc. Also appeared in the latter play in New York at the Schubert, 1930. Then appeared in London in *I Lived With You, Proscenium, Murder In Mayfair, Glamorous Night, The Happy Hypocrite, Careless Rapture, The Crest Of The Wave, Henry V* and *The Dancing Years* (which ran intermittently from 1939 until 1944). Also appeared in *Ladies Into Action* (Lyric, 1940). Recently appeared in *Perchance To Dream* (Hippodrome, 1945-46). Among his plays are *The Rat* (with Constance Collier), *The Truth Game, I Lived With You, Fresh Fields, Glamorous Night, Full House, Careless Rapture, Crest Of The Wave, Comedienne, The Dancing Years, Ladies Into Action* and *Perchance To Dream*.

O'BRIEN, TERENCE. Actor and producer. Born Dublin, 1887. Made his first appearance on the stage in *Twelfth Night*, Woking, 1908, then in London in *Hamlet* (Lyceum, 1909). Subsequently on tour in South Africa, India and China with Matheson Lang Company, until 1913. Then in London in *The Merchant Of Venice, Mr. Wu* and *Othello, Hamlet, Henry V*, etc. (for the Old Vic Company in 1916). Also in *The School For Scandal, A Midsummer Night's Dream, Henry IV* and others at the Court, 1918-19. Then on tour with the Bernard Shaw Repertory Company until 1924 when he acted in London in *Back To Methuselah, Cæsar And Cleopatra, Hamlet, The White Devil* and many others. Then on tour with his own company in the provinces and in the Far East, 1928-29. Also acted in London in *Othello, The Merchant Of Venice, Clear All Wires, Coriolanus* (for the Old Vic, 1938), *Glorious Morning, The Jews Of York*, etc. Since the war has been producing and acting on tour with the Rock Theatre. Also appeared in London in *Case 27 V.C.* (Comedy, 1942). Recently producing and appearing in *Man And Superman* and *The Father*, on tour, and Rudolph Steiner Hall, 1943-45.

O'CASEY, SEAN. Playwright. Born Dublin, 1884. Among his plays are *Juno And The Paycock, The Plough And The Stars, The Shadow Of A Gunman, The Silver Tassie, Within The Gates, The End Of The Beginning*, etc. In 1940 wrote *The Star Turns Red* for production at Unity Theatre. His more recent plays include *Red Roses For Me* and *Purple Dust*. The latter play was first produced at Liverpool by the Old Vic Company in 1945, the former at the Embassy, 1946.

O'DOHERTY, MIGNON. Actress. Born Brisbane, 1890. Studied for the stage at the Academy of Dramatic Art, making her first appearance in *Lady Frederick* (Globe, 1913). Subsequently in London in *The Recruiting Officer, Damaged Goods, Twelfth Night, The Lost Leader, The Government Inspector*, etc. Made her first appearance in New York in *Secrets* (Fulton, 1922). Then in London in *The Green Hat, The Spook Sonata, Fame, Frolic Wind, Call It A Day* and many others. Also in *To Have And To Hold, The Last Trump*, etc. In 1940 appeared in *His Majesty's Guest* (Shaftesbury). Recently acted in *Lottie Dundass* (Vaudeville, 1943), *How Are They At Home ?* (Lyric, 1944), *Irene* (His Majesty's, 1944-45), etc.

OLIVER, VIC. Actor. Born Vienna, 1898. Educated University of Vienna. Made his first appearance on the stage in vaudeville in Indianopolis, U.S.A., 1926, then in New York at the Palace, 1929. First appeared in London in variety at the Palladium, 1931, subsequently on tour in music hall. In 1936 appeared in Cochran's revue, *Follow The Sun* (Adelphi), then on tour in *Idiot's Delight*, 1938. In 1939 appeared in *Black And Blue*, then in *Black Velvet* (Hippodrome, 1940-41), *Get A Load Of This* (Hippodrome, 1942-43), *The Night And The Music* (Coliseum, 1945-46).

OLIVIER, LAURENCE. Actor and producer. Born Dorking, 1907. Married to Vivien Leigh. Studied for the stage under Elsie Fogerty, making his first appearance in *The Taming Of The Shrew*, Stratford-on-Avon, 1922. Then acted in London in *Byron* (Century, 1924), subsequently in *Henry IV, Henry VIII* and *The Cenci*. With Birmingham Repertory Company, 1926-28. Appeared in London in *The Adding Machine, Back To Methuselah, The Taming Of The Shrew, Bird In Hand, Beau Geste, The Circle Of Chalk*, etc. Made his first appearance in New York in *Murder On The Second Floor* (Eltinge, 1929). Then in London in *After All, Private Lives* (also in New York, 1931), *The Rats Of Norway, Biography, Queen Of Scots, Theatre Royal*, etc. Also in the West End in *Ringmaster, Romeo And Juliet, Bees On The Boatdeck*, etc. In 1937 joined the Old Vic, appearing in *Hamlet, Twelfth Night, Henry V, Macbeth* (and as Hamlet at Elsinore). With the Old Vic in 1938 acted in *Othello, The King Of Nowhere, Coriolanus*, after which he appeared in New York in *No Time For Comedy*, 1939. Returned to England 1940, to join the Fleet Air Arm. Released in 1944 to act in the Old Vic Season, when he appeared in *Richard III, Peer Gynt, Arms And The Man* and *Uncle Vanya* (New, 1944-45). Also toured the Continent in the above. 1945-46 with the Old Vic, he appeared in *Henry IV* (*Parts I and II*), *Œdipus* and *The Critic* (New). In 1945 produced *The Skin Of Our Teeth* (Phœnix).

O'NEILL, MAIRE. Actress. Born Dublin. Made her first appearance on the stage in Dublin in 1905, then in London in *The Playboy Of The Western World* (Kingsway, 1907). Then with the Irish National Theatre Company on tour until 1913, when she joined Birmingham Repertory Company. Made her first appearance in New York in *General John Regan* (Hudson, 1913). Then acted in London in *The Merchant Of Venice*, *The White Headed Boy* and many others. Also appeared frequently in Dublin and again in New York, 1921. Also in the West End in *The Insect Play*, *Pollyanna*, *Juno And The Paycock*, *The Plough And The Stars*, *The Shadow Of A Gunman*, *Things That Are Cæsar's*, *Other Men's Wives*, *Mrs. McConaghy's Money*, *Storm In A Teacup* and many others. Also played in the West End in *Moonshine*, *The Playboy Of The Western World*, *John Bull's Other Island*, etc. Recently : *The Playboy Of The Western World* (Mercury, 1940), *Under One Roof* (St. Martin's, 1941), *The Nutmeg Tree* (Lyric, 1941), *Laura* (St. Martin's, 1945), *Kiss And Tell* (Phœnix, 1945), etc.

OSCAR, HENRY. Actor and producer. Born London, 1891. Made his first appearance on the stage in *A Midsummer Night's Dream*, Stratford-on-Avon, 1911, subsequently with various repertory companies. First appeared in the West End in *Romance* (Lyric, 1916), thenceforth in *The Aristocrat*, *A Little Bit Of Fluff*, *Julius Cæsar*, *Romeo And Juliet*, *The Blue Peter*, *Mirandolina*, *Mine Hostess* and many others. Also in London in *Potiphar's Wife*, *The Lady With A Lamp*, *The First Mrs. Fraser*, *A Doll's House*, *Measure For Measure*, *Six Characters In Search Of An Author*, *Othello*, *Jonah And The Whale*, *Wild Justice*, *Henry IV*, *As You Like It*, *Thank You, Mr. Pepys*, *The Sun Never Sets*, etc. Made his first appearance in New York in *Waltz In Goose Step* (Hudson, 1938). In 1939 appeared in London in *Jitta's Atonement*. Since the war has been Director of ENSA Drama Section ; also appearing in a number of plays in the West End, including *War And Peace* (Phœnix, 1943), *The Assassin* (Savoy, 1945). He has also produced a considerable number of plays in London, including *Double Door*, *Saturday's Children*, *Green Waters*, *Climbing*, etc. In 1945-46 he toured the Continent in *Julius Cæsar*.

OUGHTEN, WINIFRED. Actress. Born London. Made her first appearance on the stage in *The Merchant Of Venice* (Old Vic, 1915), and remained with this company until 1920. Then in London in *St. Joan*, *The Madras House*, *The Lie*, *Henry VIII*, *Macbeth*, etc. With the Lyric, Hammersmith, Company, 1927-28, acting in *Henry V*, *The Taming Of The Shrew*, *Much Ado About Nothing*. Also in London in *Mariners*, *Dance With No Music*, *The Improper Duchess*, *Another Language*, *Nymph Errant*, *The Dark Tower*, *Grief Goes Over*, *Mary Tudor*, *Night Must Fall*, *Wanted For Murder*, *Grouse In June* and many others. In 1941 in *The Nutmeg Tree* (Lyric). Recently : *Scandal At Barchester* (Lyric and Wyndham's, 1944), *Quality Street* (Embassy, 1945), etc.

OULD, HERMAN. Playwright and poet. Born London, 1886. Was at one time associated with the Everyman Theatre (with Norman McDermott). Among his plays are *Between Sunset And Dawn*, *The Dance Of Life*, *The Moon Rides High*, *The Shadow And The Substance*, etc. Has also adapted *Hoppla* (from the German). Was formerly joint editor of " Theatrecraft," and is now general secretary of the P.E.N.

PALMER, LILLI. Actress. Born Austria, 1914. Married to Rex Harrison. Studied for the stage in Berlin, making her first appearance on the stage in Berlin, 1932 ; subsequently acted in Frankfurt and Paris. Made her first appearance in London in *The Road To Gandahar* (Garrick, 1938). Has also appeared in the

West End in *The Tree Of Eden, Little Ladyship*, etc. Then in *Ladies Into Action* (Lyric, 1940). Appeared in *No Time For Comedy* (Haymarket, 1940-41). In 1945 she went to America.

PARKER, CECIL. Actor. Born Hastings, 1897. Made his first appearance on the stage in *The Merchant Of Venice*, Eastbourne, 1922 ; then with Charles Doran's Company and at Huddersfield and Dublin Abbey. With Liverpool Repertory Company, 1924-26, making his first appearance in London in *Interference* (Everyman, 1925). Also in London in *The Yellow Streak, Full Moon, The Likes Of 'Er, Lady Windermere's Fan, Wonder Bar*, etc. Also in *The Young Idea, The Makropulos Secret, Lady In Waiting*, etc. With Embassy Theatre, 1931-32, then in the West End in *Tonight Or Never, The Rats Of Norway, Reunion In Vienna, Moonlight Is Silver, Golden Arrow, Nina, Mademoiselle, The Constant Wife, Bonnet Over The Windmill* and many others. More recently in *Lot's Wife, Official Secret, Little Ladyship*, etc. In 1940 acted in *French For Love* (Criterion). In 1941 appeared in *Blithe Spirit*, (Piccadilly) and later at the Duchess until 1944. Appeared in *The Skin Of Our Teeth* (Phœnix, 1945).

PARKS, GOWER. Designer. Born 1904. Studied at the Central School of Arts and Crafts ; formerly an advertising artist, interior decorator and book illustrator. Decor for *Marriage A La Mode* (Lyric, Hammersmith, 1930), and has since designed more than fifty productions in the West End and at Stratford. Recently designed *Brighton Rock, While The Sun Shines, Three Waltzes*, etc., in London, and *Antony And Cleopatra, Much Ado About Nothing* and *She Stoops To Conquer* (all at Stratford). In 1945 designed settings for *Henry IV* for the Old Vic (New).

PARRISH, JAMES. Playwright. Born London. Among his better-known plays are *Distinguished Gathering* and *Forty-Eight Hours Leave*. In 1945 his play, *Letters To A Lady* was produced at the Embassy. He produced a number of plays for ENSA overseas during the war, including some plays for the ENSA Festival Company, Rome, 1945-46.

PATRICK, NIGEL. Actor. Born London, 1913. Made his first appearance on the stage in *The Life Machine* (Regent, 1932), then touring provinces and Egypt, before appearing in repertory at Birmingham, Worthing and Northampton. First appeared in the West End in *Daddy Long Legs* (Victoria Palace, 1934), then in *The Immortal Garden, Half-A-Crown, Ringmaster, Roulette, Children To Bless You, The Lady Of La Paz, Mademoiselle*, etc. More recently in *George And Margaret* and *Tony Draws A Horse*. Since the outbreak of war in H.M. Forces. In 1946 he re-appeared in *Tomorrow's Child* (Lyric, Hammersmith).

PAVLOW, MURIEL. Actress. Born Kent, 1921. Made her first stage appearance on tour in *The Old Maid*. 1939-41, acted in *Dear Octopus* (Globe) and *Dear Brutus* (Globe). In 1942 in *Old Acquaintance* (Apollo). Recently in *There Shall Be No Night* (Aldwych, 1944-46), *While The Sun Shines* (Globe).

PAYN, GRAHAM. Actor. Born South Africa, 1918. First appeared in South Africa in concerts, then came to London and appeared in *Peter Pan* and toured in variety. Recently acted, 1941-43, in *Up And Doing* (Saville), *Fine And Dandy* (*Saville*), *Magic Carpet* (Princes), *The Lilac Domino* (His Majesty's). In 1944 appeared in *Alice In Wonderland* (Palace), 1944-45 *Gaieties* (Winter Garden). Then in *Sigh No More* (Piccadilly, 1945-46).

PAYNE, LAURENCE. Actor. Born London, 1919. Married to Sheila Burrell. Was formerly actor and producer with his own Shakespearean Company in London. Studied for the stage at the Old Vic School and made his first appearance in *An Enemy Of The People* (Old Vic, 1939). Then in *Romeo And Juliet* on tour, and in *King Lear* and *The Tempest* (Old Vic, 1940). 1940-44 with the Old Vic in Liverpool and London, appearing in *The Seagull, Romeo And Juliet, The Rivals*,

Great Expectations, The Sulky Fire and others. Also appearing in 1942 in *Othello* (New). Joined the Greta Douglas Company in 1944 as actor-producer, appearing in *He Must Return, The Man With The Flower In His Mouth, Happily Ever After, When We Dead Awaken, John Gabriel Borkman, Great Catherine.* Among the plays he produced here were *Love And How To Cure It,* and *The Taming Of The Shrew* (in Liverpool). 1944-45 : In *The Breadwinner, Anna Christie* and *Leonce And Lena* (all at the Arts). Touring the Continent, 1946.

PEARCE, VERA. Actress. Born Australia. First appeared on the stage in Melbourne, then on tour in Australia ; subsequently acting in London in *Love's Awakening* (Empire, 1922). Then in *Leap Year, No No Nanette, Castles In The Air, That's A Good Girl, The New Moon* and many others. Made her first appearance in New York in *Artists And Models* (Majestic, 1930). Also in London in *Stand Up And Sing, Yes Madam, Please Teacher, Big Business, Wild Oats,* etc. Recently : *Shephard's Pie* (Princes, 1940), *Fine And Dandy* (Saville). In 1944 on tour in *Staff Dance.* Then in *Three's A Family* (Saville and Winter Garden, 1944-45).

PEARSON, LLOYD. Actor. Born Yorkshire, 1897. Studied for the stage at Lady Benson's School ; making his first appearance on the stage in *Diana Of Dobson's,* Brighton, 1919. Then appeared in London in *Pompey The Great* (St. Martin's, 1920), and subsequently with the Benson Company until 1927. Was then with Birmingham and Liverpool Repertory Companies, remaining at the latter until 1937. Has also acted in London in *Dodsworth, Nanny, When We Are Married,* etc. In 1940 appeared in *Women Aren't Angels* (Strand), *Lifeline* (Duchess, 1942), *Skylark* (Duchess, 1942). Recently : *Living Room* (Garrick, 1943), *Crisis In Heaven* (Lyric, 1944), *Arsenic And Old Lace* (Strand, 1944-46).

PEEL, DAVID. Actor. Born London, 1920. Studied for the stage at R.A.D.A., making his first appearance in *Come Out To Play* (Kingsway, 1937). Also in *Goodbye, Mr. Chips* (Shaftesbury), etc. Joined H.M. Forces in 1939, invalided out in 1942. Then appeared in *Macbeth* (Piccadilly, 1942), *Landslide* (Westminster, 1943), *There Shall Be No Night* (Aldwych, 1944). Joined Stratford-on-Avon Festival Company, 1945, to appear in *Romeo And Juliet, Much Ado About Nothing, Antony And Cleopatra* and *Twelfth Night.* Adapted (with Dorothy Albertyn) the play *Landslide* from the French. In 1946 he appeared in *Marriage a La Mode* and *The King-Maker,* etc., (St. James's).

PEISLEY, FREDERICK. Actor. Born London, 1904. Studied for the stage under Italia Conti, making his first appearance, as a child, in *Eyes Of Youth* (St. James's, 1918). Subsequently on tour, then in London in *Carnival, Macbeth, A Midsummer Night's Dream,* etc. Also in London in *The Great God Brown, Contraband, Young Woodley* (in Paris, 1928), *The Love Game, She Passed Through Lorraine, Alice In Wonderland,* etc. With Manchester Repertory Company, 1934-35, then in the West End in *St. Helena, Careless Rapture, You Never Can Tell, Marriage, Heaven And Charing Cross, The Ascent Of F.*6 and others. Since the outbreak of war with H.M. Forces. In 1945 he appeared in *Trilby,* on tour.

PEMBERTON, REECE. Designer. Born 1912. Worked with Paul Shelving at Birmingham Repertory Theatre, 1934-40, and designed for the Malvern Festivals, 1938-40. Designed season of plays, Barn, Dartington Hall, 1940-41, designed sets and costumes for *What Every Woman Knows* (Lyric, 1942), *The Bartered Bride* (Sadlers Wells, 1943), *Thérèse Raquin* (for Old Vic) (Lyric, Hammersmith, 1944), *Peer Gynt* (for Old Vic) (New, 1944-45).

PERCHERON, DOREEN. Born London. Married to Antony Verney. Made her first appearance on the stage in the chorus of a Jack Buchanan show, later graduating to be one of Cochran's Young Ladies. In 1940 appeared in *Lights Up*

British Theatre

(Adelphi). In 1942 appeared in *Jam To-day* (St. Martin's), then on tour in *Distant Point* (for CEMA), in 1943 in *Flying Colours* (Lyric) and 1944-45, *Irene* (His Majesty's).

PERCY, ESME. Actor and producer. Born London, 1887. Studied for the stage at the Brussells Conservatoire, making his first appearance on the stage with F. R. Benson's Company in Nottingham, 1904. First appeared in London in *Romeo And Juliet* (Royalty, 1905), subsequently in *Nero, Henry IV, Julius Cæsar,* after which he toured South Africa in 1907. Then joined Miss Horniman's Company at Manchester, 1908-11, after which he formed his own travelling repertory company. Appeared in *Hamlet* in London in 1914. Then served with H.M. Forces until 1923. Acted in the West End in *Hassan,* after which he acted and produced with Charles Macdona's Bernard Shaw Repertory Company in *Don Juan In Hell, The Showing Up Of Blanco Posnet, Pygmalion, Androcles And The Lion, The Doctor's Dilemma,* etc. Then in London in *Man And Superman, The White Devil, The Private Secretary, Byron, The Amorists, Colonel Satan* and many others. Also in *The Admirable Crichton, Vile Bodies,* etc., before making his first appearance in New York in *Red Planet,* 1932. Among the other West End productions in which he has appeared are *Clear All Wires, This Side Idolatry, Success Story, Lady Precious Stream, The Apple Cart, Behind Your Back, The Scarlet Pimpernel,* etc. Also in *The Showing Up Of Blanco Posnet, The Taming Of The Shrew* and many others. In 1939 appeared in *Lady Precious Stream* (Kingsway), *All's Well That Ends Well* and *Henry IV* (Vaudeville). Then on tour in *Pygmalion,* 1941, *Distant Point* (Westminster, 1941), *Tales Of Hoffman* (Strand, 1942), *Blow Your Own Trumpet* (for the Old Vic), 1943. Recently in *An Ideal Husband* (Westminster, 1943-44), *Easter* (Gateway, 1944), *Jacobowsky And The Colonel* (Piccadilly, 1945), *Rosmersholm* (Torch, 1945), *Tomorrow Will Be Different* (Lindsey). Appeared in *The Fountain Of Youth* (Lindsey, 1946).

PERRINS, LESLIE. Actor. Born Birmingham. Studied for the stage at the Royal Academy of Dramatic Art, making his first appearance in *The Rattlesnake* (Shaftesbury, 1922). Subsequently in London in *The Limpet, R.U.R., Blessed Are The Rich, Treasure Island, The Donovan Affair, Outward Bound,* etc. Then in *The Road To Rome, Coquette, Insult,* etc., before making his first appearance in New York in the latter, 1930. Then in London in *Elizabeth Of England, Dinner At Eight,* etc. 1933-39 engaged in film-acting. From the outbreak of war until 1944, working as an announcer for the B.B.C. European Service. Recently appeared in the West End in *Halfway To Heaven* (Princes, 1943), *The Assassin* (Savoy, 1945).

PETTINGELL, FRANK. Actor. Born Liverpool, 1891. Made his first appearance on the stage in *The Taming Of The Shrew,* Blackpool, 1910, then on tour in the provinces until 1914. After war service he made his first appearance in London in *Lass O' Laughter* (Queen's, 1922); subsequently in the West End in *What Every Woman Knows, Macbeth, Back To Methuselah, Yellow Sands, The Good Companions* and many others. Then in *Pleasure Cruise, A Present From Margate, Spring, 1600, Magnolia Street, Touch Wood, The Black Eye, The Frog, He Was Born Gay, Sussanah And The Elders, When We Are Married,* etc. In 1942 appeared in *Lifeline* (Duchess), *Jam To-day* (St. Martin's). Then in *Arsenic And Old Lace* (Strand, 1942-44). Appeared in *Fifty-Fifty* (Strand, 1946).

PHIPPS, NICHOLAS. Actor and dramatic author. Born London, 1913, educated at Winchester. Made his first stage appearance with the Old Vic Company in *Julius Cæsar,* 1931, then in repertory at Northampton and Oxford, after which he toured South Africa in 1935. Then in London in *Spring Meeting,* 1937, *The Gate Revue* (Gate and Ambassadors, 1939). With H.M. Forces 1940-43, returning to the stage in *Crisis In Heaven* (Lyric, 1944). 1944-45 appeared in *Blithe Spirit*

318

(Duchess), Is the author of the play *First Stop North* and revue material in *Scoop, Sweeter And Lower, The New Ambassadors Revue, Gaieties*, and many others.

PILBEAM, NOVA. Actress. Born /London, 1919. Studied for the stage under Gertrude Burnett, making her first appearance on the stage in *Toad Of Toad Hall* (Savoy, 1931). Then in London in *Francis Thompson, Gallows Glorious, Peter Pan* (in 1935), *As You Like It* (for O.U.D.S.), *The Lady Of La Paz* and *Peter Pan* (again at the Palladium, 1938). From 1941-43 with the Old Vic Company at Liverpool Playhouse, appearing in *Romeo And Juliet, Ah, Wilderness* and many others. In 1944 appeared in *This Was A Woman* (Comedy).

POLLOCK, ELLEN. Actress and producer. Married to James Proudfoot. Born Heidelberg, 1903. Educated St. Mary's College, London. Made her first appearance on the stage in *Romeo And Juliet* (Everyman, 1920), subsequently toured South Africa, 1923-24. Then toured Australia, with Maurice Moscovitch, 1926-27. Has appeared in London in *Hit The Deck, The Lady Of The Camelias, The Good Companions, Too True To Be Good, Potash And Perlmutter, Finished Abroad, On The Rocks, French Salad, The Dominant Sex* and many others. Then in *The New School For Scandal, People In Love, It's A Wise Child, Lysistrata, As You Like It*, etc. In 1940 acted in *The Bare Idea* (Comedy). In 1943 appeared in *Sleeping Out* (Piccadilly), *This Time It's Love* (Comedy). In 1944 produced and appeared in the Bernard Shaw Repertory Season, Lyric, Hammersmith (in *Too True To Be Good, Pygmalion, Candida, The Dark Lady Of The Sonnets*). In 1945 produced and appeared in a season of Grand Guignol, Granville, also in *Tomorrow Will Be Different* (Lindsey).

POOLEY, OLAF. Actor. Born London, 1916. Educated Gresham School and in Paris and Freiberg. Made his first appearance on the stage in *Peter Pan* in 1922, and has since appeared in a number of repertory theatres in England. Soon after the outbreak of war joined Vivienne Bennett's Market Theatre on tour until 1943, when he joined Norman Marshall's Company. Has appeared in London in *Uncle Vanya* (Westminster, 1943); *Don Abel Wrote A Tragedy* (Arts, 1944), *The Winter's Tale* (Open Air, 1944). In 1944 joined Old Vic Company at Liverpool and appeared in *The Alchemist, Uneasy Laughter*, etc. Recently in *The Venetian* (Chanticleer, 1944), *Jacobowsky And The Colonel* (Piccadilly, 1945), *The Circle Of Chalk* (Arts, 1945), *Fit For Heroes* (Embassy, 1945), *Zoo In Silesia* (Embassy). Appeared in *The Fountain Of Youth* (Lindsey, 1946).

PORTMAN, ERIC. Actor. Born Bradford, 1903. Made his first appearance on the stage with Henry Baynton's Company in 1924, at Sunderland. First appeared in London in *The Comedy Of Errors* (Savoy, 1924); subsequently in *Richard III, White Cargo, Electra*, etc. With Old Vic Company, 1927-28, playing in *The Taming Of The Shrew, The Merchant Of Venice, Henry V, The School For Scandal, Romeo And Juliet, King Lear, Everyman, Hamlet*, etc. Also appeared in the West End in *Major Barbara, The Roof, Hamlet, Misalliance, She Stoops To Conquer, The Beaux' Stratagem, Desire Under The Elms, The Master Builder* and many others. Also in London in *The Rivals, Diplomacy, Sheppey, Richard Of Bordeaux, Napoleon, Chase The Ace, Bitter Harvest, The Great Romancer, Julius Cæsar*, etc. Made his first appearance in New York in *Madame Bovary* (Broadhurst, 1937), returning to London in *The Masque Of The Kings*, followed by *Give Me Yesterday*. To New York again in 1938 to appear in *I Have Been Here Before*. In 1939 acted in *The Intruder* (Wyndham's). In 1940 acted in *Julius Cæsar* (Embassy and His Majesty's). In 1940-41 appeared in *Jeannie* (Torch and Wyndham's). Then on tour in *Uncle Harry*, 1943. Recently: *Zero Hour* (Lyric, 1944).

POWER, HARTLEY. Actor. Born New York, 1894. Made his first appearance on the stage in *Her Past Redeemed* (Belfast, 1911). Then first appeared in London in *Kismet* (Garrick, 1911). Returned to America and made his first appearance in New York in *The Dragon's Claw* (New Amsterdam, 1914) and in a number of plays until 1916. Then in French Army until 1919, when he toured in Australia. Then in New York until 1926, after which he again acted in London in *Broadway*. Thenceforth in the West End in *The Squeaker, Dishonoured Lady, The Improper Duchess, Sweet Aloes* and many others. In 1941 in *Lady Behave* (His Majesty's). In 1942 appeared in *No Orchids For Miss Blandish* (Prince of Wales). Then in *The Petrified Forest* (Globe, 1942-43). *Under The Counter* (Phœnix, 1945), etc.

PRICE, DENNIS. Actor. Born London, 1915. Educated at Oxford. Studied for the stage at the Embassy School of Acting, making his first appearance with the John Gielgud Company in *Richard II* (Queen's, 1937), then with Croydon Repertory Company, 1938-39. In H.M. Forces, 1940-42. On being invalided out appeared with Windsor Repertory Company, then in *The Springtime Of Others* (Arts, 1943). Joined Noel Coward's Company and appeared in *This Happy Breed* and *Present Laughter* (Haymarket, 1943). Recently in *Hamlet* (for Old Vic) (New, 1944), *Scandal At Barchester* (Lyric and Wyndham's, 1945), *Blithe Spirit* (Duchess, 1945).

PRIESTLEY, J. B. Playwright and novelist. Born Bradford, 1894. Educated at Cambridge. Among his plays are *The Good Companions* (with Edward Knoblock), *Dangerous Corner, Laburnum Grove, Eden's End, Duet In Floodlight, Cornelius, Bees On The Boatdeck, Time And The Conways, I Have Been Here Before, People At Sea, When We Are Married, Johnson Over Jordan*, etc. In 1938 he became a director of the London Mask Theatre, which operated at the Westminster until 1940. His play *Music At Night*, was produced here during this period. His other, more recent, plays include *The Long Mirror* (not yet produced in the West End), *Goodnight Children* (New, 1942), *They Came To A City* (Globe, 1942-43), *Desert Highway* (produced by A.B.C.A. Play Unit) (Playhouse, 1944), *How Are They At Home?* (Lyric, 1944-45), *The Golden Fleece* (not yet seen in London) ; *The Inspector Calls, Jenny Villiers*, etc.

PRIMROSE, DOROTHY. Actress. Born Edinburgh. Made her first appearance on the stage in *The Manxman*, then in repertory at Worthing and Oxford. First acted in London in *After The Dance* (St. James's, 1939). Toured Canada in 1939 with Maurice Colbourne. Made her first appearance in New York in *Geneva*, 1940. Returned to England and went on tour in *Saloon Bar*, 1941. In 1942 toured with *Lottie Dundass*. Joined the Arts Festival Company, 1943, and appeared in *The Constant Couple, The Rivals* and *The Watched Pot*. Joined Donald Wolfit Company, 1944, and appeared in *Twelfth Night, The Merchant Of Venice*, etc., at the Scala. Recently appeared in *The Magistrate* (St. Martin's, 1944). Joined Arts Theatre Festival Company, 1945, and appeared in *The Thunderbolt, The Constant Couple, Hamlet, Getting Married* (Arts, 1945-46).

PURCELL, HAROLD. Playwright and lyricist. For some years he has been engaged in films, as screenwriter, director and producer. Among his plays are *The Lisbon Story* and *The Rest Is Silence*. He has also composed lyrics for such shows as *Something In The Air, Under The Counter, Here Come The Boys* and many others.

QUARTERMAINE, CHARLES. Actor. Born Richmond, 1877. Made his first appearance on the stage in *Sowing The Wind*, Tunbridge Wells, 1896 ; then in F. R. Benson's Company—making his first London appearance in *Henry V*, (Lyceum, 1900). Then with Beerbohm Tree, Oscar Asch and Ben Greet, before making his first appearance, with Charles Wyndham's Company in New York in *Mrs. Gorringe's Necklace* (Lyceum, 1904). Acted in London in dozens of plays thereafter, including *Hamlet, Antony And Cleopatra, Julius Cæsar, The Tempest, Twelfth Night, King Lear*, etc. Toured America and Australia, 1911-13 ; then in London in *David Copperfield, Squibs*, etc., before going to India, 1920-21. Returned to London and played in *Hedda Gabler, Twelve Hours, The Gay Adventure, Road House* and many others. Also in the West End in *Once Upon*

A Time, The Miracle Man, Judgment Day, Goodbye, Mr. Chips, etc. He has recently been acting with the Donald Wolfit Company on tour and in his seasons at the St. James's, Scala and Winter Garden. Also, in 1945, he appeared in *The Last Stone* (Phœnix) and *The Assassin* (Savoy, 1945). Since then with the Donald Wolfit Company on tour in the provinces and on the Continent.

QUARTERMAINE, LEON. Actor. Born Richmond, 1876. Made his first appearance on the stage in *A Thousand Pound Reward*, Sheffield, 1894 ; then in London in the same part, 1894. Subsequently on tour with Ben Greet, Martin Harvey and with Forbes-Robertson in England and in America. Made his first appearance in New York in *The Light That Failed* (Knickerbocker, 1903). Then in London in *Samson, The Winter's Tale, Twelfth Night, Androcles And The Lion, The Doctor's Dilemma,* etc. Also in the West End in *Ghosts, Henry VIII, The Mayor Of Troy, Bella Donna, Romance, The School For Scandal, Romeo And Juliet, Napoleon, Mary Rose, The Circle, Quality Street, Secrets, The Man With A Load Of Mischief, Trelawney Of The Wells* and many others. Among the other plays in which he has appeared in London are *The Crooked Billet, Mrs. Moonlight, Journey's End* (and in New York, 1929-30), *The Judgment Of Dr. Johnson, Heartbreak House,* etc. Joined Old Vic Company, 1933, and played in *Twelfth Night* and *The Cherry Orchard.* Then in West End in *Escape Me Never* (also in New York, 1934), *The Seagull, Antony And Cleopatra, Yes, My Darling Daughter,* etc. With John Gielgud Company, 1937-38, appearing in *Richard II, The School For Scandal, Three Sisters, The Merchant Of Venice* (Queen's). Also in *Dear Octopus* (Adelphi, 1940), *The Importance Of Being Earnest* (Globe, 1940), and others. 1941, appeared in *Dear Brutus* (Globe). Then in *Macbeth* (Piccadilly). Joined John Gielgud Company in 1943 to appear in *Love For Love* (Phœnix). Later (in the Gielgud Repertory Season) acted in the latter, *Hamlet, The Duchess Of Malfi, A Midsummer Night's Dream* (Haymarket, 1944-45).

QUAYLE, ANTHONY. Actor. Born September 7th, 1913, Liverpool. Educated Rugby. Made his first appearance on the stage in 1931. His London appearances include *Hamlet, Richard II* (with John Gielgud's Company), *Pride And Prejudice, The Silent Knight, Elizabeth,* etc. Made his first appearance in New York in *Country Wife,* 1936. In 1938-39 he appeared in London with the Old Vic Company. From 1939-45 in H.M. Forces, making his return to the stage in *The Rivals* (Criterion, 1945-46). In 1946 he produced *Crime And Punishment.*

QUINN, TONY. Actor. Born County Kildare, Ireland, 1899. Studied for the stage at the Abbey Theatre School of Acting, making his first appearance on the stage in *The Mineral Workers* (Abbey, 1919). Remained with this company until 1927, making his first appearance in London in *The Shadow Of A Gunman* (Vaudeville, 1927). First acted in New York in *The Plough And The Stars* (Hudson, 1927). With the Irish Players, 1928-30. Has appeared in London in *The Plough And The Stars, The Playboy Of The Western World, General John Regan, Ourselves Alone* and many others. Also in the West End in *The Big House, The Moon In The Yellow River, Juno And The Paycock, Death On The Table.* In 1939 joined the London Mask Theatre Company and appeared in *Desire Under The Elms* and *Abraham Lincoln* (Westminster). In H.M. Forces, 1940-43. On being invalided out appeared in *The Well Of The Saints* (Arts, 1943), followed by *Shadow And Substance* (Duke of York's), *Don Abel Wrote A Tragedy* (Arts), *The Last Of Summer* (Phœnix, 1944), *Happy Few* (Cambridge, 1944), *The Critic* (Arts, 1944). Recently joined the Embassy Theatre Company and has appeared in *Quality Street, The Two Mrs. Carrolls, Father Malachy's Miracle* and *No Room At The Inn,* 1945.

RADFORD, BASIL. Actor. Born Chester, 1897. Studied for the stage at the Royal Academy of Dramatic Art, making his first stage appearance in *Bulldog Drummond,* Hastings, 1922. Then in London in *Collusion* (Ambassadors, 1924) :

and on tour in the provinces and in Australia, 1925-28. With the British Guild
Company in Vancouver, 1929-31. Has also acted in London in *The Love Pirate,
The Outskirts, Private Room, The Dark Tower, Chase The Ace, Night Must Fall,*
and a number of others. Also in the West End in *Spring Tide, The Astonished
Ostrich, To Have And To Hold, Blondie White, The Innocent Party,* etc. In 1942
acted in *Warn That Man* (Garrick). 1943-44, appeared in *She Follows Me About*
(Garrick), etc. In 1946 appeared in *The Astonished Ostrich* (St. James's).

RAGHAN, MICHAEL. Actor and producer. Born London, 1892. Made his
first appearance on the stage in 1907 in a tour with Ellen Terry in *Captain
Brassbound's Conversion.* First appeared in London in *The House Of Temperley*
(Adelphi, 1910), then in many plays in London. After the war he appeared at
the Everyman; then founded Mirror Theatre. In 1925 he joined the Gate
Theatre, appearing in *Hedda Gabler, The Adding Machine,* etc. Following this he
produced for some years at Leeds Arts Theatre; then producing at Leicester,
Buxton, etc. Recently: Joined Arts Theatre Group of Actors in 1942, appearing
in *Awake And Sing, The Magistrate, The Constant Couple, The Rivals, On Life's
Sunny Side, Don Abel Wrote A Tragedy* and many others. In 1944 he joined the
Old Vic Company, appearing in *Peer Gynt, Richard III* at the New, afterwards
on tour in Europe. Then he appeared, for the Old Vic, in *Henry IV (Parts I
and II)* (New, 1945-46).

RAMAGE, CECIL. Actor. Born Edinburgh, 1895. Educated Edinburgh Academy
and Oxford. Made his first appearance on the stage in *The Last Enemy,* New
York, 1930, then in London acted in *The Pelican* (Playhouse, 1931), followed by
The Young Idea, Napoleon, Twelfth Night, etc. Also in the West End in *Loyalties,
Justice, When Ladies Meet, Henry IV (Part I),* and many others. With the Old
Vic Company on tour in the Mediterranean, 1939, appearing in *Henry V, Justice,*
etc. Joined Open Air Theatre Company, 1939, and appeared in *Much Ado About
Nothing, Pericles,* etc. Recently: In *The Two Children* (Arts, 1944), *Emma*
(St. James's, 1945), etc. Toured the Continent in *Julius Cæsar,* 1945-46.

RANDOLPH, ELSIE. Actress. Born London, 1904. Made her first appearance
on the stage on tour in 1916; then first appeared in London in *The Girl For The
Boy* (Duke of York's, 1919). Then in London in *The Naughty Princess, Battling
Butler, Toni, Sunny, That's A Good Girl, Follow Through, The Co-Optimists Of
1930, Wonder Bar, Stand Up And Sing, Mr. Whittington, This'll Make You Whistle,
Room For Two* and many others. In 1940-41 toured in *The Body Was Well
Nourished,* then appeared in *It's Time To Dance* (Winter Garden, 1943), *The Maid
Of The Mountains* (Coliseum, 1943-44), *Great Day* (Playhouse, 1945), *Is Your
Honeymoon Really Necessary?* (Duke of York's, 1945-46).

RANKIN, MOLLY. Actress. Born Scotland. Studied for the stage at R.A.D.A.,
making her first appearance on the stage in *Caroline,* Oxford, 1925. Then appeared
at the Festival, Cambridge, and also at Stratford-on-Avon; before making her
first appearance in London in *A Doll's House* (Kingsway, 1928). Has also appeared
in London in *Nine Till Six, Children In Uniform, Ladies-In-Waiting,* 1066 *And
All That, Time And The Conways, Ghost For Sale,* etc. In 1938 joined Liverpool
Repertory Company, acting here until she joined the B.B.C. Repertory Company
in 1940, where she has remained since that time.

RATTIGAN, TERENCE. Playwright. Born London, 1912. Educated Harrow
and Oxford. Among his plays are *First Episode,* 1934, *French Without Tears,*
1937, *After The Dance,* 1939 and *Follow My Leader,* 1940. Recently: *Flare Path*
(Apollo, 1942-43), *Love In Idleness* (Lyric, 1944-45) and *While The Sun Shines*
(Globe, 1943-46). In 1945-46 he wrote *The Winslow Boy.*

RAWLINGS, MARGARET. Born Japan, 1906. Educated at Oxford. Married
to Sir Robert Barlow. Made her first appearance on the stage in *The Doctor's
Dilemma,* Croydon, 1927, with the Charles Macdona Company, with whom she

PHOTO : CECIL BEATON

★ *John Gielgud* in Congreve's "Love For Love", which he produced in 1943, and later for his 1944-45 Repertory Season.

PHOTO : CECIL BEATON

★ *John Gielgud* as Hamlet, and Miles Malleson as Polonius in George Rylands' production of Shakespeare's tragedy, for the Gielgud Repertory Season, 1944-45.

★ *John Gielgud* as Hamlet, Leslie Banks as Claudius and Marian Spencer as Gertrude in the final episode of the Play Scene, in "Hamlet", 1944-45.

★ **_Yvonne Arnaud_** and John Gielgud in Somerset Maugham's comedy "The Circle", produced by William Armstrong for Gielgud's Repertory Season, 1944-45.

★ *Claire Luce* as Cleopatra, in Shakespeare's "Antony And Cleopatra", produced by Robert Atkins at Stratford Memorial Theatre, 1945.

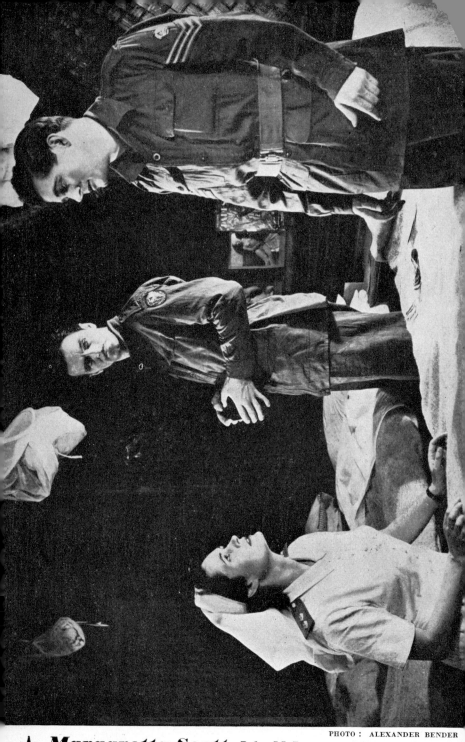

PHOTO : ALEXANDER BENDER

★ *Margaretta Scott*, John McLaren and Emrys Jones in John Patrick's "The Hasty Heart", produced by Murray Macdonald, 1945.

PHOTO : JOHN VICKERS

★ *Cecil Parker,* Terry Morgan, Pamela Conroy, Joan Young and Vivien Leigh in Thornton Wilder's "The Skin Of Our Teeth", produced by Laurence Olivier, 1945.

★ *Sybil Thorndike* as Jocasta and Laurence Olivier as
Œdipus, in Michel St. Denis' production of the Sophocles
drama, for the Old Vic, 1945-46.

remained until 1928. Made her first appearance in London in *Jordan* (Strand, 1928). Toured Canada and the United States, 1929-30 and on her return appeared in *The Last Chapter,* followed by *Betrayal, The Venetian* and *Salome.* Made her first appearance in New York in *The Venetian* (Masque, 1931), after which she toured in Australia until 1933. Among the plays in which she has appeared in the West End are *This Side Idolatry, Napoleon, The Greeks Had A Word For It, Man And Superman, Pygmalion,* etc. Appeared in New York in *Parnell,* 1935, and again in London, 1936, and also appeared in the West End in *Antony And Cleopatra, Macbeth, Black Limelight, The Trojan Women, The Flashing Stream* (In London and New York, 1939) and *The Showing Up Of Blanco Posnet,* etc. Then appeared in *Pygmalion* (Haymarket, 1939), *A House In The Square* (St. Martin's, 1940), *Dear Brutus* (Globe, 1941).

RAWSON, TRISTAN. Actor. Born London, 1888. Made his first appearance on the stage in opera at Cologne, 1910. Then first appeared in London on the legitimate stage in *As You Like It* (Lyric, Hammersmith, 1920), followed by *The Beggar's Opera, If Four Walls Told, Amphytrion, East Lynne, The Square Peg, Where The Rainbow Ends* and many others. Also in London in *Journey's End, Little Eyolf, Hamlet, Richard III, The Merry Wives Of Windsor, Julius Cæsar, Napoleon* and *Dinner At Eight.* Also in the West End in *The Rose Without A Thorn, Escape Me Never, Theatre Royal, St. Helena, Whiteoaks, The Amazing Dr. Clitterhouse, You Can't Take It With You* and many others. Joined the Old Vic Company, 1938, and appeared in *Othello,* then with the Open Air Theatre, playing in *A Midsummer Night's Dream, As You Like It, Twelfth Night* and *Lysistrata.* Again played with the Open Air Theatre in 1939 in *Much Ado About Nothing* and *Pericles.* In 1942 appeared in *Salt Of The Earth* (Vaudeville), *Abraham Lincoln* (for the Old Vic), (Playhouse, 1943), followed by *Tobias And The Angel* (Open Air, 1943), *The Rest Is Silence* (Prince of Wales, 1944), and *The Two Children* (Arts, 1944). In 1945 he joined Stratford-on-Avon Festival Company and appeared in *Antony And Cleopatra, The Merry Wives Of Windsor, Much Ado About Nothing,* etc. Appeared in *Red Roses For Me* (Embassy, 1946).

RAY, RENE. Actress. Born London, 1912. Made her first appearance on the legitimate stage in *Wonder Bar* (Savoy, 1930). Also appeared in London in *The Dominant Sex, Private Company, Bees On The Boatdeck, Climbing* and others. Then in the West End in *Yes And No, Three Blind Mice* and *They Walk Alone.* Has recently appeared on tour in *They Walk Alone,* 1940-41, *Other People's Houses* (Ambassadors, 1941-42), *Night Of The Garter* (Strand, 1943), etc. In 1945 toured the Continent in *June Mad,* then in *The Cure For Love* (Westminster, 1945-46). In 1946 appeared in *Patricia's Seven Houses* (Granville).

RAYE, CAROL. Actress. Born London, 1923. Studied to be a dancer and first appeared on the stage in *Bobby Get Your Gun* (Savoy, 1938), followed by *Funny Side Up,* etc. Recently appeared in *Fun And Games* (Princes, 1941), *The Merry Widow* (His Majesty's, 1943), *The Love Racket* (Victoria Palace, 1944) and *Big Boy* (Saville, 1945).

RAYMOND, CYRIL. Born London. Studied for the stage at R.A.D.A., making his first appearance in *Bluff King Hal* (Garrick, 1914). Then in London in *Trilby, Summertime, Threads, Welcome Stranger, The Little Minister,* etc. Toured South Africa in 1925 and made his first appearance in New York in *Red Blinds* (Maxine Elliott, 1936). Has also appeared in London in *After All, The Calendar, There's Always Juliet* (in New York and London, 1931), *Clear All Wires* and many others. Appeared in New York in *The Shining Hour,* 1934 and then in London in *Short Story, No Exit, The Constant Wife, To Have And To Hold, No Sky So Blue, Tony Draws A Horse,* etc. Since the outbreak of war, with H.M. Forces. In 1945 he reappeared in London in *Under The Counter* (Phœnix).

READ, DAVID. Actor. Educated Cheltenham College. Made his first stage appearance in *Parnell* (Gate, 1938), after which he appeared in repertory in many provincial towns. He appeared in *Uncle Harry* on tour, 1943, then for a season at the Intimate, Palmers Green. He appeared at the Memorial Theatre, Stratford-on-Avon in 1944, and again in 1945, in *Volpone, The Merchant Of Venice, Hamlet* and *Macbeth*; also in *Twelfth Night, Antony And Cleopatra, Much Ado About Nothing, The Merry Wives Of Windsor* and *Othello*. In 1945 he appeared in *King John* (Birmingham Repertory Theatre). In 1946 he appeared in *Golden Eagle* (Westminster).

REDGRAVE, MICHAEL. Actor and producer. Born Bristol, 1908. Educated at Cambridge. Married to Rachel Kempson. Made his appearance on the stage at Stratford-on-Avon in 1921. Acted considerably while still at Cambridge and in 1934 he decided to act professionally, joining Liverpool Repertory Company, where he first appeared in *Counsellor At Law*. He spent two years with this Company, and then made his first professional appearance in London, with the Old Vic Company, in *Love's Labour's Lost*, 1936. With the Old Vic Company, 1936-37, appeared in *The Country Wife, As You Like It, The Witch Of Edmonton* and *Hamlet*. Then appeared in the West End in *As You Like It, The Bat, Henry V, A Ship Comes Home, Three Set Out*, etc. With John Gielgud's Company, 1937-38, appearing in *Richard II, The School For Scandal* and *The Three Sisters* (Queen's). Then joined the Michel St. Denis Company and appeared in *The White Guard* and *Twelfth Night* (Phœnix, 1938). In 1939 joined the London Mask Theatre Company and appeared in *The Family Reunion* (Westminster). Recently appeared in *The Beggar's Opera* (Haymarket, 1940), *Thunder Rock* (Neighbourhood and Globe, 1940), *The Duke In Darkness* (St. James's, 1942), *A Month In The Country* (St. James's, 1943). Then in *Parisienne* (St. James's, 1943), *Uncle Harry* (Garrick, 1944-45), *Jacobowsky And The Colonel* (Piccadilly, 1945). He has also produced a number of plays in London, including *Lifeline, The Wingless Victory, Blow Your Own Trumpet* (for the Old Vic), *Uncle Harry* (with William Armstrong), *Jacobowsky And The Colonel*, etc.

REDMAN, JOYCE. Actress. Born London, 1919. She made her first appearance on the stage in *Alice Through The Looking Glass* (Playhouse, 1935), followed by appearances in London in *The Insect Play, Lady Precious Stream, The King's Pirate* and *Thou Shalt Not——*. Also in the West End in *The Western Chamber, Asmodée, Drawing Room*, etc. In 1940 appeared in *Lady Precious Stream* (Kingsway), then in *Twelfth Night* (Arts, 1942). In 1943 appeared in *Peter Pan* (Winter Garden), *Shadow And Substance* (Duke of York's), and *Claudia* (St. Martin's, 1943-44). In 1944 she joined the Old Vic Company and appeared in *Peer Gynt, Richard III, Arms And The Man* and *Uncle Vanya* (New). In 1945 toured the Continent with the Old Vic and rejoined the Company, appearing in *Henry IV (Part II), Œdipus* and *The Critic* (New, 1945-46).

REEVE, ADA. Actress. Born London, 1876. Made her first appearance on the stage in *East Lynne*, Dewsbury, 1882. First appeared in London in *Sinbad The Sailor*, 1883, since then has appeared in London in *The Shop Girl, The Gay Parisienne, Florodora, Kitty Grey*, etc. From 1906-15 she toured extensively in the provinces and also in South Africa and Australia, then after a short spell in England she again continued her Australian tours until 1935. In 1936 she reappeared in London in *Follow The Sun* (Adelphi), after which she toured in variety until 1942. In 1943 she appeared in *They Came To A City* (Globe). Then in *The Last Of Summer* (Phœnix) and in *Residents Only* (St. James's, 1944), *The Shop At Sly Corner* (St. Martin's, 1945-46).

REEVES, KYNASTON. Actor. Born London, 1893. Studied for the stage at R.A.D.A., making his first appearance on tour in 1920. From 1922-28 with the Lena Ashwell Players, making his first appearance in the West End in *The Unquiet*

Spirit (Apollo, 1928), then on tour in the provinces and in the United States. Also appeared in London in *Vile Bodies, The School For Scandal, Never Come Back, The Lake, La Prisonnière*, etc. Then in the West End in *Housemaster, A Midsummer Night's Dream, Glorious Morning* and others. Recently on tour in *The Man With A Load Of Mischief* for CEMA, 1942, then appeared in *Alice In Wonderland* (Palace, 1944-45). Subsequently joined the London Theatre Group to appear in *Rosmersholm* (Torch, 1945). Appeared in *So Brief The Spring*, 1945-46.

RELPH, GEORGE. Actor. Born Northumberland, 1888. Made his first appearance on the stage in *Othello*, Grimsby, 1905, then first appeared in London in *Hamlet* (Lyceum, 1909). Toured Australia in 1909 and made his first appearance in New York in *Kismet* (Knickerbocker, 1911), afterwards he appeared in London in *Joseph And His Brethren* before acting in America from 1914-16. After the war, he appeared in London in *Salome, Cæsar's Wife, The Man Who Came Back, The Bat, The Green Goddess, Is Zat So?* and many others. Then in the West End in *The Squeaker, Symphony In Two Flats, Once In A Lifetime, Living Dangerously, Chase The Ace*, and *The Squeaker* (in 1937), etc. Recently appeared in *Judgment Day* (Phœnix, 1940), *The Doctor's Dilemma* (Haymarket, 1942-43). Joined the Old Vic Company in 1944, appearing in *Peer Gynt, Richard III*. Toured with the Old Vic on the Continent, 1945, and rejoined this company to appear in *Henry IV (Parts I and II), Œdipus* and *The Critic* (New, 1945-46).

RELPH, MICHAEL. Designer. Born Broadstone, Dorset, 1915. Educated Bembridge School. Entered the film industry in 1932 as assistant art director under Alfred Junge at Gaumont British Studios. Then designed thirty films for Warner Brothers Studios and is now art director at Ealing Studios. Combines stage designing with his film work and among the West End productions for which he has designed in the past few years are : *Saloon Bar* (Wyndham's), *The Doctor's Dilemma* (Haymarket), *A Month In The Country* (St. James's), *The Petrified Forest* (Globe), *Heartbreak House* (Cambridge), *Watch On The Rhine* (Aldwych), *Up And Doing* (Saville), *The Last Of Summer* (Phœnix), *The Man Who Came To Dinner* (Savoy), *The Years Between* (Wyndham's), *Love In Idleness* (Lyric).

REYNOLDS, DOROTHY. Actress. Born Waikiki, 1913. Educated Royal Orphanage, Wolverhampton. Made her first appearance on the stage in *Payment Deferred* (Festival Theatre, Cambridge). Has appeared in repertory in various parts of England, and recently with Harry Hanson Company, Penge. Then appeared in London with the Arts Theatre Company in many plays, 1943-45, including *On Life's Sunny Side, The Critic, Anna Christie, The Simpleton Of The Unexpected Isles*. Also *The Trojan Women*, on tour with Norman Marshall Company. In 1945 with the Arts Festival Company appearing in *The Thunderbolt, The School For Scandal, Getting Married*, etc. (Arts).

RICHARDS, SUSAN. Actress. Born Blaenau Ffestiniog, North Wales. Educated St. Margaret's School, Bushey. Made her first appearance on the stage in Fred Terry's Company in 1921, remaining with him until 1923. Since then she has appeared in repertory theatres in various parts of the country, and in a number of tours. Recently *George And Margaret* on tour, *Ladies In Retirement* on tour, etc. In 1943 she joined the Arts Theatre Festival Company, appearing in *The Constant Couple, The Watched Pot*, etc. Appeared in *Uncle Harry* (Garrick, 1944-45), *The Late Christopher Bean*, on tour in India. 1945-46 : Joined the Middle East Festival Company, on tour in India, etc.

RICHARDSON, RALPH. Actor. Born Cheltenham, 1902. Married to Meriel Forbes. Made his first appearance on the stage in *The Merchant Of Venice*, Brighton, 1921 ; then on tour in the provinces for four years. With Birmingham Repertory Company, 1926, making his first appearance in London in *Yellow Sands* (Haymarket, 1926), followed by *Back To Methuselah* and *The Taming Of The Shrew*. Toured South Africa in 1929, after which he joined the Old Vic

Company, appearing in *The Jealous Wife, The Tempest, Henry IV (Part I),
Richard II,* and *Antony And Cleopatra.* Continued with this Company until
1931, acting also in *Arms And The Man, King Lear* and *Much Ado About Nothing.*
Rejoined the Old Vic 1931-32, acting in *King John, The Taming Of The Shrew,
Abraham Lincoln, Henry V, A Midsummer Night's Dream, Hamlet* and *Othello.*
Appeared at Malvern Festival in 1931 and again in 1932 ; also acted in London
in *Too True To Be Good, For Services Rendered, Sheppey, Wild Decembers, Peter
Pan, Eden End* and many others. Made his first appearance in New York in
Romeo And Juliet (Martin Beck, 1935), then again in London acted in *Promise,
Bees On The Boatdeck, The Amazing Dr. Clitterhouse* and *The Silent Night.*
Again joined the Old Vic Company in 1938, appearing in *A Midsummer Night's
Dream* and *Othello.* In 1939 acted in *Johnson Over Jordan* (New and Saville).
From 1939-43 with the Fleet Air Arm. Was released in 1944 to join the Old Vic
Company, subsequently appearing in *Peer Gynt, Arms And The Man, Richard III*
and *Uncle Vanya* (New, 1944-45). Toured with this company on the Continent
in 1945, rejoining to appear in *Henry IV (Parts I And II), The Critic* and *Œdipus*
(New, 1945-46).

RICHMOND, SUSAN. Actress. Born London, 1894. Studied for the stage
with the Benson Company, making her first appearance in *The Brothers Karamazov*
(Aldwych, 1912). First appeared in London in *Pygmalion* (Coliseum, 1917), then
in repertory with Birmingham and Liverpool. Toured Australia in 1925-26,
and on her return appeared in London in *Yellow Sands, Mr. Pickwick, The Barretts
Of Wimpole Street, Dinner At Eight, Son Of Man, Jane Eyre* and many others.
1933-39, was co-director of the Webber-Douglas School of Acting, and in 1939
became chief drama instructor at the Royal College of Music. Recently has
appeared in London in *Whiteoaks* (Intimate, 1943), *The Dark River* (Whitehall,
1943), *A Soldier For Christmas* (Wyndham's, Vaudeville and Playhouse, 1944).
In 1945 appeared in *Yellow Sands* (Westminster).

RIETTY, ROBERT. Actor. Born London, February 8th, 1923. Studied under
Victor Rietty, making his first appearance on the stage at the age of eight in *Poil
De Carotte* (Fortune, 1935). He has since appeared in many productions of the
Drama Players Theatre, including *The Father, The Devil, If I Were Young Again,*
etc. Also in London in *The Boy David, The Insect Play,* etc. Then in *Desire
Under The Elms,* on tour, *The School For Scandal* (Malvern), *The Prodigal Son*
(Mercury, 1940). Since 1942 he has been in H.M. Forces (acting with the " Central
Pool of Artists ").

RIETTY, VICTOR. Actor and producer. Born Ferrara, Italy, 1888. Educated
Bologna. Studied music and was formerly a concert violinist. Came to London
in 1919, shortly afterwards forming the Drama Players Theatre, to produce little-
known European plays in London. With this group produced and appeared in,
among others, *Gioconda, The Man Who Met Himself, Poil De Carotte, The Crescent
Moon, Sicilian Limes, The Father, The Devil* and *If I Were Young Again.* He has
also appeared in London in *Piccola, Hell For Leather,* etc., and on tour in *There
Shall Be No Night, My Sister Eileen, Claudia,* etc. Also in London in *Hay Fever*
(Everyman, 1941), *Father Malachy's Miracle* (Embassy, 1945), etc. Recently
A Bell For Adano (Phœnix, 1945).

RISCOE, ARTHUR. Born Yorkshire, 1896. Made his first appearance on the
stage in a concert party in Australia, making his first appearance in England on
tour in 1919. Then in London he acted in *French Leave, Sky High,* after which
he toured the provinces, 1925-30. Then in London in *Nippy, For The Love Of
Mike, Out Of The Bottle, Jill Darling, Going Places, Wild Oats,* etc. Recently
appeared in *Shephard's Pie* (Princes, 1941), *Fun And Games* (Princes, 1941),
Dubarry Was A Lady (His Majesty's, 1942), *Jill Darling* (Saville, 1944), *Irene*
(His Majesty's, 1944-45).

RITCHARD, CYRIL. Actor. Born Sydney, Australia, 1898. Educated Sydney University. Married to Madge Elliott. Made his first appearance on the stage in *A Waltz Dream*, Sydney, 1917, and was continuously engaged playing for J. C. Williamson until 1924, when he went to America, making his first appearance in New York in *Puzzles Of* 1925 (Fulton). Then first appeared in London in *Bubbly* (Duke of York's, 1925), followed by *Charlot's Revue*, 1925, *Lady Luck*, *Love Lies*, *The Co-Optimists Of* 1930, *The Love Race* and many others. From 1932-36 acting in Australia. Then in London in *Spread It Abroad, The Constant Sinner*, *People In Love, Bedtime Story, Nine Sharp*, etc. 1939-40, appeared in *The Little Revue* (Little), *The Importance Of Being Earnest* (Phœnix, 1940), *Up And Doing* (Saville, 1940-41), *Big Top* (His Majesty's, 1942), *The Merry Widow* (His Majesty's, 1943-44). Recently appeared in *Gay Rosalinda* (Palace, 1945), and *Sigh No More* (Piccadilly, 1945-46).

ROBERTS, J. H. Actor. Born London, 1884. Made his first appearance on the stage in *The March Hare*, Birkenhead, 1909, then joined Miss Horniman's Company at Manchester until 1911. From 1911-13 with the Liverpool Repertory Company, making his first appearance in London in *A Conversation At The Styx* (Court, 1913). Then in the Army until 1919, when he reappeared in London in *Sacred And Profane Love, Loyalties, The Lilies Of The Field, London Life, A Kiss For Cinderella*, etc. Also in the West End in *Rain, A Man With Red Hair, The Moon Rides High, Mary Rose, The Roof, Charlot's Masquerade, A Murder Has Been Arranged, Lean Harvest, Service, A Sleeping Clergyman, Hyde Park Corner, Housemaster, Lot's Wife, To Kill A Cat* and many others. In 1939-40 appeared in *The Importance Of Being Earnest* (Globe), also in *Heartbreak House* (Cambridge, 1943), *Halfway To Heaven* (Princes, 1944), etc. Recently in *The Vicar Of Wakefield*, 1945.

ROBSON, FLORA. Actress. Born South Shields, 1902. Studied for the stage at R.A.D.A., making her first appearance in *Will Shakespeare* (Shaftesbury, 1921). Then with Ben Greet, and at Oxford Playhouse under J. B. Fagan. In 1929 she joined Anmer Hall at Cambridge Festival, after which she appeared in London in *Betrayal* in 1931, followed by *Desire Under The Elms, Salome, The Anatomist, Othello, Dangerous Corner, For Services Rendered, All God's Chillun*, etc. Then with Old Vic Company, 1933-34, appearing in *The Cherry Orchard, Henry VIII, Measure For Measure, The Importance Of Being Earnest, The Tempest, Love For Love, Macbeth*, etc. Afterwards appeared in London in *Touch Wood, Mary Read, Close Quarters, Mary Tudor, Anna Christie, Satyr, Autumn* and many others. From 1939-43 acting in America. Recently appeared in *Guilty* (for the Old Vic), (Lyric, Hammersmith, 1944), *Ethel Fry*, 1945 ; *Man About The House*, 1946.

ROSMER, MILTON. Actor and producer. Born Southport, 1881. Educated Manchester Grammar School. Made his first appearance on the stage on tour in *Don Quixote*, 1899, after which he toured until 1903, when he made his first appearance in London in *The Breed Of The Treshams* (Kennington). Then with Martin Harvey for three years, and also toured in America. From 1910-15 with Miss Horniman's Company at Manchester. Then in London in *The Tragedy Of Nan, The Heritage, Julius Cæsar, Arms And The Man, Getting Married, The Philanderer, Mary Stuart, As You Like It, St. Joan, The Wild Duck* and many others. Also in the West End in *A Doll's House, Widower's Houses, He Who Gets Slapped, Many Waters, The Last Enemy, The Wild Duck, Getting Married, As You Like It, The Masque Of Kings*. More recently in *A Party For Christmas, Gaslight*, etc. In 1939-40 appeared in and produced *The Devil's Disciple* (Piccadilly). Also in *Music At Night* (Westminster, 1940). Then on tour with John Gielgud's Company in *Macbeth*. In 1942 in *Salt Of The Earth* (Vaudeville). Producer at Stratford-on-Avon Memorial Theatre, 1943, then in *Scandal At Barchester* (Lyric and Wyndham's, 1944-45). In 1945 on tour in *Ethel Fry*. Appeared in *A Doll's House*, on tour, 1945-46.

ROSS, HARRY. Actor. Born London, 1913. Made his first appearance on the stage in *Waiting For Lefty* (Unity, 1935), subsequently playing in a number of productions at this theatre, including *Plant In The Sun* and *Crisis*. Made his first professional appearance in London in *Awake And Sing* (Arts, 1942), then with B.B.C. Repertory Company, after which he appeared in the West End in *Twelfth Night* (Arts, 1942), *The Petrified Forest* (Globe, 1942-43), *Mr. Bolfry* (Westminster, 1943), *My Sister Eileen* (Savoy, 1943-44). Since 1944 in H.M. Forces, attached to Central Pool of Artists, touring Italy and Greece, etc.

ROSS, ORIEL. Actress. Born London, 1907. Married to Earl Poulett. Studied for the stage at the Royal College of Music, making her debut in *The Insect Play* (Regent, 1923). Then in London in *Mr. Pepys, Just A Kiss*, etc., before making her first appearance on the New York stage in *This Year Of Grace* (Selwyn, 1928). She remained in America until 1931. Then acted in London in *Vile Bodies, Acropolis, Touch Wood, The Mask Of Virtue*, etc. Also in *The Apple Cart, A Mid-Summer Night's Dream, Troilus And Cressida, On A Summer's Day* and others. 1939-40, with the Old Vic Company in *The Tempest*, etc. In 1942 appeared in *The Streets Of London* (Cambridge). Recently in *Trilby*, on tour, 1945-46.

ROTHA, WANDA. Actress. Born Vienna. Married to Manning Whiley. Studied for the stage at the Viennese Academy of Dramatic Art, making her first appearance in *Six Characters In Search Of An Author* (Vienna, 1926). Then acted in Frankfurt, Hamburg, Berlin and in Czechoslovakia. Came to England and made her first appearance in London in *The Astonished Ostrich* (Duke of York's, 1937). Then acted in the West End in *The Road To Damascus, Queen Christine, Elizabeth Of Austria*, etc. Recently : *Rain* (St. Martin's, 1941-42), *The Wingless Victory* (Phœnix, 1943).

ROWBOTHAM, BILL. Actor and dramatic author. Born London, 1915. Studied for the stage at the Neilson-Terry Guild. Formerly in vaudeville. He made his first appearance in London at the Unity Theatre, 1938, in *Babes In The Wood*. During the war he acted at Unity and wrote much revue material for Unity revues and pantomimes. With H.M. Forces, 1941-43. On being invalided out he made his first appearance on the profesional stage in *Mr. Bolfry* (Playhouse, 1944). In 1945 appeared in *Desert Rats* (Adelphi). His political pantomime, *Alice In Thunderland*, was produced at Unity Theatre in 1945. He has also collaborated on *Winkles And Champagne, Swinging To The Left*, etc. In 1945 he appeared at the Players' Theatre. Recently in *Now The Day Is Over*, 1945-46.

ROWE, FRANCES. Actress. Born Preston, June 26th, 1913. Educated Channing School, Highgate, and Cambridge. She made her first appearance on the stage in *Muted Strings* (Daly's, 1936), thereafter in a number of London productions. Recently : *They Came To A City* (Globe, 1943), *The Last Of Mrs. Cheyney* (Savoy, 1944-45). Joined the John Clements-Kay Hammond Repertory Company, appearing in *The Kingmaker* and *Marriage a La Mode* (St. James's, 1946).

ROYSTON, ROY. Actor. Born London, 1899. Made his first stage appearance in *The Blue Bird* (Haymarket, 1910). Then in *Hide And Seek, Betty, Follow The Crowd, Peter Pan, The Boy, The Shop Girl, Little Nellie Kelly* and many others. Made his first appearance in New York in *Peg O' My Dreams* (Jolson, 1924), after which he played in London in *The Blue Kitten, Happy-Go-Lucky, Lucky Girl, Cochran's 1930 Revue, The One Girl, After Dark*, etc. More recently in the West End in *Seeing Stars, Swing Along, Going Greek, Running Riot*, etc. From 1940-43 : With the R.A.F. Then reappeared in London in *The Love Racket* (Victoria Palace, 1943-44).

RUDDOCK, JOHN. Actor. Born Peru, 1897. Married to Avril Voules. Educated St. Lawrence College, Ramsgate. Made his first appearance on the stage in *Brown Sugar*, 1922, after which he appeared in repertory at Norwich, Windsor, Manchester, Coventry, Croydon, and extensively on the Continent with the British Repertory

Company. Was formerly a member of the Ben Greet Shakespearean Company and has acted with the Old Vic, Stratford-on-Avon Festival Company (on tour in America), etc. Recently appeared in *The Man In Half Moon Street*. In 1942 played in *The House Of Regrets* (Arts), then in *A Month In The Country* (St. James's, 1943-44), *The Sulky Fire* (Arts, 1944), *The Glass Slipper* (St. James's, 1944-45).

RUTHERFORD, MARGARET. Actress. Born London, 1892. Studied for the stage at the Old Vic, where she made her first appearance in *Little Jack Horner*, 1925. Subsequently in repertory at Oxford, Croydon, etc. Then in London in *Wild Justice, The Master Builder, Hervey House, Short Story, Farewell Performance, The Melody That Got Lost, Spring Meeting*, etc. In 1939 appeared with the John Gielgud Company in *The Importance Of Being Earnest* (Globe). Recently : In 1940 appeared in *Rebecca* (Queen's). Appeared in *Blithe Spirit* (Piccadilly and Duchess, 1941-43), *Alice In Wonderland* (Scala, 1943, and Palace, 1944), *Perchance To Dream* (Hippodrome, 1945).

ST. DENIS, MICHEL. Actor and producer. Born Beauvais, France, 1897. Was formerly an actor, first appearing in *Twelfth Night* (Theatre du Vieux Colombier, 1922), remaining with this theatre until 1930, as actor, stage director, then assistant producer. In 1930 he founded La Compagnie des Quinze and produced and acted here in a number of plays. He made his first appearance in London in 1927 in *Le Medecin Malgre Lui* (St. James's). From 1935 onwards he divided his time between London and Paris. Among the plays he produced in London were *Noah, The Witch Of Edmonton, Macbeth, Three Sisters*. In 1938 he formed his own company in London and produced *The White Guard* and *Twelfth Night* at the Phœnix. He has also toured with his own companies all over the Continent. In 1935 he founded the London Theatre Studio, which functioned until the outbreak of war. From then onwards he worked continuously with the B.B.C. French Section. In 1945 he produced *Œdipus* for the Old Vic, at the New.

SACHS, LEONARD. Actor and producer. Born South Africa, 1909. Educated University of Johannesburg. Acted in South Africa with Phyllis Neilson-Terry, Sybil Thorndike, etc. Came to England in 1929 and appeared in repertory at Windsor and Croydon. First appeared in London in *Tunnel Trench*, 1926, followed by appearances in *Street Scene, Dr. Bernhardi, Storm In A Teacup* and others. In 1937, with Peter Ridgeway, founded The Players' Theatre in Covent Garden, where he was producer-director-actor, until the theatre moved to Albermarle Street in 1940. In H.M. Forces, 1940-44. On being invalided out resumed directorship of Players' Theatre and in 1945 produced *The Breadwinner* (Arts). In 1946 the Players' moved to Villiers Street, where a new play-producing policy was inaugurated.

SAGAN, LEONTINE. Actress and producer. Born Austria, 1895. Educated in Vienna and Johannesburg. Studied for the stage under Max Reinhardt and appeared as an actress in Vienna, Berlin and Frankfurt, where she also commenced to produce. She made her first production on the London stage with *Children In Uniform* (Duchess, 1932). Her subsequent productions include *Murder In Mayfair, Glamorous Night, Vicky, Careless Rapture, Balalaika, The Crest Of The Wave, Paprika*, etc. Recently : *The Dancing Years, Arc De Triomphe, Six Pairs Of Shoes, Gay Rosalinda* and others.

SAMSON, IVAN. Actor. Born Brighton, 1894. Made his first appearance on the stage in repertory at Woolwich, 1914, then served in the Army, 1915-19. Afterwards appeared in *As You Like It, Madame Sand, Brown Sugar* and other plays in London. Toured South Africa in 1921, then made his first appearance in New York in *Romance* (89th Street, 1921). Also played in the West End in *Bluebeard's Eighth Wife, The Street Singer, The Czarina, Outward Bound, And So To Bed, Bed Rock*, etc. Then in *The Immortal Lady, She Passed Through Lorraine, Miracle At Verdun, When Ladies Meet, Someone At The Door,*

Distinguished Gathering, Careless Rapture, The Gusher, Comedienne, Dracula, etc.
From 1939-42 with B.B.C. Drama Repertory Company. Then appeared in *Flare
Path* (Apollo, 1942-44). Recently in *Young Mrs. Barrington* (Winter Garden,
1945).

SALEW, JOHN. Actor. Born February 28th, 1902, Barielly, India. Formerly
on the stage in a concert party, he made his first appearance on the legitimate stage
as a member of the chorus. He toured in *Journey's End* in India and China,
returning to England and appearing in various repertory companies for four years.
Recently toured in *Six Men Of Dorset,* then appeared in London in *Death On
The Table, To Kill A Cat,* etc. In 1942 appeared in *Saloon Bar* (Wyndham's),
then in *How Are They At Home?* (Apollo, 1944).

SARNER, ALEXANDER. Actor. Born London, 1892. Educated London University.
Studied for the stage at R.A.D.A., making his first appearance in *Othello* (His
Majesty's, 1912), where he remained under Sir Herbert Tree until 1914. After
the war he acted in London in *Oliver Cromwell, The Green Goddess, Silence, The
Crooked Billet, The Matriarch* and many others. Made his first appearance in
New York in *Jew Süss* (Erlanger's, 1930). Then in London in *Grand Hotel, Othello,
The Merchant Of Venice, A Sleeping Clergyman, Magnolia Street, Biography,
No More Peace, Thank You Mr. Pepys, Henry V* and many others. In 1939
appeared in *The Professor From Peking,* Malvern Festival. Since 1941 has been
acting with the B.B.C. Drama Repertory Company.

SARRON, BERNARD. Designer. Born London, 1915. Was formerly an
architect. Made his first appearance as an actor at Unity Theatre in *Waiting For
Lefty,* 1938. Then made his first professional appearance in *Thunder Rock*
(Neighbourhood, 1940). Designed the setting (with Herbert Marshall) of *Thunder
Rock,* 1940; after which he became designer for the Alexandra Repertory Theatre,
Birmingham, 1940-42. Has designed sets and costumes for a number of
productions at Unity, including *Fuente Ovejuna, Winkles And Champagne, Robin
Of England* and *Yellow Star.* In 1945 designed setting for the *Rochdale Pioneers,*
on tour, and *Father Malachy's Miracle* (Embassy). Now Art Director, Pathé
Pictures. In 1945 produced and designed *Swinging To The Left* (Unity).

SCOTT, HAROLD. Actor. Born London, 1891. Educated St. Paul's School.
Made his first appearance on the stage in *The Merchant Of Venice* (Court, 1919).
Then in *John Bull's Other Island, Justice,* etc., before joining the Everyman
Theatre Company in 1922. He acted here in *Getting Married, Misalliance, The
Doctor's Dilemma,* etc., until 1923, after which he acted in the West End in *Twelfth
Night, The Way Of The World, Peter Pan, St. Joan, The Long Voyage Home,
The Wild Duck, Henry VIII, Riverside Nights,* etc. Also in London in *The
Constant Nymph, Major Barbara, Captain Brassbound's Conversion, Charles And
Mary, Grand Hotel, Rose And Glove, The Beggar's Opera, This Desirable Residence,*
etc. Made his first appearance in New York in *Pride And Prejudice* (Music Box,
1935). Has since acted in London in *Peter Pan, The Great Romancer, Thank
You Mr. Pepys, The Masque Of Kings, Serena Blandish, A Doll's House,* etc. In
1939 appeared in *Sixth Floor,* and at the Open Air Theatre in *Pericles.* At the
outbreak of war he acted with B.B.C. Drama Repertory Company until 1942,
then produced *The Drunkard* (Arts). Joined the Norman Marshall Company
appearing in *The Wild Duck* and *Uncle Vanya,* the latter produced at the
Westminster, 1943. In 1945 in *A Doll's House* (Arts), and *The Circle Of Chalk*
(Arts), then on tour in *Madame Bovary,* 1945-46. In *Lady From The Sea* (Arts,
1946).

SCOTT, MARGARETTA. Actress. Born London, 1912. Studied for the
stage at R.A.D.A., making her first appearance in *Romeo And Juliet* (Strand,
1926). Then in repertory at Hull, after which she appeared in London in *The
First Mrs. Fraser, Hamlet, A Murder Has Been Arranged, Elizabeth Of England,*

Dirty Work, etc. Also in the West End in *Twelfth Night, Loyalties, The Streets Of London*, etc. With the Open Air Theatre, 1933, played in *As You Like It, The Tempest, A Midsummer Night's Dream*, etc., and again in 1934, appearing in *The Comedy Of Errors, Androcles And The Lion, Twelfth Night*, etc. Also in London in *The Miracle Man, The Man In Dress Clothes, The Dumb Wife, Love's Labour's Lost, The Silent Knight, Flood Tide, Traitor's Gate*, etc. In 1939 appeared in *To Kill A Cat*, then in *Alien Corn* (Wyndham's, 1939-40). Recently : With Stratford-on-Avon Festival Company, 1941, and again in 1942. Then in *Holy Isle* (Arts, 1943), followed by *Watch On The Rhine* (Aldwych, 1943-44) In 1945 acted in *The Hasty Heart* (Aldwych).

SCOTT, ROSEMARY. Actress. Born Sunderland, 1914. Studied for the stage at R.A.D.A., making her first appearance in *Elizabeth Of England* (Cambridge, 1931). Then with Sheffield Repertory Company, 1932, and with Rochester Repertory Company, 1933-35. Has appeared in London in *Murder In Motley, The Merchant Of Venice, Macbeth, Dr. Jekyll And Mr. Hyde*, etc. In 1936 appeared in repertory at Edinburgh and Glasgow, in 1937 in repertory at Croydon. Then in London in *Time And The Conways, Without Motive*, etc. In 1941 in *Berkeley Square* (Vaudeville), then in *Jupiter Laughs* (New, 1941-42). Recently : In 1942 appeared in *The House Of Jeffreys* (Playhouse). Played in *An Ideal Husband* (Westminster, 1943-44), *The Little Foxes* (Intimate) and several plays at Q Theatre, etc. Appeared in *Mr. Bowling Buys A Newspaper* (Embassy, 1946).

SCUDAMORE, MARGARET. Actress. Born Portsmouth, 1884. Made her first appearance on the stage in *Aladdin*, Aberdeen, 1898, then in London in *The Fire Screen* (Garrick, 1912). From 1916-17 with H. B. Irving, then in London in *Once Upon A Time, Quarantine, Secrets, The Importance Of Being Earnest, The Merry Wives Of Windsor, Arms And The Man* and many others. Also in *Trelawney Of The Wells, Major Barbara, Michael And Mary, The Silver Box, Glass Houses, Robert's Wife, No More Music*, etc. Among the plays in which she has recently appeared are *The Young And Lovely* (Arts, 1943) and *The Last Of Mrs. Cheyney* (Savoy, 1944-45). Appeared in *The Long Mirror* (Lindsey, 1946).

SEIDL, LEA. Actress. Born Vienna, 1902. Made her first appearance on the stage in *Rastelbinder*, Vienna, 1917, afterwards playing in Zurich, and then extensively in Berlin. First appeared in London in *Frederica* (Palace, 1930), followed by *White Horse Inn, A Waltz Dream, Dancing City, No Sky So Blue*, etc. Recently : Acted in *Claudia* (St. Martin's, 1942-43).

SEYLER, ATHENE. Actress. Born London, 1889. Educated Bedford College. Studied for the stage at the Academy of Dramatic Art, making her first appearance in *The Truants* (Kingsway, 1909). Then in London in *The Blue Bird, Lady Patricia, Mrs. Dane's Defence, The Great Adventure, The Debt, Mavourneen, Roxana, As You Like It*, and many others. Also in the West End in *The New Morality, Love For Love, The Dover Road, A Midsummer Night's Dream, The Mask And The Face, Much Ado About Nothing, The Country Wife, One More River, Red Sunday*, etc. Among the other West End plays in which she has appeared are *The Last Enemy, The Importance Of Being Earnest, The Circle, A Pair Of Spectacles, Othello*, etc. Joined the Old Vic Company, 1933, acting in *Twelfth Night, The Cherry Orchard, Measure For Measure, Love For Love, Macbeth*, etc. Then in London also in *The Country Wife, Family Affairs, Love And How To Cure It, Candida, The School For Scandal, People Of Our Class, The Corn Is Green*, etc. Recently : In *French For Love* (Criterion, 1940). With Old Vic Company, 1940-41, appeared in *The Cherry Orchard* (New). Then in *Watch On The Rhine* (Aldwych, 1942-44), *The Last Of Mrs. Cheyney* (Savoy, 1944-45). In 1945 she appeared in *Lady Windermere's Fan* (Haymarket).

SHAW, ANTHONY. Actor. Born 1897. Acted in provinces for a number of years before appearing in London in *The Black Spider* (Lyric, 1928). Subsequently with Liverpool Repertory Theatre, 1929-31. Then acted in London in *Loyalties, Justice, The Private Road, Petticoat Fever, Bulldog Drummond Hits Out, The Island, Juggernaut,* etc. Recently: Appeared in *The Body Was Well Nourished* (Lyric, 1940), *War Fare* (Torch, 1941). In 1944 appeared in *The Last Of Mrs. Cheyney* (Savoy). In *Mr. Bowling Buys A Newspaper* (Embassy, 1946).

SHAW, GEORGE BERNARD. Playwright. Born Dublin, 1856. His first play, *Widower's Houses*, was produced by J. T. Grein's Independent Theatre in London in 1892. Since then he has written, among others, *The Philanderer, Mrs. Warren's Profession, Arms And The Man, Candida, The Man Of Destiny, You Never Can Tell, The Devil's Disciple, Cæsar And Cleopatra, Captain Brassbound's Conversion, The Admirable Bashville, Man And Superman, John Bull's Other Island, How He Lied To Her Husband, Major Barbara, The Doctor's Dilemma, Getting Married, The Showing Up Of Blanco Posnet, The Dark Lady Of The Sonnets, Misalliance, Fanny's First Play, Androcles And The Lion, Pygmalion, Heartbreak House, Back To Methuselah, St. Joan, The Apple Cart, Too True To Be Good, Village Wooing, On The Rocks, The Simpleton Of The Unexpected Isles, The Millionairess, Geneva, The Six Of Calais, In Good King Charles's Golden Days,* etc.

SHAW, GLEN BYAM. Actor and producer. Born London, 1904. Educated Westminster School. Married to Angela Baddeley. Made his first appearance on the stage in *At Mrs. Beam's*, Torquay, 1923. Subsequently appeared in London in *The Cherry Orchard* (Lyric, Hammersmith, 1925), after which he acted with J. B. Fagan's Company at Oxford, 1926. Then in London in *Downhill* and *The Spook Sonata,* before making his first appearance in New York in *And So To Bed* (Shubert, 1927). Also acted in London in *The Truth Game, The Lady From The Sea, Portrait Of A Lady, The Seagull, The Three Sisters, The Lady Of The Camelias, Punchinello, The Miracle, As You Desire Me, This Side Idolatry, Queen Of Scots, Hamlet, Ghosts, Romeo And Juliet, Parnell,* etc. With John Gielgud's Company, 1937-38, appearing in *Richard II, The School For Scandal, The Three Sisters, The Merchant Of Venice* (Queen's). Joined Michel St. Denis Company and played in *The White Guard* (Phœnix, 1938). In 1939 appeared in *Hamlet* in London and in Elsinore. Among the plays he has produced in the West End are *The Island, Dear Octopus, The Merchant Of Venice* and *Rhondda Roundabout.* Since the outbreak of war in H.M. Forces, leaving the Army in August, 1945. He produced *The Winslow Boy* in 1946.

SHAW, SEBASTIAN. Actor. Born Norfolk, 1905. Studied for the stage at R.A.D.A., making his first appearance in *The Cockyolly Bird* (Court, 1914). Then in repertory at Bristol, Liverpool and Hull, before appearing in London in *The Sign In The Sun* (Regent, 1925). Afterwards acted in *Come With Me, The Constant Nymph, The Sacred Flame, Rope* (also in New York, 1929), *The Outsider, Who Goes Next, Measure For Measure, Romeo And Juliet, Precious Bane, Party, Double Door,* etc. Also in London in *Hervey House, The Old Maid, Green Waters, Beyond The Horizon.* In 1939 appeared in *Goodness, How Sad!* (Vaudeville). Since the outbreak of war with the R.A.F., until October, 1945, when he produced *The Gambler* (Embassy).

SHELLEY, FRANK. Actor. Born London, 1912. Formerly a journalist, studying journalism at University College. Afterwards studied for the stage at the Embassy School of Acting, and made his first appearance in *An Enemy Of The People* (Embassy), 1936. After appearing in several other productions at this theatre he toured with Dame Sybil Thorndike in *Six Men Of Dorset*. In 1938 appeared in *The Tiger* (Embassy). Made his first appearance in the West End in *Henry V* (Drury Lane, 1938). Then joined the London Mask Theatre Company and appeared in *Desire Under The Elms* (Westminster, 1939). Also in *His Majesty's Guest* (Shaftesbury, 1940). 1940-44: In H.M. Forces. Since being invalided out has acted and produced for Perth, Leeds and Oxford Repertory Companies.

Appeared in *The Circle Of Chalk* (Arts, 1945). Among his plays are *Postman's Knock*, produced at Perth, 1944. In 1945 on tour in *Desert Highway*.

SHELLEY, NORMAN. Actor. Born London, 1903. Married to Monica Bratt. Educated Merchant Taylors' School. Studied for the stage under Rosina Fillipi, making his first appearance at the Old Vic in 1919. From 1919-26, appeared on tour in Shakespeare with Charles Doran, Alexander Marsh, Ben Greet, etc. Joined the Gate Company in 1926 and appeared here in forty-seven productions. In 1927 he became designer for the Children's Theatre, and between 1927-32 he acted and designed continuously at the Gate and at the Children's Theatre, Endell Street. 1932-33, on tour with Sybil Thorndike and Lewis Casson. Among the plays in which he has appeared in London are *Search, Swords For Utopia, Closing At Sunrise, From Morn To Midnight, The White Chateau, The Painted Veil* and many others. 1940-42 : Served as a ferry pilot in Air Transport Auxiliary. Since being invalided out he has appeared on the stage in *Holy Isle* (Arts, 1943), *They Came To A City* (Globe, 1943-44).

SHELTON, JOY. Actress. Born London, 1922. Married to Sydney Tafler. Studied for the stage at the Royal Academy of Dramatic Art, making her first appearance in a tour of Shakespeare's plays with Leon M. Lion, 1939-40. Subsequently in repertory at Brighton and at the Intimate, Palmers Green. Made her first appearance in the West End in *Other People's Houses* (Ambassadors, 1942). Then in *Murder Without Crime* (Comedy, 1942-43). Recently in *Three's A Family* (Saville, 1944-45).

SHEPLEY, MICHAEL. Actor. Born Plymouth, 1907. Educated Westminster and Oxford. Married to Veronica Rose. Made his first appearance on the stage in *Charley's Aunt*, Hull, 1927, after which he toured Canada, 1927-28. First acted in London in *Justice* (Wyndham's, 1928), followed by *The Silver Box, Scrooge, Exiled, The Middle Watch* (also in New York, 1929), *Lady Windermere's Fan, The Midshipmaid, A Present From Margate*, etc. Also in the West End in *Baby Austin, Strange Barrier, Bats In The Belfry, Flood Tide, Goodbye Mr. Chips*. In 1939 appeared in *The Man In Half Moon Street* (New), *A House In The Square* (St. Martin's), *His Majesty's Guest* (Shaftesbury, 1940), *Love In A Mist* (St. Martin's, 1942). Recently : In *Scoop* (Vaudeville, 1942), *A Month In The Country* (St. James's, 1943) and *The Druid's Rest* (St. Martin's, 1944). *The Banbury Nose* (Wyndham's, 1944), *Another Love Story* (Phœnix, 1944-45), etc. In 1945 acted in *Lady Windermere's Fan* (Haymarket).

SHEPPARD, GUY. Designer. Born London, May 15th, 1912. Educated St. Dunstan's College, Catford, and University College, London. He worked for two years with a firm of stage lighting engineers, and afterwards became well-known for his work in connection with puppets and model theatres. In 1936 he was stage designer at the Tavistock Little Theatre. In 1937-38 he designed *Awake And Sing, Queen Christina* and others (for the Stage Society). Recently he has designed the following : *Mandragola* (Mercury), *Who's Taking Liberty* (Whitehall), *Peter And The Wolf* and *Enigma Variations* (for the Ballet Rambert) (Arts, 1941-42), etc. In 1943 he was designer for the Travelling Repertory Theatre ; in 1944 for the Stratford Memorial Theatre ; 1945 for York Festival Company, etc. In 1946 he designed *Romeo And Juliet* (King's, Hammersmith), *Macbeth* and *The Seagull* (both for the Old Vic) (Theatre Royal, Bristol), etc.

SHERWIN, MANNING. Composer. Born Philadelphia, 1906. He has composed music for a number of stage musicals in New York and in London. From 1936-38 he composed for films in Hollywood ; since 1938 he has composed music for many British musical films. Among the stage shows in which his music has been heard are *Magyar Melody* (His Majesty's), *Shephard's Pie* (Princes), *Fun And Games* (Princes), *Rise Above It* (Comedy), *New Faces* (Comedy and Apollo), *Get A Load Of This* (Hippodrome), *Something In The Air* (Palace), *Under The Counter* (Phœnix), *Here Come The Boys* (Saville), etc.

SHERWOOD, LYDIA. Actress. Born London,·1906. Studied for the stage at R.A.D.A., making her first appearance in *Lavender Ladies* (Comedy, 1925). Then on tour, and with Stratford-on-Avon Company in 1927. In London then acted in *Paul I, Come With Me, Red Sunday, The Roof, She Stoops To Conquer, The Last Chapter*, etc. Made her first appearance in New York in *Insult* (49th Street, 1930). Also in London in *Othello, The Merchant Of Venice, The Brontës, The King Of Rome, Nina, St. Helena, Uncle Vanya, Bats In The Belfry, You Never Can Tell*, etc. Acted in New York again in 1938 in *I Have Been Here Before*, returning to London in *To Love And To Cherish*, followed by *The Doctor's Dilemma*, etc. In 1940 in *Music At Night* (Westminster). In 1941 appeared in *Forty-Eight Hours' Leave* (Apollo). Recently : Touring extensively for CEMA etc. In 1943 acted in *Twelfth Night* (Open Air). In 1944 appeared in *Daughter Janie* (Apollo). In 1945 in *Little Eyolf* (Embassy).

SHINE, BILL. Actor. Born London, 1911. Married to Julia Lang. Made his first appearance on the stage in pantomime at New Brighton, 1917. From 1929-39 engaged principally in film acting. Then in 1941 joined the Market Theatre (on tour under the auspices of CEMA), continuing with this Company until 1943, when he joined the Arts Theatre Group of Actors to appear in *The Old Foolishness*. He also acted at this theatre in *The Constant Couple, The Rivals, The Magistrate* and *Misalliance*, 1943. Recently appeared in *Happy Few* (Cambridge, 1944), *The Magistrate* (St. Martin's, 1944), and *The Simpleton Of The Unexpected Isles* (Arts, 1945). Then joined the Birmingham Repertory Company and has appeared in *Juno And The Paycock*, etc.

SHINER, RONALD. Actor and producer. Born London, June 8th, 1903. Made his first appearance on the West End stage in *Down Our Street* (Vaudeville, 1930). Then stage director for Stage Society and the People's National Theatre, after which he appeared in all Walter Hackett's plays in London, 1931-34. Also in the West End in *The Amazing Dr. Clitterhouse* (Haymarket, 1937), *Bulldog Drummond* (Savoy, 1938), *Third Party Risk* (St. Martin's, 1939), etc. Recently : *Something In The Air* (Palace, 1943-44), *Worm's Eye View* (which he also produced) (Embassy and Whitehall, 1945-46).

SILVER, CHRISTINE. Actress. Born London, 1883. Made her first appearance on the stage in *The New Idol* (Royalty, 1902), subsequently appearing in London in *Peter Pan, Alice-Sit-By-The-Fire, An Englishman's Home, The Master Builder, Fanny's First Play, Kipps* and many others. Also in the West End in *The Yellow Jacket, A Midsummer Night's Dream, The Dragon*, and acted in extensive tours, 1915-24. Also in London in *The Perfect Wife, The Merchant Of Venice, Nine Till Six, Behind The Blinds, The Comedy Of Good And Evil, Double Door* and many others. More recently in *Barnet's Folly, Busman's Honeymoon* and *The Corn Is Green* (Duchess, 1938, and Piccadilly, 1940). In 1941 she appeared in *Room V* (Garrick). Recently has appeared in *The Old Foolishness* (Arts, 1943), *The Master Builder* (Westminster, 1944), and on tour in *Hatter's Castle*, 1944-45, etc.

SIM, ALASTAIR. Actor and producer. Born Edinburgh, 1900. Made his appearance on the stage in *Othello* (Savoy, 1930), after which he appeared in *Caviare, Betrayal* and *The Venetian*, making his appearance in New York in this play, 1931. With the Old Vic Company, 1932-33 ; also acted in London in *As You Desire Me, The Rose Without A Thorn, Murder Trial, Youth At The Helm, Lady Precious Stream* and *Alice In Wonderland*. Among the other plays in which he has appeared are *The Squeaker* and *The Gusher*. In 1939 appeared at Malvern Festival. Recently : In *Cottage To Let* (Wyndham's, 1941-42), *Peter Pan* (Winter Garden, 1942), *Holy Isle* (Arts, 1943), *Mr. Bolfry* (Westminster and Playhouse, 1944). In 1945 appeared in *It All Depends What You Mean* (Westminster). Has produced a number of plays in London, including *Holy Isle, Mr. Bolfry* and *It All*

Depends What You Mean. In 1945 he produced and appeared in *The Forrigan Reel* (Sadlers Wells). Appeared in *Death Of A Rat* (Lyric, Hammersmith, 1946).

SIM, SHEILA. Actress. Married to Richard Attenborough. Born Liverpool, 1922. Studied for the stage at the R.A.D.A., making her first appearance on the stage in 1066 *And All That* (Croydon Repertory, 1941). Then appeared for a season in repertory at Intimate, Palmers Green. In 1943 on tour with Noel Coward's Company in *This Happy Breed*. Made her first appearance in the West End in *Landslide* (Westminster, 1943). Recently appeared in *This Was A Woman* (Comedy, 1944), *Zero Hour* (Lyric, 1944). In *Tomorrow's Child* (Lyric, 1946).

SIMPSON, PEGGY. Actress. Born London, 1913. Made her first appearance on the stage in *Peter Pan* (Gaiety, 1927), then in London in *Roof, London Wall, This Desirable Residence, Lady Precious Stream* and many others. Made her first appearance in New York in *The Housemaster*. Recently appeared in *Junior Miss* (Saville, 1943-44), *Private Lives* (Apollo, 1944-46).

SIMPSON, RONALD. Actor. Born Acton, 1896. Educated Charterhouse. Studied for the stage at R.A.D.A., making his first appearance in *Abraham Lincoln*, Swansea, 1920. First appeared in London in *Hanky-Panky John* (Playhouse, 1921), subsequently on tour and then appeared in London in *Brewster's Millions, The Great Adventure, No. 17, March Hares, The Taming Of The Shrew*, etc. Also in *She Stoops To Conquer, The Critic*, then made his first appearance in New York in *Many Waters* (Maxine Elliott, 1929). Then in London in *The Limping Man, Counsel's Opinion, See Naples And Die, Wild Justice, No More Ladies, Mary Read, The Unguarded Hour* and *No Exit*. In 1936 appeared in *Whiteoaks*, then in *The Taming Of The Shrew, The Great Romancer, Goodbye Mr. Chips*, etc. In 1939 acted in *The Doctor's Dilemma* (Westminster). Since the outbreak of war has acted with the B.B.C. Repertory Company, and in the following plays, among others : *The Dark River* (Whitehall, 1943), *Halfway To Heaven* (Princes, 1943), *Daughter Janie* (Lyric, 1944), *See How They Run* (Comedy, 1945-46).

SINCLAIR, ARTHUR. Actor. Born Dublin, 1883. Made his first appearance on the stage in *On Baile's Strand* (Abbey, Dublin, 1904). Then first appeared in London in *Spreading The News*, 1905. Made his first appearance in New York in *The Rising Of The Moon* (Maxine Elliott, 1911). From 1904-11 played a variety of parts with the Abbey Theatre and from 1911-14 toured America and Canada. In 1916, formed his own company and toured Great Britain. Among the many plays in which he has appeared in London are *Fox And Geese, The White-Headed Boy, The Playboy Of The Western World, Juno And The Paycock, The Plough And The Stars, Professor Tim, The Shadow Of A Gunman, The Coiner* and *Old Man Murphy*. Toured extensively in America and made several appearances in New York, 1921-30. In addition he has also appeared in London in *The Key, Spring Tide, The Orchard Walls, The Taming Of The Shrew, Wanted For Murder, Moonshine*, etc. In 1938-39 acted in *Spring Meeting*. Recently appeared in *Peter Pan* (Stoll, 1944-45), *The Crime Of Margaret Foley* (Embassy, 1945), *The Vicar Of Wakefield*, 1945, etc.

SINCLAIR, HUGH. Actor. Born London, 1903. Educated Charterhouse. Married to Valerie Taylor. Studied for the stage at R.A.D.A., making his first appearance in *Pygmalion*, Portsmouth, 1922, with the Macdona Players, with whom he remained until 1923. Made his first appearance in London in *The Rose And The Ring* (Wyndham's, 1923), subsequently in *Charlot's Revue Of 1924*. Made his first appearance in New York in *Charlot's Revue Of 1926* (Selwyn), remaining on the Broadway stage in the following plays : *The Play's The Thing, Mariners, Our Betters, The Lady Of The Orchids, Serena Blandish, Other Men's Wives, Getting Married, The Good Companions, Too True To Be Good* and many others. Returned to London in 1933 and appeared in *The Key* and *Escape Me Never*. Again acted in New York in the latter play ; then appeared in London in *The Orchard Walls* and in *Goodness, How Sad*. Recently appeared in *Skylark* (Duchess, 1941-42), *Claudia* (St. Martin's, 1942-43), etc. In 1945 he appeared in *Private Lives* (Apollo).

SKILLAN, GEORGE. Actor. Born Woodford, 1893. Made his first appearance on the stage in *A White Man* (Lyceum, 1910), subsequently on tour with Oscar Asch and Matheson Lang, etc. Appeared in London in *The Dumb Man Of Manchester, Dandy Dick, The Ugly Duchess, The Wild Duck, Othello, The Merry Wives Of Windsor, Julius Cæsar, The Merchant Of Venice, The Wandering Jew*, etc. Also in London in *Good Friday, Pippa Passes, The Hangman, Dr. Jekyll And Mr. Hyde, Richard II, Dracula, Coriolanus* and *Henry V*, etc. In 1940 appeared in *The Venetian* and *The House Of Women* at the Torch, then joined Stratford-on-Avon Festival Company to appear in *Hamlet, King John* and *Measure For Measure*. In 1941 on tour in *Little Women*, then rejoined Stratford-on-Avon Festival Company, playing in *Macbeth, The School For Scandal, The Merchant Of Venice*, etc. In 1943 on tour in *Damaged Goods*. Joined Birmingham Repertory Theatre, 1944, and appeared in *Too Clever By Half, Six Characters In Search Of An Author, You Never Can Tell, Viceroy Sarah*, etc. In 1945 with Stratford-on-Avon Company, playing in *Othello, Henry VIII* and *Much Ado About Nothing*. Toured the Continent in *Julius Cæsar*, 1945-46.

SLATER, JOHN. Actor. Born London, 1916. Was on the amateur stage since 1927, later appearing with *The Taverners*. In 1938 appeared in *Waiting For Lefty* (Unity). Then engaged in broadcasting for a number of years. In 1943 he toured in *No Orchids For Miss Blandish*. First appeared in West End in *How Are They At Home?* (Lyric, 1944); also in *The Last Stone* (Phœnix), *Byron* (Playhouse, Amersham), *Till The Day I Die* (Unity), etc. In 1945 appeared in *Happy Few* (Cambridge). Recently in *The Shouting Dies* (Lyric, Hammersmith, 1945).

SMITH, CYRIL. Born Peterhead, Scotland, 1892. Made his first appearance on the stage in *A Midsummer Night's Dream*, 1900, and later played in London in *Gulliver's Travels, Cousin Kate*, etc., before making his first appearance in New York in *Alice-Sit-By-The-Fire* (Criterion, 1905). 1910-11, toured with H. B. Irving, and then from 1917-1923 engaged in film production. Following this he appeared in London in *Fata Morgana, Blue Skies, The Flying Squad, Counsel's Opinion, Spacetime Inn, Between Friends, The Frog, The Gusher*. In 1939 appeared in *Heaven And Charing Cross* (St. Martin's). Recently appeared in *Black Vanities* (Victoria Palace, 1942), then in *Arsenic And Old Lace* (Strand, 1943-46).

SMITH, DODIE. Playwright. Born Whitefield, Lancs. Studied for the stage at R.A.D.A., making her first appearance on the stage in 1915. Among her plays are *Autumn Crocus, Service, Touch Wood, Call It A Day, Bonnet Over The Windmill* and *Dear Octopus*.

SOFAER, ABRAHAM. Actor. Born Rangoon, 1896. Made his first appearance on the stage in *The Merchant Of Venice*, Newark, 1921. Toured with Charles Doran, Alexander Marsh and Harold Neilson until 1925, when he made his first appearance in London in *Gloriana* (Little); also acted in *Scotch Mist, Israel, The Beetle, Black Velvet, The Man In Dress Clothes, The Matriarch*. Made his first appearance in New York in the latter play (Longacre, 1930), returning to London in *Twelfth Night*, followed by *Hamlet, Street Scene, The Mask And The Face, Volpone, Julius Cæsar, Love's Labour's Lost, Miracle At Verdun, Success Story*, etc. With the Old Vic Company, 1934-35, appearing in *Antony And Cleopatra, Richard II, St. Joan, Othello, Hamlet, The Taming Of The Shrew*, etc. Also in London in *The Great Experiment, Professor Bernhardi*, etc. From 1936-39 acting in America with Helen Hayes in *Victoria Regina* and *The Merchant Of Venice*. In 1940 appeared in *Macbeth* on tour with Old Vic, later appearing in *King John* and *Medea* (New, 1941). With B.B.C. Repertory Company in 1942, later appearing in *Macbeth* (Piccadilly). Joined Stratford-on-Avon in 1943, appearing in *King Lear, Othello, Twelfth Night, The Merry Wives Of Windsor,* etc. Appeared in *The Witch* (Arts, 1944), and on tour with his own company for CEMA in *I Have Been Here Before*. In 1945 joined John Gielgud's Company, to appear in *Hamlet* (Haymarket). Then in *The Skipper Next To God* (Windsor and Embassy, 1945) ; *A Doll's House* (Winter Garden, 1946).

SOKOLOVA, NATASHA. Actress and designer. Born San Paulo, Brazil, 1917. Educated in France and England. Studied dancing and made her first appearance on the stage in 1931. Toured North and South America as principal dancer in Clifford Fisher Revues, 1937-39. Made her first appearance in London in *Rise Above It* (Comedy, 1940-41), then in *It's About Time* (Comedy, 1942), *Flying Colours* (Lyric, 1943), *Cinderella* (His Majesty's, 1944). Toured Orkneys and Shetlands in 1944, in the revue *All Adrift*, subsequently appearing in *The Simpleton Of The Unexpected Isles* (Arts, 1945), followed by *The Italian Straw Hat* and *The Government Inspector* (both at Arts). Appeared in *Here Come The Boys* (Saville, 1946).

SOMERS, JULIAN. Actor. Born London, 1905. Made his first appearance on the stage in the chorus of the Old Vic Opera Company in 1927, becoming a professional actor when he joined Croydon Repertory Company in 1934. Made his first appearance in London in *King Lear* (Westminster, 1935), after which he appeared in repertory at Croydon, Margate, York and Altrincham. In 1940 in *King Lear* (Old Vic). Recently appeared in *Awake And Sing* (Arts, 1942), produced and appeared in *Mask Of Virtue* (Mercury, 1943), then in *War And Peace* (Phœnix, 1943), *Alice In Wonderland* (Scala, 1943-44). In 1945 in *The Assassin* (Savoy), *The Skipper Next To God* (Windsor), *Mrs. Warren's Profession* (Torch), etc. Joined Stratford-on-Avon Festival Company, 1946.

SPEAIGHT, ROBERT. Actor. Born Dover, 1904. Educated Haileybury and Oxford. Made his first appearance on the stage in *Portrait Of A Gentleman*, Liverpool, 1926, then first appeared in London in *The Duchess Of Alba* (Arts, 1927). Also appeared in London in *Harold, Paul Among The Jews, Journey's End, The Conspiracy, Hamlet, Little Eyolf, King Lear, Salome,* etc. With the Old Vic Company, 1931-32, playing in *Henry V, Twelfth Night, Othello* and *Hamlet*, etc. Then in London in *Getting Married, Cæsar's Friend, If I Were You, The Rose Without A Thorn, Nurse Cavell, Viceroy Sarah, Two Kingdoms* and *Murder In The Cathedral*. He played in the latter in London, and on tour in Great Britain, 1935-37. Made his first appearance in America in the same play (Ritz, 1938). Then in London, acting in *Troilus And Cressida*. Since the outbreak of war has been with the B.B.C. In 1945 appeared in *The Old Man Of The Mountain* (Mercury), *This Way To The Tomb*! (Mercury), etc.

SPENCER, JESSICA. Actress. Born Birkenhead, 1919. Educated Gravesend High School, Kent. Studied for the stage at the Central School of Dramatic Art, making her first appearance in repertory in Aberdeen, 1939. During the war she left the stage for a time, returning in a tour with the Pilgrim Players. Then in several CEMA tours, after which she appeared in *A Trip To Scarborough* (Arts, 1944). Recently in *The Skin Of Our Teeth* (Phœnix, 1945), *The Wind Of Heaven* (St. James's, 1945), *Spring 1600* (Lyric, Hammersmith, 1945-46).

SPENCER, MARIAN. Actress. Married to Steuart West. Has recently appeared in London in *A House In The Square* (St. Martin's, 1940), *Old Acquaintance* (Apollo, 1942), *Love For Love* (Phœnix, 1943). She then joined the John Gielgud Company appearing in *Love For Love, Hamlet, A Midsummer Night's Dream, The Duchess Of Malfi* (Haymarket, 1944-45).

SQUIRE, RONALD. Actor. Born Tiverton, 1886. Educated at Wellington. Made his first appearance on the stage in *An Englishman's Home*, Eastbourne, 1909. First appeared in London in *Nobody's Daughter* (Wyndham's, 1910). Then with Liverpool Repertory Company, 1911-12, after which he appeared in London in *The Schoolmistress, Account Rendered, Are You A Mason ?, The Laughter Of Fools, The Ware Case* and many others. Made his first appearance in New York in *Gamblers All* (Maxine Elliott, 1917). Has also acted in London in *East Is West, Bulldog Drummond, Dear Brutus, Our Betters, The Last Of Mrs. Cheyney, On Approval, By Candlelight,* etc. Then in *Canaries Sometimes Sing, The Breadwinner, Springtime For Henry, All Rights Reserved, Laughter In Court, Plan For A Hostess, Sugar Plum,* etc. In 1941, appeared in *Home And Beauty*, (Playhouse, 1942), *Ducks And Drakes* (Apollo, 1942). Then in *A Month In The Country* (St. James's, 1943), followed by *While The Sun Shines* (Globe, 1944), and on tour, 1945-46.

STANLEY, PHYLLIS. Actress. Born London, 1914. Made her first appearance on the stage with George Balanchine's Ballet Company (Alhambra, 1930), then appeared in London in *The Miracle, Words And Music, Lucky Break, Not For Children, The Town Talks,* etc. Also in *Charlot's Revue Of* 1937, *Oh ! You Letty !* and *Happy Returns,* etc. In 1940 appeared in *All Clear* (Queen's). In 1943 in *It's Foolish But It's Fun* (Coliseum). In 1945 in *Me And My Girl* (Victoria Palace).

STEPANEK, KAREL. Actor. Born Czechoslovakia, October 29th, 1899. Acted for many years on the Continent, in Berlin, Prague and Vienna. Since coming to England has appeared in *Close Quarters* (Apollo, 1941), also in *The Moon Is Down* (Whitehall, 1943), *The Rest Is Silence* (Prince of Wales, 1944), *Jacobowsky And The Colonel* (Piccadilly, 1945), etc.

STERNDALE-BENNETT, JOAN. Actress. Born London, March 5th, 1914. Studied for the stage at R.A.D.A., making her first appearance in *Strange Orchestra,* at Worthing Repertory Theatre, 1933, followed by repertory in various provincial towns. In 1938 she made her first appearance at the Players' Theatre and has remained there since, also appearing in the West End in such productions as *Nine Sharp* (Little, 1940), *In Town Again* (Criterion, 1940), *Diversion* (Wyndham's, 1941), *Light And Shade* (Ambassadors, 1942), etc. Recently in *Mine Hostess* (Arts, 1944), *The Forrigan Reel* (Sadlers Wells), *The Glass Slipper* (St. James's, 1945-46).

STEWART, SOPHIE. Actress. Born Crieff, Scotland, 1908. Married to Ellis Irving. Studied for the stage at R.A.D.A., making her first appearance in *His Highness Below Stairs,* Oxford, 1925, then in repertory at Plymouth, after which she toured in *Marigold.* Made her first appearance in London in this play, (Kingsway, 1929), and appeared in New York in the same play in 1930. 1931-32 : Toured Canada with Sir Barry Jackson, then acted in London in *A Sleeping Clergyman, No Way Back, The Maitlands, Young Mr. Disraeli, Marigold* (Royalty, 1936), *The Orchard Walls,* etc. Also acted in London in *Black Swan* and *Trelawney Of The Wells.* 1938-40 acting in America. Recently appeared in London in *Mr. Bolfry* (Westminster and Playhouse, 1944), and *The Lady From Edinburgh* (Playhouse, 1945-46).

STIRLING, EDWARD. Actor and producer. Born Birmingham, May 26th, 1891. Made his first appearance on the stage in *The Merchant Of Venice,* Wolverhampton, 1909, then on tour, after which he made his first appearance in London in *Anna Karenina* (Scala, 1914). Then acted in London and on tour extensively. In 1922 he formed, with Henry Oscar, the London Players and since that time he has played in every European country. Founded the English Theatre in Paris in 1922, where he remained until 1940, when he returned to England. Among the plays he has directed in London since that time are *Jam To-day, They Walk Alone* (on tour), *Other People's Houses, Old Chelsea, Damaged Goods,* etc. Produced *Bird Of Passage* and appeared in this on tour, 1944. In September, 1944, he returned to Paris, to direct Allied entertainments for ENSA.

STOCKFIELD, BETTY. Actress. Born Sydney, Australia, 1905. Made her first appearance on the stage in *London Calling* (Duke of York's, 1924). Made her first appearance in New York in *Charlot's Revue Of* 1926 (Selwyn). Has also appeared in London in *The Phantom Fear, Paris Bound, Bees And Honey, Art And Mrs. Bottle, The Sign Of The Seven Dials*, etc. In 1942 appeared in *Why Not Tonight?* (Ambassadors). Recently appeared in London in *Halfway To Heaven* (Princes, 1943), *How Are They At Home?* (Lyric, 1944).

STONE, MARY. Actress. Born London, 1924. Studied for the stage at the Royal Academy of Dramatic Art. Made her first appearance on the stage in *After October* (Intimate Theatre, 1942). Then toured in CEMA production of *The Merchant Of Venice*, 1942-43. From 1943 has been acting at the Intimate Theatre. Recently in *The Corn Is Green, The Importance Of Being Earnest, Morning Star, This Was A Woman, Getting Married, Pink String And Sealing Wax, Hundred Years Old*, etc. In 1946 she joined John Clements' Company and appeared in *The King-Maker, Marriage a La Mode* (St. James's), etc.

STORM, LESLEY. Playwright. Born Aberdeenshire, 1903. Educated Aberdeen University. Among her plays are *Dark Horizon, Follow Your Saint, Tony Draws A Horse*, and *Great Day*.

STUART, AIMEE. Playwright. Born Glasgow, 1890. She has collaborated with her husband, Philip Stuart, on the following plays : *The Cat's Cradle, Nine Till Six, Supply And Demand, Sixteen, Love Of Women, Full Circle*, etc. With L. Arthur Rose she has written *The Lady From Edinburgh*, and is the sole author of *Summer Snow, Jeannie*, etc.

STUART, JEANNE. Actress. Born London, 1908. Made her first appearance on the stage in *Nine Till Six* (Ritz, New York, 1930). First appeared in London in *After All* (Criterion, 1931), then in *It's A Girl, Roadhouse, Hyde Park Corner, Espionage, The King's Leisure, A Spot Of Bother, Talk Of The Devil, Sixth Floor*, etc. Recently appeared in *Quiet Week-End* (Wyndham's, 1941-44). Then in *Under The Counter* (Phœnix, 1945-46).

SULLIVAN, FRANCIS L. Actor. Born London, 1903. Made his first appearance on the stage with the Old Vic in *Richard III*, 1921, remaining with this company until 1922, after which he toured with Charles Doran and with Matheson Lang. Then with Manchester Repertory Company, and also with the Stratford-on-Avon Festival Company, 1928. Made his first appearance in New York in *Many Waters* (Maxine Elliott, 1929). Also appeared in London in *The Last Chapter, Home And Beauty, The Witch, Black Coffee, Late Night Final, The Judgment Of Dr. Johnson, The Cathedral, Cæsar's Friend*, etc. Then in *The Dark Tower, Tovarich, Hamlet, Oscar Wilde*, etc. In 1940 appeared in *Follow My Leader* (Apollo, 1940), *Peril At End House* (Vaudeville, 1941), *A Midsummer Night's Dream* (Open Air). In 1941 toured in *Peril At End House*. In 1942 played in *A Man With Red Hair* (Ambassadors), in 1943 on tour in *Kiss The Girls*. Recently on tour in *Hidden Horizon*, 1945.

SWEDEN, MORRIS. Actor. Born London, 1911. Had considerable amateur experience and acted at Unity Theatre in *The Star Turns Red*, 1940, before joining Basil C. Langton's Travelling Repertory Theatre, with whom he toured until 1943, also acting in seasons at the Birmingham Repertory Theatre and with the Old Vic at Liverpool Playhouse. In 1943 acted in *Androcles And The Lion* (Arts). In 1944 on tour in *The Merry Widow*, then joined Old Vic Company to appear in *Peer Gynt, Arms And The Man* and *Richard III* (New, 1944-45). Recently appeared in *The Government Inspector* (Arts, 1945), *Merrie England* (Princes, 1945-46).

SWINBURNE, MERCIA. Actress. Born Australia, 1900. Married to George Relph. Made her first appearance on the stage at Newcastle, 1915, then first appeared in London in *Tonight's The Night* (Gaiety, 1915). Also acted in *A Night*

Out, Welcome Stranger, East Of Suez, The Grand Duchess, Exiles, The Fall Guy, The Crooked Billet, etc. Then in the West End in *The Mulberry Bush, Almost A Honeymoon, The Love Game, Queen Of Scots, Sweet Aloes, The Squeaker, Guest At Random* and many others. Since the outbreak of war has toured extensively for CEMA, mostly with the Walter Hudd Company. In 1940 appeared on tour in *Heroes Don't Care* and *Fair And Warmer.* Then in *Under One Roof* (St. Martin's, 1940). Also on tour for CEMA in *Napoleon* and *A Man Of Destiny.* In 1943 on tour in *The Wind And The Rain,* etc. In 1944 acted in *Daughter Janie* (Apollo). In 1945 appeared in *The New Morality* (Embassy).

SWINBURNE, NORA. Actress. Born Bath, 1902. Studied for the stage at R.A.D.A., making her first appearance in London in *Paddly Pools* (New, 1916). Then in *Suzette, Tilly Of Bloomsbury, The Bat,* etc. Made her first appearance in New York in *The Mountebank* (Lyceum, 1923), returning to England to appear in *In The Next Room,* followed by *No. 17, The Best People, Outward Bound, Fame, Murder On The Second Floor* and many others. Also in London in *The Gay Adventure, It's You I Want, Lover's Leap, The King's Leisure, The Astonished Ostrich, Wise Tomorrow, The Laughing Cavalier, Dodsworth, Lot's Wife, Third Party Risk,* etc. In 1941 appeared in *Dear Brutus* (Globe), *Ducks And Drakes* (Apollo, 1942). Recently appeared in *Watch On The Rhine* (Aldwych, 1943), *A Month In The Country* (St. James's, 1943), *Full Swing* (Palace). In 1945 in *The Years Between* (Wyndham's).

SWINSTEAD, JOAN. Actress. Born Chalgrove, Oxfordshire, 1903. Studied for the stage at R.A.D.A., making her first appearance in *Emma* (St. James's, 1921). Appeared in London in *Quality Street, A Girl's Best Friend, Cynara, Lean Harvest, Party, Wild Decembers,* etc. Also in *These Mortals, Lysistrata, The Happy Hypocrite* and others. Made her first appearance in New York in *Tonight At 8.30* (National, 1936), reappeared in London in *Gertie Maud,* followed by *Crest Of The Wave, Henry V,* etc. In 1939 appeared in *The Gate Revue* (Ambassadors), then in *Swinging The Gate* (Ambassadors, 1940-41). Recently has also appeared in *The New Ambassador Revue,* 1942. 1943-45 : With Norman Marshall's Company, appearing in London in *Uncle Vanya* (Westminster, 1944), etc. Appeared in *Trilby,* on tour, 1945-46, *Better Late* (Garrick, 1946).

SYDNEY, BASIL. Actor. Born St. Osyth, 1894. Made his first appearance on the stage in 1909, then first appeared in London in *Westward Ho !* (Palladium, 1913). Then on tour in England and the United States, after which he appeared in London in *The Double Dealer, Ghosts, Romance, Romeo And Juliet,* etc. Made his first appearance in New York in *Romance* (Playhouse, 1921), continuing to act on Broadway in *The Devil's Disciple, She Stoops To Conquer, The Taming Of The Shrew, Becky Sharp* and many others. In London has also appeared in *Strange Interlude, Dinner At Eight, The Dark Tower, Blondie White, Traitor's Gate,* etc. In 1939 appeared in *Pygmalion* (Haymarket). Recently : In 1943 appeared in *Hamlet* (for the Old Vic) (New) ; *Man About The House,* 1946.

SYLVAINE, VERNON. Actor and playwright. Born Manchester, 1897. Made his first appearance on the stage in *Mr. Wu,* Glasgow, 1917, then first appeared in London in *Cash On Delivery* (Palace, 1917). Subsequently on tour in England and in South Africa, 1921-25, after which made his first appearance in New York in *Courting* (49th Street, 1925). Has also appeared in London in *Hedda Gabler, The Doctor's Dilemma, A Doll's House, Peg O' My Heart, Windfall, The Roof, Napoleon, An Enemy Of The People* and many others. Among his plays are *The Road Of Poplars, And A Woman Passed By, Aren't Men Beasts, A Spot Of Bother, Worth A Million, Banana Ridge, Down In The Forest, Madame Louise,* etc. Has also acted in and produced many of his own plays.

TAFLER, SYDNEY. Actor. Born London, 1916. Married to Joy Shelton. Studied for the stage at R.A.D.A., making his first appearance in *The Man In*

Dress Clothes (Victoria Palace, 1936). Then in repertory at York and Birmingham, before appearing in *Charley's Aunt* (Haymarket, 1939). From 1940-44 acted with B.B.C. Drama Repertory Company. In 1944 joined the Old Vic Company, appearing in *Richard III, Peer Gynt* and *Arms And The Man* (New, 1944-45). In 1945 toured the Continent with the Old Vic, and at the New appeared in *Henry IV* (*Parts I And II*), *Œdipus* and *The Critic*, 1945-46.

TATE, REGINALD. Actor. Born Garforth, Yorks, 1896. Studied for the stage under Lady Benson, making his first appearance in *The Will*, (Leeds Art Theatre, 1922), where he remained producing and acting until 1927. First appeared in London in *Romeo And Juliet* (Strand, 1926), followed by *The Yellow Mask, The Perfect Wife, Her Past, Caviare, Farewell To Love, The Life Machine, Evensong* and many others. Also acted in London in *Eight Bells, The World Of Light, The Rose Without A Thorn, Biography, Journey's End, The House Of Borgia, Jane Eyre* and many others. More recently in *Mourning Becomes Electra, Glorious Morning, Bridge Of Sighs*, etc. From 1939-44 with H.M. Forces. Then on tour in a repertory of Edgar Wallace plays. In 1945 appeared in *Sweet Yesterday* (Adelphi). He produced *The Astonished Ostrich* (St. James's, 1946).

TAYLOR, PAT. Actress. Born London, 1918. She first appeared on the stage with a dancing troupe in 1930, subsequently appearing in variety. Then acted on the West End stage in *Big Business*, followed by *Happy Returns, Let's Pretend*, and others. In 1940 she appeared in *Shephard's Pie* (Princes), *Fine And Dandy* (Saville, 1941), then appeared in *Show Boat* (Stoll, 1943). In 1944 she appeared in *The Lilac Domino* (His Majesty's). In 1945 appeared in *Irene* (His Majesty's).

TAYLOR, VALERIE. Actress. Born London, 1902. Married to Hugh Sinclair. Studied for the stage at R.A.D.A., making her first appearance in *French Leave,* Mentone, France, 1922. Then in London acted in *Storm* (Royalty, 1924), followed by *The Show, The Seagull, Cobra, Androcles And The Lion, The Showing Up Of Blanco Posnet, The Marvellous History Of St. Bernard, Berkeley Square, On Approval* and many others. Also in *The Seagull*, after which she made her first appearance in New York in *Berkeley Square* (Lyceum, 1929). Subsequently acted in America until 1932. Then in London in *The Man With A Load Of Mischief, La Prisonnière, Call It A Day, The Children's Hour, The Orchard Walls, Surprise Item, Dear Octopus* and a number of others. In 1940 appeared in a revival of *Dear Octopus* (Adelphi). Then in *Skylark* (Duchess, 1942). Recently : In *Watch On The Rhine* (Aldwych, 1944). Also in *A Month In The Country* (St. James's, 1943-44), etc. In 1945 appeared in *The Wind Of Heaven* (St. James's). Joined Stratford-on-Avon Festival Company, 1946.

TEARLE, GODFREY. Actor. Born New York, 1884. Made his first appearance on the stage in *Richard III*, Burnley, 1893, then on tour in the provinces and in South Africa until 1906, when he made his first appearance on the London stage in *Mary Queen Of Scots* (King's, Hammersmith). Then in London in *Atilla, The School For Scandal, Julius Cæsar, The Tenth Man, The Easiest Way, Quality Street* and many others. In 1913 appeared in the West End in *Peter Pan*, followed by *Quinneys, Henry VIII, Tiger Rose*, etc. Made his first appearance in New York in *Carnival* (49th Street, 1919). Then in London in *Othello, The Faithful Heart, The Way Of An Eagle, Bluebeard's Eighth Wife, Silence, Salomy Jane, The Fate, White Cargo*, etc. Also in *Aloma, Seventh Heaven, The Way Of The World, Jealousy, The Berg, Hamlet, The Beaux' Stratagem, Late Night Final* and a number of others. More recently in London in *Road House, Henry V, Sixteen, Living Dangerously, Hyde Park Corner, The Unguarded Hour, The Boy David*, etc. In 1938 appeared in *The Island*. In 1939 he acted in *The Flashing Stream* in London and in New York. In 1940 appeared in *The Light Of Heart* (Apollo and Globe). Since 1941 he has been extensively engaged in films. In 1945, with Barry Jones, went to Rome with an ENSA Festival Company, appearing in *The Light Of Heart, The Rivals, The Circle*, etc.

THATCHER, BILLY. Actor. Born London, 1921. Made his first stage appearance as a child in *Emil And The Detectives* (Vaudeville, 1933), then in London in *Yours Tunefully, What Happened To George, Eskimos Ahoy*, Herbert Farjeon's *Children's Variety Show*, etc. Recently appeared in *Diversion* (Wyndham's, 1941), *Rise Above It* (Comedy, 1941), *Whitehall Follies* (Whitehall, 1942). Joined Noel Coward Company and appeared in *This Happy Breed* and *Present Laughter* (Haymarket, 1943), then appeared in *Flare Path* (Apollo, 1943), *Alice In Wonderland* (Palace, 1944), *Ethel Fry*, on tour, 1945, and *Tomorrow's Eden* (Embassy, 1945).

THESIGER, ERNEST. Actor. Born London, 1879. Educated Marlborough College. First appeared on the stage in *Colonel Smith* (St. James's, 1909). Subsequently in the West End in *Lady Windermere's Fan, Othello, A Little Bit Of Fluff, The Merry Wives Of Windsor, Peter Pan, The Second Mrs. Tanqueray, The Jews Of Malta, The Painted Lady, The Country Wife, St. Joan, The Ware Case* and many others. Also in London in *On With The Dance, Dr. Faustus, Sybarites, Hamlet, Lady Windermere's Fan* (Everyman, 1930), *A Trip To Scarborough, Vile Bodies*, etc. Made his first appearance in New York in *The Devil Passes* (Selwyn, 1932). Then in London in *Too True To Be Good, A Sleeping Clergyman, The Golden Toy, The Country Wife* and many others. More recently in *Flood Tide, Geneva, Scandal In Assyria*, etc. Also acted at the Malvern Festival, 1933, 1936 and 1938, playing in *St. Joan, Pygmalion, Music At Night, Geneva*, etc. In 1941 in *In Good King Charles's Golden Days* (New). Recently appeared in *Macbeth* (Piccadilly, 1942), *This Time It's Love* (Comedy, 1943), *Twelfth Night* (Open Air, 1943), *Crisis In Heaven* (Lyric, 1944). Then joined Old Vic Company and appeared in *Hamlet* (Liverpool, 1944). In *Man About The House*, 1946.

THORNDIKE, RUSSELL. Actor and playwright. Born Rochester, 1885. Studied for the stage with Ben Greet, making his first appearance in *The Merry Wives Of Windsor*, Cambridge, 1904. Then acted in London in *The Eternal City* (Marlborough), after which he made his first appearance in New York in *Henry V*, 1905. With Ben Greet Company until 1909. Then in London in *Romeo And Juliet, Twelfth Night, The Fires Of Fate* and many others. Joined the Old Vic Company, 1916, appearing in *Julius Cæsar, Othello, The School For Scandal, Romeo And Juliet, Twelfth Night* and others, until 1918, when he appeared in the West End in *The Loving Heart*. Subsequently as actor and producer with the Old Vic, 1919-20. Then in *Peer Gynt, St. Joan, Thérèse Raquin*, etc., before touring America, 1929-32. Returned to London and acted in *Grand Guignol, Everyman, The Admirable Crichton, The Tempest, The House Of Borgia* and many others. Among his plays are *Oh Hell!*, *The Tragedy Of Punch* (with Reginald Arkell) and *The House Of Jeffreys*. He has also adapted *The Christmas Carol* and *Oliver Twist*. Recently appeared on the stage in *The House Of Jeffreys* (Playhouse, 1942), *Abraham Lincoln* (Playhouse, 1943). Also in *Twelfth Night* (Arts, 1942). Then acted in *The Russians* (for the Old Vic) (Playhouse, 1943), etc. In 1945 appeared on tour in *Thirteen To The Gallows*.

THORNDIKE, DAME SYBIL. Actress. Born Gainsborough, 1882. Married to Sir Lewis Casson. Studied for the stage with Ben Greet, making her first appearance on the stage in *The Merry Wives Of Windsor*, Cambridge, 1904. From 1904-08 toured in the U.S.A. with Ben Greet. 1908-09 with Miss Horniman's Company, Manchester. Made her first appearance in London in *The Marquis* (Scala, 1908). Subsequently acted in *Hindle Wakes, Jane Clegg*, etc. Made her first appearance in New York in *Smith*, 1910. She joined the Old Vic Company in 1914, remaining until 1918 and acting all the leading feminine parts in Shakespeare's plays. Also acted in London in *The Chinese Puzzle, The Trojan Women, Napoleon, Candida, Medea*, etc. 1920-21 in *Grand Guignol* (Little). Thereafter in the West End in *The Scandal, The Cenci, Cymbeline, The Lie, St. Joan, As You Like It, Henry VIII, Hamlet, Granite, Macbeth* and dozens of others. Again with the Old Vic, 1927-28, then toured South Africa, 1928-29.

Afterwards in London in *The Silver Cord, Major Barbara, The Devil, Phèdre, Ghosts, Othello, The Knight Of The Burning Pestle,* etc. 1932-33 : Toured in Egypt, Palestine and Australia. Subsequently acted in London in *The Distaff Side* (also in New York, 1934), *Mrs. Siddons, Double Door, Village Wooing, Grief Goes Over, Short Story, Kind Lady* and many others. In 1937 she toured in *Six Men Of Dorset,* after which she appeared in London in *Yes, My Darling Daughter* and *The Trojan Women* (Adelphi, 1937). In 1938 she acted in New York in *Time And The Conways,* returning to London in *Coriolanus* (Old Vic), followed by *The Corn Is Green* (Duchess, 1938-39). With the Old Vic Company in 1940 she toured in Wales and Durban, also appearing in London in *King John* and *Medea* (for the Old Vic) (New, 1940-41). In 1942 acted in *The House Of Jeffreys* (Playhouse). Then in *Lottie Dundass* (Vaudeville, 1943) and *Alice In Wonderland* (Scala, 1943-44 and Palace, 1944-45). In 1944 she rejoined the Old Vic Company, appearing in *Peer Gynt, Arms And The Man, Richard III* and *Uncle Vanya* (New 1944-45). In 1945 toured the Continent with the Old Vic, subsequently appearing in *Henry IV (Parts I And II), The Critic, Œdipus* (New, 1945-46).

TICKLE, FRANK. Actor. Born London, 1893. Educated John Lyon's School, Harrow. Made his first appearance on the stage in *The Comedy Of Errors* (Open Air, 1934). Then appeared in London in *A Midsummer Night's Dream, King Lear, Hamlet, The Tempest, Henry IV, St. Joan, Man And Superman, Anything Goes, The Island* and many others. Recently appeared in *Great Expectations* (Rudolf Steiner, 1939-40), *Rebecca* (Lyric, 1940-41), *The Merry Widow* (His Majesty's, 1943), etc. In 1945 appeared in *The Government Inspector* (Arts).

TODD, ANN. Actress. Born Hartford, 1909. Studied for the stage at the Central School of Dramatic Art, making her first appearance in *The Land Of Heart's Desire* (Arts, 1928). Subsequently acted in London in *A Damsel In Distress, The Middle Watch, Honours Easy, Cynara, Flat To Let, Service* and many others. Also in London in *When Ladies Meet, No More Ladies, Man Of Yesterday, Promise, Flood Tide,* etc. In 1939 appeared in *The Man In Half Moon Street* (New). Recently in *Love In A Mist* (St. Martin's, 1942). Also in *Peter Pan* (Winter Garden, 1942-43), *Lottie Dundass* (Vaudeville, 1943), *The Rest Is Silence* (Prince of Wales, 1944).

TOONE, GEOFFREY. Actor. Born Dublin, 1910. Educated at Charterhouse and Cambridge. Made his first appearance with the Old Vic Company in 1930, subsequently on tour in the provinces and in the West Indies. In 1934 appeared at the Malvern Festival, after which he appeared in repertory at Liverpool and Oxford. Joined John Gielgud Company and appeared in *Hamlet* and *Romeo And Juliet,* then in *Dodsworth.* 1940-43, in H.M. Forces. On being invalided out, appeared in *Watch On The Rhine* (Aldwych, 1943), *The Last Of Summer* (Phœnix, 1944), *Hamlet* (for Old Vic), (New, 1944). In 1945 on tour in *The First Gentleman,* then appeared in *Lady Windermere's Fan* (Haymarket, 1945-46).

TOTTENHAM, MERLE. Actress. Born Quetta, India, January 22nd, 1901. Educated Greenway School, Tiverton. Made her first appearance on the stage in *The Goldfish* (West Pier, Brighton, 1913). She first appeared in the West End in *Happy Family* (Prince of Wales Theatre, 1916), after which she studied at the Central School of Dramatic Art. Among the other plays she has appeared in, in London, are *Cavalcade, Nine Till Six, After October,* etc. Recently : In *Duet For Two Hands* (Lyric, 1945-46).

TOYE, WENDY. Actress, dancer and choreographer. Born London, 1917. Made her first appearance on the stage in *A Midsummer Night's Dream* (Old Vic, 1929) ; subsequently in *Toad Of Toad Hall, The Miracle, Ballerina, The Golden Toy* and others. Also in *Tulip Time, Love And How To Cure It,* etc. Arranged the dances for *These Foolish Things, Black And Blue, Hi De Hi,* etc. In 1943 appeared in and arranged dances for *Strike A New Note* (Prince of Wales), also

Strike It Again (Prince of Wales, 1944-45), etc. In 1945 collaborated on the dances for *Sigh No More* (Piccadilly). Then appeared in *Follow The Girls* (His Majesty's, 1945-46). Produced *Big Ben* for C. B. Cochran, 1946.

TRAVERS, BEN. Playwright. Born London, 1886. Among his plays are *A Cuckoo In The Nest, Rookery Nook, Thark, Plunder, Mischief, A Cup Of Kindness, Dirty Work, Turkey Time*, etc. More recently : *Banana Ridge, Spotted Dick, She Follows Me About*, and others.

TREVOR, AUSTIN. Actor. Born Belfast, 1897. Studied for the stage at R.A.D.A., making his first appearance in *Hamlet*, Richmond, U.S.A., 1915. After the war appeared in England with the Stratford-on-Avon Festival Company ; then with the Old Vic, 1920-22. First acted in the West End in *Loyalties,* (St. Martin's, 1924), subsequently in *The Lilies Of The Field, Old English, Fallen Angels, Escape*, etc. Made his first appearance in New York in the latter play (Booth, 1927). Also in London in *Justice, High Treason, Bitter Sweet, Hamlet, The Cat And The Fiddle, Wild Decembers, Nymph Errant, A Doll's House, Libel* and many others. Then in *The Alchemist, Call It A Day, Wanted For Murder, Paprika, Nora*, etc. Recently appeared in *The Doctor's Dilemma* (Haymarket, 1942-43), *The Last Of Mrs. Cheyney* (Savoy, 1944-45).

TROUNCER, CECIL. Actor. Born Southport, 1898. Made his first appearance on the stage in *The Man Who Stayed At Home*, Isle of Wight, 1920, then acted in London in *The Circle* (Haymarket, 1921). Subsequently in *Quality Street, Secrets, Old English* and others. From 1925 to 1928, toured in the provinces, in South Africa and Egypt, with Lena Ashwell, the Macdona Players and Robert Atkins, respectively. Then in London in *The Merchant Of Venice, She Passed Through Lorraine, Romeo And Juliet, Fanfare*, etc. Acted with Croydon Repertory Company, 1932-34, then 1934-36 with Old Vic Company, playing in *Much Ado About Nothing, St. Joan, Othello, Major Barbara, The School For Scandal, The Three Sisters, Richard III*, etc. With the Westminster Theatre Company, 1936-37, appearing in *A Month In The Country, The Wild Duck, Waste, Heartbreak House, Uncle Vanya, Hamlet*, etc. Also in London in *The Last Trump* and in 1938-39 acted in *Geneva* (Saville). In 1940 appeared in *In Good King Charles's Golden Days* (New). From 1940-42 with the B.B.C. Drama Repertory Company. Then joined John Gielgud's Company and appeared in *Love For Love* (Phœnix and Haymarket, 1943-44). Recently in *The Circle, Hamlet* and *The Duchess Of Malfi* (Haymarket, 1944-45). Appeared in *The Guinea Pig* (Criterion, 1946).

TUDOR, VALERIE. Actress. Born Neath, 1910. Educated Bedford High School. Studied for the stage under Laura Smithson, making her first appearance for the Old Vic in *King John* (Sadlers Wells, 1931). She remained with this company until 1933, appearing in *As You Like It, Henry V, The Merchant Of Venice, Cæsar And Cleopatra, Macbeth, The School For Scandal, Romeo And Juliet*, etc. From 1933 to 1935 with the Liverpool Repertory Company. From 1936-38 with the Stratford-on-Avon Festival Company, appearing in *Hamlet, A Midsummer Night's Dream, The Merry Wives Of Windsor, Romeo And Juliet, The Two Gentleman Of Verona, Henry VIII*, etc. Then in London in *Okay For Sound, Man And Superman*, etc. Recently : With Stratford-on-Avon Festival Company, 1942 and 1943. In 1944 she appeared in *Fanny's First Play* (Arts).

TYLER, GRANT. Actor. Born London, April 12th, 1929. Formerly a photographer's model, making his first appearance on the stage in *Whiteoaks* (Comedy, 1940). Then in *The Dancing Years* (Adelphi, 1941-43), *Staff Dance*, on tour, 1944, *Watch On The Rhine*, on tour, 1944, etc. Recently in *Sigh No More* (Piccadilly, 1945-46) ; *Better Late* (Garrick, 1946).

USTINOV, PETER. Actor and playwright. Born London, 1921. Married to Isolde Denham. Educated Westminster School. Made his first appearance on the stage in *The Wood Demon* (Barn, Shere) (under John Burrell). Then trained with Michel St. Denis at London Theatre Studio, making his first London appearance at the Players' Theatre in 1939. Then in *First Night* (Richmond, 1940), *Swinging The Gate* (Ambassadors, 1940), *Fishing For Shadows* (Threshold, 1940), *Diversion* (Wyndham's, 1941). Since 1942 has been in H.M. Forces. In 1941 produced *Squaring The Circle* (Vaudeville) and in 1944 produced and appeared in *The Rivals* (Garrison Theatre, Salisbury). His play *House Of Regrets* was produced at the Arts, 1942, as also was *Beyond*, 1943. His other plays include *Blow Your Own Trumpet* (produced by Old Vic, 1943), *The Banbury Nose* (produced at Wyndham's, 1944), *The Tragedy Of Good Intentions, The Man Behind The Statue* (produced by the Old Vic, at Liverpool), etc. In 1946 he appeared in *Crime and Punishment*.

VALK, FREDERICK. Actor. Born Germany. Married to Diana Quirk. Acted extensively in Germany and Czechoslovakia, before coming to England. Acting in London since 1939 in *Thunder Rock* (Neighbourhood and Globe, 1940 and St. Martin's, 1941), after which he joined the Old Vic Company on tour, also appearing in *Othello* (New, 1942) and *The Merchant Of Venice* (New, 1943). In 1943 he appeared in *War And Peace* (Phœnix) and *Watch On The Rhine* (Aldwych). In 1944 in *Point Valaine* (Liverpool). In 1945 he appeared in *The Gay Pavilion* (Piccadilly, 1945), *More Than Science* (Chanticleer) and *A Bell For Adano* (Phœnix). Appeared in *The Time Of Your Life*, and *Othello*, 1946.

VAN GYSEGHEM, ANDRE. Actor and producer. Born Eltham, 1906. Married to Jean Forbes-Robertson. Studied for the stage at R.A.D.A., making first appearance in *The Constant Nymph*, Bognor, 1927. Then first appeared in London in *A King's Daughter*, 1928, after which he appeared in repertory at Hull, 1928-30. From 1930-34, acting and producing at the Embassy. Among the plays he appeared in are *The House Of Pretence, The Liar, The Witch, Black Coffee, The Second Man, Strange Orchestra, The Macropulos Secret*, etc. Among the plays he has produced in London are *Black Coffee, Behind The Blinds, See Naples And Die, Dance With No Music, Miracle At Verdun, The Cathedral, All God's Chillun, The Tudor Wench, Windfall, The Roof, Napoleon, Stevedore, Profit And Loss, Open Verdict* and many others. In 1940 produced Priestley's *The Long Mirror*, on tour. 1940-41 produced and appeared in *Berkeley Square* (Vaudeville), then produced and appeared in *Forty-Eight Hours Leave* (Apollo). In 1941 produced and appeared in *Distant Point* (Westminster). In 1942 formed his own company in association with CEMA and produced and appeared in *Twelfth Night* and *Distant Point* on tour. In 1942 also produced *The Witch* (for Old Vic), on tour. Recently toured in *Days Without End* for CEMA, 1943, then appeared in *Wingless Victory* (Phœnix, 1943), and *The Fur Coat* (Comedy, 1943). In 1944 produced at Kettering Repertory Theatre. Since then in H.M. Forces, producing for ABCA Play Unit.

VANBRUGH, IRENE. Actress. Born Exeter, 1872. Studied for the stage under Sarah Thorne, making her first appearance on the stage in *As You Like It*, Margate, 1888. First appeared in London in *Alice In Wonderland* (Globe, 1888 ; subsequently in *The Merchant Of Venice, The Upper Crust, The Tempter, Guy Domville, The Importance Of Being Earnest, The Second Mrs. Tanqueray, The Liars* and many others. Joined Arthur Bourchier and accompanied him to America, making her first appearance in New York in *The Chili Widow* (Bijou, 1896). Then in London in *Trelawney Of The Wells*, etc. after which she joined John Hare, playing with him in London and in New York. From 1901-14 she appeared under the management of Charles Frohman in the following : *The Gay Lord Quex, The Admirable Crichton, Letty, His House In Order, The Man Of Destiny, Smith, The Twelve Pound Look*, and many others. Also acted in London in *The School For Scandal, His Excellency The Governor, Belinda, Mr. Pym Passes By, The Truth About Blayds, Mid-Channel*, etc. 1923-26 on tour in South Africa, Australia and New Zealand, reappearing in London in *All The King's Horses*.

Then in *Art And Mrs. Bottle, Misalliance, Hamlet, Dinner At Eight, Viceroy Sarah, The Old Maid,* etc. More recently in *The Orchard Walls, The Merry Wives Of Windsor, Operette, The Jealous God, Only Yesterday,* etc. In 1940 appeared in *In Good King Charles's Golden Days* (New). In 1941 in *The Merry Wives Of Windsor* (Strand) and in *Forty-Eight Hours Leave* (Apollo), followed by *What Every Woman Knows* (Lyric, 1943). Recently appeared in *An Ideal Husband* (Westminster, 1943-44), then on tour in *Appointment With Death.* In 1945 appeared in *Fit For Heroes* (Embassy). Joined John Clements' Co., 1946.

VARNEL, MARCEL. Producer. Born Paris, 1894. Educated College Chaptal and Charterhouse in London. Studied for the stage at the Paris Conservatoire of Dramatic Art and was formerly an actor and director on the Paris stage. From 1925 to 1935 producing plays and directing films in America. Since 1935 directing films in England. Recently produced the following plays in London : *The Man Who Came To Dinner* (Savoy), *Arsenic And Old Lace* (Strand), *Junior Miss* (Saville), *My Sister Eileen* (Savoy), *The Assassin* (Savoy), etc.

VENNING, UNA. Actress. Born Bedford, 1893. Studied for the stage at R.A.D.A., making her first appearance in *The Flag Lieutenant,* Ipswich, 1911. Then on tour in the provinces and in America, making her first appearance in London in *The Queen's Champion* (Aldwych, 1914). Then in London in *Outcast, The Betrothal, The Dancers, To Have The Honour, The Last Of Mrs. Cheyney, Common People, Fame* and many others. Made her first appearance in New York in *Symphony In Two Flats* (Shubert, 1930), then in London in *Fresh Fields, Theatre Royal, Hervey House, Short Story* and *Dear Octopus.* On tour in *Dear Octopus,* 1940-41, then appeared in *The Nutmeg Tree* (Lyric and St. James's, 1941-42) Retired from the stage, 1942-45, making her reappearance in *The First Gentleman* (New and Savoy, 1945-46).

VERE, JOHN. Actor. Born London, July 7th, 1915. Educated Clifton College, Bristol. Studied for the stage at R.A.D.A., making his first appearance in *The Skin Game* (Coventry Repertory Theatre, 1934). Then made his first West End appearance in *Espionage* (Apollo, 1935), subsequently in *The First Legion,* etc., after which he appeared for a season at the Open Air in 1939. In H.M. Forces, 1939-41, after which he reappeared on the stage in *A Midsummer Night's Dream* (Westminster, 1942). Also in *What Every Woman Knows* (Lyric, 1943), *An Ideal Husband* (Westminster, 1943-44), *Jacobowsky And The Colonel* (Piccadilly, 1945). Recently : *Mrs. Warren's Profession* (Torch, 1945).

VERNEY, ANTONY. Actor. Born London, 1917. Married to Doreen Percheron. Made his first appearance on the stage at the age of twelve in *Peter Pan.* Has since appeared often on the London stage in the following, among others : *This Side Idolatry, Once In A Lifetime, Red Night, Judgment Day,* etc. Has also appeared in repertory at Northampton, Nottingham, Bexhill and the Intimate, Palmers Green. From 1940-43 with the R.A.F. Has recently appeared in *The Merchant Of Venice* (Intimate), *War And Peace* (Phœnix, 1943), *The Assassin* (Savoy, 1945). Touring the Continent, 1946.

VERNEY, GUY. Actor. Born London, 1915. Married to Joan Clarkson. Made his first appearance on the stage at Ramsgate in 1919, then appeared in London in *Where The Rainbow Ends* (Holborn Empire, 1927). This was followed by *Peter Pan, Third Time Lucky, Badger's Green, The Judgment Of Dr. Johnson, The Miracle* and other plays in London. Toured with Ben Greet, 1932 and 1933. Has since appeared in London in *R.U.R., The Cathedral, The Wandering Jew, Hamlet, Spring, 1600,* etc. In 1934 appeared in *The Marvellous History Of St. Bernard,* Malvern Festival, after which he appeared in London in *Miracle At Verdun, The Barretts Of Wimpole Street,* etc. 1935-36, in repertory at Nottingham, York and Birmingham. After two years' illness, he returned to the stage in *The Sun Never Sets* (Drury Lane, 1938), followed by *George And Margaret, Heaven*

And Charing Cross, Juggernaut, The Gate Revue. Also in *Swinging The Gate* (Ambassadors, 1940), *Distant Point* (Westminster, 1941), *Rise Above It* (Comedy, 1941), *Lifeline* (Duchess, 1942). In 1943 joined the Norman Marshall Company and appeared on tour in *The School For Scandal* and *Major Barbara.* In 1944 he toured in *Ten Little Niggers* and also produced at Worthing Repertory Theatre. Recently appeared in *The Assassin* (Savoy) and *The Circle Of Chalk* (Arts, 1945). Appeared in *Stage Door* (Saville, 1946).

VERNO, JERRY. Actor. Born London, 1895. Made his first appearance in variety in 1907, spent many years in variety in England and on tour in the Far East. Made his first appearance in London on the legitimate stage in *Alf's Button* (New Oxford, 1925). Then in the West End in *Song Of The Sea, Beau Geste, Paris Bound, The Three Musketeers, The Maid Of The Mountains,* etc. Also in *Wild Violets, The Merchant Of Venice, Magyar Melody,* etc. Recently appeared in *Wednesday After The War* (New, 1940), *Chu Chin Chow* (Palace, 1940-41), *The Man Who Came To Dinner* (Savoy, 1942-43), *A Night In Venice* (Cambridge, 1944-45). Then appeared in *The Hasty Heart* (Aldwych, 1945-46).

VINES, MARGARET. Actress. Born Lourenco Marques, Africa, 1910. Educated in Johannesburg. Studied for the stage at R.A.D.A., making her first appearance in *Mr. Abdulla*, Brixton, 1926. Then in the West End in *The Constant Nymph, Down Wind,* etc., after which she appeared in repertory at Hull, 1928-29. Then in London, appearing in *Jew Süss, An Object Of Virtue,* before appearing with the Birmingham Repertory Theatre in 1931. Also in London in *The Faithful Heart, Rudolph Of Austria, Party, Dinner At Eight,* etc. Made her first appearance in New York in *Richard Of Bordeaux* (Empire, 1934), then in London again in *Theatre Royal, A Midsummer Night's Dream, Much Ado About Nothing* and *Pericles.* In 1940 appeared in *A Midsummer Night's Dream* (Open Air). Recently appeared in *Emma* (St. James's, 1944-45), then joined the Arts Theatre Festival Company and appeared in *The Constant Couple, The School For Scandal* and *The Thunderbolt* (Arts, 1945-46).

WAKEFIELD, HUGH. Actor. Born Wanstead, Essex, 1888. Made his first appearance on the stage in *In Days Of Old* (St. James's, 1899), thenceforth in London in *The Noble Lord, The Belle Of Bohemia, Bluebell In Fairyland, Charley's Aunt, Baby Mine, Gypsy Love,* etc. Served in the war, 1914-20, reappearing in the West End in *London, Paris And New York.* Subsequently in *The Silver Box, Bluebeard's Eighth Wife, Storm,* etc. Made his first appearance in New York in *Louis XIV* (Cosmopolitan, 1925). In London has also appeared in *Quest, Knight Errant, 77 Park Lane, Take A Chance, Sitting On A Fence, Gay Masquerade, Room For Two* and many others. From 1940-44 : in H.M. Forces. Appeared in *While The Sun Shines* (Globe, 1944-46).

WALBROOK, ANTON. Actor. Born Vienna, 1900. Made his appearance on the stage in Vienna, 1920, and subsequently played in every Continental city. Made his first stage appearance in London in *Design For Living* (Haymarket, 1939). This ran until 1940; then in 1942 he appeared in *Watch On The Rhine* (Aldwych), which ran for two years. Recently appeared in *Another Love Story* (Phœnix, 1944-45).

WALDOCK, DENIS. Dramatic author. Born Cambridge, 1911. Educated Perse School and Cambridge. Formerly a screenwriter, he has contributed to the following West End revues : *New Faces, Rise Above It, Whitehall Follies, Sky High, Apple Sauce, Black Velvet, New Ambassadors Revue, Scoop, Sweet And Low, Henson's Gaieties* and *Sweeter And Lower.* Among his plays are *Comfort Me With Apples, Three Made Their Bed ;* and *Jam To-day* (in collaboration with Roger Burford), produced at St. Martin's, 1942. During the war he has been working in the B.B.C. European Section. He has recently contributed to *Better Late* (Garrick, 1946), *Sweetest And Lowest* (Ambassadors, 1946), *Make It a Date,* etc.

WALKER, MARTIN. Actor. Born Harrow, 1901. Made his first appearance on the stage in *The Boy* (Adelphi, 1917), subsequently in London in *Brown Sugar, The Faithful Heart, The Muddler*, etc. Toured Australia and South Africa, 1923-27, making his first appearance in New York in *The Silver Box* (Morosco, 1928). Then appeared in London at the Everyman, in *The Passing Of The Third Floor Back, The Ship* and others. Also in the West End in *The Flying Fool, The Storm, The Beaux' Stratagem, The Man From Blankley's, The Painted Veil, The Cat And The Fiddle, The Left Bank* and many others. Then in *Command Performance, Living Dangerously, Indian Summer, Behind Your Back, No Sleep For The Wicked, People At Sea*, etc. In 1939 appeared in *After The Dance* (St. James's). Recently appeared in *Forty-Eight Hours Leave* (Apollo, 1941), *Ladies Into Action* (Lyric, 1940), *Flare Path* (Apollo, 1942-44), *The Rest Is Silence* (Prince of Wales, 1944), then in *Residents Only* (St. James's, 1945). Appeared in *Trilby*, on tour, 1945-46.

WALLS, TOM. Actor and producer. Born Kingsthorpe, 1883. Made his first appearance on the stage in *Aladdin*, Glasgow, 1905, subsequently on tour in the provinces and the United States, 1906-07. First appeared in London in *Sir Roger De Coverley* (Empire, 1907). Has appeared in London also in *The Sunshine Girl, A Country Girl, Betty, High Jinks, Kissing Time,* and many others. Then in *Tons Of Money, It Pays To Advertise*, after which he appeared at the Aldwych, 1925-31 in the following : *A Cuckoo In The Nest, Rookery Nook, Thark, Plunder, A Cup Of Kindness, A Night Like This, Marry The Girl, Turkey Time*, most of which he also produced. From 1931-38 acting in films. In 1939 he ran the Alexandra, Stoke Newington, as a repertory theatre until the outbreak of war. Recently has appeared in *His Majesty's Guest* (Shaftesbury, 1940), also in *Why Not Tonight?* (Ambassadors, 1941).

WALSH, PERCY. Actor. Born Luton, 1888. Educated Mill Hill and in Switzerland. Made his first appearance on the stage in *The Prisoner Of Zenda*, Scarborough, 1911, and has since appeared with the companies of H. B. Irving and Sir John Martin Harvey. Was with the Old Vic Company for two seasons. Among the recent plays in which he has appeared in London are *The Farmer's Wife, Journey's End* and *French Without Tears*. Appeared in *Ten Little Niggers* (St. James's, 1943), *Appointment With Death* (Piccadilly, 1945).

WALTER, WILFRID. Actor and playwright. Born Ripon, 1882. Was formerly a designer and painter, designing with the Old Vic, 1919-22. Made his first appearance on the stage with the Old Vic in 1919, remaining here until 1924 and appearing in many plays, including *Othello, A Midsummer Night's Dream, Henry IV (Parts I And II), Henry V*, etc. Then in London acting in *The Tyrant, The Wild Goose Chase*, after which he appeared at Stratford-on-Avon, 1927 and 1928, also touring in England and the United States, 1928-30. Then in London in *Happy And Glorious, The Venetian* (also in New York, 1931), *The Judgment Of Dr. Johnson, Let Sleeping Dogs Lie, The Wandering Jew, Mary Read, Othello, Love's Labour's Lost, Green Waters* and many others. Appeared in New York in 1936 in *Hamlet*, after which he toured the United States and Canada. In 1939 he appeared at the Old Vic in *An Enemy Of The People* and at the Open Air Theatre in *Pericles*. Also appeared in *Misalliance* (Embassy) and *The Venetian* (St. Martin's). From 1940-43 served with the R.A.F. Regiment. On being invalided out, appeared in *The Tempest* and *As You Like It* (Open Air, 1943), and in *The Dark River* (Whitehall, 1943). In 1944 on tour in *Tomorrow's Eden*. Then appeared in *Doctor's Delight* at Birmingham Repertory Theatre and *The First Gentleman* (New and Savoy, 1945). Is the author of a number of plays, including *Happy And Glorious, Oh Hang!* and *Let Sleeping Dogs Lie*.

WALTERS, THORLEY. Actor. Educated Moncton Combe School, Bath. He made his first appearance on the stage with the Old Vic Company in 1933, remaining until 1935. He made his first appearance in the West End in *St. Helena* (Daly's, 1936), subsequently in *Gentle Rain, Do You Remember ?, Mary Goes To See*, etc.

Recently : *Cottage To Let* (Wyndham's, 1942), *Escort* (Lyric, 1942), *Claudia* (St. Martin's, 1942-43). From 1943-45 he appeared with Cicely Courtneidge's musical unit for ENSA in Britain and overseas. Recently : *Under The Counter* (Phœnix, 1945-46).

WARD, MACKENZIE. Actor. Born Eastbourne, 1903. Made his first appearance on the stage in *Alice In Wonderland*, Manchester, 1918. Then first appeared in London in *Make Your Fortune*, 1925. Made his first appearance in New York in *Red Blinds* (Maxine Elliott, 1926), remaining on Broadway in various plays until 1929, when he returned to London in *The Father*. Subsequently appeared in London in *The Cannibal, Clear All Wires, The Wind And The Rain, Certainly, Sir !, The Astonished Ostrich, The Sun Never Sets, French Without Tears*, etc. During the war served with H.M. Forces. Appeared at the Granville, 1946.

WARD, PENELOPE. Actress. Born London, 1914. Made her first appearance on the stage in 1935 in *The Wind And The Rain* (Liverpool Repertory Theatre), where she remained until 1936. Then in repertory at Brighton, after which she made her first appearance in London in *Ladies And Gentlemen* (Strand, 1937), followed by *Victoria Regina*. Made her first appearance in New York in *French Without Tears* (Henry Miller, 1937). Has also appeared in London in *Counter Attraction*, and in 1939 again acted in New York in *Set To Music*. Recently appeared in *Magic* (Arts, 1942), then 1944-45 appeared in *Blithe Spirit* (Duchess).

WARD, RONALD. Actor. Born Eastbourne, 1901. Made his first appearance on the stage in *Theodore And Co.*, Islington, 1916, subsequently on tour in the provinces, Australia and New Zealand. Has appeared in London in *Bed And Breakfast, The Young Idea* and *Merton Of The Movies*. Made his first appearance in New York in *André Charlot's Revue Of* 1924, after which he toured in Australia extensively until 1929, when he returned to London in *The Bachelor Father*. Subsequently in *Let Us Be Gay, Behold We Live, The Mocking Bird, Distinguished Gathering* and many others. Also in *The Orchard Walls, George And Margaret, The Importance Of Being Earnest* and *We At The Crossroads*. In 1941 appeared in *Dear Brutus* (Globe), *Rebecca* (Queen's), *Old Acquaintance* (Apollo, 1942), then in the *Little Foxes* (Piccadilly, 1942), *Junior Miss* (Saville, 1943-44), *The Years Between* (Wyndham's, 1945-46).

WARING, BARBARA. Actress. Born London, August 1st, 1917. Educated Hastings, Sussex. Made her first appearance on the stage in Ireland in 1923 ; after which she appeared in a number of productions in Dublin and in London. Recently : *The Well Of The Saints* (Arts, 1943), *The Old Foolishness* (Arts, 1943), *Pink String And Sealing Wax* (Phœnix, 1944), etc. In 1945 she appeared with the York Festival Company, at the King's, Hammersmith, etc.

WARRE, MICHAEL. Actor and designer. Born London, 1922. Educated at Eton. From 1938-39 ran the Barn Theatre in Dorset ; after which he studied for the stage at the London Mask Theatre, 1939-40. Then appeared in London at the Intimate (under John Clements) and at Coventry, 1940-41. In 1941 appeared on tour in *Desire Under The Elms* and played in *The Taming Of The Shrew* (Theatre Royal, York). Made his first appearance in London in *Blow Your Own Trumpet* (for the Old Vic) (Playhouse, 1943), after which he acted in *The Judgment Of Dr. Johnson* (Arts). He then played *Hamlet* at York, 1943, after which he joined the Citizen's Theatre, Glasgow, as actor and designer, appearing in (and designing) *Drama At Irish, The Showing Up Of Blanco Posnet* and *Bull Market*. In 1944 joined the Old Vic Company and appeared in *Richard III* and *Peer Gynt* (New, 1944-45). Recently appeared on tour in *Romeo And Juliet* (which he also designed). Rejoined Old Vic, 1945, to appear in *Henry IV* (*Parts I And II*) and *The Critic* (New, 1945-46). Among the plays which he has designed in London are *Fishing For Shadows, Holy Isle, The Judgment Of Dr. Johnson, Mr. Bolfry, It Depends What You Mean, Scandal At Barchester, The Simpleton Of The Unexpected Isles*, etc. and *Hamlet* (Arts Theatre Festival of Drama, 1945).

WARREN, BETTY. Actress. Born Fareham, 1905. Made her first appearance on the stage in *The Forty Thieves*, Southsea, 1924, then in London in *The London Revue* (Lyceum, 1925). Subsequently on tour in the provinces in *On With The Show*, etc. Then in London in *Balalaika*, 1936-38, *Paprika*, *Magyar Melody*, etc. In 1940 appeared in *Fig Leaves* (Adelphi), *Present Arms* (Prince of Wales), *Waltz Without End* (Cambridge, 1942-43). Recently in *Magic Carpet* (Princes, 1943), etc. In 1944 on tour in *Golden Fleece*. In 1945 on tour in *Three's A Family*. Appeared in *Dear Ruth* (St. James's, 1946).

WARRENDER, HAROLD. Actor. Born London, 1903. Educated at Cambridge. Made his first appearance on the stage in *Charlot's Revue* (Golders Green, 1925). Made his first appearance in New York in *The Charlot Revue* (Earl Carroll, 1927). Then acted in London in *Shake Your Feet, Rookery Nook, Thark, Mischief, The Old Man, The Case Of The Frightened Lady*, etc. Also in the West End in *The Night Of The Garter, The Streets Of London, Other People's Lives, Indoor Fireworks, Anthony And Anna, Lady With Designs, The Shoemaker's Holiday, Juggernaut* and many others. Since the outbreak of war in the Royal Navy.

WATSON, HENRIETTA. Actress. Born Dundee, 1873. Made her first appearance on the stage in *East Lynne*, 1888. First acted in London in *A Royal Divorce* (Olympic, 1891). From 1891-94 acting in Australia. Then in London in *Thoroughbred, The School For Scandal*, etc., before touring U.S.A., 1896-97. Also in London in *The Happy Life, Quality Street, The Voysey Inheritance, You Never Can Tell, The Bondman, The Hypocrites, Waste, The Price, An Ideal Husband* and many others. Also in *The Silver King, His House In Order, The Passing Of The Third Floor Back, Nothing But The Truth, Little Women, The Laughing Lady* and many other plays. Made her first appearance in New York in *The Swan* (Empire, 1924), thenceforth in London in *The Best People, Blackmail, Tell Her The Truth, Indoor Fireworks*, etc. Also in *Frolic Wind, Dodsworth, Lot's Wife* and many others. Recently : *Ten Little Niggers* (St. James's, 1943-44), *The Years Between* (Wyndham's, 1945-46), etc.

WATTS, LYONEL. Actor. Born Cheadle, Cheshire, September 5th, 1884. Educated Winchester and Oxford. Made his first appearance on the stage in *The Flag Lieutenant*, 1908, subsequently in many productions in London and the provinces from 1909 to 1929. Went to America for eight years, returning to London in *Pride And Prejudice* (St. James's, 1938), followed by *It Happened In September* (St. James's, 1942), etc. Recently : *This Was A Woman* (Comedy, 1944-45).

WAYNE, NAUNTON. Actor. Born Llanwonno, 1901. Made his first appearance on the stage in a concert party, Barry, 1920. Thereafter in concert parties until 1928, when he first appeared in London in music-hall, Victoria Palace. Subsequently appeared in *Chelsea Follies, Streamline, 1066 And All That, All Wave*, etc. Made his first appearance in a straight part in *Wise Tomorrow* (Lyric) (in London and in New York, 1937). Recently : In *Black Vanities* (Victoria Palace, 1941), *Goodnight Children* (New, 1942), *Sky High* (Phœnix, 1942), *Arsenic And Old Lace* (Strand, 1942-46).

WEBB, ALAN. Actor. Born York, 1906. Made his first appearance on the stage in *The Devil's Disciple* (Century, 1924), with Lena Ashwell Players, with whom he remained until 1926. Then 1926-28 with J. B. Fagan at Oxford, 1929-31 with Liverpool Repertory Company, 1932-33 Croydon Repertory Company. Has appeared in the West End in *The Brontës, As You Desire Me*, etc. With Old Vic Company, 1934-35. Then in London in *Hervey House, Arms And The Man, The Wind And The Rain, Tonight At 8.30* (also in New York, 1936), *Comedienne, She, Too, Was Young*, etc. In 1939 appeared in *Design For Living* (Haymarket). Since the outbreak of war with H.M. Forces. In 1946 he appeared in *Blithe Spirit* (Duchess) ; *The Years Between* (Wyndham's), etc.

WEIGHT, MICHAEL. Designer. Born Cape Town, South Africa, May 31st, 1906. Educated University of Cape Town. Came to England and has since designed many London play productions. In 1930 : *Dandy Dick* and *The Importance Of Being Earnest* for Sir Nigel Playfair, after which he designed, among others, *Faust, A Doll's House, Piccola, The Naughty Nineties, Cochran's* 1931 *Revue, Hi-Diddle-Diddle, Shall We Reverse?, Stop—Go, And On We Go, The Corn Is Green, Adults Only, The Light Of Heart* and many others. From 1940-45 : in the Royal Navy. Since being released from the Navy he has designed the following : *The Shouting Dies, The Trojan Women, Spring* 1600 (all at Lyric, Hammersmith). In 1946 : *Dear Evelyn, The Winslow Boy*, etc.

WELCH, ELIZABETH. Actress. Born New York City, 1904. Made her first appearance on the stage in *The Chocolate Dandies* (Colonial, 1924). Then first appeared in London in *Dark Doings* (Leicester Square, 1933). Subsequently in London in *Nymph Errant, Glamorous Night, Let's Raise The Curtain, It's In The Bag* and many others. Recently : Appeared in *No Time For Comedy* (Haymarket, 1941). Also in *Sky High* (Phœnix, 1942), *Arc De Triomphe* (Phœnix, 1944), *Happy And Glorious* (Palladium, 1944-46), etc.

WELLS, DEERING. Actor. Born London, 1896. Educated at City of London School. Studied for the stage at R.A.D.A., making his first appearance at Drury Lane in 1913. After the war he appeared in Egypt and Palestine, then with Liverpool Repertory Company, 1919-20. Toured America, 1922-25. Then on stage in London for many years. Recently in *The Importance Of Being Earnest* (Phœnix, 1940), *Crisis In Heaven* (Lyric, 1944), *Jenny Jones* (Hippodrome, 1945), *Lady Windermere's Fan* (Haymarket, 1945-46), etc.

WHATMORE, A. R. Actor and producer. Born Much Marcle, Glos., 1899. Made his first appearance on the stage in *Milestones*, Kennington, 1913, then on tour and in the Army from 1915-19. He founded Hull Repertory Company in 1923, continuing here as actor and producer until 1930, when he took over the Embassy (with Alec L. Rea) until 1932. Here he produced *The Liar, The Witch, The Torchbearers, The Crime At Blossoms, The Second Man, Strange Orchestra* and many others. He has also acted in London in *Man Overboard, Escape, Loyalties, Justice, Dusty Ermine, After October, Sarah Simple* and others. Has produced a number of plays in London including *Wild Justice, The Greeks Had A Word For It, Dusty Ermine, After October, Bats In The Belfry, Sarah Simple* etc. In 1940 produced at Aberdeen Repertory Theatre and *Peril At End House* (Vaudeville). In 1941 produced at Dundee Repertory Theatre and a tour of *Ambrose Applejohn's Adventure* and *Peril At End House*. Since 1942 has been director of Dundee Repertory Theatre.

WHEATLEY, ALAN. Actor. Born Tolworth, 1907. Made his first appearance on the stage in *Heartbreak House*, Cambridge, 1928, continuing with the Festival Company until 1929. Then at Hull, 1929-30, after which he appeared in London at the Grafton, remaining here until 1931. Also appeared in London in *Britannia Of Billingsgate, Miracle At Verdun, The Witch, Wild Justice, Within The Gates, Rose And Glove*, etc. More recently in the West End in *The Impresario From Smyrna, St. Helena, Professor Bernhardi*, etc. Made his first appearance in New York in *St. Helena* (Lyceum, 1936), then in London in *Othello, Judgment Day, Mr. Gladstone, Volpone, Oscar Wilde, Walk In The Sun, The Doctor's Dilemma* and others. From 1940-45 with the B.B.C. European Service, reappearing on the stage in a Continental tour of *Village Wooing* (with the Pilgrim Players for CEMA). Then on tour in *Romeo And Juliet* for CEMA, after which he appeared in *The Vicar Of Wakefield*, 1945. On tour in *The Petrified Forest*, 1945-46. Appeared in *This Way To The Tomb!* and *The Shadow Factory* (Mercury, 1946).

WHILEY, MANNING. Actor. Born 1915. Married to Wanda Rotha. Educated Highgate and the Continent. Studied for the theatre under Alexander Moissi and Benno MacKay. In 1939-40 with the Old Vic Company on tour in *St. Joan, Romeo And Juliet, Viceroy Sarah*, etc. In 1941 appeared in London in *Rain* (St. Martin's), *Squaring The Circle* (Vaudeville, 1941), *Goodnight Children* (New, 1942), *The Wingless Victory* (Phœnix, 1943), *An Ideal Husband* (Westminster, 1943-44), *Desert Rats* (Adelphi, 1945).

WHITBY, GWYNNE. Actress. Born Leamington, 1903. Studied for the stage at R.A.D.A., making her first appearance in *Shakespeare's Dream* (Princes, 1912). Also in London in *Chu Chin Chow, Christopher Sly, Mr. Wu, Charley's Aunt, The Lilies Of The Field, The Likes Of 'Er, The Will*, etc. With Liverpool Repertory Company, 1925-26, then with the Old Vic Company, 1926-27. From 1927-28 toured in Australia. Has also appeared in London in *Sweet Lavender, Magic Marble, People Of Our Class* and *Quiet Wedding*. In addition she has appeared at Stratford-on-Avon in 1934 and again in 1935. In 1940 in *The Women* (Strand), then appeared in a season at the Barn, Dartington Hall, until 1941, when she played in *Quiet Week-End* (Wyndham's) until 1944. Recently acted in *The Gay Pavilion* (Piccadilly, 1945).

WHITE, JOAN. Actress. Born Alexandria, 1909. Studied for the stage at R.A.D.A., making her first appearance in *Tobias And The Angel* (Cambridge, 1930). First appeared in London in *Betrayal* (Little, 1931), thenceforth with the Westminster Theatre Company in *The Anatomist, The Kingdom Of God, Love's Labour's Lost, Jonah And The Whale*, etc., remaining at this theatre until 1933. Also acted in London in *The Golden Toy, The Barretts Of Wimpole Street, The Black Eye, Children To Bless You, Housemaster* and others. More recently in *Susannah And The Elders* and *Little Ladyship*. Recently: 1943-44, in *Junior Miss* (Saville), then in *The Cure For Love* (Westminster, 1945-46).

WHITTAKER, MICHAEL. Actor and designer. Born London, 1918. Educated in London and Brussels. Studied as an industrial designer, then made his first appearance on the stage in repertory at Bournemouth, 1939. Also acted at Oxford before making his first appearance in London in *Their Finest Hour* (Comedy, 1940). Since then has played in *Baby Mine* (Westminster, 1941), *The Admirable Crichton* (His Majesty's, 1943), *The Rest Is Silence* (Prince of Wales, 1944), *Residents Only* (St. James's, 1944). In 1945 appeared in *Desert Rats* (Adelphi), and *Elizabeth Sleeps Out* (King's, Hammersmith). He has also designed costumes for *Their Finest Hour, Tradesmen's Entrance* and *Big Boy*, and designed sets and costumes for *Residents Only*.

WILDING, MICHAEL. Actor. Born London, 1913. Studied to be an artist at St. Martin's Art School, later worked as a technician in films. Made his first appearance on the stage in repertory. Then made his first appearance on the West End stage in *Chase The Ace* (Daly's). Subsequently appeared in London in *Spread It Abroad, Home And Beauty*, etc., after which he toured Australia with Fay Compton in *Victoria Regina*. He returned to London in 1938 and appeared in *The Gate Revue* (Ambassadors). In 1940 appeared in *The Chanticleer Revue*, after which he appeared in *Quiet Week-End* (Wyndham's, 1941-42), *Men In Shadow* (Vaudeville, 1943). Recently in *While The Sun Shines* (Globe, 1944-45).

WILLARD, EDMUND. Actor. Born Brighton, 1884. Made his first appearance on the stage in *Punchinello*, Boston, U.S.A., 1899, then on tour in America and Europe until 1906, during which time he came to London and made his first appearance here in *The Cardinal* (St. James's, 1903). For the next ten years he toured in England, subsequently appearing in London in *Macbeth, The Insect Play, Robert E. Lee, Richard III, The Fool, The Cherry Orchard, Granite, Princess Charming* and many others. Also appeared in the West End in *Our Idols, Quest, Beau Geste, Cape Forlorn, The Silver Box, The Ship, The Dubarry, The Country Wife, Treasure Island*, followed by *The Insect Play* at the Little, in 1936. Then appeared in *Chinese White, And The Music Stopped, The Shoemaker's Holiday,*

The Showing Up Of Blanco Posnet and many others. Recently appeared in *Distant Point* (Westminster, 1941), then in *Arsenic And Old Lace* (Strand, 1942-46).

WILLIAMS, EMLYN. Actor, playwright and producer. Born Mostyn, Wales, 1905. Educated at Oxford. Made his first appearance on the stage in *And So To Bed* (Savoy, 1927), also making his first appearance in New York with this play later on in the same year. Subsequently in London acted in *Glamour, Thérèse Raquin, The Mock Emperor, The Silver Tassie, Tunnel Trench, On The Spot, The Case Of The Frightened Lady, The Man I Killed, Man Overboard* and many others. Also in London in *Wild Decembers, Rose And Glove, Night Must Fall* (also in New York, 1936), *He Was Born Gay,* etc. With the Old Vic in 1937 he appeared in *Ghosts, Measure For Measure* and *Richard III.* Then appeared in *The Corn Is Green,* which ran at the Duchess and Piccadilly until after the outbreak of war. Among his plays are *Glamour, A Murder Has Been Arranged, Port Said, Spring 1600, Night Must Fall, He Was Born Gay* and *The Corn Is Green.* In 1940 he wrote and produced *The Light Of Heart* (Apollo) and in 1941 played, when Godfrey Tearle had to leave the cast. 1941-43, wrote, produced and appeared in *Morning Star* (Globe), wrote and produced *Druid's Rest* (St. Martin's). In 1944 he played in *Blithe Spirit* for more than a year to troops abroad. In 1945, wrote, produced and appeared in *Wind Of Heaven* (St. James's). Among the other plays which he has produced recently are *Watch On The Rhine, The Little Foxes, A Month In The Country,* etc. Among his adaptations are *Josephine* and *The Late Christopher Bean.* In 1945 he also produced a new version of his play, *Spring 1600* (Lyric, Hammersmith). Produced *Dear Evelyn,* 1946; and appeared in *The Winslow Boy.*

WILLIAMS, HARCOURT. Actor and producer. Born Croydon, 1880. Made his first appearance on the stage in *Henry V,* Belfast, 1897 with F. R. Benson's Company, with whom he remained until 1902. First appeared in London in *Henry V* (Lyceum, 1900). Then in many West End plays, including *Electra, Measure For Measure, You Never Can Tell, As You Like It, The Builder Of Bridges, The Bells, Salome, The Master Builder, Fanny's First Play,* etc. Also in London in *How He Lied To Her Husband, John Bull's Other Island, Romeo And Juliet, The Wild Duck, The Three Musketeers, The Merchant Of Venice, Richard III,* etc. From 1919-29 appeared in such West End plays as *Abraham Lincoln, Napoleon, Mary Stuart, Magic, The Dark Lady Of The Sonnets, Hamlet, A Doll's House, Israel, The Winter's Tale, Such Men Are Dangerous* and others. From 1929-34 he produced fifty plays at the Old Vic. From 1934 onwards he appeared in London in *The Voysey Inheritance, Days Without End, Viceroy Sarah, Cornelius, Timon Of Athens, Waste, Uncle Vanya, Richard II, The School For Scandal, The Zeal Of Thy House* (which he also produced). In 1939 in *The Devil To Pay.* In 1940 in *King Lear* (Old Vic). Recently appeared in London in *Abraham Lincoln* (for the Old Vic) (Playhouse, 1943); *Brighton Rock* (Garrick, 1943). In 1944 joined the Old Vic Company and appeared in *Richard III, Peer Gynt* (New, 1944-45). In 1945 toured with the Old Vic on the Continent, rejoining this company to appear in *Henry IV (Parts I And II), Œdipus* and *The Critic* (New, 1945-46).

WILLIAMS, HUGH. Actor. Born Bexhill, 1904. Educated at Haileybury. Married to Margaret Vyner. Studied for the stage at R.A.D.A., making his first appearance in *The Charm School,* Margate, 1921. First appeared in London in *Yellow Jacket* (Kingsway, 1922), subsequently on tour and then with the Liverpool Repertory Company, 1923-25. Then acted in London in *The Tyrant, The Best People, The Garden Of Eden, The Great God Brown,* before touring Australia, 1927-28. On his return appeared in London in *The Ship, The Offence* and *The Matriarch,* before touring America, 1929-30. Then in London in *Twelve Hours, Who Goes Next?, Grand Hotel, While Parents Sleep, Firebird, Strange Orchestra, The Green Bay Tree, Pride And Prejudice, Old Music, We At The Crossroads,* etc.

In 1939 appeared in *Dear Octopus* (Globe). Since the outbreak of war, has been in H.M. Forces. In 1945 he appeared in *Zoo In Silesia* (Embassy).

WILLIAMSON, HUGH ROSS. Playwright. Born London, 1901. Educated at London University. Among his plays are *The Adventurer, In A Glass Darkly, Rose And Glove, The Seven Deadly Virtues, Mr. Gladstone* and *Various Heavens.* Recently wrote *Paul, A Bond Slave.*

WILLIS, TED. Playwright. Born London, 1914. Had his plays first produced at Unity Theatre, King's Cross, the first being *Calling Erna Kramer,* in 1941. Among his other plays are *Buster,* produced at the Arts, 1943, *Sabotage, All Change Here* and *The Yellow Star* (which he also produced at Unity and at Grand Palais, Whitechapel, 1945). 1943-46, dramatic critic for " Daily Worker." Is now engaged in writing screenplays. Also wrote (in collaboration) such plays as *Where Do We Go From Here ?* and *Lend Lease* for ABCA Play Unit (produced on tour of Army camps, and at the Arts, 1945). In 1946 he became Director of the first professional Unity Theatre, producing *All God's Chillun, Casey Jones,* etc.

WILLMAN, NOEL. Actor. Born Ireland, August 4th, 1918. Educated in Ireland and France. Studied for the stage under Michel St. Denis at the London Theatre Studio, making his first appearance in *Hamlet* (Lyceum, 1939). Then in *The Beggar's Opera* (Haymarket, 1940), *The Witch,* on tour, and *The Merchant Of Venice* (New) (both for the Old Vic Company). In 1942 appeared in *Light And Shade* (Ambassadors), *House Of Regrets* (Arts), after which he joined the Old Vic Company at Liverpool, appearing in *Dr. Faustus, The Alchemist, Uneasy Laughter,* etc. He also produced here *Ah Wilderness, The Rivals, Noah,* etc. In 1945 he produced *A Doll's House* (Winter Garden, 1946).

WILSHIN, SUNDAY. Actress. Born London, 1905. Made her first appearance in *Where The Rainbow Ends* (Garrick, 1915), subsequently in London in *A Kiss For Cinderella, The Aristocrat, Quality Street, Peter Pan,* etc. Made her first appearance in New York in *Charlot's Revue Of* 1926 (Earl Carroll). Then in London in *The Golden Calf, The Eternal Flame, Nine Till Six, Napoleon, The Left Bank, Road House, No More Ladies, The Greeks Had A Word For It, First Night,* etc. Since the outbreak of war has been acting and producing for the B.B.C.

WINSTON, BRUCE. Actor. Born Liverpool, 1879. Made his first appearance on the stage in *Oh ! I Say !* (Criterion, 1913). Subsequently appeared in London in *The Spring Song, Cyrano De Bergerac, St. Joan, Dr. Syn,* etc. Made his first appearance in New York in *Katja* (Empire, 1926). Then appeared in London in *The Circle Of Chalk, The Land Of Smiles, Volpone,* etc., before touring Egypt and Australia, 1932-33. Then in London in *Nymph Errant, Mrs. Siddons, The Alchemist, Fritzi, A Kiss For Cinderella, The Melody That Got Lost* and a number of others. Recently, has appeared in *Lottie Dundass* (Vaudeville, 1943), *Three Waltzes* (Princes, 1944-45).

WITHERS, GOOGIE. Actress. Born March 12th, 1917, Karachi, India. Educated Frenville Park, Kent, and the Convent of the Holy Trinity, London. Studied for the stage under Italia Conti, making her first appearance in the chorus of *Nice Goings On* (Strand, 1933), subsequently in *Happy Week-End, Duet In Floodlight, Gate Theatre Revue, Ladies And Gentlemen, Hand In Glove,* etc. Recently : *They Came To A City* (Globe, 1943-44), *Private Lives* (Apollo, 1945-46).

WOLFIT, DONALD. Actor and producer. Born Newark-on-Trent, 1902. Made his first appearance on the stage in *The Taming Of The Shrew,* York, 1920, then on tour until 1924, when he made his first appearance in London in *The Wandering Jew* (New). 1925-26, acting and producing with the Arts League of Service, then with Sheffield Repertory Company. Played in London in *The Enemy, Such Men Are Dangerous* and *The Chinese Bungalow,* before joining the Old Vic Company in 1929 to appear in *Julius Cæsar, Romeo And Juliet, As You Like It, Macbeth,* etc. Also acted in London in *Topaze, The Witch, Black Coffee* and *Precious Bane.*

★ *Vivien Leigh* as Sabina, in Wilder's "The Skin of Our Teeth".

★ ***Ralph Richardson*** as Falstaff in John Burrell's production of Shakespeare's "Henry IV—Parts I and II", for the Old Vic Repertory Season, 1945-46.

PHOTO : JOHN VICKERS

★ *Ralph Richardson* as Burleigh, and Laurence Olivier as Puff in Miles Malleson's production of Sheridan's "The Critic", for the Old Vic Repertory Season, 1945-46.

PHOTO : ANGUS MCBEAN

★ *Alec Clunes* as Hamlet, in Judith Furse's production, for the Arts Theatre Festival of English Drama, 1945-46.

★ ***Laurence Olivier*** as Œdipus in the Michel St.
Denis production, Old Vic, 1945-46.

★ *John Mills* and Elwyn Brook-Jones in Mary Hayley Bell's "Duet For Two Hands", produced by John Mills and Anthony Pelissier, 1945.

★ *Robert Beatty* and Bonar Colleano, Jr., in "A Bell For Adano", dramatised by Paul Osborn from John Hersey's novel, and produced by H. C. Potter, 1945.

★ ***Diana Wynyard*** and Emlyn Williams in Williams'
play "The Wind Of Heaven", which he himself produced,
1945

Toured in Canada with Sir Barry Jackson, 1931-32. Then played in London in *Too True To Be Good, Richard Of Bordeaux, Hamlet, The Master Builder, The Sulky Fire, The Moon In The Yellow River, She Stoops To Conquer, Major Barbara,* etc. Appeared at the Shakespeare Memorial Theatre in 1936, and again in 1937, after which he founded his own company to produce the plays of Shakespeare. In 1938 he appeared in London in *Volpone,* and in 1939 in *Geneva,* but from 1937 until the present time he has been mainly concerned with the production of Shakespeare's plays on tour. Since 1940 he has appeared in seasons of Shakespeare in London at the Strand, St. James's, Westminster, Scala and Winter Garden, and has produced most of the plays in his repertoire. Among his many productions during the war years have been *The Merchant Of Venice, Macbeth, King Lear, Twelfth Night, The Merry Wives Of Windsor, The Imaginary Invalid, Othello, The Master Builder, Hamlet, Volpone, As You Like It, Cymbeline.*

WONTNER, ARTHUR. Actor. Born London, 1875. Made his first appearance on the stage in *The Sorrows Of Satan,* Ryde, 1897, subsequently on tour in the provinces with Mrs. Lewis Waller, Edward Compton and others. Thenceforth toured Australia with Sir Herbert Tree, after which he appeared in London in *Raffles, The Great Conspiracy, An Englishman's Home, Madame X, Hamlet, The Witch, Salome,* etc. Also in London in *Ben Hur, Twelfth Night, Diplomacy, An Ideal Husband, On Trial, Peter Pan, The Maid Of The Mountains* and many others. Then in *Woman To Woman, The Bat, Catherine, The Ware Case, The Lady From The Sea, Henry VIII,* etc. Made his first appearance in New York in *The Captive* (Empire, 1926), then in London in *The Man They Buried, The Three Musketeers, Napoleon, Twelfth Night, Good Friday, Village Wooing, Justice, The Great Experiment* and many others. Appeared in *Sons Of Adam* (Arts, 1939), *The Immortal Garden* (Westminster, 1942), etc. In 1944 on tour in *Ten Little Niggers.* Appeared in *The Great Adventure,* on tour, 1945-46. Also in *Golden Eagle* (Westminster, 1946).

WOOD, VICTOR. Actor. Born Dublin, 1914. Educated Wesley College, Dublin. Made his first appearance on the stage in variety in Ireland. Came to England and studied with Neilson-Terry Guild of Dramatic Art. Made his first London appearance at the Open Air, in the Robert Atkins Company, 1939. Then in *Heartbreak House,* on tour, 1942-43, *Fighters Calling,* on tour, 1944, *Three's A Family* (Saville, 1944-45). In 1945 produced and appeared in *The Adventures Of O'Rierdon* (Gateway), etc. Appeared in *Red Roses For Me* (Embassy, 1946).

WOODBRIDGE, GEORGE. Actor. Born Exeter, 1907. Made his first appearance on the stage in *Cæsar And Cleopatra* (Festival, Cambridge, 1928), then first played in London in *Spread Eagle* (New, 1928). Subsequently appeared in *77 Park Lane, Hamlet,* etc., after which he toured in a Shakespearean repertory company until 1934, when he joined the Old Vic Company, appearing in *St. Joan, The Winter's Tale, King Lear, St. Helena, Peer Gynt,* etc., remaining here until 1936. Then in London in *Muted Strings, Judgment Day, Chu The Sinner, Cymbeline, Last Train South,* etc. With the London Mask Theatre Company in 1938-39, acting in *Troilus And Cressida, Marco Millions, Miss Julie, The Doctor's Dilemma, The Family Reunion, Bridge Head,* all at the Westminster. 1939-40 appeared in *Desire Under The Elms* (Westminster). In 1942 appeared in *Macbeth* (Piccadilly), then joined John Gielgud's Company and appeared in *Love For Love* (Phœnix, 1943), after which he acted in the latter play and *Hamlet* in the Gielgud Festival Season (Haymarket, 1944-45).

WORDSWORTH, RICHARD. Actor. Appeared in London at the Threshold Theatre in 1940; subsequently joined the Old Vic on tour, also appearing in *King John* (New, 1940), and *Othello* (New, 1942) (both for the Old Vic). In 1943 he appeared in *A Trip To Scarborough* (Arts) and *The Witch* (Arts). Then in *The Banbury Nose* (Wyndham's, 1944). In 1945, acting and producing at the Colchester Repertory Theatre. Joined the Norman Marshall Company in 1945.

WRAY, MAXWELL. Producer. Born Doncaster, 1898. Made his first appearance on the stage in *The Merry Wives Of Windsor* (Old Vic, 1919), where he remained until 1923, when he joined Basil Dean as stage-manager until 1925. 1926-30, producing at Sheffield Repertory Theatre. 1930-32, producing for the Birmingham Repertory Theatre, such plays as *See Naples And Die, The Macropulos Secret, Bird In Hand, The Playboy Of The Western World, Street Scene* and many others. Has also produced a number of plays in London, including *Other People's Lives, The Streets Of London, If I Were You, The Six Of Calais, Young Mr. Disraeli, The Mask Of Virtue, Children To Bless You, The Two Bouquets,* etc. 1936-39, engaged in film production. Since 1939 he has produced in London such plays as *St. Joan, A Woman's Privilege, The Two Bouquets, The Vagabond King, The Streets Of London, Sunny River, The Lilac Domino, Hi De Hi,* etc.

WYNDHAM-LEWIS, ANGELA. Actress. Born London. Educated Badmington School. Studied for the stage at R.A.D.A., making her first stage appearance in repertory at Oxford Playhouse, 1940, followed by repertory at the Alexandra, Birmingham. First appeared in London with the Old Vic Company in *The Merchant Of Venice* (New, 1943), then in *How Are They At Home?* (Apollo, 1944), *Peter Pan* (Stoll, 1944-45), *The Golden Fleece,* on tour, 1945.

WYNYARD, DIANA. Actress. Born London, 1906. Married to Carol Reed. Made her first appearance on the stage in *The Grand Duchess* (Globe, 1925). Then on tour until 1927 when she joined the Liverpool Repertory Company, remaining for two years. From 1929 onwards she has appeared in London in *Sorry You've Been Troubled, The Devil, Petticoat Influence, Lean Harvest, The Old Bachelor,* etc. Made her first appearance in New York in *The Devil Passes* (Selwyn, 1932), then in London in *Wild Decembers, Sweet Aloes, The Ante-Room, Heart's Content, Candida, Pygmalion, The Silent Knight,* etc. In 1939 appeared in *Design For Living* (Savoy), which ran until 1940. Recently appeared in *No Time For Comedy* (Haymarket, 1941), *Watch On The Rhine* (Aldwych, 1942-44), *The Wind Of Heaven* (St. James's, 1945). Appeared in *Portrait In Black,* 1946.

WYSE, JOHN. Actor and producer. Born Henley, 1904. Studied for the stage at R.A.D.A., making his first appearance in *The Dancers* (Wyndham's, 1923), subsequently in London in *The Flame, The Round Table, Beggar On Horseback, Raleigh* and others. From 1925-27 with the Old Vic Company and in 1927 acted with the Liverpool Repertory Company. Then in London in *Cyrano De Bergerac, Hamlet, The Skin Game, Androcles And The Lion, Jealousy, John O' Dreams, The Iron Woman, The Merchant Of Venice, The Silver King* and others. With the Stratford-on-Avon Festival Company in 1933 and again in 1934, playing in *The Tempest, Much Ado About Nothing, Julius Cæsar, Henry V, Romeo And Juliet,* etc. Then in London in *Love's Labour's Lost, Comus, You Never Can Tell, Hundreds And Thousands, Third Party Risk* and others. He has produced a number of plays in London, including *Frolic Wind, Fritzi* and *Ride-A-Cock-Horse.* From 1940-45 with H.M. Forces. During this period he acted with the Drama Unit of Army Welfare, appearing in London in *Desert Highway* (Playhouse, 1943). In 1945 he was invalided out of the Army and produced *Desert Highway* on tour.

YOUNG, ARTHUR, Actor. Born Bristol, 1898. Studied for the stage at R.A.D.A., making his first appearance in *Hamlet,* Bristol, 1914. Then on tour, 1914-16, after which he served in H.M. Forces, 1916-19. From 1919-25 on tour with Charles Doran; then made his first appearance in London in *Georges Dandin* (Gate, 1925). Toured Australia, 1928-29, then appeared in London in *The Immortal Lady, Champion North, The Enemy, This Side Idolatry, Reunion In Vienna, The Ghost Train, A Comedy Of Good And Evil, Parnell, Antony And Cleopatra, Good And Proper, Elizabeth Of Austria* and many others. Appeared in *Judgment Day* (Phœnix, 1940), then in *The Duke In Darkness* (Garrison Theatre, Salisbury) and *Residents Only* (St. James's, 1944). Recently appeared in *The Assassin* (Savoy, 1945), *The Gambler* (Embassy, 1945), etc.

YOUNG, JOAN. Actress. Born Newcastle, 1903. Educated in France and at the Convent of the Cross, Bournemouth. Was formerly an actress on the music halls, touring extensively until 1934, when she began working exclusively for the B.B.C. She wrote the book and lyrics for several radio revues, and appeared in musicals, variety, drama and features. In June, 1943, she appeared in Cochran's *Seventy Years Of Song* (Albert Hall). Made her first appearance in London in a straight play in *Our Town* (for the American Army Drama Unit), (Playhouse, 1944). Recently appeared in *The Skin Of Our Teeth* (Phœnix, 1945), *The Shouting Dies* (Lyric, Hammersmith, 1945), *The Happy Journey* (Lyric, Hammersmith, 1945), etc. Appeared in *Big Ben*, 1946.

OUTSTANDING PRODUCTIONS ON THE LONDON STAGE

Autumn 1939 to Spring 1946

(An asterisk indicates that the play was presented in association with CEMA—now the Arts Council)

1939-40.

MUSIC AT NIGHT, by J. B. Priestley. Produced by *Michael MacOwan*, for the London Mask Theatre, at the Westminster. Decor by David Homan. Stephen Murray, Robert Harris, Catherine Lacey, Michael Denison, Mark Dignam, Lydia Sherwood, Milton Rosmer, Jean Cadell, Jenny Laird, Richard Littledale, Marie Ault, Kay Bannerman, Wilson Coleman, Nicholas Meredith.

THE PLAYBOY OF THE WESTERN WORLD, by J. M. Synge. Produced by *John Chandos*, at the Mercury. Stephen Murray, John Chandos, Moya Devlin, Elspeth March, Brefni O'Rorke.

THE IMPORTANCE OF BEING EARNEST, by Oscar Wilde. Produced by *John Gielgud*, at The Globe. Decor by Motley. John Gielgud, Edith Evans, Jack Hawkins, George Howe, Peggy Ashcroft, Gwen Ffrangcon-Davies, Margaret Rutherford.

MAJOR BARBARA, by Bernard Shaw. Produced by *John Fernald* for the London Mask Theatre, at the Westminster. Decor by David Homan. Catherine Lacey, Stephen Murray, Robert Harris, Mark Dignam, Michael Denison.

BOYS IN BROWN, by Reginald Beckwith. Produced by *Norman Marshall*, at the Gate. Decor by Hedley Briggs. John Carol, Julian Somers, Derek Blomfield, Arthur Ridley.

REBECCA, by Daphne du Maurier. Produced by *George Devine*, at the Queen's. Decor by Roger Furse. Celia Johnson, Owen Nares, Margaret Rutherford, Raymond Huntley, Ronald Ward, Edith Sharpe, George Thorpe, Douglas Jeffries, Richard George.

THE DONALD WOLFIT SEASON : Hamlet, Othello, Much Ado About Nothing, The Merchant of Venice and Twelfth Night. Decor by Ernest Stern and Donald Wolfit. Produced by *Donald Wolfit*, at the Kingsway. Donald Wolfit, Rosalinde Fuller, Jay Laurier, Clare Harris, Nigel Clarke, Donald Layne, Rosalind Iden.

DESIRE UNDER THE ELMS, by Eugene O'Neill. Produced by *Henry Cass*, for the London Mask Theatre, at the Westminster. Decor by David Homan. Beatrix Lehmann, Stephen Murray, Mark Dignam, Richard George, George Woodbridge, Frank Shelley, Georgia Mackinnon, Marie Ault, Wilson Coleman, Robert Marsden, Sarah Galbraith, George Dillon, J. Hwfa Pryse.

KING LEAR, by William Shakespeare. Produced by *Lewis Casson* and *Harley Granville-Barker*, at the Old Vic. Decor by Roger Furse. John Gielgud, Nicholas Hannen, Robert Harris, Stephen Haggard, Lewis Casson, Fay Compton, Cathleen Nesbitt, Jessica Tandy, Julian Somers, Jack Hawkins, Harcourt Williams.

THE BEGGAR'S OPERA, by John Gay. Produced by *John Gielgud*, at the Haymarket. Decor by Motley. Michael Redgrave, Audrey Mildmay, Rachel Kempson, Linda Gray, Noel Willman, Frank Napier.

NEW FACES, a revue by Eric Maschwitz and Jack Strachey. Produced by *Hedley Briggs*, at the Comedy (and Apollo). July Campbell, Charles Hawtrey, Betty Ann Davies, Zoë Gail, Anne Allan, Bill Fraser, Frith Banbury, Edmund Bailey, Eric Micklewood, Joan Alexis, Edmund Gray, Peggy Willoughby, Moira Kennett, Madalyn Arnold, Feithlenn McGurk, Audrey Boyes, Mary Barton.

THE DEVIL'S DISCIPLE, by Bernard Shaw. Produced by *Milton Rosmer*, at the Piccadilly. Decor by Sydney Gausden. Robert Donat, Roger Livesey, Rosamund John, Joyce Redman, Milton Rosmer, Jonathan Field, Edgar K. Bruce, Janet Barrow.

JEANNIE, by Aimée Stuart. Produced by *Irene Hentschel*, at the Torch and Wyndham's. Eric Portman, Barbara Mullen, Albert Lieven, Dorothy Hamilton, Tatiana Lieven, James Woodburn, Leo de Pokorny.

SWINGING THE GATE (a second edition of **The Gate Revue**), a revue by Diana Morgan, Robert MacDermott, and others. Produced by *Norman Marshall*, at the Ambassadors. Decor by William Chappell. Hermione Gingold, Walter Crisham, Roberta Huby, Derek Farr, Carole Lynne, Guy Verney, Reginald Beckwith, Ronald Millar, Robert Helpmann, David Evans, Kay Young, Hedley Briggs, Joan Swinstead.

THE TEMPEST, by William Shakespeare. Produced by *Marius Goring* and *George Devine*, at the Old Vic. Decor by Oliver Messel. John Gielgud, Jack Hawkins, Marius Goring, Alec Guiness, Peggy Ashcroft, Marne Maitland, Renée Asherson, Lewis Casson, Vera Lindsay, Oriel Ross, André Morell, Andrew Cruikshank, James Donald, Frank Tickle, W. G. Fay, Vera Lindsay, Laurence Payne, Felicity Lyster.

*THUNDER ROCK, by Robert Ardrey. Produced by *Herbert Marshall*, at the Neighbourhood and Globe. Decor by Herbert Marshall and Bernard Sarron. Michael Redgrave, Frederick Valk, Bernard Miles, Fredda Brilliant, Robert Sansom, Selma Vaz Dias, Percy Parsons, Bernard Sarron.

DIVERSION, a revue by Herbert Farjeon and Walter Leigh. Produced by *George Benson*, at Wyndham's. Decor by John Guthrie. Edith Evans, Walter Crisham, Dorothy Dickson, Bernard Miles, Vida Hope, Peter Ustinov, Joyce Grenfell, Joanna Horder, Billy Thatcher, Joan Sterndale-Bennett, Archie Harradine, Dilys Rees, Derek Bogaerde, Irene Eisinger, Mischa Spoliansky, Elsie French, John Mott. (This was followed by **Diversion No. 2,** with the same company, this time produced by *Walter Crisham*).

1941.

DEAR BRUTUS, by J. M. Barrie. Produced by *John Gielgud*, at the Globe. Decor by Ruth Keating. John Gielgud, Roger Livesey, Margaret Rawlings, Ursula Jeans, Leon Quartermaine, Ronald Ward, George Howe, Muriel Pavlow, Mary Jerrold, Nora Swinburne, Zena Dare.

NO TIME FOR COMEDY, by S. N. Behrman. Produced by *Harold French*, at the Haymarket. Decor by G. E. Calthrop. Diana Wynyard, Rex Harrison, Lilli Palmer, Elizabeth Welch, Arthur Macrae, Denys Blakelock, Walter Fitzgerald.

RISE ABOVE IT, a revue by Leslie Julian Jones, Manning Sherwin, Val Guest, and others. Produced by *Henry Kendall*, at the Comedy. Decor by Berkeley Sutcliffe. Hermione Gingold, Hermione Baddeley, Henry Kendall, Walter

Crisham, Natasha Sokolova, Billy Thatcher, Wilfred Hyde-White, Carole Lynne, Guy Verney, Eric Micklewood, Prudence Hyman, Georgina Cookson, Virginia Winter.

THE STAR TURNS RED, by Sean O'Casey. Produced by *John Allan*, at Unity Theatre.

*THE CHERRY ORCHARD, by Anton Tchekov. Produced by *Tyrone Guthrie*, for the Old Vic Company, at the New. Athene Seyler, Walter Hudd, Rosalind Atkinson, James Donald, James Dale.

BLITHE SPIRIT, by Noel Coward. Produced by *Noel Coward*, at the Piccadilly. Decor by G. E. Calthrop. Fay Compton, Cecil Parker, Kay Hammond, Margaret Rutherford, Ruth Reeves, Moya Nugent.

DISTANT POINT, by Afinogenov. Produced by *André van Gyseghem*, at the Westminster. Decor by P. I. Peache. Edmund Willard, Mary Morris, Guy Verney, Esme Percy, Christine Silver, Josephine Wilson, Arthur Hambling, Christopher Willard, Tarver Penna.

1942.

THE MAN WHO CAME TO DINNER, by Moss Hart and George Kaufmann. Produced by *Marcel Varnel*, at the Savoy. Decor by Michael Relph. Robert Morley, Coral Browne, Edward Cooper, Mary Alice Collins, Jerry Verno, Peter de Greef, Daphne Courtney, David Laing, Viola Lyel, Cliff Gordon.

WATCH ON THE RHINE, by Lilian Hellman. Produced by *Emlyn Williams*, at the Aldwych. Decor by Michael Relph. Anton Walbrook, Diana Wynyard, Judy Campbell, Charles Goldner, Athene Seyler, Peter Murray-Hill, Brian Nissen, Betty Hardy, Norris Smith, Irmgard Spoliansky, Yvan Deley.

THE DOCTOR'S DILEMMA, by Bernard Shaw. Produced by *Irene Hentschel*, at the Haymarket. Decor by Michael Relph. Vivien Leigh, Frank Allenby, Charles Goldner, Austin Trevor, Cyril Cusack, George Relph, Morland Graham, Peter Glenville, John Turnbull, Paul Demel, Geoffrey Edwards, Peter Jones, William Murray, Courtney Bromet.

AWAKE AND SING, by Clifford Odets. Produced by *Alec Clunes*, for the Arts Theatre Group of Actors, at the Arts and Cambridge. Decor by Rolf Gerard. Lily Kann, Martin Miller, Vivienne Bennett, Denys Blakelock, John Ruddock, Richard Attenborough, Julian Somers, Harry Ross, Michael Raghan, Fred Berger.

*MACBETH, by William Shakespeare. Produced by *John Gielgud*, at the Piccadilly. Decor by John Minton and Michael Ayrton. John Gielgud, Gwen Ffrangcon-Davies, Nicholas Hannen, Leon Quartermaine, Ernest Thesiger, George Woodbridge, Abraham Sofaer, Francis Lister, Emrys Jones, David Peel.

THE DUKE IN DARKNESS, by Patrick Hamilton. Produced by *Michael Redgrave*, at the St. James's. Decor by Ernest Stern. Michael Redgrave, Leslie Banks, Walter Fitzgerald, Hugh Burden, Charles Deane, Richmond Nairne. Humphrey Heathcote, D. J. Williams, Fred Groves, Ian Morris.

ARSENIC AND OLD LACE, by Joseph Kesselring. Produced by *Marcel Varnel*, at the Strand. Decor by Roger Furse. Lilian Braithwaite, Mary Jerrold, Edmund Willard, Martin Miller, Naunton Wayne, Frank Pettingell, Eileen Bennett, Cyril Smith, Clarence Bigge, E. J. Kennedy, Wilfrid Caithness.

HOUSE OF REGRETS, by Peter Ustinov. Produced by *Alec Clunes*, for the Arts Theatre Group of Actors, at the Arts. Decor by Nadia Benois. John Ruddock, Max Adrian, Noel Willman, Julian Dallas, David Bird, Lalage Lewis, Christine Silver, Barbara Carswell, Gibb McLaughlin, Susan Richards, Josephine Middleton, Miki Iveria.

*OTHELLO, by William Shakespeare. Produced by *Julius Gellner*, for the Old Vic Company, at the New. Decor by Frederick Crooke. Frederick Valk, Bernard Miles, Hermione Hannen, Freda Jackson, Laurence Payne, Richard Wordsworth, Renée Asherson, Frederick Horrey, Ernest Hare, Clement Ashby, Basil Coleman, Frank Petley, Felicity Lyster.

1943.

*A MONTH IN THE COUNTRY, by Ivan Turghenev. Adapted and produced by *Emlyn Williams*, at the St. James's. Decor by Michael Relph. Michael Redgrave, Valerie Taylor, Michael Shepley, Tom Gill, Isolde Denham, Ronald Squire, John Ruddock, Alban Blakelock, Frederick Schiller, Annie Esmond, Winifred Hindle, Jacqueline Clarke.

BRIGHTON ROCK, by Frank Harvey, Jr. (from the novel by Graham Greene). Produced by *Richard Bird*, at the Garrick. Decor by Gower Parks. Richard Attenborough, Dulcie Gray, Hermione Baddeley, William Hartnell, Harcourt Williams, Norman Pierce, Charles Lamb, Lyn Evans, Becket Bould, Virginia Winter, Sheila Keith, Anna Burden, Daphne Newton, Alec Faversham.

STRIKE A NEW NOTE, a revue by Nicholas Phipps, Kenneth Leslie Smith, Hubert Gregg and others. Produced by *Robert Nesbitt*, at the Prince of Wales'. Decor by George Ramon. Sid Field, Zoë Gail, Triss Henderson, Derek Roy, Marianne Lincoln, Theresa Langfield, Alec Pleon, Bernard Hunter, John Brandon, Tom Linden, Margaret McGrath, Donald Reed, Kenneth Carten, Jerry Desmonde, Jill Manners, Leni Lynn, Maureen Stanley.

HEARTBREAK HOUSE, by Bernard Shaw. Produced by *John Burrell*, at the Cambridge. Decor by Michael Relph. Robert Donat, Edith Evans, Deborah Kerr, J. H. Roberts, Isabel Jeans, George Merritt, Philip Godfrey, Vernon Kelso, Amy Veness, Francis Lister.

WAR AND PEACE, adapted by Robert Lucas from the novel by Tolstoy. Produced by *Julius Gellner*, at the Phoenix. Decor by Hein Heckroth. Frederick Valk, Henry Oscar, Barry Morse, Peter Illing, Paulette Preney, Frederick Lloyd, David Dawson, Ronald Millar, Julian Somers, Yvonne Marling, Dorothy Hammond, John Nicolson, Deering Wells, Lucielle Gray, Maurice Bannister, Antony Verney, Peter Cushing, Peter Bennett, Alexander Pashkoff.

*THEY CAME TO A CITY, by J. B. Priestley. Produced by *Irene Hentschel*, at the Globe. Decor by Michael Relph. John Clements, Googie Withers, Norman Shelley, Ada Reeve, Raymond Huntley, A. E. Mathews, Mabel Terry-Lewis, Frances Rowe, Renée Gadd.

*HEDDA GABLER, by Henrik Ibsen. Produced by *Walter Hudd*, for the Mercury Players, at the Westminster. Decor by Andrée Howard. Sonia Dresdel, Walter Hudd, Elwyn Brook-Jones, Julian Randall, Helen Burns, Irene Arnold, Amy Dalby.

THE OLD FOOLISHNESS, by Paul Vincent Carroll. Produced by *Dennis Arundell*, for the Arts Theatre Group of Actors, at the Arts. Decor by Maise Meiklejohn. Michael Golden, Bill Shine, Barbara Waring, John Varley, Christine Silver, Chris Castor.

*LOVE FOR LOVE, by William Congreve. Produced by *John Gielgud*, at the Phoenix, and Haymarket. Decor by Rex Whistler. John Gielgud, Yvonne Arnaud, Cecil Trouncer, Miles Malleson, Naomi Jacob, George Woodbridge, Angela Baddeley, Rosalie Crutchley, Marian Spencer, Max Adrian, Leslie Banks, Leon Quartermaine, D. J. Williams, Isabel Dean, Alec Mason, John Byron.

*THE RUSSIANS, by Konstantin Simonov. Produced by *Tyrone Guthrie*, for the Old Vic Company, at the Playhouse. Decor by Frederick Crooke. Michael

Golden, Freda Jackson, Olga Lindo, Russell Thorndike, David Carr, Frederick Horrey, Rosalind Atkinson, Roy Malcolm, Ferdy Mayne, Clement Ashby, James Pugh, Ruth Dunning, Franklin Dyall, Arthur Hambling, Ronald Long, Robert Beaumont.

LIVING ROOM, by Esther McCracken. Produced by the author, at the Garrick. Decor by Hamish Wilson. Louise Hampton, Nellie Bowman, Jane Baxter, Philip Cunningham, Lloyd Pearson, Charles Lamb, Eileen Beldon, Dorothy Millar, Keith Shepherd, Fred Groves.

SWEET AND LOW, a revue by Alan Melville, Geoffrey Wright, Denis Waldock, Nicholas Phipps, John Jowett, and others. Decor by Berkeley Sutcliffe. Produced by *Charles Hickman*, at the Ambassadors. Hermione Gingold, Walter Crisham, Edna Wood, Bonar Colleano Jr., Ilena Sylva, George Carden, Graham Penley, Mary Irwin, Brenda Bruce, Richard Curnock (and, later, as **Sweeter and Lower**, with the addition of Henry Kendall, Christopher Hewitt, Gretchen Franklin).

GHOSTS, by Henrik Ibsen (English version by Norman Ginsbury). Produced by *Dennis Arundell*, at the Duke of York's. Decor by Joseph Carl. Beatrix Lehmann, John Carol, Elizabeth Hunt, Harry Herbert, Edward Byrne.

LOTTIE DUNDASS, by Enid Bagnold. Produced by *Irene Hentschel*, at the Vaudeville, and Cambridge. Decor by Joseph Carl. Ann Todd, Sybil Thorndike, Renée Asherson, Bruce Winston, Mignon O'Doherty, John Jarvis, Miki Iveria, Frederick Cooper, Janet Barrow.

SHADOW AND SUBSTANCE, by Paul Vincent Carroll. Produced by *Hugh Hunt*, at the Duke of York's. Decor by Clifford Pember. Joyce Redman, Malcolm Keen, Edward Byrne, Harry Hutchinson, Denis Carey, Megs Jenkins, Tony Quinn, Mona Harrison, Maude Lambert.

THE IMAGINARY INVALID, by Molière. Produced by *Donald Wolfit*, at the Westminster. Decor by Donald Wolfit. Donald Wolfit, Rosalind Iden, Peter Jones, Eric Adeney, Roy Dean, Richard Lyndhurst, Joan Peart, Adza Vincent, Michael Blythe, Audrey Teesdale, Henry Fielding, Alexander Brownlow.

*TOBIAS AND THE ANGEL, by James Bridie. Produced by *Ruth Spalding*, at the Open Air Theatre. Milo Sperber, James Dale, Tristan Rawson, Eliot Makeham, Patricia Hicks.

THE FESTIVAL OF ENGLISH COMEDY, at the Arts. A Repertory Season consisting of the following plays : **The Constant Couple,** by George Farquhar. Decor by Rolf Gerard. **The Magistrate,** by Arthur Wing Pinero. Decor by Maise Meiklejohn. **The Watched Pot,** by H. H. Munro and Charles Maude. Decor by Maise Meiklejohn. **Misalliance,** by Bernard Shaw. Decor by Maise Meiklejohn. All produced by *Alec Clunes*, for the Arts Theatre Group of Actors ; and **The Rivals,** by Richard Brinsley Sheridan. Produced by *Noel Illiff* for the ATGA. Decor by Maise Meiklejohn. Alec Clunes, Denys Blakelock, Bill Shine, Peter Jones, Robert Marsden, Michael Raghan, Harold Lang, David Bird, Avice Landone, Dorothy Primrose, Ruth Buchanan, Yvonne Coulette, Magda Kun, Susan Richards, Derek Birch, Malya Nappi, Newton Blick, John Shackell, Rosemary Freeland.

MR. BOLFRY, by James Bridie. Produced by *Alastair Sim*, at the Westminster, and Playhouse. Decor by Michael Warre. Alastair Sim, Sophie Stewart, Raymond Lovell, Walter Fitzgerald, Harry Ross, Ronald Millar, Jenny Laird, Bill Rowbotham, Alfie Bass, Sheila Brownrigg, Dorothy Smith.

AN IDEAL HUSBAND, by Oscar Wilde. Produced by *Jack Minster*, at the Westminster. Decor by Rex Whistler. Irene Vanbrugh, Martita Hunt, Roland Culver, Esme Percy, Manning Whiley, Rosemary Scott, Peggy Bryan, Townsend

Whitling, Ian Lubbock, Rosamund Greenwood, Joan Haythorne, John Baker, John Vere, Ian Morris.

THE RECRUITING OFFICER, by George Farquhar. Produced by *Alec Clunes*, for the Arts Theatre Group of Actors, at the Arts. Decor by Maise Meiklejohn. Trevor Howard, Helen Cherry, Elwyn Brook-Jones, Edward Byrne, Michael Raghan, Gibb McLaughlin, Dorothy Gordon, Gillian Adams, Robert Marsden.

1944.

THERE SHALL BE NO NIGHT, by Robert Sherwood. Produced by *Alfred Lunt*, at the Aldwych. Decor by G. E. Calthrop. Alfred Lunt, Lynne Fontanne, Muriel Pavlow, Terry Morgan, Frederick Lloyd, Norman Williams, Charles Lamb, David Peel, Harvey Golden, Lance Hamilton, Eric Rutherford, Charles Russell, Kathleen Kent, Gerard Kempinski, Alexander Pashkoff, Alan Sedgwick.

WINKLES AND CHAMPAGNE—the story of the music halls—an extravaganza written by Terry Newman and Bill Rowbotham. Produced by *Bill Rowbotham*, at Unity Theatre. Decor by Bernard Sarron. Frank Godwin, Doris Levenson, David Kossoff, Joe Levene, Frederick Billany, Henry Webb, Roger Bull, Anne Elvey, Audrey Hale, Norman Howard.

OUR TOWN, by Thornton Wilder. Produced by *Gene Jeroski* for the Theatre Unit of the Special Service Section, United States Army, at the Playhouse. John Sweet, Joan Young, Kay Lewis, Thomas Palmer, Jordan Miller and other members of the U.S. Army and U.S. Red Cross Services.

*HAMLET, by William Shakespeare. Produced by *Tyrone Guthrie* and *Michael Benthall*, for the Old Vic Company, at the New. Decor by Leslie Hurry. Robert Helpmann, Pamela Brown, Basil Sydney, Margot Grahame, Dennis Price, Geoffrey Toone, Lawrence Hanray, David Carr, Gus McNaughton, Charles Hickman, Charles Deane, Harold Lang, Frederick Horrey, Lalage Lewis, David Ralph, Robert Beaumont, John Fitzgerald, Marione Everall.

THE WITCH, by John Masefield (from the Dutch of Weirs-Jenssen). Produced by *Catherine Lacey*, for the Arts Theatre Group of Actors, at the Arts. Decor by Jan Kurzke and Maise Meiklejohn. Mary Morris, Abraham Sofaer, Nell Carter, Richard Wordsworth, Chris Castor, Ernest Hare, Wilfred Fletcher, Michael Raghan, Gibb McLaughlin, John Maxwell, Edward Byrne, Newton Blick, Dorothy Reynolds.

*DESERT HIGHWAY, by J. B. Priestley. Produced by *Major Michael MacOwan*, for the Play Unit of the Army Bureau of Current Affairs, at the Playhouse. Decor by George Ramon. Stephen Murray, John Wyse, Stanley Rose, George Cooper, Emlyn James and Peter Tuddenham.

THE DONALD WOLFIT SEASON OF REPERTORY, at the Scala. **Richard The Third,** by William Shakespeare. Decor by Donald Wolfit. **King Lear,** by William Shakespeare. Decor by Ernest Stern. **Volpone,** by Ben Jonson. Decor by Donald Wolfit. All produced by *Donald Wolfit*. Donald Wolfit, Rosalind Iden, Dorothy Primrose, Eric Adeney, Anne Chalkley, Richard Goolden, Charles Quartermaine, Lionel Stevens, Richard Lyndhurst, Brown Derby, Roy Dean, Elisabeth Bayley.

UNCLE HARRY, by Thomas Job. Produced by *Michael Redgrave* and *William Armstrong*, at the Garrick. Michael Redgrave, Beatrix Lehmann, Ena Burrill, Rachel Kempson, Susan Richards, Lee Fox, Hugh Stewart, Ian Colin, Keith Campbell, John Garside, John Clevedon, Harrop Allin, Margery Bryce.

A HUNDRED YEARS OLD, by the Quintero Brothers. Produced by *Greta Douglas*, at the Chanticleer. Decor by E. B. Harker. Audrey Fildes, John Lindsay, Margaret Gordon, Joy Harvey, Roy Siddons, Joan Veale, Edward Rutherfoord, Simon Taylor, Meg Maxwell, Martin Benson, Judy Tomlin.

British Theatre

*THE SHOEMAKER'S HOLIDAY, by Thomas Dekker. Produced for CEMA by Walter Hudd, at the Lyric, Hammersmith. Walter Hudd, Andrew Leigh, John Raffan, Sheila Macintosh, Fanny Carby.

TOMORROW THE WORLD, by James Gow and Arnaud d'Usseau. Produced by *Marcel Varnel*, at the Aldwych. Decor by Henderson Storie. Robert Harris, Elizabeth Allan, David O'Brien, Angela Glynne, Lilly Kann, Jean Cadell, Julien Mitchell.

THE BANBURY NOSE, by Peter Ustinov. Produced by *Norman Marshall*, at Wyndham's. Decor by Michael Relph. Roger Livesey, Ursula Jeans, Hugh Burden, Michael Shepley, Christine Silver, Lyn Evans, Richard Wordsworth, Alan Trotter, Eric Maturin, Eric Messiter, Marione Everall, Richard Hart, Isolde Denham, Philip Hillman.

THE BERNARD SHAW SEASON OF REPERTORY, at the Lyric, Hammersmith : **Too True To Be Good, Candida, Pygmalion, The Dark Lady of the Sonnets, Village Wooing.** Produced by *Ellen Pollock* and *Michael Golden*. Decor by Riette Sturge Moore. Ellen Pollock, Michael Golden, Patricia Hilliard, Nigel Clarke, Edward Byrne, John Leather, Margaret Halstan, Richard Goolden, Wallas Eaton, Joan Craft.

THE OLD VIC COMPANY SEASON OF REPERTORY, at the New. **Peer Gynt,** by Henrik Ibsen (English version by Norman Ginsbury). Produced by *Tyrone Guthrie*. Decor by Reece Pemberton. **Richard the Third,** by William Shakespeare. Decor by Morris Kestelman. **Arms and the Man,** by Bernard Shaw. Decor by Doris Zinkeisen. Both plays produced by *John Burrell*. Laurence Olivier, Ralph Richardson, Sybil Thorndike, Nicholas Hannen, George Relph, Joyce Redman, Margaret Leighton, Sydney Tafler, Michael Warre, Vida Hope, Morris Sweden, Harcourt Williams, David Kentish, Charles Leno, Maurice Nicholas, Michael Hitchman, Humphrey Heathcote, Nancy Nevinson, Diana Maddox, Michael Raghan, Bay White, Pauline Wynn, George Rose.

THE JOHN GIELGUD COMPANY SEASON OF REPERTORY, at the Haymarket. **Hamlet,** by William Shakespeare. Produced by *George Rylands*. Decor by Ruth Keating. **Love For Love,** by William Congreve. Produced by *John Gielgud*. Decor by Rex Whistler. **The Circle,** by Somerset Maugham. Produced by *William Armstrong*. Decor by Sybil Colefax and John Fowler. John Gielgud, Peggy Ashcroft, Leslie Banks, Yvonne Arnaud, Miles Malleson, Cecil Trouncer, Rosalie Crutchley, Max Adrian, Marian Spencer, Peggy Ashcroft, Leon Quartermaine, Francis Lister, Ernest Hare, George Woodbridge, Patrick Crean, Annie Esmond, John Blatchley, Isabel Dean, D. J. Williams, Donald Bain, Michael Lynd, Dorothy Lane.

1945—Spring, 1946.

UNCLE VANYA, by Anton Tchekov. Produced by *John Burrell*, for the Old Vic Company, at the New. Decor by Tanya Moiseiwitsch. Sybil Thorndike, Laurence Olivier, Ralph Richardson, Harcourt Williams, Margaret Leighton, Joyce Redman, George Relph, Betty Hardy, Humphrey Heathcote.

A MIDSUMMER NIGHT'S DREAM, by William Shakespeare. Produced by *Nevill Coghill*, at the Haymarket. John Gielgud, Peggy Ashcroft, Leslie Banks, Max Adrian, Francis Lister, Marian Spencer, Miles Malleson, Leon Quartermaine, Rosalie Crutchley, Patrick Crean, Isabel Dean, Ernest Hare, John Blatchley, George Woodbridge, Francis Drake, Patricia Dainton, George Bryden.

THE INFERNAL MACHINE, by Jean Cocteau. Produced by *Peter Brook*, at the Chanticleer. Decor by Peter Brook. Sigrid Lanstad, Frederick Horrey, Roger Trafford, Frank Tregear, Ronald Long, Robert Marsden, Joy Harvey, Joan Veale, Betty Linton, Ronald Bowman.

380

THE WIND OF HEAVEN, by Emlyn Williams. Produced by the author and *William Armstrong*, at the St. James's. Decor by Alick Johnstone. Emlyn Williams, Diana Wynyard, Megs Jenkins, Dorothy Edwards, Clifford Huxley, Arthur Hambling, Herbert Lomas, Barbara Couper.

THE DUCHESS OF MALFI, by John Webster. Produced by *George Rylands*, at the Haymarket. Decor by Roger Furse. John Gielgud, Peggy Ashcroft, Leon Quartermaine, Leslie Banks, Max Adrian, Cecil Trouncer, Miles Malleson, Ernest Hare, John Blatchley, Patrick Crean, Francis Drake, George Bryden, Joy Harvey, Marian Spencer, Tom Colmer, Shaun Noble.

THE SKIN OF OUR TEETH, by Thornton Wilder. Produced by *Laurence Olivier*, at the Phoenix. Decor by Roger Furse. Vivien Leigh, Cecil Parker, Sydney Monckton, Joan Young, Michael Lynd, Pamela Conroy, Terry Morgan, Peter Lord, Anthony Wallis, Maurice Bannister, Norman Webb, Meg Maxwell, Hugh Stewart, Ena Burrill, Wallas Eaton, John Murphy, David Carr, Charles Doran, Daphne Newton, Ann Wilton, Jessica Spencer.

DUET FOR TWO HANDS, by Mary Hayley Bell. Produced by *John Mills* and *Anthony Pelissier*, at the Lyric. Decor by Anthony Pelissier. John Mills, Mary Morris, Elwyn Brook-Jones, Elspeth March, Merle Tottenham.

SWINGING TO THE LEFT, a revue by Bill Rowbotham. Produced by *Bernard Sarron*, at the Unity. Decor by Helen Biggar. Frank Godwin, Una Brandon-Jones, Audrey Hale, Ann Godwin, Mark Chaney, Joe Levine, Howard Mann, Elsie Chisnall, Mary Clifton, Henry Marshall, Charles Warren, Hazel Wallace, Anna Ponsford, Bob Goreley.

NO ROOM AT THE INN, by Joan Temple. Produced by *Anthony Hawtrey*, at the Embassy. Decor by Lucienne Gow. Freda Jackson, Ursula Howells, Joan Dowling, Mary Kimber, Tony Quinn, David Laing, Ruth Dunning, Valerie Forest, Billie Brook, John Potter, Neville Brook, Doris Rogers, Alfred Hirst, Christopher Steele.

THE FIRST GENTLEMAN, by Norman Ginsbury. Produced by *Norman Marshall*, at the Savoy. Decor by Laurence Irving. Robert Morley, Wendy Hiller, Amy Frank, Wilfrid Walter, Una Venning, Brown Derby, Robert Beaumont, Sigrid Lanstad, Ian Sadler, Guy le Feuvre, John Baker, Helen Stirling, Frances Waring, Philip Friend, Madge Compton.

THE HASTY HEART, by John Patrick. Produced by *Murray Macdonald*, at the Aldwych. Decor by Henderson Storie. Emrys Jones, Margaretta Scott, Frank Leighton, Jerry Verno, Orlando Martins, John McLaren, Nicholas Parsons, Verne Morgan, Roy Russell.

WHERE DO WE GO FROM HERE? a Living Newspaper by Bridget Boland, Ted Willis and Jack Lindsay. Produced by *Stephen Murray*, at the Arts. Acted by the Play Unit of the Army Bureau of Current Affairs, including: John Boxer, Derek Benfield, Guest James, Tristram Butt, Jack Hancock, Joyce Latham, Sheila Ronald, Gilbert Cour, John Boddington, Jack Wood, John Horsley, Brian Oulten, Natalie Jordan, Louise Gainsborough, Frederick Bennett, Charles Wade.

A BELL FOR ADANO, by Paul Osborn, from the novel by John Hersey. Produced by *H. C. Potter*, at the Phoenix. Decor by Motley. Robert Beatty, Bonar Colleano Jr., Milo Sperber, Macdonald Parke, Andrea Malandrinos, Maurice Bannister, Nicholas Stuart, John Fitzgerald, Victor Rietti, Martin Murphy, Clement Ashby, Philip O'Brien, Jessie Evans, Philip Morant, Selma Vaz Dias, Frederick Valk, Thomas Palmer, Sebastian Cabot, Arnold Marlé, Gerard Kempinski, Lilly Molnar.

THE ARTS THEATRE GROUP OF ACTORS FESTIVAL OF ENGLISH DRAMA, at the Arts. **Getting Married,** by Bernard Shaw. Produced by *Judith Furse*. Decor by Jan Kurzke. **The Thunderbolt,** by Sir Arthur Wing

Pinero. Produced by *Peter Streuli.* Decor by Maise Meiklejohn. **The School For Scandal,** by Richard Brinsley Sheridan. Produced by *Christopher Fry.* Decor by Fanny Taylor. **The Constant Couple,** by George Farquhar. Produced by *Alec Clunes.* Decor by Rolf Gerard. **Hamlet,** by William Shakespeare. Produced by *Judith Furse.* Decor by Michael Warre. Alec Clunes, Margaret Vines, Mark Dignam, Olga Lindo, Dorothy Primrose, Peter Streuli, Dorothy Reynolds, Allan McClelland, Roy Malcolm, Leonard Trollope, Newton Blick, Derek Birch, Gordon Davies, Brian Haines, Bertram Shuttleworth, Marcus Insley, Ramon Kilby, Elizabeth Clifford, June Charlier, Julian d'Albie, Chris Castor, Anne Jenkins, Charles Cox.

THE OLD VIC COMPANY SEASON OF REPERTORY, at the New. **Henry IV,** Parts One and Two, by William Shakespeare. Produced by *John Burrell.* Decor by Gower Parks. **Oedipus,** by Sophocles (English version by W. B. Yeats). Produced by *Michel St. Denis.* Decor by John Piper. **The Critic,** by Richard Brinsley Sheridan. Produced by *Miles Malleson.* Decor by Tanya Moiseiwitsch. (**Uncle Vanya** and **Arms and the Man** were later added to the repertory). Laurence Olivier, Ralph Richardson, Sybil Thorndike, Nicholas Hannen, Michael Warre, Joyce Redman, Margaret Leighton, Peter Copley, Sydney Tafler, George Curzon, George Relph, Miles Malleson, David Kentish, William Monk, Harcourt Williams, Paul Stephenson, Michael Raghan, George Rose, Diana Maddox, John Garley, Joseph James, Maxwell Reed, George Cooper, Nicolette Bernard, Max Brent, Kenneth Edwards, Brian Parker.

THIS WAY TO THE TOMB! by Ronald Duncan. With music by Benjamin Britten. Produced by *E. Martin Browne,* at the Mercury. Robert Speaight, Frank Napier, Norman Tyrrell, Pamela Alan, Jean Powell, Sehri Saklatvala, Gwen Nelson, Henzie Raeburn, Stuart Latham, Leonard Thompson, David Pruen, Eileen Vine, Eric Shilling.

THE TIME OF YOUR LIFE, by William Saroyan. Produced by *Peter Glenville,* at the Lyric, Hammersmith. Decor by Tanya Moiseiwitsch. Walter Crisham, Margaret Johnston, Arthur Sager, Frederick Valk, Arnold Marle, George Pembroke, Antony Baird, Donald Finlay, Donald Reed, Willie Wilson, Richard Nelson, Irene Worth, Miriam Karlin, Eileen Herlie, Russell Shad, Danny Green, Lilly Molnar, Molly Gay, Prudence Hyman, John Perrin, Donald Bain, William Macguire, Charles Calvert, Margery Caldicott, Christopher Page, Denise de Faudel.

RED ROSES FOR ME, by Sean O'Casey. Produced by *Ria Mooney,* at the Embassy. Decor by Henry Bird. Ethel O'Shea, Kieron O'Hanrahan, Nora O'Mahony, Sheila Carty, Norrie Duff, Maureen Pook, Eddie Byrne, Dermot MacDowell, Alex Dignam, Victor Wood, Tristan Rawson, Robert Mooney, Michael Healey, Harry Webster, Meric Dobson, Tom Hurley, Charles Blair, Terry Wilson, Robert Mooney.

THE WISE HAVE NOT SPOKEN, by Paul Vincent Carroll. Produced by *Basil C. Langton* for the Travelling Repertory Theatre at the King's, Hammersmith. Decor by Peter Goffin. Renee Asherson, Alan Judd, Basil C. Langton, Ann Casson, Frank Foster, Lewis Casson, Stanford Holme, W. E. Holloway, Charles Staite, Douglas Wilmer.

THE GUINEA PIG, by Warren Chetham Strode. Produced by *Jack Minster,* at the Criterion. Derek Blomfield, Robert Flemyng, Cecil Trouncer, Rachel Gurney, Edith Sharpe, Joan Hickson, Duncan Lewis.

THE KINGMAKER, by Margaret Luce. Produced by *John Clements,* at the St. James's. Decor by Harold Melvill. John Clements, Kay Hammond, Irene Vanbrugh, Robert Eddison, Frances Rowe, David Peel, Moira Lister, Mary Stone, Russell Napier, Brian Hayes, John Harvey, Charles Lloyd Pack, Howieson Culff, Graham Stuart, James E. Mills, Keith Pyott, Michael Wayne, Harold Gardener, David Bird, Laurence Goodwin, Rosemary Davis, John Gatrell, Honor Shepherd, Alwyn Whatsley, Robert del Kyrke, Gerald Vane, Dennis Fraser, Rita Daniel.

THE LONDON THEATRES

ADELPHI THEATRE, Strand, W.C.2
   Box Office—Temple Bar 7611   Stage Door—Temple Bar 9578

ALDWYCH THEATRE, Aldwych, W.C.2
   Box Office—Temple Bar 6404   Stage Door—Temple Bar 3271

AMBASSADORS THEATRE, West Street, W.C.2
   Box Office—Temple Bar 1171   Stage Door—Temple Bar 4105

APOLLO THEATRE, Shaftesbury Avenue, W.1
   Box Office—Gerrard 2663   Stage Door—Gerrard 3435

ARTS THEATRE, Great Newport Street, W.C.2
   Box Office—Temple Bar 7542   Stage Door—Temple Bar 7541

CAMBRIDGE THEATRE, Earlham Street, W.C.2
   Box Office—Temple Bar 6056   Stage Door—Temple Bar 3093

CHANTICLEER THEATRE, Clareville Street, S.W.7
   Box Office—Kensington 5845

COLISEUM THEATRE, St. Martin's Lane, W.C.2
   Box Office—Temple Bar 3161   Stage Door—Temple Bar 1416

COMEDY THEATRE, Panton Street, W.C.2
   Box Office—Whitehall 2578   Stage Door—Whitehall 2620

COVENT GARDEN OPERA HOUSE
   Box Office—Temple Bar 7961

CRITERION THEATRE, Piccadilly Circus, W.1
   Box Office—Whitehall 3216

DRURY LANE THEATRE, Drury Lane, W.C.2
   Stage Door—Temple Bar 1575

DUCHESS THEATRE, Catherine Street, W.C.2
   Stage Door—Temple Bar 6867   Box Office—Temple Bar 8243

DUKE OF YORK'S THEATRE, St. Martin's Lane, W.C.2
   Stage Door—Temple Bar 2991   Box Office—Temple Bar 5122

EMBASSY THEATRE, Eton Avenue, N.W.3
   Stage Door—Primrose 2353   Box Office—Primrose 2211

FORTUNE THEATRE, Covent Garden, W.C.2

GARRICK THEATRE, Charing Cross Road, W.C.2
   Box Office—Temple Bar 4601   Stage Door—Temple Bar 8271

GATEWAY THEATRE, Chepstow Villas, Notting Hill Gate
   Box Office—Bayswater 7444

GLOBE THEATRE, Shaftesbury Avenue, W.1
   Stage Door—Gerrard 6003   Box Office—Gerrard 1592

GRANVILLE THEATRE, Walham Green, S.W.6
  Box Office—Fulham 3477

HAYMARKET THEATRE, Haymarket, S.W.1
  Stage Door—Whitehall 8890   Box Office—Whitehall 9832

HIPPODROME THEATRE, Charing Cross Road, W.C.2
  Stage Door—Gerrard 2284   Box Office—Gerrard 3272

HIS MAJESTY'S THEATRE, Haymarket, S.W.1
  Stage Door—Whitehall 6435   Box Office—Whitehall 6606

INTIMATE THEATRE, Green Lanes, Palmers Green, N.13
  Stage Door—Palmers Green 4090   Box Office—Palmers Green 3798

KING'S THEATRE, Hammersmith, W.6
  Stage Door—Riverside 4947   Box Office—Riverside 5094

LINDSEY THEATRE, Palace Gardens Terrace, Notting Hill Gate, W.11
  Bayswater 2512

LYRIC THEATRE, Shaftesbury Avenue, W.C.2
  Stage Door—Gerrard 5443   Box Office—Gerrard 3686

LYRIC THEATRE, Hammersmith, W.6
  Stage Door—Riverside 4432-3   Box Office—Riverside 4432-3

MERCURY THEATRE, 2 Ladbroke Road, W.11
  Stage Door—Park 7233   Box Office—Park 5700

NEW THEATRE, St. Martin's Lane, W.C.2
  Stage Door—Temple Bar 5650   Box Office—Temple Bar 3878

PALACE THEATRE, Cambridge Circus, W.C.2
  Stage Door—Gerrard 4144   Box Office—Gerrard 6834

PALLADIUM THEATRE, 8 Argyll Street, W.1
  Stage Door—Gerrard 1278   Box Office—Gerrard 7373

PHOENIX THEATRE, Charing Cross Road, W.C.2
  Stage Door—Temple Bar 7431   Box Office—Temple Bar 8611

PICCADILLY THEATRE, Piccadilly Circus, W.1
  Stage Door—Gerrard 1757   Box Office—Gerrard 4506

PLAYERS' THEATRE, 13 Albermarle Street, W.1
  Box Office—Regent 0996
  (Now moved to the premises formerly occupied by the Forum Cinema,
  Villiers Street, W.C.2)

PLAYHOUSE THEATRE, Charing Cross, W.C.2
  Stage Door—Whitehall 3970   Box Office—Whitehall 7774

PRINCE OF WALES' THEATRE, Cranbourne Street, W.C.2
  Stage Door—Whitehall 1432   Box Office—Whitehall 8681

PRINCES THEATRE, Shaftesbury Avenue, W.C.2
  Stage Door—Temple Bar 8200   Box Office—Temple Bar 6956

Q THEATRE, Kew Bridge, Brentford
  Stage Door—Chiswick 2877   Box Office—Chiswick 2920

RUDOLF STEINER HALL, Baker Street, N.W.1
Box Office—Paddington 8219

ST. JAMES'S THEATRE, King Street, S.W.1
Stage Door—Whitehall 3944   Box Office—Whitehall 3903

ST. MARTIN'S THEATRE, West Street, W.C.2
Stage Door—Temple Bar 1086   Box Office—Temple Bar 1443

SADLER'S WELLS THEATRE, Rosebery Avenue, E.C.

SAVILLE THEATRE, 135 Shaftesbury Avenue, W.C.2
Stage Door—Temple Bar 5518   Box Office—Temple Bar 4011

SAVOY THEATRE, Strand, W.C.2
Stage Door—Temple Bar 8117   Box Office—Temple Bar 8888

SCALA THEATRE, Charlotte Street, W.1
Stage Door—Museum 6911   Box Office—Museum 5731

STOLL THEATRE, Kingsway, W.C.2
Stage Door—Chancery 5357   Box Office—Holborn 3703

STRAND THEATRE, Aldwych, W.C.2
Stage Door—Temple Bar 4144   Box Office—Temple Bar 4143

TAVISTOCK LITTLE THEATRE, Tavistock Place, Russell Square,
W.C.1   Box Office—Euston 2796

TORCH THEATRE, Wilton Place, Knightsbridge
Box Office—Sloane 9967

TWENTIETH CENTURY THEATRE, Westbourne Grove, W.11

UNITY THEATRE, Goldington Street, N.W.1
Box Office—Euston 5391   Stage Door—Euston 2381

VAUDEVILLE THEATRE, Strand, W.C.2
Stage Door—Temple Bar 3191   Box Office—Temple Bar 4871

VICTORIA PALACE, Victoria Street, S.W.1
Stage Door—Victoria 2781   Box Office—Victoria 1317

WESTMINSTER THEATRE, Palace Street, S.W.1
Stage Door—Victoria 7882-3   Box Office—Victoria 0283-4

WHITEHALL THEATRE, 14 Whitehall, S.W.1
Stage Door—Whitehall 8011   Box Office—Whitehall 6692

WIMBLEDON THEATRE, S.W.19
Box Office—Liberty 1166

WINDMILL THEATRE
Stage Door—Gerrard 4841   Box Office—Gerrard 7413

WINTER GARDEN THEATRE, Drury Lane, W.C.2
Stage Door—Holborn 8882-3   Box Office—Holborn 8881

WYNDHAM'S THEATRE, Charing Cross Road, W.C.2
Stage Door—Temple Bar 4106   Box Office—Temple Bar 3028

LONDON THEATRICAL MANAGEMENTS

A. A. SHENBURN, Granville Theatre, Walham Green, S.W.6
  Fulham 3477

ADVANCE PLAYERS ASSOCIATION (Donald Wolfit Company),
  c/o Winter Garden Theatre, Drury Lane, W.C.2
  Holborn 8882

ALFRED ESDAILE, Garrick Theatre, Charing Cross Road, W.C.2
  Temple Bar 8271

ANTHONY HAWTREY, Embassy Theatre, Swiss Cottage, N.W.3
  Primrose 5577

ASSOCIATED ARTISTS, LTD., 54, New Cavendish Street, W.1
  Welbeck 7236

BARRY O'BRIEN, 18 Charing Cross Road, W.C.2
  Temple Bar 6447, 2602

BERNARD DELFONT, Astoria House, 62 Shaftesbury Avenue, W.1
  Gerrard 2712-3, 3336-7, 2673

BRONSON ALBERY, Wyndhams' Theatre Offices, Charing Cross Road,
  W.C.2
  Temple Bar 4106

EMILE LITTLER, Coliseum Theatre, St. Martin's Lane, W.C.2
  Temple Bar 6160, 9873-4

FARNDALE, 45 Clarges Street, W.1
  Grosvenor 3312-3-4

FIRTH SHEPHARD, Gloucester House, 19 Charing Cross Road, W.C.2
  Abbey 6292-3

GEORGE BLACK (VAL PARNELL), Cranbourn Mansions, Cranbourn
  Street, W.C.2
  Gerrard 2274

GEORGE T. SMITH, Duke of York's Theatre, W.C.2

GILBERT MILLER, St. James's Theatre, King Street, S.W.1
  Whitehall 3944

HARRY HANSON, 16 Old Bond Street, W.1
  Regent 6508

HENRY SHEREK, 49 Old Bond Street, W.1
  Regent 0424

H. M. TENNENT LTD., Globe Theatre, Shaftesbury Avenue, W.1
  Gerrard 3647-8-9

HOWARD AND WYNDHAM LTD., Standbrook House, 2-5 Old Bond
  Street, W.1
  Regent 2341-2

JACK BUCHANAN, Lyric Theatre, Shaftesbury Avenue, W.1
Gerrard 3694

JACK DE LEON, Q Theatre, Kew Bridge, Brentford
Chiswick 2921-2

JACK HYLTON, His Majesty's Theatre, Haymarket, S.W.1
Whitehall 7241-2

JACK WALLER, 52 Haymarket, London, S.W.1
Whitehall 5961

**JAMES LAVALL, LESLIE JULIAN JONES AND ANTHONY
WICKHAM LTD.,** Piccadilly House, Piccadilly Circus, W.1
Regent 2865

JAY POMEROY (PRODUCTIONS LTD.), 120 Pall Mall, S.W.1
Abbey 4856-7

J. W. PEMBERTON, Ambassador's Theatre, West Street, W.C.2
Temple Bar 4797, 4105

LEE EPHRAIM, Palace Theatre, Shaftesbury Avenue, W.1
Gerrard 4248

LINNIT AND DUNFEE LTD., 28 Brook Street, New Bond Street, W.1
Mayfair 0111 (10 lines)

LUPINO LANE, Victoria Palace, Victoria Street, S.W.1
Victoria 5741

M.E.E.C. PRODUCTIONS, Arts Theatre Club, Gt. Newport Street,
W.C.2
Temple Bar 7541

MILES BYRNE, 41, Charing Cross Road, W.C.2

OLD VIC AND SADLER'S WELLS, 9 St. Martin's Court, W.C.2
Temple Bar 5787

OVERTURE PRODUCTIONS LTD., 19 Charing Cross Road, W.C.2

PATRICK DESMOND, 43 Bedford Street, Strand, W.C.2
Temple Bar 0407

PEOPLES' ENTERTAINMENT SOCIETY LTD., Pioneer House,
Wicklow Street, Gray's Inn Road, W.C.1

PETER DAUBENY, Garrick House, 27 Southampton Street
Temple Bar 0607

PETER DEARING, 34 South Molton Street, W.1

PRINCE LITTLER, Aldwych Theatre Offices, Aldwych Theatre, W.C.2
Temple Bar 3271

REANDCO (Alec L. Rea and E. P. Clift), 29 Manfield House, Strand,
W.C.2
Temple Bar 7226

REUNION THEATRE, c/o " Connies " Ltd., 92, Regent Street, W.1

ROBERT DONAT, Westminster Theatre, Palace Street, S.W.1
Victoria 7881

ROCK THEATRE COMPANY LTD., 9 South Parks Road, Oxford
Oxford 3880

ROY LIMBERT, Panton House, 25 Haymarket, S.W.1
Whitehall 3332

STANBROOK PRODUCTIONS LTD., 15a Hay Hill, Berkeley Square,
W.1
Regent 3827

THEATRE '46, c/o Derek Glynne, 115, Shaftesbury Avenue, W.1
Temple Bar 6916

THE COMPANY OF FOUR, Lyric Theatre, Hammersmith, W.6
Riverside 4432

THE COVENT GARDEN OPERA TRUST, Covent Garden Opera
House
Temple Bar 7961

TOM ARNOLD, 125 Shaftesbury Avenue, W.C.1
Temple Bar 6151-2-3

T.R.T. PRODUCTIONS LTD., 7 New Square, Lincoln's Inn, W.C.2
U N A PLAYS, Standbrook House, 2-5 Old Bond Street, W.1
Regent 2341-2

UNITY THEATRE PRODUCTIONS, 9 Great Newport Street, W.C.2
Temple Bar 4818-9

WILLIAM WATT, Gloucester House, 19 Charing Cross Road, W.C.2
Abbey 2759